Differential Privacy in Artificial Intelligence

From, Theory to Practice

Ferdinando Fioretto and
Pascal Van Hentenryck
(Editors)

now
the essence of knowledge

Published, sold and distributed by:
now Publishers Inc.
PO Box 1024
Hanover, MA 02339
United States
Tel. +1-781-985-4510
www.nowpublishers.com
sales@nowpublishers.com

Outside North America:
now Publishers Inc.
PO Box 179
2600 AD Delft
The Netherlands
Tel. +31-6-51115274

ISBN: 978-1-63828-476-5
E-ISBN: 978-1-63828-477-2
DOI: 10.1561/9781638284772

Suggested citation: Ferdinando Fioretto and Pascal Van Hentenryck (eds.). (2023). *Differential Privacy in Artificial Intelligence: From Theory to Practice*. Boston–Delft: Now Publishers

Table of Contents

Part I

Foundation

DOI: 10.1561/9781638284772.ch1

Chapter 1

Overview and Fundamental Techniques

By Ferdinando Fioretto, Pascal Van Hentenryck and Juba Ziani

1.1 Introduction

Data is continuously harvested from nearly every facet of our lives by corporations, service providers, and public institutions. Whether through smartphones, social media interactions, internet use, healthcare visits, or financial transactions, information is continuously gathered, shaping the foundation of the modern economy. Private companies leverage this vast pool of data to evaluate loan candidates, optimize transportation networks, improve supply chains, personalize services, and predict market demands, all to enhance decision making. Similarly, public policies and government initiatives rely heavily on this data, guiding resource distribution, monitoring public health crises, and driving urban development and sustainability efforts.

However, these datasets also contain a large array of sensitive information, including health, financial, or location data. Major privacy violations and breaches are commonplace, and can have severe negative impacts, not only on consumers and online users, but also on entire organizations and governments. For instance, the 2017 Equifax data breach [Wik24a] exposed the personal information of 147 million individuals, including social security numbers, birth dates, and addresses, leaving millions vulnerable to identity theft, fraud, and long-term financial harm. Similarly, the 2016 Facebook-Cambridge Analytica scandal [Wik24b], in which the personal data of up to 87 million Facebook users was harvested without consent for political advertising purposes, raised concerns about its possible influence on the outcome of the 2016 presidential election.

Privacy concerns have become central in today's society, driving significant changes in government policy. Various regulatory frameworks have been established, with the United States and Europe leading efforts toward stronger privacy practices. In Europe, the General Data Protection Regulation (GDPR) sets strict standards for data management, focusing on consent and data minimization [PE16], while in the U.S., regulations like Title 13 [Uni98] govern the handling of census data and laws like the Health Insurance Portability and Accountability Act (HIPAA) and the California Consumer Privacy Act (CCPA) offer protections for health and consumer data [Cen96; Leg18]. This movement was further emphasized in October 2023 when the Biden administration issued an Executive Order on AI, ensuring the enforcement of consumer protection laws and introducing safeguards against privacy violations in AI systems. Government actions, such as the release of the AI Bill of Rights Blueprint [Hou23] in the US, underscore the increasing focus on privacy in both policy and technology.

Public policy has also devoted extensive research into technical solutions for privacy. Over the past three decades, this research has explored a wide range of privacy definitions and techniques, but one has emerged as a pivotal framework: *Differential Privacy* (DP) [Dwo+06]. DP has gained widespread recognition and adoption, not only by leading technology companies like Apple, Meta, Google, and LinkedIn, but also by the U.S. government, most notably in its landmark 2020 Census data release.

Differential Privacy is now widely regarded as the gold standard for privacy protection in statistical analyses and dataset releases. Its strength lies in providing a *formal* and *mathematical* definition of privacy, offering *precise* and *provable* guarantees. This is in stark contrast to historically ad-hoc and loosely defined privacy methods, which have repeatedly failed under attacks aimed at reconstructing part of the original dataset or identifying individuals in said datasets. As privacy challenges evolve, so too does Differential Privacy, expanding across diverse fields to meet new demands. This book aims at providing a comprehensive introduction to DP, particularly within the novel challenges brought by AI applications. It explores its foundational theories, applications in machine learning, and practical implementations, equipping readers with the knowledge to leverage this critical technology effectively.

Overview of the Chapter

This chapter is structured to provide an introduction to Differential Privacy. It begins by illustrating various attempts to protect data privacy, emphasizing where and why they failed, and providing the key desiderata of a robust privacy definition (Section 1.2). It then defines the key actors, tasks, and scopes that make up the domain of privacy-preserving data analysis (Section 1.3). Following that, Section 1.4, formalizes the definition of DP and its inherent properties, including composition, post-processing immunity, and group privacy. The chapter also reviews the basic techniques and mechanisms commonly used to implement Differential Privacy in Sections 1.4 to 1.6. Finally, Section 1.8 concludes with an overview of Differential Privacy applications and some future directions in this field.

1.2 A Historical Perspective on Privacy

This section begins by posing a fundamental question: *What are the key desiderata and properties that a robust privacy definition must guarantee?* To address this, it examines historical failures of previous and current privacy definitions, highlighting the necessity for well-defined and formal guarantees. This section first outlines the main properties satisfied by Differential Privacy—these properties will be formally detailed later in this chapter. It then delves into specific examples of major privacy breaches over the past 30 years, identifying for each how adherence to certain privacy desiderata could have prevented the failure.

A central argument of this book is the importance of *well-defined and formal privacy guarantees*. A major weakness in many privacy techniques arises when the protections themselves are poorly specified, particularly when they fail to clearly define the classes of attacks they are designed to resist. Over the past three decades, numerous privacy attacks have exploited such ambiguities, often by applying privacy notions beyond their intended use cases. To address these challenges, this chapter focuses on four main *desiderata* that a strong privacy definition should satisfy:

1. **Desiderata 1: Compositionality.** A good privacy definition should ensure that its protections gracefully degrade when applied multiple times, whether across several datasets or through repeated private data analyses. In a data-driven world, where datasets are frequently analyzed multiple times and may contain overlapping information about individuals, composition is crucial. Without it, repeated analyses can cumulatively erode privacy safeguards and ultimately compromise individual privacy.
2. **Desiderata 2: Post-processing immunity.** Once data has been privatized using a privacy-preserving mechanism, any further data analyses should not degrade its privacy guarantees, provided that the original, non-privatized data remains inaccessible. This property assures that subsequent steps or transformations applied to the privatized output cannot compromise privacy.

Post-processing immunity offers a strong guarantee that allows data analysts to abstract away potential attack models, effectively providing *future-proof protection* against privacy violations.

3. **Desiderata 3: Group privacy.** Group privacy aims at controlling how privacy guarantees degrade when considering groups of individuals rather than single individuals. It ensures that a privacy mechanism does not arbitrarily fail to protect privacy beyond the individual level when data from multiple users is combined. While it is inevitable that privacy guarantees weaken as group sizes increase, since more information is encoded about them, the degradation should be controlled and quantifiable.
4. **Desiderata 4: Quantifiable privacy-accuracy trade-offs.** There is no free lunch in privacy: releasing accurate information about a group of people must necessarily and statistically encode some information about individuals. As privacy protection increases the accuracy of insights derived from the data may decrease. A good privacy definition should provide quantifiable trade-offs, allowing data analysts, decision-makers, and model builders to measure how much accuracy is sacrificed for a given level of privacy. This enables them to balance privacy and utility according to specific needs.

The following sections provide historical examples illustrating why privacy is complex, where traditional methods have failed, and how the above desiderata are essential for guaranteeing robust privacy.

1.2.1 Data Anonymization

A standard technique for privacy protection in various domains is *anonymization*. It involves the removal or masking of any identifying details to prevent the recovery of personal identities. Anonymization has been employed in areas such as the release of medical datasets under the Health Insurance Portability and Accountability Act (HIPAA) standards. In the mid-1990s, the Massachusetts Group Insurance Commission (GIC), a government agency responsible for purchasing health insurance for state employees, sought to promote medical research by releasing anonymized health data. The GIC approach involved removing what they considered "explicit" identifiers such as names, addresses, and social security numbers, while retaining hundreds of other attributes deemed non-identifiable. Supported by then-Governor William Weld, this initiative aimed at balancing data utility with privacy protection. However, in 1997, Dr. Latanya Sweeney, then a graduate student at MIT, set out to challenge the effectiveness of this anonymization. Using publicly available information, she re-identified Governor Weld's medical records within the dataset and sent them to his office, starkly demonstrating the vulnerability of supposedly anonymized data.

How was Dr. Sweeney able to uncover Governor Weld's personal medical information from the GIC's released data? One might assume that such an attack required sophisticated techniques and significant resources. In reality, her de-anonymization attack cost only $20 and limited time. The GIC's dataset included three crucial attributes for each individual: sex, zip code, and date of birth. Dr. Sweeney purchased voter registration records from Cambridge, Massachusetts, which contained names, addresses, zip codes, and dates of birth. By cross-referencing these two datasets, she found that only six people in Cambridge shared Governor Weld's birth date. Of those, only three were male, and just one resided in his zip code—uniquely identifying his medical records. This type of attack, known as a *linkage attack*, re-identifies individuals by linking anonymized data with external public records. In a subsequent report [Swe00], Dr. Sweeney demonstrated that her attack extended far beyond a single high-profile individual. She found that "87% of the population in the United States had reported characteristics that likely made them unique based only on 5-digit ZIP, gender, date of birth." Even at broader geographic levels, significant portions of the population could be uniquely identified with minimal information. "About half of the U.S. population are likely to be uniquely identified by only place, gender, date of birth, where place indicates the city, town, or municipality in which the individual resides."

Why Did Anonymization Fail?

Anonymization failed because it lacked formal privacy guarantees. Dr. Sweeney's attack was remarkably simple, yet unanticipated due to the absence of a precise attack model. The lack of *post-processing immunity* meant that, once the anonymized data was released, combining it with other publicly available datasets could reveal more information than intended. If the privacy mechanism had been robust to post-processing, additional analyses or data combinations would not have compromised individual privacy beyond what was already publicly accessible. This example motivates the need for formal privacy definitions that account for all potential avenues of data exploitation.

1.2.2 K-Anonymity

At this point, one might argue that the previous example does not represent a fundamental failure of anonymization as a privacy technique, but rather a misapplication in that specific instance. Is it possible to thwart de-anonymization attacks by simply withholding more attributes? For instance, would not releasing someone's zip code, date of birth, or gender resolve the issue? However, a significant challenge emerges in determining which combinations of publicly available attributes could uniquely identify an individual. As the number of features in a dataset grows, it becomes practically impossible for modern computing to predict and guard against all potential attack vectors. Moreover, sensitive attributes often correlate statistically with non-sensitive ones, rendering anonymization susceptible to statistical attacks that can probabilistically reconstruct sensitive information through these correlations—for a particularly sensitive example involving genomic data, refer to [Hom+08].

Despite decades of deployment, anonymization has consistently failed to provide robust privacy protection. Other high-profile failures include the AOL search data release [BZH06], the Netflix Prize dataset [NS06], and studies demonstrating that individuals can be uniquely identified using just a few mobile phone location points [DHVB13]. So, what is the next step? Can the concept of anonymization be refined to address its shortcomings? A promising strategy might be to release only partial information about each attribute. For example, in demographic or medical analyses, knowing that an individual falls within a certain age *range*, such as "between 18 and 35," might suffice. By revealing less precise information, can re-identification attacks be made more difficult?

In 1998, Prof. Pierangela Samarati and Dr. Latanya Sweeney (the same Dr.Sweeney who highlighted the failures of basic anonymization) introduced a generalization called *k-anonymity* [SS98; Swe02]. A dataset satisfies k-anonymity if, for every record, there are at least $k - 1$ other records with identical values in a set of quasi-identifiers—attributes that could potentially be linked to external data to re-identify individuals. In this framework, it should be impossible to distinguish between any of the k individuals sharing the same quasi-identifiers. In particular, the larger the value of k, the stronger the privacy guarantee. Consider, for example, the dataset in Table 1.1 (left), containing information about state employees. One approach is to release this dataset by replacing sensitive names with random identifiers (see Table 1.1 (middle)). This technique provides only

Table 1.1. Three levels of anonymization on a demographic dataset. **Left:** original dataset. **Center:** masking the sensitive names for 1-anonymity. **Right:** generalizing Zip codes and age attributes for 4-anonymity.

Original Data

Name	Zip Code	Age
Rick	19456	67
Nathan	30309	33
Yani	19445	64
Xiao	30457	35
Luciana	19456	67
Anastasia	30271	38
Marcia	19456	31
Yuki	19456	62

Anonymized Data

ID	Zip Code	Age
1	19456	67
2	30309	33
3	19445	64
4	30457	35
5	19456	67
6	30271	38
7	19456	31
8	19456	62

4-anonymized Data

ID	Zip Code	Age
1	19***	60-70
2	30***	30-40
3	19***	60-70
4	30***	30-40
5	19***	60-70
6	30***	30-40
7	30***	30-40
8	19***	60-70

1-anonymity, which is essentially standard anonymization. However, each individual still has a unique combination of zip code and age, making them vulnerable to singling-out attacks [Swe00; Swe02]. In contrast, the table on the right demonstrates 4-anonymity: entries #1, 3, 5, and 8 are indistinguishable from each other, as are entries #2, 4, 6, and 7. Individuals are grouped into clusters of four, where each group shares the same generalized (zip code, age) attributes, significantly enhancing privacy.

Remark 1.1 (Privacy vs. Utility). *In k-anonymization, increasing the value of k enhances* privacy *by making it more difficult to distinguish between individuals, as they are grouped into larger clusters with identical quasi-identifiers. However, this comes at the expense of* utility. *As k increases, the information becomes less precise, reducing the dataset's usefulness for analysis. For instance, in the 4-anonymized version of our dataset, the details about individuals' zip codes and ages are less specific compared to the 1-anonymized version. This trade-off between privacy and utility is a central theme in privacy research and will be addressed in the context of Differential Privacy in subsequent chapters.*

Where Does *k*-anonymization Fail? Reason #1: Lack of Group Privacy

At first glance, *k*-anonymity appears to address the shortcomings of basic anonymization by preventing the singling out of any specific individual within a dataset. In fact, for years, it was considered the state-of-the-art solution for preventing re-identification attacks. However, *k*-anonymity suffers from a significant limitation concerning the leakage of sensitive information, even when individuals are not directly identified. The core issue is not merely the potential to link a data subject to a specific record. Instead, the real problem lies in the exposure of sensitive information associated with individuals without explicit re-identification, as highlighted in [Des17]. In essence, one does not need to pinpoint a specific person to infer personal, sensitive details about them. Consider the previous example, but now suppose the dataset includes a sensitive attribute, such as credit scores (see Table 1.2, Left). Even without directly identifying anyone, an adversary could learn sensitive information about individuals based on the available data. Using the same linkage approach that Dr. Sweeney employed in her de-anonymization of the GIC medical records, one could cross-reference publicly available data to deduce that entries #2, 4, 6, and 7 correspond to Nathan, Xiao, Anastasia, and Marcia. Although it is impossible to match each person to their exact record, one can still infer that all four individuals have a credit score in the "Fair" category. This represents a significant privacy breach, as sensitive information is disclosed without explicit identification. Here, the property of *group privacy* is violated—the privacy guarantee collapses when aggregating data from as few as four individuals—leading to both group-level and *individual-level* harms.

Table 1.2. Two k-anonymized datasets augmented with credit score information. **Left:** State Employee Dataset. **Right:** The Dataset of Company Z.

ID	Zip Code	Age	Credit Score
1	19***	60-70	797
2	30***	30-40	650
3	19***	60-70	755
4	30***	30-40	590
5	19***	60-70	767
6	30***	30-40	597
7	30***	30-40	613
8	19***	60-70	775

ID	Zip Code	Age	Credit Score
A	30***	30-40	815
B	30***	30-40	613
C	30***	30-40	376
D	30***	30-40	727

Where Does k-anonymization Fail? Reason #2: Lack of Composition

A more subtle issue with k-anonymity arises from the concept of *composition*, described earlier in this chapter. Unfortunately, k-anonymity lacks fundamental composition guarantees and fails when multiple datasets are released. In fact, even releasing just two k-anonymized datasets can be sufficient to break its privacy protections in the worst-case scenario. To illustrate this, imagine a situation where it is known that Marcia is a state employee included in a dataset that has been 4-anonymized. Additionally, suppose that Marcia is a client of Company Z , which aims at helping individuals improve their credit scores. Company Z sells a separate 4-anonymized dataset about its customers (see Table 1.2, Right). Knowing that Marcia is present in both datasets, an adversary can cross-reference the state records with Company Z's records to find a *unique* match: the only individual appearing in both datasets is someone in the 30-40 age range, residing in zip code 30***, and having a credit score of 613. This individual must be Marcia, thereby uniquely identifying her. This scenario demonstrates a failure of *composition*: the privacy guarantees of k-anonymity break down when datasets are combined. While this example is simplified for clarity, extensive practical evidence has shown that the issues with k-anonymity are real and pervasive [NS08]. These limitations underscore the need for more robust privacy definitions that can withstand linkage attacks, data aggregation, and the release of multiple datasets.

1.2.3 Any Perfectly Accurate and Deterministic Privacy Notion Must Fail

Various strategies have been proposed to address the shortcomings k-anonymity without significantly reducing the utility of data for demographic and population-level analyses. One such method is *data swapping*, which involves exchanging parts of dataset entries among individuals to ensure that no single row corresponds directly to one person, while still preserving overall demographic counts like the "number of people in dataset X that have property Y." This technique was employed in the release of U.S. Census data products prior 2020. Another approach is *data minimization*, which focuses on collecting as little data as necessary and discarding it after it has served its purpose. Despite these efforts, the challenge of ensuring that privacy guarantees degrade gracefully and predictably under repeated queries remains unresolved. To address this, it is important to highlight a *fundamental* property that must be satisfied by any robust privacy definitions, helping us narrow down the search for effective solutions. Specifically, the claim is that *no perfectly accurate and deterministic privacy technique can satisfy our requirements*, and that *randomization is essential for privacy*.

This crucial point can be illustrated with a simple example where the lack of randomness leads to a failure in *composition*. Imagine a hypothetical company named Gluble, which has 25 employees. Gluble publicly announces that the average salary of its employees is $500,000, perhaps to attract top talent with its competitive compensation. After hiring a 26th employee named Rick, the company updates its public average salary to $505,000. From these two pieces of information, one can deduce Rick's salary. Using basic arithmetic, Rick's salary x is obtained by solving $\frac{(x+25\times 500{,}000)}{26} = 505,000$, i.e., $x = \$630,000$. This amount is significantly higher than his colleagues' salaries. This scenario shows a *failure of composition*: while each individual data release seems innocuous, combining them allows an adversary to infer sensitive information about an individual. Even with access to just two queries, a differential attack reconstructed private data. Although this example is simplified, Dinur and Nissim [DN03] have shown that such differential attacks can be executed in far more complex settings, even when the query language is restricted. Importantly, the attack used no information about how the data was privatized. This vulnerability arises because the average salary at Gluble was released deterministically and exactly. What would happen if noise was added to Gluble's salary reports? Suppose that the average salary before hiring Rick was reported as approximately $500,000, and after hiring, it was approximately $505,000. It is no longer clear question whether the change is due to Rick's salary or simply a result of the added randomness. After all, the introduction of noise creates uncertainty, preventing exact inference of individual salaries. This concept of adding randomness to data releases is a cornerstone of Differential Privacy.

Observe that providing Differential Privacy is more complex than "just" adding noise. At a high level, the more noise is added, the better our privacy guarantees are going to be; however, adding too much noise is undesirable, as it destroys the utility of privately-released datasets and statistics. Therefore, noise must be carefully calibrated to balance privacy protection with data utility, enabling us to provide formal and provable privacy guarantees alongside precise *privacy-utility trade-offs*.

In fact, three years before Differential Privacy was formally introduced by Dwork et al. [DMNS06], Dinur and Nissim [DN03] laid the groundwork for understanding these trade-offs when incorporating privacy noise. Readers can consult their work, as well as subsequent studies [CNSU20b; CNSU20a], for a deeper exploration of the challenges in calibrating noise to protect against reconstruction attacks. The following sections delve deeper into Differential Privacy, what it protects against, its formal definition, guarantees, and the basic mechanisms to achieve it, providing a comprehensive understanding of the crucial role played by randomization in safeguarding privacy.

1.2.4 A Side Note: Other Types of Privacy Breaches

The discussion above highlights the importance of our privacy desiderata and illustrates how previous techniques that failed to meet these criteria have led to significant privacy failures. So far, the presentation relied on simple examples involving variants of anonymization techniques and the challenges associated with privatizing and releasing datasets. However, with the advent of increasingly complex models and large-scale machine learning applications, privacy failures have begun to emerge in more intricate and subtle ways—even when privatized datasets are never directly released. In particular, recent research has demonstrated that privacy can be compromised not only through released statistics but also via the models themselves. A notable example is *Federated Learning (FL)* [LSTS20], discussed in Chapter 8. The goal of FL frameworks is to protect privacy through decentralization: each user retains their data on their local device, performs computations locally, and only transmits aggregated updates (such as gradient information) to a central server. The intent is that no central entity ever accesses individual user data, thereby preserving privacy. Yet, recent work has shown that this is insufficient: the gradient updates themselves often encode sufficient information to be able to guess the original user data with high accuracy [ZLH19]. This is the topic of Chapter 8.

This issue is not confined to the training of machine learning models. Even after a model is trained and the original data is ostensibly deleted, the released models can still encapsulate information about the training data. This can lead to privacy breaches where models inadvertently memorize and reproduce parts of their training datasets, as discussed in Chapter 5. For instance, large language models trained on extensive text corpora have been found to occasionally output verbatim snippets from the training data when prompted in specific ways [Car+21]. A real-world example involves a South Korean AI company Scatter Lab [Dob21]. Scatter Lab used text and messaging data from users on South Korea's biggest test messaging company, KakaoTalk, to train a chatbot service. Despite efforts to remove personally identifiable information, the chatbot reproduced memorized conversations from the training data when users interacted with it, inadvertently disclosing private and sensitive information about KakaoTalk users. These examples illustrate that privacy breaches can occur even without direct access to the underlying datasets. Thus there is a need for privacy-preserving techniques that extend beyond data anonymization and address the inherent risks in modern machine learning practices. Differential Privacy offers a framework to mitigate these risks by providing formal guarantees that limit the potential for information leakage, even when models are trained on sensitive data and released publicly. Part II of this book explores how Differential Privacy can be applied to machine learning and optimization tasks to safeguard individual privacy for increasingly complex data analysis.

1.3 What Protections Does Differential Privacy Provide?

1.3.1 What Does Differential Privacy Promise?

This section examines and defines what Differential Privacy does and does not protect against. It considers the scenario of an analyst or data curator who aims at collecting and aggregate personal and sensitive data for release in a privacy-preserving manner. This release can take various forms, such as a synthetic version of the dataset that masks private information, a set of sensitive population-level statistics about individuals in the dataset, or a model trained on the sensitive data. The common objective in all these cases is to release data that carefully conceal sensitive attributes at the *individual* and *group* level while retaining sufficient information to provide useful statistics or models at the *population* level. For example, an analyst might wish to determine the fraction of a population with a particular disease or calculate the average salary of employees in a company. In these instances, the data pertaining to each individual is private and sensitive, and individuals may prefer to keep it confidential.

First Attempt: No Information Leakage

Ideally, no information about any specific individual should be leaked through the data release, i.e., "nobody can learn *any* information about a specific individual from the privatized computation." Achieving this level of privacy is theoretically straightforward: simply do not collect or use any data at all. However, this is impractical, as it precludes any meaningful data analysis. *Herein lies a fundamental tension highlighted earlier in this chapter: using more data enhances the accuracy and usefulness of the models and statistics but potentially compromises individual privacy.*

Second Attempt: *Almost* No Information Leakage

Rather than requiring that one learns *nothing* about any individual when conducting useful statistical analyses, perhaps one can accept learning *as little as possible* or *almost nothing* about them. Recall the example from the introduction concerning Rick's salary and the addition of noise for privacy. If the company Rick works for is large enough, adding a small amount of noise to the average salary can allow for releasing an approximate estimate of the average salary, while making it difficult to deduce Rick's specific salary. However, the problem here is subtle. It may still be possible to learn significant information about Rick, for instance, that he likely has a high salary because he works at a company where the average salary is close to \$500,000. This may seem innocuous if Rick is expected to hold a high-paying position. But consider a more sensitive scenario: imagine that, in the early 1950s, Rick is a smoker participating in a novel medical study investigating the link between smoking and cancer. The study concludes that smoking does cause lung cancer. As a result, anyone who knows that Rick smokes now knows he is at a higher risk of developing lung cancer. His insurance company might increase his premiums or refuse coverage for cancer treatment, citing a pre-existing condition due to his smoking. Clearly, Rick has been *harmed* by the outcome of the study.

Refining the Definition of Privacy

The perspective adopted in this book and by Differential Privacy is that the above scenario does not constitute a privacy violation. Consider a counterfactual world where Rick did not participate in the study. The medical study would still have concluded that smoking causes cancer, and Rick would have faced the same potential harms. Rick's decision to share his data had *(almost) no impact* on the released statistical inference that smoking causes cancer. This outcome is unavoidable: *any* accurate statistical analysis revealing that smoking causes cancer would have had the same effect on Rick. This book takes the point of view that it is important to distinguish between harms arising from the ethical implications of certain statistical inferences and *privacy harms* that result specifically from the collection and use of an individual's data. This redefines what good statistical privacy guarantees should ensure and the refined desiderata: the goal is to ensure that *one can learn almost nothing new about an individual that could not have been inferred had they not shared their data.* It is important to emphasize that Differential Privacy is not an algorithm; it is a *definition* or *requirement* for privacy. The remainder of this chapter aims at accomplishing two goals: *(i)* to carefully formalize the definition and guarantees provided by Differential Privacy, and *(ii)* to cover basic algorithmic techniques and building blocks for achieving Differential Privacy.

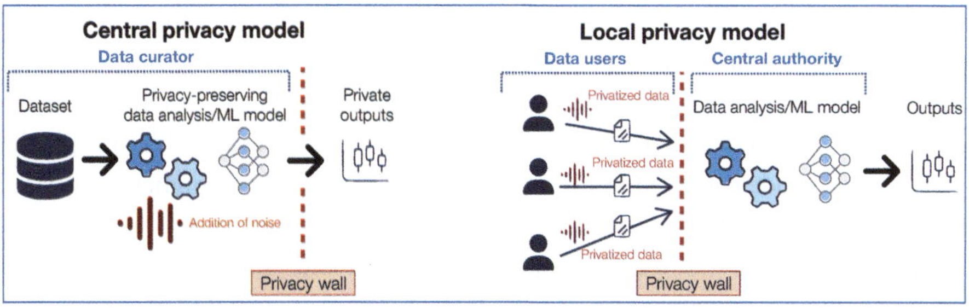

Figure 1.1. Actors and models in the Privacy Preserving data processing pipeline. Central privacy model (left) and Local privacy model (right).

1.3.2 Where to Guarantee Differential Privacy? Local vs Central Models

Implementing Differential Privacy requires careful consideration of the context in which privacy guarantees are applied, particularly regarding the underlying trust model. The degree of trust placed in data curators or aggregators significantly influences the design and effectiveness of privacy-preserving mechanisms. This book examines the two primary frameworks within privacy-preserving ecosystems: the *centralized* model and the *distributed* (or local) model, each with distinct characteristics and implications for privacy management.

In a *centralized* framework, all data collection, storage, and processing occur at a single, central location managed by a trusted data curator. This central entity has direct access to the raw data and is responsible for implementing and monitoring all privacy-preserving mechanisms. The assumption here is that the data curator will faithfully protect individual privacy and handle data responsibly. This setup represents the *central model* in Differential Privacy, as illustrated in Figure 1.1 (left). Conversely, a *distributed* framework keeps data decentralized, residing at its point of origin—such as personal devices or local databases. Privacy-preserving algorithms are executed locally by the data contributors themselves, and only essential, processed information is communicated to a central authority. For instance, in a typical federated learning setup, raw user data remains on their devices, and only privatized versions of the data—such as noisy data points or gradient updates—are sent to the central aggregator. This approach embodies the *local model* in Differential Privacy, depicted in Figure 1.1 (right). Both centralized and distributed frameworks offer distinct advantages and challenges concerning privacy.

Centralized systems concentrate data in one location, creating a single point of failure. If the central entity fails to protect the data—due to a breach or misuse—it can lead to widespread privacy violations affecting all users. Moreover, centralized frameworks require users to *trust* that the platform will implement privacy measures correctly and not exploit the data for unintended purposes. However, the centralized setting offers significant advantages in terms of data utility and algorithmic flexibility. Because the data curator has access to the raw data, they can inject carefully calibrated noise at the aggregate level, often requiring much less noise to achieve the same privacy guarantees compared to the local setting. This means that analyses and models derived in the centralized setting can be of higher quality and accuracy. Additionally, the centralized model allows for the development of more complex algorithms that require inspecting the data and estimating joint statistics before adding noise—a process that is often challenging or infeasible in the local model.

In contrast, *the distributed model reduces the need for trust in a central authority since privacy is enforced locally by each user*. Even if the central aggregator is compromised, the attacker gains access only to the noisy, privacy-protected data that users have shared. This mitigates the risk associated with a central point of failure and enhances individual control over personal data. However, while the distributed model enhances privacy by minimizing trust requirements, it also introduces additional complexity in implementing privacy-preserving protocols. Each user must correctly execute the algorithms, which may involve sophisticated computations. Additionally, because each user adds noise to their data independently, the aggregated results may suffer from reduced accuracy due to the accumulation of noise. The centralized model, on the other hand, allows for more efficient privacy-utility trade-offs. Since the data curator has access to the raw data, they can add carefully calibrated noise at the aggregate level, achieving the desired privacy guarantees with potentially less impact on data utility. This centralized addition of noise can result in higher-quality data analyses compared to the distributed approach. An in-depth discussion of the local model of DP is provided in Chapter 2.

Distinguishing Data Privacy From Data Security

It is important to differentiate between *data privacy* and *data security* within the landscape of privacy-preserving technologies. Data *security* focuses on preventing unauthorized access to data, implementing measures such as encryption, authentication protocols, and intrusion detection systems to safeguard against breaches and cyber threats. These measures are designed to protect data from external attackers and unauthorized insiders. However, security alone is insufficient to prevent the *inference* of individual-level sensitive information from released data. In contrast, data *privacy*, as addressed in this book, aims at preventing *inference* of individual information when data, statistics, or machine learning models are released. Even when cryptographic security is fully implemented, computing a statistic or training a machine learning model can still allow an attacker to infer individual-level information from the computed statistics or the released model alone, without ever breaching the system or accessing the original data. How this can occur was illustrated through our earlier example of a differential attack recovering Rick's salary or health status. Differential Privacy thus provides an *orthogonal and complementary* layer of protection to traditional data security techniques. *While data security aims at preventing unauthorized data access, Differential Privacy limits the potential harm from running inference or reconstruction attacks on released databases, statistics, and models.*

1.4 Differential Privacy: Formal Definition, Techniques, and Properties

Differential Privacy is a mathematical framework for measuring and bounding the individuals' privacy risks in a computation. The concept, first introduced in 2006 by Dwork, McSherry, Nissim, and Smith in [DMNS06], informally states that the presence or absence of any individual record in a dataset should not significantly affect the outcome of a mechanism. In this book, a *mechanism* is defined as any computation that can be performed on the data. Differential Privacy deals with randomized mechanisms, and a mechanism is considered *differentially private* if the probability of any outcome occurring is nearly the same for any two datasets that differ in only one record.

In this context, an adversary is any entity attempting to infer sensitive information about individuals from the output of a data analysis. Remarkably, the privacy guarantee of Differential Privacy holds even if the adversary possesses unlimited computing power and complete knowledge of the algorithm and system used to collect and analyze the data. Thus, even if the adversary were to develop new and sophisticated methods, including the attack methods discussed earlier, as well as new attacks that do not yet exist today, or even if new additional external information becomes available, Differential Privacy provides the exact same level of protection. In this sense, Differential Privacy is considered *future-proof.*

The section, next, reviews *Randomized Response*, a classic method adopted in surveys for ensuring the privacy of respondents. Originally developed as a survey technique to encourage honest responses to sensitive questions, Randomized Response leverages randomness to protect individual privacy while still allowing researchers to estimate population characteristics accurately. This method serves as a foundational example of how randomness can be systematically used to achieve Differential Privacy, illustrating the principles that guide more complex privacy-preserving mechanisms discussed later in this section, and throughout the book.

Randomized Response

Randomized response [War65] was proposed by Warner in 1965 to privately survey respondents for a potentially sensitive property. The setup is as follows: one wishes to test for how many individuals in a set of respondents have a certain property, $\mathcal{P}$, which might be a controversial one to possess, and this might ordinarily lead to a subset of respondents becoming what Warner described as a "non-cooperative" group, who might refuse to be surveyed or provide a dishonest answer, introducing unwanted bias in the survey results. To simultaneously ensure that respondents answer honestly (and, as a result, avoid bias due to the aforementioned non-cooperation) and that their privacy is not violated, randomized response provides respondents the ability to deny their response while also preserving the quality of the summary statistics inferred. This is ensured by introducing randomness into the process of surveying as follows.

1. The respondent takes a fair coin and flips it;
2. If *tails* is obtained, then the respondent answers truthfully, and if *heads* is obtained, the respondent flips the coin again and
   (a) Responds affirmatively if the outcome is heads;
   (b) Responds negatively if the outcome is tails.

Note that here the outcomes and numbers of coin flips are only known to the respondent. The property of *plausible deniability* allows respondents to be able to deny their responses, and this provides them with privacy guarantees (as it will be elaborated later). While the responses are partly perturbed due to this process, an analyst can recover the expected number of "Yes" responses accurately as follows,

$$\mathbb{E}[\text{Yes}] = \frac{3}{4}n(\text{has } \mathcal{P}) + \frac{1}{4}n(\text{does not have } \mathcal{P}),$$

where $\mathbb{E}[\text{Yes}]$ is the expected number of affirmative responses, and $n(X)$ is the number of respondents who claimed to satisfy property X.

As will become clear later in this section, the plausible deniability property of randomized response has a strong connection with Differential Privacy.

1.4.1 Differential Privacy, Formally

Prior to defining Differential Privacy formally, this section formalizes what this privacy notion aims at protecting (dataset) and the means by which an analyst interacts with data (queries).

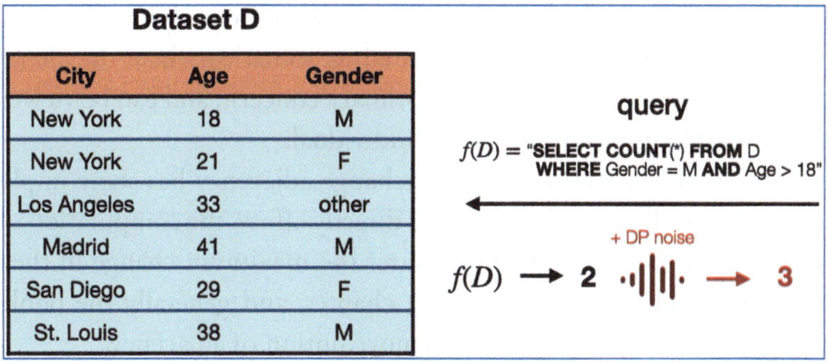

Figure 1.2. Example dataset and query.

Datasets and Queries

A *dataset* D is a multi-set of elements in the *data universe* $\mathcal{U}$. The set of every possible dataset is denoted $\mathcal{D}$. The data universe $\mathcal{U}$ is a cross product of multiple *attributes* $U_1, \ldots, U_n$ and has *dimension* n. For example, Figure 1.2, illustrates a dataset D with three attributes: city, age, and gender. If C is the set of all cities considered, the interval $A = [0, 100]$ the set of all ages considered, and $G = \{\text{M}, \text{F}, \text{other}\}$, then $\mathcal{U} = \mathcal{C} \times \mathcal{A} \times \mathcal{G}$. A *numeric query* is a function $f : \mathcal{D} \to \mathcal{R} \subseteq \mathbb{R}^r$ that maps a dataset in some real vector space. For instance, the query $f(D)$ could be an *SQL statement* that counts the number of male individuals over the age of 18 in dataset D, as illustrated in Figure 1.2.

The concept of *adjacency* is fundamental in DP. It frames the *unit of change* that Differential Privacy seeks to protect against, ensuring that the presence or absence of any single individual's data does not significantly alter the outcomes of data analysis. There are two common ways to define adjacency in the context of Differential Privacy, reviewed next.

Definition 1.2 (Add/remove adjacency). *Two datasets D and D' are said adjacent under the add/remove notion, denoted as $D \sim D'$, if $|D \Delta D'| = 1$, where $\triangle$ is the symmetric difference of two sets.*

In other words, two datasets are defined as adjacent if one can be obtained from the other by either adding or removing the data of a single individual. This model is particularly relevant when considering the impact of an individual's participation or absence in the dataset.

Definition 1.3 (Exchange adjacency). *Two datasets D and D' are said* adjacent *under the exchange notion, denoted as $D \sim_{\rightleftarrows} D'$, if D' is obtained from D by successively removing one record and then adding a (possibly different) record. That is, there exist elements $d \in D$ and $d' \in \mathcal{U}$ such that: $D' = (D \setminus \{d\}) \cup \{d'\}$. This implies that $|D| = |D'|$ and $|D \triangle D'| = 2$.*

In this notion, adjacent datasets differ in the data of exactly one individual but have the same size. This definition is suited to scenarios where the alteration of data within a constant-size dataset is the primary concern, and can be viewed as the removal followed by the addition of one individual.

The choice between add/remove or exchange adjacency has some implications for how Differential Privacy is applied as it directly affects the computation of global sensitivity, introduced next, which measures the maximum change in the output of a function for adjacent datasets. This chapter, and generally the book unless specified otherwise, adhere to the add/remove notion of adjacency.

Global Sensitivity

The impact of a single individual's data on the overall analysis is measured through the concept of *global sensitivity*. Formally, the global sensitivity of a function $f : \mathcal{D} \to \mathcal{R}$ is defined as the maximum difference in the output of f over all pairs of adjacent datasets $D \sim D' \in \mathcal{D}$, measured with respect to the ℓ_p norm:

$$\Delta_p f = \max_{D \sim D'} \|f(D) - f(D')\|_p. \tag{1.1}$$

In simpler terms, it measures how much the output of a function can change when an individual's data is added or removed from the dataset. This measurement provides a basis for determining the amount of noise that needs to be added to the function's output to achieve privacy. For example, the query considered in Figure 1.2 that counts the number of individuals satisfying a certain property in a dataset has global sensitivity 1, since adding or removing a single individual in the dataset can affect the final count by at most 1. Suppose instead that the task is to compute the average age of all individuals in the dataset. Then the global sensitivity of this average function would be

$$\Delta_p f = \frac{\max(A) - \min(A)}{|D|} = \frac{100}{|D|},$$

where A represents the range of possible ages (assuming ages range from 0 to 100). In this chapter, the ℓ_1-sensitivity $\Delta_1 f$ is denoted with Δf.

Differential Privacy

These examples illustrate how a single individual's data can influence the output of a function applied to a dataset. This influence is central to the concept of Differential Privacy. The impact of adding or removing an individual's data varies depending on the type of function in question—whether it's calculating sums, averages, or any other measure of the data. This sensitivity measurement tells us how much the output of the target function need to be adjusted in order to protect an individual's privacy. Differential Privacy achieves this by adding noise to the function's output, by an amount calibrated to the function sensitivity. This approach ensures that the presence or absence of any single individual's data does not significantly alter the output, thereby masking their participation.

Definition 1.4 (Differential Privacy [DMNS06]). *A randomized mechanism $\mathcal{M} : \mathcal{D} \to \mathcal{R}$ with domain $\mathcal{D}$ and range $\mathcal{R}$ is* (ε, δ)-differentially private *if, for any event $S \subseteq \mathcal{R}$ and any pair $D, D' \in \mathcal{D}$ of adjacent datasets:*

$$Pr[\mathcal{M}(D) \in S] \leq \exp(\varepsilon) Pr[\mathcal{M}(D') \in S] + \delta, \tag{1.2}$$

where the probability is calculated over the randomness of $\mathcal{M}$.

A differentially private mechanism maps a dataset to a distribution over the possible outputs because, e.g., it adds random noise or makes randomized choices. The released DP output is a single random sample drawn from this distribution. The level of privacy is controlled by the parameter $\varepsilon \geq 0$, called the *privacy loss*, with values close to 0 denoting strong privacy, and a secondary parameter δ which can be loosely interpreted as a margin of error.

First, observe that the inequality:

$$Pr[\mathcal{M}(D) \in S] \leq \exp(\varepsilon) Pr[\mathcal{M}(D') \in S],$$

(here with $\delta = 0$ for simplicity of exposition) holds for any D and D'. In particular, since it holds for any pair of neighboring databases, it also holds when *swapping* the roles of D and D' in the above definition. Hence, an $(\varepsilon, 0)$-differentially private algorithm must also satisfy

$$Pr[\mathcal{M}(D') \in S] \leq \exp(\varepsilon) Pr[\mathcal{M}(D) \in S].$$

This directly implies the "stronger" inequality below:

$$\exp(-\varepsilon) Pr[\mathcal{M}(D') \in S] \leq Pr[\mathcal{M}(D) \in S] \leq \exp(\varepsilon) Pr[\mathcal{M}(D') \in S], \tag{1.3}$$

which highlights that the probabilities of any event S under $\mathcal{M}$ applied to D and D' are close to each other, controlled by ε.

To intuitively understand these parameters, think of ε as a knob controlling the level of privacy. Lowering ε enhances privacy by making the outputs less sensitive to changes in any individual's data. As ε approaches zero (with $\delta = 0$), the inequality in Equation (1.3) forces the distributions $\mathcal{M}(D)$ and $\mathcal{M}(D')$ to become nearly identical. This means *more* privacy, as distinguishing between D and D', which is necessary to recover the data of the individual that differs across both databases, becomes harder. When $\varepsilon = 0$, $Pr[\mathcal{M}(D) \in S] = Pr[\mathcal{M}(D') \in S]$ for all S; i.e., the output is independent of and does not use the input dataset, providing *perfect* privacy, but *no utility*—mathematically, an easy implication of $\varepsilon = 0$ is that

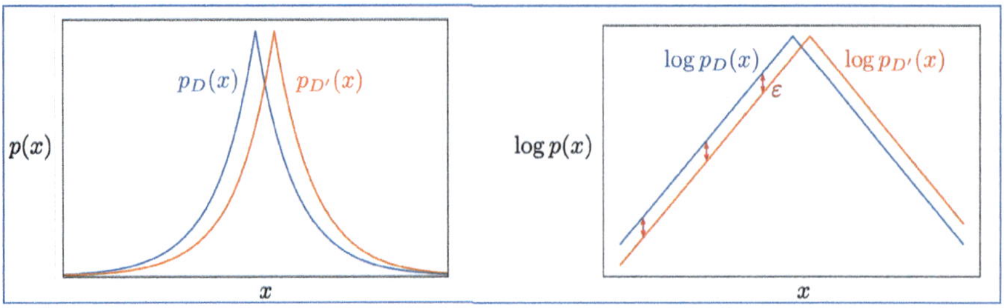

Figure 1.3. An illustration of the ε-DP guarantee (here, using the Laplace mechanism of Section 1.4.3). The log-probability of a value to be output by a mechanism given two neighboring datasets is bounded by ε.

our mechanism must have a (trivially) constant output across all datasets. When $\varepsilon \to +\infty$, the inequality is always satisfied by any mechanism and *no privacy* is guaranteed.

The parameter δ serves as a margin of error. It is typically a small number close to zero that defines a *failure threshold* allowing the DP guarantee not to hold with a probability of up to δ[i]. In practice, δ is chosen to be a negligible value, often much smaller than $\frac{1}{N}$, where N is the size of the dataset. This ensures that the likelihood of disclosing sensitive information about any individual remains extremely low. A mechanism satisfying $(\varepsilon, 0)$-differential privacy is said to satisfy *pure* Differential Privacy or ε-Differential Privacy.

The guarantees of Differential Privacy are illustrated in Figure 1.2, which shows the distribution of outputs from a differentially private mechanism applied to two adjacent datasets D and D'. The blue and red curves represent the probability distributions of the outputs for D and D', respectively. The left figure shows how the probability distributions over outputs must be close to each other for adjacent datasets. The right figure quantifies the difference between the probabilities, showing that the log-probabilities of any outcome x differ by at most ε. This means that the ratio of probabilities is bounded by e^{ε}, as required by the definition. One can see that requiring a smaller ε forces the distributions to be closer to each other across D and D', making it harder to distinguish between the two databases and hence providing stronger privacy protections.

1.4.2 Formal Properties of Differential Privacy

This section formalizes the properties guaranteed by Differential Privacy, and how they match the desirata described in Section 1.2. The composition, group privacy,

i. $(\varepsilon, 0)$-DP most of the time, except with probability δ, and (ε, δ)-DP are closely related but not exactly equivalent.

and post-processing properties are derived directly from the direction of Differential Privacy, and do not assume a specific mechanism like Randomized Response. As such, composition. group privacy, and post-processing hold for *any* differentially private mechanism, i.e. *any mechanism that satisfies requirement* (1.2).

Composition

Composition ensures that a combination of differentially private mechanisms (whether the mechanisms release privatized data, statistics on data, or learning models) preserves Differential Privacy. Composition is a key concept that enables the construction of complex algorithms by combining simpler primitives. It facilitates *privacy accounting*, the rigorous analysis of the overall privacy loss of a composite and potentially complex algorithm by aggregating the privacy guarantees of individual primitives. More formally, it can be stated as follows [DR14]:

Theorem 1.5 (Composition). *Let $\mathcal{M}_i : \mathcal{D} \to \mathcal{R}_i$ be an ε_i-differentially private mechanism for $i \in \{1, 2\}$. Then, their composition, defined as $\mathcal{M}(D) = (\mathcal{M}_1(D), \mathcal{M}_2(D))$, is $(\varepsilon_1 + \varepsilon_2)$-differentially private.*

Proof. For any $(R_1, R_2) \subseteq \mathcal{R}_1 \times \mathcal{R}_2$ and any two neighboring datasets $D \sim D'$,

$$\begin{aligned}
\frac{Pr[\mathcal{M}(D) \in (R_1, R_2)]}{Pr[\mathcal{M}(D') \in (R_1, R_2)]} &= \frac{Pr[\mathcal{M}_1(D) \in R_1] Pr[\mathcal{M}_2(D) \in R_2]}{Pr[\mathcal{M}_1(D') \in R_1] Pr[\mathcal{M}_2(D') \in R_2]} \\
&= \left(\frac{Pr[\mathcal{M}_1(D) \in R_1]}{Pr[\mathcal{M}_1(D') \in R_1]}\right)\left(\frac{Pr[\mathcal{M}_2(D) \in R_2]}{Pr[\mathcal{M}_2(D') \in R_2]}\right) \\
&\leq \exp(\varepsilon_1)\exp(\varepsilon_2) \\
&= \exp(\varepsilon_1 + \varepsilon_2).
\end{aligned}$$

□

This argument can be generalized to for k differentially private mechanisms by induction. More precisely, if $\mathcal{M}_i : \mathcal{D} \to \mathcal{R}_i$ is an ε_i-differentially private mechanism for $i = 1, \ldots, k$. Then, the composition $\mathcal{M}(D) = (\mathcal{M}_1(D), \ldots, \mathcal{M}_k(D))$ is $(\sum_{i=1}^{k} \varepsilon_i)$-differentially private. The result above is also called *simple composition*, as it deals with pure Differential Privacy mechanisms. An extensive treatment of composition in Differential Privacy is deferred to Chapter 3.

Group Privacy

The Differential Privacy notions discussed so far bound differences in output distributions of the mechanism for any pairs of adjacent datasets, i.e. for datasets D, D' such that $|D \Delta D'| = 1$. However, what is not immediately clear is the case when two datasets differ in more than one individual's data. Fortunately, Differential Privacy yields group privacy guarantees that bound this difference for datasets that differ in k entries, for $k > 0$:

Theorem 1.6 (Group privacy). *Let $\mathcal{M} : \mathcal{D} \to \mathcal{R}$ be an ε-differentially private algorithm. Suppose D and D' are two datasets that differ in exactly k entries. Then, for all $S \subseteq \mathcal{R}$:*

$$Pr[\mathcal{M}(D) \in S] \leq \exp(k\varepsilon) Pr[\mathcal{M}(D') \in S].$$

Proof. Let $D^{(0)} \triangleq D$ and $D^{(k)} \triangleq D'$, and let $D^{(0)}, D^{(1)}, \ldots, D^{(k-1)}, D^{(k)}$ be a sequence of datasets where $D^{(i)} \sim D^{(i+1)}$ for $i = 0, 1, \ldots, k-1$. The datasets in this sequence can be thought of as "intermediate" datasets when trying to obtain D' by starting with D and changing one entry at a time successively. Then by the DP guarantee of $\mathcal{M}$, for any $R \subseteq \mathcal{R}$ and $i \in [k-1]$,

$$Pr[\mathcal{M}(D^{(i)}) \in R] \leq \exp(\varepsilon) Pr[\mathcal{M}(D^{(i+1)}) \in R].$$

Then, for any $R \subseteq \mathcal{R}$,

$$\begin{aligned} Pr[\mathcal{M}(D) \in R] &= Pr[\mathcal{M}(D^{(0)}) \in R] \\ &\leq \exp(\varepsilon) Pr[\mathcal{M}(D^{(1)}) \in R] \\ &\leq \exp(2\varepsilon) Pr[\mathcal{M}(D^{(2)}) \in R] \\ &\vdots \\ &\leq \exp(k\varepsilon) Pr[\mathcal{M}(D^{(k)}) \in R] \\ &= \exp(k\varepsilon) Pr[\mathcal{M}(D') \in R]. \end{aligned}$$

□

Post-processing

Another key property of Differential Privacy is post-processing immunity. It ensures that privacy guarantees are preserved by arbitrary data-independent post-processing steps [DR14]:

Theorem 1.7 (Post-Processing Immunity). *Let $\mathcal{M} : \mathcal{D} \to \mathcal{R}$ be a mechanism that is ε-differentially private and $g : \mathcal{R} \to \mathcal{R}'$ be a data-independent mapping. The mechanism $g \circ \mathcal{M}$ is ε-differentially private.*

Proof. The proof first considers a deterministic mapping $g : \mathcal{R} \to \mathcal{R}'$. Let $\tilde{S} \triangleq \{r \in \mathcal{R} : g(r) \in S\}, \forall S \subseteq \mathcal{R}'$. Then for any two neighboring datasets $D \sim D'$,

$$\begin{aligned} Pr[g \circ \mathcal{M}(D) \in S] &= Pr[\mathcal{M}(D) \in \tilde{S}] \\ &\leq \exp(\varepsilon) Pr[\mathcal{M}(D') \in \tilde{S}] \\ &= \exp(\varepsilon) Pr[g \circ \mathcal{M}(D') \in S]. \end{aligned}$$

This proves post-processing immunity for deterministic functions. To extend this guarantee to randomized functions, note that randomized functions can be viewed as a distribution over deterministic functions, and, in particular as a convex combination of deterministic functions. Given that a convex combination of differentially private mechanisms (here each mechanism is obtained by composing each deterministic function with the mechanism $\mathcal{M}$) is also differentially private, the result follows. □

This property ensures that, once Differential Privacy guarantees are applied, any further analysis or manipulation of the protected results will not compromise its privacy guarantees. Post-processing significantly expands the scope and applicability of Differential Privacy algorithms in real-world applications, as shown in Part III.

Quantifiable Privacy-accuracy Trade-offs

The last important property, mentioned in Section 1.2, the trade-off between privacy and accuracy can be quantified exactly. Privacy-accuracy trade-offs are *mechanism-level* properties: each mechanism has its own trade-off. The privacy-accuracy trade-offs of the main building blocks are described later in this section, including the privacy-accuracy trade-offs of *Randomized Response* in Section 1.7, of the *Laplace Mechanism* in Section 1.4.3, and of the *Gaussian Mechanism* in Section 1.5.1.

1.4.3 The Laplace Mechanism

The Laplace Distribution with 0 mean and scale b has a probability density function $\text{Lap}(x|b) = \frac{1}{2b}e^{-\frac{|x|}{b}}$. The Laplace mechanism is a differentially private mechanism based on the Laplace distribution for answering numeric queries [DMNS06]. It is a fundamental building block for many DP algorithms described in this book, and itfunctions by simply computing the output of the query f and then perturbing each coordinate with noise drawn from the Laplace distribution. The scale b of the noise is calibrated to the query sensitivity Δf divided by ε:

Definition 1.8 (The Laplace Mechanism). *Let $f : \mathcal{D} \to \mathcal{R} \subseteq \mathbb{R}^d$ be a numerical query, with d being a positive integer. The Laplace mechanism is defined as*

$\mathcal{M}_{Lap}(D; f, \varepsilon) = f(D) + Z$ *where* $Z \in \mathcal{R}$ *is a vector of i.i.d. samples drawn from* $Lap(\frac{\Delta f}{\varepsilon})$.

The Laplace mechanism adds random noise drawn from the Laplace distribution independently to each of the d dimensions of the query response.

Theorem 1.9 (Differential Privacy of The Laplace Mechanism)**.** *The Laplace mechanism,* $\mathcal{M}_{Lap}$*, achieves* $(\varepsilon, 0)$*-Differential Privacy.*

Proof. Let $D \sim D'$ be any two neighboring datasets in $\mathcal{D}$, and let p_D and $p_{D'}$ be the probability density functions of $\mathcal{M}_{\text{Lap}}(D; f, \varepsilon)$ and $\mathcal{M}_{\text{Lap}}(D'; f, \varepsilon)$, respectively. Then for any $r \in \mathcal{R}$,

$$
\begin{aligned}
\frac{p_D(r)}{p_{D'}(r)} &= \prod_{i=1}^{d} \left(\frac{\exp\left(-\frac{\varepsilon |f(D)_i - r_i|}{\Delta f}\right)}{\exp\left(-\frac{\varepsilon |f(D')_i - r_i|}{\Delta f}\right)} \right) \\
&= \prod_{i=1}^{d} \exp\left(\frac{\varepsilon(|f(D')_i - r_i| - |f(D)_i - r_i|)}{\Delta f} \right) \\
&\leq \prod_{i=1}^{d} \exp\left(\frac{\varepsilon(|f(D')_i - f(D)_i|)}{\Delta f} \right) && \text{(By the triangle inequality.)} \\
&= \prod_{i=1}^{d} \exp\left(\frac{\varepsilon \cdot (\|f(D) - f(D')\|_1)}{\Delta f} \right) && \text{(By the definition of } \Delta f\text{.)} \\
&\leq \exp(\varepsilon).
\end{aligned}
$$

The proof is similar for $\frac{p_{D'}(r)}{p_D(r)} \leq \exp(\varepsilon)$. □

A graphical representation of the densities and log density of two Laplace distributions associated with neighboring datasets D and D' are provided in Figure 1.3, respectively. Note how the difference between the log probabilities for x for each of the neighboring datasets $D \sim D'$ is bounded by ε.

Accuracy Guarantee of the Laplace Mechanism

The accuracy guarantees of the Laplace Mechanism is characterized by the following result.

Theorem 1.10. *For any numerical query* $f : \mathcal{D} \to \mathcal{R} \subseteq \mathbb{R}^d$*, and any database* $D \in \mathcal{D}$*,*

$$
Pr\left[\left| f(D) - \mathcal{M}_{Lap}(D; f; \varepsilon) \right| \geq \ln\left(\frac{d}{\beta}\right) \cdot \left(\frac{\Delta f}{\varepsilon}\right) \right] \leq \beta.
$$

Proof. The proof is for $d = 1$ for simplicity, but it generalizes for $d > 1$. The proof follows from characterizations of the tails of the Laplace distribution. For a random variable $Z \sim Lap(b)$ and a real number $\alpha > 0$,

$$Pr\left[|Z| \geq \alpha\right] = \exp\left(-\alpha/b\right).$$

Therefore, given that $f(D) - \mathcal{M}_{Lap}(D; f; \varepsilon)$ is Laplace with parameter $b = \frac{\Delta f}{\varepsilon}$, it follows that

$$Pr\left[\left|f(x) - \mathcal{M}_{Lap}(D; f; \varepsilon)\right| \geq \alpha\right] = \exp\left(-\alpha \cdot \frac{\varepsilon}{\Delta f}\right) \triangleq \beta.$$

Solving for α in $\exp\left(-\alpha \cdot \frac{\varepsilon}{\Delta f}\right) = \beta$ leads to

$$\alpha \cdot \frac{\varepsilon}{\Delta f} = \ln\left(\frac{1}{\beta}\right),$$

hence

$$\alpha = \ln\left(\frac{1}{\beta}\right) \cdot \left(\frac{\Delta f}{\varepsilon}\right).$$

This conclude the proof. □

The accuracy guarantee of the Laplace Mechanism provides a practical way to understand how the added noise affects the utility of the released data while ensuring differential privacy. Essentially, it quantifies the expected deviation between the true value of a numerical query and the noisy output produced by the mechanism.

1.4.4 Answering Private Queries in Practice

Next, we present two examples to illustrate how the Laplace Mechanism can be applied in practice.

Example 1: Computing the Average Age

Consider a dataset containing the ages of 10,000 individuals, with ages ranging from 0 to 100 years. The task is to compute the average age while ensuring differential privacy. A practical procedure follows the following steps:

1. *Determine the query function and its sensitivity.* In this task the query function is the average age,

$$f(\text{data}) = \frac{1}{n}\sum_{i=1}^{n} \text{age}_i,$$

where n is the number of individuals in the dataset. The global sensitivity Δf of the average function is the maximum change in the output when one individual is added or removed. Since the age can vary between 0 and 100, adding the data about a single individual can affect the sum by at most 100 units. Therefore, the sensitivity is:

$$\Delta f = \frac{\text{max age} - \text{min age}}{n} = \frac{100 - 0}{10{,}000} = 0.01.$$

2. *Apply the Laplace Mechanism.* The next step is to select the privacy parameter ε and add noise drawn from the Laplace distribution with scale parameter $\frac{\Delta f}{\varepsilon}$. Selecting $\varepsilon = 0.5$ to obtain a strong privacy guarantee adds the following noise:

$$\text{noise} \sim \text{Lap}\left(\frac{\Delta f}{\varepsilon}\right) = \text{Lap}\left(\frac{0.01}{0.5}\right) = \text{Lap}(0.02).$$

The private query thus reports $f(\text{data}) + \text{noise}$.
3. *Analyze the error bound.* Additionally, by setting a confidence level $\beta = 0.05$ (meaning that one is 95% confident in the error bound), the error bound can be computed as,

$$\text{Error Bound} = \frac{\Delta f}{\varepsilon} \ln\left(\frac{1}{\delta}\right) = \frac{0.01}{0.5} \ln\left(\frac{1}{0.05}\right) \approx 0.06 \text{ years.}$$

This means that, with 95% confidence, the noisy average age returned by the Laplace Mechanism will differ from the true average age by no more than approximately 0.06 years. If the privacy parameter is set to $\varepsilon = 1$, allowing for slightly less privacy in exchange for greater accuracy, the error bound decreases to about 0.03 years. Thus, selecting ε and β appropriately ensures that the released data remains both useful and privacy-preserving.

Example 2: Releasing a Histogram

Suppose a statistical agency wants to release a histogram showing the number of individuals in different age groups, segmented by gender and region, from a dataset containing a large number of respondents. The age groups could be categorized in intervals (e.g., 0–9, 10–19, …, 90+). The goal is to release this histogram while ensuring differential privacy. Note that this is different from the previous task where a single quantity wasreleased. The procedure again follows the the three same steps:

1. *Determine the query function and its sensitivity.* The query function is the count of individuals in each combination of age group, gender, and region. For count queries, the global sensitivity Δf is 1 because adding or removing one individual can change the count in one category by at most 1.

2. *Apply the Laplace Mechanism.* The next step consists in selecting a privacy parameter $\varepsilon = 0.5$ for each count in the histogram and adding independent Laplace noise to each cell (i.e., each combination of age group, gender, and region) in the histogram. Let $c_{i,j,k}$ be the true count for age group i, gender j, and region k, and $\tilde{c}_{i,j,k}$ is the private counterpart to be released. The counts are linked by the following formula:

$$\tilde{c}_{i,j,k} = c_{i,j,k} + \text{Noise}_{i,j,k}, \quad \text{where Noise}_{i,j,k} \sim \text{Laplace}\left(\frac{\Delta f}{\varepsilon}\right) = \text{Laplace}(2).$$

3. *Post-processing to ensure valid counts.* Notice that the application of real-valued noise to each count may render the resulting privacy-preserving counterpart negative or non-integers, thus producing invalid ouputs. These issues can be corrected by applying a post-processing step, that set any negative noisy counts to zero and round the noisy counts to the nearest integer. Such post-processing steps do not alter the privacy guarantees of the original release and are commonly applied in deployments [CDMS21].
4. *Analyze privacy and utility.* Each count is ε-differentially private with $\varepsilon = 0.5$. Since each individual's data affects only one count, and the counts are disjoint, the overall privacy guarantee remains $\varepsilon = 0.5$. The added Laplace noise has a mean of zero and a scale of 2 and thus the expected absolute error for each count is 2. For categories with large counts, this noise has a relatively small impact. However, for categories with small counts, especially in less populated age groups or regions, the noise can significantly affect the accuracy. A further analysis on disparate impacts of Differential Privacy on different subpopulations is discussed in Chapter 17.

Note that other mechanisms can produce integer counts directly without additional rounding, by using discrete noise mechanisms, such as the Geometric mechanism [GRS12] and the discrete Laplace mechanism [KS12].

1.5 Approximate Differential Privacy

The discussion in the previous section focused on pure Differential Privacy and the mechanisms and guarantees associated with it. The case where $\delta > 0$ for (ε, δ)-DP constitutes a variant of Differential Privacy known as *Approximate Differential Privacy*. Recall that $\delta \in (0, 1)$ is the failure probability of the privacy loss bound in the relaxed variant of pure DP, and is meant to be a cryptographically low quantity—that is, so small it is considered negligible for practical purposes, often much less than $\frac{1}{N}$ where N is the dataset size. This allows practitioners to apply other mechanisms which yields better utility than the Laplace mechanism in exchange for a marginal failure probability. Importantly, approximate Differential Privacy retains the composition, group privacy, and post-processing immunity properties provided by pure Differential Privacy.

1.5.1 The Gaussian Mechanism

The canonical mechanism for (ε, δ)-DP is the Gaussian mechanism [DR14]. Where the Laplace mechanism adds noise proportionally to the ℓ_1 sensitivity of a query f, Δf, the Gaussian mechanism uses the ℓ_2 sensitivity, denoted by $\Delta_2 f$, and defined as in Equation (1.1) with $p = 2$. The ℓ_2 and ℓ_1 norms enjoy the following relationship: for a vector $x \in \mathbb{R}^d$, $\|x\|_2 \leq \|x\|_1 \leq \sqrt{d}\|x\|_2$. Thus, the ℓ_2 sensitivity can be up to a factor $\sqrt{d}$ less than the ℓ_1 sensitivity. The Gaussian distribution with 0 mean and standard deviation σ has the probability density function $\mathcal{N}(x|\sigma) = \frac{1}{\sigma\sqrt{2\pi}} \exp\left(-\frac{(x-\mu)^2)}{2\sigma^2}\right)$.

Definition 1.11 (Gaussian Mechanism). *Let $f : \mathcal{D} \to \mathcal{R}$ be a numerical query. The Gaussian mechanism is defined as $\mathcal{M}_{Gauss}(D; f, \varepsilon) = f(D) + z$ where $z \in \mathcal{R}$ is a vector of i.i.d. samples drawn from $\mathcal{N}\left(0, \sigma^2 I\right)$ where $\sigma \geq \sqrt{2\ln(\frac{1.25}{\delta})}(\Delta_2 f/\varepsilon)$.*

As with the Laplace mechanism, the numerical query response is d-dimensional for some integer $d > 0$ as well. Gaussian noise is added to each dimension of the query response independently by the Gaussian mechanism. To highlight a key distinction between the Laplace and Gaussian mechanisms, consider the context of computing the mean of a multivariate dataset, revisited from [Kam20]. Consider a dataset $D \in \{0, 1\}^{n \times d}$ aiming to compute the mean in a privacy-preserving manner, denoted by $f(D) = \frac{1}{n}\sum_{i=1}^{n} D_i$. The maximum discrepancy in f across adjacent datasets is $\frac{1}{n}1$, yielding a vector with ℓ_1 norm of $\frac{d}{n}$ and ℓ_2 norm of $\sqrt{d/n}$ as the ℓ_1 and ℓ_2 sensitivities. The following theorem defines the (ε, δ)-DP guarantees for the Gaussian mechanism.

Theorem 1.12. *The Gaussian mechanism, $\mathcal{M}_{Gauss}$, achieves (ε, δ)-Differential Privacy, for $\varepsilon \in (0, 1]$ and $\delta \in [0, 1]$.*

For the proof of this theorem, see Appendix A of [DR14]. Notice that, in the original proposition, also reviewed in [DR14], the mechanism is restricted to use ε within $(0, 1]$. However, it is not uncommon to see values of $\varepsilon > 1$ in practice, including in various discussions in this book. This restriction was studied and overcome in [BW18], which provided a more general *analytical Gaussian mechanism* that holds for $\varepsilon > 1$ as well. While the details of the DP guarantee of the analytical Gaussian mechanism are beyond the scope of this text, the mechanism and the associated (ε, δ)-DP is defined as follows.

Theorem 1.13. *(Analytical Gaussian Mechanism [BW18]). Let* $f : \mathcal{D} \to \mathcal{R}$ *be a numerical query with global* ℓ_2 *sensitivity* $\Delta_2 f$. $\forall \varepsilon > 0$ *and* $\delta \in [0, 1]$*, the Gaussian mechanism* $\mathcal{M}_{Gauss}(D; f, \varepsilon) = f(D) + z$ *with* $z \sim \mathcal{N}(0, \sigma^2 I)$ *satisfies* (ε, δ)*-Differential Privacy if and only if*

$$\Phi\left(\frac{\Delta_2 f}{2\sigma} - \frac{\varepsilon\sigma}{\Delta_2 f}\right) - e^{\varepsilon}\Phi\left(-\frac{\Delta_2 f}{2\sigma} - \frac{\varepsilon\sigma}{\Delta_2 f}\right) \leq \delta.$$

Where $\Phi(t) = Pr[\mathcal{N}(0,1) \leq t] = \frac{1}{\sqrt{2\pi}} \int_{-\infty}^{t} e^{-y^2/2} dy$ *is the CDF of the standard univariate Gaussian distribution.*

The reader is referred to [BW18] for the details on the analytical Gaussian mechanism.

Discussion of Accuracy

The exact formal accuracy guarantees is left as an exercise to the reader. The proof is similar to that of the accuracy guarantee for the Laplace mechanism, simply quantifying tails on the Gaussian distribution. Note that, in high-dimensions, the Laplace mechanism introduces noise scaled by $\frac{d}{n\varepsilon}$ to each dimension, providing an ε-DP estimate of f with an ℓ_2 error scaling as $O(\frac{d^{3/2}}{n\varepsilon})$. In contrast, the Gaussian mechanism introduces noise with a scale of $O(\sqrt{\frac{d \log(1/\delta)}{n\varepsilon}})$ per dimension, resulting in an (ε, δ)-DP estimate of f with ℓ_2 error approximately $O(\frac{d}{n\varepsilon})$. Thus the Gaussian mechanism shaves of a factor of $O(\sqrt{d})$ from the noise, improving accuracy significantly for large d at a slight cost to the privacy guarantee, positing it as a potentially more effective approach for multi-variate estimations.

1.6 Beyond Statistical Queries: Differentially Private Selection

Numerical queries form an important class of computations over which privacy can be enforced. However, in many natural situations, *the goal may be to output an object selected according to certain criteria among other objects, rather than just a numerical value.* Consider the following example, adapted from [DR14]. Suppose that a retailer is selling an amount of items for which there are 3 potential buyers A, B, and C. Each buyer has a maximum price they are willing to pay for the item, known as their *valuation.* The buyers wish to keep their valuations private, to avoid disclosing sensitive information about their purchasing strategies or financial standing. *Hence the task of the retailer is to set a sale price to maximize their total revenue without revealing the valuations of the buyers in the process.*

Assume that the valuations of buyers A, B and C are, respectively \$1.00, \$1.01, and \$3.01. Consider the possible pricing options:

- **Price at \$1.00**: All three buyers are willing to purchase at this price, thus the total revenue is \$1.00 × 3 buyers = **\$3.00**.
- **Price at \$1.01**: Buyers B and C are willing to purchase, thus the total revenue is \$1.01 × 2 buyers = **\$2.02**.
- **Price at \$3.01**: Only buyer C is willing to purchase, thus the total revenue is \$3.01 × 1 buyer = **\$3.01**.

To maximize revenue, the retailer should set the price at \$3.01. However, since the buyers' valuations are private, the seller cannot directly know the optimal price. The seller needs to select a price in a privacy-preserving manner. One naive approach might be for the seller to add random noise to the buyers' valuations to preserve their privacy. Suppose the seller adds noise to buyer C's valuation, and it becomes, say, \$3.02. Based on this noisy valuation, the seller decides to set the price at \$3.02 apiece. However, this approach leads to a problem: at a price of \$3.02, none of the buyers are willing to purchase the item, since their true valuations are all below this price. Consequently, the total revenue would be **\$0**, which is worse than any of the previous pricing options. This illustrates that simply adding noise to the valuations is not suitable for such a setting. Adding noise to the valuations can lead to suboptimal pricing decisions. Small changes in the valuations (due to noise) can result in significant differences in the optimal price, which may drastically reduce the seller's revenue or eliminate it altogether. This is particularly problematic when the output is an object selection (the optimal price) rather than a simple numerical query.

1.6.1 The Exponential Mechanism

To be able to perform selection privately while also preserving the quality of the selection made, McSherry and Talwar defined the exponential mechanism [MT07]. Given a set of objects $\mathcal{H}$, a dataset $D \in \mathcal{D}$, and a score function $s : \mathcal{D} \times \mathcal{H} \to \mathbb{R}$, the exponential mechanism chooses an object $h \in \mathcal{H}$ that maximizes the score function in a differentially private manner.

Definition 1.14 (Exponential Mechanism). *The exponential mechanism, denoted by $\mathcal{M}_{exp}$, takes as input a dataset $D \in \mathcal{D}$, a set of objects $\mathcal{H}$, and a score function $s : \mathcal{D} \times \mathcal{H} \to \mathbb{R}$ and outputs $h \in \mathcal{H}$ with probability proportional to $\exp\left(\frac{\varepsilon s(D,h)}{2\Delta s}\right)$, where $\Delta s \triangleq \max_{h \in \mathcal{H}} \max_{D \sim D'} |s(D,h) - s(D',h)|$.*

In this pricing example, the seller defines a utility function $u(D,p)$ that calculates the total revenue generated by setting a price p, given the buyers' valuations in the dataset D. The exponential mechanism then selects a price p with probability *proportional* – the actual probability needs to be renormalized to sum to 1 – to:

$$\exp\left(\frac{\varepsilon \cdot u(D,p)}{2\Delta u}\right),$$

where ε is the privacy parameter controlling the level of privacy, and Δu is the global sensitivity of the utility function—that is, the maximum change in $u(D,p)$ when a single individual's valuation in D is modified. The seller thus probabilistically chooses a price that is likely to yield high revenue. The probability of selecting a particular price is influenced by the total revenue it generates, but is also smoothed to prevent any single buyer's data from having too much impact on the computation. This smoothing out is controlled by ε. When $\varepsilon \to 0$, all prices become equally likely independently of the buyers' valuations D and the revenue $u(D,p)$, leading to perfect privacy. As ε increases, the mechanism introduces less smoothing out and gives more importance to the revenue $u(D,p)$, providing more utility—by putting more mass on higher revenues—but less privacy. This mechanism thus allows the seller to achieve a balance between maximizing revenue and preserving the privacy of the buyers. The exponential mechanism provides Differential Privacy.

Theorem 1.15. *The exponential mechanism, $\mathcal{M}_{exp}$, achieves $(\varepsilon,0)$-Differential Privacy.*

Proof. The proof assumes that $\mathcal{H}$ is a finite set. For any two neighbouring datasets $D \sim D'$ and some outcome $h \in \mathcal{H}$,

$$\begin{aligned}
\frac{Pr[\mathcal{M}_{\exp}(D) = h]}{Pr[\mathcal{M}_{\exp}(D') = h]} &= \frac{\left(\frac{\exp(\varepsilon s(D,h)/2\Delta_s)}{\sum_{h'\in\mathcal{H}}\exp(\varepsilon s(D,h')/2\Delta_s)}\right)}{\left(\frac{\exp(\varepsilon s(D',h)/2\Delta_s)}{\sum_{h'\in\mathcal{H}}\exp(\varepsilon s(D',h')/2\Delta_s)}\right)} \\
&= \exp\left(\frac{\varepsilon(s(D,h) - s(D',h))}{2\Delta s}\right)\frac{\sum_{h'\in\mathcal{H}}\exp\left(\varepsilon s(D',h')/2\Delta_s\right)}{\sum_{h'\in\mathcal{H}}\exp\left(\varepsilon s(D,h')/2\Delta_s\right)} \\
&\le \exp\left(\frac{\varepsilon}{2}\right)\exp\left(\frac{\varepsilon}{2}\right)\frac{\sum_{h'\in\mathcal{H}}\exp\left(\varepsilon s(D,h')/2\Delta_s\right)}{\sum_{h'\in\mathcal{H}}\exp\left(\varepsilon s(D,h')/2\Delta_s\right)} \\
&= \exp(\varepsilon).
\end{aligned}$$

The inequality follows due to the definition of Δs. □

Accuracy Guarantee

For the exponential mechanism, accuracy is not measured in terms of how close the mechanism is to the optimal hypothesis h. Rather, the objective is to guarantee that, with high probability, the output by the mechanism has a high score, as close as possible to optimality.

Theorem 1.16. *Let us fix a database D, and let* $\mathcal{H}_{OPT} = \{h^* \in \mathcal{H} \text{ s.t. } s(D,h) = \max_h s(D,h)\}$ *be the set of elements in* $\mathcal{H}$ *that achieve the maximum possible utility score. Then, the exponential mechanism guarantees*

$$Pr\left[s(D, \mathcal{M}_{exp}(D)) \geq OPT - \frac{2\Delta s}{\varepsilon}(\ln(|\mathcal{H}|/\beta))\right] \geq 1 - \beta.$$

where $OPT = \max_h s(D,h)$.

Proof. Take any $c \in \mathbb{R}$. It follows that

$$\begin{aligned} Pr\left[s(D, \mathcal{M}_{\text{exp}}(D) \leq c\right] &= \frac{\sum_{h:\ s(D,h)\leq c} \exp\left(\varepsilon s(D,h)/2\Delta s\right)}{\sum_{r\in\mathcal{H}} \exp(\varepsilon s(D,h)/2\Delta s)} \\ &\leq \frac{\sum_{r:\ s(D,h)\leq c} \exp\left(\varepsilon c/2\Delta s\right)}{\sum_{r\in\mathcal{H}_{\text{OPT}}} \exp(\varepsilon \text{OPT}/2\Delta s)} \\ &\leq \frac{|\mathcal{H}| \exp(\varepsilon c/2\Delta s)}{|\mathcal{H}_{\text{OPT}}| \exp(\varepsilon \text{OPT}/2\Delta s)} \\ &= \frac{|\mathcal{H}|}{|\mathcal{H}_{\text{OPT}}|} \exp\left(\frac{\varepsilon(c - \text{OPT})}{2\Delta s}\right) \\ &\leq |\mathcal{H}| \exp\left(\frac{\varepsilon(c - \text{OPT})}{2\Delta s}\right). \end{aligned}$$

The result follows by plugging in

$$c \triangleq \text{OPT} - \frac{2\Delta s}{\varepsilon} \ln\left(|\mathcal{H}|/\delta\right).$$

□

Practically, this means that, although the mechanism introduces randomness to protect individual privacy (e.g., the buyers' valuations in our example), it still ensures that the selected output (the price) will yield a utility (the revenue) that is close to the best possible. E.g., in our example, the maximum possible revenue was \$3.01 at price \$3.01). Moreover, the utility loss due to privacy is limited and can be controlled by adjusting the privacy parameters.

1.7 Randomized Response, Revisited

Before concluding this chapter, it is useful to revisit the concept of randomized response. Consider Figure 1.4: its left side presents a pixelated version of the Mona Lisa, where each pixel is represented by either an 'M' or a '.' character. By implementing a random process that flips each pixel with a probability of 0.25,

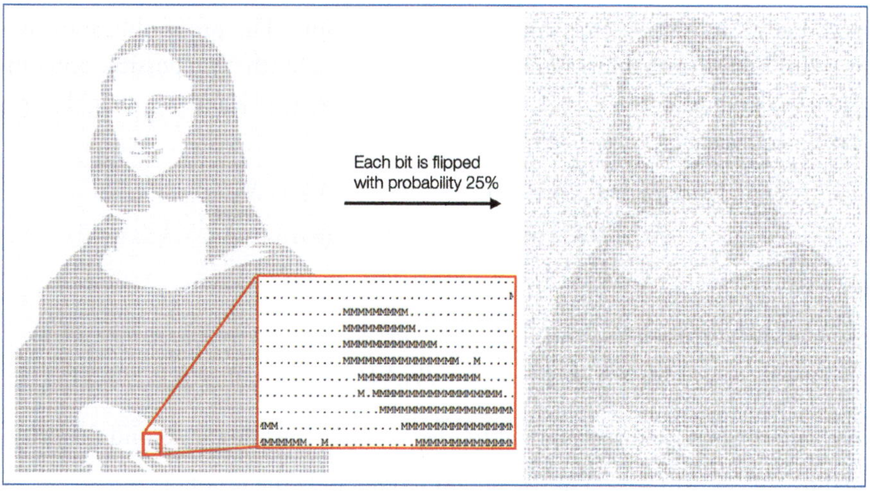

Figure 1.4. A metaphor for private data analysis: Perturbing each bit of the image on the left by flipping it with a random probability of 25% prevents inferring with high probability whether each single bit was originally an "M" or a ".", while still allowing to observe conclusions from the big picture. Figure adapted from slides presentation of Ulfar Erlingsson [Nam17].

the figure on the right emerges as locally perturbed yet retains the overall image, enabling recognition of the iconic Mona Lisa painting. This metaphor demonstrates that, although plausible deniability is afforded for the original value of each pixel, the outcomes of data analysis can still be preserved with considerable accuracy.

Revisiting Randomized Response

Figure 1.4 happens to be an instance of using randomized response to obscure individual responses while providing accurate summary statistics. Indeed, there is an equivalent formulation of randomized response that satisfies ε-DP in a stronger setting called *local Differential Privacy*, where instead of having a trusted curator that perturbs raw data to provide Differential Privacy, each data contributor perturbs its own data prior to its release. The topic of local DP is the subject of study of Chapter 2. Given $\varepsilon > 0$, for every private bit X, the mechanism is defined as follows:

$$\mathcal{M}(X) = \begin{cases} X, \text{ with probability} = \frac{\exp(\varepsilon)}{1+\exp(\varepsilon)}; \\ 1 - X, \text{ with probability} = \frac{1}{1+\exp(\varepsilon)}. \end{cases}$$

Privacy Guarantees

Randomized response has the following Differential Privacy guarantees.

Theorem 1.17. *Randomized Response is* $(\varepsilon, 0)$*-differentially private.*

Proof. Let $p = \frac{\exp(\varepsilon)}{1+\exp(\varepsilon)}$ for simplicity of exposition. The proof obligation is to upper bound the probability of ratios of probabilities for the two possible outcomes $\mathcal{M}(X) = X$ and $\mathcal{M}(X) = 1 - X$ for any $X \in \{0, 1\}$ and the neighbouring $X' = 1 - X$, i.e.,

$$\frac{Pr[\mathcal{M}(X) = X]}{Pr[\mathcal{M}(X') = X]} = \frac{Pr[\mathcal{M}(X) = X]}{Pr[\mathcal{M}(1 - X) = X]},$$

and

$$\frac{Pr[\mathcal{M}(X) = 1 - X]}{Pr[\mathcal{M}(X') = 1 - X]} = \frac{Pr[\mathcal{M}(X) = 1 - X]}{Pr[\mathcal{M}(1 - X) = 1 - X]}.$$

Note that the first quantity is equal to $\frac{p}{1-p} = \exp(\varepsilon)$, while the second quantity is equal to $\frac{1-p}{p} = \exp(-\varepsilon)$. This is enough to conclude the proof. □

Accuracy of Randomized Response

To provide the accuracy guarantee of Randomized Response, consider a collection of n data points $X_1, \ldots, X_n$. The goal is to compute the average of these data points, given by $\mu \triangleq \frac{1}{N}\sum_{i=1}^{n} X_i$. Consider the following simple linear estimator that corrects for the bias introduced by flipping X to the wrong answer, $1 - X$, with probability $p \triangleq \frac{\exp(\varepsilon)}{1+\exp(\varepsilon)}$:

$$\hat{X} = \frac{1}{(2p-1)N}\left(\sum_{i=1}^{n} \mathcal{M}(X_i) + p - 1\right).$$

Lemma 1.18. *$\hat{X}$ is an unbiased estimator of $\mu = \frac{1}{n}\sum_{i=1}^{n} X_i$. Further, with probability at least $1 - \beta$,*

$$\left|\hat{X} - \mu\right| \leq \frac{\sqrt{1/\beta}}{2(2p-1)\sqrt{n}}.$$

Before providing the proof of this accuracy bound, consider what Differential Privacy promises. Remember that $p \triangleq \frac{\exp(\varepsilon)}{1+\exp(\varepsilon)}$. Plugging this in the bound above,

$$\left|\hat{X} - \mu\right| = O\left(\frac{(1 + e^{\varepsilon})}{2\,(e^{\varepsilon} - 1)\,\sqrt{n}}\right).$$

As $\varepsilon \to 0$, the $1 + \exp(\varepsilon)$ term goes to 1; the $1 - \exp(\varepsilon)$ term can be approximated by ε given a first-order Taylor expansion. Hence, it follows that, as ε is small,

$$\left|\hat{X} - \mu\right| = O\left(\frac{1}{\varepsilon\sqrt{n}}\right).$$

In particular, given a small ε, to obtain an accuracy of α, requires that $n \sim \frac{1}{\varepsilon^2\alpha^2}$ samples.

Proof. Note that

$$\begin{aligned}\mathbb{E}[\mathcal{M}(X)] &= Pr[\mathcal{M}(X) = X] \cdot X + Pr[\mathcal{M}(X) = 1 - X] \cdot (1 - X) \\ &= pX + (1-p)(1-X) \\ &= (2p-1)X + (1-p).\end{aligned}$$

Therefore,

$$\mathbb{E}[\mathcal{M}(X)] = (2p-1)\mu + (1-p),$$

immediately implying unbiasedness of $\hat{X}$. Now note that the variance of estimator $\hat{X}$ is given by

$$\text{Var}\left[\hat{X}\right] = \frac{1}{(2p-1)^2N^2}\sum_{i=1}^{N}\text{Var}\left[\mathcal{M}(X_i)\right] \leq \sum_{i=1}^{N}\frac{1}{4(2p-1)^2N^2} = \frac{1}{4(2p-1)^2N},$$

where the first equality follows from the fact that $\text{Var}[cX] = c^2\text{Var}[X]$ and $\text{Var}[X + c] = \text{Var}[X]$ for a constant c, and the inequality follows from the fact that $\mathcal{M}(X)$ is a Bernoulli random variable and has variance at most $1/4$. Using Chebyshev's inequality with $k = \frac{1}{\sqrt{\beta}}$, it follows that

$$Pr\left[\left|\hat{X} - \mu\right| \geq \frac{\sqrt{1/\beta}}{2(1-2p)\sqrt{n}}\right] \leq \beta.$$

□

The above bound is an example of privacy-accuracy trade-off. To obtain an accuracy level of α (i.e., the estimator does not mis-estimate μ by more than α) with high probability $1 - \beta$, one needs to pick the value of p such that

$$\frac{\sqrt{1/\beta}}{2(1-2p)\sqrt{n}} \leq \alpha.$$

This immediately gives the desired value of ε, given us a trade-off between the accuracy level α and the privacy level ε. Here, decreasing ε towards 0 (or equivalently decreasing p towards $1/2$) yields a worse accuracy guarantee, as the denominator decreases and eventually goes to 0. This goes in the expected direction: the more privacy is required, the more the accuracy suffers.

1.8 Concluding Remarks

This chapter discussed foundational concepts and mechanisms that are the bedrock of Differential Privacy. Since its conceptual introduction, Differential Privacy has seen considerable evolution, both in theoretical development and practical applications. Researchers have refined the mathematical guarantees, offering tighter bounds on privacy leakage and more effective mechanisms for trading utility with privacy. Practically, Differential Privacy has been applied across diverse sectors, from healthcare to social science, to engineering systems, as reviewed in Part III. These applications demonstrate the flexibility and robustness of Differential Privacy in safeguarding personal information while maintaining data utility. The implications of adopting Differential Privacy extends beyond the technical realm, influencing regulatory policies around data privacy [Exe23], as also discussed in Part V of this book. As organizations increasingly rely on data-driven decision-making, the implementation of DP can help build trust with stakeholders by demonstrating a commitment to privacy-preserving practices. This trust is crucial for compliance with international data protection regulations and for fostering a more privacy-conscious data ecosystem. Furthermore, the principles of Differential Privacy can guide ethical considerations in data usage, promoting a balance between innovation and individual rights to privacy.

Acknowledgements

This work was partially supported by NSF grants SaTC-2345483, CAREER RI-2401285, CAREER HCC-2336236, and by a Google Scholar Research Award. Its view and conclusions are those of the authors only.

References

[BW18] B. Balle and Y.-X. Wang. "Improving the Gaussian Mechanism for Differential Privacy: Analytical Calibration and Optimal Denoising". In: International Conference on Machine Learning. 2018. URL: https://api.semanticscholar.org/CorpusID:21713075 (cit. on pp. 30, 31).

[BZH06] M. Barbaro, T. Zeller, and S. Hansell. "A face is exposed for AOL searcher no. 4417749". In: New York Times 9.2008 (2006), p. 8 (cit. on p. 8).

[Car+21] N. Carlini, F. Tramer, E. Wallace, M. Jagielski, A. Herbert-Voss, K. Lee, A. Roberts, T. Brown, D. Song, U. Erlingsson, et al. "Extracting training data from large language models". In: 30th USENIX Security Symposium (USENIX Security 21). 2021, pp. 2633–2650 (cit. on p. 12).

[CDMS21] A. Cohen, M. Duchin, J. Matthews, and B. Suwal. "Census TopDown: The Impacts of Differential Privacy on Redistricting". In: Proceedings of the 2nd Symposium on Foundations of Responsible Computing. Ed. by K. Ligett and S. Gupta. FORC '21. 2021, 5:1–22 (cit. on p. 29).

[Cen96] Centers for Medicare & Medicaid Services. The Health Insurance Portability and Accountability Act of 1996 (HIPAA). Online at http://www.cms.hhs.gov/hipaa/. 1996 (cit. on p. 4).

[CNSU20a] A. Cohen, A. Nikolov, Z. Schutzman, and J. Ullman. Reconstruction Attacks in Practice. DifferentialPrivacy.org. https://differentialprivacy.org/diffix-attack/. Oct. 2020 (cit. on p. 12).

[CNSU20b] A. Cohen, A. Nikolov, Z. Schutzman, and J. Ullman. The Theory of Reconstruction Attacks. DifferentialPrivacy.org. https://differentialprivacy.org/reconstruction-theory/. Oct. 2020 (cit. on p. 12).

[Des17] D. Desfontaines. k-anonymity, the parent of all privacy definitions. https://desfontain.es/blog/k-anonymity.html. Ted is writing things (personal blog). Aug. 2017 (cit. on p. 9).

[DHVB13] Y.-A. De Montjoye, C. A. Hidalgo, M. Verleysen, and V. D. Blondel. "Unique in the crowd: The privacy bounds of human mobility". In: Scientific reports 3.1 (2013), pp. 1–5 (cit. on p. 8).

[DMNS06] C. Dwork, F. McSherry, K. Nissim, and A. Smith. "Calibrating noise to sensitivity in private data analysis". In: Theory of cryptography conference. Springer. 2006, pp. 265–284 (cit. on pp. 12, 17, 21, 25).

[DN03] I. Dinur and K. Nissim. "Revealing information while preserving privacy". In: Proceedings of the twenty-second ACM SIGMOD-SIGACT-SIGART symposium on Principles of database systems. 2003, pp. 202–210 (cit. on pp. 11, 12).

[Dob21] L. Dobberstein. Korean app-maker Scatter Lab fined for using private data to create homophobic and lewd chatbot. 2021. URL: https://www.theregister.com/2021/04/29/scatter_lab_fined_for_lewd_chatbot/ (cit. on p. 12).

[DR14] C. Dwork and A. Roth. "The Algorithmic Foundations of Differential Privacy". In: Found. Trends Theor. Comput. Sci. 9 (2014), pp. 211–407. URL: https://api.semanticscholar.org/CorpusID:207178262 (cit. on pp. 23, 24, 30, 31).

[Dwo+06] C. Dwork, K. Kenthapadi, F. McSherry, I. Mironov, and M. Naor. "Our Data, Ourselves: Privacy Via Distributed Noise Generation". In: Advances in Cryptology - EUROCRYPT. Vol. 4004. Lecture Notes in Computer Science. Springer, 2006, pp. 486–503. URL: https://doi.org/10.1007/11761679%5C_29 (cit. on p. 4).

[Exe23] Executive Office of the President. Safe, Secure, and Trustworthy Development and Use of Artificial Intelligence. Federal Register. Available online: https://www.federalregister.gov/documents/2023/11/01/2023-24283/safe-secure-and-trustworthy-development-and-use-of-artificial-intelligence. Nov. 2023 (cit. on p. 38).

[GRS12] A. Ghosh, T. Roughgarden, and M. Sundararajan. "Universally Utility-Maximizing Privacy Mechanisms". In: SIAM Journal on Computing 41.6 (2012), pp. 1673–1693 (cit. on p. 29).

[Hom+08] N. Homer, S. Szelinger, M. Redman, D. Duggan, W. Tembe, J. Muehling, J. V. Pearson, D. A. Stephan, S. F. Nelson, and D. W. Craig. "Resolving individuals contributing trace amounts of DNA to highly complex mixtures using high-density SNP genotyping microarrays". In: PLoS genetics 4.8 (2008), e1000167 (cit. on p. 8).

[Hou23] T. W. House. Blueprint for an AI Bill of Rights. Nov. 2023. URL: https://www.whitehouse.gov/ostp/ai-bill-of-rights/ (cit. on p. 4).

[Kam20] G. Kamath. Approximate Differential Privacy. CS 860: Algorithms for Private Data Analysis - Fall 2020 Lecture Notes. Available online at: http://www.gautamkamath.com/courses/CS860-fa2022-files/lec5.pdf. 2020 (cit. on p. 30).

[KS12] V. Karwa and A. B. Slavković. "Differentially Private Graphical Degree Sequences and Synthetic Graphs". In: Privacy in Statistical Databases. Ed. by J. Domingo-Ferrer and I. Tinnirello. Vol. 7556. Lecture Notes in Computer Science. Springer, 2012, pp. 273–285 (cit. on p. 29).

[Leg18] C. S. Legislature. California Consumer Privacy Act (CCPA) — oag.ca.gov. Online at https://oag.ca.gov/privacy/ccpa. 2018 (cit. on p. 4).

[LSTS20] T. Li, A. K. Sahu, A. Talwalkar, and V. Smith. "Federated learning: Challenges, methods, and future directions". In: IEEE signal processing magazine 37.3 (2020), pp. 50–60 (cit. on p. 12).

[MT07] F. McSherry and K. Talwar. "Mechanism Design via Differential Privacy". In: 48th Annual IEEE Symposium on Foundations of Computer Science (FOCS'07). 2007, pp. 94–103 (cit. on p. 32).

[Nam17] A. Name. RAPPOR Talk for DIMACS Workshop, April 2017. Slide presentation at the DIMACS Workshop on Big Data Integration. Available online at: http://archive.dimacs.rutgers.edu/Workshops/BigDataHub/Slides/RAPPOR-talk-for-DIMACS-workshop-April-2017.pdf. DIMACS, Apr. 2017. URL: http://archive.dimacs.rutgers.edu/Workshops/BigDataHub/Slides/RAPPOR-talk-for-DIMACS-workshop-April-2017.pdf (cit. on p. 35).

[NS06] A. Narayanan and V. Shmatikov. "How To Break Anonymity of the Netflix Prize Dataset". In: ArXiv abs/cs/0610105 (2006). URL: https://api.semanticscholar.org/CorpusID:1086763 (cit. on p. 8).

[NS08] A. Narayanan and V. Shmatikov. "Robust de-anonymization of large sparse datasets". In: 2008 IEEE Symposium on Security and Privacy (sp 2008). IEEE. 2008, pp. 111–125 (cit. on p. 10).

[PE16] E. Parliament and C. of the European Union. Regulation (EU) 2016/679 of the European Parliament and of the Council of 27 April 2016 on the protection of natural persons with regard to the processing of personal data and on the free movement of such data, and repealing Directive 95/46/EC (General Data Protection Regulation) (Text with EEA relevance). May 2016 (cit. on p. 4).

[SS98] P. Samarati and L. Sweeney. "Protecting Privacy When Disclosing Information: k-Anonymity and Its Enforcement through Generalization and Suppression". In: Proceedings of the IEEE Symposium on Research in Security and Privacy. 1998 (cit. on p. 8).

[Swe00] L. Sweeney. "Simple Demographics Often Identify People Uniquely". Working paper. 2000. URL: http://dataprivacylab.org/projects/identifiability/ (cit. on pp. 7, 9).

[Swe02] L. Sweeney. "k-anonymity: a model for protecting privacy". In: Int. J. Uncertain. Fuzziness Knowl.-Based Syst. 10.5 (Oct. 2002), pp. 557–570. ISSN: 0218-4885. URL: https://doi.org/10.1142/S0218488502001648 (cit. on pp. 8, 9).

[Uni98] United States Census Bureau. Title 13 of the United States Code: Census. https://www.census.gov/about/history/bureau-history/agency-history-timeline/title-13.html. Accessed: 2024-04-27. 1998 (cit. on p. 4).

[War65] S. L. Warner. "Randomized Response: A Survey Technique for Eliminating Evasive Answer Bias". In: Journal of the American Statistical Association 60.309 (1965), pp. 63–69. ISSN: 01621459. URL: http://www.jstor.org/stable/2283137 (cit. on p. 18).

[Wik24a] Wikipedia. 2017 Equifax data breach — Wikipedia, The Free Encyclopedia. Online at http://en.wikipedia.org/w/index.php?title=2017-Equifax-data-breach&oldid=1241882235. 2024 (cit. on p. 3).

[Wik24b] Wikipedia. Facebook–Cambridge Analytica data scandal — Wikipedia, The Free Encyclopedia. Online at https://en.wikipedia.org/wiki/FacebookâŁ"Cambridge_Analytica_data_scandal#Governmental_actions. 2024 (cit. on p. 3).

[ZLH19] L. Zhu, Z. Liu, and S. Han. "Deep leakage from gradients". In: Advances in neural information processing systems 32 (2019) (cit. on p. 12).

DOI: 10.1561/9781638284772.ch2

Chapter 2

Local Differential Privacy for Privacy-preserving Machine Learning

By Graham Cormode

2.1 Introduction

As discussed in the previous chapter, Differential Privacy (DP) provides a widely-accepted model of privacy based on introducing carefully calibrated random noise to information revealed about private data. In the standard presentation, the DP model assumes the existence of a trusted aggregator: an entity who holds a collection of information about a population of individuals, and applies differentially private mechanisms to information computed from this data collection. This allows accurate statistics and models to be derived, but comes at a cost: we must be satisfied that we can indeed trust this aggregator to handle the collected data responsibly. In practical applications, this data aggregator is likely to be a powerful entity, such as an internet service provider, technology company, or government, who may collect the private information of millions of individuals. Hence the potential for misuse may be of some concern, even if we have no prior reason to suspect the motives of the aggregator.

In response to this, a number of other models of privacy have been considered which aim to reduce or eliminate the trust placed on the central entity. These can include decentralization – dividing the data among multiple aggregators, so no single one sees the entire information – or cryptographic techniques – which restrict the view of the aggregator of the raw data. In this chapter, we survey an approach known as Local Differential Privacy, or LDP. The LDP approach directly provides a differential privacy guarantee on the results of the computation, and entirely eliminates the need for a trusted aggregator to hold the private data. However, the LDP approach comes at some cost: more computational work is needed, and the results achieve a weaker tradeoff between accuracy and privacy than in the traditional, "centralized" differential privacy model.

The essence of LDP is that each user who holds some private data is now an active participant in the data release process. Instead of passively sending their data to the aggregator and retiring, each user now runs a randomized procedure on their input. The requirement is that the distribution of the message(s) sent by each user individually should satisfy the DP guarantee. Formally, let x_i and x_i' be two possible inputs that user i might hold, let $\mathcal{R}$ denote the (randomized) protocol that user i will apply to generate their messages, and let ε be the desired privacy parameter. We require that for all possible transcripts T of user i's communication, we should have

$$\frac{\mathbf{Pr}[\mathcal{R}(x_i) = T]}{\mathbf{Pr}[\mathcal{R}(x_i') = T]} \leq \exp(\varepsilon) \tag{2.1}$$

Note that this definition is symmetrical in the roles of x_i and x_i'. This is exactly the standard (pure) differential privacy definition (see Section 1.4.1 of Chapter 1), applied to the inputs of a single user i.

On first glance, attempting to obtain useful results under this restrictive definition may seem doomed to failure. The noise introduced in differentially private mechanisms is calibrated so as to effectively "mask out" the contribution of any single user. Specifically, we usually expect the magnitude of any (numeric) noise added to a function of users' data to be approximately equivalent (in expectation) to the weight of any individual user's data. So we would expect that applying this to the contribution of just a single user would entirely hide the information they are contributing, and prevent any subsequent use of it. Indeed, the first part of this intuition is true: the noisy response of a user should indeed mask out their contribution, and so make it impractical to learn anything about their individual information. However, if we aggregate the reports over a large enough population of users, we can still draw accurate conclusions about the overall population behavior: the signal emerges from the noise. The explanation for this apparent paradox is that since each user independently chooses how to add noise, the noise tends to cancel out as we combine all the user reports, leaving the true answer masked by a smaller magnitude of total noise.

2.1.1 A First LDP Protocol

We illustrate this phenomenon with a simple example drawing on standard DP mechanisms from the centralized case. Suppose we have a population of $N = 1$ million users, who each hold a secret binary value (0 or 1), which encodes some private attribute – say, their opinion on a contentious issue (pro or anti), or some other feature. We would like to learn what is the population-level value of this statistic, i.e., what percentage of our population hold a '1' value. The standard centralized DP approach is to add noise sampled from a Laplace distribution with parameter $1/\varepsilon$. The variance of this distribution is then $2/\varepsilon^2$, and so the expected magnitude of this noise is around $1/\varepsilon$.

This approach can be adapted to the local setting by having each user add this quantity of noise independently to their input. The resulting distribution would have variance $2N/\varepsilon^2$, and hence absolute magnitude proportional to $\sqrt{N}/\varepsilon$. Concretely, consider our case with $N = 1$ million, and $\varepsilon = 1$. Then the local case allows us to estimate the population *fraction* with additive error around 0.001. This is certainly good enough to easily distinguish large values from small, and comparable to the error due to sampling which people to ask. However, the corresponding error in the centralized case is vastly smaller — closer to 10^{-6} in this case.

This small example serves to show that we can obtain sufficient accuracy in the local model of differential privacy, albeit weaker than in the centralized case. To get good results for more complex analysis tasks requires a large population of users participating (honestly) in the protocol, and carefully tuned protocols to maximize the accuracy obtained.

The naive approach of taken an existing method from the centralized setting does not always work. Consider for example trying to produce a clustering of some input data points. If each user holds a single point (representing their data), then a central DP algorithm is unlikely to produce a very meaningful output for them. Moreover, it is unclear how to combine the results if each user produces a noisy clustering of their single point. Instead, for this and other problems, we would seek novel methods better suited to the local model.

The key properties that we aim to understand for different problems are the tradeoff between accuracy and privacy, as a function of the privacy parameter ε, and the number of participating users, N. Secondarily, we are also concerned about the other computational costs – the time and space required by users to run their part of the protocol, and the time and space needed by the aggregator to interpret all their messages. Lastly, we may also seek to minimize the size of the messages sent by the users, and the number of rounds of interaction between users and the aggregator.

2.1.2 A Brief History of LDP

As will be discussed in subsequent sections, the antecedents of Local Differential Privacy date back at least fifty years, to the work on Randomized Response in survey design [War65]. More recently, a notion equivalent to local different privacy was introduced by Evfimievski, Gehrke and Srikant [EGS03], around the same time that the foundations of differential privacy were being laid [DN03]. The connection between randomized response and differential privacy has been observed in texts on the differential privacy model [DR14]. However, the current interest in LDP can be traced to recent developments in theory and practice. Duchi, Jordan and Wainwright coined the label of "local differential privacy", and studied problems of statistical inference under this model [DJW13]. This led to much subsequent interest in the theoretical underpinnings of LDP and its variants. Around the same time, Google published a paper on its RAPPOR system, which is based on LDP [EPK14], used to collect browsing statistics privately. Papers on deployments by Apple [Tea17], Microsoft [DKY17] and Snap [Pih+18] on related problems demonstrated a strong interest in LDP as a practical model for private data collection.

Overview of the Chapter

Following the interest in Local Differential Privacy from both theory and practice, in this chapter we survey a sampling of the developments in LDP. Since its formal introduction less than a decade ago (at time of writing), there have been many hundreds of papers published on the topic, and this chapter provides a very partial view of this topic. We begin by introducing the foundational notion of Randomized Response in Section 2.2, for revealing information about a binary choice. In Section 2.3, we show how randomized response has been extended and enhanced to provide the notion of a "Frequency Oracle", which gathers information about the distribution of values held by a collection of users. The Frequency Oracle is the basis for many of the applications of LDP. Some of the basic statistical collection tasks, such as finding frequent items, and capturing the cumulative distribution, are described in Section 2.4. We move on to more advanced data analysis and modelling tasks in Section 2.5. Finally, we conclude by reflecting on the limitations on LDP protocols, and describe some alternate related models which attempt to remedy these deficiencies in Section 2.6.

2.2 Randomized Response

In this section, we return to the problem stated in the introduction of this chapter, to estimate the proportion of individuals whose binary input is a 1 value. We will describe a simple approach that provides an accurate answer, and show its analysis in some detail. This approach, known as Randomized Response, is at the heart of many LDP algorithms that we will discuss subsequently (albeit in less detail).

The approach from Section 2.1.1, of adding noise drawn from a Laplace distribution, certainly works, but has some disadvantages. It produces potentially large real numerical values. Since the inputs are binary, it is natural to ask whether we can restrict the messages from each user to the same domain.

If we do so, then we can immediately derive the description of a protocol. For a user with input value $b \in \{0, 1\}$, their only option is to report either b truthfully, or lie, and report $1 - b$. Suppose we set the probability of truthtelling to be p, and hence the probability of lying is $1 - p$. We can assume without loss of generality that $p > \frac{1}{2} > 1 - p$. To ensure that the (local) differential privacy property (2.1) holds, we require that the probability of seeing the same output in the two cases that $b = 0$ and $b = 1$ satisfies

$$\frac{p}{1-p} \leq \exp(\varepsilon).$$

That is, the ratio between (correctly) observing a 1 on input 1, and (erroneously) seeing a 1 on input 0, should not exceed the bound of $\exp(\varepsilon)$. For utility, we would like p to be as large as possible, which means setting $\frac{p}{1-p} = \exp(\varepsilon)$. Rearranging, we obtain that $p = \frac{\exp(\varepsilon)}{1+\exp(\varepsilon)}$.

Suppose we apply this protocol over a large population where a ϕ fraction of users have input 1, and the rest have input 0. Then, for each user, the expected observed value o is given by

$$\mathsf{E}[o] = p\phi + (1 - p)(1 - \phi).$$

From this, we can form an unbiased estimate for the (unknown) parameter ϕ by rearranging: we write

$$\hat{\phi} = \frac{o - (1 - p)}{2p - 1}.$$

We can observe that the observed value o is equal to the input x with probability p, otherwise they are different. In the former case, the error of $\hat{\phi}$ is $\frac{p-1}{2p-1}$, and in the latter it is $\frac{p}{2p-1}$. Hence, we can also compute the variance of this (unbiased) estimator, as

$$\mathsf{Var}[\hat{\phi}] = \mathsf{E}[(\phi - \hat{\phi})^2] = \frac{p(p-1)^2 + (1-p)p^2}{(2p-1)^2} = \frac{p(1-p)}{(2p-1)^2}.$$

Using our setting of $p = \exp(\varepsilon)/(1 + \exp(\varepsilon))$, we obtain

$$\mathsf{Var}[\hat{\phi}] = \frac{\exp(\varepsilon)}{1 + \exp(\varepsilon)} \cdot \frac{1}{1 + \exp(\varepsilon)} \frac{(1 + \exp(\varepsilon))^2}{(\exp(\varepsilon) - 1)^2} = \frac{\exp(\varepsilon)}{(\exp(\varepsilon) - 1)^2}.$$

We can approximate this quantity when ε is small, in which case $\exp(\varepsilon) \approx 1 + \varepsilon$ and so $\mathsf{Var}[\hat{\phi}] \approx \frac{1}{\varepsilon^2}$.

Equipped with this understanding, we can observe that the average of N unbiased estimates for a population of N users will have a variance proportional to N/ε^2, and so an expected absolute error proportional to $\sqrt{N}/\varepsilon$. This is comparable in scale to the cruder method based on adding Laplace noise, but comes with a tighter understanding of the behavior (variance less by constant factors), and reduced communication costs (the protocol sends noisy bits instead of noisy real values).

The notion of randomized response was first introduced by Warner [War65], as a method of providing plausible deniability for survey respondents answering potentially embarrassing questions. It was subsequently observed to provide differential privacy, and has been used as the foundation for many other protocols achieving local differential privacy.

2.3 Frequency Oracles

The Randomized Response protocol in the previous section allows us to estimate the fraction of population satisfying a certain property. Equivalently, it can be viewed as providing an estimate of the parameter of a binomial distribution, when each user samples from the same global Bernoulli distribution. More generally, we might want to estimate the distribution when each user has one out of d possible categorical values. This problem has been widely studied in the context of local differential privacy, and the techniques developed for this problem have been used in the solution of other problems discussed subsequently.

Across a variety of different approaches, some similarities emerge: each user sends a message noisily encoding information about their input, which can be aggregated to provide an estimate of the number of occurrences of a particular category. That is, if each user i has an input value $x_i \in [d]$, we seek to build an estimate for $f(x) = |\{i : x_i = x\}|$. The estimate of $f(x)$ will be a random variable, whose randomness derives from the random choices of the users in adding noise to their input. We refer to the randomized algorithm that can produce an estimate $\hat{f}(x)$ of $f(x)$ for any $x \in [d]$ as a *frequency oracle*. The aim is to minimize the variance of the estimate, as well as keeping the other computational costs low. In this section, we describe the operation of several different frequency oracles, and summarize their properties.

2.3.1 Direct Encoding

A natural first attempt to build a frequency oracle is to generalize the notion of randomized response to d possible values. As with (binary) randomized response, each user can report their input truthfully with probability p, or pick each of the other possible inputs with probability $(1-p)/(d-1)$ each. Satisfying the LDP property (2.1) leads to choosing $p = \exp(\varepsilon)/(\exp(\varepsilon)+d-1)$. Here, the expression for the variance of this estimator is a little more complex, so we focus on the variance conditioned on reporting an erroneous value, which tends to dominate the cost. We write this variance bound as Var^*, which is given by $\mathsf{Var}^* = \frac{\exp(\varepsilon)+d-2}{(\exp(\varepsilon)-1)^2}$. We can observe that this agrees exactly with the variance for binary randomized response when setting $d = 2$. This analysis of Direct Encoding, and the definition of Var^*, is due to Wang et al. [WBLJ17].

2.3.2 Unary Encoding

An alternative generalization of randomized response is to use a unary encoding of the input, and apply randomized response independently to each bit. That is, we express user i's input as a d-bit "one-hot" encoding, where we set the x_i'th bit to be a 1, and the remaining bits to 0. We then flip each bit independently, and report the noisy result. We can observe that in order to ensure the differential privacy condition (2.1), we only need to consider that pairs of inputs can change in at most two location: between two possible inputs, there is one location where a 1 is replaced by a 0, and one where a 0 is replaced by a 1.

To improve the accuracy, we can observe that we can choose different probabilities for flipping a 0 to a 1 than for flipping a 1 to a 0. We obtain better accuracy if the former is lower and the latter is higher, since there are more 0s to preserve than 1s in this sparse encoding. Optimizing this choice subject to the DP condition leads to picking the probability of flipping a 1 to 0 as $\frac{1}{2}$, while 0s are flipped to 1s with lower probability of $\frac{1}{1+\exp(\varepsilon)}$. This choice minimizes $\mathsf{Var}^* = \frac{4\exp(\varepsilon)}{(\exp(\varepsilon)-1)^2}$. Observe that this improves over direct encoding for larger d, when $d > 3\exp(\varepsilon)+2$, which is typically the case for moderate values of ε and d. However, this comes at the cost of sending d bit messages, which can become excessive for large values of d. The notion of "optimized" unary encoding is due to Wang et al. [WBLJ17].

2.3.3 Hash Encoding

When the domain size d gets moderately large, it can be useful to use hashing techniques to reduce the effective domain size, while still providing enough information to encode the frequency distribution. The idea of hash encoding is for each user to (independently) pick a random hash function, and to use a method such as direct encoding to privately encode the noisy value of the hash of the user's input. Given the noisy encoding and the description of each hash function, an aggregator can build up an accurate picture of the overall population distribution. Analyzing this procedure shows it suffices to use relatively simple hash functions (specifically, hash functions that meet the condition of "pairwise independence"), onto a small domain of possibilities. Optimizing the parameters leads to choosing the range of hash values to be $\exp(\varepsilon) + 1$, so that the true hash value is reported with probability $\frac{1}{2}$, while the other choices are each selected with probability $\frac{1}{1+\exp(\varepsilon)}$ — mirroring the probabilities from unary encoding. Following similar calculations, we find $\mathsf{Var}^* = \frac{4\exp(\varepsilon)}{(\exp(\varepsilon)-1)^2}$. Now the messages sent are just $\log_2(\exp(\varepsilon) + 1)$ bits to encode the hash value, plus $O(\log d)$ to specify the hash function. However, the work required by the aggregator to build estimators from the N messages is quite large – $O(Nd)$. This optimized local hashing approach is also due to Wang et al. [WBLJ17].

2.3.4 Hadamard Encoding

The approach of Hadamard encoding is quite similar to the hashing approach, where the hash function is drawn based on a structured set of possibilities. This allows the decoding of messages to be performed more quickly, while achieving similar accuracy. Specifically, we consider a hash function which maps onto two possible values, -1 and $+1$. The j'th hash function is specified by $h_j(x) = (-1)^{\langle j,x\rangle}$, where $\langle j, x\rangle$ denotes the inner product of the binary representations of j and x. The hash value can be encoded by standard binary randomized response over the two possibilities of -1 and $+1$.

This special set of hash functions can be interpreted as encoding the *Hadamard transform* of the input. The Hadamard transform is an instance of a Fourier transform, and possesses a fast algorithm to transform and invert a vector of values. Consequently, the aggregator can use the Fast Hadamard (inverse) transform to accumulate and compute the frequency estimates in time proportional to $O(N + d \log d)$, assuming d is a power of 2. The message size is 1 bit to encode the noisy value, plus $\log d$ bits to send the value of j that defines the hash function. The resulting variance bound is $\frac{(\exp(\varepsilon)+1)^2}{(\exp(\varepsilon)-1)^2}$. This is close to optimal when $\exp(\varepsilon)$ is close to 1. For larger values of $\exp(\varepsilon)$, variations can be applied, such as sending multiple hash values, to reduce the variance to $O\left(\frac{\exp(\varepsilon)}{(\exp(\varepsilon)-1)^2}\right)$. The idea of using Hadamard encoding to build a frequency oracle appears in a variety of places [Tea17; Ngu+16; ASZ19].

2.3.5 Domain Size Reduction

The above approaches work well as d ranges up to moderate size – say, from single digits up to thousands of possibilities. However, when d is huge, all the methods lessen in usefulness, due to increased cost to maintain, and reduced accuracy. Such large domains arise in practice, for example when capturing information about words typed by users, or websites visited, where the set of possibilities easily ranges into the millions.

To cope with this high domain size, protocols can take advantage of dimensionality reduction techniques. Essentially, the protocol specifies a randomly chosen projection of the input items into a lower dimensional space, so that frequencies in the lower dimensional space can be used to provide frequency estimates for items in the original space. Such dimensionality reduction techniques are often referred to as "sketches". Common examples used in the LDP setting include the Bloom Filter, Count sketch and Count-Min sketch [CY20]. Importantly, these techniques are all *sparsity preserving*: if we apply them to a single input item, represented as a one-hot vector, then the resulting sketch is also mostly zero, having only a few non-zero values, and adhering to some additional structural restrictions. This means that we can apply the above frequency oracles to a sketch representation of user inputs in an almost black-box fashion. The cost now depends on the (smaller) d' value representing the size of the sketch, instead of the much larger original d value. Papers that pursued this approach provide further details of how to guarantee privacy and accuracy with the Bloom Filter [EPK14], Count-Min sketch [Tea17] and Count sketch [BNST20].

2.4 Heavy Hitters, Marginals, and Range Queries

Once we have a frequency oracle, we can apply it to numerous other related statistics-gathering problems. In this section, we describe how this can be done in the case of finding frequent items from a large domain (heavy hitters), computing marginal distributions within multidimensional data, and answering range queries and quantile queries.

2.4.1 Heavy Hitters

The "heavy hitters" within a distribution are those items whose frequency is large. This problem is naturally closely tied to the use of frequency oracles. The difference is that a frequency oracle allows us to test the frequency of a single item, whereas finding the heavy hitters potentially requires ranging over a very large set of possibilities. In the LDP setting, a number of approaches have been suggested to make this search procedure efficient and accurate.

The naive approach is simply to perform a frequency estimation query for every item in the domain. The disadvantages of this are primarily the computational cost: heavy hitters are often sought over a very large domain of possibilities. For example, the domain may consist of words typed by users on mobile devices, or URLs visited. Considering the number of valid strings of characters to consider, this can easily reach billions or trillions of possibilities. Enumerating all such possibilities can be very time consuming indeed. Moreover, even though each query to a frequency oracle may be quite accurate, over this many probes, there will be some errors, where infrequent items are reported as having a high frequency. Thus, we would expect some amount of false positives.

To reduce the number of queries, and hence false positives, we can seek ways to prune the search space, using ideas from information theory and error-correcting codes. For instance, suppose we knew that there were no heavy hitter items beginning with the letter 'z': then we could save ourselves the effort of testing any sequence of characters starting 'z', and so cut off this part of the search space. For our running example, we will consider inputs that are six letter words over the Roman alphabet, e.g. "apples" or "banana", where each user holds one such word, and we want to find which words are most common.

Some of the first approaches proposed to find heavy hitters were based on breaking the input strings into shorter substrings, and finding which substrings are frequent. In our running example, we could consider all two letter substrings – say, "ba" (the first two characters of banana), or "pl" (the middle two characters of apples). Each user can split their input word into its (disjoint) substrings, and report each of these through a frequency oracle. So, apples is split into ap, pl and es. Once the frequency oracle has been built from all the user submissions, a data analyst can try to find the heavy hitters. They can query the frequency oracle for all heavy substrings: note that posing $26^2 = 676$ queries for all character pairs is much smaller than the 308 million strings of length 6. This then gives a "jigsaw puzzle" to solve: how to recombine the heavy substrings into the correct set of heavy words?

A first approach proposed is to use statistical inference over pairs of substrings [FPE16], although this can potentially get fooled into outputting infrequent combinations. Subsequent approaches seek instead to perform a more reliable search over the space of possibilities. The "sequence fragment puzzle" (SFP) approach tags each substring with more information [Tea17]. It first concatenates each substring with a hash value of the whole string, to avoid substrings of different strings getting mixed up with each other. It also tags each substring with the location of the substring within the whole string, which is not private information. So in our example, if the hash value of apples was 7, then pl would be reported via a frequency oracle as (pl7, 3), i.e., the string pl occurs at index 3, and is concatenated with the hash value 7. If the string apples were a heavy hitter, then the analyst would recover the tuples (ap7, 1), (pl7, 3), (es7, 5), and so have enough information to recover the full string. Another frequency oracle can be kept over the full strings to provide an additional check that the reconstructed strings are indeed heavy.

Instead of collecting all the pieces in one go and putting them back together, hierarchical approaches to solving the heavy hitters problem incrementally build up the strings of heavy items. In this case, each user reports prefixes of their input (via a frequency oracle). In our example, the prefixes of apples in multiples of two characters are ap, appl and apples. The data analyst can first test all two character prefixes, and collect only those that appear heavy – e.g., aa to zz. They can then test only those four character prefixes that extend a heavy prefix – so in our example, this would test from apaa to apzz, to identify appl as heavy. The search proceeds until the full set of heavy hitters has been found. Although this requires a little more work than the SFP approach, since more candidates are considered, the accuracy is increased, as no hash functions are needed. This idea and its variations has appeared under various names – TreeHistogram [BNST20], Prefix Extending Method [WLJ21], and PrivTrie [Wan+18]. Across these variants, some recommendations have emerged. For example, it is preferable for each user to only report a single substring, rather than all substrings of their input, as this gives a better tradeoff of accuracy against privacy guarantees. It is also natural to keep information about each prefix length in a separate frequency oracle, to reduce noise.

Last, other approaches have been suggested in the theoretical literature which achieve slightly better results at the expense of rather more complex constructions making use of error correcting codes [BNS18; BS15; BNST20]. However, these do not seem to have seen use in practice. In practical deployments, the RAPPOR system has used the statistical expectation-maximization approach [FPE16], while Apple's implementation uses their Sequence Fragment Puzzle algorithm [Tea17].

2.4.2 Marginals

Given inputs represented as d-dimensional feature vectors, it is often desirable to learn statistics about combinations of k features. For example, given inputs recording sex, height and weight of individuals, the three *2-way marginals* capture information about sex and height; sex and weight; and height and weight, respectively.

Naively, we could directly apply frequency oracles to solve this, by having each user report information about their values for each k-way marginal. However, as k and d grow, this quickly becomes unsuitable. For $d = 10$ and $k = 3$, there are $\binom{10}{3} = 120$ distinct 3-way marginals. Maintaining this many frequency oracles (one for each marginal) will quickly lose accuracy. At the other extreme, we could simply maintain a single frequency oracle to capture the full d-way distribution, then project the desired k-way marginal by "marginalizing" the unwanted dimensions. This also incurs a lot of inaccuracy, as noise is added up.

Various approaches have been suggested to handle this approach. A first approach, drawing on insights from the theory of representing functions, and techniques used in the centralized privacy setting, is to make further use of the Hadamard transform of the input, as described by Cormode et al. [CKS18]. It is observed that any marginal distribution over binary data can be expressed as a linear combination of only $\binom{d}{k}$ Hadamard coefficients, which can be much smaller than the 2^d coefficients needed to represent the full binary data. This allows each Hadamard coefficient to be found more accurately, since we can ignore those Hadamard coefficients not needed for any k-way marginal.

The LoPub approach proposed by [Ren+18] captures information about lower degree marginals (say, $k = 2$), then uses various statistical approaches as postprocessing to build up a picture of the higher order marginals. This involves expectation maximization to infer the marginals, and lasso regression to enforce sparsity in the resulting distributions.

An alternative approach is to select a subset of marginal distributions to materialize, so that any desired marginal can be found by marginalizing a larger distribution. The "Consistent Adaptive Local Marginal" (CALM) approach presented by Zhang et al. [Zha+18] defines how to pick such a set of marginals to materialize of a fixed size, chosen to minimize the (squared) error incurred. Additional postprocessing is applied to improve accuracy by removing inconsistencies among the overlapping marginals.

2.4.3 Range Queries and Quantiles

Often, private data is drawn from an ordered domain — say, salary values, or exam scores. A frequency oracle allows us to learn the distribution of individual values, but more often we would also like to learn the cumulative distribution of values. This captures notions such as the median value, or the fraction of user inputs that fall within a specified range. Broadly, we describe these problems as range queries (what fraction of inputs fall between x and y?), and quantiles (for which input value x does a q fraction of inputs fall below?). Both can be answered by reducing to prefix queries, which ask what fraction of user inputs fall below a given value x.

There are two popular approaches to answering prefix queries that have been described in the LDP setting. Hierarchical approaches impose a regular hierarchy over the (discrete) input domain — such as a binary tree of height h. Then any prefix can be answered by summing up the weights associated with at most h nodes of the (binary) tree. These weights can be found by having each user report information about the items within the imposed binary tree, via a frequency oracle. Tradeoffs can be achieved by varying the depth of the hierarchy, and its branching factor. Transformation based approaches apply an appropriate (linear) transformation to the input — the most relevant being the Haar wavelet transform. This transforms a user's input into a (sparse) set of Haar coefficient values, which can also be collected and aggregated via frequency oracles. The data analyst can then answer prefix queries based on the noisy (but unbiased) wavelet coefficients. Similar approaches have been evaluated in the centralized setting. Studies under the LDP model found that the accuracy of both approaches is very similar in practice [CKS19], and that the hierarchical approach can naturally extend to multi-dimensional range queries with good accuracy [Wan+19].

2.5 Local Differential Privacy in Applications

Building on the above techniques for gathering statistics on arbitrary data distributions, there has been much work on solving various modeling and machine learning tasks under the LDP guarantee. In this section, we survey some of the approaches used, across a range of different settings, such as location and network-based data.

2.5.1 Text and Language Modeling

There are many reasons to want to analyze text. For example, we may wish to understand the evolving use of language. More pragmatically, operating system developers may wish to build better models to help mobile users type more accurately, by automatically correcting spelling errors. Equally, there are strong reasons to consider the text typed by users on their devices to be highly private, so it is not suitable to ship it in bulk to an analyst. Current deployments of LDP have often focused on text and text-like data. For example, Apple's implementation focuses on building custom dictionaries based on currently popular words, and highlighting popular emoji in lists. Meanwhile, Google's collection has focused on popular URLs, which can be represented as long text strings from a large domain.

An instructive example of how this modeling can be combined with LDP is due to Chang and Thakurta [CT18], in their work on autocompletion under local differential privacy. Absent of privacy, language modelling relies on building large, high dimensional models. For example, we might seek to predict the next word based on looking at the most recent *k* words typed, for some moderate choice of *k* (say, 4-5). However, when we apply the constraints of privacy, we encounter a challenge: the noise for privacy will typically dominate the low-frequencies associated with such rare combinations.

Instead, Chang and Thakurta propose a simpler "tag and words" model. Each word in some text is tagged with its part of speech (noun, verb, adverb etc.), and the tag for the next word is predicted based on the tags of the two most recent words. Then, options for the next word are predicted based on the predicted tag and the last word. This model can be instantiated in LDP by building a frequency oracle of the distributions of tag triples, and word-tag-word triples. Importantly, the size of these distributions is kept relatively low, so the statistics required to instantiate them have higher support, and the privacy noise is reduced. The lesson for LDP protocol design is to prefer simpler models whose parameters can be learned with higher confidence.

2.5.2 Spatial Data

Information associated with people's location can naturally be very sensitive. Protecting people's location is widely agreed to be a strict requirement of private data handling. A canonical (hypothetical) example often referred to is a person attending a sexual health clinic: any data release which reveals their attendance violates their privacy, and potentially threatens their status and well-being. Nevertheless, revealing suitably private views of location and movement data of populations is considered a valuable aim. It can inform planning for amenities and businesses, as well as influencing political districting and government fund allocations.

A first attempt to handle spatial data is to impose a simple division of space, such as a grid, and to reveal (noisy) counts of the occupancy of each cell. Such approaches have been proposed in the centralized model of privacy, with moderate success. In this case, the aim is to find heavy regions, and can be addressed using frequency oracles. In the local setting, the drawbacks of this approach are that it can be hard to determine the appropriate granularity of the grid. Sparsely populated rural areas may suit coarse cells (of the order of kilometres in size), but densely populated urban areas require much finer representations to best describe them, perhaps only tens of metres in size.

To make progress on this problem, it may be appropriate to relax the privacy constraints. In particular, while individuals may not wish their exact location to be revealed, it may be acceptable to reveal the country that an individual is within. That is, we might be more likely to perturb someone's location within a smaller radius, but much less likely to impose a very large perturbation.

The approach of private spatial data aggregation of Chen et al. [Che+16] defines such a relaxation of local differential privacy, based on a hierarchy over locations. This can be based on public geographic features, such as countries divided into states, which are further subdivided into cities and quarters. Each user can then decide at what level they are comfortable to be placed in – for example, they may allow the true city to be revealed, but not exactly where in the city they are located. Location distributions can then be revealed via an appropriately generalized frequency oracle. The user's location may be perturbed, but locations outside their specified "safe zone" are constrained to be empty. The system as described can be further extended: users can also choose a "personalized" privacy parameter ε_i; the system can try to group users together to run fewer invocations of a frequency oracle.

2.5.3 Graphs and Social Network Data

Data emerging from social interactions can naturally be subject to some privacy concerns. While some online social networks expose a certain amount of information to the world, such as lists of "friends" or "followers", other information is more restricted. Most social network systems do not reveal which users have been in close communication, or information about the frequency and intensity of these interactions. Nevertheless, to sociologists and other students of human behavior, learning accurate information about people's actions within (online) social network*s* is of great interest.

Most work on private graph data analysis takes the approach of (explicitly or implicitly) revealing information in the form of a mathematical model. That is, we consider the input to describe a member of a family of graphs, and we aim to extract certain information about the graph in order to instantiate a statistical graph model. The parameters of the model can be revealed under a suitable model of privacy. Then analysis can be performed, either directly on these noisy parameters, or by sampling new graphs according the graph model, and studying their properties. This approach has proved challenging to guarantee useful results even in the centralized model of differential privacy, so only becomes more difficult in the local regime, where higher volumes of noise are required.

A first question for this setting is how to define a suitable notion of privacy to graph data. In particular, what is the appropriate notion of "neighboring inputs" to apply the DP definition to? In the node privacy model, two graphs are considered to be neighboring if they differ in the adjacency pattern of a single node — that is, the connections from one node in the graph can be completely rewritten. In the edge privacy model, neighboring graphs differ only in the presence or absence of a single edge. The edge privacy definition holds the edge relationship to be the unit of privacy, while the node privacy model focuses on the node as the basic unit. Clearly, edge privacy requires less perturbation of information to achieve, since one node may correspond to a large number of edge links. Arguably, node privacy is the definition to aspire to, since in many social network graphs, the node represents all the information of a single user. This puts it closest to definitions of differential privacy, which seek to bound information based on the addition or removal of an individual (person) from the dataset. Nevertheless, most work has addressed the more tractable edge (LDP) case.

Given a social network graph, where each user has a list of other nodes that they are linked to in the graph, there are two natural approaches to consider first as baselines. First, one might try to reveal the full adjacency list of a user — perhaps, treated as a (relatively sparse) binary vector indicating which links are present. This can be performed under LDP by applying randomized response to each bit in the adjacency vector. However, it will of necessity introduce a very large number of false neighbors for any node. Instead, we may seek a model to instantiate where the parameters have more support, and hence give greater confidence. Second, we could provide very simple information about each node, such as its degree. Under the model of edge privacy, this can be done quite effectively: the average noise will be a small constant, compared to degrees in social networks which are typically hundreds on average. This can be used to instantiate graph models which require only degree information. However, this can be unsatisfying, since node degrees do not capture any useful information about how pairs of nodes interact with others, say. Consequently, we find that the adjacency list approach is too detailed and subject to noise, while the degree approach is too coarse and uninformative. Instead, we seek a graph model which falls in between these two.

Qin et al. [Qin+17] propose such an approach, which is learned iteratively under LDP. It aims to build a description of the graph in terms of the pattern of connections between each node and a set of possible partners. That is, we would like to define a small set of "clusters" of nodes, and describe how many links each individual node has to each of the clusters. The two previous approaches can be viewed as extremes within this setting: trying to reveal the adjacency list can be seen as the case when each cluster is a single other node; revealing degrees corresponds to having a single cluster containing all the nodes. Ideally, we would be given a suitable clustering of nodes (e.g., each cluster could represent the continent on which people live). However, in general no such clustering is available, and so it must be learned from scratch.

Qin et al. describe a way to build a clustering over a set of iterations. In the first iteration, each node is randomly assigned to one of k clusters. Each user can then release a noisy histogram of how their neighbors fall into these clustering. Each histogram is of size k, and is noised by adding values sampled from a Laplace distribution to each entry, sufficient to provide edge privacy. The next stage is to derive a new set of clusters. This is done by applying a clustering procedure to the (noisy) histograms, to find a new set of k clusters. Each node is then assigned to the new cluster in which its histogram is placed. The new cluster assignments are (implicitly) shared with neighbors, and the procedure can be iterated for a fixed number of steps. The intent is that the final set of clusters provide a representative set of different patterns of connection which help to describe the nodes. Finally, once the final (noisy) representation is built, it can be released publicly, and used as the basis of a sampling procedure to sample synthetic graphs with similar connection patterns. Experiments on this approach show that the sampled graphs do well at preserving various graph properties (clustering coefficient, mutual information, etc.) of the original input, while providing an LDP guarantee.

2.5.4 Classification and Regression

Building accurate predictive models via classification (for predicting categoric values) and regression (for numeric values) is at the heart of the recent explosion of interest in machine learning. In the private data setting, we can think of each user holding one (or a few) different training examples, with the goal being to build an accurate model from these distributed examples. The LDP requirement ensures that we should not be able to learn the private information of any user (although, of course, the learned model may nevertheless allow us to make inferences about individuals and their data).

Minimizing a Loss Function

Although there are many and varied models and learning procedures described in the literature, there are some similarities that allow a common approach to be proposed. Specifically, the training of many ML models can be expressed as minimizing a loss function over user examples, with features x (as a vector) and label y. The exact form of the loss function depends on the model type being learned, and the regularization being applied, but in many cases the loss is expressed as a sum over a loss from each example under the current model. That is, we can write the objective as trying to minimize the function

$$\sum_i \text{Loss}(\Theta, x_i, y_i) + \lambda N \|\Theta\|_2^2,$$

where, i indexes the N examples (x_i, y_i); Θ are the model parameters to vary; λ is a regularization parameter; and Loss is a function that gives the loss for each example under the current parameters. Two cases that can be expressed under this framework are linear regression, where the loss function is $\text{Loss}(\Theta, x_i, y_i) = (x_i^T \Theta - y_i)^2$;

and support vector machines with hinge loss, where $\text{Loss}(\Theta, x_i, y_i) = \max(0, 1 - y_i x_i^T \Theta)$.

Although certain models may admit a specific or closed-form solution, a more general approach is to optimize the loss function via stochastic gradient descent. That is, starting from some randomly chosen initial Θ, we choose a new Θ' by evaluating the gradient of the loss function on an appropriate subset of data points, and taking a step in the direction to reduce the loss function. The key aspect that makes this suitable for the LDP model is that, since the total loss is a sum over the loss of each data point, so also is the gradient of the loss function. Hence, we can start to build a protocol in the LDP model: a user i will receive a current value of Θ (which is non-private), and will reveal information about the gradient of the loss function with Θ and x_i, y_i.

Vector Release

To complete the description of the protocol, we need to determine how to output this gradient privately. We refer to the problem of publishing a vector with appropriate (local) differential privacy guarantees as "Vector Release". A first challenge for vector release is that gradient values could be arbitrarily large. This would make it hard to guarantee privacy, since we need to ensure that large values are protected by correspondingly large noise. A standard solution is "clipping": we ensure that the magnitude of each entry in the gradient vector is clipped to the range $[-1, +1]$. It is now possible to adapt existing LDP mechanisms to solve the vector release problem. For an individual coordinate in the range $[-1, +1]$, one can apply a variant of randomized response. A simple approach due to Duchi et al. [DJW13] is to first randomly round the input to $\{-1, +1\}$: given $r \in [-1, +1]$, map to $+1$ with probability $(r + 1)/2$, otherwise map to -1. We can then apply randomized response to the two inputs $\{-1, +1\}$ based on the parameter ε.

In order to handle d dimensional vector inputs, there are alternate approaches to consider. We could apply this rounding to every coordinate in the vector, after reducing the privacy parameter to ε/d, invoking a privacy composition result for LDP. Or, we could pick one (or a few) coordinates to release with a larger privacy budget. This latter approach is advocated in the work of [Ngu+16], who show that it gives preferable results. Taking the mean of the unbiased responses from the users is used to give a gradient update, and compute a new set of parameters Θ'.

Putting it All Together

Finally, we need to consider multiple steps of the gradient descent algorithm. Again, we could have each user participate in multiple rounds, by dividing their privacy budget up into smaller pieces; or divide the users into groups ("minibatches"), and have each user participate in one round only. Analysis due to Nguyen et al.

[Ngu+16], who proposed and analyzed this protocol, demonstrates that the mini-batch approach is clearly preferable. This means that obtaining accurate results can be a challenge, since the population of users is spread out over a number of rounds, and a large number of users is needed to ensure accuracy. This motivates working with a small model dimension d when possible, perhaps by using random projection techniques to reduce the dimensionality.

The need for multiple rounds of interaction means that convergence may be slow, due to the need to wait to receive responses from a large population of distributed users, perhaps using relatively impoverished mobile devices. There has been some theoretical study of whether multiple rounds of interaction are necessary for LDP machine learning tasks. Smith et al. [STU17] show constant-round protocols for simple problems like least-squares regression; Zheng et al. [ZMW17] incorporate dimensionality reduction and approximation theory to learn in a single round; and Wang et al. [WGX18] use polynomial approximations for smooth loss functions to further improve on these.

2.5.5 Recommender Systems

Recommender systems form another compelling use-case for Local Differential Privacy. They abstract the problem of providing meaningful recommendations to users, based on their previously expressed interest in items. Recommender systems are already widely used in the non-private setting, to recommend products from an e-commerce site based on past purchases, or to recommend music or movies.

Formally, we imagine that user preferences can be represented by an $n \times m$ matrix R, where n is the number of users and m is the number of items. The value of $R_{i,j}$ is the rating given by user i to item j. The rating system can be a scale (0 to 5), or binary (indicating whether or not the user has bought that item). Typically the matrix R is large and sparse. A common approach to recommender systems is to try to approximately factor R into UV, where U is an $n \times \ell$ matrix and V is $\ell \times m$. The parameter ℓ captures the number of "latent factors". Then the (predicted) ranking for item j for user i is given by $(UV)_{i,j}$.

If we introduce $y_{i,j}$ to indicate whether user i has entered a rating for item j, we can write an objective function for this in order to minimize a loss, $\sum_{i,j} y_{i,j}(r_{i,j} - U_i^T V_j)^2$, which is the squared error in predictions compared to the known ratings. As in the previous section, this can be solved by gradient descent, alternating over updating U and V.

For Local Differential Privacy, Shin et al. [SKSX18] proposed an approach that offers a guarantee per user, across their entire data. It makes use of a protocol for "vector release", as described in the previous section, over multiple iterations. Informally, each user will maintain their presence in U as a vector u_i, which is not shared with anyone else, and their ratings, as a vector r_i. Given a current choice of matrix V, each user will compute a gradient vector based on minimizing their contribution to the loss function, i.e., based on $\text{Loss}(V, u_i, r_i) = \sum_j y_{i,j}((r_i)_j - u_i^T V_j)^2$. As before, clipping can be used to ensure that the gradients stay within $[-1, 1]^m$. These (noisy) gradients are returned to the data analyst, who averages them to obtain a new matrix V', and the procedure is repeated, up to some fixed number k of iterations. The final matrix V_k is then shared with users for them to make future predictions with. The result is effective in practice, although is somewhat static, since it is not convenient to add new users i or items j after the initial training is complete.

2.5.6 Common Themes for LDP in Machine Learning Applications

Across these various examples of combining modeling and machine learning with local differential privacy, some common themes emerge due to the interaction of privacy requirements with ML models.

Finding a Good Class of Models

In non-private machine learning and data analytics, there is a trend towards bigger and more complex models: larger volumes of training data mean that we can fit richer models, and capture behaviors exhibited by only a small fraction of the training examples. This is not uniformly the case under models of privacy, and particularly so under local differential privacy. Firstly, fitting parts of the model to a small number of examples contradicts the aims of privacy, where we seek to protect the information of individuals or small groups. Moreover, the model of LDP works against this: the noise added must be such that if a parameter is only supported by a small number of individuals, then the recovered value will be completely distorted by the noise. To obtain accurate values, we should ensure that they are supported by a large enough fraction of the users. This is most clearly seen in the text prediction model (Section 2.5.1): the model is chosen to be compact, and is factored into two small pieces, rather than explicitly trying to learn a larger joint distribution. However, the same phenomenon guides other tasks: the work on graphs described in Section 2.5.3 seeks a model where each user contributes to a low-degree model (captured by the parameter k) that is much smaller than the number of nodes, n. The works on other ML tasks in Sections 2.5.4 and 2.5.5 are similarly affected by the dimensionality d, and it is suggested to choose d relatively small, or to use techniques like random projections to reduce the dimensionality.

Collect Data That can be Combined Linearly

A common thread across all the examples discussed is that the data collected from users is combined in a way that is fundamentally *linear*. That is, we can sum up the debiased user reports. This is clearest for the earlier examples of gathering statistics on frequencies and distributions (Section 2.4), where the data — whether in the form of histograms or Hadamard/Wavelet coefficients — are simple linear transforms of the users' inputs that can be added together by the data analyst. However, our other examples, of text, spatial data, graphs, classification and recommender systems, can all be viewed as combining data linearly, in the form of vectors, matrices, histograms or distributions.

Note that this does not preclude the use of non-linear models, just that the data collected is most conveniently handled in a linear form. Consider the highly non-linear models that emerge when using (deep) neural networks. We can consider learning the weights for such models under LDP. Many optimization techniques are non-linear, and so are hard to implement under LDP. But various gradient descent methods are feasible here. The computation of the gradient itself is a non-linear function of the input. Nevertheless, as described in Section 2.5.4, it can be decomposed into the gradient due to each user's input. We can therefore delegate the (non-linear) local gradient computation to the user, who can then use an appropriate LDP mechanism to release information about the gradient vector to the analyst. By ensuring that non-linear tasks are performed either by users or by the analyst, in such a way that the messages sent can be combined linearly, we obtain solutions that can be practical under LDP.

Reduce to Well-understood Problems

Although we have considered quite a varied range of applications, there are only a few different abstract problems solved by the central parts of the LDP protocol. In many of the cases seen above, the problem reduces either to that of Frequency Oracle, or Vector Release. These two primitives, and some of their generalizations, form the backbone of many LDP protocols. This is a helpful abstraction, since it means that LDP protocol designers do not have to re-solve these basic problems, but can adopt one of the optimized solutions from the literature. It also helps to focus on a feasible design for a new application: we should first attempt to reduce the problem to a model that can be instantiated by one or other of these methods, before turning to think about other possible solution methods.

Noise Reduction Techniques

In the centralized differential privacy case, the existence of composition theorems make it commonplace to build compound mechanisms using various steps. It is common to treat the overall privacy parameter ε as a "privacy budget", and to divide this budget among subtasks. This also allows protocols to be spread across multiple iterations, where the budget is further subdivided across each iteration. While corresponding composition results hold for LDP, the mathematics of the analysis tend to encourage different approaches to building protocols. Specifically, rather than asking each user to answer multiple questions about their input, it is usually better to partition the users into groups, and ask each group one of the questions. Or, somewhat equivalently, we may ask each user to sample one question to answer out of the set of possibilities. Roughly speaking, this is because LDP protocols built on top of frequency oracles typically have an error behavior that scales with $\frac{1}{\varepsilon\sqrt{n}}$. If we are trying to measure d quantities, then dividing the error budget ε into d pieces produces an error for each quantity of $(d/\varepsilon) \cdot 1/\sqrt{n}$. However, asking groups of (n/d) users to answer each question yields an error proportional to $1/\varepsilon \cdot \sqrt{d/n}$, better by a factor of $\sqrt{d}$. Similar reasons mean that when running a protocol over multiple iterations, it is preferable to have each user participate in only one of the k iterations, rather than devote (ε/k) privacy budget to each round. As noted above, we are also incentivized to pick d and k as small as possible, to further reduce these error bounds.

Data Representation

Last, we note that various methods described above have used various (linear) transformations on the users' data. Hadamard transforms are used in the construction of frequency oracles and in gathering marginal statistics, to help maximize the information in data that would otherwise be sparse. Haar wavelet transforms rotate the user data to answer queries related to ranges and quantile queries. Random projections are advocated to reduce the dimensionality of data that may be large and sparse. Finally, histograms can be viewed as a data transformation to reduce the domain size in a structured way. The lesson here is that a transformation like these may help to capture the essence of the data needed to solve a particular problem, and reduce the error.

2.6 LDP Limitations and Related Models

In this closing section, we reflect on some of the limitations of the Local Differential Privacy model, and some of the variant models that have been proposed as a consequence.

2.6.1 LDP Limitations

Budget Management

A key parameter of any differentially private procedure is the "privacy budget", ε. Despite its centrality to the DP model, there is still much discussion and disagreement around how to set and interpret this parameter (see, for example, [DKM20]).

In LDP this is a particularly knotty question, since many of the applications aim to make repeated measurements of user data over time. The data collection in Apple operating systems has been criticized, due to the high values of ε used, and the fact that the budget "resets" every day to allow fresh collection, as analyzed by Tang et al. [Tan+17]. Other implementations have tried to address this issue, by using "fixed random values" and memoization techniques, but these only provide a partial solution [EPK14; DKY17]. Providing meaningful privacy guarantees over long periods of time remains an open problem.

Strength of ML Models

As discussed in the previous section, much work on implementing machine learning models under LDP has focused on models that may be considered more at the more simplistic end: linear regression, or models like SVM and decision trees. Many state-of-the-art results in machine learning are achieved with larger and more complex models, particularly deep neural networks. As noted above, the tradeoff with LDP is different, meaning that large and complex models cannot always be handled well. Work is ongoing to combine the accuracy of deep models with the privacy guarantees of LDP.

Accuracy Guarantees

We return to the first example in the introduction: releasing the number of people that hold a particular attribute. We saw that the error in LDP scales with $\sqrt{n}/\varepsilon$, while the error for centralized DP scales with $1/\varepsilon$. The additional dependence on $\sqrt{n}$ may be an Achilles heel for LDP: as we consider increasingly complex tasks, the overall error from privacy quickly stacks up. There are two basic ways to decrease the error of an arbitrary LDP protocol: increase ε or increase n.

Increasing ε means taking an increasingly relaxed notion of privacy, to the point where the precise statement of the guarantee may be statistically meaningless. Growing ε from 1 to 10, say, may look relatively tame, but the consequence is that probabilities of different outcomes are bounded by factors of $\exp(\varepsilon)$, which for $\varepsilon = 10$ is over 22,000. For protocols based on Randomized Response, the probability of reporting a false answer is $1/(\exp(\varepsilon) + 1)$. For ε values of this magnitude, almost every user is reporting their true information, and the guarantees of LDP are consequently quite weak.

Increasing n is perhaps more defensible, but comes at a cost. The error rate decreases only with $\sqrt{n}$, so to halve the error, we need to quadruple the number of participants. For more complex protocols, this means that much larger user populations must be engaged to participate (honestly) in the protocol. Concretely, in Google's deployment, it was noted that at least 10,000 users must report a phenomenon before a clear enough signal could be observed [EPK14]. Access to tens of thousands, if not millions, of users may be feasible for large technology companies, but is out of reach for lesser groups. This may mean that LDP is primarily of interest only to a minority of organizations.

Vulnerability to 'Poisoning'

So-called "poisoning" attacks on machine learning systems are based on the idea of manipulating a small amount of the training data to force the resulting classifier to achieve poor results. Within the context of local differential privacy, this question asks what influence a small number of colluding users can have on the results? It has been observed that LDP is particularly vulnerable to data poisoning, more so than centralized DP [CJG19]. The intuition for this is that the random perturbations of randomized response and similar techniques lead us to reweight the averaged responses accordingly, to compensate for the cancellation of the random noise. Input poisoning can take advantage of this reweighting, by throwing all this weight in a particular direction. Different mechanisms vary in their susceptibility to such poisoning [CSU19], and while some mitigations exist, all LDP methods are vulnerable to poisoning to some extent.

2.6.2 Alternate Models

Federated Learning

The model of Federated Learning is similar to some of the LDP protocols for model training we have seen. In Federated Learning, a central server shares a current model with all users, who each evaluate the model on their local training data, and reply with their suggested updates to the model. Most commonly, these updates are in the form of gradients, which the server can combine by averaging to build the new model. In this form, no effort is made to mask or manipulate the messages from the users. The idea is that, since the users' data remains under their control and is not directly shared with the server, they remain private. However, the revealed gradients can inform on the users' data, particularly if the model is crafted adversarially. This leakage can be limited to just the server if the users establish a secure channel to the server. In order to provide a stronger guarantee, some form of (differential) privacy can additionally be enforced, and research is ongoing into how to achieve the best balance between privacy and utility – see the recent extensive survey due to Kairouz et al. [Kai+21]. An in-depth exploration of the topic of privacy-preserving federated learning is presented in Chapter 8.

Distributed Noise Generation and Secure Multiparty Computation

The goal of the LDP model can be summarized as protecting the input of each user through an appropriate privacy guarantee, and ensuring that the view and output of a data analyst meets a differential privacy guarantee. LDP achieves both simultaneously by enforcing the DP property for each user individually. This implies that DP also holds at the analyst, but as we have seen the accuracy guarantee is weaker than in the centralized DP model. An alternate approach is to use cryptographic techniques to provide privacy for the users, so that the output of the analyst is DP [Dwo+06]. We compare against the centralized DP model, where a typical approach has the analyst compute the exact solution, and add noise from an appropriate distribution (say, Laplace or Gaussian noise). In the "distributed noise generation" approach, each user adds a small fraction (or "share") of that noise, so that the sum of these shares is distributed according to the overall target noise level. This requires the target noise distribution to be "infinitely divisible", but fortunately many distributions appropriate for differential privacy have this property [AKL21; Bag+21; Gha+21; PS22]. To put this into effect, "secure sum" techniques can be used so that the analyst can derive the sum of the submitted (noisy) values, without observing any of the inputs. We could delegate this task to a trusted entity (with a secure hardware implementation), or via a distributed protocol using cryptographic techniques to compute the sum [Bon+17; Bel+20]. The key here is to ensure that the protocol is robust to attempts to evade it, such as if some users collude with the analyst to try to discover the value of one targeted user, and to handle cases when some users may drop out of the protocol (e.g., mobile users moving out of communication range, or running out of battery).

Shuffling

The shuffling model of privacy alters the model of trust by introducing an intermediate step between the users and the data analyst. The intuition is that if we can break the link between the message sent by a user and the identity of that user, then it becomes harder to draw any inference about them, and we can obtain a higher level of (differential) privacy. In the shuffle model, we imagine that there is a "shuffler" who sits between the users and the analyst, and who receives all messages, removes all identifying information about the source, and reveals the multiset of messages to the analyst. Under this model, it is possible to prove "privacy amplification" results: that messages sent with a low privacy guarantee nevertheless provide a stronger privacy guarantee at the analyst. As well as general amplification theorems, results have been shown giving tight bounds for specific problems such as sums and counts [Bit+17; Erl+19; BBGN19; Che+19]. An in-depth discussion on privacy amplification is provided in Section 3.6 of Chapter 3. Importantly, it is observed that users can follow an ε-local DP protocol to determine their (private) messages to the shuffler, and be assured of a stronger ε' DP guarantee for the overall outcome of the shuffled protocol. This motivates further development of LDP protocols which can then be used as a building block within the shuffle model.

To realize the shuffler in practice, we could instantiate a trusted entity to act as the shuffler, who is relied upon to act independently of the analyst. However, this relies on a certain level of trust, so we could instead seek to build a distributed shuffler via cryptographic "mix" networks. There are close connections between distributed noise generation and shuffling: many protocols in the shuffle protocol can be viewed as generating distributed noise, and vice-versa. This implies that secure aggregation techniques can often be applied to build the histogram of outputs from a shuffling protocol [Bel+20].

2.7 Concluding Remarks

Local Differential Privacy provides a clean definition of privacy that is appropriate for many computations over large, distributed populations who wish to share their data under a suitable privacy guarantee. Several large-scale deployments have demonstrated that LDP is practical for data collection and analysis. However, since accurate and usable results require large populations and larger values of privacy parameter ε, current approaches are reaching the limits of what can be achieved effectively, and generalizations or extensions of the model may be required for more advanced machine learning tasks with fewer participants while still giving strong privacy guarantees.

Acknowledgements

This chapter is based on a tutorial developed in collaboration with Somesh Jha, Tejas Kulkarni, Ninghui Li, Divesh Srivastava and Tianhao Wang [Cor+18]. Special thanks to Tianhao Wang for detailed comments and suggestions.

References

[AKL21] N. Agarwal, P. Kairouz, and Z. Liu. "The Skellam Mechanism for Differentially Private Federated Learning". In: Advances in Neural Information Processing Systems 34: Annual Conference on Neural Information Processing Systems 2021, NeurIPS 2021, December 6-14, 2021, virtual. 2021, pp. 5052–5064. URL: https://proceedings.neurips.cc/paper/2021/hash/285baacbdf8fda1de94b19282acd23e2-Abstract.html (cit. on p. 67).

[ASZ19] J. Acharya, Z. Sun, and H. Zhang. "Hadamard Response: Estimating Distributions Privately, Efficiently, and with Little Communication". In: International Conference on Artificial Intelligence and Statistics, AISTATS. Vol. 89. Proceedings of Machine Learning Research. PMLR, 2019, pp. 1120–1129. URL: http://proceedings.mlr.press/v89/acharya19a.html (cit. on p. 51).

[Bag+21] E. Bagdasaryan, P. Kairouz, S. Mellem, A. Gascón, K. A. Bonawitz, D. Estrin, and M. Gruteser. "Towards Sparse Federated Analytics: Location Heatmaps under Distributed Differential Privacy with Secure Aggregation". In: CoRR abs/2111.02356 (2021). arXiv: 2111.02356. URL: https://arxiv.org/abs/2111.02356 (cit. on p. 67).

[BBGN19] B. Balle, J. Bell, A. Gascón, and K. Nissim. "The Privacy Blanket of the Shuffle Model". In: Advances in Cryptology - CRYPTO. Vol. 11693. Lecture Notes in Computer Science. Springer, 2019, pp. 638–667. URL: https://doi.org/10.1007/978-3-030-26951-7%5C_22 (cit. on p. 67).

[Bel+20] J. H. Bell, K. A. Bonawitz, A. Gascón, T. Lepoint, and M. Raykova. "Secure Single-Server Aggregation with (Poly)Logarithmic Overhead". In: ACM SIGSAC Conference on Computer and Communications Security. ACM, 2020, pp. 1253–1269. URL: https://doi.org/10.1145/3372297.3417885 (cit. on pp. 67, 68).

[Bit+17] A. Bittau, Ú. Erlingsson, P. Maniatis, I. Mironov, A. Raghunathan, D. Lie, M. Rudominer, U. Kode, J. Tinnés, and B. Seefeld. "Prochlo: Strong Privacy for Analytics in the Crowd". In: Proceedings of the 26th Symposium on Operating Systems Principles. ACM, 2017, pp. 441–459. URL: https://doi.org/10.1145/3132747.3132769 (cit. on p. 67).

[BNS18] M. Bun, J. Nelson, and U. Stemmer. "Heavy Hitters and the Structure of Local Privacy". In: Proceedings of ACM SIGMOD-SIGACT-SIGAI Symposium on Principles of Database Systems. Ed. by J. V. den Bussche and M. Arenas. ACM, 2018, pp. 435–447. URL: https://doi.org/10.1145/3196959.3196981 (cit. on p. 53).

[BNST20] R. Bassily, K. Nissim, U. Stemmer, and A. Thakurta. "Practical Locally Private Heavy Hitters". In: J. Mach. Learn. Res. 21 (2020),

16:1–16:42. URL: http://jmlr.org/papers/v21/18-786.html (cit. on pp. 51, 53).

[Bon+17] K. A. Bonawitz, V. Ivanov, B. Kreuter, A. Marcedone, H. B. McMahan, S. Patel, D. Ramage, A. Segal, and K. Seth. "Practical Secure Aggregation for Privacy-Preserving Machine Learning". In: ACM SIGSAC Conference on Computer and Communications Security. ACM, 2017, pp. 1175–1191. URL: https://doi.org/10.1145/3133956.3133982 (cit. on p. 67).

[BS15] R. Bassily and A. D. Smith. "Local, Private, Efficient Protocols for Succinct Histograms". In: Proceedings of the Forty-Seventh Annual ACM on Symposium on Theory of Computing. ACM, 2015, pp. 127–135. URL: https://doi.org/10.1145/2746539.2746632 (cit. on p. 53).

[Che+16] R. Chen, H. Li, A. K. Qin, S. P. Kasiviswanathan, and H. Jin. "Private spatial data aggregation in the local setting". In: IEEE International Conference on Data Engineering, ICDE. IEEE Computer Society, 2016, pp. 289–300. URL: https://doi.org/10.1109/ICDE.2016.7498248 (cit. on p. 57).

[Che+19] A. Cheu, A. D. Smith, J. R. Ullman, D. Zeber, and M. Zhilyaev. "Distributed Differential Privacy via Shuffling". In: Advances in Cryptology - EUROCRYPT. Vol. 11476. Lecture Notes in Computer Science. Springer, 2019, pp. 375–403. URL: https://doi.org/10.1007/978-3-030-17653-2%5C_13 (cit. on p. 67).

[CJG19] X. Cao, J. Jia, and N. Z. Gong. "Data Poisoning Attacks to Local Differential Privacy Protocols". In: CoRR abs/1911.02046 (2019). arXiv: 1911.02046. URL: http://arxiv.org/abs/1911.02046 (cit. on p. 66).

[CKS18] G. Cormode, T. Kulkarni, and D. Srivastava. "Marginal Release Under Local Differential Privacy". In: Proceedings of the International Conference on Management of Data, SIGMOD. Ed. by G. Das, C. M. Jermaine, and P. A. Bernstein. ACM, 2018, pp. 131–146. URL: https://doi.org/10.1145/3183713.3196906 (cit. on p. 54).

[CKS19] G. Cormode, T. Kulkarni, and D. Srivastava. "Answering Range Queries Under Local Differential Privacy". In: Proc. VLDB Endow. 12.10 (2019), pp. 1126–1138. URL: http://www.vldb.org/pvldb/vol12/p1126-cormode.pdf (cit. on p. 55).

[Cor+18] G. Cormode, S. Jha, T. Kulkarni, N. Li, D. Srivastava, and T. Wang. Privacy at Scale: Local Differential Privacy in Practice. Tutorial at SIGMOD and KDD. 2018 (cit. on p. 68).

[CSU19] A. Cheu, A. D. Smith, and J. R. Ullman. "Manipulation Attacks in Local Differential Privacy". In: CoRR abs/1909.09630 (2019). arXiv: 1909.09630. URL: http://arxiv.org/abs/1909.09630 (cit. on p. 66).

[CT18] J. C.-N. Chang and A. Thakurta. "Autocompletion in Local Differential Privacy". In: IEEE Symposium on Security and Privacy. 2018, p. 2 (cit. on p. 55).

[CY20] G. Cormode and K. Yi. Small Summaries for Big Data. CUP, 2020 (cit. on p. 51).

[DJW13] J. C. Duchi, M. I. Jordan, and M. J. Wainwright. "Local Privacy and Statistical Minimax Rates". In: 54th Annual IEEE Symposium on Foundations of Computer Science, FOCS. IEEE Computer Society, 2013, pp. 429–438. URL: https://doi.org/10.1109/FOCS.2013.53 (cit. on pp. 46, 60).

[DKM20] C. Dwork, N. Kohli, and D. Mulligan. "Differential Privacy in Practice: Expose Your Epsilons!" In: Journal of Privacy and Confidentiality 9.2 (2020) (cit. on p. 64).

[DKY17] B. Ding, J. Kulkarni, and S. Yekhanin. "Collecting Telemetry Data Privately". In: Advances in Neural Information Processing Systems. 2017, pp. 3571–3580. URL: https://proceedings.neurips.cc/paper/2017/hash/253614bbac999b38b5b60cae531c4969-Abstract.html (cit. on pp. 46, 65).

[DN03] I. Dinur and K. Nissim. "Revealing information while preserving privacy". In: Proceedings of the ACM SIGACT-SIGMOD-SIGART Symposium on Principles of Database Systems. Ed. by F. Neven, C. Beeri, and T. Milo. ACM, 2003, pp. 202–210. URL: https://doi.org/10.1145/773153.773173 (cit. on p. 46).

[DR14] C. Dwork and A. Roth. "The Algorithmic Foundations of Differential Privacy." In: Foundations and Trends in Theoretical Computer Science 9.3-4 (2014), pp. 211–407. URL: http://dblp.uni-trier.de/db/journals/fttcs/fttcs9.html#DworkR14 (cit. on p. 46).

[Dwo+06] C. Dwork, K. Kenthapadi, F. McSherry, I. Mironov, and M. Naor. "Our Data, Ourselves: Privacy Via Distributed Noise Generation". In: Advances in Cryptology - EUROCRYPT. Vol. 4004. Lecture Notes in Computer Science. Springer, 2006, pp. 486–503. URL: https://doi.org/10.1007/11761679%5C_29 (cit. on p. 67).

[EGS03] A. V. Evfimievski, J. Gehrke, and R. Srikant. "Limiting privacy breaches in privacy preserving data mining". In: Proceedings of the ACM SIGACT-SIGMOD-SIGART Symposium on Principles of Database Systems. Ed. by F. Neven, C. Beeri, and T. Milo. ACM, 2003, pp. 211–222. URL: https://doi.org/10.1145/773153.773174 (cit. on p. 46).

[EPK14] Ú. Erlingsson, V. Pihur, and A. Korolova. "RAPPOR: Randomized Aggregatable Privacy-Preserving Ordinal Response". In: Proceedings of the 2014 ACM SIGSAC Conference on Computer and Communications Security. ACM, 2014, pp. 1054–1067. URL: https://doi.org/10.1145/2660267.2660348 (cit. on pp. 46, 51, 65).

[Erl+19] Ú. Erlingsson, V. Feldman, I. Mironov, A. Raghunathan, K. Talwar, and A. Thakurta. "Amplification by Shuffling: From Local to Central Differential Privacy via Anonymity". In: Proceedings of ACM-SIAM Symposium on Discrete Algorithms, SODA. SIAM, 2019, pp. 2468–2479. URL: https://doi.org/10.1137/1.9781611975482.151 (cit. on p. 67).

[FPE16] G. C. Fanti, V. Pihur, and Ú. Erlingsson. "Building a RAPPOR with the Unknown: Privacy-Preserving Learning of Associations and Data Dictionaries". In: Proc. Priv. Enhancing Technol. 2016.3 (2016), pp. 41–61. URL: https://doi.org/10.1515/popets-2016-0015 (cit. on pp. 52, 53).

[Gha+21] B. Ghazi, N. Golowich, R. Kumar, R. Pagh, and A. Velingker. "On the Power of Multiple Anonymous Messages: Frequency Estimation and Selection in the Shuffle Model of Differential Privacy". In: Advances in Cryptology - EUROCRYPT 2021 - 40th Annual International Conference on the Theory and Applications of Cryptographic Techniques, Zagreb, Croatia, October 17-21, 2021, Proceedings, Part III. Vol. 12698. Lecture Notes in Computer Science. Springer, 2021, pp. 463–488. URL: https://doi.org/10.1007/978-3-030-77883-5%5C_16 (cit. on p. 67).

[Kai+21] P. Kairouz et al. "Advances and Open Problems in Federated Learning". In: Found. Trends Mach. Learn. 14.1-2 (2021), pp. 1–210. URL: https://doi.org/10.1561/2200000083 (cit. on p. 66).

[Ngu+16] T. T. Nguyên, X. Xiao, Y. Yang, S. C. Hui, H. Shin, and J. Shin. "Collecting and Analyzing Data from Smart Device Users with Local Differential Privacy". In: CoRR abs/1606.05053 (2016). arXiv: 1606.05053. URL: http://arxiv.org/abs/1606.05053 (cit. on pp. 51, 60, 61).

[Pih+18] V. Pihur, A. Korolova, F. Liu, S. Sankuratripati, M. Yung, D. Huang, and R. Zeng. "Differentially-Private "Draw and Discard" Machine Learning". In: CoRR abs/1807.04369 (2018). arXiv: 1807.04369. URL: http://arxiv.org/abs/1807.04369 (cit. on p. 46).

[PS22] R. Pagh and N. M. Stausholm. "Infinitely Divisible Noise in the Low Privacy Regime". In: International Conference on Algorithmic Learning Theory. Vol. 167. Proceedings of Machine Learning Research. PMLR, 2022, pp. 881–909. URL: https://proceedings.mlr.press/v167/pagh22a.html (cit. on p. 67).

[Qin+17] Z. Qin, T. Yu, Y. Yang, I. Khalil, X. Xiao, and K. Ren. "Generating Synthetic Decentralized Social Graphs with Local Differential Privacy". In: Proceedings of ACM SIGSAC Conference on Computer and Communications Security, CCS. ACM, 2017, pp. 425–438. URL: https://doi.org/10.1145/3133956.3134086 (cit. on p. 58).

[Ren+18] X. Ren, C. Yu, W. Yu, S. Yang, X. Yang, J. A. McCann, and P. S. Yu. "LoPub: High-Dimensional Crowdsourced Data Publication With Local Differential Privacy". In: IEEE Trans. Inf. Forensics Secur. 13.9 (2018), pp. 2151–2166. URL: https://doi.org/10.1109/TIFS.2018.2812146 (cit. on p. 54).

[SKSX18] H. Shin, S. Kim, J. Shin, and X. Xiao. "Privacy Enhanced Matrix Factorization for Recommendation with Local Differential Privacy". In: IEEE Trans. Knowl. Data Eng. 30.9 (2018), pp. 1770–1782. URL: https://doi.org/10.1109/TKDE.2018.2805356 (cit. on p. 61).

[STU17] A. D. Smith, A. Thakurta, and J. Upadhyay. "Is Interaction Necessary for Distributed Private Learning?" In: IEEE Symposium on Security and Privacy. IEEE Computer Society, 2017, pp. 58–77. URL: https://doi.org/10.1109/SP.2017.35 (cit. on p. 61).

[Tan+17] J. Tang, A. Korolova, X. Bai, X. Wang, and X. Wang. "Privacy Loss in Apple's Implementation of Differential Privacy on MacOS 10.12". In: CoRR abs/1709.02753 (2017). arXiv: 1709.02753. URL: http://arxiv.org/abs/1709.02753 (cit. on p. 65).

[Tea17] A. Team. Apple differential privacy technical overview. Online at https://www.apple.com/privacy/docs/DifferentialPrivacyOverview.pdf. 2017 (cit. on pp. 46, 51–53).

[Wan+18] N. Wang, X. Xiao, Y. Yang, T. D. Hoang, H. Shin, J. Shin, and G. Yu. "PrivTrie: Effective Frequent Term Discovery under Local Differential Privacy". In: 34th IEEE International Conference on Data Engineering. IEEE Computer Society, 2018, pp. 821–832. URL: https://doi.org/10.1109/ICDE.2018.00079 (cit. on p. 53).

[Wan+19] T. Wang, B. Ding, J. Zhou, C. Hong, Z. Huang, N. Li, and S. Jha. "Answering Multi-Dimensional Analytical Queries under Local Differential Privacy". In: Proceedings of the ACM International Conference on Management of Data. 2019, pp. 159–176. ISBN: 9781450356435. URL: https://doi.org/10.1145/3299869.3319891 (cit. on p. 55).

[War65] S. L. Warner. "Randomized Response: A Survey Technique for Eliminating Evasive Answer Bias". In: Journal of the American Statistical Association 60.309 (1965), pp. 63–69. ISSN: 01621459. URL: http://www.jstor.org/stable/2283137 (cit. on pp. 46, 48).

[WBLJ17] T. Wang, J. Blocki, N. Li, and S. Jha. "Locally Differentially Private Protocols for Frequency Estimation". In: 26th USENIX Security Symposium, USENIX Security. USENIX Association, 2017, pp. 729–745. URL: https://www.usenix.org/conference/usenixsecurity17/technical-sessions/presentation/wang-tianhao (cit. on pp. 49, 50).

[WGX18] D. Wang, M. Gaboardi, and J. Xu. "Empirical Risk Minimization in Non-interactive Local Differential Privacy Revisited". In: Advances in Neural Information Processing Systems. 2018, pp. 973–982. URL: https://proceedings.neurips.cc/paper/2018/hash/13f320e7b5ead1024ac95c3b208610db-Abstract.html (cit. on p. 61).

[WLJ21] T. Wang, N. Li, and S. Jha. "Locally Differentially Private Heavy Hitter Identification". In: IEEE Transactions on Dependable and Secure Computing 18.2 (2021), pp. 982–993 (cit. on p. 53).

[Zha+18] Z. Zhang, T. Wang, N. Li, S. He, and J. Chen. "CALM: Consistent Adaptive Local Marginal for Marginal Release under Local Differential Privacy". In: Proceedings of ACM SIGSAC Conference on Computer and Communications Security, CCS. Ed. by D. Lie, M. Mannan, M. Backes, and X. Wang. ACM, 2018, pp. 212–229. URL: https://doi.org/10.1145/3243734.3243742 (cit. on p. 54).

[ZMW17] K. Zheng, W. Mou, and L. Wang. "Collect at Once, Use Effectively: Making Non-interactive Locally Private Learning Possible". In: Proceedings of International Conference on Machine Learning, ICML. Vol. 70. Proceedings of Machine Learning Research. PMLR, 2017, pp. 4130–4139. URL: http://proceedings.mlr.press/v70/zheng17c.html (cit. on p. 61).

DOI: 10.1561/9781638284772.ch3

Chapter 3

Composition of Differential Privacy & Privacy Amplification by Subsampling

By Thomas Steinke

3.1 Introduction

Our data is subject to many different uses. Many entities will have access to our data, including government agencies, healthcare providers, employers, technology companies, and financial institutions. Those entities will perform many different analyses that involve our data and those analyses will be updated repeatedly over our lifetimes. The greatest risk to privacy is that an attacker will combine multiple pieces of information from the same or different sources and that the combination of these will reveal sensitive details about us. Thus we cannot study privacy leakage in a vacuum; it is important that we can reason about the accumulated privacy leakage over multiple independent analyses.

As a concrete example to keep in mind, consider the following simple differencing attack: Suppose your employer provides healthcare benefits. The employer pays for these benefits and thus may have access to summary statistics like how many employees are currently receiving pre-natal care or currently are being treated for cancer. Your pregnancy or cancer status is highly sensitive information, but intuitively the aggregated count is not sensitive as it is not specific to you. However, this count may be updated on a regular basis and your employer may notice that the count increased on the day you were hired or on the day you took off for a medical appointment. This example shows how multiple pieces of information – the date of your hire or medical appointment, the count before that date, and the count afterwards – can be combined to reveal sensitive information about you, despite each piece of information seeming innocuous on its own. Attacks could combine many different statistics from multiple sources and hence we need to be careful to guard against such attacks, which leads us to differential privacy.

Differential privacy has strong composition properties – if multiple independent analyses are run on our data and each analysis is differentially private on its own, then the combination of these analyses is also differentially private. This property is key to the success of differential privacy. Composition enables building complex differentially private systems out of simple differentially private subroutines. Composition allows the re-use data over time without fear of a catastrophic privacy failure. And, when multiple entities use the data of the same individuals, they do not need to coordinate to prevent an attacker from learning private details of individuals by combining the information released by those entities. To prevent the above differencing attack, we could independently perturb each count to make it differentially private; then taking the difference of two counts would be sufficiently noisy to obscure your pregnancy or cancer status.

Composition is quantitative. The differential privacy guarantee of the overall system will depend on the number of analyses and the privacy parameters that they each satisfy. The exact relationship between these quantities can be complex. There are various composition theorems that give bounds on the overall parameters in terms of the parameters of the parts of the system. In this chapter, we will study several composition theorems (including the relevant proofs) and we will also look at some examples that demonstrate how to apply the composition theorems and why we need them.

Composition theorems provide privacy bounds for a given system. A system designer must use composition theorems to design systems that simultaneously give good privacy and good utility (i.e., good statistical accuracy). This process often called "privacy budgeting" or "privacy accounting." Intuitively, the system designer has some privacy constraint (i.e., the overall system must satisfy some final privacy guarantee) which can be viewed as analogous to a monetary budget that must be divided amongst the various parts of the system. Composition theorems provide the accounting rules for this budget. Allocating more of the budget to some part of the system makes that part more accurate, but then less budget is available for other parts of the system. Thus the system designer must also make a value judgement about which parts of the system to prioritize.

Overview of the Chapter

This chapter provides an in-depth discussion of composition theorems and privacy amplification techniques in Differential Privacy. It begins by introducing the basic composition theorem in Section 3.2, and examining whether basic composition strategies achieve optimal privacy guarantees. Next, in Section 3.3, it reviews the concept of privacy loss distributions and offers a statistical hypothesis testing perspective to understand approximate Differential Privacy. The chapter then discusses advanced composition via the privacy loss distribution, in Section 3.4, revisiting basic composition and exploring composition through Gaussian approximation. It reviews the notion of Concentrated Differential Privacy, adaptive composition, and post-processing, and examines the composition of approximate Differential Privacy. Then, the chapter focuses on privacy amplification by subsampling, in Section 3.6, covering subsampling techniques for pure and approximate Differential Privacy, the differences between addition/removal and replacement for neighboring datasets, and how subsampling interacts with composition. Here, the concept of Rényi Differential Privacy is introduced, along with analytic bounds for privacy amplification and practical guidance on the use of privacy amplification by subsampling in real-world applications. Finally, the chapter concludes, in Section 3.7, with a reflection on the historical development of the discussed concepts and provides further reading for a deeper understanding of these concepts.

3.2 Basic Composition

The simplest composition theorem is what is known as basic composition. This applies to pure ε-DP (although it can be extended to approximate (ε, δ)-DP). Basic composition says that, if we run k independent ε-DP algorithms, then the composition of these is $k\varepsilon$-DP. More generally, we have the following result.

Theorem 3.1 (Basic Composition). *Let $M_1, M_2, \cdots, M_k : \mathcal{X}^n \to \mathcal{Y}$ be randomized algorithms. Suppose M_j is ε_j-DP for each $j \in [k]$. Define $M : \mathcal{X}^n \to \mathcal{Y}^k$ by $M(x) = (M_1(x), M_2(x), \cdots, M_k(x))$, where each algorithm is run independently. Then M is ε-DP for $\varepsilon = \sum_{j=1}^{k} \varepsilon_j$.*

Proof. Fix an arbitrary pair of neighboring datasets $x, x' \in \mathcal{X}^n$ and output $y \in \mathcal{Y}^k$. To establish that M is ε-DP, we must show that $e^{-\varepsilon} \le \frac{\mathbb{P}[M(x)=y]}{\mathbb{P}[M(x')=y]} \le e^{\varepsilon}$. By independence, we have

$$\frac{\mathbb{P}\left[M(x) = y\right]}{\mathbb{P}\left[M(x') = y\right]} = \frac{\prod_{j=1}^{k} \mathbb{P}\left[M_j(x) = y_j\right]}{\prod_{j=1}^{k} \mathbb{P}\left[M_j(x') = y_j\right]}$$

$$= \prod_{j=1}^{k} \frac{\mathbb{P}\left[M_j(x) = y_j\right]}{\mathbb{P}\left[M_j(x') = y_j\right]} \le \prod_{j=1}^{k} e^{\varepsilon_j} = e^{\sum_{j=1}^{k} \varepsilon_j} = e^{\varepsilon},$$

where the inequality follows from the fact that each M_j is ε_j-DP and, hence, $e^{-\varepsilon_j} \le \frac{\mathbb{P}[M_j(x)=y_j]}{\mathbb{P}[M_j(x')=y_j]} \le e^{\varepsilon_j}$. Similarly, $\prod_{j=1}^{k} \frac{\mathbb{P}[M_j(x)=y_j]}{\mathbb{P}[M_j(x')=y_j]} \ge \prod_{j=1}^{k} e^{-\varepsilon_j}$, which completes the proof. □

Basic composition is already a powerful result, despite its simple proof; it establishes the versatility of differential privacy and allows us to begin reasoning about complex systems in terms of their building blocks. For example, suppose we have k functions $f_1, \cdots, f_k : \mathcal{X}^n \to \mathbb{R}$ each of sensitivity 1. For each $j \in [k]$, we know that adding Laplace$(1/\varepsilon)$ noise to the value of $f_j(x)$ satisfies ε-DP. Thus, if we add independent Laplace$(1/\varepsilon)$ noise to each value $f_j(x)$ for all $j \in [k]$, then basic composition tells us that releasing this vector of k noisy values satisfies $k\varepsilon$-DP. If we want the overall system to be ε-DP, then we should add independent Laplace(k/ε) noise to each value $f_j(x)$.

3.2.1 Is Basic Composition Optimal?

If we want to release k values each of sensitivity 1 (as above) and have the overall release be ε-DP, then, using basic composition, we can add Laplace(k/ε) noise to each value. The variance of the noise for each value is $2k^2/\varepsilon^2$, so the standard deviation is $\sqrt{2}k/\varepsilon$. In other words, the scale of the noise must grow linearly with the number of values k if the overall privacy and each value's sensitivity is fixed. It is natural to wonder whether the scale of the Laplace noise can be reduced by improving the basic composition result. We now show that this is not possible.

For each $j \in [k]$, let $M_j : \mathcal{X}^n \to \mathbb{R}$ be the algorithm that releases $f_j(x)$ with Laplace(k/ε) noise added. Let $M : \mathcal{X}^n \to \mathbb{R}^k$ be the composition of these k algorithms. Then M_j is ε/k-DP for each $j \in [k]$ and basic composition tells us that M is ε-DP. The question is whether M satisfies a better DP guarantee than this – i.e., does M satisfy ε_*-DP for some $\varepsilon_* < \varepsilon$? Suppose we have neighboring datasets $x, x' \in \mathcal{X}^n$ such that $f_j(x) = f_j(x') + 1$ for each $j \in [k]$. Let $y = (a, a, \cdots, a) \in \mathbb{R}^k$ for some $a \ge \max_{j=1}^{k} f_j(x)$. Then

$$\begin{aligned}
\frac{\mathbb{P}\left[M(x)=y\right]}{\mathbb{P}\left[M(x')=y\right]} &= \frac{\prod_{j=1}^{k} \mathbb{P}\left[f_j(x)+\text{Laplace}(k/\varepsilon)=y_j\right]}{\prod_{j=1}^{k} \mathbb{P}\left[f_j(x')+\text{Laplace}(k/\varepsilon)=y_j\right]} \\
&= \prod_{j=1}^{k} \frac{\mathbb{P}\left[\text{Laplace}(k/\varepsilon)=y_j-f_j(x)\right]}{\mathbb{P}\left[\text{Laplace}(k/\varepsilon)=y_j-f_j(x')\right]} \\
&= \prod_{j=1}^{k} \frac{\frac{\varepsilon}{2k}\exp\left(-\frac{\varepsilon}{k}|y_j-f_j(x)|\right)}{\frac{\varepsilon}{2k}\exp\left(-\frac{\varepsilon}{k}|y_j-f_j(x')|\right)}
\end{aligned}$$

$$= \prod_{j=1}^{k} \frac{\exp\left(-\frac{\varepsilon}{k}(y_j - f_j(x))\right)}{\exp\left(-\frac{\varepsilon}{k}(y_j - f_j(x'))\right)} \qquad (y_j \geq f_j(x) \text{ and } y_j \geq f_j(x'))$$

$$= \prod_{j=1}^{k} \exp\left(\frac{\varepsilon}{k}\left(f_j(x) - f_j(x')\right)\right)$$

$$= \exp\left(\frac{\varepsilon}{k}\sum_{j=1}^{k}\left(f_j(x) - f_j(x')\right)\right) = e^{\varepsilon}.$$

This shows that basic composition is optimal. For this example, we cannot prove a better guarantee than what is given by basic composition.

Is there some other way to improve upon basic composition that circumvents this example? Note that we assumed that there are neighboring datasets $x, x' \in \mathcal{X}^n$ such that $f_j(x) = f_j(x') + 1$ for each $j \in [k]$. In some settings, no such worst case datasets exist. In that case, instead of scaling the noise linearly with k, we can scale the Laplace noise according to the ℓ_1 sensitivity $\Delta_1 := \sup_{\substack{x,x' \in \mathcal{X}^n \\ \text{neighboring}}} \sum_{j=1}^{k} |f_j(x) - f_j(x')|$.

Instead of adding assumptions to the problem, we will look more closely at the example above. We showed that there exists some output $y \in \mathbb{R}^d$ such that $\frac{\mathbb{P}[M(x)=y]}{\mathbb{P}[M(x')=y]} = e^{\varepsilon}$. However, such outputs y are very rare, as we require $y_j \geq \max\{f_j(x), f_j(x')\}$ for each $j \in [k]$ where $y_j = f_j(x) + \text{Laplace}(k/\varepsilon)$. Thus, in order to observe an output y such that the likelihood ratio is maximal, all of the k Laplace noise samples must be positive, which happens with probability 2^{-k}. The fact that outputs y with maximal likelihood ratio are exceedingly rare turns out to be a general phenomenon and not specific to the example above.

Can we improve on basic composition if we only ask for a high probability bound? That is, instead of demanding $\frac{\mathbb{P}[M(x)=y]}{\mathbb{P}[M(x')=y]} \leq e^{\varepsilon_*}$ for all $y \in \mathcal{Y}$, we demand $\underset{Y \leftarrow M(x)}{\mathbb{P}}\left[\frac{\mathbb{P}[M(x)=Y]}{\mathbb{P}[M(x')=Y]} \leq e^{\varepsilon_*}\right] \geq 1 - \delta$ for some $0 < \delta \ll 1$. Can we prove a better bound $\varepsilon_* < \varepsilon$ in this relaxed setting? The answer turns out to be yes.

The limitation of pure ε-DP is that events with tiny probability – which are negligible in real-world applications – can dominate the privacy analysis. This motivates us to move to relaxed notions of differential privacy, such as approximate (ε, δ)-DP and concentrated DP, which are less sensitive to low probability events. In particular, these relaxed notions of differential privacy allow us to prove quantitatively better composition theorems. The rest of this chapter develops this direction further.

3.3 Privacy Loss Distributions

Qualitatively, an algorithm $M : \mathcal{X}^n \to \mathcal{Y}$ is differentially private if, for all neighboring datasets $x, x' \in \mathcal{X}^n$, the output distributions $M(x)$ and $M(x')$ are "indistinguishable" or "close." The key question is how do we quantify the closeness or indistinguishability of a pair of distributions?

Pure DP (a.k.a. pointwise DP) [DMNS06] uniformly bounds the likelihood ratio – $\frac{\mathbb{P}[M(x)=y]}{\mathbb{P}[M(x')=y]} \leq e^{\varepsilon}$ for all $y \in \mathcal{Y}$. As discussed at the end of the section on basic composition (Section 3.2), this can be too strong as the outputs y that maximize this likelihood ratio may be very rare.

We could also consider the total variation distance (a.k.a. statistical distance):

$$\mathrm{d_{TV}}\left(M(x), M(x')\right) := \sup_{S \subset \mathcal{Y}} \left(\mathbb{P}\left[M(x) \in S\right] - \mathbb{P}\left[M(x') \in S\right]\right).$$

Another option would be the KL divergence (a.k.a. relative entropy). Both TV distance and KL divergence turn out to give poor privacy-utility tradeoffs; that is, to rule out bad algorithms M, we must set these parameters very small, but that also rules out all the good algorithms. Intuitively, both TV and KL are not sensitive enough to low-probability bad events (whereas pure DP is too sensitive). We need to introduce a parameter (δ) to determine what level of low probability events we can ignore.

Approximate (ε, δ)-DP [Dwo+06] is a combination of pure ε-DP and δ TV distance. Specifically, M is (ε, δ)-DP if, for all neighboring datasets $x, x' \in \mathcal{X}^n$ and all measurable $S \subset \mathcal{Y}$, $\mathbb{P}\left[M(x) \in S\right] \leq e^{\varepsilon} \cdot \mathbb{P}\left[M(x') \in S\right] + \delta$. Intuitively, (ε, δ)-DP is like ε-DP except we can ignore events with probability $\leq \delta$. That is, δ represents a failure probability, so it should be small (e.g., $\delta \leq 10^{-6}$), while ε can be larger (e.g., $\varepsilon \approx 1$); having two parameters with very different values allows us to circumvent the limitations of either pure DP or TV distance as a similarity measure.

All of these options for quantifying indistinguishability can be viewed from the perspective of the privacy loss distribution. The privacy loss distribution also turns out to be essential to the analysis of composition. Approximate (ε, δ)-DP bounds are usually proved via the privacy loss distribution.

We now formally define the privacy loss distribution and relate it to the various quantities we have considered. Then, in Section 3.3.1, we will calculate the privacy loss distribution corresponding to the Gaussian mechanism, which is a particularly nice example. In the next Section 3.3.2, we explain how the privacy loss distribution arises naturally via statistical hypothesis testing. To conclude, in Section 3.3.3, we precisely relate the privacy loss back to approximate (ε, δ)-DP. In the next section

(Section 3.4), we will use the privacy loss distribution as a tool to analyze composition.

Definition 3.2 (Privacy Loss Distribution). *Let P and Q be two probability distributions on $\mathcal{Y}$. Define $f_{P\|Q} : \mathcal{Y} \to \mathbb{R}$ by $f_{P\|Q}(y) = \log(P(y)/Q(y))$.*[i] *The privacy loss random variable is given by $Z = f_{P\|Q}(Y)$ for $Y \leftarrow P$. The distribution of Z is denoted* $\text{PrivLoss}(P\|Q)$.

In the context of differential privacy, the distributions $P = M(x)$ and $Q = M(x')$ correspond to the outputs of the algorithm M on neighboring inputs x, x'. Successfully distinguishing these distributions corresponds to learning some fact about an individual person's data. The randomness of the privacy loss random variable Z comes from the randomness of the algorithm M (e.g., added noise). Intuitively, the privacy loss tells us which input (x or x') is more likely given the observed output ($Y \leftarrow M(\cdot)$). If $Z > 0$, then the hypothesis $Y \leftarrow P = M(x)$ explains the observed output better than the hypothesis $Y \leftarrow Q = M(x')$ and vice versa. The magnitude of the privacy loss Z indicates how strong the evidence for this conclusion is. If $Z = 0$, both hypotheses explain the output equally well, but, if $Z \to \infty$, then we can be nearly certain that the output came from P, rather than Q. A very negative privacy loss $Z \ll 0$ means that the observed output $Y \leftarrow P$ strongly supports the wrong hypothesis (i.e., $Y \leftarrow Q$).

As long as the privacy loss distribution is well-defined,[ii] we can easily express almost all the quantities of interest in terms of it:

- Pure ε-DP of M is equivalent to demanding that $\mathop{\mathbb{P}}_{Z \leftarrow \text{PrivLoss}(M(x)\|M(x'))}[Z \leq \varepsilon] = 1$ for all neighboring x, x'.[iii]

---

i. The function $f_{P\|Q}$ is called the log likelihood ratio of P with respect to Q. Formally, $f_{P\|Q}$ is the natural logarithm of the Radon-Nikodym derivative of P with respect to Q. This function is defined by the property that $P(S) = \mathop{\mathbb{E}}_{Y \leftarrow P}[\mathbb{I}[Y \in S]] = \mathop{\mathbb{E}}_{Y \leftarrow Q}\left[e^{f_{P\|Q}(Y)} \cdot \mathbb{I}[Y \in S]\right]$ for all measurable $S \subset \mathcal{Y}$. For this to exist, we must assume that P and Q have the same sigma-algebra and that P is absolutely continuous with respect to Q and vice versa – i.e., $\forall S \subset \mathcal{Y} \quad Q(S) = 0 \iff P(S) = 0$.

ii. The privacy loss distribution is not well-defined if absolute continuity fails to hold. Intuitively, this corresponds to the privacy loss being infinite. We can extend most of these definitions to allow for an infinite privacy loss. For simplicity, we do not delve into these issues.

iii. Note that, by the symmetry of the neighboring relation (i.e., if x, x' are neighboring datasets then x', x are also neighbors), we also have $\mathop{\mathbb{P}}_{Z \leftarrow \text{PrivLoss}(M(x)\|M(x'))}[Z \geq -\varepsilon] = 1$ as a consequence of $\mathop{\mathbb{P}}_{Z' \leftarrow \text{PrivLoss}(M(x')\|M(x))}\left[Z' \leq \varepsilon\right] = 1$.

- The KL divergence is the expectation of the privacy loss: $\mathrm{D}_1(P\|Q) := \mathop{\mathbb{E}}_{Z \leftarrow \mathrm{PrivLoss}(P\|Q)}[Z]$.[iv]
- The TV distance is given by

$$\begin{aligned} \mathrm{d}_{\mathrm{TV}}(P,Q) &= \mathop{\mathbb{E}}_{Z \leftarrow \mathrm{PrivLoss}(P\|Q)}\left[\max\{0, 1-\exp(-Z)\}\right] \\ &= \frac{1}{2} \mathop{\mathbb{E}}_{Z \leftarrow \mathrm{PrivLoss}(P\|Q)}\left[\left|1-\exp(-Z)\right|\right]. \end{aligned}$$

- Approximate (ε,δ)-DP of M is implied by $\mathop{\mathbb{P}}_{Z \leftarrow \mathrm{PrivLoss}(M(x)\|M(x'))}[Z \le \varepsilon] \ge 1-\delta$ for all neighboring x, x'. So we should think of approximate DP as a tail bound on the privacy loss. To be precise, (ε,δ)-DP of M is equivalent to

$$\mathop{\mathbb{E}}_{Z \leftarrow \mathrm{PrivLoss}(M(x)\|M(x'))}\left[\max\{0, 1-\exp(\varepsilon - Z)\}\right] \le \delta,$$

  for all neighboring x, x'. (See Proposition 3.7.)

3.3.1 Privacy Loss of Gaussian Noise Addition

As an example, we will work out the privacy loss distribution corresponding to the addition of Gaussian noise to a bounded-sensitivity query. This example is particularly clean, as the privacy loss distribution is also a Gaussian, and it will turn out to be central to the story of composition.

Proposition 3.3 (Privacy Loss Distribution of Gaussian). *Let* $P = \mathcal{N}(\mu, \sigma^2)$ *and* $Q = \mathcal{N}(\mu', \sigma^2)$. *Then* $\mathrm{PrivLoss}(P\|Q) = \mathcal{N}(\rho, 2\rho)$ *for* $\rho = \frac{(\mu-\mu')^2}{2\sigma^2}$.

Proof. We have $P(y) = \frac{1}{\sqrt{2\pi\sigma^2}} \exp\left(-\frac{(y-\mu)^2}{2\sigma^2}\right)$ and $Q(y) = \frac{1}{\sqrt{2\pi\sigma^2}} \exp\left(-\frac{(y-\mu')^2}{2\sigma^2}\right)$. Thus the log likelihood ratio is

$$\begin{aligned} f_{P\|Q}(y) &= \log\left(\frac{P(y)}{Q(y)}\right) \\ &= \log\left(\frac{\frac{1}{\sqrt{2\pi\sigma^2}} \exp\left(-\frac{(y-\mu)^2}{2\sigma^2}\right)}{\frac{1}{\sqrt{2\pi\sigma^2}} \exp\left(-\frac{(y-\mu')^2}{2\sigma^2}\right)}\right) \\ &= -\frac{(y-\mu)^2}{2\sigma^2} + \frac{(y-\mu')^2}{2\sigma^2} \end{aligned}$$

iv. The expectation of the privacy loss is always non-negative. Intuitively, this is because we take the expectation of the log likelihood ratio $f_{P\|Q}(Y)$ with respect to $Y \leftarrow P$ – i.e., the true answer is P, so on average the log likelihood ratio should point towards the correct answer.

$$= \frac{(y^2 - 2\mu' y + \mu'^2) - (y^2 - 2\mu y + \mu^2)}{2\sigma^2}$$
$$= \frac{2(\mu - \mu')y - \mu^2 + \mu'^2}{2\sigma^2}$$
$$= \frac{(\mu - \mu')(2y - \mu - \mu')}{2\sigma^2}.$$

The log likelihood ratio $f_{P\|Q}$ is an affine linear function. Thus the privacy loss random variable $Z = f_{P\|Q}(Y)$ for $Y \leftarrow P = \mathcal{N}(\mu, \sigma^2)$ will also follow a Gaussian distribution. Specifically, $\mathbb{E}[Y] = \mu$, so

$$\mathbb{E}[Z] = \frac{(\mu - \mu')(2\mathbb{E}[Y] - \mu - \mu')}{2\sigma^2} = \frac{(\mu - \mu')^2}{2\sigma^2} = \rho$$

and, similarly, $\mathbb{V}[Y] = \sigma^2$, so

$$\mathbb{V}[Z] = \frac{((2(\mu - \mu'))^2}{(2\sigma^2)^2} \cdot \mathbb{V}[Y] = \frac{(\mu - \mu')^2}{\sigma^2} = 2\rho.$$

□

To relate Proposition 3.3 to the standard Gaussian mechanism $M : \mathcal{X}^n \to \mathbb{R}$, recall that $M(x) = \mathcal{N}(q(x), \sigma^2)$, where q is a sensitivity-Δ query – i.e., $|q(x) - q(x')| \leq \Delta$ for all neighboring datasets $x, x' \in \mathcal{X}^n$. Thus, for neighboring datasets x, x', we have $\mathrm{PrivLoss}\left(M(x) \middle\| M(x')\right) = \mathcal{N}(\rho, 2\rho)$ for some $\rho \leq \frac{\Delta^2}{2\sigma^2}$.

The privacy loss of the Gaussian mechanism is unbounded; thus it does not satisfy pure ε-DP. However, the Gaussian distribution is highly concentrated, so we can say that with high probability the privacy loss is not too large. This is the basis of the privacy guarantee of the Gaussian mechanism.

3.3.2 Statistical Hypothesis Testing Perspective

To formally quantify differential privacy, we must measure the closeness or indistinguishability of the distributions $P = M(x)$ and $Q = M(x')$ corresponding to the outputs of the algorithm M on neighboring inputs x, x'. Distinguishing a pair of distributions is precisely the problem of (simple) hypothesis testing in the field of statistical inference. Thus it is natural to look at hypothesis testing tools to quantify the (in)distinguishability of a pair of distributions.

In the language of hypothesis testing, the two distributions P and Q would be the null hypothesis and the alternate hypothesis, which correspond to a positive or negative example. We are given a sample Y drawn from one of the two distributions and our task is to determine which. Needless to say, there is, in general, no hypothesis test that perfectly distinguishes the two distributions and, when choosing a hypothesis test, we face a non-trivial tradeoff between false positives and false negatives. There are many different ways to measure how good a given hypothesis test is.

For example, we could measure the accuracy of the hypothesis test evenly averaged over the two distributions. In this case, given the sample Y, an optimal test chooses P if $P(Y) \geq Q(Y)$ and otherwise chooses Q; the accuracy of this test is

$$\frac{1}{2} \underset{Y \leftarrow P}{\mathbb{P}} [P(Y) \geq Q(Y)] + \frac{1}{2} \underset{Y \leftarrow Q}{\mathbb{P}} [P(Y) < Q(Y)] = \frac{1}{2} + \frac{1}{2} \mathrm{d}_{\mathrm{TV}}(P, Q).$$

This measure of accuracy thus corresponds to TV distance. The greater the TV distance between the distributions, the more accurate this test is. However, as we mentioned earlier, TV distance does not yield good privacy-utility tradeoffs. Intuitively, the problem is that this hypothesis test doesn't care about how confident we are. That is, the test only asks whether $P(Y) \geq Q(Y)$, but not how big the difference or ratio is. Hence we want a more refined measure of accuracy that does not count false positives and false negatives equally.

Regardless of how we measure how good the hypothesis test is, there is an optimal test statistic, namely the log likelihood ratio. This test statistic gives a real number and thresholding that value yields a binary hypothesis test; *any* binary hypothesis test is dominated by some value of the threshold. In other words, the tradeoff between false positives and false negatives reduces to picking a threshold. This remarkable – yet simple – fact is established by the Neyman-Pearson lemma:

Lemma 3.4 (Neyman-Pearson Lemma [NP33]). *Fix distributions P and Q on $\mathcal{Y}$ and define the log-likelihood ratio test statistic $f_{P\|Q} : \mathcal{Y} \to \mathbb{R}$ by $f_{P\|Q}(y) = \log\left(\frac{P(y)}{Q(y)}\right)$. Let $T : \mathcal{Y} \to \{P, Q\}$ be any (possibly randomized) test. Then there exists some $t \in \mathbb{R}$ such that*

$$\underset{Y \leftarrow P}{\mathbb{P}} [T(Y) = P] \leq \underset{Y \leftarrow P}{\mathbb{P}} \left[f_{P\|Q}(Y) \geq t\right] \quad \textit{and}$$

$$\underset{Y \leftarrow Q}{\mathbb{P}} [T(Y) = Q] \leq \underset{Y \leftarrow Q}{\mathbb{P}} \left[f_{P\|Q}(Y) \leq t\right].$$

How is this related to the privacy loss distribution? The test statistic $Z = f_{P\|Q}(Y)$ under the hypothesis $Y \leftarrow P$ is precisely the privacy loss random variable $Z \leftarrow \mathrm{PrivLoss}(P\|Q)$. Thus the Neyman-Pearson lemma tells us that the privacy loss distribution $\mathrm{PrivLoss}(P\|Q)$ captures everything we need to know about distinguishing P from Q.

Note that the Neyman-Pearson lemma also references the test statistic $f_{P\|Q}(Y)$ under the hypothesis $Y \leftarrow Q$. This is fundamentally not that different from the privacy loss. There are two ways we can relate this quantity back to the usual privacy loss: First, we can relate it to $\mathrm{PrivLoss}(Q\|P)$ and this distribution is something we should be able to handle due to the symmetry of differential privacy guarantees.

Remark 3.5. *Fix distributions P and Q on $\mathcal{Y}$ such that the log likelihood ratio $f_{P\|Q}(y) = \log\left(\frac{P(y)}{Q(y)}\right)$ is well-defined for all $y \in \mathcal{Y}$. Since $f_{P\|Q}(y) = -f_{Q\|P}(y)$ for all $y \in \mathcal{Y}$, if $Z \leftarrow \mathrm{PrivLoss}(Q\|P)$, then $-Z$ follows the distribution of $f_{P\|Q}(Y)$ under the hypothesis $Y \leftarrow Q$.*

Second, if we need to compute an expectation of some function g of $f_{P\|Q}(Y)$ under the hypothesis $Y \leftarrow Q$, then we can still express this in terms of the privacy loss $\mathrm{PrivLoss}(P\|Q)$:

Lemma 3.6 (Change of Distribution for Privacy Loss). *Fix distributions P and Q on $\mathcal{Y}$ such that the log likelihood ratio $f_{P\|Q}(y) = \log\left(\frac{P(y)}{Q(y)}\right)$ is well-defined for all $y \in \mathcal{Y}$. Let $g : \mathbb{R} \to \mathbb{R}$ be measurable. Then*

$$\underset{Y\leftarrow Q}{\mathbb{E}}\left[g(f_{P\|Q}(Y))\right] = \underset{Z\leftarrow \mathrm{PrivLoss}(P\|Q)}{\mathbb{E}}\left[g(Z)\cdot e^{-Z}\right].$$

Proof. By the definition of the log likelihood ratio (see Definition 3.2), we have $\underset{Y\leftarrow P}{\mathbb{E}}[h(Y)] = \underset{Y\leftarrow Q}{\mathbb{E}}\left[h(Y)\cdot e^{f_{P\|Q}(Y)}\right]$ for all measurable functions h. Setting $h(y) = g(f_{P\|Q}(y))\cdot e^{-f_{P\|Q}(y)}$ yields $\underset{Z\leftarrow \mathrm{PrivLoss}(P\|Q)}{\mathbb{E}}\left[g(Z)\cdot e^{-Z}\right] = \underset{Y\leftarrow P}{\mathbb{E}}[h(Y)] = \underset{Y\leftarrow Q}{\mathbb{E}}\left[h(Y)\cdot e^{f_{P\|Q}(Y)}\right] = \underset{Y\leftarrow Q}{\mathbb{E}}\left[g(f_{P\|Q}(Y))\right]$, as required. We can also write these expressions out as an integral to obtain a more intuitive proof:

$$\begin{aligned}
\underset{Y\leftarrow Q}{\mathbb{E}}\left[g(f_{P\|Q}(Y))\right] &= \int_{\mathcal{Y}} g(f_{P\|Q}(y))\cdot Q(y)\mathrm{d}y \\
&= \int_{\mathcal{Y}} g(f_{P\|Q}(y))\cdot \frac{Q(y)}{P(y)}\cdot P(y)\mathrm{d}y \\
&= \int_{\mathcal{Y}} g(f_{P\|Q}(y))\cdot e^{-\log(P(y)/Q(y))}\cdot P(y)\mathrm{d}y \\
&= \int_{\mathcal{Y}} g(f_{P\|Q}(y))\cdot e^{-f_{P\|Q}(y)}\cdot P(y)\mathrm{d}y \\
&= \underset{Y\leftarrow P}{\mathbb{E}}\left[g(f_{P\|Q}(Y))\cdot e^{-f_{P\|Q}(Y)}\right] \\
&= \underset{Z\leftarrow \mathrm{PrivLoss}(P\|Q)}{\mathbb{E}}\left[g(Z)\cdot e^{-Z}\right].
\end{aligned}$$

□

3.3.3 Approximate DP & the Privacy Loss Distribution

So far, in this section, we have defined the privacy loss distribution, given an example, and illustrated that it is a natural quantity to consider that captures essentially everything we need to know about the (in)distinguishability of two distributions. To wrap up this section, we will relate the privacy loss distribution back to the definition of approximate (ε, δ)-DP:

Proposition 3.7 (Conversion from Privacy Loss Distribution to Approximate Differential Privacy). *Let P and Q be two probability distributions on $\mathcal{Y}$ such that the privacy loss distribution* $\text{PrivLoss}(P\|Q)$ *is well-defined. Fix $\varepsilon \geq 0$ and define*

$$\delta := \sup_{S \subset \mathcal{Y}} P(S) - e^{\varepsilon} \cdot Q(S).$$

Then

$$\begin{aligned}
\delta &= \underset{Z \leftarrow \text{PrivLoss}(P\|Q)}{\mathbb{P}}[Z > \varepsilon] - e^{\varepsilon} \cdot \underset{Z' \leftarrow \text{PrivLoss}(Q\|P)}{\mathbb{P}}\left[-Z' > \varepsilon\right] \\
&= \underset{Z \leftarrow \text{PrivLoss}(P\|Q)}{\mathbb{E}}\left[\max\{0, 1 - \exp(\varepsilon - Z)\}\right] \\
&= \int_{\varepsilon}^{\infty} e^{\varepsilon - Z} \cdot \underset{Z \leftarrow \text{PrivLoss}(P\|Q)}{\mathbb{P}}[Z > z]\mathrm{d}z \\
&\leq \underset{Z \leftarrow \text{PrivLoss}(P\|Q)}{\mathbb{P}}[Z > \varepsilon].
\end{aligned}$$

Proof. For any measurable $S \subset \mathcal{Y}$, we have

$$P(S) - e^{\varepsilon} \cdot Q(S) = \int_{\mathcal{Y}} \mathbb{I}[y \in S] \cdot \left(P(y) - e^{\varepsilon} \cdot Q(y)\right) \mathrm{d}y,$$

where $\mathbb{I}$ denotes the indicator function – it takes the value 1 if the condition is true and 0 otherwise. To maximize this expression, we want $y \in S$ whenever $P(y) - e^{\varepsilon} \cdot Q(y) > 0$ and we want $y \notin S$ when this is negative. Thus $\delta = P(S_*) - e^{\varepsilon} \cdot Q(S_*)$ for

$$S_* := \left\{y \in \mathcal{Y} : P(y) - e^{\varepsilon} \cdot Q(y) > 0\right\} = \left\{y \in \mathcal{Y} : f_{P\|Q}(y) > \varepsilon\right\}.$$

Now

$$P(S_*) = \underset{Y \leftarrow P}{\mathbb{P}}\left[f_{P\|Q}(Y) > \varepsilon\right] = \underset{Z \leftarrow \text{PrivLoss}(P\|Q)}{\mathbb{P}}[Z > \varepsilon],$$

and, by Remark 3.5,

$$Q(S_*) = \underset{Y \leftarrow Q}{\mathbb{P}}\left[f_{P\|Q}(Y) > \varepsilon\right] = \underset{Z' \leftarrow \text{PrivLoss}(Q\|P)}{\mathbb{P}}\left[-Z' > \varepsilon\right].$$

This gives the first expression in the result:

$$\delta = P(S_*) - e^\varepsilon \cdot Q(S_*) = \underset{Z \leftarrow \text{PrivLoss}(P\|Q)}{\mathbb{P}}[Z > \varepsilon] - e^\varepsilon \cdot \underset{Z' \leftarrow \text{PrivLoss}(Q\|P)}{\mathbb{P}}\left[-Z' > \varepsilon\right].$$

Alternatively, $P(S_*) = \underset{Z \leftarrow \text{PrivLoss}(P\|Q)}{\mathbb{E}}[\mathbb{I}[Z > \varepsilon]]$ and, by Lemma 3.6,

$$Q(S_*) = \underset{Y \leftarrow Q}{\mathbb{E}}\left[\mathbb{I}[f_{P\|Q}(Y) > \varepsilon]\right] = \underset{Z \leftarrow \text{PrivLoss}(P\|Q)}{\mathbb{E}}\left[\mathbb{I}[Z > \varepsilon] \cdot e^{-Z}\right],$$

which yields

$$\delta = P(S_*) - e^\varepsilon \cdot Q(S_*) = \underset{Z \leftarrow \text{PrivLoss}(P\|Q)}{\mathbb{E}}\left[(1 - e^\varepsilon \cdot e^{-Z}) \cdot \mathbb{I}[Z > \varepsilon]\right].$$

Note that $(1 - e^\varepsilon \cdot e^{-z}) \cdot \mathbb{I}[z > \varepsilon] = \max\{0, 1 - e^{\varepsilon - z}\}$ for all $z \in \mathbb{R}$. This produces the second expression in our result.

To obtain the third expression in the result, we apply integration by parts to the second expression: Let $F(z) := \underset{Z \leftarrow \text{PrivLoss}(P\|Q)}{\mathbb{P}}[Z > z]$ be the complement of the cumulative distribution function of the privacy loss distribution. Then the probability density function of Z evaluated at z is given by the negative derivative, $-F'(z)$.[v] Then

$$\begin{aligned}
\delta &= \underset{Z \leftarrow \text{PrivLoss}(P\|Q)}{\mathbb{E}}\left[\max\{0, 1 - e^{\varepsilon - Z}\}\right] \\
&= \int_{\mathbb{R}} \max\{0, 1 - e^{\varepsilon - z}\} \cdot (-F'(z))\mathrm{d}z \\
&= \int_\varepsilon^\infty (1 - e^{\varepsilon - z}) \cdot (-F'(z))\mathrm{d}z \\
&= \int_\varepsilon^\infty \left(\frac{\mathrm{d}}{\mathrm{d}z}(1 - e^{\varepsilon - z}) \cdot (-F(z))\right) - (0 - e^{\varepsilon - z} \cdot (-1)) \cdot (-F(z))\mathrm{d}z \\
&\qquad \text{(product rule)} \\
&= \lim_{z \to \infty} (1 - e^{\varepsilon - z}) \cdot (-F(z)) - (1 - e^{\varepsilon - \varepsilon}) \cdot (-F(\varepsilon)) - \int_\varepsilon^\infty e^{\varepsilon - z} \cdot (-F(z))\mathrm{d}z \\
&\qquad \text{(fundamental theorem of calculus)} \\
&= - \lim_{z \to \infty} \underset{Z \leftarrow \text{PrivLoss}(P\|Q)}{\mathbb{P}}[Z > z] + \int_\varepsilon^\infty e^{\varepsilon - z} \cdot \underset{Z \leftarrow \text{PrivLoss}(P\|Q)}{\mathbb{P}}[Z > z]\mathrm{d}z.
\end{aligned}$$

If the privacy loss is well-defined, then $\lim_{z \to \infty} \underset{Z \leftarrow \text{PrivLoss}(P\|Q)}{\mathbb{P}}[Z > z] = 0$.

---

v. In general, the privacy loss may not be continuous – i.e., F may not be differentiable. Nevertheless, the final result still holds in this case.

The final expression (an upper bound, rather than a tight characterization) is easily obtained from any of the other three expressions. In particular, dropping the second term $-e^{\varepsilon} \cdot \underset{Z' \leftarrow \text{PrivLoss}(Q\|P)}{\mathbb{P}}\left[-Z' > \varepsilon\right] \leq 0$ from the first expression yields the upper bound. □

The expression $\delta = \sup_{S \subset \mathcal{Y}} P(S) - e^{\varepsilon} \cdot Q(S)$ in Proposition 3.7 is known as the "hockey stick divergence" and it determines the smallest δ for a given ε such that $P(S) \leq e^{\varepsilon} Q(S) + \delta$ for all $S \subset \mathcal{Y}$. If $P = M(x)$ and $Q = M(x')$ for arbitrary neighboring datasets x, x', then this expression gives the best approximate (ε, δ)-DP guarantee.

Proposition 3.7 gives us three equivalent ways to calculate δ, each of which will be useful in different circumstances. To illustrate how to use Proposition 3.7, we combine it with Proposition 3.3 to prove a tight approximate differential privacy guarantee for Gaussian noise addition:

Corollary 3.8 (Tight Approximate Differential Privacy for Univariate Gaussian). *Let $q : \mathcal{X}^n \to \mathbb{R}$ be a deterministic function and let $\Delta := \sup_{\substack{x,x' \in \mathcal{X}^n \\ \text{neighboring}}} |q(x) - q(x')|$ be its sensitivity. Define a randomized algorithm $M : \mathcal{X}^n \to \mathbb{R}$ by $M(x) = \mathcal{N}(q(x), \sigma^2)$ for some $\sigma^2 > 0$. Then, for any $\varepsilon \geq 0$, M satisfies (ε, δ)-DP with*

$$\delta = \overline{\Phi}\left(\frac{\varepsilon - \rho_*}{\sqrt{2\rho_*}}\right) - e^{\varepsilon} \cdot \overline{\Phi}\left(\frac{\varepsilon + \rho_*}{\sqrt{2\rho_*}}\right),$$

where $\rho_* := \Delta^2/2\sigma^2$ and $\overline{\Phi}(z) := \underset{G \leftarrow \mathcal{N}(0,1)}{\mathbb{P}}[G > z] = \frac{1}{\sqrt{2\pi}} \int_z^{\infty} \exp(-t^2/2) \mathrm{d}t$.

Furthermore, this guarantee is optimal – for every $\varepsilon \geq 0$, there is no $\delta' < \delta$ such that M is (ε, δ')-DP for general q.

Proof. Fix arbitrary neighboring datasets $x, x' \in \mathcal{X}^n$ and $S \subset \mathcal{Y}$. Let $\mu = q(x)$ and $\mu' = q(x')$. Let $P = M(x) = \mathcal{N}(\mu, \sigma^2)$ and $Q = M(x') = \mathcal{N}(\mu', \sigma^2)$. We must show $P(S) \leq e^{\varepsilon} \cdot Q(S) + \delta$ for arbitrary $\varepsilon \geq 0$ and the value δ given in the result.

By Proposition 3.3, $\text{PrivLoss}(P\|Q) = \text{PrivLoss}(Q\|P) = \mathcal{N}(\rho, 2\rho)$, where $\rho = \frac{(\mu - \mu')^2}{2\sigma^2} \leq \rho_* = \frac{\Delta^2}{2\sigma^2}$.

By Proposition 3.7, we have $P(S) \leq e^{\varepsilon} \cdot Q(S) + \delta$, where

$$\begin{aligned}
\delta &= \underset{Z \leftarrow \text{PrivLoss}(P\|Q)}{\mathbb{P}}[Z > \varepsilon] - e^{\varepsilon} \cdot \underset{Z' \leftarrow \text{PrivLoss}(Q\|P)}{\mathbb{P}}\left[-Z' > \varepsilon\right] \\
&= \underset{Z \leftarrow \mathcal{N}(\rho, 2\rho)}{\mathbb{P}}[Z > \varepsilon] - e^{\varepsilon} \cdot \underset{Z' \leftarrow \mathcal{N}(\rho, 2\rho)}{\mathbb{P}}\left[-Z' > \varepsilon\right] \\
&= \underset{G \leftarrow \mathcal{N}(0,1)}{\mathbb{P}}\left[\rho + \sqrt{2\rho} \cdot G > \varepsilon\right] - e^{\varepsilon} \cdot \underset{G \leftarrow \mathcal{N}(0,1)}{\mathbb{P}}\left[-\rho + \sqrt{2\rho} \cdot G > \varepsilon\right] \\
&= \underset{G \leftarrow \mathcal{N}(0,1)}{\mathbb{P}}\left[G > \frac{\varepsilon - \rho}{\sqrt{2\rho}}\right] - e^{\varepsilon} \cdot \underset{G \leftarrow \mathcal{N}(0,1)}{\mathbb{P}}\left[G > \frac{\varepsilon + \rho}{\sqrt{2\rho}}\right]
\end{aligned}$$

$$= \overline{\Phi}\left(\frac{\varepsilon - \rho}{\sqrt{2\rho}}\right) - e^{\varepsilon} \cdot \overline{\Phi}\left(\frac{\varepsilon + \rho}{\sqrt{2\rho}}\right).$$

Since $\rho \leq \rho_*$ and the above expression is increasing in ρ, we can substitute in ρ_* as an upper bound.

Optimality follows from the fact that both Propositions 3.3 and 3.7 give exact characterizations. Note that we must assume that there exist neighboring x, x' such that $\rho = \rho_*$. □

The guarantee of Corollary 3.8 is exact, but it is somewhat hard to interpret. We can easily obtain a more interpretable upper bound:

$$\begin{aligned} \delta &= \overline{\Phi}\left(\frac{\varepsilon - \rho_*}{\sqrt{2\rho_*}}\right) - e^{\varepsilon} \cdot \overline{\Phi}\left(\frac{\varepsilon + \rho_*}{\sqrt{2\rho_*}}\right) \\ &\leq \overline{\Phi}\left(\frac{\varepsilon - \rho_*}{\sqrt{2\rho_*}}\right) = \underset{G \leftarrow \mathcal{N}(0,1)}{\mathbb{P}}\left[G > \frac{\varepsilon - \rho_*}{\sqrt{2\rho_*}}\right] \\ &\leq \frac{\exp\left(-\frac{(\varepsilon - \rho_*)^2}{4\rho_*}\right)}{\max\left\{2, \sqrt{\frac{\pi}{\rho_*}} \cdot (\varepsilon - \rho_*)\right\}}. \qquad \text{(assuming } \varepsilon \geq \rho_*\text{)} \end{aligned}$$

3.4 Composition via the Privacy Loss Distribution

The privacy loss distribution captures essentially everything about the (in)distinguishability of a pair of distributions. It is also the key to understanding composition. Suppose we run multiple differentially private algorithms on the same dataset and each has a well-defined privacy loss distribution. The composition of these algorithms corresponds to the convolution of the privacy loss distributions. That is, the privacy loss random variable corresponding to running all of the algorithms independently is equal to the sum of the independent privacy loss random variables of each of the algorithms:

Theorem 3.9 (Composition is Convolution of Privacy Loss Distributions). *For each $j \in [k]$, let P_j and Q_j be distributions on $\mathcal{Y}_j$ and assume* $\mathrm{PrivLoss}\left(P_j \| Q_j\right)$ *is well defined. Let $P = P_1 \times P_2 \times \cdots \times P_k$ denote the product distribution on $\mathcal{Y} = \mathcal{Y}_1 \times \mathcal{Y}_2 \times \cdots \times \mathcal{Y}_k$ obtained by sampling independently from each P_j. Similarly, let $Q = Q_1 \times Q_2 \times \cdots \times Q_k$ denote the product distribution on $\mathcal{Y}$ obtained by sampling independently from each Q_j. Then* $\mathrm{PrivLoss}\left(P \| Q\right)$ *is the convolution of the distributions* $\mathrm{PrivLoss}\left(P_j \| Q_j\right)$ *for all $j \in [k]$. That is, sampling $Z \leftarrow$* $\mathrm{PrivLoss}\left(P \| Q\right)$ *is equivalent to $Z = \sum_{j=1}^{k} Z_j$ when $Z_j \leftarrow$* $\mathrm{PrivLoss}\left(P_j \| Q_j\right)$ *independently for each $j \in [k]$.*

Proof. For all $y \in \mathcal{Y}$, the log likelihood ratio (Definition 3.2) satisfies

$$\begin{aligned} f_{P\|Q}(y) &= \log\left(\frac{P(y)}{Q(y)}\right) \\ &= \log\left(\frac{P_1(y_1)\cdot P_2(y_2)\cdot \cdots \cdot P_k(y_k)}{Q_1(y_1)\cdot Q_2(y_2)\cdot \cdots \cdot Q_k(y_k)}\right) \\ &= \log\left(\frac{P_1(y_1)}{Q_1(y_1)}\right) + \log\left(\frac{P_2(y_2)}{Q_2(y_2)}\right) + \cdots + \log\left(\frac{P_k(y_k)}{Q_k(y_k)}\right) \\ &= f_{P_1\|Q_1}(y_1) + f_{P_2\|Q_2}(y_2) + \cdots + f_{P_k\|Q_k}(y_k). \end{aligned}$$

Since P is a product distribution, sampling $Y \leftarrow P$ is equivalent to sampling $Y_1 \leftarrow P_1, Y_2 \leftarrow P_2, \cdots, Y_k \leftarrow P_k$ independently.

A sample from the privacy loss distribution $Z \leftarrow \mathrm{PrivLoss}(P\|Q)$ is given by $Z = f_{P\|Q}(Y)$ for $Y \leftarrow P$. By the above two facts, this is equivalent to $Z = f_{P_1\|Q_1}(Y_1)+f_{P_2\|Q_2}(Y_2)+\cdots+f_{P_k\|Q_k}(Y_k)$ for $Y_1 \leftarrow P_1, Y_2 \leftarrow P_2, \cdots, Y_k \leftarrow P_k$ independently. For each $j \in [k]$, sampling $Z_j \leftarrow \mathrm{PrivLoss}\left(P_j \middle\| Q_j\right)$ is given by $Z_j = f_{P_j\|Q_j}(Y_j)$ for $Y_j \leftarrow P_j$. Thus sampling $Z \leftarrow \mathrm{PrivLoss}(P\|Q)$ is equivalent to $Z = Z_1 + Z_2 + \cdots + Z_k$ where $Z_1 \leftarrow \mathrm{PrivLoss}(P_1\|Q_1)$, $Z_2 \leftarrow \mathrm{PrivLoss}(P_2\|Q_2)$, $\cdots, Z_k \leftarrow \mathrm{PrivLoss}(P_k\|Q_k)$ are independent. □

Theorem 3.9 is the key to understanding composition of differential privacy. More concretely, we should think of a pair of neighboring inputs x, x' and k algorithms $M_1, \cdots, M_k$. Suppose M is the composition of $M_1, \cdots, M_k$. Then the the differential privacy of M can be expressed in terms of the privacy loss distribution $\mathrm{PrivLoss}\left(M(x) \middle\| M(x')\right)$. Theorem 3.9 allows us to decompose this privacy loss as the sum/convolution of the privacy losses of the constituent algorithms $\mathrm{PrivLoss}\left(M_j(x) \middle\| M_j(x')\right)$ for $j \in [k]$. Thus if we have differential privacy guarantees for each M_j, this allows us to prove differential privacy guarantees for M.

Basic Composition, Revisited

We can revisit basic composition (Theorem 3.1 in Section 3.2) with the perspective of privacy loss distributions. Suppose $M_1, M_2, \cdots, M_k : \mathcal{X}^n \to \mathcal{Y}$ are each ε-DP. Fix neighboring datasets $x, x' \in \mathcal{X}^n$. This means that $\underset{Z_j \leftarrow \mathrm{PrivLoss}\left(M_j(x) \middle\| M_j(x')\right)}{\mathbb{P}}\left[Z_j \le \varepsilon\right] = 1$ for each $j \in [k]$. Now let $M : \mathcal{X}^n \to \mathcal{Y}^k$ be the composition of these algorithms. We can express the privacy loss $Z \leftarrow \mathrm{PrivLoss}\left(M(x) \middle\| M(x')\right)$ as $Z = Z_1 + Z_2 + \cdots + Z_k$ where $Z_j \leftarrow \mathrm{PrivLoss}\left(M_j(x) \middle\| M_j(x')\right)$ for each $j \in [k]$. Basic composition simply adds up the upper bounds:

$$Z = Z_1 + Z_2 + \cdots + Z_k \le \varepsilon + \varepsilon + \cdots + \varepsilon = k\varepsilon.$$

This bound is tight if each Z_j is a point mass (i.e., $\mathbb{P}\left[Z_j=\varepsilon\right] = 1$). However, this is not the case. (It is possible to prove, in general, that $\mathbb{P}\left[Z_j=\varepsilon\right] \le \frac{1}{1+e^{-\varepsilon}}$.) The way we will prove better composition bounds is by applying concentration of measure bounds to this sum of independent random variables. That way we can prove that the privacy loss is small with high probability, which yields a better differential privacy guarantee.

Intuitively, we will apply the central limit theorem. The privacy loss random variable of the composed algorithm M can be expressed as the sum of independent bounded random variables. That means the privacy loss distribution $\mathrm{PrivLoss}\left(M(x)\middle\|M(x')\right)$ is well-approximated by a Gaussian, which is the information we need to prove a composition theorem. What is left to do is to obtain bounds on the mean and variance of the summands and make this Gaussian approximation precise.

Gaussian Composition

It is instructive to look at composition when each constituent algorithm M_j is the Gaussian noise addition mechanism. In this case the privacy loss distribution is exactly Gaussian and convolutions of Gaussians are also Gaussian. This is the ideal case and our general composition theorem will be an approximation to this ideal.

Specifically, we can prove a multivariate analog of Corollary 3.8:

Corollary 3.10 (Tight Approximate Differential Privacy for Multivariate Gaussian). *Let $q:\mathcal{X}^n \to \mathbb{R}^d$ be a deterministic function and let $\Delta := \sup_{\substack{x,x'\in\mathcal{X}^n \\ \text{neighboring}}} \|q(x)-q(x')\|_2$ be its sensitivity in the 2-norm. Define a randomized algorithm $M:\mathcal{X}^n \to \mathbb{R}^d$ by $M(x)=\mathcal{N}(q(x),\sigma^2 I)$ for some $\sigma^2>0$, where I is the identity matrix. Then, for any $\varepsilon \ge 0$, M satisfies (ε,δ)-DP with*

$$\delta = \overline{\Phi}\left(\frac{\varepsilon-\rho_*}{\sqrt{2\rho_*}}\right) - e^{\varepsilon}\cdot\overline{\Phi}\left(\frac{\varepsilon+\rho_*}{\sqrt{2\rho_*}}\right),$$

where $\rho_* := \Delta^2/2\sigma^2$ and $\overline{\Phi}(z) := \underset{G\leftarrow\mathcal{N}(0,1)}{\mathbb{P}}[G>z] = \frac{1}{\sqrt{2\pi}}\int_z^\infty \exp(-t^2/2)\mathrm{d}t$.

Furthermore, this guarantee is optimal – for every $\varepsilon \ge 0$, there is no $\delta' < \delta$ such that M is (ε,δ')-DP for general q.

Proof. Fix arbitrary neighboring datasets $x,x' \in \mathcal{X}^n$ and $S \subset \mathcal{Y}$. Let $\mu = q(x), \mu' = q(x') \in \mathbb{R}^d$. Let $P = M(x) = \mathcal{N}(\mu,\sigma^2 I)$ and $Q = M(x') = \mathcal{N}(\mu',\sigma^2 I)$. We must show $P(S) \le e^{\varepsilon}\cdot Q(S)+\delta$ for arbitrary $\varepsilon \ge 0$ and the value δ given in the result.

Now both P and Q are product distributions: For $j \in [d]$, let $P_j = \mathcal{N}(\mu_j,\sigma^2)$ and $Q_j = \mathcal{N}(\mu'_j,\sigma^2)$. Then $P = P_1 \times P_2 \times \cdots P_d$ and $Q = Q_1 \times Q_2 \times \cdots \times Q_d$.

By Theorem 3.9, $\mathrm{PrivLoss}(P\|Q) = \sum_{j=1}^{d} \mathrm{PrivLoss}\left(P_j \middle\| Q_j\right)$ and $\mathrm{PrivLoss}(Q\|P) = \sum_{j=1}^{d} \mathrm{PrivLoss}\left(Q_j \middle\| P_j\right)$.

By Proposition 3.3, $\mathrm{PrivLoss}\left(P_j \middle\| Q_j\right) = \mathrm{PrivLoss}\left(Q_j \middle\| P_j\right) = \mathcal{N}(\rho_j, 2\rho_j)$, where $\rho_j = \frac{(\mu_j - \mu_j')^2}{2\sigma^2}$ for all $j \in [d]$.

Thus $\mathrm{PrivLoss}(P\|Q) = \mathrm{PrivLoss}(Q\|P) = \sum_{j=1}^{d} \mathcal{N}(\rho_j, 2\rho_j) = \mathcal{N}(\rho, 2\rho)$, where $\rho = \sum_{j=1}^{d} \rho_j = \frac{\|\mu - \mu'\|_2^2}{2\sigma^2} \leq \rho_* = \frac{\Delta^2}{2\sigma^2}$.

By Proposition 3.7, we have $P(S) \leq e^{\varepsilon} \cdot Q(S) + \delta$, where

$$\begin{aligned}
\delta &= \underset{Z \leftarrow \mathrm{PrivLoss}(P\|Q)}{\mathbb{P}} [Z > \varepsilon] - e^{\varepsilon} \cdot \underset{Z' \leftarrow \mathrm{PrivLoss}(Q\|P)}{\mathbb{P}} \left[-Z' > \varepsilon\right] \\
&= \underset{Z \leftarrow \mathcal{N}(\rho, 2\rho)}{\mathbb{P}} [Z > \varepsilon] - e^{\varepsilon} \cdot \underset{Z' \leftarrow \mathcal{N}(\rho, 2\rho)}{\mathbb{P}} \left[-Z' > \varepsilon\right] \\
&= \underset{G \leftarrow \mathcal{N}(0,1)}{\mathbb{P}} \left[\rho + \sqrt{2\rho} \cdot G > \varepsilon\right] - e^{\varepsilon} \cdot \underset{G \leftarrow \mathcal{N}(0,1)}{\mathbb{P}} \left[-\rho + \sqrt{2\rho} \cdot G > \varepsilon\right] \\
&= \underset{G \leftarrow \mathcal{N}(0,1)}{\mathbb{P}} \left[G > \frac{\varepsilon - \rho}{\sqrt{2\rho}}\right] - e^{\varepsilon} \cdot \underset{G \leftarrow \mathcal{N}(0,1)}{\mathbb{P}} \left[G > \frac{\varepsilon + \rho}{\sqrt{2\rho}}\right] \\
&= \overline{\Phi}\left(\frac{\varepsilon - \rho}{\sqrt{2\rho}}\right) - e^{\varepsilon} \cdot \overline{\Phi}\left(\frac{\varepsilon + \rho}{\sqrt{2\rho}}\right).
\end{aligned}$$

Since $\rho \leq \rho_*$ and the above expression is increasing in ρ, we can substitute in ρ_* as an upper bound.

Optimality follows from the fact that Propositions 3.3 and 3.7 and Theorem 3.9 give exact characterizations. Note that we must assume that there exist neighboring x, x' such that $\rho = \rho_*$. □

The key to the analysis of Gaussian composition in the proof of Corollary 3.10 is that sums of Gaussians are Gaussian. In general, the privacy loss of each component is not Gaussian, but the sum still behaves much like a Gaussian and this observation is the basis for improving the composition analysis.

Composition Via Gaussian Approximation

After analyzing Gaussian composition, our next step is to analyze the composition of k independent ε-DP algorithms. We will use the same tools as we did for Gaussian composition and we will develop a new tool, which is called concentrated differential privacy.

Let $M_1, \cdots, M_k : \mathcal{X}^n \to \mathcal{Y}$ each be ε-DP and let $M : \mathcal{X}^n \to \mathcal{Y}^k$ be the composition of these algorithms. Let $x, x' \in \mathcal{X}^n$ be neighboring datasets. For notational convenience, let $P_j = M_j(x)$ and $Q_j = M_j(x')$ for all $j \in [k]$ and let $P = M(x) = P_1 \times P_2 \times \cdots \times P_k$ and $Q = M(x') = Q_1 \times Q_2 \times \cdots \times Q_k$.

For each $j \in [k]$, the algorithm M_j satisfies ε-DP, which ensures that the privacy loss random variable $Z_j \leftarrow \mathrm{PrivLoss}\left(P_j \| Q_j\right) = \mathrm{PrivLoss}\left(M_j(x) \| M_j(x')\right)$ is supported on the interval $[-\varepsilon, \varepsilon]$. The privacy loss being bounded immediately implies a bound on the variance: $\mathbb{V}\left[Z_j\right] \leq \mathbb{E}\left[Z_j^2\right] \leq \varepsilon^2$. We also can prove a bound on the expectation: $\mathbb{E}\left[Z_j\right] \leq \frac{1}{2}\varepsilon^2$. We will prove this bound formally later (in Proposition 3.16). For now, we give some intuition: Clearly $\mathbb{E}\left[Z_j\right] \leq \varepsilon$ and the only way this can be tight is if $Z_j = \varepsilon$ with probability 1. But $Z_j = \log(P_j(Y_j)/Q_j(Y_j))$ for $Y_j \leftarrow P_j$. Thus $\mathbb{E}\left[Z_j\right] = \varepsilon$ implies $P_j(Y_j) = e^{\varepsilon} \cdot Q_j(Y_j)$ with probability 1. This yields a contradiction: $1 = \sum_y P_j(y) = \sum_y e^{\varepsilon} \cdot Q_j(y) = e^{\varepsilon} \cdot 1$. Thus we conclude $\mathbb{E}\left[Z_j\right] < \varepsilon$ and, with a bit more work, we can obtain the bound $\mathbb{E}\left[Z_j\right] \leq \frac{1}{2}\varepsilon^2$ from the fact that $|Z_j| \leq \varepsilon$ and $\sum_y P_j(y) = \sum_y Q_j(y) = 1$.

Our goal is to understand the privacy loss $Z \leftarrow \mathrm{PrivLoss}\,(P \| Q) = \mathrm{PrivLoss}\left(M(x) \| M(x')\right)$ of the composed algorithm. Theorem 3.9 tells us that this is the convolution of the constituent privacy losses. That is, we can write $Z = \sum_{j=1}^{k} Z_j$ where $Z_j \leftarrow \mathrm{PrivLoss}\left(P_j \| Q_j\right) = \mathrm{PrivLoss}\left(M_j(x) \| M_j(x')\right)$ independently for each $j \in [k]$.

By independence, we have

$$\mathbb{E}\,[Z] = \sum_{j=1}^{k} \mathbb{E}\left[Z_j\right] \leq \frac{1}{2}\varepsilon^2 \cdot k \quad \text{and} \quad \mathbb{V}\,[Z] = \sum_{j=1}^{k} \mathbb{V}\left[Z_j\right] \leq \varepsilon^2 \cdot k.$$

Since Z can be written as the sum of independent bounded random variables, the central limit theorem tells us that it is well approximated by a Gaussian – i.e.,

$$\mathrm{PrivLoss}\,(P \| Q) = \mathrm{PrivLoss}\left(M(x) \| M(x')\right) \approx \mathcal{N}(\mathbb{E}\,[Z], \mathbb{V}\,[Z]).$$

Are we done? Can we substitute this approximation into Proposition 3.7 to complete the proof of a better composition theorem? We must make this approximation precise. Unfortunately, the approximation guarantee of the quantitative central limit theorem (a.k.a., the Berry-Esseen Theorem) is not quite strong enough. To be precise, converting the guarantee to approximate (ε, δ)-DP would incur an error of $\delta \geq \Omega(1/\sqrt{k})$, which is larger than we want.

Our approach is to look at the moment generating function – i.e., the expectation of an exponential function – of the privacy loss distribution. To be precise, we will show that, for all $t \geq 0$,

$$\underset{Z \leftarrow \mathrm{PrivLoss}(P\|Q)}{\mathbb{E}}\left[\exp(tZ)\right] = \prod_{j=1}^{k} \underset{Z_j \leftarrow \mathrm{PrivLoss}\left(P_j \| Q_j\right)}{\mathbb{E}}\left[\exp(tZ_j)\right]$$

$$
\begin{aligned}
&\leq \exp\left(\frac{1}{2}\varepsilon^2 t(t+1)\cdot k\right)\\
&= \underset{\tilde{Z}\leftarrow\mathcal{N}(\frac{1}{2}\varepsilon^2 k,\varepsilon^2 k)}{\mathbb{E}}\left[\exp(t\tilde{Z})\right].
\end{aligned}
$$

In other words, rather than attempting to prove a Gaussian approximation, we prove a one-sided bound. Informally, this says that $\mathrm{PrivLoss}\,(P\|Q) \leq \mathcal{N}(\frac{1}{2}\varepsilon^2 k, \varepsilon^2 k)$. The expectation of an exponential function turns out to be a nice way to formalize this inequality, because, if X and Y are independent, then $\mathbb{E}\left[\exp(X+Y)\right] = \mathbb{E}\left[\exp(X)\right]\cdot\mathbb{E}\left[\exp(Y)\right]$.

To formalize this approach, we next introduce concentrated differential privacy.

3.4.1 Concentrated Differential Privacy

Concentrated differential privacy [DR16; BS16] is a variant of differential privacy (like pure DP and approximate DP). The main advantage of concentrated DP is that it composes well. Thus we will use it as a tool to prove better composition results.

Definition 3.11 (Concentrated Differential Privacy). *Let $M : \mathcal{X}^n \to \mathcal{Y}$ be a randomized algorithm. We say that M satisfies ρ-concentrated differential privacy (ρ-zCDP) if, for all neighboring inputs $x, x' \in \mathcal{X}^n$, the privacy loss distribution* $\mathrm{PrivLoss}\left(M(x)\|M(x')\right)$ *is well-defined (see Definition 3.2) and*

$$
\forall t\geq 0 \qquad \underset{Z\leftarrow\mathrm{PrivLoss}(M(x)\|M(x'))}{\mathbb{E}}\left[\exp(tZ)\right] \leq \exp(t(t+1)\cdot\rho).
$$

To contextualize this definition, we begin by showing that the Gaussian mechanism satisfies it.

Lemma 3.12 (Gaussian Mechanism is Concentrated DP). *Let $q : \mathcal{X}^n \to \mathbb{R}^d$ have sensitivity Δ – that is, $\|q(x)-q(x')\|_2 \leq \Delta$ for all neighboring $x, x' \in \mathcal{X}^n$. Let $\sigma > 0$. Define a randomized algorithm $M : \mathcal{X}^n \to \mathbb{R}^d$ by $M(x) = \mathcal{N}(q(x), \sigma^2 I_d)$. Then M is ρ-zCDP for $\rho = \frac{\Delta^2}{2\sigma^2}$.*

Proof. Fix neighboring inputs $x, x' \in \mathcal{X}^n$ and $t \geq 0$. By Proposition 3.3, for each $j \in [d]$,
$\mathrm{PrivLoss}\left(M(x)_j\|M(x')_j\right) = \mathcal{N}(\hat{\rho}_j, 2\hat{\rho}_j)$ for $\hat{\rho}_j = \frac{(q(x)_j - q(x')_j)^2}{2\sigma^2}$. By Theorem 3.9, $\mathrm{PrivLoss}\left(M(x)\|M(x')\right) = \sum_{j=1}^d \mathcal{N}(\hat{\rho}_j, 2\hat{\rho}_j) = \mathcal{N}(\hat{\rho}, 2\hat{\rho})$ for $\hat{\rho} = \sum_{j=1}^d \hat{\rho}_j = \frac{\|q(x)-q(x')\|_2^2}{2\sigma^2} \leq \rho$. Thus $\underset{Z\leftarrow\mathrm{PrivLoss}(M(x)\|M(x'))}{\mathbb{E}}\left[\exp(tZ)\right] = \exp(t(t+1)\hat{\rho}) \leq \exp(t(t+1)\rho)$, as required. □

To analyze the composition of k independent ε-DP algorithms, we will prove three results: (i) Pure ε-DP implies $\frac{1}{2}\varepsilon^2$-zCDP. (ii) The composition of k independent $\frac{1}{2}\varepsilon^2$-zCDP algorithms satisfies $\frac{1}{2}\varepsilon^2 k$-zCDP. (iii) $\frac{1}{2}\varepsilon^2 k$-zCDP implies approximate (ε', δ)-DP with $\delta \in (0,1)$ arbitrary and $\varepsilon' = \varepsilon \cdot \sqrt{2k\log(1/\delta)} + \frac{1}{2}\varepsilon^2 k$. We begin with composition, as this is the raison d'être for concentrated DP:

Theorem 3.13 (Composition for Concentrated Differential Privacy). *Let $M_1, M_2, \cdots, M_k : \mathcal{X}^n \to \mathcal{Y}$ be randomized algorithms. Suppose M_j is ρ_j-zCDP for each $j \in [k]$. Define $M : \mathcal{X}^n \to \mathcal{Y}^k$ by $M(x) = (M_1(x), M_2(x), \cdots, M_k(x))$, where each algorithm is run independently. Then M is ρ-zCDP for $\rho = \sum_{j=1}^k \rho_j$.*

Proof. Fix neighboring inputs $x, x' \in \mathcal{X}^n$. By our assumption that each algorithm M_j is ρ_j-zCDP,

$$\forall t \geq 0 \qquad \underset{Z_j \leftarrow \mathrm{PrivLoss}\left(M_j(x) \| M_j(x')\right)}{\mathbb{E}} \left[\exp(tZ_j)\right] \leq \exp(t(t+1) \cdot \rho_j).$$

By Theorem 3.9, $Z \leftarrow \mathrm{PrivLoss}\left(M(x) \| M(x')\right)$ can be written as $Z = \sum_{j=1}^k Z_j$, where $Z_j \leftarrow \mathrm{PrivLoss}\left(M_j(x) \| M_j(x')\right)$ independently for each $j \in [k]$.

Thus, for any $t \geq 0$, we have

$$\begin{aligned}
\underset{Z \leftarrow \mathrm{PrivLoss}(M(x) \| M(x'))}{\mathbb{E}} \left[\exp(tZ)\right] &= \underset{\substack{\forall j \in [k] \;\; Z_j \leftarrow \mathrm{PrivLoss}\left(M_j(x) \| M_j(x')\right) \\ \text{independent}}}{\mathbb{E}} \left[\exp\left(t \sum_{j=1}^k Z_j\right)\right] \\
&= \prod_{j=1}^k \underset{Z_j \leftarrow \mathrm{PrivLoss}\left(M_j(x) \| M_j(x')\right)}{\mathbb{E}} \left[\exp(tZ_j)\right] \\
&\leq \prod_{j=1}^k \exp(t(t+1) \cdot \rho_j) \\
&= \exp\left(t(t+1) \cdot \sum_{j=1}^k \rho_j\right) \\
&= \exp(t(t+1) \cdot \rho).
\end{aligned}$$

Since x and x' were arbitrary, this proves that M satisfies ρ-zCDP, as required. □

Next we show how to convert from concentrated DP to approximate DP, which applies the tools we developed earlier.

Proposition 3.14 (Conversion from Concentrated DP to Approximate DP). *For any $M : \mathcal{X}^n \to \mathcal{Y}$ and any $\varepsilon, t \geq 0$, M satisfies (ε, δ)-DP with*

$$\begin{aligned}\delta &= \sup_{\substack{x,x' \in \mathcal{X}^n \\ \text{neighboring}}} \underset{Z \leftarrow \mathrm{PrivLoss}(M(x)\|M(x'))}{\mathbb{E}} \left[\exp(tZ)\right] \cdot \frac{\exp(-\varepsilon t)}{t+1} \cdot \left(1 - \frac{1}{t+1}\right)^t \\ &\leq \sup_{\substack{x,x' \in \mathcal{X}^n \\ \text{neighboring}}} \underset{Z \leftarrow \mathrm{PrivLoss}(M(x)\|M(x'))}{\mathbb{E}} \left[\exp(t(Z-\varepsilon))\right].\end{aligned}$$

In particular, if M satisfies ρ-zCDP, then M satisfies (ε, δ)-DP for any $\varepsilon \geq \rho$ with

$$\begin{aligned}\delta &= \inf_{t>0} \exp(t(t+1)\rho - \varepsilon t) \cdot \frac{1}{t+1} \cdot \left(1 - \frac{1}{t+1}\right)^t \\ &\leq \exp(-(\varepsilon - \rho)^2/4\rho).\end{aligned}$$

Proof. Fix arbitrary neighboring inputs x, x'. Fix $\varepsilon, t \geq 0$. We must show that for all S we have $\mathbb{P}\left[M(x) \in S\right] \leq e^{\varepsilon} \cdot \mathbb{P}\left[M(x') \in S\right] + \delta$ for the value of δ given in the statement above.

Let $Z \leftarrow \mathrm{PrivLoss}\left(M(x)\middle\|M(x')\right)$. By Proposition 3.7, it suffices to show

$$\mathbb{E}\left[\max\{0, 1 - \exp(\varepsilon - Z)\}\right] \leq \delta,$$

for the value of δ given in the statement above.

Let $c > 0$ be a constant such that, with probability 1,

$$\max\{0, 1 - \exp(\varepsilon - Z)\} \leq c \cdot \exp(tZ).$$

Taking expectations of both sides we have $\mathbb{E}\left[\max\{0, 1 - \exp(\varepsilon - Z)\}\right] \leq c \cdot \mathbb{E}\left[\exp(tZ)\right]$, which is the kind of bound we need. It only remains to identify the appropriate value of c to obtain the desired bound.

We trivially have $0 \leq c \cdot \exp(tZ)$ as long as $c > 0$. Thus we only need to ensure $1 - \exp(\varepsilon - Z) \leq c \cdot \exp(tZ)$. That is, for any value of $t > 0$, we can set

$$\begin{aligned}c &= \sup_{z \in \mathbb{R}} \frac{1 - \exp(\varepsilon - z)}{\exp(tz)} \\ &= \sup_{z \in \mathbb{R}} \exp(-tz) - \exp(\varepsilon - (t+1)z) \\ &= \frac{\exp(-\varepsilon t)}{t+1} \cdot \left(1 - \frac{1}{t+1}\right)^t,\end{aligned}$$

where the final equality follows from using calculus to determine that $z = \varepsilon + \log(1 + 1/t)$ is the optimal value of z. Thus $\mathbb{E}\left[\max\{0, 1 - \exp(\varepsilon - Z)\}\right] \leq \mathbb{E}\left[\exp(tZ)\right] \cdot \frac{\exp(-\varepsilon t)}{t+1} \cdot \left(1 - \frac{1}{t+1}\right)^t$, which proves the first part of the statement.

Now assume M is ρ-zCDP. Thus

$$\forall t \geq 0 \quad \mathbb{E}\left[\exp(tZ)\right] \leq \exp(t(t+1)\cdot\rho),$$

which immediately yields the equality in the second part of the statement.

To obtain the inequality in the second part of the statement, we observe that

$$\max\{0, 1-\exp(\varepsilon - Z)\} \leq \mathbb{I}[Z > \varepsilon] \leq \exp(t(Z-\varepsilon)),$$

whence $c \leq \exp(-\varepsilon t)$. Substituting in this upper bound on c and setting $t = (\varepsilon - \rho)/2\rho$ completes the proof $\square$

Remark 3.15. *Proposition 3.14 shows that ρ-zCDP implies $(\varepsilon, \delta = \exp(-(\varepsilon-\rho)^2/4\rho))$-DP for all $\varepsilon \geq \rho$. Equivalently, ρ-zCDP implies $(\varepsilon = \rho + 2\sqrt{\rho\cdot\log(1/\delta)}, \delta)$-DP for all $\delta > 0$. Also, to obtain a given a target (ε, δ)-DP guarantee, it suffices to have ρ-zCDP with*

$$\frac{\varepsilon^2}{4\log(1/\delta)+4\varepsilon} \leq \rho = \left(\sqrt{\log(1/\delta)+\varepsilon} - \sqrt{\log(1/\delta)}\right)^2 \leq \frac{\varepsilon^2}{4\log(1/\delta)}.$$

This gives a sufficient condition; tighter bounds can be obtained from Proposition 3.14.

The final piece of the puzzle is the conversion from pure DP to concentrated DP.

Proposition 3.16. *Suppose M satisfies ε-DP, then M satisfies $\frac{1}{2}\varepsilon^2$-zCDP.*

Proof. Fix neighboring inputs x, x'. Let $Z \leftarrow \mathrm{PrivLoss}\left(M(x)\|M(x')\right)$. By our ε-DP assumption, Z is supported on the interval $[-\varepsilon, +\varepsilon]$. Our task is to prove that $\mathbb{E}\left[\exp(tZ)\right] \leq \exp(\frac{1}{2}\varepsilon^2 t(t+1))$ for all $t > 0$.

The key additional fact is the following consequence of Lemma 3.6

$$\begin{aligned}\underset{Z\leftarrow\mathrm{PrivLoss}(P\|Q)}{\mathbb{E}}\left[e^{-Z}\right] &= \underset{Y\leftarrow P}{\mathbb{E}}\left[e^{-f_{P\|Q}(Y)}\right] \\ &= \underset{Y\leftarrow Q}{\mathbb{E}}\left[e^{f_{P\|Q}(Y)}\cdot e^{-f_{P\|Q}(Y)}\right] = \underset{Y\leftarrow Q}{\mathbb{E}}[1] = 1.\end{aligned}$$

We can write this out as an integral to make it clear:

$$\begin{aligned}\underset{Z\leftarrow\mathrm{PrivLoss}(P\|Q)}{\mathbb{E}}\left[\exp(-Z)\right] &= \underset{Y\leftarrow P}{\mathbb{E}}\left[\exp(-f_{P\|Q}(Y))\right] \\ &= \underset{Y\leftarrow P}{\mathbb{E}}\left[\exp(-\log(P(Y)/Q(Y)))\right] \\ &= \underset{Y\leftarrow P}{\mathbb{E}}\left[\frac{Q(Y)}{P(Y)}\right] \\ &= \int_{\mathcal{Y}} \frac{Q(y)}{P(y)} P(y)\mathrm{d}y\end{aligned}$$

$$= \int_{\mathcal{Y}} Q(y) \mathrm{d}y$$
$$= 1.$$

The combination of these two facts – $Z \in [-\varepsilon, \varepsilon]$ and $\mathbb{E}\left[\exp(-Z)\right] = 1$ – is all we need to know about Z to prove the result. The technical ingredient is Hoeffding's lemma [Hoe63]:

Lemma 3.17 (Hoeffding's lemma). *Let Z be a random variable supported on the interval $[-\varepsilon, +\varepsilon]$. Then for all $t \in \mathbb{R}$, $\mathbb{E}\left[\exp(tZ)\right] \leq \exp(t\mathbb{E}[Z] + t^2\varepsilon^2/2)$.*

Proof. To simplify things, we can assume without loss of generality that Z is supported on the discrete set $\{-\varepsilon, +\varepsilon\}$. To prove this claim, let $\tilde{Z} \in \{-\varepsilon, +\varepsilon\}$ be a randomized rounding of Z. That is, $\mathop{\mathbb{E}}_{\tilde{Z}}\left[\tilde{Z} \middle| Z = z\right] = z$ for all $z \in [-\varepsilon, +\varepsilon]$. By Jensen's inequality, since $\exp(tz)$ is a convex function of $z \in \mathbb{R}$ for any fixed $t \in \mathbb{R}$, we have

$$\mathop{\mathbb{E}}_{Z}\left[\exp(tZ)\right] = \mathop{\mathbb{E}}_{Z}\left[\exp\left(t\mathop{\mathbb{E}}_{\tilde{Z}}\left[\tilde{Z}\middle|Z\right]\right)\right] \leq \mathop{\mathbb{E}}_{Z}\left[\mathop{\mathbb{E}}_{\tilde{Z}}\left[\exp(t\tilde{Z})\middle|Z\right]\right] = \mathop{\mathbb{E}}_{\tilde{Z}}\left[\exp(t\tilde{Z})\right].$$

Note that $\mathbb{E}\left[\tilde{Z}\right] = \mathbb{E}[Z]$. Thus it suffices to prove $\mathbb{E}\left[\exp(t\tilde{Z})\right] \leq \exp(t\mathbb{E}\left[\tilde{Z}\right] + \frac{1}{2}\varepsilon^2 t^2)$ for all $t \in \mathbb{R}$.

The final step in the proof is some calculus: Let $p := \mathbb{P}\left[\tilde{Z} = \varepsilon\right] = 1 - \mathbb{P}\left[\tilde{Z} = -\varepsilon\right]$. Then $\mathbb{E}[Z] = \mathbb{E}\left[\tilde{Z}\right] = \varepsilon p - \varepsilon(1-p) = \varepsilon(2p-1)$. Define $f : \mathbb{R} \to \mathbb{R}$ by

$$f(t) := \log \mathbb{E}\left[\exp(t\tilde{Z})\right] = \log(p \cdot e^{t\varepsilon} + (1-p) \cdot e^{-t\varepsilon}) = \log(1-p+p \cdot e^{2t\varepsilon}) - t\varepsilon.$$

For all $t \in \mathbb{R}$,

$$f'(t) = \frac{2\varepsilon p \cdot e^{2t\varepsilon}}{1-p+p \cdot e^{2t\varepsilon}} - \varepsilon,$$

and

$$\begin{aligned} f''(t) &= \frac{(2\varepsilon)^2 p \cdot e^{2t\varepsilon} \cdot (1-p+p \cdot e^{2t\varepsilon}) - (2\varepsilon p \cdot e^{2t\varepsilon})^2}{(1-p+p \cdot e^{2t\varepsilon})^2} \\ &= (2\varepsilon)^2 \cdot \frac{p \cdot e^{2t\varepsilon}}{1-p+p \cdot e^{2t\varepsilon}} \cdot \left(1 - \frac{p \cdot e^{2t\varepsilon}}{1-p+p \cdot e^{2t\varepsilon}}\right) \\ &= (2\varepsilon)^2 \cdot x \cdot (1-x) \leq (2\varepsilon)^2 \cdot \frac{1}{4} = \varepsilon^2. \end{aligned}$$

The final line sets $x = \frac{p \cdot e^{2t\varepsilon}}{1-p+p \cdot e^{2t\varepsilon}}$ and uses the fact that the function $x \cdot (1-x)$ is maximized at $x = \frac{1}{2}$.

Note that $f(0) = 0$ and $f'(0) = 2\varepsilon p - \varepsilon = \mathbb{E}\left[\tilde{Z}\right] = \mathbb{E}[Z]$. By the fundamental theorem of calculus, for all $t \in \mathbb{R}$,

$$f(t) = f(0) + f'(0) \cdot t + \int_0^t \int_0^s f''(r) \mathrm{d}r \mathrm{d}s \leq 0 + \mathbb{E}[Z] \cdot t$$
$$+ \int_0^t \int_0^s \varepsilon^2 \mathrm{d}r \mathrm{d}s = \mathbb{E}[Z] \cdot t + \frac{1}{2}\varepsilon^2 t^2.$$

This proves the lemma, as $\mathbb{E}\left[\exp(tZ)\right] \leq \mathbb{E}\left[\exp(t\tilde{Z})\right] = \exp(f(t)) \leq \exp(\mathbb{E}[Z] \cdot t + \frac{1}{2}\varepsilon^2 t^2)$. □

If we substitute $t = -1$ into Lemma 3.17, we have

$$1 = \mathbb{E}\left[\exp(-Z)\right] \leq \exp(-\mathbb{E}[Z] + \frac{1}{2}\varepsilon^2),$$

which rearranges to $\mathbb{E}[Z] \leq \frac{1}{2}\varepsilon^2$.

Substituting this bound on the expectation back into Lemma 3.17 yields the result: For all $t > 0$, we have

$$\mathbb{E}\left[\exp(tZ)\right] \leq \exp\left(t \cdot \mathbb{E}[Z] + \frac{1}{2}\varepsilon^2 t^2\right) \leq \exp\left(\frac{1}{2}\varepsilon^2 t(t+1)\right).$$

□

Combining these three results lets us prove what is known as the advanced composition theorem where we start with each individual algorithm satisfying pure DP [DRV10]:

Theorem 3.18 (Advanced Composition Starting with Pure DP). *Let $M_1, M_2, \cdots, M_k : \mathcal{X}^n \to \mathcal{Y}$ be randomized algorithms. Suppose M_j is ε_j-DP for each $j \in [k]$. Define $M : \mathcal{X}^n \to \mathcal{Y}^k$ by $M(x) = (M_1(x), M_2(x), \cdots, M_k(x))$, where each algorithm is run independently. Then M is (ε, δ)-DP for any $\delta > 0$ with*

$$\varepsilon = \frac{1}{2}\sum_{j=1}^{k} \varepsilon_j^2 + \sqrt{2\log(1/\delta)\sum_{j=1}^{k} \varepsilon_j^2}.$$

Proof of Theorem 3.18. By Proposition 3.16, for each $j \in [k]$, M_j satisfies ρ_j-zCDP with $\rho_j = \frac{1}{2}\varepsilon_j^2$. By composition of concentrated DP (Theorem 3.13), M satisfies

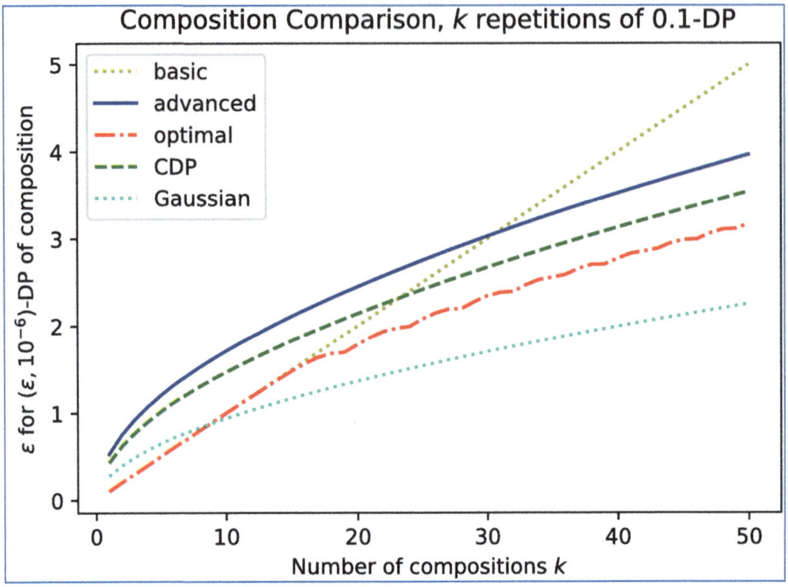

Figure 3.1. Comparison of different composition bounds. We compose k independent 0.1-DP algorithms to obtain a $(\varepsilon, 10^{-6})$-DP guarantee. Theorem 3.1 - *basic* composition - gives $\varepsilon = k \cdot 0.1$. For comparison, we have *advanced* composition (Theorem 3.18), an *optimal* bound [KOV15], and Concentrated DP (*CDP*) with the improved conversion from Proposition 3.14. For comparison, we also consider composing the *Gaussian* mechanism using Corollary 3.10, where the Gaussian noise is scaled to have the same variance as Laplace noise would have to attain 0.1-DP.

ρ-zCDP with $\rho = \sum_{j=1}^{k} \rho_j$. Finally, Proposition 3.14 can convert this concentrated DP guarantee to approximate DP: M satisfies (ε, δ)-DP for all $\varepsilon \geq \rho$ and $\delta = \exp(-(\varepsilon - \rho)^2/4\rho)$. We can rearrange this so that $\delta > 0$ is arbitrary and $\varepsilon = \rho + \sqrt{4\rho \log(1/\delta)}$. □

Recall that the basic composition theorem (Theorem 3.1) gives $\delta = 0$ and $\varepsilon = \sum_{j=1}^{k} \varepsilon_j$. That is, basic composition scales with the 1-norm of the vector $(\varepsilon_1, \varepsilon_2, \cdots, \varepsilon_k)$, whereas advanced composition scales with the 2-norm of this vector (and the squared 2-norm). Neither bound strictly dominates the other. However, asymptotically (in a sense we will make precise in the next paragraph) advanced composition dominates basic composition.

Suppose we have a fixed (ε, δ)-DP guarantee for the entire system and we must answer k queries of sensitivity 1. Using basic composition, we can answer each query by adding Laplace(k/ε) noise to each answer. However, using advanced composition, we can answer each query by adding Laplace$(\sqrt{k/2\rho})$ noise to each answer, where

$$\rho \geq \frac{\varepsilon^2}{4\log(1/\delta) + 4\varepsilon},$$

(per Remark 3.15). If the privacy parameters $\varepsilon, \delta > 0$ are fixed (which implies ρ is fixed) and $k \to \infty$, we can see that asymptotically advanced composition gives noise per query scaling as $\Theta(\sqrt{k})$, while basic composition results in noise scaling as $\Theta(k)$.

3.4.2 Adaptive Composition & Post-processing

Thus far we have only considered non-adaptive composition. That is, we assume that the algorithms $M_1, M_2, \cdots, M_k$ being composed are independent. More generally, adaptive composition considers the possibility that M_j can depend on the outputs of $M_1, \cdots, M_{j-1}$. This kind of dependence arises very often, either in an iterative algorithm, or an interactive system where a human chooses analyses to perform sequentially. Fortunately, adaptive composition is easy to deal with.

Proposition 3.19 (Adaptive Composition of Concentrated DP)**.** *Let $M_1 : \mathcal{X}^n \to \mathcal{Y}_1$ be ρ_1-zCDP. Let $M_2 : \mathcal{X}^n \times \mathcal{Y}_1 \to \mathcal{Y}_2$ be such that, for all $y_1 \in \mathcal{Y}_1$, the algorithm $x \mapsto M(x, y_1)$ is ρ_2-zCDP. That is, M_2 is ρ_2-zCDP in terms of its first argument for any fixed value of the second argument. Define $M : \mathcal{X}^n \to \mathcal{Y}_2$ by $M(x) = M_2(x, M_1(x))$. Then M is $(\rho_1 + \rho_2)$-zCDP.*

Proposition 3.19 only considers the composition of two algorithms, but it can be extended to k algorithms by induction.

Proof. Fix neighboring inputs $x, x' \in \mathcal{X}^n$. Fix $t \geq 0$. Let $Z \leftarrow \mathrm{PrivLoss}\left(M(x) \| M(x')\right)$. We must prove $\mathbb{E}\left[\exp(tZ)\right] \leq \exp(t(t+1)(\rho_1 + \rho_2))$.

For non-adaptive composition, we could write $Z = Z_1 + Z_2$ where $Z_1 \leftarrow \mathrm{PrivLoss}\left(M_1(x) \| M_1(x')\right)$ and $Z_2 \leftarrow \mathrm{PrivLoss}\left(M_2(x) \| M_2(x')\right)$ are independent. However, we cannot do this in the adaptive case – the two privacy losses are not independent. Instead, we use the fact that, conditioned on the value of the first privacy loss Z_1, the privacy loss Z_2 still satisfies the bound on the moment generating function. That is, for all z_1, we have $\mathbb{E}\left[\exp(tZ_2) \mid Z_1 = z_1\right] \leq \exp(t(t+1)\rho_2)$. To make this argument precise, we must expand out the relevant definitions.

For now, we make a simplifying technical assumption (which we will justify later): We assume that, given $y_2 = M(x, y_1)$, we can determine y_1. This means we can decompose $f_{M(x)\|M(x')}(y_2) = f_{M_1(x)\|M_1(x')}(y_1) + f_{M_2(x,y_1)\|M_2(x',y_1)}(y_2)$. Thus

$$\mathop{\mathbb{E}}_{Z \leftarrow \mathrm{PrivLoss}(M(x)\|M(x'))}\left[\exp(tZ)\right]$$

$$
\begin{aligned}
&= \underset{Y \leftarrow M_2(x, M_1(x))}{\mathbb{E}} \left[\exp\left(t \cdot f_{M(x)\|M(x')}(Y)\right)\right] \\
&= \underset{Y_1 \leftarrow M_1(x)}{\mathbb{E}} \left[\underset{Y_2 \leftarrow M_2(x, Y_1)}{\mathbb{E}} [\exp(t \cdot (f_{M_1(x)\|M_1(x')}(Y_1) \right. \\
&\quad \left. + f_{M_2(x,Y_1)\|M_2(x',Y_1)}(Y_2)))] \right] \\
&= \underset{Y_1 \leftarrow M_1(x)}{\mathbb{E}} \left[\exp\left(t \cdot f_{M_1(x)\|M_1(x')}(Y_1)\right) \right. \\
&\quad \left. \cdot \underset{Y_2 \leftarrow M_2(x, Y_1)}{\mathbb{E}} \left[\exp\left(t \cdot f_{M_2(x,Y_1)\|M_2(x',Y_1)}(Y_2)\right)\right] \right] \\
&\le \underset{Y_1 \leftarrow M_1(x)}{\mathbb{E}} \left[\exp\left(t \cdot f_{M_1(x)\|M_1(x')}(Y_1)\right)\right] \\
&\quad \cdot \sup_{y_1} \underset{Y_2 \leftarrow M_2(x, y_1)}{\mathbb{E}} \left[\exp\left(t \cdot f_{M_2(x,y_1)\|M_2(x',y_1)}(Y_2)\right)\right] \\
&= \underset{Z_1 \leftarrow \mathrm{PrivLoss}(M_1(x)\|M_1(x'))}{\mathbb{E}} \left[\exp\left(t \cdot Z_1\right)\right] \\
&\quad \cdot \sup_{y_1} \underset{Z_2 \leftarrow \mathrm{PrivLoss}\left(M_2(x,y_1)\middle\|M_2(x',y_2)\right)}{\mathbb{E}} \left[\exp\left(t \cdot Z_2\right)\right] \\
&\le \exp(t(t+1)\rho_1) \cdot \exp(t(t+1)\rho_2) \\
&= \exp(t(t+1)(\rho_1 + \rho_2)),
\end{aligned}
$$

as required. All that remains is to justify our simplifying technical assumption. We can perforce ensure this assumption holds by defining $\hat{M} : \mathcal{X}^n \to \mathcal{Y}_1 \times \mathcal{Y}_2$ by $\hat{M}(x) = (y_1, y_2)$ where $y_1 = M_1(x)$ and $y_2 = M_2(x, y_1)$ and proving the theorem for $\hat{M}$ in lieu of M. Since the output of $\hat{M}$ includes both outputs, rather than just the last output, the above decomposition works. The result holds in general because M is a *post-processing* of $\hat{M}$. That is, we can obtain $M(x)$ by running $\hat{M}(x)$ and discarding the first part of the output. Intuitively, discarding part of the output cannot hurt privacy. Formally, this is the post-processing property of concentrated DP, which we prove in Lemma 3.20 and Corollary 3.21. □

Lemma 3.20 (Post-processing for Concentrated DP)**.** *Let $\hat{P}$ and $\hat{Q}$ be distributions on $\hat{\mathcal{Y}}$ and let $g : \hat{\mathcal{Y}} \to \mathcal{Y}$ be an arbitrary function. Define $P = g(\hat{P})$ and $Q = g(\hat{Q})$ to be the distributions on $\mathcal{Y}$ obtained by applying g to a function from $\hat{P}$ and $\hat{Q}$ respectively. Then, for all $t \ge 0$,*

$$
\underset{Z \leftarrow \mathrm{PrivLoss}(P\|Q)}{\mathbb{E}} \left[\exp(tZ)\right] \le \underset{\hat{Z} \leftarrow \mathrm{PrivLoss}\left(\hat{P}\middle\|\hat{Q}\right)}{\mathbb{E}} \left[\exp(t\hat{Z})\right].
$$

Proof. To generate a sample from $Y \leftarrow Q$, we sample $\hat{Y} \leftarrow \hat{Q}$ and set $Y = g(\hat{Y})$. We consider the reverse process: Given $y \in \mathcal{Y}$, define $\hat{Q}_y$ to be the conditional distribution of $\hat{Y} \leftarrow \hat{Q}$ conditioned on $g(\hat{Y}) = y$. That is, $\hat{Q}_y$ is a distribution such that we can generate a sample $\hat{Y} \leftarrow \hat{Q}$ by first sampling $Y \leftarrow Q$ and then sampling $\hat{Y} \leftarrow \hat{Q}_Y$. Note that if g is an injective function, then $\hat{Q}_y$ is a point mass.

We have the following key identity. Formally, this relates the Radon-Nikodym derivative of the postprocessed distributions (P with respect to Q) to the Radon-Nikodym derivative of the original distributions ($\hat{P}$ with respect to $\hat{Q}$) via the conditional distribution $\hat{Q}_y$.

$$\forall y \in \mathcal{Y} \quad \frac{P(y)}{Q(y)} = \underset{\hat{Y} \leftarrow \hat{Q}_y}{\mathbb{E}}\left[\frac{\hat{P}(\hat{Y})}{\hat{Q}(\hat{Y})}\right].$$

To see where this identity comes from, write

$$\begin{aligned}
\underset{\hat{Y} \leftarrow \hat{Q}_y}{\mathbb{E}}\left[\frac{\hat{P}(\hat{Y})}{\hat{Q}(\hat{Y})}\right] &= \int_{\{\hat{y}:g(\hat{y})=y\}} \frac{\hat{P}(\hat{y})}{\hat{Q}(\hat{y})} \cdot \hat{Q}_y(\hat{y})\mathrm{d}\hat{y} \\
&= \int_{\{\hat{y}:g(\hat{y})=y\}} \frac{\hat{P}(\hat{y})}{\hat{Q}(\hat{y})} \cdot \frac{\hat{Q}(\hat{y})}{\int_{\{\tilde{y}:g(\tilde{y})=y\}} \hat{Q}(\tilde{y})\mathrm{d}\tilde{y}} \mathrm{d}\hat{y} \\
&= \frac{\int_{\{\hat{y}:g(\hat{y})=y\}} \hat{P}(\hat{y})\mathrm{d}\hat{y}}{\int_{\{\tilde{y}:g(\tilde{y})=y\}} \hat{Q}(\tilde{y})\mathrm{d}\tilde{y}} \\
&= \frac{P(y)}{Q(y)}.
\end{aligned}$$

Finally, we have

$$\begin{aligned}
\underset{Z \leftarrow \mathrm{PrivLoss}(P\|Q)}{\mathbb{E}}\left[\exp(tZ)\right] &= \underset{Y \leftarrow P}{\mathbb{E}}\left[\exp(t \cdot f_{P\|Q}(Y))\right] \\
&= \underset{Y \leftarrow Q}{\mathbb{E}}\left[\exp((t+1) \cdot f_{P\|Q}(Y))\right] && \text{(Lemma 3.6)} \\
&= \underset{Y \leftarrow Q}{\mathbb{E}}\left[\left(\frac{P(Y)}{Q(Y)}\right)^{t+1}\right] \\
&= \underset{Y \leftarrow Q}{\mathbb{E}}\left[\left(\underset{\hat{Y} \leftarrow \hat{Q}_Y}{\mathbb{E}}\left[\frac{\hat{P}(\hat{Y})}{\hat{Q}(\hat{Y})}\right]\right)^{t+1}\right] \\
&\leq \underset{Y \leftarrow Q}{\mathbb{E}}\left[\underset{\hat{Y} \leftarrow \hat{Q}_Y}{\mathbb{E}}\left[\left(\frac{\hat{P}(\hat{Y})}{\hat{Q}(\hat{Y})}\right)^{t+1}\right]\right] && \text{(Jensen)}
\end{aligned}$$

$$
\begin{aligned}
&= \underset{\hat{Y} \leftarrow \hat{Q}}{\mathbb{E}}\left[\left(\frac{\hat{P}(\hat{Y})}{\hat{Q}(\hat{Y})}\right)^{t+1}\right] \\
&= \underset{\hat{Y} \leftarrow \hat{Q}}{\mathbb{E}}\left[\exp((t+1) \cdot f_{\hat{P} \| \hat{Q}}(\hat{Y}))\right] \\
&= \underset{\hat{Y} \leftarrow \hat{P}}{\mathbb{E}}\left[\exp(t \cdot f_{\hat{P} \| \hat{Q}}(\hat{Y}))\right] \qquad \text{(Lemma 3.6)} \\
&= \underset{\hat{Z} \leftarrow \mathrm{PrivLoss}\left(\hat{P} \| \hat{Q}\right)}{\mathbb{E}}\left[\exp(t\hat{Z})\right],
\end{aligned}
$$

where the inequality follows from Jensen's inequality and the convexity of the function $v \mapsto v^{t+1}$. □

Corollary 3.21. *Let $\hat{M} : \mathcal{X}^n \to \hat{\mathcal{Y}}$ satisfy ρ-zCDP. Let $g : \hat{\mathcal{Y}} \to \mathcal{Y}$ be an arbitrary function. Define $M : \mathcal{X}^n \to \mathcal{Y}$ by $M(x) = g(\hat{M}(x))$. Then M is also ρ-zCDP.*

Proof. Fix neighboring inputs $x, x' \in \mathcal{X}^n$. Let $P = M(x)$, $Q = M(x')$, $\hat{P} = \hat{M}(x)$, and $\hat{Q} = \hat{M}(x')$. By Lemma 3.20 and the assumption that $\hat{M}$ is ρ-zCDP, for all $t \geq 0$,

$$
\begin{aligned}
\underset{Z \leftarrow \mathrm{PrivLoss}(M(x) \| M(x'))}{\mathbb{E}}\left[\exp(tZ)\right] &= \underset{Z \leftarrow \mathrm{PrivLoss}(P \| Q)}{\mathbb{E}}\left[\exp(tZ)\right] \\
&\leq \underset{\hat{Z} \leftarrow \mathrm{PrivLoss}\left(\hat{P} \| \hat{Q}\right)}{\mathbb{E}}\left[\exp(t\hat{Z})\right] \\
&= \underset{\hat{Z} \leftarrow \mathrm{PrivLoss}\left(\hat{M}(x) \| \hat{M}(x')\right)}{\mathbb{E}}\left[\exp(t\hat{Z})\right] \\
&\leq \exp(t(t+1)\rho),
\end{aligned}
$$

which implies that M is also ρ-zCDP. □

3.4.3 Composition of Approximate (ε, δ)-DP

Thus far we have only considered the composition of pure DP mechanisms (Theorems 3.1 & 3.18) and the Gaussian mechanism (Corollary 3.10). What about approximate (ε, δ)-DP?

We have the following result which extends Theorems 3.1 & 3.18 to approximate DP and to adaptive composition.

Theorem 3.22 (Advanced Composition Starting with Approximate DP). *For $j \in [k]$, let $M_j : \mathcal{X}^n \times \mathcal{Y}_{j-1} \to \mathcal{Y}_j$ be randomized algorithms. Suppose M_j is $(\varepsilon_j, \delta_j)$-DP for each $j \in [k]$. For $j \in [k]$, inductively define $M_{1 \cdots j} : \mathcal{X}^n \to \mathcal{Y}_j$ by $M_{1 \cdots j}(x) =$*

$M_j(x, M_{1\cdots(j-1)}(x))$, where each algorithm is run independently and $M_{1\cdots 0}(x) = y_0$ for some fixed $y_0 \in \mathcal{Y}_0$. Then $M_{1\cdots k}$ is (ε, δ)-DP for any $\delta > \sum_{j=1}^k \delta_j$ with

$$\varepsilon = \min \left\{ \sum_{j=1}^k \varepsilon_j, \frac{1}{2}\sum_{j=1}^k \varepsilon_j^2 + \sqrt{2\log(1/\delta') \sum_{j=1}^k \varepsilon_j^2} \right\},$$

where $\delta' = \delta - \sum_{j=1}^k \delta_j$.

Intuitively, if you consider the privacy loss $\text{PrivLoss}\left(M(x) \| M(x')\right)$ (where $x, x' \in \mathcal{X}^n$ are arbitrary neighboring inputs), then M being (ε, δ)-DP is equivalent to the privacy loss being in $[-\varepsilon, +\varepsilon]$ with probability at least $1 - \delta$; otherwise the privacy loss can be arbitrary (including possibly infinite). Informally, the proof of Theorem 3.22 uses a union bound to show that with probability at least $1 - \sum_{j=1}^k \delta_j$ all of the privacy losses of the k algorithms are bounded by their respective ε_js. Once we condition on this event, the proof proceeds as before.

Formally, rather than reasoning about possibly infinite privacy losses, we use the following decomposition result.

Lemma 3.23. *Let P and Q be probability distributions over $\mathcal{Y}$. Fix $\varepsilon, \delta \geq 0$. Suppose that, for all measurable $S \subset \mathcal{Y}$, we have $P(S) \leq e^{\varepsilon} \cdot Q(S) + \delta$ and $Q(S) \leq e^{\varepsilon} P(S) + \delta$.*

Then there exist distributions P', Q', P'', Q'' over $\mathcal{Y}$ with the following properties. We can express P and Q as convex combinations of these distributions, namely $P = (1-\delta)P' + \delta P''$ and $Q = (1-\delta)Q' + \delta Q''$. And, for every measurable $S \subset \mathcal{Y}$, we have $e^{-\varepsilon} \cdot Q'(S) \leq P'(S) \leq e^{\varepsilon} \cdot Q'(S)$.

Proof. Fix $\varepsilon_1, \varepsilon_2 \in [0, \varepsilon]$ to be determined later. Define distributions P', P'', Q', and Q'' as follows.[vi] For all points $y \in \mathcal{Y}$,

$$P'(y) = \frac{\min\{P(y), e^{\varepsilon_1} \cdot Q(y)\}}{1 - \delta_1},$$

$$P''(y) = \frac{P(y) - (1 - \delta_1)P'(y)}{\delta_1} = \frac{\max\{0, P(y) - e^{\varepsilon_1} \cdot Q(y)\}}{\delta_1},$$

$$Q'(y) = \frac{\min\{Q(y), e^{\varepsilon_2} \cdot P(y)\}}{1 - \delta_2},$$

$$Q''(y) = \frac{Q(y) - (1 - \delta_2)Q'(y)}{\delta_2} = \frac{\max\{0, Q(y) - e^{\varepsilon_2} \cdot P(y)\}}{\delta_2},$$

vi. Formally, $P(y)$, $P'(y)$, $P''(y)$, $Q(y)$, $Q'(y)$, and $Q''(y)$ denote the Radon-Nikodym derivative of these distributions with respect to some base measure – usually either the counting measure (in which case these quantities are probability mass functions) or Lebesgue measure (in which case these quantities are probability density functions) – in any case, we can take $P + Q$ to be the base measure.

where δ_1 and δ_2 are appropriate normalizing constants.

By construction, $(1-\delta_1)P' + \delta_1 P'' = P$ and $(1-\delta_2)Q' + \delta_2 Q'' = Q$.

If $\delta_1 = \delta_2 = \delta$, then we have the appropriate decomposition and, for all $y \in \mathcal{Y}$, we have

$$e^{-\varepsilon} \le e^{-\varepsilon_2} \le \frac{P'(y)}{Q'(y)} = \frac{\min\{P(y), e^{\varepsilon_1} \cdot Q(y)\}}{\min\{Q(y), e^{\varepsilon_2} \cdot P(y)\}} \le e^{\varepsilon_1} \le e^{\varepsilon},$$

as required. If $\delta_1 = \delta_2 < \delta$, we can change the decomposition to

$$P = (1-\delta)P' + (\delta - \delta_1)P' + (1-\delta_1)P'' = (1-\delta)P' + \delta \cdot \left(\frac{\delta - \delta_1}{\delta} P' + \frac{\delta_1}{\delta} P'' \right),$$

and likewise for Q, which also yields the result.

It only remains to show that we can ensure that $\delta_1 = \delta_2 \le \delta$ by appropriately setting $\varepsilon_1, \varepsilon_2 \in [0, \varepsilon]$. We have

$$\delta_1 = \int_{\mathcal{Y}} \max\{0, P(y) - e^{\varepsilon_1} \cdot Q(y)\} \mathrm{d}y = \int_S P(y) - e^{\varepsilon_1} \cdot Q(y) \mathrm{d}y = P(S) - e^{\varepsilon_1} Q(S),$$

where $S = \{y \in \mathcal{Y} : P(y) \ge e^{\varepsilon_1} \cdot Q(y)\}$. If $\varepsilon_1 = \varepsilon$, then $\delta_1 \le \delta$ by the assumptions of the Lemma. If $\varepsilon_1 = 0$, then $\delta_1 = \mathrm{d_{TV}}(P, Q)$. By decreasing ε_1, we continuously increase δ_1. Thus we can pick $\varepsilon_1 \in [0, \varepsilon]$ such that $\delta_1 = \min\{\delta, \mathrm{d_{TV}}(P, Q)\}$. Similarly, we can pick $\varepsilon_2 \in [0, \varepsilon]$, such that $\delta_2 = \min\{\delta, \mathrm{d_{TV}}(P, Q)\}$. □

The proof of Theorem 3.22 is, unfortunately, quite technical. Most of the steps are the same as we have seen in the pure DP case. The only novelty is applying the decomposition of Lemma 3.23 inductively; this requires cumbersome notation, but is otherwise straightforward.

Proof of Theorem 3.22. Fix neighboring datasets $x, x' \in \mathcal{X}^n$. We inductively define distributions P_j and Q_j on $\mathcal{Y}_0 \times \mathcal{Y}_1 \times \cdots \times \mathcal{Y}_j$ as follows. For $j \in [k]$, $P_j = (Y_0, Y_1, \cdots, Y_{j-1}, M_j(x, Y_{j-1}))$, where $(Y_1, \cdots, Y_{j-1}) \leftarrow P_{j-1}$, and $Q_j = (Y_0, Y_1, \cdots, Y_{j-1}, M_j(x', Y_{j-1}))$, where $(Y_1, \cdots, Y_{j-1}) \leftarrow Q_{j-1}$. We define $P_0 = Q_0$ to be the point mass on y_0.

We will prove by induction that, for each $j \in [k]$, there exist distributions P'_j, P''_j, Q'_j, and Q''_j on $\mathcal{Y}_0 \times \mathcal{Y}_1 \times \cdots \times \mathcal{Y}_j$ such that

$$P_j = \prod_{\ell=1}^{j} (1-\delta_\ell) P'_j + \left(1 - \prod_{\ell=1}^{j} (1-\delta_\ell) \right) P''_j$$

and

$$Q_j = \prod_{\ell=1}^{j}(1-\delta_\ell)Q_j' + \left(1 - \prod_{\ell=1}^{j}(1-\delta_\ell)\right)Q_j''$$

and, for all $t \geq 0$,

$$\mathop{\mathbb{E}}_{Z_j' \leftarrow \mathrm{PrivLoss}\left(P_j' \| Q_j'\right)}\left[\exp(tZ_j')\right] \leq \exp\left(\frac{t(t+1)}{2}\sum_{\ell=1}^{j}\varepsilon_\ell^2\right)$$

and, for all measurable $S \subset \mathcal{Y}_0 \times \mathcal{Y}_1 \times \cdots \times \mathcal{Y}_j$, $P_j'(S) \leq \exp\left(\sum_{\ell=1}^{j}\varepsilon_\ell\right) \cdot Q_j'(S)$.

Before proving the inductive claim, we show that it suffices to prove the result. Fix an arbitrary measurable $S \subset \mathcal{Y}_k$ and let $\tilde{S} = \mathcal{Y}_0 \times \mathcal{Y}_1 \times \cdots \times \mathcal{Y}_{k-1} \times S$. We have

$$\begin{aligned}
\mathbb{P}\left[M(x) \in S\right] &= P_k(\tilde{S}) && \text{(Postprocessing)}\\
&= \prod_{\ell=1}^{k}(1-\delta_\ell)P_k'(\tilde{S}) + \left(1 - \prod_{\ell=1}^{k}(1-\delta_\ell)\right)P_k''(\tilde{S})\\
&\leq \prod_{\ell=1}^{k}(1-\delta_\ell)P_k'(\tilde{S}) + \sum_{j=1}^{k}\delta_j\\
& && \left(P_k''(\tilde{S}) \leq 1 \text{ and } 1 - \textstyle\prod_{\ell=1}^{k}(1-\delta_\ell) \leq \sum_{j=1}^{k}\delta_j\right)\\
&\leq \prod_{\ell=1}^{k}(1-\delta_\ell)\left(e^{\varepsilon} \cdot Q_k'(\tilde{S}) + \delta'\right) + \sum_{j=1}^{k}\delta_j && (*)\\
&\leq e^{\varepsilon} \cdot \prod_{\ell=1}^{k}(1-\delta_\ell) \cdot Q_k'(\tilde{S}) + \delta && \left(\delta = \delta' + \textstyle\sum_{j=1}^{k}\delta_j\right)\\
&\leq e^{\varepsilon} \cdot Q_k(\tilde{S}) + \delta\\
& && \left(Q_k = \textstyle\prod_{\ell=1}^{k}(1-\delta_\ell)Q_k' + \left(1 - \prod_{\ell=1}^{k}(1-\delta_\ell)\right)Q_k''\right)\\
&= e^{\varepsilon} \cdot \mathbb{P}\left[M(x') \in S\right] + \delta.
\end{aligned}$$

The inequality $P_k'(\tilde{S}) \leq e^{\varepsilon} \cdot Q_k'(\tilde{S}) + \delta'$ (*) follows the proof we have seen before. Our inductive conclusion includes a pure DP result – $P_j'(\tilde{S}) \leq \exp\left(\sum_{\ell=1}^{j}\varepsilon_\ell\right) \cdot Q_j'(\tilde{S})$ – and a concentrated DP result – for all $t \geq 0$, we have

$$\underset{Z'_j \leftarrow \mathrm{PrivLoss}\left(P'_j \middle\| Q'_j\right)}{\mathbb{E}}\left[\exp(tZ'_j)\right] \leq \exp\left(\tfrac{t(t+1)}{2}\textstyle\sum_{\ell=1}^{j}\varepsilon_\ell^2\right), \text{ which implies}$$

$$\begin{aligned}
P'_k(\tilde{S}) &\leq e^{\varepsilon}\cdot Q'_k(\tilde{S}) + \underset{Z'_k \leftarrow \mathrm{PrivLoss}(P'_k\|Q'_k)}{\mathbb{P}}\left[Z'_k > \varepsilon\right] && \text{(Proposition 3.7)}\\
&\leq e^{\varepsilon}\cdot Q'_k(\tilde{S}) + \underset{Z'_k \leftarrow \mathrm{PrivLoss}(P'_k\|Q'_k)}{\mathbb{E}}\left[\exp(t(Z'_k-\varepsilon))\right]\\
& && (\mathbb{I}[Z'_k > \varepsilon] \leq \exp(t(Z'_k-\varepsilon)))\\
&\leq e^{\varepsilon}\cdot Q'_k(\tilde{S}) + \exp\left(\frac{t(t+1)}{2}\sum_{j=1}^{k}\varepsilon_j^2\right)\cdot\exp(-t\varepsilon)\\
& && \text{(Induction conclusion)}\\
&\leq e^{\varepsilon}\cdot Q'_k(\tilde{S}) + \delta',
\end{aligned}$$

where the final inequality holds for the case $\varepsilon = \frac{1}{2}\sum_{j=1}^{k}\varepsilon_j^2 + \sqrt{2\log(1/\delta')\sum_{j=1}^{k}\varepsilon_j^2}$ and requires setting $t = \frac{\varepsilon}{\sum_{j=1}^{k}\varepsilon_j^2} - \frac{1}{2} = \sqrt{\frac{2\log(1/\delta')}{\sum_{j=1}^{k}\varepsilon_j^2}}$.

It only remains for us to perform the induction. The base case ($j = 0$) is trivial. Fix $j \in [k]$ and assume the induction hypothesis holds for $j-1$. The distribution P_j is defined as a mixture (i.e., convex combination) of $P_j|_Y$ for $Y \leftarrow P_{j-1}$, where $P_j|_Y := (Y, M_j(x, Y_{j-1}))$. For every y, we apply Lemma 3.23 to the conditional distribution $P_j|_y$ and then we take the convex combination of these decompositions to obtain a decomposition of P_j. Of course, we must also decompose Q_j at the same time.

For each $y \in \mathcal{Y}_0 \times \mathcal{Y}_1 \times \cdots \mathcal{Y}_{j-1}$, the conditional distributions satisfy $\forall S\ P_j|_y(S) \leq e^{\varepsilon_j}Q_j|_y(S)+\delta_j$ and vice versa. Thus Lemma 3.23 allows us to decompose the conditional distributions $P_j|_y$ and $Q_j|_y$ as $P_j|_y = (1-\delta_j)P'_j|_y + \delta_j P''_j|_y$ and $Q_j|_y = (1-\delta_j)Q'_j|_y + \delta_j Q''_j|_y$ where $e^{-\varepsilon_j}\cdot Q'_j|_y(S) \leq P'_j|_y(S) \leq e^{\varepsilon_j}\cdot Q'_j|_y(S)$ for all S. This gives us the desired decomposition:

$$\begin{aligned}
P_j &= \underset{Y\leftarrow P_{j-1}}{\mathbb{E}}\left[P_j|_Y\right]\\
&= \underset{Y\leftarrow P_{j-1}}{\mathbb{E}}\left[(1-\delta_j)P'_j|_Y + \delta_j P''_j|_Y\right]\\
&= \prod_{\ell=1}^{j-1}(1-\delta_\ell)\underset{Y\leftarrow P'_{j-1}}{\mathbb{E}}\left[(1-\delta_j)P'_j|_Y+\delta_j P''_j|_Y\right]+\left(1-\prod_{\ell=1}^{j-1}(1-\delta_\ell)\right)\\
&\quad\times \underset{Y\leftarrow P''_{j-1}}{\mathbb{E}}\left[(1-\delta_j)P'_j|_Y+\delta_j P''_j|_Y\right]
\end{aligned}$$

$$= \prod_{\ell=1}^{j}(1-\delta_\ell) \underset{Y \leftarrow P'_{j-1}}{\mathbb{E}}\left[P'_j|_Y\right] + \delta_j \prod_{\ell=1}^{j-1}(1-\delta_\ell) \underset{Y \leftarrow P'_{j-1}}{\mathbb{E}}\left[P''_j|_Y\right]$$
$$+ \left(1 - \prod_{\ell=1}^{j-1}(1-\delta_\ell)\right)(1-\delta_j) \underset{Y \leftarrow P''_{j-1}}{\mathbb{E}}\left[P'_j|_Y\right]$$
$$+ \left(1 - \prod_{\ell=1}^{j-1}(1-\delta_\ell)\right)\delta_j \underset{Y \leftarrow P''_{j-1}}{\mathbb{E}}\left[P''_j|_Y\right].$$

Thus we define the new decomposition as $P'_j = P'_j|_Y$ for $Y \leftarrow P'_{j-1}$ and $Q'_j = Q'_j|_Y$ for $Y \leftarrow Q'_{j-1}$. The "weight" of P'_j is the product of the weight of P'_{j-1} (i.e., $\prod_{\ell=1}^{j-1}(1-\delta_\ell)$) and the weight of $P'_j|_Y$ (i.e., $1-\delta_j$), as required. The remaining parts of the decomposition are combined to define $P''_j =$ and Q''_j; note that P''_j includes both $P'_j|_Y$ for $Y \leftarrow P''_{j-1}$ and $P''_j|_Y$ for $Y \leftarrow P_{j-1}$. It is easy to verify that this decomposition satisfies the requirements of the induction:

$$\underset{Z'_j \leftarrow \mathrm{PrivLoss}\left(P'_j \middle\| Q'_j\right)}{\mathbb{E}}\left[\exp(tZ'_j)\right]$$
$$= \underset{Y'_j \leftarrow P'_j}{\mathbb{E}}\left[\exp\left(t \cdot f_{P'_j \| Q'_j}(Y'_j)\right)\right]$$
$$= \underset{Y'_{j-1} \leftarrow P'_{j-1}}{\mathbb{E}}\left[\underset{Y'_j \leftarrow P'_j|_{Y_{j-1}}}{\mathbb{E}}\left[\exp\left(t \cdot \left(f_{P'_{j-1}\|Q'_{j-1}}(Y'_{j-1}) + f_{P'_j|_{Y_{j-1}}\|Q'_j|_{Y_{j-1}}}(Y'_j)\right)\right)\right]\right]$$
$$= \underset{Y'_{j-1} \leftarrow P'_{j-1}}{\mathbb{E}}\left[\exp\left(t \cdot f_{P'_{j-1}\|Q'_{j-1}}(Y'_{j-1})\right)\right.$$
$$\left.\cdot \underset{Y'_j \leftarrow P'_j|_{Y_{j-1}}}{\mathbb{E}}\left[\exp\left(t \cdot f_{P'_j|_{Y_{j-1}}\|Q'_j|_{Y_{j-1}}}(Y'_j)\right)\right]\right]$$
$$= \underset{Y'_{j-1} \leftarrow P'_{j-1}}{\mathbb{E}}\left[\exp\left(t \cdot f_{P'_{j-1}\|Q'_{j-1}}(Y'_{j-1})\right)\right.$$
$$\left.\cdot \underset{Z'_j \leftarrow \mathrm{PrivLoss}\left(P'_j|_{Y_{j-1}} \middle\| Q'_j|_{Y_{j-1}}\right)}{\mathbb{E}}\left[\exp\left(t \cdot Z'_j\right)\right]\right]$$
$$\le \underset{Y'_{j-1} \leftarrow P'_{j-1}}{\mathbb{E}}\left[\exp\left(t \cdot f_{P'_{j-1}\|Q'_{j-1}}(Y'_{j-1})\right) \cdot \exp\left(t(t+1)\frac{1}{2}\varepsilon_j^2\right)\right]$$

(Proposition 3.16 & $|Z'_j| \le \varepsilon_j$)

$$\leq \exp\left(\frac{t(t+1)}{2}\sum_{\ell=1}^{j-1}\varepsilon_\ell^2\right)\cdot\exp\left(t(t+1)\frac{1}{2}\varepsilon_j^2\right) \qquad \text{(Induction hypothesis)}$$

$$= \exp\left(\frac{t(t+1)}{2}\sum_{\ell=1}^{j}\varepsilon_\ell^2\right).$$

And, for pure DP, we have $P_j'(S) = \underset{Y_{j-1}'\leftarrow P_{j-1}'}{\mathbb{E}}\left[P_j'|_{Y_{j-1}}(S)\right] \leq \underset{Y_{j-1}'\leftarrow P_{j-1}'}{\mathbb{E}}\left[e^{\varepsilon_j} Q_j'|_{Y_{j-1}}(S)\right] \leq \exp\left(\sum_{\ell=1}^{j-1}\varepsilon_\ell\right)\cdot \underset{Y_{j-1}'\leftarrow Q_{j-1}'}{\mathbb{E}}\left[e^{\varepsilon_j} Q_j'|_{Y_{j-1}}(S)\right] = \exp\left(\sum_{\ell=1}^{j}\varepsilon_\ell\right)\cdot Q_j'(S)$ for all measurable S. □

3.5 Asymptotic Optimality of Composition

Is the advanced composition theorem optimal? That is, could we prove a result that is stronger? This is an important question, but we first need to think about what optimality even means. Recall that, in Section 3.2.1, we proved that basic composition is optimal, but then we showed that we could do better by relaxing the requirement from pure DP to approximate DP or concentrated DP. To prove asymptotic optimality of advanced composition, we will show that no algorithm can provide better accuracy than advanced composition gives (except for constant factors) subject to approximate DP. Furthermore, we will see that the analysis is not specific to approximate DP.

Combining advanced composition (Theorem 3.18 or 3.22) with Laplace noise addition shows that we can answer k bounded sensitivity queries (e.g., counting queries) with noise scale $\Theta(\sqrt{k/\rho})$ for each query, where ρ only depends on the privacy parameters, e.g., $\rho = \Theta(\varepsilon^2/\log(1/\delta))$ for (ε,δ)-DP. (Gaussian noise addition also gives the same asymptotics, per Corollary 3.10.)

We can prove that this asymptotics – average error per query $\Omega(\sqrt{k})$ – is optimal. Formally, we have the following result.

Theorem 3.24 (Negative Result for Error of Private Mean Estimation). *Let $\mathcal{X} = \{0,1\}^k$ and $\mathcal{Y} = [0,1]^k$. Let $M : \mathcal{X}^n \to \mathcal{Y}$ satisfy (ε,δ)-DP. If $\delta \leq 1/100n$ and $k \geq 200(e^\varepsilon - 1)^2 n$, then there exists some $x \in \mathcal{X}^n$ such that*

$$\sqrt{\mathbb{E}\left[\frac{1}{k}\|M(x)-\overline{x}\|_2^2\right]} \geq \min\left\{\frac{\sqrt{k}}{16\cdot n\cdot(e^\varepsilon-1)}, \frac{1}{10}\right\},$$

where $\overline{x} = \frac{1}{n}\sum_{i=1}^n x_i \in [0,1]^k$ is the mean of input dataset.

Theorem 3.24 shows that any DP algorithm answering k queries must have error per query scaling with $\Omega(\sqrt{k})$, which matches the guarantees of the advanced composition theorem. We briefly remark on some of the properties of this theorem:

First, M could just output $\frac{1}{2}$ for each coordinate; this is trivially private and has root mean square error at most $\frac{1}{2}$. The theorem must apply to such an algorithm too, which is the fundamental reason why the lower bound in the conclusion of Theorem 3.24 cannot be larger than a constant $\frac{1}{10}$.

Second, the assumption $\delta \leq 1/100n$ is also necessary, up to constant factors. If $\delta \gg 1/n$, then M could sample $n\delta$ of the inputs and return the sample mean. This would be $(0, \delta)$-DP and would give accuracy $\sqrt{\mathbb{E}\left[\frac{1}{k}\|M(x) - \overline{x}\|_2^2\right]} \leq \frac{1}{\sqrt{n\delta}} \ll 1$. Note that the advanced composition theorem includes a $\sqrt{\log(1/\delta)}$ term. It is possible to extend the negative results to include such a term too [SU15] (see also Lemma 2.3.6 of Bun [Bun16]), but we do not do this here for simplicity.

Third, the assumption $k \geq 200(e^{\varepsilon} - 1)^2 n$ is not really necessary; it is an artifact of our analysis. If $k \ll \varepsilon^2 n$, then the privacy error is lower than the sampling error (if we think of x as consisting of n samples from some distribution). A different analysis is possible in this case.

Fourth, Theorem 3.24 has $e^{\varepsilon} - 1$ in the denominator, where our positive results have ε. For small ε, we have $e^{\varepsilon} - 1 \approx \varepsilon$. But, for large ε, there is an exponential difference. Surprisingly, this is inherent; by using discrete noise [CKS20] in place of continuous Laplace noise it is possible to improve the positive results to yield this asymptotic behavior. However, we are generally not interested in the large ε setting.

Finally, fifth, this theorem is not merely an esoteric impossibility result. It corresponds to realistic attacks, which are known as "tracing attacks" [DSSU17] or "membership inference attacks" [SSSS17], which are the subject of Chapter 5 of this book.

Proof of Theorem 3.24. The theorem guarantees that there exists a specific input x on which M has high error. In general, x must depend on M. To prove this we show that, for a random input from a carefully chosen distribution, any M must have high error. It follows that for each specific M there must exist some fixed input with high error.

For $p \in [0, 1]^k$, let $\mathcal{D}_p$ be the product distribution over $\{0, 1\}^k$ with mean p. Our random input $X \in \mathcal{X}^n$ will consist of n independent draws from $\mathcal{D}_p$. Furthermore, we select the mean parameter randomly too. That is, $P \in [0, 1]^d$ is uniformly random and X consists of n conditionally independent draws from $\mathcal{D}_P$.

We analyze the quantity

$$Z := \sum_{i=1}^{n} \langle M(X) - P, X_i - P \rangle .$$

Applying Lemma 3.25 with $f(x) = \mathbb{E}\left[M(X)_j | X_j = x\right]$ and summing over the coordinates $j \in [k]$ shows that

$$\begin{aligned}&\mathop{\mathbb{E}}_{\substack{P \leftarrow \text{Uniform}([0,1]^k) \\ X \leftarrow \mathcal{D}_P^n}}\left[Z + \|M(X) - \overline{X}\|_2^2\right] \\ &= \sum_{j=1}^{k} \mathop{\mathbb{E}}_{\substack{P \leftarrow \text{Uniform}([0,1]^k) \\ X \leftarrow \mathcal{D}_P^n}}\left[(M(X)_j - P_j) \cdot \sum_{i=1}^{n}(X_{i,j} - P_j)\right] \geq \frac{k}{12}.\end{aligned}$$

Denoting $\alpha^2 k = \mathbb{E}\left[\|M(X) - \overline{X}\|_2^2\right]$, we have $\mathbb{E}[Z] \geq \frac{k}{12} - \alpha^2 k$. Intuitively, Z measures the total correlation between the output of M and its inputs. What Lemma 3.25 shows is that, if M is accurate – i.e., $\mathbb{E}\left[\|M(X) - \overline{X}\|_2^2\right] \leq o(k)$ – then this correlation must be large.

The punchline of the proof is that we show that differential privacy means the correlation must be small, which conflicts with the fact that we have proven it must be large. Ergo, we will obtain the desired impossibility result.

For $i \in [n]$, define

$$Z_i = \langle M(X) - P, X_i - P \rangle,$$

so that $Z = \sum_{i=1}^{n} Z_i$. Let X_0 be a fresh sample from $\mathcal{D}_P$ that is (conditionally) independent from $X_1, \cdots, X_n$. Let $M(X_0, X_{-i})$ denote running M on the dataset X where X_i has been replaced by X_0 and define

$$\tilde{Z}_i = \langle M(X_0, X_{-i}) - P, X_i - P \rangle.$$

By differential privacy, $M(X_0, X_{-i})$ is indistinguishable from $M(X)$, even if we condition on $X_0, X_1, \cdots, X_n$. Thus the distributions of $\tilde{Z}_i$ and Z_i are also indistinguishable.

Since $M(X_0, X_{-i})$ and X_i are independent (conditioned on P) and $\mathbb{E}[X_i - P] = \vec{0}$, $\mathbb{E}\left[\tilde{Z}_i\right] = 0$ and

$$\begin{aligned}\mathop{\mathbb{E}}_{P,X,M}\left[\tilde{Z}_i^2\right] &= \sum_{j=1}^{k} \mathop{\mathbb{E}}_{P}\left[P_j(1 - P_j) \cdot \mathop{\mathbb{E}}_{X,M}\left[(M(X_0, X_{-i})_j - P_j)^2\right]\right] \\ &\leq \frac{1}{4} \mathop{\mathbb{E}}_{P,X,M}\left[\|M(X) - P\|_2^2\right].\end{aligned}$$

Now $\mathbb{E}\left[\|M(X)-P\|_2^2\right] \le 2\mathbb{E}\left[\|M(X)-\overline{X}\|_2^2\right]+2\mathbb{E}\left[\|\overline{X}-P\|_2^2\right] \le 2\alpha^2 k+\frac{k}{3n}$.[vii]

Lemma 3.26, $|Z_i| \le k$, $|\tilde{Z}_i| \le k$, and $\mathbb{E}\left[|\tilde{Z}_i|\right] \le \sqrt{\mathbb{E}\left[\tilde{Z}_i^2\right]}$ (i.e., Jensen's inequality) gives

$$\mathbb{E}[Z_i] \le \mathbb{E}\left[\tilde{Z}_i\right] + (e^{\varepsilon}-1)\mathbb{E}\left[|\tilde{Z}_i|\right] + 2\delta k \le \frac{e^{\varepsilon}-1}{2}\sqrt{2\alpha^2 k + \frac{k}{3n}} + 2\delta k.$$

Putting things together, we have

$$\frac{k}{12} - \alpha^2 k \le \mathbb{E}[Z] = \sum_{i=1}^{n} \mathbb{E}[Z_i] \le n \cdot \left(\frac{e^{\varepsilon}-1}{2}\sqrt{2\alpha^2 k + \frac{k}{3n}} + 2\delta k\right).$$

Ignoring terms that are (hopefully) low order, this is $\Omega(k) \le O(n\cdot\varepsilon\sqrt{\alpha^2 k})$, which rearranges to $\alpha = \sqrt{\mathbb{E}\left[\frac{1}{k}\|M(X)-\overline{X}\|_2^2\right]} \ge \Omega\left(\frac{\sqrt{k}}{n\varepsilon}\right)$, which is the desired asymptotic result. To be precise, this rearranges to

$$\alpha \ge \sqrt{\left(\frac{1}{6} - 2\alpha^2 - 4n\delta\right)^2 \cdot \frac{k}{2n^2\cdot(e^{\varepsilon}-1)^2} - \frac{1}{6n}}.$$

If $\alpha \le 1/10$ and $\delta \le 1/100n$, then $\frac{1}{6} - 2\alpha^2 - 4n\delta \ge \frac{1}{10}$. If $k \ge 200(e^{\varepsilon}-1)^2 n$, then $\left(\frac{1}{10}\right)^2 \cdot \frac{k}{2n^2(e^{\varepsilon}-1)^2} \ge \frac{1}{n}$. If all three of these conditions hold, then

$$\sqrt{\mathbb{E}\left[\frac{1}{k}\|M(X)-\overline{X}\|_2^2\right]} = \alpha \ge \sqrt{\frac{k}{200\cdot n^2\cdot(e^{\varepsilon}-1)^2}\left(1-\frac{1}{6}\right)} \ge \frac{\sqrt{k}}{16n(e^{\varepsilon}-1)}.$$

Hence, if $\delta \le 1/100n$ and $k \ge 200(e^{\varepsilon}-1)^2 n$, then either $\alpha > 1/10$ or $\alpha \ge \sqrt{k}/16n(e^{\varepsilon}-1)$, as required. □

Now we prove the two lemma that were used to prove Theorem 3.24. We begin with the lemma showing that the correlation Z must be large if M is accurate.

The lemma only contemplates one coordinate and then we sum over the k coordinates in the proof of Theorem 3.24. That is, the function f in the theorem is simply one coordinate of M and we average out the randomness of M and the other coordinates.

Lemma 3.25. *Let $f : \{0,1\}^d \to [0,1]$ be an arbitrary function. Let $P \in [0,1]$ be uniformly random and, conditioned on P, let $X_1, \cdots, X_n \in \{0,1\}$ be independent*

---

vii. $\mathbb{E}\left[\|\overline{X}-P\|_2^2\right] = \sum_{j=1}^{k} \underset{P_j \leftarrow \mathrm{Uniform}([0,1])}{\mathbb{E}}\left[\underset{Y_j \leftarrow \mathrm{Binomial}(n,P_j)}{\mathbb{E}}\left[(\frac{1}{n}Y_j - P_j)^2\right]\right] = k\cdot\int_0^1 \frac{p(1-p)}{n}\mathrm{d}p = \frac{k}{6n}$.

with $\mathbb{E}[X_i] = P$ *for each* $i \in [n]$. *Then*

$$\mathop{\mathbb{E}}_{X,P}\left[(f(X) - P) \cdot \sum_{i=1}^{n}(X_i - P)\right] + \mathop{\mathbb{E}}_{P}\left[\mathop{\mathbb{E}}_{X}\left[f(X) - \overline{X}\right]^2\right] \geq \frac{1}{12}.$$

By Jensen's inequality $\mathop{\mathbb{E}}_{P}\left[\mathop{\mathbb{E}}_{X}\left[f(X) - \overline{X}\right]^2\right] \leq \mathop{\mathbb{E}}_{P,X}\left[\left(f(X) - \overline{X}\right)^2\right]$. Thus

$$\mathop{\mathbb{E}}_{X,P}\left[(f(X) - P) \cdot \sum_{i=1}^{n}(X_i - P) + \left(f(X) - \overline{X}\right)^2\right] \geq \frac{1}{12}.$$

To gain some intuition for the lemma statement, suppose $f(x) = \overline{x} = \frac{1}{n}\sum_{i=1}^{n} x_i$. Then

$$\begin{aligned}\mathbb{E}\left[(f(X) - P, X_i - P)\right] &= \mathbb{E}\left[(\overline{X} - P) \cdot \left(\sum_{i=1}^{n} X_i - P\right)\right] \\ &= \frac{1}{n}\sum_{i=1}^{n}\mathbb{E}\left[(X_i - P)^2\right] = \frac{1}{6}.\end{aligned}$$

The constant $\frac{1}{6} = \int_0^1 p(1-p)\mathrm{d}p$ in this example is slightly better than the constant $\frac{1}{12}$ in the general result. However, if $f(x) = \frac{1}{2}$ is a constant function, then the constant is tight, as $\mathop{\mathbb{E}}_{P}\left[\mathop{\mathbb{E}}_{X}\left[f(X) - \overline{X}\right]^2\right] = \mathop{\mathbb{E}}_{P}\left[\left(\frac{1}{2} - P\right)^2\right] = \frac{1}{12}$.

Proof of Lemma 3.25. Define $g : [0, 1] \to [0, 1]$ by $g(p) = \mathop{\mathbb{E}}_{X \leftarrow \mathcal{D}_p^n}\left[f(X)\right]$, where $\mathcal{D}_p^n$ denotes the product distribution over $\{0, 1\}^n$ with each coordinate having mean p. Then

$$\begin{aligned}g'(p) &= \frac{\mathrm{d}}{\mathrm{d}p}\mathop{\mathbb{E}}_{X \leftarrow \mathcal{D}_p^n}\left[f(X)\right] \\ &= \sum_{x \in \{0,1\}^n} f(x) \frac{\mathrm{d}}{\mathrm{d}p}\prod_{\ell=1}^{n}\left(x_\ell \cdot p + (1 - x_\ell) \cdot (1 - p)\right) \\ &= \sum_{x \in \{0,1\}^n} f(x) \prod_{\ell=1}^{n}\left(x_\ell \cdot p + (1 - x_\ell)\right. \\ &\quad \left.\cdot (1 - p)\right) \sum_{i=1}^{n} \frac{\frac{\mathrm{d}}{\mathrm{d}p}(px_i \cdot p + (1 - x_i) \cdot (1 - p))}{x_i \cdot p + (1 - x_i) \cdot (1 - p)} \qquad \text{(Product rule)}\end{aligned}$$

$$= \sum_{x\in\{0,1\}^n} f(x) \prod_{\ell=1}^{n} \big(x_\ell \cdot p + (1-x_\ell)$$

$$\cdot (1-p)\big) \sum_{i=1}^{n} \frac{2x_i - 1}{x_i \cdot p + (1-x_i)\cdot(1-p)}$$

$$= \sum_{x\in\{0,1\}^n} f(x) \prod_{\ell=1}^{n} \big(x_\ell \cdot p + (1-x_\ell)\cdot(1-p)\big) \sum_{i=1}^{n} \frac{x_i - p}{p(1-p)}$$

(Case analysis for $x_i \in \{0,1\}$)

$$= \mathop{\mathbb{E}}_{X\leftarrow\mathcal{D}_p^n}\left[f(X)\cdot \sum_{i=1}^{n} \frac{X_i - p}{p(1-p)}\right].$$

Now we apply integration by parts to this derivative:

$$\mathop{\mathbb{E}}_{P\leftarrow[0,1]}\left[\mathop{\mathbb{E}}_{X\leftarrow\mathcal{D}_P^n}\left[f(X)\cdot\sum_{i=1}^{n}(X_i - P)\right]\right]$$

$$= \int_0^1 g'(p)\cdot p(1-p)\mathrm{d}p$$

$$= \int_0^1 \left(\frac{\mathrm{d}}{\mathrm{d}p} g(p)\cdot p(1-p)\right) - g(p)\cdot(1-2p)\mathrm{d}p$$

$$= g(1)\cdot 1(1-1) - g(0)\cdot 0(1-0) + \int_0^1 g(p)\cdot(2p-1)\mathrm{d}p$$

$$= 2\mathop{\mathbb{E}}_{P\leftarrow[0,1]}\left[g(P)\cdot\left(P-\frac{1}{2}\right)\right].$$

Using the fact that $\mathop{\mathbb{E}}_{P\leftarrow[0,1]}\left[P-\frac{1}{2}\right] = 0$ and $\mathop{\mathbb{E}}_{X\leftarrow\mathcal{D}_p^n}\left[X_i - p\right] = 0$, we can center these expressions:

$$\mathop{\mathbb{E}}_{\substack{P\leftarrow[0,1]\\ X\leftarrow\mathcal{D}_P^n}}\left[(f(X)-P)\cdot\sum_{i=1}^{n}(X_i - P)\right]$$

$$= 2\mathop{\mathbb{E}}_{P\leftarrow[0,1]}\left[\left(g(P)-\frac{1}{2}\right)\cdot\left(P-\frac{1}{2}\right)\right]$$

$$= \mathop{\mathbb{E}}_{P\leftarrow[0,1]}\left[\left(g(P)-\frac{1}{2}\right)^2+\left(P-\frac{1}{2}\right)^2-\left(\left(g(P)-\frac{1}{2}\right)-\left(P-\frac{1}{2}\right)\right)^2\right]$$

$$\geq \mathop{\mathbb{E}}_{P\leftarrow[0,1]}\left[0+\left(P-\frac{1}{2}\right)^2-(g(P)-P)^2\right]$$

$$= \frac{1}{12} - \underset{P \leftarrow [0,1]}{\mathbb{E}}\left[\left(g(P) - P\right)^2\right]$$
$$= \frac{1}{12} - \underset{P \leftarrow [0,1]}{\mathbb{E}}\left[\underset{X \leftarrow \mathcal{D}_P^n}{\mathbb{E}}\left[f(X) - \overline{X}\right]^2\right].$$

□

Lemma 3.26. *Let X and Y be random variables supported on $[-\Delta, \Delta]$ satisfying $\mathbb{P}[X \in S] \leq e^{\varepsilon} \cdot \mathbb{P}[Y \in S] + \delta$ and $\mathbb{P}[Y \in S] \leq e^{\varepsilon} \cdot \mathbb{P}[X \in S] + \delta$ for all measurable S. Then*

$$\mathbb{E}[X] \leq \mathbb{E}[Y] + (e^{\varepsilon} - 1)\mathbb{E}[|Y|] + 2\delta\Delta.$$

Proof.

$$\begin{aligned}
\mathbb{E}[X] &= \int_0^{\Delta} \mathbb{P}[X > t] - \mathbb{P}[X < -t]\mathrm{d}t \\
&\leq \int_0^{\Delta} e^{\varepsilon} \cdot \mathbb{P}[Y > t] + \delta - e^{-\varepsilon} \cdot (\mathbb{P}[Y < -t] - \delta)\mathrm{d}t \\
&= \int_0^{\Delta} (\mathbb{P}[Y > t] - \mathbb{P}[Y < -t]) + (e^{\varepsilon} - 1) \cdot \mathbb{P}[Y > t] + (1 - e^{-\varepsilon}) \\
&\quad \cdot \mathbb{P}[Y < -t] + (1 + e^{-\varepsilon})\delta\mathrm{d}t \\
&= \mathbb{E}[Y] + (e^{\varepsilon} - 1)\mathbb{E}[\max\{0, Y\}] + (1 - e^{-\varepsilon})\mathbb{E}[\max\{0, -Y\}] \\
&\quad + (1 + e^{-\varepsilon})\delta\Delta \\
&\leq \mathbb{E}[Y] + (e^{\varepsilon} - 1)\mathbb{E}[|Y|] + 2\delta\Delta,
\end{aligned}$$

as $1 - e^{-\varepsilon} \leq e^{\varepsilon} - 1$ and $1 + e^{-\varepsilon} \leq 2$. □

Remark 3.27. *The only part of the proof of Theorem 3.24 that uses differential privacy is Lemma 3.26. Thus, if we were to consider a different definition of differential privacy, as long as an analog of Lemma 3.26 holds for this alternative definition, an analog of Theorem 3.24 would still apply. That is to say, this negative result is robust to our choice of privacy definition (unlike the the negative result in Section 3.2.1).*

3.6 Privacy Amplification by Subsampling

Thus far we have considered the composition of Gaussian mechanisms, and generic mechanisms satisfying pure or approximate DP. We now turn our attention to subsampled privacy mechanisms. These mechanisms introduce some additional quirks into the picture, which will force us to develop new tools.

The premise of privacy amplification by subsampling is that we run a DP algorithm on some random subset of the data. The subset introduces additional uncertainty, which benefits privacy. In particular, there is some probability that your data is not included in the analysis, which can only enhance your privacy. Furthermore, a potential attacker does not know whether or not your data was dropped; this uncertainty can benefit your privacy even when your data is included. Privacy amplification by subsampling theorems make this intuition precise.

Subsampling arises naturally. We often would like to collect the data of the entire population, but this is impractical. Thus we collect the data of a subset of the population and use statistical methods to generalize from this sample to the entire population. In particular, in deep learning applications, we will use stochastic gradient descent. That is, we choose a random subset of our training data (called a minibatch) and compute the gradient of the loss function with respect to this subset, rather than the entire dataset. This method reduces the computational cost for training. If we want to make deep learning differentially private, then we will add noise to the gradients and we should exploit privacy amplification by subsampling to analyze the privacy properties of this algorithm.

In this section we will analyze subsampling precisely and we will show how it interacts with composition.

3.6.1 Subsampling for Pure or Approximate DP

We begin by analyzing privacy amplification by subsampling under pure or approximate differential privacy. This is a relatively simple result, but it will be instructive as we later attempt to derive more precise bounds.

Theorem 3.28 (Privacy Amplification by Subsampling for Approximate DP). *Let $U \subset [n]$ be a random subset. For a dataset $x \in \mathcal{X}^n$, let $x_U \in \mathcal{X}^n$ denote the entries of x indexed by U. That is, $(x_U)_i = x_i$ if $i \in U$ and $(x_U)_i = \perp$ if $i \notin U$, where $\perp \in \mathcal{X}$ is some null value.*

Assume that, for all $i \in [n]$, we can define $U_{-i} \subset [n] \setminus \{i\}$ such that the following two conditions hold.

- *For all $x \in \mathcal{X}^n$ and $i \in [d]$, x_U and $x_{U_{-i}}$ are always neighboring datasets.*
- *For all $i \in [n]$, the marginal distribution of U_{-i} conditioned on $i \in U$ is equal to the marginal distribution of U conditioned on $i \notin U$.*

Let $M : \mathcal{X}^n \to \mathcal{Y}$ satisfy (ε, δ)-DP. Define $M^U : \mathcal{X}^n \to \mathcal{Y}$ by $M^U(x) = M(x_U)$.

Let $p = \max_{i \in [n]} \underset{U}{\mathbb{P}}[i \in U]$. Then M^U is (ε', δ')-DP for $\varepsilon' = \log(1 + p(e^\varepsilon - 1))$ and $\delta' = p \cdot \delta$.

For small values of ε, we have $\varepsilon' = \log(1 + p(e^\varepsilon - 1)) \approx p \cdot \varepsilon$. More precisely, $\varepsilon' = \log(1+p(e^\varepsilon - 1)) \le p \cdot (e^\varepsilon - 1)$ and, for $\varepsilon \le 1$, we have $e^\varepsilon - 1 \le \varepsilon + \varepsilon^2 \le 2\varepsilon$.

The technical assumption about U in the theorem statement is satisfied by many natural subsampling distributions: If U is a uniformly random subset of $[n]$ of a fixed size m, then U_{-i} can be obtained by replacing i with a a uniformly random element that is not in U. If U is Poisson subsampled – i.e., each $i \in [n]$ is independently included in U with probability p – then, by independence, we can simply remove i, namely $U_{-i} = U \setminus \{i\}$.

The technical assumption should be thought of as an independence assumption. For example, it rules out distributions of the form $\underset{U}{\mathbb{P}}[U = [n]] = p$ and $\mathbb{P}[U = \emptyset] = 1 - p$, which do not yield meaningful privacy amplification.

Proof of Theorem 3.28. Fix neighboring inputs $x, x' \in \mathcal{X}^n$ and some measurable $S \subset \mathcal{Y}$. Let $i \in [n]$ be the index on which they differ (i.e., $x_j = x'_j$ for all $j \in [n]\setminus\{i\}$) and let $p_i = \underset{U}{\mathbb{P}}[i \in U]$. We have

$$\begin{aligned}
\underset{M^U}{\mathbb{P}}\left[M^U(x) \in S\right] &= \underset{U}{\mathbb{E}}\left[\underset{M}{\mathbb{P}}[M(x_U) \in S]\right] \\
&= (1 - p_i) \cdot \underset{U}{\mathbb{E}}\left[\underset{M}{\mathbb{P}}[M(x_U) \in S] \mid i \notin U\right] \\
&\quad + p_i \cdot \underset{U}{\mathbb{E}}\left[\underset{M}{\mathbb{P}}[M(x_U) \in S] \mid i \in U\right] \\
&= (1 - p_i) \cdot \underset{U}{\mathbb{E}}\left[\underset{M}{\mathbb{P}}\left[M(x'_U) \in S\right] \mid i \notin U\right] \\
&\quad + p_i \cdot \underset{U}{\mathbb{E}}\left[\underset{M}{\mathbb{P}}[M(x_U) \in S] \mid i \in U\right] \\
&= (1 - p_i) \cdot a + p_i \cdot b, \\
\underset{M^U}{\mathbb{P}}\left[M^U(x') \in S\right] &= (1 - p_i) \cdot \underset{U}{\mathbb{E}}\left[\underset{M}{\mathbb{P}}\left[M(x'_U) \in S\right] \mid i \notin U\right] \\
&\quad + p_i \cdot \underset{U}{\mathbb{E}}\left[\underset{M}{\mathbb{P}}\left[M(x'_U) \in S\right] \mid i \in U\right] \\
&= (1 - p_i) \cdot a + p_i \cdot b',
\end{aligned}$$

where $a = \underset{U}{\mathbb{E}}\left[\underset{M}{\mathbb{P}}[M(x_U) \in S] \mid i \notin U\right] = \underset{U}{\mathbb{E}}\left[\underset{M}{\mathbb{P}}\left[M(x'_U) \in S\right] \mid i \notin U\right]$, $b = \underset{U}{\mathbb{E}}\left[\underset{M}{\mathbb{P}}[M(x_U) \in S] \mid i \in U\right]$, and $b' = \underset{U}{\mathbb{E}}\left[\underset{M}{\mathbb{P}}\left[M(x'_U) \in S\right] \mid i \in U\right]$.

Note that x_U and x'_U are always neighboring datasets. And, if $i \notin U$, then $x_U = x'_U$. Since M is (ε, δ)-DP, we have $\underset{M}{\mathbb{P}}[M(x_U) \in S] \leq e^{\varepsilon} \cdot \underset{M}{\mathbb{P}}\left[M(x'_U) \in S\right] + \delta$ for all values of U; thus

$$b = \underset{U}{\mathbb{E}}\left[\underset{M}{\mathbb{P}}[M(x_U) \in S] \mid i \in U\right] \leq \underset{U}{\mathbb{E}}\left[e^{\varepsilon} \cdot \underset{M}{\mathbb{P}}\left[M(x'_U) \in S\right] + \delta \mid i \in U\right]$$
$$= e^{\varepsilon} \cdot b' + \delta.$$

However, this inequality alone is not sufficient to prove the claim. We also need to show that $b \leq e^{\varepsilon} \cdot a + \delta$. Using our technical assumption, we have

$$\begin{aligned}
b &= \underset{U}{\mathbb{E}}\left[\underset{M}{\mathbb{P}}[M(x_U) \in S] \mid i \in U\right] \\
&\leq \underset{U}{\mathbb{E}}\left[e^{\varepsilon} \cdot \underset{M}{\mathbb{P}}\left[M(x_{U_{-i}}) \in S\right] + \delta \mid i \in U\right] && (x_{U_{-i}} \text{ is a neighbour of } x_U) \\
&= \underset{U}{\mathbb{E}}\left[e^{\varepsilon} \cdot \underset{M}{\mathbb{P}}[M(x_U) \in S] + \delta \mid i \notin U\right] \\
& && (U_{-i}|_{i \in U} \text{ has the same distribution as } U|_{i \notin U}) \\
&= e^{\varepsilon} \cdot a + \delta.
\end{aligned}$$

Now we can complete the proof: For any $\lambda \in [0, 1]$,

$$\begin{aligned}
\underset{M^U}{\mathbb{P}}\left[M^U(x) \in S\right] &= (1 - p_i) \cdot a + p_i \cdot b \\
&\leq (1 - p_i) \cdot a + p_i \cdot ((1 - \lambda) \cdot (e^{\varepsilon} \cdot a + \delta) + \lambda \cdot (e^{\varepsilon} \cdot b' + \delta)) \\
&= (1 - p_i + e^{\varepsilon} \cdot (1 - \lambda) \cdot p_i) \cdot a + p_i \cdot e^{\varepsilon} \cdot \lambda \cdot b' + p_i \cdot \delta.
\end{aligned}$$

Set $\lambda = p_i + (1 - p_i) \cdot e^{-\varepsilon}$ to obtain

$$\begin{aligned}
\underset{M^U}{\mathbb{P}}\left[M^U(x) \in S\right] &\leq (1 - p_i + e^{\varepsilon} \cdot (1 - \lambda) \cdot p_i) \cdot a + p_i \cdot e^{\varepsilon} \cdot \lambda \cdot b' + p_i \cdot \delta \\
&= \left(1 + p_i \cdot (e^{\varepsilon} - 1)\right) \cdot \left((1 - p_i) \cdot a + p_i \cdot b'\right) + p_i \cdot \delta \\
&= \left(1 + p_i \cdot (e^{\varepsilon} - 1)\right) \cdot \underset{M^U}{\mathbb{P}}\left[M_U(x') \in S\right] + p_i \cdot \delta \\
&\leq e^{\varepsilon'} \cdot \underset{M^U}{\mathbb{P}}\left[M_U(x') \in S\right] + \delta'.
\end{aligned}$$

□

Theorem 3.28 is tight: Consider an algorithm $M : \{0, 1, \perp\}^n \to \{0, 1\}$ that sums its input (excluding $\perp$ values) and performs randomized response on whether or not the sum is 0.[viii] That is, if $y \in \{0,1,\perp\}^n$ satisfies $\sum_{i:y_i \neq \perp} y_i = 0$, then $\mathbb{P}\left[M(y)=0\right] = \frac{e^\varepsilon}{e^\varepsilon=1}$ and $\mathbb{P}\left[M(y)=1\right] = \frac{1}{e^\varepsilon=1}$ and, if $y \in \{0,1,\perp\}^n$ satisfies $\sum_{i:y_i \neq \perp} y_i > 0$, then $\mathbb{P}\left[M(y)=1\right] = \frac{e^\varepsilon}{e^\varepsilon=1}$ and $\mathbb{P}\left[M(y)=0\right] = \frac{1}{e^\varepsilon-1}$. This algorithm satisfies ε-DP.

Let $U \subset [n]$ be random and let $M^U : \{0,1\}^n \to \{0,1\}$ be as in Theorem 3.28. Consider neighboring datasets $x = (0,0,\cdots,0)$ and $x' = (1,0,0,\cdots,0)$. We have

$$\begin{aligned}
\mathbb{P}\left[M^U(x)=0\right] &= \frac{e^\varepsilon}{e^\varepsilon+1},\\
\mathbb{P}\left[M^U(x)=1\right] &= \frac{1}{e^\varepsilon+1},\\
\mathbb{P}\left[M^U(x')=1\right] &= \frac{\mathbb{P}\left[1 \in U\right]\cdot e^\varepsilon + \mathbb{P}\left[1 \notin U\right]}{e^\varepsilon+1},\\
\mathbb{P}\left[M^U(x')=0\right] &= \frac{\mathbb{P}\left[1 \in U\right] + \mathbb{P}\left[1 \notin U\right]\cdot e^\varepsilon}{e^\varepsilon+1},\\
e^{\varepsilon'} \geq \frac{\mathbb{P}\left[M^U(x')=1\right]}{\mathbb{P}\left[M^U(x)=1\right]} &= 1 + \mathbb{P}\left[1 \in U\right]\cdot(e^\varepsilon - 1),
\end{aligned}$$

where ε' is the pure DP parameter satisfied by M^U. We can assume without loss of generality that $p = \max_i \mathbb{P}\left[i \in U\right] = \mathbb{P}\left[1 \in U\right]$. Thus this bound matches the guarantee of Theorem 3.28. (This example can be extended to approximate DP too.)

3.6.2 Addition or Removal versus Replacement for Neighboring Datasets

For this discussion of subsampling, we need to be careful about what it means for datasets to be neighboring. There are three common definitions of what qualifies as neighboring datasets: (i) addition or removal of one person's data, (ii) replacement of one person's data, or (iii) both. Each of these three options is a reasonable choice. Work on differential privacy often glosses over this choice – often the choice is irrelevant. But it becomes relevant if we want sharp analyses of privacy amplification by subsampling.

For the discussion of composition so far in this chapter, it does not matter at all how we define neighboring datasets, as long as we are consistent. In general, it only matters slightly which we choose: A replacement can be accomplished by a

viii. Alternatively (and equivalently), consider an algorithm that adds discrete Laplace noise to the sum of its non-null inputs.

combination of a removal and an addition. Thus, by group privacy, if the algorithm is (ε, δ)-DP with respect to addition or removal, then it is $(2\varepsilon, (1 + e^{\varepsilon})\delta)$-DP with respect to replacement. Conversely, we can simulate a removal or addition by replacing the record with a "null" value ($\perp$ in the formalism of Theorem 3.28). Thus DP with respect to replacement entails DP with respect to addition or removal with the same parameters, unless the semantics of the algorithm forbids null values.

This subtlety already arises in Theorem 3.28. Let's take a close look at the technical assumption: Theorem 3.28 assumes that, for all $i \in [n]$, we can define $U_{-i} \subset [n] \setminus \{i\}$ such that the following two conditions hold.

- For all $x \in \mathcal{X}^n$ and $i \in [d]$, x_U and $x_{U_{-i}}$ are always neighboring datasets.
- For all $i \in [n]$, the marginal distribution of U_{-i} conditioned on $i \in U$ is equal to the marginal distribution of U conditioned on $i \notin U$.

Suppose $U \subset [n]$ is a uniformly random subset of a fixed size $|U| = m$. Then we would define U_{-i} to be U with i replaced by a uniformly random element that is not already in U. Thus, for x_U and $x_{U_{-i}}$ to be neighboring datasets, our neighboring relation must allow replacement, not just addition or removal.

However, if U corresponds to Poisson subsampling (i.e., each $i \in [n]$ is included in U independently with probability p), then U_{-i} would just correspond to removing i. In that case, for x_U and $x_{U_{-i}}$ to be neighboring datasets, our neighboring relation must allow addition and removal.

It turns out to be easier to work with Poisson subsampling and assuming the neighboring relation is addition or removal. In this case, the proof of Theorem 3.28 simplifies to the following.

Proof of Theorem 3.28 for the special case of Poisson sampling and addition or removal. Let $U \subset [n]$ independently include each element with probability p. Let $x, x' \in \mathcal{X}^n$ be neighboring datasets in terms of addition or removal. Without loss of generality, assume x' is x with x_i removed (or, rather, replaced by $x'_i = \perp$).[ix] For any measurable $S \subset \mathcal{Y}$,

$$\begin{aligned}\underset{M^U}{\mathbb{P}}\left[M^U(x) \in S\right] &= \underset{U}{\mathbb{E}}\left[\underset{M}{\mathbb{P}}\left[M(x_U) \in S\right]\right] \\ &= (1-p) \cdot \underset{U}{\mathbb{E}}\left[\underset{M}{\mathbb{P}}\left[M(x_U) \in S\right] \mid i \notin U\right] \\ &\quad + p \cdot \underset{U}{\mathbb{E}}\left[\underset{M}{\mathbb{P}}\left[M(x_U) \in S\right] \mid i \in U\right]\end{aligned}$$

ix. To be formal, we assume $\perp \in \mathcal{X}$ is a null value that is equivalent to removing the item. In particular, for $x \in \mathcal{X}^n$ and $U \subset [n]$ we can define $x_U \in \mathcal{X}^n$ such that $(x_U)_i = x_i$ if $i \in U$ and $(x_U)_i = \perp$ if $i \in [n] \setminus U$.

$$
\begin{aligned}
&= (1-p) \cdot \underset{U}{\mathbb{E}}\left[\underset{M}{\mathbb{P}}\left[M(x'_U) \in S\right] \mid i \notin U\right] \\
&\quad + p \cdot \underset{U}{\mathbb{E}}\left[\underset{M}{\mathbb{P}}[M(x_U) \in S] \mid i \in U\right] \\
&= (1-p) \cdot \underset{U}{\mathbb{E}}\left[\underset{M}{\mathbb{P}}\left[M(x'_U) \in S\right]\right] \\
&\quad + p \cdot \underset{U}{\mathbb{E}}\left[\underset{M}{\mathbb{P}}[M(x_U) \in S] \mid i \in U\right] \\
&\leq (1-p) \cdot \underset{U}{\mathbb{E}}\left[\underset{M}{\mathbb{P}}\left[M(x'_U) \in S\right]\right] \\
&\quad + p \cdot \underset{U}{\mathbb{E}}\left[e^{\varepsilon} \cdot \underset{M}{\mathbb{P}}\left[M(x'_U) \in S\right] + \delta \mid i \in U\right] \\
&= (1-p) \cdot \underset{U}{\mathbb{E}}\left[\underset{M}{\mathbb{P}}\left[M(x'_U) \in S\right]\right] \\
&\quad + p \cdot \underset{U}{\mathbb{E}}\left[e^{\varepsilon} \cdot \underset{M}{\mathbb{P}}\left[M(x'_U) \in S\right] + \delta\right] \\
&= (1-p+p \cdot e^{\varepsilon}) \cdot \underset{M^U}{\mathbb{P}}\left[M^U(x') \in S\right] + p \cdot \delta
\end{aligned}
$$

and, by the same calculation,

$$
\begin{aligned}
\underset{M^U}{\mathbb{P}}\left[M^U(x) \in S\right] &= (1-p) \cdot \underset{U}{\mathbb{E}}\left[\underset{M}{\mathbb{P}}\left[M(x'_U) \in S\right]\right] \\
&\quad + p \cdot \underset{U}{\mathbb{E}}\left[\underset{M}{\mathbb{P}}[M(x_U) \in S] \mid i \in U\right] \\
&\geq (1-p) \cdot \underset{U}{\mathbb{E}}\left[\underset{M}{\mathbb{P}}\left[M(x'_U) \in S\right]\right] \\
&\quad + p \cdot \underset{U}{\mathbb{E}}\left[e^{-\varepsilon} \cdot (\underset{M}{\mathbb{P}}\left[M(x'_U) \in S\right] - \delta) \mid i \in U\right] \\
&= (1-p+p \cdot e^{-\varepsilon}) \cdot \underset{M^U}{\mathbb{P}}\left[M^U(x') \in S\right] - p \cdot e^{-\varepsilon} \cdot \delta \\
&\geq \frac{1}{1-p+p \cdot e^{\varepsilon}} \cdot (\underset{M^U}{\mathbb{P}}\left[M^U(x') \in S\right] - p \cdot \delta).
\end{aligned}
$$

(Lemma 3.35)

The key step in the proof is the equality $\underset{U}{\mathbb{E}}\left[\underset{M}{\mathbb{P}}\left[M(x'_U) \in S\right] \mid i \notin U\right] = \underset{U}{\mathbb{E}}\left[\underset{M}{\mathbb{P}}\left[M(x'_U) \in S\right] \mid i \in U\right] = \underset{U}{\mathbb{E}}\left[\underset{M}{\mathbb{P}}\left[M(x'_U) \in S\right]\right]$. This holds because $x'_i =$

$\perp$, so whether or not $i \in U$ is irrelevant for x'_U, and because the event $i \in U$ is independent from $U \setminus \{i\}$. □

For the rest of this section, we will restrict our attention to Poisson subsampling and assume that the neighboring relation corresponds to addition or removal of one individual's data.

3.6.3 Subsampling & Composition

How does composition work with subsampling? Of course, we can combine the advanced composition theorem (Theorem 3.22) with our privacy amplification by subsampling result (Theorem 3.28). However, it turns out this is not the best way to analyze many realistic systems.

Consider the following algorithm (which arises in differentially private deep learning applications). Let $x \in \mathcal{X}^n$ be the private input. Iteratively, for $t = 1, \cdots, T$, we pick some function $q_t : \mathcal{X}^n \to \mathbb{R}^d$ and randomly sample a subset $U_t \subset [n]$; then we reveal $\mathcal{N}(q_t(x_{U_t}), \sigma^2 I_d)$.

This algorithm interleaves composition with privacy amplification by subsampling. That is, we combine multivariate Gaussian noise addition (which is a form of composition over the d coordinates) with subsampling and then we compose over the T iterations.

We can use Corollary 3.10 to show that releasing $\mathcal{N}(q_t(x), \sigma^2 I_d)$ satisfies $(\varepsilon_0, \delta_0)$-DP for $\varepsilon_0 = O\left(\sqrt{\frac{\Delta_2^2}{\sigma^2}\log(1/\delta_0)}\right)$, where $\Delta_2 = \sup_{\substack{x,x' \in \mathcal{X}^n \\ \text{neighboring}}} \|q_t(x) - q_t(x')\|_2$ is the sensitivity of q_t. Then we can use Theorem 3.28 to show that, if U_t is a Poisson sample which contains each element with probability p, then $\mathcal{N}(q_t(x_{U_t}), \sigma^2 I_d)$ is $(\varepsilon_1, \delta_1)$-DP where $\varepsilon_1 = \log(1 + p \cdot (e^{\varepsilon_0} - 1)) = O(p \cdot \varepsilon_0)$ and $\delta_1 = p \cdot \delta_0$. Finally, Theorem 3.22 tells us that the composition over T iterations satisfies (ε, δ)-DP with $\varepsilon = O\left(\varepsilon_1 \cdot \sqrt{T \log(1/\delta_2)}\right)$ and $\delta = \delta_2 + T \cdot \delta_1$. Overall, we have

$$\varepsilon = O\left(\frac{\Delta_2}{\sigma} \cdot p \cdot \sqrt{T} \cdot \log(T/\delta)\right).$$

This result is asymptotically suboptimal because we have picked up two $\sqrt{\log(1/\delta)}$ terms. We obtained one from the Gaussian noise addition (Corollary 3.10) and another from the composition (Theorem 3.22). Both arise from bounding the tails of the privacy loss distribution. This is redundant; we should only need to bound the tails of the privacy loss distribution once.

Intuitively, we started with a Gaussian privacy loss; then we applied a tail bound to obtain a $(\varepsilon_0, \delta_0)$-DP guarantee to which we applied the subsampling theorem; and then we converted this back into a concentrated DP guarantee to apply advanced composition and finally we applied a tail bound to convert this back to (ε, δ)-DP.

We are going to avoid this redundancy by analyzing privacy amplification by subsampling directly in terms of the privacy loss distribution, rather than needing to go via approximate DP. To do so, we need to introduce a new tool.

3.6.4 Rényi Differential Privacy

Rényi differential privacy was introduced by Mironov [Mir17] and was motivated by analyzing privacy amplification by subsampling interleaved with composition, which arises in differentially private deep learning [Aba+16].

Definition 3.29 (Rényi Differential Privacy). *Let $M : \mathcal{X}^n \to \mathcal{Y}$ be a randomized algorithm. We say that M satisfies (α, ε)-Rényi differential privacy ((α, ε)-RDP) if, for all neighboring inputs $x, x' \in \mathcal{X}^n$, the privacy loss distribution* $\text{PrivLoss}\left(M(x) \middle\| M(x')\right)$ *is well-defined (see Definition 3.2) and*

$$\underset{Z \leftarrow \text{PrivLoss}(M(x)\|M(x'))}{\mathbb{E}} \left[\exp((\alpha - 1)Z)\right] \leq \exp((\alpha - 1) \cdot \varepsilon).$$

Rényi DP is closely related to concentrated DP (Definition 3.11). Specifically, ρ-zCDP is equivalent to satisfying $(\alpha, \alpha \cdot \rho)$-RDP for all $\alpha \in (1, \infty)$. Rényi DP inherits the nice composition properties of concentrated DP:

Lemma 3.30. *Let $M_1 : \mathcal{X}^n \to \mathcal{Y}_1$ be (α, ε_1)-RDP. Let $M_2 : \mathcal{X}^n \times \mathcal{Y}_1 \to \mathcal{Y}_2$ be such that, for all $y_1 \in \mathcal{Y}_1$, the algorithm $x \mapsto M(x, y_1)$ is (α, ε_2)-RDP. Define $M : \mathcal{X}^n \to \mathcal{Y}_2$ by $M(x) = M_2(x, M_1(x))$. Then M is $(\alpha, \varepsilon_1 + \varepsilon_2)$-RDP.*

The proof of Lemma 3.30 is identical to that of Proposition 3.19. Note that, while the ε parameter adds up, the α parameter does not change. More generally, composing an $(\alpha_1, \varepsilon_1)$-RDP algorithm with an $(\alpha_2, \varepsilon_2)$-RDP algorithm yields $(\min\{\alpha_1, \alpha_2\}, \varepsilon_1 + \varepsilon_2)$-RDP.

It is helpful to think of ε in (α, ε)-RDP as a function of α, rather than a single number. This function can encode a rich variety of privacy guarantees. (Concentrated DP corresponds to a linear function.) In particular, it allows us to more precisely represent the kinds of guarantees obtained by subsampling.

Concentrated DP corresponds to the privacy loss being subgaussian (i.e., ρ-zCDP implies $\underset{Z \leftarrow \text{PrivLoss}(M(x)\|M(x'))}{\mathbb{P}} [Z > \tilde{\varepsilon}] \leq \exp(-(\tilde{\varepsilon} - \rho)^2/4\rho)$ for all $\tilde{\varepsilon} \geq \rho$ and all neighboring inputs x and x'), whereas Rényi DP corresponds to the privacy loss being subexponential (i.e., (α, ε)-RDP implies $\underset{Z \leftarrow \text{PrivLoss}(M(x)\|M(x'))}{\mathbb{P}} [Z > \tilde{\varepsilon}] \leq \exp(-(\alpha - 1)(\tilde{\varepsilon} - \varepsilon))$). That is, Rényi DP is more appropriate for analyzing privacy loss distributions with slightly heavier tails than Gaussian. In contrast, pure DP corresponds to the privacy loss being bounded (i.e., ε-DP implies $\underset{Z \leftarrow \mathrm{PrivLoss}(M(x)\|M(x'))}{\mathbb{P}}[Z > \varepsilon] = 0$). So we can view concentrated DP as a relaxation of pure DP and, in turn, Rényi DP is a relaxation of concentrated DP.

Rényi DP is typically formulated in terms of Rényi divergences [Rén61], which were studied in the information theory literature long before differential privacy was discovered.

Definition 3.31 (Rényi Divergences). *Let P and Q be distributions over $\mathcal{Y}$.*[x] *For $\alpha \in (1, \infty)$, define*

$$\begin{aligned}
\mathrm{D}_\alpha(P\|Q) &= \frac{1}{\alpha - 1}\log \underset{Z \leftarrow \mathrm{PrivLoss}(P\|Q)}{\mathbb{E}}\left[\exp((\alpha - 1)Z)\right] \\
&= \frac{1}{\alpha - 1}\log \underset{Y \leftarrow P}{\mathbb{E}}\left[\left(\frac{P(Y)}{Q(Y)}\right)^{\alpha-1}\right] \\
&= \frac{1}{\alpha - 1}\log \underset{Y \leftarrow Q}{\mathbb{E}}\left[\left(\frac{P(Y)}{Q(Y)}\right)^{\alpha}\right].
\end{aligned}$$

Also, define

$$\begin{aligned}
\mathrm{D}_1(P\|Q) &= \lim_{\alpha \to 1} \mathrm{D}_\alpha(P\|Q) \\
&= \underset{Z \leftarrow \mathrm{PrivLoss}(P\|Q)}{\mathbb{E}}[Z] \\
&= \underset{Y \leftarrow P}{\mathbb{E}}\left[\log\left(\frac{P(Y)}{Q(Y)}\right)\right], \\
\mathrm{D}_\infty(P\|Q) &= \lim_{\alpha \to \infty} \mathrm{D}_\alpha(P\|Q) \\
&= \sup\left\{\log\left(\frac{P(S)}{Q(S)}\right) : S \subset \mathcal{Y}, Q(S) > 0\right\}.
\end{aligned}$$

Thus an equivalent definition of M satisfying (α, ε)-RDP is that $\mathrm{D}_\alpha\left(M(x)\middle\|M(x')\right) \le \varepsilon$ for all neighboring x, x'.

We now state several key properties of Rényi divergences; most of these are properties we have proved earlier, but we now restate them in a new language.

x. We make the usual measure theoretic disclaimers: We assume the P and Q have the same sigma-algebra. We assume P is absolutely continuous with respect to Q – i.e., $\forall S \;\; Q(S) = 0 \implies P(S) = 0$ – so that the Radon-Nikodym derivative is well-defined; we denote the Radon-Nikodym derivative of P with respect to Q evaluated at y by $P(y)/Q(y)$. More generally, if the absolute continuity assumption does not hold, then we define $\mathrm{D}_\alpha(P\|Q) = \infty$ for all $\alpha \in [1, \infty]$.

Lemma 3.32. *Let P, Q be probability distributions over $\mathcal{Y}$ with a common sigma-algebra such that P is absolutely continuous with respect to Q.*

1. ***Post-processing (a.k.a. data processing inequality) & non-negativity:*** *Let $f : \mathcal{Y} \to \mathcal{Z}$ be a measurable function. Let $f(P)$ denote the distribution on $\mathcal{Z}$ obtained by applying f to a sample from P; define $f(Q)$ similarly. Then $0 \leq \mathrm{D}_\alpha\left(f(P)\middle\|f(Q)\right) \leq \mathrm{D}_\alpha\left(P\|Q\right)$ for all $\alpha \in [1, \infty]$.*
2. ***Composition:*** *If $P = P' \times P''$ and $Q = Q' \times Q''$ are product distributions, then $\mathrm{D}_\alpha\left(P\|Q\right) = \mathrm{D}_\alpha\left(P'\middle\|Q'\right) + \mathrm{D}_\alpha\left(P''\middle\|Q''\right)$ for all $\alpha \in [1, \infty]$.*

   More generally, suppose P and Q are distributions on $\mathcal{Y} = \mathcal{Y}' \times \mathcal{Y}''$. Let P' and Q' be the marginal distributions on $\mathcal{Y}'$ induced by P and Q respectively. For $y' \in \mathcal{Y}'$, let $P''_{y'}$ and $Q''_{y'}$ be the conditional distributions on $\mathcal{Y}''$ induced by P and Q respectively. That is, we can generate a sample $Y = (Y', Y'') \leftarrow P$ by first sampling $Y' \leftarrow P'$ and then sampling $Y'' \leftarrow P''_{Y'}$ and similarly for Q. Then $\mathrm{D}_\alpha\left(P\|Q\right) \leq \mathrm{D}_\alpha\left(P'\middle\|Q'\right) + \sup_{y' \in \mathcal{Y}'} \mathrm{D}_\alpha\left(P''_{y'}\middle\|Q''_{y'}\right)$ for all $\alpha \in [1, \infty]$.
3. ***Monotonicity:*** *For all $1 \leq \alpha \leq \alpha' \leq \infty$, $\mathrm{D}_\alpha\left(P\|Q\right) \leq \mathrm{D}_{\alpha'}\left(P\|Q\right)$.*
4. ***Gaussian divergence:*** *For all $\mu, \mu', \sigma \in \mathbb{R}$ with $\sigma > 0$ and all $\alpha \in [1, \infty)$,*

$$\mathrm{D}_\alpha\left(\mathcal{N}(\mu, \sigma^2)\middle\|\mathcal{N}(\mu', \sigma^2)\right) = \alpha \cdot \frac{(\mu - \mu')^2}{2\sigma^2}.$$

5. ***Pure DP to Concentrated DP:*** *For all $\alpha \in [1, \infty)$,*

$$\mathrm{D}_\alpha\left(P\|Q\right) \leq \frac{\alpha}{8} \cdot \left(\mathrm{D}_\infty\left(P\|Q\right) + \mathrm{D}_\infty\left(Q\|P\right)\right)^2.$$

6. ***Quasi-convexity:*** *Let P' and Q' be probability distributions over $\mathcal{Y}$ such that P' is absolutely continuous with respect to Q'. For $s \in [0, 1]$, let $(1-s) \cdot P + s \cdot P'$ denote the convex combination of the distributions P and P' with weighting s. For all $\alpha \in (1, \infty)$ and all $s \in [0, 1]$,*

$$\begin{aligned}
&\mathrm{D}_\alpha\left((1-s) \cdot P + s \cdot P'\middle\|(1-s) \cdot Q + s \cdot Q'\right) \\
&\leq \frac{1}{\alpha - 1} \log\left((1-s) \cdot \exp\left((\alpha - 1)\mathrm{D}_\alpha\left(P\|Q\right)\right)\right. \\
&\quad \left.+ s \cdot \exp\left((\alpha - 1)\mathrm{D}_\alpha\left(P'\middle\|Q'\right)\right)\right) \\
&\leq \max\left\{\mathrm{D}_\alpha\left(P\|Q\right), \mathrm{D}_\alpha\left(P'\middle\|Q'\right)\right\}
\end{aligned}$$

   and $\mathrm{D}_1\left((1-s) \cdot P + s \cdot P'\middle\|(1-s) \cdot Q + s \cdot Q'\right) \leq (1-s) \cdot \mathrm{D}_1\left(P\|Q\right) + s \cdot \mathrm{D}_1\left(P'\middle\|Q'\right)$.
7. ***Triangle-like inequality (a.k.a. group privacy):*** *Let R be a distribution on $\mathcal{Y}$ and assume that Q is absolutely continuous with respect to R. For all $1 < \alpha <$*

$\alpha' < \infty$,

$$\mathrm{D}_{\alpha}\left(P\|R\right) \leq \frac{\alpha'}{\alpha'-1} \cdot \mathrm{D}_{\alpha \cdot \frac{\alpha'-1}{\alpha'-\alpha}}\left(P\|Q\right) + \mathrm{D}_{\alpha'}\left(Q\|R\right).$$

In particular, if $\mathrm{D}_{\alpha}(P\|Q) \leq \rho_1 \cdot \alpha$ *and* $\mathrm{D}_{\alpha}(Q\|R) \leq \rho_2 \cdot \alpha$ *for all* $\alpha \in (1,\infty)$, *then* $\mathrm{D}_{\alpha}(P\|R) \leq (\sqrt{\rho_1} + \sqrt{\rho_2})^2 \cdot \alpha$ *for all* $\alpha \in (1,\infty)$.

8. ***Conversion to approximate DP:*** *For all measurable* $S \subset \mathcal{Y}$, *all* $\alpha \in (1,\infty)$, *and all* $\tilde{\varepsilon} \geq \mathrm{D}_{\alpha}(P\|Q)$,

$$\begin{aligned} P(S) &\leq e^{\tilde{\varepsilon}} \cdot Q(S) + e^{-(\alpha-1)(\tilde{\varepsilon}-\mathrm{D}_{\alpha}(P\|Q))} \cdot \frac{1}{\alpha} \cdot \left(1 - \frac{1}{\alpha}\right)^{\alpha-1} \\ &\leq e^{\tilde{\varepsilon}} \cdot Q(S) + e^{-(\alpha-1)(\tilde{\varepsilon}-\mathrm{D}_{\alpha}(P\|Q))}. \end{aligned}$$

Proof. 1. *Post-processing (a.k.a. data processing inequality) & non-negativity:* See Lemma 3.20. Non-negativity follows from setting f to be a constant function and noting that the divergence between two point masses is zero.

2. *Composition:* See Proposition 3.19.
3. *Monotonicity:* Let $1 < \alpha \leq \alpha' < \infty$. (The cases where $\alpha = 1$ and $\alpha' = \infty$ follow from continuity.) Let $f(x) = x^{\frac{\alpha'-1}{\alpha-1}}$. Then f is convex and, by Jensen's inequality,

$$\begin{aligned} e^{(\alpha'-1)\mathrm{D}_{\alpha}(P\|Q)} &= f\left(\underset{Y \leftarrow P}{\mathbb{E}}\left[\left(\frac{P(Y)}{Q(Y)}\right)^{\alpha-1}\right]\right) \\ &\leq \underset{Y \leftarrow P}{\mathbb{E}}\left[f\left(\left(\frac{P(Y)}{Q(Y)}\right)^{\alpha-1}\right)\right] = e^{(\alpha'-1)\mathrm{D}_{\alpha'}(P\|Q)}, \end{aligned}$$

which implies $\mathrm{D}_{\alpha}(P\|Q) \leq \mathrm{D}_{\alpha'}(P\|Q)$.

4. *Gaussian divergence:* See Lemma 3.12.
5. *Pure DP to Concentrated DP:* See Proposition 3.16.
6. *Quasi-convexity:* See Lemma B.6 of Bun and Steinke [BS16].
7. *Triangle-like inequality (a.k.a. group privacy):* Let $\alpha \in (1,\infty)$. Let $p, q \in (1,\infty)$ satisfy $\frac{1}{p} + \frac{1}{q} = 1$. By Hölder's inequality,

$$\begin{aligned} e^{(\alpha-1)\mathrm{D}_{\alpha}(P\|R)} &= \underset{Y \leftarrow P}{\mathbb{E}}\left[\left(\frac{P(Y)}{R(Y)}\right)^{\alpha-1}\right] = \underset{Y \leftarrow R}{\mathbb{E}}\left[\left(\frac{P(Y)}{R(Y)}\right)^{\alpha}\right] \\ &= \underset{Y \leftarrow Q}{\mathbb{E}}\left[\frac{P(Y)}{Q(Y)} \cdot \left(\frac{P(Y)}{Q(Y)} \cdot \frac{Q(Y)}{R(Y)}\right)^{\alpha-1}\right] \end{aligned}$$

$$
\begin{aligned}
&= \mathop{\mathbb{E}}_{Y \leftarrow Q}\left[\left(\frac{P(Y)}{Q(Y)}\right)^{\alpha} \cdot \left(\frac{Q(Y)}{R(Y)}\right)^{\alpha-1}\right] \\
&\leq \mathop{\mathbb{E}}_{Y \leftarrow Q}\left[\left(\frac{P(Y)}{Q(Y)}\right)^{\alpha p}\right]^{1/p} \cdot \mathop{\mathbb{E}}_{Y \leftarrow Q}\left[\left(\frac{Q(Y)}{R(Y)}\right)^{(\alpha-1)q}\right]^{1/q} \\
&= e^{\frac{\alpha p-1}{p}\mathrm{D}_{\alpha p}(P\|Q)} \cdot e^{\frac{(\alpha-1)q}{q}\mathrm{D}_{(\alpha-1)q+1}(Q\|R)}.
\end{aligned}
$$

This rearranges to

$$
\begin{aligned}
\mathrm{D}_{\alpha}\left(P\|R\right) &\leq \frac{\alpha p - 1}{(\alpha-1)p}\mathrm{D}_{\alpha p}\left(P\|Q\right) + \mathrm{D}_{(\alpha-1)q+1}\left(Q\|R\right) \\
&= \left(1 + \frac{1}{(\alpha-1)q}\right) \cdot \mathrm{D}_{\alpha p}\left(P\|Q\right) + \mathrm{D}_{(\alpha-1)q+1}\left(Q\|R\right) \\
&= \frac{\alpha'}{\alpha'-1} \cdot \mathrm{D}_{\alpha \cdot \frac{\alpha'-1}{\alpha'-\alpha}}\left(P\|Q\right) + \mathrm{D}_{\alpha'}\left(Q\|R\right),
\end{aligned}
$$

where the final equality sets $p = \frac{\alpha'-1}{\alpha'-\alpha}$ and $q = \frac{\alpha'-1}{\alpha-1}$.

Now assume $\mathrm{D}_{\alpha}\left(P\|Q\right) \leq \rho_1 \cdot \alpha$ and $\mathrm{D}_{\alpha}\left(Q\|R\right) \leq \rho_2 \cdot \alpha$ for all $\alpha \in (1, \infty)$. Then

$$
\begin{aligned}
\mathrm{D}_{\alpha}\left(P\|R\right) &\leq \inf_{\alpha'>\alpha} \frac{\alpha'}{\alpha'-1} \cdot \mathrm{D}_{\alpha \cdot \frac{\alpha'-1}{\alpha'-\alpha}}\left(P\|Q\right) + \mathrm{D}_{\alpha'}\left(Q\|R\right) \\
&\leq \inf_{\alpha'>\alpha} \frac{\alpha'}{\alpha'-1} \cdot \alpha \cdot \frac{\alpha'-1}{\alpha'-\alpha} \cdot \rho_1 + \alpha' \cdot \rho_2 \\
&= \inf_{x>0} \alpha \cdot \frac{x+1}{x} \cdot \rho_1 + \alpha \cdot (x+1) \cdot \rho_2 \\
&\qquad\qquad\qquad\qquad \text{(Reparameterize } \alpha' = (x+1) \cdot \alpha\text{)} \\
&= \alpha \cdot \inf_{x>0} \rho_1 + \rho_2 + \frac{1}{x}\rho_1 + x \cdot \rho_2 \\
&= \alpha \cdot (\rho_1 + \rho_2 + 2\sqrt{\rho_1 \cdot \rho_2}) \qquad\qquad (x = \sqrt{\rho_1/\rho_2}) \\
&= \alpha \cdot (\sqrt{\rho_1} + \sqrt{\rho_2})^2.
\end{aligned}
$$

8. *Conversion to approximate DP:* See Proposition 3.14.

□

3.6.5 Sharp Privacy Amplification by Poisson Subsampling for Rényi DP

Now we analyze privacy amplification by subsampling under Rényi DP. We start with a Rényi DP guarantee and we obtain an amplified Rényi DP guarantee. The goal is to obtain a sharp analysis that avoids converting to approximate DP and back.

For mathematical simplicity, we restrict our attention to Poisson subsampling and assume that neighboring datasets correspond to addition or removal of one person's data.

Theorem 3.33 (Tight Privacy Amplification by Subsampling for Rényi DP). *Let $U \subset [n]$ be a random set that contains each element independently with probability p. For $x \in \mathcal{X}^n$ let $x_U \in \mathcal{X}^n$ be given by $(x_U)_i = x_i$ if $i \in U$ and $(x_U)_i = \perp$ if $i \notin U$, where $\perp \in \mathcal{X}$ is some fixed value.*

Let $\varepsilon : \mathbb{N}_{\geq 2} \to \mathbb{R} \cup \{\infty\}$ be a function. Let $M : \mathcal{X}^n \to \mathcal{Y}$ satisfy $(\alpha, \varepsilon(\alpha))$-RDP for all $\alpha \in \mathbb{N}_{\geq 2}$ with respect to addition or removal – i.e., $x, x' \in \mathcal{X}^n$ are neighboring if, for some $i \in [n]$, we have $x_i = \perp$ or $x'_i = \perp$, and $\forall j \neq i \ x_j = x'_j$.

Define $M^U : \mathcal{X}^n \to \mathcal{Y}$ by $M^U(x) = M(x_U)$. Then M^U satisfies $(\alpha, \varepsilon'_p(\alpha))$-RDP for all $\alpha \in \mathbb{N}_{\geq 2}$ where

$$\varepsilon'_p(\alpha) = \frac{1}{\alpha - 1} \log\Bigg((1-p)^{\alpha-1}(1 + (\alpha - 1)p) + \sum_{k=2}^{\alpha} \binom{\alpha}{k} (1-p)^{\alpha-k} p^k \cdot e^{(k-1)\varepsilon(k)} \Bigg).$$

Note that $(1-p)^{\alpha-1}(1+(\alpha-1)p) \leq 1$. It is easy to see from the proof that this analysis is tight. That is, if the assumption that M satisfies $(\alpha, \varepsilon(\alpha))$-RDP for all α is tight for some fixed pair of neighboring inputs, then the conclusion that M^U satisfies $(\alpha, \varepsilon'_p(\alpha))$-RDP is also tight.

Theorem 3.33 only considers Rényi DP with orders $\alpha \in \mathbb{N}_{\geq 2} = \{2, 3, 4, \cdots\}$. This restriction arises because the proof uses a binomial expansion, which only works for integer exponents. In certain cases, it is possible to obtain an expression all $\alpha \in (1, \infty)$ using an infinite binomial series [MTZ19]. In general, we can use Monotonicity (part 3 of Lemma 3.32) to bound non-integer α, namely for all $\alpha \in (1, \infty)$, M^U satisfies $(\alpha, \varepsilon'_p(\lceil \alpha \rceil))$-RDP.

Proof of Theorem 3.33. Fix neighboring datasets $x, x' \in \mathcal{X}^n$. Without loss of generality, assume that x' is x with one element removed – i.e., $\exists i \in [n] \ (x'_i = \perp) \wedge (\forall j \in [n] \setminus \{i\} \ x_j = x'_j)$. Fix this i.

Let $Q = M(x'_U) = M^U(x')$. Let $P = M(x_U)|_{i \in U}$ be the conditional distribution of $M(x_U)$ with $i \in U$. Note that $M(x_U)|_{i \notin U} = Q$ because $x_U = x'_U$ when $i \notin U$ and the event $i \in U$ is independent from $U \setminus \{i\}$. (This is where we use the Poisson subsampling assumption.)

Thus we can express the distribution of $M^U(x)$ as a convex combination: $M(x_U) = p \cdot P + (1-p) \cdot Q$, since $p = \mathbb{P}[i \in U]$.

For all $\alpha \in \mathbb{N}_{\geq 2}$, M is assumed to be $(\alpha, \varepsilon(\alpha))$-RDP, so we have $\mathrm{D}_\alpha(P\|Q) \leq \varepsilon(\alpha)$ and $\mathrm{D}_\alpha(Q\|P) \leq \varepsilon(\alpha)$.

To complete the proof we must show that

$$\mathrm{D}_\alpha\left(p \cdot P + (1-p) \cdot Q \middle\| Q\right) \leq \varepsilon_p'(\alpha)$$

and

$$\mathrm{D}_\alpha\left(Q \middle\| p \cdot P + (1-p) \cdot Q\right) \leq \varepsilon_p'(\alpha)$$

for all $\alpha \in \mathbb{N}_{\geq 2}$.

Fix $\alpha \in \mathbb{N}_{\geq 2}$. We have

$$\begin{aligned}
e^{(\alpha-1)\mathrm{D}_\alpha(p \cdot P+(1-p)\cdot Q\|Q)} &= \mathop{\mathbb{E}}_{Y \leftarrow Q}\left[\left(\frac{p \cdot P(Y) + (1-p) \cdot Q(Y)}{Q(Y)}\right)^\alpha\right] \\
&= \mathop{\mathbb{E}}_{Y \leftarrow Q}\left[\left(1 - p + p \cdot \frac{P(Y)}{Q(Y)}\right)^\alpha\right] \\
&= \mathop{\mathbb{E}}_{Y \leftarrow Q}\left[\sum_{k=0}^{\alpha}\binom{\alpha}{k}(1-p)^{\alpha-k}p^k\left(\frac{P(Y)}{Q(Y)}\right)^k\right] \\
&\qquad \text{(Binomial expansion)} \\
&= \sum_{k=0}^{\alpha}\binom{\alpha}{k}(1-p)^{\alpha-k}p^k \mathop{\mathbb{E}}_{Y \leftarrow Q}\left[\left(\frac{P(Y)}{Q(Y)}\right)^k\right] \\
&= (1-p)^\alpha + \alpha(1-p)^{\alpha-1}p \\
&\quad + \sum_{k=2}^{\alpha}\binom{\alpha}{k}(1-p)^{\alpha-k}p^k \cdot e^{(k-1)\mathrm{D}_k(P\|Q)} \\
&\qquad \left(\mathop{\mathbb{E}}_{Y \leftarrow Q}\left[\frac{P(Y)}{Q(Y)}\right] = 1\right) \\
&\leq (1-p)^{\alpha-1}(1 + (\alpha-1)p) \\
&\quad + \sum_{k=2}^{\alpha}\binom{\alpha}{k}(1-p)^{\alpha-k}p^k \cdot e^{(k-1)\varepsilon(k)} \\
&\qquad (\mathrm{D}_k(P\|Q) \leq \varepsilon(k)) \\
&= e^{(\alpha-1)\varepsilon_p'(\alpha)}.
\end{aligned}$$

Note that $(1-p)^{\alpha-1}(1+(\alpha-1)p) \leq (e^{-p})^{\alpha-1}e^{(\alpha-1)p} = 1$.

An identical calculation shows that

$$\mathrm{D}_\alpha\left(p \cdot Q + (1-p) \cdot P \middle\| P\right) \le \varepsilon'_p(\alpha).$$

Finally, Theorem 3.34 gives

$$\mathrm{D}_\alpha\left(Q \middle\| pP + (1-p)Q\right) \le \max\left\{ \begin{array}{c} \mathrm{D}_\alpha\left(pP + (1-p)Q \middle\| Q\right), \\ \mathrm{D}_\alpha\left(pQ + (1-p)P \middle\| P\right) \end{array} \right\} \le \varepsilon'_p(\alpha).$$

□

The following result shows that, in terms of subsampling for Rényi DP, it suffices to analyze one side of the add/remove neighboring relation.

Theorem 3.34. *Let P and Q be probability distributions that are absolutely continuous with respect to each other. Let $p \in [0,1]$ and $\alpha \in (1,\infty)$. Set $\lambda = \frac{(2\alpha-1)p}{(2\alpha-1)p+3(1-p)}$. Then*

$$\begin{aligned} e^{(\alpha-1)\mathrm{D}_\alpha(Q\|pP+(1-p)Q)} &\le (1-\lambda)\cdot e^{(\alpha-1)\mathrm{D}_\alpha(pP+(1-p)Q\|Q)} \\ &\quad + \lambda \cdot e^{(\alpha-1)\mathrm{D}_\alpha(pQ+(1-p)P\|P)}. \end{aligned}$$

Since $\lambda \in [0,1]$, this implies

$$\mathrm{D}_\alpha\left(Q \middle\| pP + (1-p)Q\right) \le \max\left\{ \begin{array}{c} \mathrm{D}_\alpha\left(pP + (1-p)Q \middle\| Q\right), \\ \mathrm{D}_\alpha\left(pQ + (1-p)P \middle\| P\right) \end{array} \right\}.$$

Proof. Define $f : (0,\infty) \to \mathbb{R}$ by

$$f(x) = (1-\lambda)(1-p+p\cdot x)^\alpha + \lambda \cdot x \cdot \left(1 - p + \frac{p}{x}\right)^\alpha - \left(1 - p + p \cdot x\right)^{1-\alpha}.$$

We have

$$\begin{aligned} &(1-\lambda)\cdot e^{(\alpha-1)\mathrm{D}_\alpha(pP+(1-p)Q\|Q)} + \lambda \cdot e^{(\alpha-1)\mathrm{D}_\alpha(pQ+(1-p)P\|P)} \\ &\quad - e^{(\alpha-1)\mathrm{D}_\alpha(Q\|pP+(1-p)Q)} \\ &= (1-\lambda)\cdot \mathop{\mathbb{E}}_{Y\leftarrow Q}\left[\left(\frac{pP(Y)+(1-p)Q(Y)}{Q(Y)}\right)^\alpha\right] \\ &\quad + \lambda \cdot \mathop{\mathbb{E}}_{Y\leftarrow P}\left[\left(\frac{pQ(Y)+(1-p)P(Y)}{P(Y)}\right)^\alpha\right] \\ &\quad - \mathop{\mathbb{E}}_{Y\leftarrow Q}\left[\left(\frac{Q(Y)}{pP(Y)+(1-p)Q(Y)}\right)^{\alpha-1}\right] \\ &= (1-\lambda)\cdot \mathop{\mathbb{E}}_{Y\leftarrow Q}\left[\left(p\frac{P(Y)}{Q(Y)} + (1-p)\right)^\alpha\right] \end{aligned}$$

$$
\begin{aligned}
&+\lambda \cdot \underset{Y \leftarrow P}{\mathbb{E}}\left[\left(p\left(\frac{P(Y)}{Q(Y)}\right)^{-1}+1-p\right)^{\alpha}\right] \\
&-\underset{Y \leftarrow Q}{\mathbb{E}}\left[\left(p \frac{P(Y)}{Q(Y)}+(1-p)\right)^{1-\alpha}\right] \\
=&(1-\lambda) \cdot \underset{Y \leftarrow Q}{\mathbb{E}}\left[\left(p \frac{P(Y)}{Q(Y)}+(1-p)\right)^{\alpha}\right] \\
&+\lambda \cdot \underset{Y \leftarrow Q}{\mathbb{E}}\left[\frac{P(Y)}{Q(Y)} \cdot\left(p\left(\frac{P(Y)}{Q(Y)}\right)^{-1}+1-p\right)^{\alpha}\right] \\
&-\underset{Y \leftarrow Q}{\mathbb{E}}\left[\left(p \frac{P(Y)}{Q(Y)}+(1-p)\right)^{1-\alpha}\right] \\
&\qquad\qquad\qquad\qquad \left(\text{For any } g, \underset{Y \leftarrow Q}{\mathbb{E}}\left[\frac{P(Y)}{Q(Y)} g(Y)\right]=\underset{Y \leftarrow P}{\mathbb{E}}[g(Y)]\right) \\
=&\underset{Y \leftarrow Q}{\mathbb{E}}\left[(1-\lambda) \cdot\left(1-p+p \cdot \frac{P(Y)}{Q(Y)}\right)^{\alpha}\right. \\
&\left.+\lambda \cdot \frac{P(Y)}{Q(Y)} \cdot\left(1-p+\frac{p}{\frac{P(Y)}{Q(Y)}}\right)^{\alpha}-\left(1-p+p \cdot \frac{P(Y)}{Q(Y)}\right)^{1-\alpha}\right] \\
=&\underset{X}{\mathbb{E}}[f(X)],
\end{aligned}
$$

where $X=\frac{P(Y)}{Q(Y)}$ for $Y \leftarrow Q$. Thus our objective is to show that $\underset{X}{\mathbb{E}}[f(X)] \geq 0$.[xi]

We claim that f is convex. Convexity implies $f(x) \geq f(1)+f'(1) \cdot (x-1)$ for all $x \in (0, \infty)$. Since $f(1)=0$ and $\mathbb{E}[X]=\underset{Y \leftarrow Q}{\mathbb{E}}\left[\frac{P(Y)}{Q(Y)}\right]=1$, this implies $\mathbb{E}[f(X)] \geq f(1)+f'(1)\mathbb{E}[X-1]=0$, as required.

It only remains to prove that f is convex. We have, for all $x>0$,

$$
\begin{aligned}
f(x) &= (1-\lambda)(1-p+p \cdot x)^{\alpha}+\lambda \cdot x \cdot\left(1-p+\frac{p}{x}\right)^{\alpha}-(1-p+p \cdot x)^{1-\alpha}, \\
f'(x) &= (1-\lambda) \alpha p(1-p+p \cdot x)^{\alpha-1}+\lambda \cdot\left(1-p+\frac{p}{x}\right)^{\alpha} \\
&\quad -\lambda \alpha \frac{p}{x}\left(1-p+\frac{p}{x}\right)^{\alpha-1}+(\alpha-1) p(1-p+p \cdot x)^{-\alpha} \\
f''(x) &= (1-\lambda) \alpha(\alpha-1) p^{2}(1-p+p \cdot x)^{\alpha-2}
\end{aligned}
$$

xi. Note that we assume P and Q are absolutely continuous with respect to each other – i.e., $\forall S\ P(S)=0 \iff Q(S)=0$. This ensures that the Radon-Nikodym derivative $\frac{P(y)}{Q(y)}$ is well-defined and, further that $\underset{Y \leftarrow Q}{\mathbb{P}}\left[\frac{P(Y)}{Q(Y)} \leq 0\right]=0$. Thus the function f need only be defined on $(0, \infty)$.

$$
\begin{aligned}
& - \lambda\alpha \frac{p}{x^2}\left(1 - p + \frac{p}{x}\right)^{\alpha-1} + \lambda\alpha \frac{p}{x^2}\left(1 - p + \frac{p}{x}\right)^{\alpha-1} \\
& + \lambda\alpha(\alpha - 1)\frac{p^2}{x^3}\left(1 - p + \frac{p}{x}\right)^{\alpha-2} - \alpha(\alpha - 1)p^2\left(1 - p + p \cdot x\right)^{-\alpha-1} \\
&= \alpha(\alpha - 1)p^2\left((1 - \lambda)(1 - p + px)^{\alpha-2} + \lambda\frac{1}{x^3}\left(1 - p + \frac{p}{x}\right)^{\alpha-2}\right. \\
& \left. -(1 - p + px)^{-\alpha-1}\right) \\
&= \frac{\alpha(\alpha - 1)p^2}{(1 - p + px)^{\alpha+1}}\left((1 - \lambda)(1 - p + px)^{2\alpha-1} + \lambda\frac{1}{x^3}\left(1 - p + \frac{p}{x}\right)^{\alpha-2}\right. \\
& \left. \cdot(1 - p + px)^{\alpha+1} - 1\right) \\
&= \frac{\alpha(\alpha-1)p^2}{(1-p+px)^{\alpha+1}}\left((1-\lambda)(1-p+px)^{2\alpha-1} + \lambda\left(\frac{1-p+px}{x}\right)^3\right. \\
& \left. \cdot\left(1-p+\frac{p}{x}\right)^{\alpha-2} \cdot (1-p+px)^{\alpha-2} - 1\right) \\
&\geq \frac{\alpha(\alpha - 1)p^2}{(1 - p + px)^{\alpha+1}} \\
& \times\left((1 - \lambda)(1 - p + px)^{2\alpha-1} + \lambda\left(\frac{1 - p + px}{x}\right)^3 \cdot 1 - 1\right) \\
& \hspace{20em} \text{(Lemma 3.35)} \\
&= \frac{\alpha(\alpha - 1)p^2}{(1 - p + px)^{\alpha+1}}\left(\frac{\begin{array}{c} 3(1 - p)(1 - p + px)^{2\alpha-1} \\ +(2\alpha - 1)p\left(\frac{1-p}{x} + p\right)^3 \\ -3(1 - p) - (2\alpha - 1)p \end{array}}{3(1 - p) + (2\alpha - 1)p}\right) \\
& \hspace{14em} \left(\lambda = \tfrac{(2\alpha-1)p}{(2\alpha-1)p+3(1-p)}\right) \\
&\geq 0. \hspace{18em} \text{(Lemma 3.36)}
\end{aligned}
$$

□

We now give the auxiliary lemmata used in the proof of Theorem 3.34.

Lemma 3.35. *For all* $p \in [0, 1]$ *and* $x \in (0, \infty)$,

$$\frac{1}{1 - p + p/x} \leq 1 - p + p \cdot x.$$

Proof. Let $f(t) = t + 1/t$. Then $f'(t) = 1 - 1/t^2$ and $f''(t) = 2/t^3 > 0$ for all $t > 0$. Thus $f'(t) = 0 \iff t = 1$ and $f(x) \geq f(1) = 2$. Now

$$\begin{aligned}(1 - p + p \cdot x) \cdot (1 - p + p/x) &= p^2 + (1-p)^2 + p(1-p)(x + 1/x) \\ &\geq p^2 + (1-p)^2 + p(1-p) \cdot 2 \\ &= (p + (1-p))^2 = 1.\end{aligned}$$

Rearranging yields the result. □

Lemma 3.36. *For all $v \geq 1$, $p \in [0,1]$, and $x \in (0, \infty)$,*

$$3(1-p)(1-p+px)^v + vp\left(\frac{1-p}{x} + p\right)^3 \geq 3(1-p) + vp.$$

Proof. Define $f : (0, \infty) \to \mathbb{R}$ by

$$f(x) = 3(1-p)(1-p+px)^v + vp\left(\frac{1-p}{x} + p\right)^3.$$

Our goal is to prove that $f(x) \geq f(1) = 3(1-p) + vp$ for all $x \in (0, \infty)$. It suffices to prove that f is convex and that $f'(1) = 0$. We have

$$\begin{aligned}f'(x) &= 3vp(1-p)\left((1-p+px)^{v-1} - \frac{1}{x^2}\left(\frac{1-p}{x} + p\right)^2\right), \\ f''(x) &= 3vp(1-p)\left((v-1)p(1-p+px)^{v-2} + \frac{2}{x^3} \cdot \left(\frac{1-p}{x} + p\right)^2\right. \\ &\qquad \left. + \frac{2}{x^2} \cdot \frac{1-p}{x^2} \cdot \left(\frac{1-p}{x} + p\right)\right).\end{aligned}$$

From these expressions, it is easy to see that $f'(1) = 0$ and $f''(x) \geq 0$ for all $x \in (0, \infty)$. □

3.6.6 Analytic Rényi DP Bound for Privacy Amplification by Poisson Subsampling

Theorem 3.33 gives a tight RDP bound for privacy amplification by Poisson subsampling. However, the bound is in the form of a series. This is adequate for numerical purposes, but it is helpful for our understanding to have a simpler closed-form expression.

In this subsection we will provide a simpler expression and attempt to build some understanding of how privacy amplification by subsampling applies to Rényi DP.

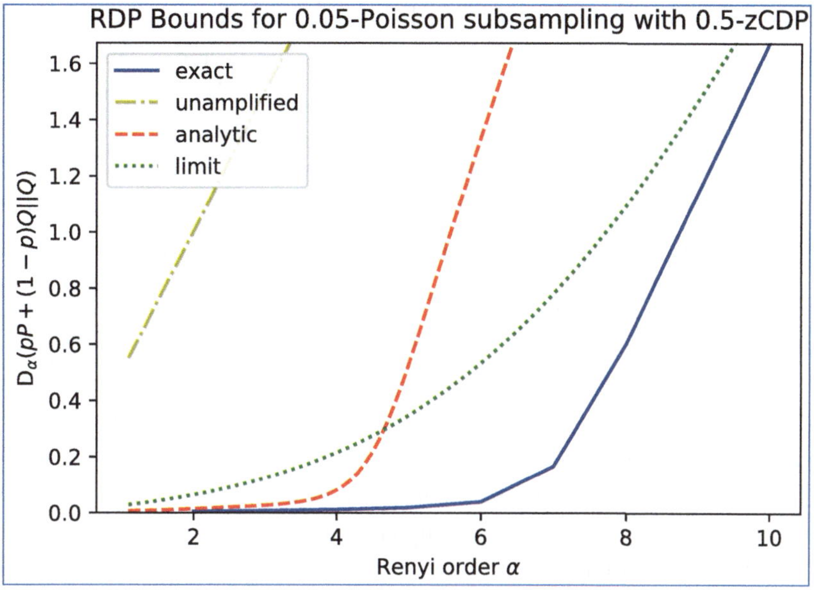

Figure 3.2. Comparison of Rényi divergence guarantees for Poisson subsampling - i.e., including each person with probability $p = 0.05$. The *unamplified* algorithm satisfies 0.5-zCDP. The *exact* bound is given by Theorem 3.33. For comparison, we have the *analytic* upper bound from Proposition 3.40 as well as the behavior in the *limit* given by Proposition 3.41.

Theorem 3.37 (Asymptotic Privacy Amplification by Subsampling for Rényi DP). *Let $p \in [0, 1/2]$ and $\rho \in (0, 1]$. Define $\omega = \min\left\{\frac{\log(1/p)}{4\rho}, 1 + p^{-1/4}\right\}$. Assume $\omega \geq 3 + 2\frac{\log(1/\rho)}{\log(1/p)}$.*

Let $M : \mathcal{X}^n \to \mathcal{Y}$ satisfy ρ-zCDP with respect to addition or removal.[xii]

Define $M^U : \mathcal{X}^n \to \mathcal{Y}$ by $M^U(x) = M(x_U)$, where $U \subset [n]$ be a random set that contains each element independently with probability p and, for $x \in \mathcal{X}^n$, $x_U \in \mathcal{X}^n$ is given by $(x_U)_i = x_i$ if $i \in U$ and $(x_U)_i = \perp$ if $i \notin U$.

Then M^U satisfies $(\alpha, 10p^2\rho\alpha)$-RDP for all $\alpha \in (1, \omega)$.

There are many caveats in the statement of Theorem 3.37, but the high level message is that Poisson subsampling a p fraction of the dataset amplifies ρ-zCDP to something like $O(p^2 \cdot \rho)$-zCDP. We will discuss these caveats in a moment, but, ignoring these caveats and the constant factor in the guarantee, this is exactly the kind of guarantee we would hope for.

xii. I.e., $x, x' \in \mathcal{X}^n$ are neighboring if, for some $i \in [n]$, we have $x_i = \perp$ or $x'_i = \perp$, and $\forall j \neq i\ x_j = x'_j$, where $\perp \in \mathcal{X}$ is some fixed value.

Consider the following example, which illustrates what kind guarantee we would hope for. Suppose we have a query $q : \mathcal{X} \to [0,1]$ and a sensitive dataset $x \in \mathcal{X}^n$ and our goal is to estimate $q(x) := \frac{1}{n}\sum_i^n q(x_i)$. We could release a sample from $\mathcal{N}(q(x), \sigma^2)$, which satisfies $\frac{1}{2n^2\sigma^2}$-zCDP and has mean squared error σ^2. However, perhaps due to computational constraints, we might instead select a random p fraction $U \subset [n]$ and instead release a sample from $M^U(x) = \mathcal{N}\left(\frac{1}{pn}\sum_{i\in U} q(x_i), \sigma^2\right)$. We can calculate that the mean squared error of this algorithm is at most $\sigma^2 + \frac{1-p}{pn}$. Without amplification this satisfies $(\rho = \frac{1}{2p^2n^2\sigma^2})$-zCDP. With amplification, Theorem 3.37 tells us that this satisfies $(\alpha, O(p^2 \cdot \rho))$-RDP for α not too large. Now $p^2 \cdot \rho = \frac{1}{2n^2\sigma^2}$ is exactly the guarantee that we obtained by simply evaluating q on the entire dataset and avoiding subsampling. We cannot hope to do better than this.

The constant factor of 10 in the theorem can be improved, but a constant factor loss is the price we pay for having a simpler expression; if we want tight constants we should apply Theorem 3.33.

The main caveat in Theorem 3.37 is the requirement that $\alpha \le \omega \le \frac{\log(1/p)}{4\rho}$. This is necessary, as the $(\alpha, \varepsilon(\alpha))$-RDP guarantee qualitatively changes when $\alpha \ge O(\log(1/p)/\rho)$. It changes from $\varepsilon(\alpha) = O(p^2\rho\alpha)$ to $\varepsilon(\alpha) = \rho\alpha - O(\log(1/p))$. To see why this is inherent, consider the following lower bound. For all $p \in [0,1]$, all $\alpha \in (1,\infty)$, and all absolutely continuous probability distributions P and Q, we have

$$\begin{aligned} e^{(\alpha-1)\mathrm{D}_\alpha(pP+(1-p)Q\|Q)} &= \mathop{\mathbb{E}}_{Y\leftarrow Q}\left[\left(1-p+p\cdot\frac{P(Y)}{Q(Y)}\right)^\alpha\right] \\ &\ge \mathop{\mathbb{E}}_{Y\leftarrow Q}\left[\left(p\cdot\frac{P(Y)}{Q(Y)}\right)^\alpha\right] = p^\alpha \cdot e^{(\alpha-1)\mathrm{D}_\alpha(P\|Q)}. \end{aligned}$$

Thus $\mathrm{D}_\alpha\left(pP+(1-p)Q\middle\|Q\right) \ge \mathrm{D}_\alpha\left(P\|Q\right) - \frac{\alpha}{\alpha-1}\log(1/p)$. This tells us that, for large α, we cannot have more than an additive improvement in the RDP guarantee, whereas for small α we have a multiplicative improvement. Proposition 3.41 shows that this lower bound is tight.

We now proceed to prove Theorem 3.37.

Lemma 3.38. *Let $\alpha \in (1,\infty)$, $p \in \left[0, 1-e^{-1}\right]$, and $x \in [0,\infty)$. If either $\alpha \le 2$ or $\alpha > 2$ and $px \le \max\left\{p, \frac{1-p}{\alpha-2}\right\}$, then*

$$(1-p+p\cdot x)^\alpha \le 1 + \alpha p(x-1) + \frac{e}{2}\alpha(\alpha-1)p^2(x-1)^2.$$

Proof. We assume $p > 0$. Otherwise the result is trivial.

Define $f : [0, \infty) \to \mathbb{R}$ by

$$f(x) = (1 - p + px)^{\alpha}.$$

For all $x \in [0, \infty)$, we have

$$\begin{aligned}
f'(x) &= \alpha p(1 - p + px)^{\alpha-1}, \\
f''(x) &= \alpha(\alpha - 1)p^2(1 - p + px)^{\alpha-2}, \\
f'''(x) &= \alpha(\alpha - 1)(\alpha - 2)p^3(1 - p + px)^{\alpha-3}.
\end{aligned}$$

By Taylor's theorem, for all $x \in [0, \infty)$, there exists $\xi_x \in [\min\{1, x\}, \max\{1, x\}]$ such that

$$\begin{aligned}
f(x) &= f(1) + f'(1)(x - 1) + \frac{1}{2}f''(\xi_x)(x - 1)^2 \\
&= 1 + \alpha p(x - 1) + \frac{1}{2}f''(\xi_x)(x - 1)^2.
\end{aligned}$$

To complete the proof is suffices to show that $f''(\xi) \leq e \cdot \alpha(\alpha - 1)p^2$ in two cases: First, for all $\xi \in [0, \infty)$ assuming $\alpha \leq 2$. Second, for all $\xi \in \left[0, \max\left\{1, \frac{1-p}{p}\frac{1}{\alpha-2}\right\}\right]$ assuming $\alpha > 2$. (Note that, $\xi_x \in \left[0, \max\left\{1, \frac{1-p}{p}\frac{1}{\alpha-2}\right\}\right]$ is implied by the assumptions $px \leq \max\left\{p, \frac{1-p}{\alpha-2}\right\}$ and $p > 0$.)

First, suppose $\alpha \leq 2$. Then $f'''(x) \leq 0$ for all $x \in [0, \infty)$. Thus f'' is decreasing (or constant) and, for all $\xi \in [0, \infty)$, we have

$$\begin{aligned}
f''(\xi) &\leq f''(0) \\
&= \alpha(\alpha - 1)p^2(1 - p)^{\alpha-2} \\
&\leq \alpha(\alpha - 1)p^2\frac{1}{1 - p} && (\alpha > 1) \\
&\leq \alpha(\alpha - 1)p^2 \cdot e. && (p \leq 1 - e^{-1})
\end{aligned}$$

Second, assume $\alpha > 2$ and $px \leq \max\left\{p, \frac{1-p}{\alpha-2}\right\}$, which implies $\xi_x \leq \max\left\{1, \frac{1-p}{p}\frac{1}{\alpha-2}\right\}$.

We have $f'''(x) > 0$ for all $x \in [0, \infty)$. Thus f'' is increasing and, for all $\xi \in \left[0, \max\left\{1, \frac{1-p}{p}\frac{1}{\alpha-2}\right\}\right]$, we have

$$\begin{aligned}
f''(\xi) &\leq f''\left(\max\left\{1, \frac{1-p}{p}\frac{1}{\alpha - 2}\right\}\right) \\
&= \alpha(\alpha - 1)p^2\left(1 - p + p \cdot \max\left\{1, \frac{1-p}{p}\frac{1}{\alpha - 2}\right\}\right)^{\alpha-2}
\end{aligned}$$

$$
\begin{aligned}
&= \alpha(\alpha-1)p^2 \max\left\{1, (1-p)^{\alpha-2} \cdot \left(1 + \frac{1}{\alpha-2}\right)^{\alpha-2}\right\} \\
&\leq \alpha(\alpha-1)p^2 \max\left\{1, (1-p)^0 \cdot \left(e^{\frac{1}{\alpha-2}}\right)^{\alpha-2}\right\} \\
&= \alpha(\alpha-1)p^2 \cdot e.
\end{aligned}
$$

□

Lemma 3.39. *Let $\alpha, \omega \in (1, \infty)$ with $\alpha \leq \omega$, $p \in \left[0, 1 - e^{-1}\right]$, and $x \in [0, \infty)$. Then*

$$
(1 - p + p \cdot x)^\alpha \leq 1 + \alpha p(x-1) + \frac{e}{2}\alpha(\alpha-1)p^2(x-1)^2 + \left((\alpha-1)px\right)^\omega.
$$

Proof. We can assume $p > 0$, as otherwise the result is trivial.

If $\alpha \leq 2$ or if $\alpha > 2$ and $x \leq \max\left\{1, \frac{1-p}{p}\frac{1}{\alpha-2}\right\}$, then the result follows from Lemma 3.38, as $\left((\alpha-1)px\right)^\omega \geq 0$.

Thus we assume $\alpha > 2$ and $x \geq \max\left\{1, \frac{1-p}{p}\frac{1}{\alpha-2}\right\}$.

Since $x \geq 1$, we have $\alpha p(x-1) + \frac{e}{2}\alpha(\alpha-1)p^2(x-1)^2 \geq 0$. Therefore it suffices to prove that $(1-p+px)^\alpha \leq ((\alpha-1)px)^\omega$.

The assumption $x \geq 1$ implies $1-p+px \geq 1$ and, hence, that $(1-p+px)^\alpha \leq (1-p+px)^\omega$, as we have $\alpha \leq \omega$. The assumption $x \geq \frac{1-p}{p}\frac{1}{\alpha-2}$ rearranges to $1-p \leq px(\alpha-2)$, which implies $1-p+px \leq (\alpha-1)px$ and, hence, $(1-p+px)^\omega \leq ((\alpha-1)px)^\omega$, as required. □

Proposition 3.40 (Analytic Privacy Amplification by Subsampling for Rényi Divergence). *Let P and Q be probability distributions with P absolutely continuous with respect to Q. Let $p \in \left[0, 1-e^{-1}\right]$ and $\alpha, \omega \in (1, \infty)$ with $\alpha \leq \omega$. Then*

$$
\begin{aligned}
&\mathrm{D}_\alpha\left(pP + (1-p)Q \| Q\right) \\
&\quad \leq \frac{1}{\alpha-1}\log\left(1 + \frac{e}{2}\alpha(\alpha-1)p^2\left(e^{\mathrm{D}_2(P\|Q)} - 1\right)\right. \\
&\qquad \left. + ((\alpha-1)p)^\omega \cdot e^{(\omega-1)\mathrm{D}_\omega(P\|Q)}\right) \\
&\quad \leq \alpha \cdot \frac{e}{2} \cdot p^2 \cdot \left(e^{\mathrm{D}_2(P\|Q)} - 1\right) + p \cdot \left((\alpha-1) \cdot p \cdot e^{\mathrm{D}_\omega(P\|Q)}\right)^{\omega-1}.
\end{aligned}
$$

Proof. We have

$$
e^{(\alpha-1)\mathrm{D}_\alpha\left(pP+(1-p)Q\|Q\right)}
$$

$$
\begin{aligned}
&= \mathop{\mathbb{E}}_{Y \leftarrow Q}\left[\left(\frac{p \cdot P(Y) + (1-p) \cdot Q(Y)}{Q(Y)}\right)^{\alpha}\right] \\
&= \mathop{\mathbb{E}}_{Y \leftarrow Q}\left[\left(1 - p + p \cdot \frac{P(Y)}{Q(Y)}\right)^{\alpha}\right] \\
&\leq \mathop{\mathbb{E}}_{Y \leftarrow Q}\left[1 + \alpha p \left(\frac{P(Y)}{Q(Y)} - 1\right) + \frac{e}{2}\alpha(\alpha-1)p^2\left(\frac{P(Y)}{Q(Y)} - 1\right)^2\right. \\
&\quad \left. + \left((\alpha-1)p\frac{P(Y)}{Q(Y)}\right)^{\omega}\right] \qquad \text{(Lemma 3.39)} \\
&= 1 + \alpha p (1 - 1) + \frac{e}{2}\alpha(\alpha-1)p^2\left(e^{\mathrm{D}_2(P\|Q)} - 1\right) \\
&\quad + \left((\alpha-1)p\right)^{\omega} \cdot e^{(\omega-1)\mathrm{D}_{\omega}(P\|Q)}.
\end{aligned}
$$

The second inequality in the result follows from the fact that $\log(1+u) \leq u$ for all $u > -1$. □

We also have the following simpler result that provides better bounds when the Rényi order α is large.

Proposition 3.41. *Let P and Q be probability distributions with P absolutely continuous with respect to Q. Let $p \in [0, 1]$ and $\alpha \in (1, \infty)$. Then*

$$
\begin{aligned}
&\mathrm{D}_{\alpha}\left(pP + (1-p)Q \| Q\right) \\
&\quad \leq \frac{\alpha}{\alpha - 1}\log\left(1 - p + p \cdot e^{(1-1/\alpha)\mathrm{D}_{\alpha}(P\|Q)}\right) \\
&\quad = \mathrm{D}_{\alpha}\left(P\|Q\right) - \frac{\alpha}{\alpha-1}\log(1/p) + \frac{\alpha}{\alpha-1}\log\left(1 + \frac{1-p}{p} \cdot e^{-\frac{\alpha-1}{\alpha}\mathrm{D}_{\alpha}(P\|Q)}\right) \\
&\quad \leq \mathrm{D}_{\alpha}\left(P\|Q\right) - \frac{\alpha}{\alpha-1}\log(1/p) + \frac{\alpha}{\alpha-1} \cdot \frac{1-p}{p} \cdot e^{-\frac{\alpha-1}{\alpha}\mathrm{D}_{\alpha}(P\|Q)}
\end{aligned}
$$

Proof. We assume $0 < p < 1$, as the result is immediate otherwise. By Jensen's inequality and the convexity of $v \mapsto v^{\alpha}$, for all $x \in [0, \infty)$ and all $\lambda \in (0, 1)$,

$$
(1-p+px)^{\alpha} = \left((1-\lambda) \cdot \frac{1-p}{1-\lambda} + \lambda \cdot \frac{px}{\lambda}\right)^{\alpha} \leq (1-\lambda) \cdot \left(\frac{1-p}{1-\lambda}\right)^{\alpha} + \lambda \cdot \left(\frac{px}{\lambda}\right)^{\alpha}.
$$

Now, for all $\lambda \in (0, 1)$, we have

$$
e^{(\alpha-1)\mathrm{D}_{\alpha}\left(pP+(1-p)Q\|Q\right)} = \mathop{\mathbb{E}}_{Y \leftarrow Q}\left[\left(1 - p + p\frac{P(Y)}{Q(Y)}\right)^{\alpha}\right]
$$

$$\leq \mathop{\mathbb{E}}_{Y \leftarrow Q}\left[(1-\lambda)\cdot\left(\frac{1-p}{1-\lambda}\right)^{\alpha} + \lambda\cdot\left(\frac{p}{\lambda}\cdot\frac{P(Y)}{Q(Y)}\right)^{\alpha}\right]$$
$$= (1-\lambda)^{1-\alpha}\cdot(1-p)^{\alpha} + \lambda^{1-\alpha}\cdot p^{\alpha}\cdot e^{(\alpha-1)\mathrm{D}_\alpha(P\|Q)}.$$

We can choose λ to minimize this expression. It turns out to be optimal to set $\lambda = \frac{1}{1+\frac{1-p}{p}\cdot e^{-(1-1/\alpha)\mathrm{D}_\alpha(P\|Q)}}$. Now we have

$$\begin{aligned}
&e^{(\alpha-1)\mathrm{D}_\alpha(pP+(1-p)Q\|Q)}\\
&\leq (1-\lambda)^{1-\alpha}\cdot(1-p)^{\alpha} + \lambda^{1-\alpha}\cdot p^{\alpha}\cdot e^{(\alpha-1)\mathrm{D}_\alpha(P\|Q)}\\
&= \left(1+\frac{p}{1-p}e^{(1-1/\alpha)\mathrm{D}_\alpha(P\|Q)}\right)^{\alpha-1}\cdot(1-p)^{\alpha}\\
&\quad + \left(1+\frac{1-p}{p}\cdot e^{-(1-1/\alpha)\mathrm{D}_\alpha(P\|Q)}\right)^{\alpha-1}\cdot p^{\alpha}\cdot e^{(\alpha-1)\mathrm{D}_\alpha(P\|Q)}\\
&= \left(1-p+p\cdot e^{(1-1/\alpha)\mathrm{D}_\alpha(P\|Q)}\right)^{\alpha-1}\cdot(1-p)\\
&\quad + \left(p+(1-p)\cdot e^{-(1-1/\alpha)\mathrm{D}_\alpha(P\|Q)}\right)^{\alpha-1}\cdot p\cdot e^{(\alpha-1)\mathrm{D}_\alpha(P\|Q)}\\
&= \left(1-p+p\cdot e^{(1-1/\alpha)\mathrm{D}_\alpha(P\|Q)}\right)^{\alpha-1}\cdot(1-p)\\
&\quad + \left(p\cdot e^{(1-1/\alpha)\mathrm{D}_\alpha(P\|Q)}+(1-p)\right)^{\alpha-1}\cdot p\cdot e^{(1-1/\alpha)\mathrm{D}_\alpha(P\|Q)}\\
&= \left(1-p+p\cdot e^{(1-1/\alpha)\mathrm{D}_\alpha(P\|Q)}\right)^{\alpha}.
\end{aligned}$$

Rearranging yields the result. □

Proof of Theorem 3.37. Fix neighboring inputs $x, x' \in \mathcal{X}^n$. Fix some $\alpha \in (1, \omega)$ with $\omega = \min\left\{\frac{\log(1/p)}{4\rho}, 1+p^{-1/4}\right\} \geq 3 + 2\frac{\log(1/\rho)}{\log(1/p)}$.

Without loss of generality x' is x with some element removed. That is, we can fix some $i \in [n]$ such that $x'_i = \perp$ and $x'_j = x_j$ for all $j \neq i$.

Let $P = M(x_U)|_{i\in U}$ and let $Q = M(x_U)|_{i\notin U}$. Then $M^U(x) = M(x_U) = pP + (1-p)Q$. Also $M(x') = Q$

Thus we must prove that $\mathrm{D}_\alpha\left(pP+(1-p)Q\middle\|Q\right) \leq 10p^2\rho\alpha$ and $\mathrm{D}_\alpha\left(Q\middle\|pP+(1-p)Q\right) \leq 10p^2\rho\alpha$. Since M is assumed to be ρ-zCDP, we have $\mathrm{D}_{\alpha'}(P\|Q) \leq \rho\alpha'$ and $\mathrm{D}_{\alpha'}(Q\|P) \leq \rho\alpha'$ for all $\alpha' \in (1, \infty)$.

By Proposition 3.40,

$$\begin{aligned}
\mathrm{D}_\alpha\left(pP+(1-p)Q\middle\|Q\right) &\leq \alpha\cdot\frac{e}{2}\cdot p^2\cdot\left(e^{\mathrm{D}_2(P\|Q)}-1\right)\\
&\quad + p\cdot\left((\alpha-1)\cdot p\cdot e^{\mathrm{D}_\omega(P\|Q)}\right)^{\omega-1}
\end{aligned}$$

$$
\begin{aligned}
&\leq \alpha \cdot \frac{e}{2} \cdot p^2 \cdot \left(e^{2\rho} - 1\right) + p \cdot \left((\alpha - 1) \cdot p \cdot e^{\omega\rho}\right)^{\omega - 1} \\
&\leq \alpha \cdot \frac{e}{2} \cdot p^2 \cdot \left(e^{2\rho} - 1\right) + p \cdot \left(p^{-1/4} \cdot p \cdot p^{-1/4}\right)^{\omega - 1} \\
&\qquad\qquad (\alpha \leq \omega = \min\{1 + p^{-1/4}, \log(1/p)/4\rho\}) \\
&= \alpha \cdot \frac{e}{2} \cdot p^2 \cdot \left(e^{2\rho} - 1\right) + p^{\frac{1+\omega}{2}} \\
&\leq \alpha \cdot \frac{e}{2} \cdot p^2 \cdot \left(e^{2\rho} - 1\right) + p^2 \cdot \rho \\
&\qquad\qquad (\omega \geq 3 + 2\log(1/\rho)/\log(1/p)) \\
&= \alpha \cdot p^2 \cdot \rho \cdot \left(\frac{e}{2} \cdot \frac{e^{2\rho} - 1}{\rho} + \frac{1}{\alpha}\right) \\
&\leq \alpha \cdot p^2 \cdot \rho \cdot 10. \qquad\qquad (\rho \in (0,1) \text{ and } \alpha \in (1, \omega))
\end{aligned}
$$

Symmetrically, we have $\mathrm{D}_\alpha\left(pQ + (1-p)P \middle\| P\right) \leq \alpha \cdot p^2 \cdot \rho \cdot 10$. By Theorem 3.34,

$$
\mathrm{D}_\alpha\left(Q \middle\| pP + (1-p)Q\right) \leq \max\left\{\begin{matrix}\mathrm{D}_\alpha\left(pP + (1-p)Q \middle\| Q\right), \\ \mathrm{D}_\alpha\left(pQ + (1-p)P \middle\| P\right)\end{matrix}\right\} \leq \alpha \cdot p^2 \cdot \rho \cdot 10.
$$

□

3.6.7 How to Use Privacy Amplification by Subsampling

The most common use case for privacy amplification by subsampling is analyzing noisy stochastic gradient descent. That is, we repeatedly sample a small subset of the data, compute a function on this subset, and add Gaussian noise. To be precise, let $x \in \mathcal{X}^n$ be the private input. Iteratively, for $t = 1, \cdots, T$, we pick some function $q_t : \mathcal{X}^n \to \mathbb{R}^d$ and randomly sample a subset $U_t \subset [n]$; then we reveal $\mathcal{N}(q_t(x_{U_t}), \sigma^2 I_d)$.

The addition of Gaussian noise satisfies concentrated DP. Specifically, Lemma 3.12 shows that releasing $\mathcal{N}(q_t(x), \sigma^2 I_d)$ satisfies $\frac{\Delta_2^2}{2\sigma^2}$-zCDP, where $\Delta_2 = \sup_{\substack{x,x' \in \mathcal{X}^n \\ \text{neighboring}}} \|q_t(x) - q_t(x')\|_2$ is the sensitivity of q_t. We can thus apply Theorem 3.33 to obtain a tight Rényi DP guarantee for $\mathcal{N}(q_t(x_{U_t}), \sigma^2 I_d)$, where U_t is a Poisson sample. Finally, we can apply the composition property of Rényi DP (Lemma 3.30) over the T rounds and we can convert this final Rényi DP guarantee to approximate DP using Proposition 3.14. This is how differentially private deep learning is analyzed in practice by libraries such as TensorFlow Privacy [Goo18; McM+18].

We can also obtain an asymptotic analysis: Theorem 3.37 shows that $\mathcal{N}(q_t(x_{U_t}), \sigma^2 I_d)$ with $U_t \subset [n]$ including each element independently with probability p satisfies $\left(\alpha, 5\alpha p^2 \Delta_2^2/\sigma^2\right)$-RDP for all $\alpha \in (1, \omega)$. Composition over T rounds yields $\left(\alpha, 5\alpha T p^2 \Delta_2^2/\sigma^2\right)$-RDP for all $\alpha \in (1, \omega)$, which implies (ε, δ)-DP for all $\delta > 0$ and

$$\varepsilon = O\left(\frac{\Delta_2}{\sigma} \cdot p \cdot \sqrt{T \cdot \log(1/\delta)}\right).$$

This bound is directly comparable to the bound from Section 3.6.3, which was derived by converting back and forth between concentrated DP and approximate DP. The difference is that here we have a $\sqrt{\log(1/\delta)}$ whereas there we had a $\log(T/\delta)$ term. This is the asymptotic improvement obtained by keeping the analysis within RDP. This asymptotic improvement also translates into a significant improvement in practice.

We have only analyzed Poisson subsampling, where the size of the sample is random. (Specifically, it follows a binomial distribution.) Naturally, other subsampling schemes may arise in practice. In particular, a fixed size sample is common. As discussed in Section 3.6.2, this corresponds to neighboring datasets allowing the replacement of one individual's data, rather than addition or removal. In terms of Rényi divergences, we must analyze $\mathrm{D}_\alpha\left(pP + (1-p)Q \middle\| pP' + (1-p)Q\right)$, whereas addition and removal correspond to $\mathrm{D}_\alpha\left(pP + (1-p)Q \middle\| Q\right)$ and $\mathrm{D}_\alpha\left(Q \middle\| pP' + (1-p)Q\right)$. However, we can apply group privacy (part 7 of Lemma 3.32) to reduce the analysis to the case we have already analyzed: For all $\alpha' > \alpha$, we have

$$\begin{aligned}&\mathrm{D}_\alpha\left(pP+(1-p)Q \middle\| pP'+(1-p)Q\right)\\ &\quad\le \frac{\alpha'}{\alpha'-1} \cdot \mathrm{D}_{\alpha \cdot \frac{\alpha'-1}{\alpha'-\alpha}}\left(pP+(1-p)Q \middle\| Q\right) + \mathrm{D}_{\alpha'}\left(Q \middle\| pP'+(1-p)Q\right).\end{aligned}$$

3.7 Concluding Remarks

Composition

Differential privacy (specifically, pure DP) was introduced by Dwork, McSherry, Nissim, and Smith [DMNS06].[xiii] The original paper gives a form of basic composition (Theorem 3.1), but does not state it in full generality; rather it states a result specific to Laplace noise addition. Approximate DP was introduced by Dwork,

xiii. The name "differential privacy" does not appear in the original paper. It is attributed to Michael Schroeder [DMNS17] and first appeared in a talk by Dwork [Dwo06].

Kenthapadi, McSherry, Mironov, and Naor [Dwo+06] and this work gave a more general statement of the basic composition result, as well as an analysis of the Gaussian mechanism (although not as tight as Corollary 3.8). The tight analysis of the Gaussian mechanism (Corollaries 3.8 & 3.10) is due to Balle and Wang [BW18].

The advanced composition theorem (Theorem 3.22) was proved by Dwork, Rothblum, and Vadhan [DRV10].[xiv] The key concepts of privacy loss distributions and concentrated DP were implicit in this proof, but they were only made explicit in a separate paper by Dwork and Rothblum [DR16]. Bun and Steinke [BS16] refined the notion of concentrated DP and presented the definition that we use here (Definition 3.11).

Kairouz, Oh, and Viswanathan [KOV15] proved an optimal composition theorem for approximate differential privacy. Specifically, the k-fold composition of (ε, δ)-differential privacy satisfies (ε', δ')-differential privacy if and only if

$$\frac{1}{(1+e^{\varepsilon})^k} \sum_{\ell=0}^{k} \binom{k}{\ell} \cdot e^{\ell\varepsilon} \cdot \max\left\{0, 1 - e^{\varepsilon' - (2\ell - k)\varepsilon}\right\} \leq 1 - \frac{1-\delta'}{(1-\delta)^k}.$$

This expression is rather complex, but the proof is relatively intuitive. The key insight is that we can reduce the analysis to the k-fold composition of a specific worst-case (ε, δ)-DP mechanism. With probability δ, this mechanism has infinite privacy loss. With probability $(1-\delta) \cdot \frac{e^{\varepsilon}}{1+e^{\varepsilon}}$, it has privacy loss ε. And, with probability $(1-\delta) \cdot \frac{1}{1+e^{\varepsilon}}$, it has privacy loss $-\varepsilon$. The privacy loss of the k-fold composition is the convolution of k of these privacy losses. Thus, with probability $1-(1-\delta)^k$ the privacy loss of the composition is infinite. Otherwise – i.e., with probability $(1-\delta)^k$ – the privacy loss has a shifted binomial distribution. Namely, for all $\ell \in [k] \cup \{0\}$,

$$\mathbb{P}\left[Z = \varepsilon \cdot \ell - \varepsilon \cdot (k-\ell)\right] = (1-\delta)^k \cdot \binom{k}{\ell} \cdot \left(\frac{e^{\varepsilon}}{e^{\varepsilon}+1}\right)^{\ell} \cdot \left(\frac{1}{e^{\varepsilon}+1}\right)^{k-\ell},$$

where Z is the privacy loss of the k-fold composition of the worst-case (ε, δ)-DP mechanism. Applying Proposition 3.7 to this distribution yields the expression for the optimal composition theorem.

Kairouz, Oh, and Viswanathan [KOV15] also considered *heterogeneous* optimal composition. That is, the composition of k mechanisms where each mechanism $j \in [k]$ has a different $(\varepsilon_j, \delta_j)$-DP guarantee. However, the expression becomes more complicated. Intuitively, this is because the privacy loss distribution can be

xiv. The original proof showed that the k-fold composition of (ε, δ)-DP algorithms satisfies $(\varepsilon', k\delta + \delta')$-DP with $\delta' > 0$ arbitrary and $\varepsilon' = k\varepsilon(e^{\varepsilon} - 1) + \varepsilon \cdot \sqrt{2k \log(1/\delta')}$. The first term $k\varepsilon(e^{\varepsilon} - 1)$ is slightly worse than Theorem 3.22, which gives $\frac{1}{2}k\varepsilon^2$ instead.

supported on 2^k points in the heterogeneous case, whereas, in the homogeneous case, it is supported on only $k+1$ points. Thus it takes exponential time to compute the privacy loss distribution. To be precise, Murtagh and Vadhan [MV16] showed that exactly computing the optimal composition is #P-complete, even if $\delta_j = 0$ for each $j \in [k]$. However, Murtagh and Vadhan also showed that the optimal composition theorem could be approximated to arbitrary precision in polynomial time.

Although these composition results [KOV15; MV16] are optimal, they are limited in that they begin by assuming some $(\varepsilon_j, \delta_j)$-DP guarantees about the algorithms being composed. However, we usually know more about the algorithms being composed than simply these two parameters. For example, we may know that the algorithms being composed are Gaussian noise addition. Incorporating this additional information allows us to prove even better bounds than optimal composition. This was the main impetus for the development of concentrated DP and Rényi DP, which we have discussed.

A recent line of work [MM18; KJH20; KJPH21; KH21; GLW21; DRS19; ZDW22; CKS20; GKKM22] has explored optimal composition guarantees whilst incorporating additional information about the mechanisms being composed. To make these computations efficient they consider the (discrete) Fourier transform of the privacy loss.[xv] That is, where concentrated DP and Rényi DP consider the moment generating function of the privacy loss $\underset{Z \leftarrow \mathrm{PrivLoss}(M(x)\|M(x'))}{\mathbb{E}}\left[\exp(tZ)\right]$, these works look at the characteristic function $\underset{Z \leftarrow \mathrm{PrivLoss}(M(x)\|M(x'))}{\mathbb{E}}\left[\exp(itZ)\right]$, where $i^2 = -1$. These methods provide composition guarantees which are arbitrarily close to optimal, which are thus better than what is attainable via concentrated DP or Rényi DP.

The optimality of advanced composition (Theorem 3.24) is due to Bun, Ullman, and Vadhan [BUV14]. We present the analysis following Kamath and Ullman [KU20].

The composition results we have presented all assume that the privacy parameters of the algorithms being composed (i.e., $(\varepsilon_j, \delta_j)$ for $j \in [k]$ in the language of Theorem 3.22) are fixed. It is natural to consider the setting where these parameters are chosen adaptively [RRUV16] – i.e., $(\varepsilon_j, \delta_j)$ could depend on the output of M_{j-1}. For the most part, the composition results carry over seamlessly to the setting of adaptively-chosen privacy parameters. In particular, for Concentrated or Rényi DP, as long as the sum of the adaptively-chosen privacy parameters remains

xv. To apply a *discrete* Fourier transform, we must first discretize the privacy loss distribution, e.g., by rounding it to a grid. The choice of discretization determines the tightness of the final guarantee, and the computational complexity of computing it.

bounded, we attain privacy with that bound [FZ21]. Another extension is "concurrent composition" [VW21], which applies when an adversary may simultaneously access multiple interactive DP systems. Fortunately, the standard composition results readily extend to this setting [VZ22; Lyu22].

Privacy Amplification by Subsampling

The first explicit statement of differential privacy amplification by subsampling was in a blog post by Smith [Smi09], although it appeared implicitly earlier [Kas+11] and the privacy effects of sampling on its own had also been studied [CM06].

For approximate DP, Balle, Barthe, and Gaborardi [BBG18] provide a thorough analysis of privacy amplification by subsampling (cf. Theorem 3.28). They present tight results for Poisson sampling (i.e., including each element independently), sampling a subset of a fixed size (without replacement), and also sampling with replacement, which means a person's data may appear *multiple* times in the subsampled dataset.

As discussed in Sections 3.6.3 and 3.6.7, subsampling arises in differentially private versions of stochastic gradient descent [CMS11; BST14]. Abadi, Chu, Goodfellow, McMahan, Mironov, Talwar, and Zhang [Aba+16] applied this in the context of deep learning. To obtain better analyses, they developed the "Moments Accountant" – i.e., Rényi DP (although the connection to Rényi divergences was only made later [Mir17; BS16]).

Abadi et al. [Aba+16] obtained asymptotic Rényi DP bounds for the Poisson subsampled Gaussian mechanism, but they used numerical integration for their implementation. Mironov, Talwar, and Zhang [MTZ19] improved these asymptotic results and gave a better numerical method for exact computation (cf. Theorem 3.33); our presentation in Section 3.6.5 largely follows theirs. Bun, Dwork, Rothblum, and Steinke [BDRS18] prove asymptotic Rényi DP bounds for Poisson subsampling applied to a concentrated DP mechanism (cf. Theorem 3.37). Zhu and Wang [ZW19] gave generic Rényi DP bounds for Poisson subsampling.[xvi]

Moving away from Poisson subsampling, Wang, Balle, and Kasiviswanathan [WBK19] provide Rényi DP results for sampling a fixed-size set without replacement.

Koskela, Jälkö, and Honkela [KJH20] provide expressions for the privacy loss distribution of the subsampled Gaussian (under both Poisson subsampling and sampling a fixed size set with or without replacement) which can be numerically integrated to obtain optimal composition results.

xvi. Mironov, Talwar, and Zhang [MTZ19] and Zhu and Wang [ZW19] both provide analogs of Theorem 3.34. However, to the best of our knowledge, Theorem 3.34 is novel.

Closely related to privacy amplification by subsampling is privacy amplification by *shuffling* [Bit+17; Erl+19; Che+19; BBGN19; FMT21; FMT22]. Privacy amplification by shuffling is usually presented in terms of local differential privacy [Kas+11]. That is, there are n individuals who independently generate random messages that satisfy local ε-DP. Those messages are then "shuffled" so that the potential adversary/attacker cannot identify which message originated from which individual. The additional randomness of the shuffling amplifies the privacy to $\left(O\left(\varepsilon \cdot \sqrt{\frac{\log(1/\delta)}{n}}\right), \delta\right)$-DP.

Intuitively, shuffling is similar to subsampling with composition. Suppose we repeatedly sample one individual uniformly at random and perform an ε-DP computation on their data and the number of repetitions is equal to the number of individuals n. We can analyze this as subsampling a $1/n$ fraction (fixed size set) composed n times. Privacy amplification by subsampling (Theorem 3.28) says each repetition is ε'-DP for $\varepsilon' = \log(1 + \frac{1}{n}(e^{\varepsilon} - 1)) = O(\varepsilon/n)$. Advanced composition (Theorem 3.18) over the n repetitions yields (ε'', δ)-DP for $\varepsilon'' = O(\sqrt{n \log(1/\delta)} \cdot \varepsilon') = O\left(\varepsilon \cdot \sqrt{\frac{\log(1/\delta)}{n}}\right)$.

In contrast, for shuffling, we sample without replacement, so no individual is sampled more than once. This means the samples are not independent, so we cannot appeal to the subsampling plus composition analysis. Nevertheless, this intuition leads to the correct result.

References

[Aba+16] M. Abadi, A. Chu, I. Goodfellow, H. B. McMahan, I. Mironov, K. Talwar, and L. Zhang. "Deep Learning with Differential Privacy". In: Proceedings of the 2016 ACM SIGSAC Conference on Computer and Communications Security. CCS '16. Vienna, Austria: Association for Computing Machinery, 2016, pp. 308–318. ISBN: 9781450341394. URL: https://doi.org/10.1145/2976749.2978318 (cit. on pp. 126, 147).

[BBG18] B. Balle, G. Barthe, and M. Gaboardi. "Privacy Amplification by Subsampling: Tight Analyses via Couplings and Divergences". In: Advances in Neural Information Processing Systems. Ed. by S. Bengio, H. Wallach, H. Larochelle, K. Grauman, N. Cesa-Bianchi, and R. Garnett. Vol. 31. Curran Associates, Inc., 2018. URL: https : / / proceedings . neurips . cc / paper / 2018 /

file / 3b5020bb891119b9f5130f1fea9bd773 - Paper. pdf (cit. on p. 147).

[BBGN19] B. Balle, J. Bell, A. Gascón, and K. Nissim. "The Privacy Blanket of the Shuffle Model". In: Advances in Cryptology – CRYPTO 2019. Ed. by A. Boldyreva and D. Micciancio. Cham: Springer International Publishing, 2019, pp. 638–667. ISBN: 978-3-030-26951-7. URL: https://arxiv.org/abs/1903.02837 (cit. on p. 148).

[BDRS18] M. Bun, C. Dwork, G. N. Rothblum, and T. Steinke. "Composable and Versatile Privacy via Truncated CDP". In: Proceedings of the 50th Annual ACM SIGACT Symposium on Theory of Computing. STOC 2018. Los Angeles, CA, USA: Association for Computing Machinery, 2018, pp. 74–86. ISBN: 9781450355599. URL: https://doi.org/10.1145/3188745.3188946 (cit. on p. 147).

[Bit+17] A. Bittau, Ú. Erlingsson, P. Maniatis, I. Mironov, A. Raghunathan, D. Lie, M. Rudominer, U. Kode, J. Tinnes, and B. Seefeld. "Prochlo: Strong privacy for analytics in the crowd". In: Proceedings of the 26th symposium on operating systems principles. 2017, pp. 441–459 (cit. on p. 148).

[BS16] M. Bun and T. Steinke. "Concentrated differential privacy: Simplifications, extensions, and lower bounds". In: Theory of Cryptography Conference. Springer. 2016, pp. 635–658. URL: https://arxiv.org/abs/1605.02065 (cit. on pp. 96, 129, 145, 147).

[BST14] R. Bassily, A. Smith, and A. Thakurta. "Private empirical risk minimization: Efficient algorithms and tight error bounds". In: 2014 IEEE 55th annual symposium on foundations of computer science. IEEE. 2014, pp. 464–473 (cit. on p. 147).

[Bun16] M. M. Bun. "New Separations in the Complexity of Differential Privacy". PhD thesis. 2016 (cit. on p. 113).

[BUV14] M. Bun, J. Ullman, and S. Vadhan. "Fingerprinting Codes and the Price of Approximate Differential Privacy". In: Proceedings of the Forty-Sixth Annual ACM Symposium on Theory of Computing. STOC '14. New York, New York: Association for Computing Machinery, 2014, pp. 1–10. ISBN: 9781450327107. URL: https://arxiv.org/abs/1311.3158 (cit. on p. 146).

[BW18] B. Balle and Y.-X. Wang. "Improving the gaussian mechanism for differential privacy: Analytical calibration and optimal denoising". In: International Conference on Machine Learning. PMLR. 2018, pp. 394–403 (cit. on p. 145).

[Che+19] A. Cheu, A. Smith, J. Ullman, D. Zeber, and M. Zhilyaev. "Distributed differential privacy via shuffling". In: Annual International Conference on the Theory and Applications of Cryptographic Techniques. Springer. 2019, pp. 375–403. URL: https://arxiv.org/abs/1808.01394 (cit. on p. 148).

[CKS20] C. L. Canonne, G. Kamath, and T. Steinke. "The discrete gaussian for differential privacy". In: Advances in Neural Information Processing Systems 33 (2020), pp. 15676–15688. URL: https://journalprivacyconfidentiality.org/index.php/jpc/article/view/784 (cit. on pp. 113, 146).

[CM06] K. Chaudhuri and N. Mishra. "When Random Sampling Preserves Privacy". In: Proceedings of the 26th Annual International Conference on Advances in Cryptology. CRYPTO'06. Santa Barbara, California: Springer-Verlag, 2006, pp. 198–213. ISBN: 3540374329. URL: https://doi.org/10.1007/11818175_12 (cit. on p. 147).

[CMS11] K. Chaudhuri, C. Monteleoni, and A. D. Sarwate. "Differentially Private Empirical Risk Minimization". In: J. Mach. Learn. Res. 12.null (July 2011), pp. 1069–1109. ISSN: 1532-4435 (cit. on p. 147).

[DMNS06] C. Dwork, F. McSherry, K. Nissim, and A. Smith. "Calibrating noise to sensitivity in private data analysis". In: Theory of cryptography conference. Springer. 2006, pp. 265–284 (cit. on pp. 82, 144).

[DMNS17] C. Dwork, F. McSherry, K. Nissim, and A. Smith. "Calibrating Noise to Sensitivity in Private Data Analysis". In: Journal of Privacy and Confidentiality 7.3 (May 2017), pp. 17–51. URL: https://journalprivacyconfidentiality.org/index.php/jpc/article/view/405 (cit. on p. 144).

[DR16] C. Dwork and G. N. Rothblum. "Concentrated differential privacy". In: arXiv preprint arXiv:1603.01887 (2016). URL: https://arxiv.org/abs/1603.01887 (cit. on pp. 96, 145).

[DRS19] J. Dong, A. Roth, and W. J. Su. "Gaussian differential privacy". In: arXiv preprint arXiv:1905.02383 (2019) (cit. on p. 146).

[DRV10] C. Dwork, G. N. Rothblum, and S. Vadhan. "Boosting and differential privacy". In: 2010 IEEE 51st Annual Symposium on Foundations of Computer Science. IEEE. 2010, pp. 51–60 (cit. on pp. 101, 145).

[DSSU17] C. Dwork, A. Smith, T. Steinke, and J. Ullman. "Exposed! a survey of attacks on private data". In: Annu. Rev. Stat. Appl 4.1 (2017), pp. 61–84 (cit. on p. 113).

[Dwo+06] C. Dwork, K. Kenthapadi, F. McSherry, I. Mironov, and M. Naor. "Our data, ourselves: Privacy via distributed noise generation". In: Annual International Conference on the Theory and Applications of Cryptographic Techniques. Springer. 2006, pp. 486–503 (cit. on pp. 82, 145).

[Dwo06] C. Dwork. "Differential Privacy". In: Automata, Languages and Programming. Ed. by M. Bugliesi, B. Preneel, V. Sassone, and I. Wegener. Berlin, Heidelberg: Springer Berlin Heidelberg, 2006, pp. 1–12. ISBN: 978-3-540-35908-1 (cit. on p. 144).

[Erl+19] Ú. Erlingsson, V. Feldman, I. Mironov, A. Raghunathan, K. Talwar, and A. Thakurta. "Amplification by Shuffling: From Local to Central Differential Privacy via Anonymity". In: Proceedings of the 2019 Annual ACM-SIAM Symposium on Discrete Algorithms (SODA). 2019, pp. 2468–2479. eprint: https://epubs.siam.org/doi/pdf/10.1137/1.9781611975482.151. URL: https://epubs.siam.org/doi/abs/10.1137/1.9781611975482.151 (cit. on p. 148).

[FMT21] V. Feldman, A. McMillan, and K. Talwar. "Hiding Among the Clones: A Simple and Nearly Optimal Analysis of Privacy Amplification by Shuffling". In: 2021 IEEE 62nd Annual Symposium on Foundations of Computer Science (FOCS). 2021, pp. 954–964. URL: https://arxiv.org/abs/2012.12803 (cit. on p. 148).

[FMT22] V. Feldman, A. McMillan, and K. Talwar. "Stronger Privacy Amplification by Shuffling for R\'enyi and Approximate Differential Privacy". In: arXiv preprint arXiv:2208.04591 (2022). URL: https://arxiv.org/abs/2208.04591 (cit. on p. 148).

[FZ21] V. Feldman and T. Zrnic. "Individual Privacy Accounting via a Rényi Filter". In: Advances in Neural Information Processing Systems. Ed. by M. Ranzato, A. Beygelzimer, Y. Dauphin, P. Liang, and J. W. Vaughan. Vol. 34. Curran Associates, Inc., 2021, pp. 28080–28091. URL: https://proceedings.neurips.cc/paper/2021/file/ec7f346604f518906d35ef0492709f78-Paper.pdf (cit. on p. 147).

[GKKM22] B. Ghazi, P. Kamath, R. Kumar, and P. Manurangsi. "Faster Privacy Accounting via Evolving Discretization". In: International Conference on Machine Learning. PMLR. 2022, pp. 7470–7483 (cit. on p. 146).

[GLW21] S. Gopi, Y. T. Lee, and L. Wutschitz. "Numerical Composition of Differential Privacy". In: Advances in Neural Information Processing Systems. Ed. by M. Ranzato, A. Beygelzimer, Y. Dauphin, P. Liang, and J. W. Vaughan. Vol. 34. Curran Associates, Inc., 2021, pp. 11631–11642. URL: https://proceedings.neurips.cc/paper/2021/file/6097d8f3714205740f30debe1166744e-Paper.pdf (cit. on p. 146).

[Goo18] Google. TensorFlow Privacy Library. https://github.com/tensorflow/privacy & https://github.com/google/differential-privacy. 2018 (cit. on p. 143).

[Hoe63] W. Hoeffding. "Probability for sums of bounded random variables". In: J. Am. Stat. Assoc 58 (1963) (cit. on p. 100).

[Kas+11] S. P. Kasiviswanathan, H. K. Lee, K. Nissim, S. Raskhodnikova, and A. Smith. "What Can We Learn Privately?" In: SIAM Journal on Computing 40.3 (2011), pp. 793–826. eprint: https://doi.org/10.1137/090756090. URL: https://doi.org/10.1137/090756090 (cit. on pp. 147, 148).

[KH21] A. Koskela and A. Honkela. "Computing differential privacy guarantees for heterogeneous compositions using fft". In: arXiv preprint arXiv:2102.12412 (2021) (cit. on p. 146).

[KJH20] A. Koskela, J. Jälkö, and A. Honkela. "Computing Tight Differential Privacy Guarantees Using FFT". In: Proceedings of the Twenty Third International Conference on Artificial Intelligence and Statistics. Ed. by S. Chiappa and R. Calandra. Vol. 108. Proceedings of Machine Learning Research. PMLR, Aug. 2020, pp. 2560–2569. URL: https://proceedings.mlr.press/v108/koskela20b.html (cit. on pp. 146, 147).

[KJPH21] A. Koskela, J. Jälkö, L. Prediger, and A. Honkela. "Tight Differential Privacy for Discrete-Valued Mechanisms and for the Subsampled Gaussian Mechanism Using FFT". In: Proceedings of The 24th International Conference on Artificial Intelligence and Statistics. Ed. by A. Banerjee and K. Fukumizu. Vol. 130. Proceedings of Machine Learning Research. PMLR, Apr. 2021, pp. 3358–3366.

URL: https://proceedings.mlr.press/v130/koskela21a.html (cit. on p. 146).

[KOV15] P. Kairouz, S. Oh, and P. Viswanath. "The composition theorem for differential privacy". In: International conference on machine learning. PMLR. 2015, pp. 1376–1385 (cit. on pp. 102, 145, 146).

[KU20] G. Kamath and J. Ullman. "A primer on private statistics". In: arXiv preprint arXiv:2005.00010 (2020). URL: https://arxiv.org/abs/2005.00010 (cit. on p. 146).

[Lyu22] X. Lyu. "Composition Theorems for Interactive Differential Privacy". In: arXiv preprint arXiv:2207.09397 (2022) (cit. on p. 147).

[McM+18] H. B. McMahan, G. Andrew, U. Erlingsson, S. Chien, I. Mironov, N. Papernot, and P. Kairouz. "A general approach to adding differential privacy to iterative training procedures". In: arXiv preprint arXiv:1812.06210 (2018) (cit. on p. 143).

[Mir17] I. Mironov. "Rényi differential privacy". In: 2017 IEEE 30th computer security foundations symposium (CSF). IEEE. 2017, pp. 263–275 (cit. on pp. 126, 147).

[MM18] S. Meiser and E. Mohammadi. "Tight on Budget? Tight Bounds for r-Fold Approximate Differential Privacy". In: Proceedings of the 2018 ACM SIGSAC Conference on Computer and Communications Security. CCS '18. Toronto, Canada: Association for Computing Machinery, 2018, pp. 247–264. ISBN: 9781450356930. URL: https://doi.org/10.1145/3243734.3243765 (cit. on p. 146).

[MTZ19] I. Mironov, K. Talwar, and L. Zhang. "R\'enyi differential privacy of the sampled gaussian mechanism". In: arXiv preprint arXiv:1908.10530 (2019) (cit. on pp. 131, 147).

[MV16] J. Murtagh and S. Vadhan. "The complexity of computing the optimal composition of differential privacy". In: Theory of Cryptography Conference. Springer. 2016, pp. 157–175 (cit. on p. 146).

[NP33] J. Neyman and E. S. Pearson. "IX. On the problem of the most efficient tests of statistical hypotheses". In: Philosophical Transactions of the Royal Society of London. Series A, Containing Papers of a Mathematical or Physical Character 231.694-706 (1933), pp. 289–337 (cit. on p. 86).

[Rén61] A. Rényi. "On measures of entropy and information". In: Proceedings of the fourth Berkeley symposium on mathematical statistics and probability. Vol. 1. 547-561. Berkeley, California, USA. 1961. URL: https://projecteuclid.org/proceedings/berkeley-symposium-on-mathematical-statistics-and-probability/Proceedings-of-the-Fourth-Berkeley-Symposium-on-Mathematical-Statistics-and/Chapter/On-Measures-of-Entropy-and-Information/bsmsp/1200512181 (cit. on p. 127).

[RRUV16] R. Rogers, A. Roth, J. Ullman, and S. Vadhan. "Privacy Odometers and Filters: Pay-as-You-Go Composition". In: Proceedings of the 30th International Conference on Neural Information Processing Systems. NIPS'16. Barcelona, Spain: Curran Associates Inc., 2016, pp. 1929–1937. ISBN: 9781510838819 (cit. on p. 146).

[Smi09] A. Smith. Differential privacy and the secrecy of the sample. https://adamdsmith.wordpress.com/2009/09/02/sample-secrecy/. 2009 (cit. on p. 147).

[SSSS17] R. Shokri, M. Stronati, C. Song, and V. Shmatikov. "Membership inference attacks against machine learning models". In: 2017 IEEE symposium on security and privacy (SP). IEEE. 2017, pp. 3–18 (cit. on p. 113).

[SU15] T. Steinke and J. Ullman. "Between pure and approximate differential privacy". In: arXiv preprint arXiv:1501.06095 (2015) (cit. on p. 113).

[VW21] S. Vadhan and T. Wang. "Concurrent Composition of Differential Privacy". In: Theory of Cryptography Conference. Springer. 2021, pp. 582–604 (cit. on p. 147).

[VZ22] S. Vadhan and W. Zhang. "Concurrent Composition Theorems for all Standard Variants of Differential Privacy". In: arXiv preprint arXiv:2207.08335 (2022) (cit. on p. 147).

[WBK19] Y.-X. Wang, B. Balle, and S. P. Kasiviswanathan. "Subsampled Renyi Differential Privacy and Analytical Moments Accountant". In: Proceedings of the Twenty-Second International Conference on Artificial Intelligence and Statistics. Ed. by K. Chaudhuri and M. Sugiyama. Vol. 89. Proceedings of Machine Learning Research. PMLR, Apr. 2019, pp. 1226–1235. URL: https://proceedings.mlr.press/v89/wang19b.html (cit. on p. 147).

[ZDW22] Y. Zhu, J. Dong, and Y.-X. Wang. "Optimal Accounting of Differential Privacy via Characteristic Function". In: Proceedings of The 25th International Conference on Artificial Intelligence and Statistics. Ed. by G. Camps-Valls, F. J. R. Ruiz, and I. Valera. Vol. 151. Proceedings of Machine Learning Research. PMLR, Mar. 2022, pp. 4782–4817. URL: https://proceedings.mlr.press/v151/zhu22c.html (cit. on p. 146).

[ZW19] Y. Zhu and Y.-X. Wang. "Poission Subsampled Rényi Differential Privacy". In: Proceedings of the 36th International Conference on Machine Learning. Ed. by K. Chaudhuri and R. Salakhutdinov. Vol. 97. Proceedings of Machine Learning Research. PMLR, June 2019, pp. 7634–7642. URL: https://proceedings.mlr.press/v97/zhu19c.html (cit. on p. 147).

DOI: 10.1561/9781638284772.ch4

Chapter 4

Data Release and Synthetic Data

By Yuchao Tao, David Pujol and Ashwin Machanavajjhala

4.1 Introduction

Organizations and researchers often need to extract valuable insights from sensitive datasets while ensuring the privacy of individuals. As discussed in the previous chapters, Differential Privacy (DP) offers a robust mathematical framework to balance this trade-off between data utility and privacy protection. However, implementing DP in practical scenarios presents significant challenges, especially when dealing with complex queries, high-dimensional data, or large query workloads.

One of the primary challenges is answering as many queries as accurately as possible under a fixed privacy budget. Each query consumes a portion of the privacy budget, and adding noise to each query individually can accumulate excessive noise, degrading the overall utility of the results. For instance, if a statistical database is subjected to numerous queries, even with noise added to each answer, an attacker might reconstruct significant portions of the original data, leading to privacy breaches as highlighted by the fundamental law of information recovery. Consider a scenario where a government agency wants to release statistical information about its citizens, such as average income levels, education statistics, or health metrics. Directly answering each statistical query with added noise may either consume the entire privacy budget quickly or result in answers that are too noisy to be useful. Moreover, complex queries involving high sensitivity or structured data exacerbate this problem, necessitating advanced mechanisms that can efficiently manage the privacy-accuracy trade-off.

To tackle these challenges, researchers have developed a variety of DP mechanisms tailored to specific settings and tasks. There is no universal mechanism optimal for all scenarios; instead, the choice of mechanism depends on factors such as the nature of the queries, the dimensionality of the data, and whether the queries are processed in an online or offline manner. Additionally, ensuring consistency among query answers and addressing the needs of data analysts (e.g., through synthetic data generation) are crucial considerations in mechanism design. This chapter provides an overview of these challenges and solutions; it reviews some important DP mechanisms designed to balance privacy and utility under various scenarios.

Overview of the Chapter

We begin by motivating the problem and highlighting the inherent challenges in balancing query accuracy with privacy preservation in Section 4.1. Next, in Section 4.2, we examine the factors influencing privacy and utility, such as data dimensionality, query types, and the importance of consistency in query answers. We then delve into workload answering mechanisms (Section 4.3) and data-dependent algorithms that adapt to the underlying data distribution to improve accuracy (Section 4.4). The chapter then proceeds to address online query answering, focusing on mechanisms like Private Multiplicative Weights that handle sequences of adaptively chosen queries while managing the privacy budget effectively (Section 4.5). Finally, we also examine approaches for generating synthetic data under differential privacy (Section 4.6, and review how to answer non-linear queries in Section 4.7, discussing techniques like smooth sensitivity and Lipschitz extensions, which provide ways to accurately answer complex queries while maintaining differential privacy.

4.2 Problem Motivation

The fundamental law of information recovery states [DN03] that a majority of records in a database of size n can be reconstructed when $n\log(n)^2$ queries are answered by the statistical database, even if each answer has up to $O(\sqrt{n})$ error. This either limits the amount of queries that can be answered (even under differential privacy) or the maximum amount of privacy budget that can be used, since increasing either increases the risk of a privacy breach. As such, when answering queries under differential privacy, the fundamental goal of a privacy preserving mechanism is to answer as many queries as accurately as possible while satisfying differential privacy under a fixed setting of the privacy loss parameter ε.

While the Laplace and Exponential mechanisms are useful primitives for answering individual differentially private queries, they become inefficient when used to answer either queries with high (or unbounded) sensitivity, large sets of queries, structured queries, or queries on structured data. In this chapter, we describe several classes of privacy preserving mechanisms meant to answer queries in different settings. Of these, we will see mechanisms designed to answer large sets of queries by reducing them to smaller sets, mechanisms designed to generate synthetic data which may be queried infinitely many times, mechanisms designed for high dimensional sparse data or particularly dense data, and mechanisms that are designed to answer adaptive queries chosen over time among others. Each of these settings is distinct and poses their own technical problems which come with their own solutions. There is no single differentially private mechanism which is optimal in all settings [Hay+16]; instead there are mechanisms specialized for specific settings and specific tasks which are all designed to maintain privacy under a fixed privacy budget.

4.2.1 Basic Notations and Definitions

We consider a database D as a single tabular data with m attributes and n tuples. The domain for each attribute A_i is Σ_i, and the domain for a tuple t is thus $\Sigma = \Sigma_1 \times \Sigma_2 \ldots \Sigma_m$. A statistical query q takes the database D as input and output a single scalar or a vector of real numbers.

For the majority of this chapter, we focus on linear queries. A linear query can be expressed as $\sum_{t \in D} \phi(t)$, where ϕ is an arbitrary scalar function. When ϕ is in $\{0, 1\}$, this becomes a predicate counting query. When ϕ is a range, this becomes a range counting query.

A linear counting query can also be expressed as a SQL query "SELECT COUNT(*) FROM D WHERE ϕ" to count the number of tuples in D that match the predicate ϕ. A non-linear query has a non-linear transformation of the data before aggregation. For example, consider a table EDGE(from, to) and a self-join counting query "SELECT COUNT(*) FROM EDGE AS E1, EDGE AS E2 WHERE E1.to = E2.from", this query is a non-linear query since self-join is a non-linear transformation.

A workload of queries is a set of queries. When the workload is a set of predicate counting queries with disjoin predicates, this becomes a histogram query. When these disjoint predicates cover the full domain of multiple attributes, this becomes a marginal query over those attributes.

4.3 Different Dimensions of Problems

It is not yet known whether there is a single mechanism that can provide strong utility guarantee for all problems while satisfying differential privacy. These problems could vary in scope and complexity. For example, one problem is to answer a set of statistical queries, and another problem is to release a synthetic data set such that it could be used to answer a set of statistical queries. Meanwhile, these statistical queries could either be linear queries or non-linear queries. From these examples, we observe that problems could be categorized by different characteristics on different dimensions. In this section, we discuss the problems that are commonly studied in differential privacy community in different dimensions.

- **Synthetic data vs query answering.** When we are designing a system that can both protect the data privacy and provide utility for the data analysts, we are facing two choices: one is to make the system interactive, which is to take the queries from the data analysts and return direct query answers. Another is to make the system non-interactive, which is to release a synthetic data set which data analysts can use to answer queries. In the interactive setting, the system can choose a mechanism tailored to the queries of interest [KMHM17]. However, the privacy budget may run out and no future queries could be answered. When synthetic data is released, arbitrary queries or even complex learning tasks can be performed on the synthetic data set. However, the synthetic dataset will not be accurate for all query/analytics tasks.

  There is a large scope of query answering problems that are studied in the differential privacy community, such as range counting queries [Hay+16], marginal queries, graph queries, linear regressions and so on. For the synthetic data generation problem, approaches include density estimation, using domain decomposition, probabilistic graphical models, ML approaches like GANs, and more recently using GPTs/LLMs.
- **Low vs high dimension.** The dimensionality of the data dictates the type of DP algorithm one might use for answering statistical queries. In high dimensional data, the data is quite sparse. Take k-marginal queries on a table with m attributes as example. A k-marginal query is a histogram over k attributes, which lists the counts for all possible domain values for k attributes. If k is 1, this is a histogram over one attribute. When k is getting large, the histogram size is getting exponentially larger, and the count for each bin is almost zero everywhere. Adding Laplace noise to all bin counts to release the k marginal query under DP will result in a relative error that is so high as to make the noisy release useless.

For low dimensional queries such as 1- or 2-dimensional range counting queries, a variety of differentially private mechanisms exists. [Hay+16]. When the query dimension is getting larger, researchers consider a low dimensional representation of the high dimensional queries, such as graphical models [MSM19].

- **Linear vs non-linear queries.** Queries like histogram, marginal and range counting queries are all linear queries. Linear queries are queries that can be expressed as a linear combination of individual weights. The global sensitivity for a linear query is thus bounded by the maximal weight times the number of queries. However, for non-linear queries, the global sensitivity could be much higher or even unbounded. For example, a triangle counting query, which is to count the number of triangles in a graph, has global sensitivity unbounded since there always exists a graph such that adding a node or edge can increase the number of triangles by an arbitrary high number. Adding Laplace noise scaled to the global sensitivity is thus meaningless in this case, so for non-linear queries a different mechanism design should be considered.
- **Online vs offline.** Depending on whether queries arrive all at once or one by one, we separate these two cases as offline mode and online mode, respectively. In the offline mode, all queries are given as the input and the mechanism can take all queries into account to optimize the query results holistically. In the online mode, queries are given as a sequence $q_1, q_2, \ldots, q_n$ that arrives one by one. The total number of queries n may not be known in advance. The query sequence can also be adaptive; i.e., q_i may depend on the answers $a_1, \ldots, a_{i-1}$ for the past queries. Since it is unknown what the future queries are, if most of the privacy budget is spent on answering the early arriving queries accurately, future queries may be answered with poor accuracy. However, if future queries are all similar to the early arriving queries, it is not necessary to save the privacy budget for the early arriving queries. In contrast, in the offline mode, all the queries are known in advance and thus one can use that information to determine an optimal strategy to construct DP answers. Hence, the techniques used to answer queries in the online mode differ from the methods used to answer a batch of queries in the offline mode.
- **Consistency.** When answering multiple queries under DP, the answers released by a differentially private mechanism may not be consistent due to the injected noise; e.g., the noisy count of men and the noisy count of women may not add up to be equal to the noisy count of the total population. Data inconsistency reduces the utility of differential privacy as it causes conflicts in the data analysis. On the other hand, it implies that we have injected unnecessary extra noise to our query answers. Thus, in several settings, there is a need to ensure consistent query answering of multiple queries.

In some cases, enforcing consistency can both improve the utility and reduce the noise, but in some settings it can introduce bias in the released statistics [Puj+20; ZHF21].

4.4 Workload Answering Mechanisms

In this section, we consider answering a workload of linear queries under differential privacy. To simplify the analysis, we use a vector representation of the data and query. Recall that we define a database D as a collection of n tuples, where each tuple is from the domain Σ with N unique domain values. We can also represent a database D as a histogram, where each bin i corresponds to one unique domain value $t_i \in \Sigma$, and its bin count corresponds to how many tuples in D matches to that domain value. We denote this histogram as $x = [x_1, \ldots, x_N]$. The size of this histogram N is the size of the domain Σ. Given this representation of D, we can rewrite the answer of a linear query q from $\sum_{t \in D} \phi(t)$ to $\Sigma_{i=1}^{N} \phi(t_i) x_i$, which is a vector product with x. Therefore, we consider a query as a N dimensional vector. For a workload with d queries, we express it as a $d \times N$ matrix F. The answer for this workload is thus given as Fx.

4.4.1 Lower Bound of Error

Suppose the global sensitivity of the workload F is d. A typical mechanism to answer F on x in an ε-differential private way is to apply d-dimension Laplace mechanism [DMNS06] with sensitivity d. Let error be defined as the expected ℓ_2 distance of the output d-dimensional vectors from the ground truth Fx and the mechanism output. The error for Laplace mechanism in this setting is $d\sqrt{d}/\varepsilon$. A proof sketch is given as follows: Suppose $Z_1, Z_2, \ldots, Z_d$ are i.i.d random variables following the Laplace distribution $Lap(d/\varepsilon)$. The error of Laplace mechanism is thus given as $E\left[\sqrt{\sum_{i=1}^{d} Z_i^2}\right] \leq \sqrt{E\left[\sum_{i=1}^{d} Z_i^2\right]} = \sqrt{d \cdot 2 \cdot (d/\varepsilon)^2} = O(d\sqrt{d}/\varepsilon)$. The first inequality is credit to Jensen inequality.

A lower bound of error in this setting is given by Moritz, Hardt and Kunal Talwar [HT10]. They give a lower bound as $\Omega\left(\min\{d\sqrt{d}/\varepsilon, d\sqrt{\log(N/d)}/\varepsilon\}\right)$ when $d \leq N$. The proof of this lower bound is based on convex geometry. Especially, consider B_1^N as a unit ℓ_1 ball, and K as a convex polytope by $K = FB_1^N$, the lower bound of error is given as $\Omega\left(d\sqrt{d}/\varepsilon \cdot Vol(K)^{1/d}\right)$, where $Vol(K)$ is the volume of K. The idea behind the proof is as follows. Consider each database x as a point in B_1^N, and B_x is a ball centered around Fx with some radius such that the probability that x is mapped into B_x by the mechanism is more than $1/2$. To satisfy ε-differential privacy, the probability that a zero database 0 is mapped into the same B_x ball should be bounded by a constant factor, and it is held for any x. According to the packing theorem, we can have exponentially many such balls in K that are disjoint, and this number is controlled by the ball radius. Since they are disjoint, the probability that 0 is mapped into the union of these balls is bounded by 1, which means the number of such balls should be bounded. Since the number of such balls is related to the ball radius, this bound gives a lower bound on the ball radius. Intuitively, a larger ball radius indicates lager error for the mechanism, thus bounding the lower bound of the ball radius is associated with bounding the lower bound of the mechanism error.

4.4.2 Select Measure Reconstruct

When answering a workload of queries it is sometimes impractical to answer each individual query directly. Sometimes the workload has a very high sensitivity and thus requires a high amount of noise. Sometimes queries are very similar and share large amounts of data and answering each of these queries would result in a large amount of noise and some inconsistent query answers. In cases like these mechanisms often invoke a design paradigm known as the Select Measure Reconstruct Paradigm. A mechanism which invokes this paradigm first **Selects** an alternative set of queries to answer known as the strategy. This set of queries is usually smaller and having a lower sensitivity than the original workload and as such requires less noise to answer directly. The mechanism then **Measures** these strategy query answers using a differentially private primitive such as the Laplace mechanism. Then the mechanism uses the noisy answers to the strategy workload to **Reconstruct** the original workload. Mechanisms which invoke this paradigm perform well when answering large numbers of related queries.

4.4.3 The Hierarchical Mechanism

One of the first mechanisms which invoked the Select Measure Reconstruct Paradigm is the Hierarchical Mechanism [HRMS09] often called H_b for short. This mechanism was designed to answer large amounts of range queries in an efficient manner. It does so by repeatedly partitioning the domain into a tree with branching factor b, where individual counts in the databases are leaf nodes and parent nodes represent continuous ranges. The mechanism then answers the range queries represented by each individual node in the tree directly. Any additional range queries can be reconstructed using the answers directly in the tree.

In Figure 4.1 we show an example of a Hierarchical tree with branching factor 2 or H_2 for short. In this example, the database in question has domain size of 8. The

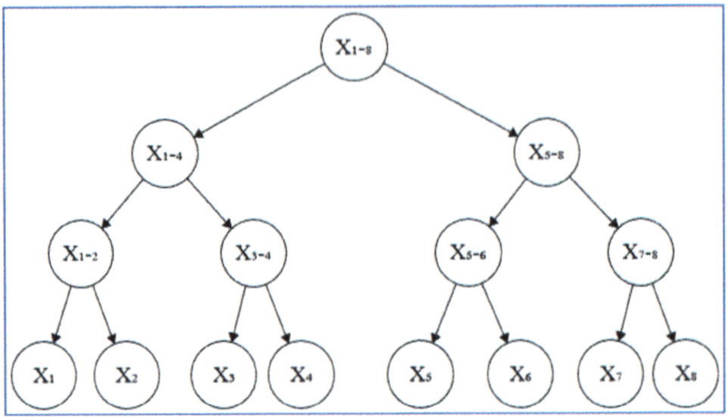

Figure 4.1. An example of an H_2 tree. The root node contains the range query over the entire domain. It's left child node contains the range query over the first half of the domain while it's right node contains the range query over the second half of the domain. The leaf nodes contain queries over single counts.

root tree here represents the range query containing all the counts in the database, the left child represents the range query containing counts 1, 2, 3, and 4 while the right child is the range query containing counts 5,6,7, and 8. The rest of the nodes are denoted similarly. When answering each the queries associated with each node, the sensitivity is the number of nodes along the path from leaf to root, $log_b(k) + 1$, where k is the domain size. Using the H_b strategy any range query can be answered using at most $2\log(k)$ of the nodes. Therefore if we use the Laplace mechanism to measure the nodes each individual node as an expected error of $O\left(\frac{\log(k)^2}{\varepsilon^2}\right)$. Then any range query using at most $2\log(k)$ nodes has an expected error of $O\left(\frac{\log(k)^3}{\varepsilon^2}\right)$ and as such the workload containing all k^2 possible range queries has an expected error of $O\left(\frac{k^2\log(k)^2}{\varepsilon^2}\right)$.

4.4.4 The Matrix Mechanism

The Matrix Mechanism [Li+15] is a more general use of the Select Measure Reconstruct paradigm, which can be used to answer any set of linear counting queries. The matrix mechanism first represents the database as a column vector, denoted x, where each element in the data vector represents the number of individuals that satisfy some property (or combination of properties). Each individual should only be counted in a single element in the data vector in order to bound sensitivity. Once the database is represented in this data vector form, a linear counting query can be represented as a row vector of the same size, and the answer to the query can be computed as the dot product of the query vector and the data vector. A workload of linear counting queries, denoted W is represented as a $k \times n$ matrix where k is the domain size and n is the number of queries. This matrix is simply constructed by

$$
\begin{aligned}
&\text{SELECT} \left\{ A = \text{Optimize}_{MM}(W) \right. \\
&\text{MEASURE} \begin{cases} a = Ax \\ y = a + \text{Lap}(\|A_1\|/\varepsilon) \end{cases} \\
&\text{RECONSTRUCT} \begin{cases} \bar{x} = A^{+}y \\ ans = a + \text{Lap}(\|A_1\|/\varepsilon) \end{cases}
\end{aligned}
$$

Figure 4.2. The SELECT MEASURE RECONSTRUCT paradigm in the matrix mechanism.

the vertical stack of each query. As such answering the entire workload W of queries can be done by the matrix multiplication Wx. Since the data vector requires that each individual be in only one count, the sensitivity of a workload is the maximum L1 column norm of the matrix denoted as $\| W\|_1$. The matrix mechanism takes in a workload W and selects a full rank strategy matrix A to instead answer. It then directly measures A by taking the vector $y = Ax$ and adding independently sampled Laplace noise. It then reconstructs the answers W by taking the pseduo-inverse of $A(\tilde{y} = A^{+}y)$, and then using the resulting noisy data vector to answer the original workload W. An instantiation of the matrix mechanism as Select Measure Reconstruct paradigm is provided in Figure 4.2.

The expected error of the matrix mechanism is as follows:

$$\frac{2}{\varepsilon^2}\|A\|_1^2\| WA^{+}\|_F^2,$$

where $\| \cdot \|_F$ is the Frobenius norm.

The matrix mechanism is a very general mechanism which can be used in many settings and which can represent many other mechanisms. For example consider answering the workload containing all possible range queries with a data vector of size 4 and a privacy budget of $\varepsilon = 1$. If you were to answer the entire workload directly you would get an expected error of 288. Alternatively you could use the hierarchical mechanism, shown as a matrix strategy in Figure 4.3, and use those queries to reconstruct the range queries. Doing so results in an expected error of 201. Originally the task of finding the optimal strategy matrix was proposed as a semi-definite program with rank constraints which could be solved in $O(k^4(n^4 + k^4))$ time. The High Dimensional Matrix Mechanism (HDMM) [MMHM18] is a variant of the matrix mechanism which restricts the possible search space in order to use a gradient decent method to select a strategy matrix. It does this by searching only the simplified p-identity space. This space includes matrices which consist of the the $n \times n$ identity matrix with an additional p rows appended to them, which are

$$\begin{bmatrix} 1 & 1 & 1 & 1 \\ 1 & 1 & 0 & 0 \\ 0 & 0 & 1 & 1 \\ 1 & 0 & 0 & 0 \\ 0 & 1 & 0 & 0 \\ 0 & 0 & 1 & 0 \\ 0 & 0 & 0 & 1 \end{bmatrix}$$

Figure 4.3. An example of an H_2 tree with domain equal to 4 represented as a strategy matrix.

then normalized to have a maximum column norm of 1. This reduces the running time of the gradient descent to be a more feasible $O(p * n^2)$.

4.5 Data Dependent Algorithms

Up until now we have considered Data independent Mechanisms whose expected error is independent of the database itself or any properties thereof. Data dependent mechanisms leverage some property of the data to reduce the overall error of the mechanism. This information can be properties of the data which are known ahead of time, such as bounds on specific values, or this data can be inferred during run time such as the distribution of the data. Any information inferred or learned at run-time must be done in a differentially private manner (using some of the privacy budget) to ensure that mechanism as a whole still satisfies differential privacy. Performance of data dependent mechanisms like the name suggests are dependent on how well the mechanism is suited for the specific data. Some mechanisms perform better on sorted or mostly homogeneous data while other mechanisms perform better on data that follows a specific distribution.

4.5.1 Data and Workload Aware Algorithm

The Data- and Workload-Aware Algorithm (DAWA) [LHMW14] is an example of a data adaptive mechanism for computing range and histogram queries. The mechanism has three major steps. First, the mechanism uses a portion of the budget, ε_1, to partition the data into approximately uniform sections; all the counts in each approximately uniform section are added to a bucket. Then it uses a noisy differentially private subroutine to measure the counts in each bucket, in a workload aware manner, similar to the matrix mechanism. Finally, it expands the buckets back into histogram form by uniformly distributing the counts in each bucket across the domain of the partition. The key point of DAWA is that instead of adding noise to each individual count in the domain, it instead buckets several points in the domain together and adds a single unit of noise to the entire bucket. In the worst case, where each point in the domain is significantly different than it's surrounding points, each point in the domain is given it's own bucket and thus independent noise for each point is required. This is no better than using the Laplace mechanism on each count using only the remainder of the privacy budget ($\varepsilon - \varepsilon_1$). However, in the best case where the data is almost completely homogeneous DAWA could add all of the histogram to a single bucket resulting in only one instance of noise being used across the entire database. Because of this Dawa performs better on databases which have large continuous sections of nearly homogeneous data or on data which is sorted.

4.5.2 PrivTree: Data Adaptive Spatial Decomposition

For a two-dimensional spatial data, e.g. coordinates in a map, a common class of queries is to ask the number of points in a rectangular range. For a single range counting query, to satisfy differential privacy, a typical solution is to add Laplace noise to the count with sensitivity equal to 1. When we have a workload of range counting queries, if we use Laplace noise to answer each query, we have to divide the privacy budget for each query, which results poor accuracy. As shown in Section 4.4 "Workload Answering Mechanisms", one workaround is to partition the domain into small ranges as defined by the range counting queries and their intersections, so that data can be transformed into a vector and the workload of range counting queries can be expressed as a matrix. Then, we can apply techniques introduced in Section 4.4 to release the query answer. However, when we have a fine-grained workload of range counting queries, we also tend to have a fine-grained partition of the domain, which results a sparse vector representation for the data.

An alternative strategy for answering a workload of range counting queries is to first find a good partition of the data so that within each sub-region, points are close to a uniform distribution and the number of them is sufficiently high comparing to the Laplace noise added in each sub-region. For each range counting queries, the count is reported as the sum of noisy counts in the sub-regions it covered and the fractional counts in the sub-regions it partially intersects. Based on these ideas, Jun Zhang, Xiaokui Xiao and Xing Xie propose PrivTree [ZXX16], which decompose the spatial domain by a quad-tree in a differentially private manner. The algorithm starts from the root, which is the entire domain, and then recursively check and decompose the node. For each node that is being checked, it computes the count of points within the region that is represented by the node, decrease the count by a certain amount according to the depth, add a Laplace noise, and then compare with a threshold. If it is above the threshold, then split the region into halves for each dimension as child nodes, and repeat the sub-routine for each child node.

The quad-tree constructed by PrivTree is totally data-driven. Unlike the traditional private spatial decomposition algorithm, this approach does not specify the limit of max depth, and the privacy loss also does not depend on the max depth of the tree. If data is very dense at a certain sub-region, PrivTree can go deeper for that sub-region without violating differential privacy. Ideally, what PrivTree returns is a spatial decomposition such that dense regions have a dense decomposition and sparse regions have a sparse decomposition. To answer range counting queries, extra Laplace noise is added to each region. For a range counting query on a dense area, it may contain many noises from the sub-regions. However, since it is a dense area, the total counts in this area is sufficiently higher than the total noise, which means the relative error is not low. Other error could come from the bias due to the uniformity assumption within each region.

4.6 Online Query Answering

So far we have assumed the entire workload of queries is known in advance and the mechanism may leverage any structure in the queries to answer them with minimum error. However, in most query answering settings, we imagine an SQL like environment where an analyst asks one query at a time adaptively choosing the next query from the answer to the previous one. This brings us to the online setting. Unlike offline DP mechanisms, where we assume all the queries are known ahead of time, in the online setting the analyst asks one query at a time and the mechanism must answer the queries as they are given before seeing subsequent queries. There are two key challenges in the online setting; budget management and query optimization.

Due to the fundamental law of information recovery we cannot answer an unlimited number of queries, even with noise added each time. Instead we must answer the entire sequence of queries using a limited and fixed privacy budget. Online differentially private mechanisms must spend the privacy budget over time while still maintaining enough budget to answer queries later. Some mechanisms do this by reusing previous query answers or maintaining a synthetic dataset to answer queries from.

Another challenge for online problems is optimizing overall error across queries. In offline query answering, all the queries are known in advance and the mechanism may optimize across the entire workload at once. By contrast, in online query answering, the mechanism only knows the queries that have already been answered, not any that will be asked in the future. Online mechanisms, however, can leverage previously answered queries when asking new ones. A mechanism can avoid spending budget on a query if it can be reconstructed from previous queries with high accuracy.

4.6.1 Private Multiplicative Weights

Private Multiplicative [HR10] weights is an example of an online query answering mechanism for linear queries. This mechanism can answer an infinite number of linear queries, even after exhausting the allotted privacy budget. The mechanism begins by creating a differentially private normalized histogram from which it can query without spending privacy budget. At initialization the histogram is created to have all values be equal. Whenever a query is asked the mechanism checks (in a differentially private manner) if the current version of the histogram can answer the query accurately. If the histogram can answer accurately the query is answered directly from the maintained histogram. Since the maintained histogram is always updated in a differentially private manner, it itself is differentially private and as such, any queries asked directly from it are differentially private without spending any additional privacy budget. If the answer from the histogram is not accurate enough, the mechanism spends part of its budget asking the query directly from the true dataset using the Laplace mechanism and uses that direct query answer to update the maintained histogram. This way, budget is only spent if the histogram cannot answer the query efficiently, at which point the histogram is updated to more closely resemble the real dataset. This process continues until the mechanism has exhausted it's entire privacy budget. Once the entire privacy budget is spent, the mechanism outputs the maintained differentially private histogram which may be used to answer the remaining queries.

We say that an online query answering mechanism is (α, β, k) adaptively accurate on database x, if for all k adaptively chosen queries $f_1, f_2 \ldots f_k$, with all but β probability $|a_t - \langle f_t, x\rangle| \leq \alpha$. Where $\langle f_t, x\rangle$ is the mechanisms noisy answer to query f_t on database x and a_t is the true answer of that same query. For any set of parameters $k, \varepsilon, \delta, \beta > 0$, Private multiplicative weights is guaranteed to be (α, β, k) adaptively accurate on any database of size n with $\alpha = O\left(\varepsilon^{-1} n^{-1/2} \cdot \log(1/\delta) \log^(1/4)(N) \cdot (\log(k) + \log(1/\beta)\right)$. Where $N = |U|$, the size of the data universe. Likewise, since this holds for adaptively chosen queries, it also holds for non-adaptively chosen queries.

4.7 Synthetic Data

A typical scenario for data analysis is that one data analyst submits some queries to the data curator, and data curator returns the query answers to the analyst. To ensure data is protected by differential privacy, these query answers are perturbed by some differentially private mechanisms. However, the data curator can also choose another strategy to respond to the request. Instead of returning the noisy query answers, the data curator can also generate a synthetic data set that satisfies differential privacy, and then return it to the data analyst. A synthetic dataset is a completely made up dataset with the same schema as the input dataset and which preserves some statistical properties from the input. The data analyst can evaluate queries on the synthetic data set to get query answers, and it satisfies differential privacy due to the post-processing rule (see Theorem 1.7 of Chapter 1.4.2). The utility of a synthetic data release is associated with a specific task or metric. For example, the utility could be associated with the expected ℓ_2 error of a set of linear queries evaluating on the original data and the synthetic data.

Avrim Blum, Katrina Ligett and Aaron Roth show that when considering answering a class of counting queries C using the synthetic data set while satisfying ε-differential privacy, the lower bound of error only depends on the VC-dimension of the query class C and the privacy factor ε [BLR13]. They define (α, δ)-usefulness for a mechanism with respect to the query class C if the max L_1 query error for any query in C is bounded by α with probability $1 - \delta$. Based on the reconstruction proof for "blatant non-privacy" [DN03], they show that given a database with size $\leq VCDIM(C)/2$, for any ε-differentially private mechanism that is (α, δ)-useful for a query class C, we have $\alpha \geq \frac{1}{2\exp(\varepsilon)+1}$. They also propose the Net mechanism [BLR13] that construct a set of candidate data sets, called α-net, such that for any ground truth data set, there always exists a candidate data set that can accurately answers any query from a fixed query class compared to the ground truth one with L1 error less than α. The Net mechanism then chooses a data set from the α-net using exponential mechanism with score function as the inverse max L1 error for all queries, and thus satisfies differential privacy. However, the size of α-net is often large. The bound given in [BLR13] shows that for any counting class C and any data domain X, the size of minimal α-net is at most $|X|^{O(VCDIM(C)log(1/\alpha)/\alpha^2)}$. It is also computationally infeasible to sample a data set from the α-net according to the exponential mechanism.

Another approach for private synthetic data generation uses generative models, which includes probabilistic graphical models and deep generative models. Approaches based on probabilistic graphical models include Bayesian networks [Zha+17] and Markov networks [CXZX15; Ber+17; MSM19; ZKKW20]. Most of these approaches first learn the probabilistic graphical model structure of the data, and then learn the parameters for the model. Approaches based on deep generative models include DP-AuGM [Che+18], DP-VaeGM [Che+18], DPGAN [Xie+18], and PATE-GAN [JYV18]. These approaches are based on training (variational) autoencoders or generative adversarial networks in a differentially private way. Other approaches includes estimating the data distribution from the noisy DP query answers, such as MWEM [HLM10] and PGM estimation [MSM19].

4.7.1 PrivBayes

PrivBayes [Zha+17] is one of several methods for generating differentially private synthetic data. It does so through three major steps. First, it splits the entire privacy budget into two separate budgets, ε_1 and ε_2. The first of these budgets is used to learn a Bayesian network capturing the important attribute correlations in the input database in a differentially private manner. The second privacy budget is used to construct noisy versions of the conditional distributions contained in the Bayesian network. From these two steps we are given a differentially private Bayesian network as well as differentially private conditional distribution for each node in the network. In combination the network and the noisy conditional distributions are then used to approximate the distribution of tuples in the original database. Sampling from this distribution creates differentially private synthetic data with a distribution approximately equivalent to the tuples in the original database. Since the first two steps satisfy ε_1 and ε_2 differential privacy respectively and since the third step is a post processing step PrivBayes algorithm as a whole satisfies $\varepsilon = \varepsilon_1 + \varepsilon_2$ differential privacy.

4.7.2 Markov network

Suppose the domain for a tuple is $\mathcal{X}$, we could express this data as a $|\mathcal{X}|$-dimensional full-domain vector, where each cell in the vector indicates the fraction of rows in the data matching a specific tuple value. Assuming N is public and fixed, this $|\mathcal{X}|$-dimensional vector is equivalent to a contingency table of the data, which lists the number of rows matched for all possible values of n attributes.

To generate a synthetic data set under differential privacy, one approach is to perturb the $|\mathcal{X}|$-dimensional full-domain vector using Laplace mechanism, post-process the noisy vector to be non-negative, normalize it to be a probability distribution and then sample a synthetic data set from it. Roughly speaking, the expected statistical distance between the sanitized distribution and the ground truth grows with the ratio $|\mathcal{X}|/N$, where $|\mathcal{X}|$ is the size of the full-domain vector and N is the data size. When $|\mathcal{X}|$ is much larger than the data size N, most cells in the full-domain vector are zero and few cells have a low non-zero counts, thus adding Laplace noise to all cells results large amount of relative error, which further makes the sanitized distribution useless.

An alternative approach is to learn several lower dimensional marginal distributions of the data using differentially private mechanisms, and then infer the full-domain distribution with some principles. Since the full-domain distribution is of high dimension, it is important to find a computationally tractable expression of the distribution. One such principle to infer the full-domain distribution is to find a distribution such that its marginal distributions are close to the sanitized ones generated by the differentially private mechanisms. Based on these ideas, Ryan McKenna, Daniel Sheldon and Gerome Miklau propose a inference principle based on the undirected graphical model of data and the space of marginal polytope [MSM19]. An undirected graphical model, or Markov network, factorizes the data distribution into a product of factor functions over the cliques of a graph with a normalization. In [MSM19], they assume all the attributes from the noisy marginal distributions given as the input for the full-domain distribution inference are the cliques of the graphical model. The goal is to find the parameters in the factor functions such that the loss of marginal distributions is minimized while the entropy of the full-domain distribution is maximized.

To achieve this goal, the first step is to find a valid set of marginals such that the loss between the found marginals and the noisy marginals are minimized, and then the factor parameters can be derived from the marginals using the maximum entropy rule. A set of marginals is valid if there exists a full-domain distribution such that its marginals match the set of marginals. The space of such valid marginals form a marginal polytope. The optimization problem is thus to find a valid set of marginals with minimum loss on this marginal polytope. The loss is defined as the negative log-likelihood in [MSM19], where the likelihood is about how likely the differentially private mechanism generates the noisy result given a specific marginal. In [MSM19], the optimization problem is solved by an algorithm based on entropic mirror descent algorithm, and further improved by Nesterov's accelerated dual averaging approach. This algorithm also generates the factor parameters at the same time. To generate a synthetic data set, one can sample from the graphical model using the inferred factor parameters.

Learning a Markov network from the noisy marginals not only provides a tractable expression of the full-domain distribution, but also ensure consistency and some accuracy for the further inference of the distribution. However, it is unknown whether a data distribution can always be factorized using a Markov network, and it is also unknown whether the maximum entropy rule is the best option to infer a Markov network given a set of marginal distributions.

4.7.3 Multiplicative Weights Exponential Mechanism

Suppose we are given some initial guess to the full-domain distribution, such as a uniform distribution, and we are also given a query result of q, which maps each tuple in the data to $[-1, +1]$ and sums up, how should we update our initial guess of the full-domain distribution according to what we have observed? One approach is to update the weight of each value in the domain using the multiplicative weight rule. Section 4.6.1 introduces this approach in on online setting, where queries are coming one by one and the distribution is updated every time if a query answered using the Laplace mechanism on the ground truth data is very different from being answered on the synthetic data set. The query answer that is released is always based on the latest synthetic data set.

Maintaining a synthetic data set or distribution in this way is also an approach to release a private synthetic data set. Here we consider an offline setting as discussed in MWEM [HLM10]. If all the queries are given at once instead of arriving one by one, we can cherry-pick the query which has the maximum error to update the distribution. This query selection is done through the Exponential mechanism, where the score function is the L1 distance between the query answer on the current distribution and the ground truth. Once a query is selected, the query is answered based on the ground truth data using the Laplace mechanism, and the distribution is updated using the multiplicative rule. The algorithm will then repeat again to select a new query and make a new update. If there are in total T such updates, then the privacy budget is divided into $2T$ pieces, one for the EM mechanism and one for the Laplace mechanism in each update. The final distribution or the synthetic data set is the average of all past distribution in the updates. Suppose the domain size of data is $|D|$, the pool size of queries is $|Q|$, the data size is n and the total privacy budget is ε, then there exists a T such that with probability at least $1 - 1/ploy(|Q|)$, the error of any query answered by the final synthetic data set is $O\left(n^{2/3}\left(\frac{\log|D|\log|Q|}{\varepsilon}\right)\right)$

Since the update of distribution is a pure post-processing step, one can apply the multiplicative weight update multiple times using the existing sanitized query answers. The initial guess of the distribution can also be replaced by some public knowledge or another private mechanism. The final distribution can also be replaced by the final updated distribution instead of the averaged one. These variants of the algorithm may improve the performance of MWEM in a practical sense.

4.8 Non-linear query Answering

Non-linear queries are queries that cannot be expressed as the weighted summation of data elements. Examples include quantile queries, join-count queries, and graph queries. Most DP mechanisms are designed for linear queries. For non-linear queries, the global sensitivity is not clear and naively applying Laplace mechanism may fail to follow DP.

4.8.1 Smooth Sensitivity

For a linear query, the global sensitivity is determined by the max weight in the query. For example, the global sensitivity is 1 for a common predicate-counting query where each weight is one or zero. To answer such a linear query under ε-differential privacy, one approach is apply the Laplace mechanism, which adds a Laplace noise scaled to the global sensitivity of the query divided by the privacy budget ε. However, for a non-linear query, the global sensitivity is often much larger. For example, for a median query on a data set with domain $[0, \Lambda]$, the global sensitivity is Λ. Consider a data set with $2n + 1$ elements such as $\{0, 0, \ldots, \Lambda, \Lambda\}$ where n are 0 and $n + 1$ are Λ. The median is this case is Λ. However, under bounded differential privacy, consider a neighboring database by changing the $n+1^{st}$ element from Λ to 0; the median drops to 0. This example shows that the global sensitivity of median is Λ, and thus releasing the median using Laplace mechanism could result in meaningless outputs when Λ is very large or the number of elements is small. This is surprising, since the median is less sensitive especially for large datasets, but the relative noise introduced by Laplace mechanism is not decreasing as we increase the data size.

One way to reduce the noise needed to achieve differential privacy is to replace global sensitivity with a measure of sensitivity on the specific database instance. Local sensitivity is the maximum query difference between the input database and all its neighboring data sets. For measures like the median, the local sensitivity varies depending on the input database. For the pathological example above, the local sensitivity is still Λ. However, for a database with $2n+1$ elements with the same value in the positions n, $n+1$ and $n+2$, then the local sensitivity is 0! However, the local sensitivity itself is a sensitive information of the data (e.g. for the case of median you can tell the values in positions n, $n+1$ and $n+2$ are the same when local sensitivity is 0). Hence, adding Laplace noise scaled to the local sensitivity is does not guarantee differentially privacy. To connect local sensitivity to differential privacy, Kobbi Nissim, Sofya Raskhodnikova, and Adam Smith propose the smooth sensitivity mechanism [NRS07]. Smooth sensitivity is a tight smooth upper bound of the local sensitivity such that itself is e^{β}-Lipschitz for some β: i.e., smooth sensitivity $SS(\cdot)$ has the following property: $SS(D) \geq LS(D)$ and $|SS(D) - SS(D')| \leq e^{\beta} \cdot d(D, D')$ for any data sets D and D', where $LS(D)$ is the local sensitivity of D and $d(D, D')$ is the hamming distance between D and D'. Calibrating noise to smooth sensitivity and adding it to the raw query result achieves (ε, δ)-differential privacy.

Deriving the smooth sensitivity S_f from the local sensitivity LS_f for the query f on some data set is not trivial. Taking the median as an example. Consider a data set with n elements and n is odd. Suppose data is ordered as $\{x_1, x_2, \ldots, x_n\}$. Denote $m = \frac{n+1}{2}$ as the index for the median. The local sensitivity LS_{med} is thus equal to

$\max(x_m - x_{m-1}, x_{m+1} - x_m)$. To derive the smooth sensitivity, [NRS07] considers an extension of local sensitivity as local sensitivity at distance k, $LS_f^{(k)}$, which is the max local sensitivity for the data set that differs by at most k rows with the ground truth data set. The smooth sensitivity of f is thus equal to the max of $e^{-k\beta} LS_f^{(k)}$ for $k \in \{0, 1, \ldots, n\}$. For the median case, its local sensitivity at distance k is given as $LS_{med}^{(k)} = \max_{0 \le t \le k+1} (x_{m+t} - x_{m+t+k-1})$, which can be further used to derive the smooth sensitivity, and the running time for computing its smooth sensitivity is thus $O(n^2)$.

It is not always clear how to efficiently compute the smooth sensitivity. A naive algorithm to find local sensitivity at distance k is to try all possible data set by changing up to k tuples, and for each data set iterate over all neighboring data sets of that data set to compute the local sensitivity. To deploy smooth sensitivity in a real application, it is important to find a computationally efficient algorithm to compute the smooth sensitivity or its approximate upper bound.

4.8.2 Lipschitz Extension

One representative class of non-linear queries is sub-graph counting queries. For example, given an un-directed graph $G(V, E)$, a triangle counting query counts number of triangles in the graph. Other sub-graph counting queries include counting the number of edges, k-stars, and so on. If we think about each node in the graph as the basic element, sub-graph counting queries cannot be expressed as a linear combination of nodes since each node may be involved in multiple sub-graphs.

To answer these queries under differential privacy, a basic solution is to apply Laplace mechanism, which adds the Laplace noise scaled to the global sensitivity. Recall that the definition of global sensitivity for a function f is $\max |f(G) - f(G')|$ for all G and G' that are neighbors. Here we consider G and G' are neighbors if they differ by a single node. This is so called node-DP. Under node-DP, for a graph query like counting the number of triangles, the global sensitivity is unbounded. Even if we assume the total number of nodes is n, the global sensitivity is $\binom{n-1}{2}$ due to a pair of neighboring graphs that are n-clique and $(n-1)$-clique.

If we assume the graph degree is bounded by D and denote this space as $\mathcal{G}^D$, then the global sensitivity of triangle counting query is $\binom{D}{2}$, which is much smaller than $\binom{n-1}{2}$ since $D \ll n$ is common. Usually D can be selected by some common knowledge or some public information, so that it is close to the real degree bound. However, we cannot guarantee this assumption is always true. When this assumption does not hold, we still want our query to be have low sensitivity like when the assumption is true. This leads to the solution based on Lipschitz extension, which is to find a new function that gives the same answer in the original scope and also has the same global sensitivity[i]. For example, suppose f is defined on graphs from G^D, we can find a new function $\hat{f}$ that takes any graph as input such that $\hat{f}(G) = f(G)$ on $G \in \mathcal{G}^D$ and the global sensitivity $GS(\hat{f}) = GS(f)$.

Finding the Lipschitz extension of graph queries is not trivial. Shiva Prasad Kasiviswanathan, Kobbi Nissim, Sofya Raskhodnikova and Adam Smith consider using max flow of a constructed flow graph for answering the number of edges and using linear programming for answering the number of sub-graphs [KNRS13]. Given a graph $G(V, E)$, a flow graph is constructed as a source s, a sink t and two copies of V as V_l and V_r such that the source s is connected to each v_l in V_l with capacity D, each v_r in V_r is connected to the sink t with capacity D and v_l is connected to v_r with unit capacity if $(v_l, v_r) \in E$. The half of the max flow in this graph is a Lipschitz extension of the number of edges for graphs from $\mathcal{G}^D$. For answering the number of a specific sub-graph in G, a Lipschitz extension based on linear programming is considered as follows: Suppose Δ_D is the global sensitivity of answering the number of sub-graph for graphs from $\mathcal{G}^D$. Create variables $x_c \in [0, 1]$ for each possible sub-graph c in G (no matter whether it exists or not). For each node in G, the sum of x_c that is adjacent to that node is bounded by Δ_D. The objective is to maximize the sum of x_c. The optimal value by solving this linear programming is a Lipschitz extension of the sub-graph counting for graphs from $\mathcal{G}^D$.

These examples of Lipschitz extension shows the applicability of Lipschitz extension to graph queries with scalar outputs. For graph queries with multi-dimensional outputs, such as degree distribution, another flow graph based solution is considered [RS16]. Other studies based on Lipschitz extension include [BBDS13; DLL16; DZBJ18]. Studies that involves the similar idea of Lipschitz extension includes [CZ13; Zha+15; Kot+19; THMR20]

4.8.3 Answering SQL Queries

SQL queries are widely existing in the real world data analysis tasks. They provide a rich model of query structures that is far beyond simple linear queries. Privately answering SQL queries is thus challenging. On the other hand, SQL queries are often asked on a relational database with multiple relations. Relations are usually associated with each other by some foreign-primary keys. In a multi-relational database, if we remove one tuple in a relation, it is nature to consider cascade delete as removing tuples in other relations that have foreign keys associated with the tuple. In this case, even for a simple linear query, the privacy analysis is not clear since removing a tuple may cause cascade deletions and the sensitivity for the linear query thus is not always a constant.

---

i. If the new global sensitivity is s times the original one, it is called Lipschitz extension with stretch s

Kotsogiannis et al. propose a system PrivateSQL for answering SQL queries privately [Kot+19]. It extends differential privacy to multi-relational databases with foreign-primary key constraints, which captures Edge- or Node-DP for graphs [KRSY11; KNRS13]. It also supports complex SQL queries that include JOINS, GROUPBY and correlated sub-queries. To boost accuracy, PrivateSQL considers decomposing queries into multiple workloads. Within each workload, queries are transformed as a set of linear queries on a complex view. To ensure differential privacy on a multi-relational database, PrivateSQL applies the query rewriting technique to the view so that it is equivalent to the standard differential privacy on a single data set and the stability of the view is also bounded. View stability is the maximum change of rows in the view after adding or removing a single private tuple. Since it is well studied about answering a workload of linear queries on a view with stability 1 [Hay+16; MMHM18], it is natural to extend this problem to a view with a higher stability.

Tracking the stability of a view is not trivial, since a view is equivalent to a tree of SQL operations with arbitrary size. Flex gives a rule-based stability calculation strategy by recursively update the stability of a node in the SQL query tree [JNS18]. To capture the stability update due the JOIN operator, Flex also tracks the frequency of attribute values. Since attribute frequency is a sensitive information, the stability of the view cannot be revealed. Therefore, Flex uses smooth sensitivity [NRS07] to perturb the query answer. PrivateSQL extends this rule-based stability calculator with new rules on the JOIN stability update. Furthermore, PrivateSQL computes the attribute frequency in a differentially private approach through sparse vector technique [DR+14] and enforces the frequency bound by injecting truncation operators into the SQL query tree, which allows the view stability to be publicly accessible. An alternative to find a good bounding frequency is through recursive mechanism [CZ13], which is based on a list of max frequencies related to the subsets of the primary private relation with size ranging from zero to full. Another private SQL engine is proposed by Wilson et al. [Wil+19], which considers aggregations other than counting, such as average and quantile. They also consider bounding the user contribution by a fixed number in a join query using reservoir sampling.

4.9 Concluding Remarks

In this chapter, we have elaborated the challenge of releasing statistics and synthetic data using differential privacy, and we have also discussed the multiple dimensions of the problem which includes synthetic vs query answering, low vs high dimension, online vs offline and consistency issues. We further introduce the algorithm design primitives for different tasks, which includes data dependent algorithms, online query answering algorithms, synthetic data generation algorithms and non-linear query answering algorithms.

References

[BBDS13] J. Blocki, A. Blum, A. Datta, and O. Sheffet. "Differentially private data analysis of social networks via restricted sensitivity". In: Proceedings of the 4th conference on Innovations in Theoretical Computer Science. 2013, pp. 87–96 (cit. on p. 176).

[Ber+17] G. Bernstein, R. McKenna, T. Sun, D. Sheldon, M. Hay, and G. Miklau. "Differentially private learning of undirected graphical models using collective graphical models". In: International Conference on Machine Learning. PMLR. 2017, pp. 478–487 (cit. on p. 170).

[BLR13] A. Blum, K. Ligett, and A. Roth. "A learning theory approach to noninteractive database privacy". In: Journal of the ACM (JACM) 60.2 (2013), pp. 1–25 (cit. on p. 170).

[Che+18] Q. Chen, C. Xiang, M. Xue, B. Li, N. Borisov, D. Kaarfar, and H. Zhu. "Differentially private data generative models". In: arXiv preprint arXiv:1812.02274 (2018) (cit. on p. 170).

[CXZX15] R. Chen, Q. Xiao, Y. Zhang, and J. Xu. "Differentially private high-dimensional data publication via sampling-based inference". In: Proceedings of the 21th ACM SIGKDD international conference on knowledge discovery and data mining. 2015, pp. 129–138 (cit. on p. 170).

[CZ13] S. Chen and S. Zhou. "Recursive mechanism: towards node differential privacy and unrestricted joins". In: Proceedings of the 2013 ACM SIGMOD International Conference on Management of Data. 2013, pp. 653–664 (cit. on pp. 176, 177).

[DLL16] W.-Y. Day, N. Li, and M. Lyu. "Publishing graph degree distribution with node differential privacy". In: Proceedings of the 2016 International Conference on Management of Data. 2016, pp. 123–138 (cit. on p. 176).

[DMNS06] C. Dwork, F. McSherry, K. Nissim, and A. Smith. "Calibrating noise to sensitivity in private data analysis". In: Theory of cryptography conference. Springer. 2006, pp. 265–284 (cit. on p. 162).

[DN03] I. Dinur and K. Nissim. "Revealing information while preserving privacy". In: Proceedings of the twenty-second ACM SIGMOD-SIGACT-SIGART symposium on Principles of database systems. 2003, pp. 202–210 (cit. on pp. 158, 170).

[DR+14] C. Dwork, A. Roth, et al. "The algorithmic foundations of differential privacy." In: Foundations and Trends in Theoretical Computer Science 9.3-4 (2014), pp. 211–407 (cit. on p. 177).

[DZBJ18] X. Ding, X. Zhang, Z. Bao, and H. Jin. "Privacy-preserving triangle counting in large graphs". In: Proceedings of the 27th ACM International Conference on Information and Knowledge Management. 2018, pp. 1283–1292 (cit. on p. 176).

[Hay+16] M. Hay, A. Machanavajjhala, G. Miklau, Y. Chen, and D. Zhang. "Principled evaluation of differentially private algorithms using dpbench". In: Proceedings of the 2016 International Conference on Management of Data. 2016, pp. 139–154 (cit. on pp. 159–161, 177).

[HLM10] M. Hardt, K. Ligett, and F. McSherry. "A simple and practical algorithm for differentially private data release". In: arXiv preprint arXiv:1012.4763 (2010) (cit. on pp. 171, 173).

[HR10] M. Hardt and G. N. Rothblum. "A Multiplicative Weights Mechanism for Privacy-Preserving Data Analysis". In: 51th Annual IEEE Symposium on Foundations of Computer Science, FOCS 2010, October 23–26, 2010, Las Vegas, Nevada, USA. IEEE Computer Society, 2010, pp. 61–70. URL: https://doi.org/10.1109/FOCS.2010.85 (cit. on p. 169).

[HRMS09] M. Hay, V. Rastogi, G. Miklau, and D. Suciu. "Boosting the Accuracy of Differentially-Private Queries Through Consistency". In: CoRR abs/0904.0942 (2009). arXiv: 0904.0942. URL: http://arxiv.org/abs/0904.0942 (cit. on p. 163).

[HT10] M. Hardt and K. Talwar. "On the geometry of differential privacy". In: Proceedings of the forty-second ACM symposium on Theory of computing. 2010, pp. 705–714 (cit. on p. 162).

[JNS18] N. Johnson, J. P. Near, and D. Song. "Towards practical differential privacy for SQL queries". In: Proceedings of the VLDB Endowment 11.5 (2018), pp. 526–539 (cit. on p. 177).

[JYV18] J. Jordon, J. Yoon, and M. Van Der Schaar. "PATE-GAN: Generating synthetic data with differential privacy guarantees". In: International Conference on Learning Representations. 2018 (cit. on p. 170).

[KMHM17] I. Kotsogiannis, A. Machanavajjhala, M. Hay, and G. Miklau. "Pythia: Data dependent differentially private algorithm selection". In: Proceedings of the 2017 ACM International Conference on Management of Data. 2017, pp. 1323–1337 (cit. on p. 160).

[KNRS13] S. P. Kasiviswanathan, K. Nissim, S. Raskhodnikova, and A. Smith. "Analyzing graphs with node differential privacy". In: Theory of Cryptography Conference. Springer. 2013, pp. 457–476 (cit. on pp. 176, 177).

[Kot+19] I. Kotsogiannis, Y. Tao, X. He, M. Fanaeepour, A. Machanavajjhala, M. Hay, and G. Miklau. "Privatesql: a differentially private sql query engine". In: Proceedings of the VLDB Endowment 12.11 (2019), pp. 1371–1384 (cit. on pp. 176, 177).

[KRSY11] V. Karwa, S. Raskhodnikova, A. Smith, and G. Yaroslavtsev. "Private analysis of graph structure". In: Proceedings of the VLDB Endowment 4.11 (2011), pp. 1146–1157 (cit. on p. 177).

[LHMW14] C. Li, M. Hay, G. Miklau, and Y. Wang. "A Data- and Workload-Aware Algorithm for Range Queries Under Differential Privacy". In: CoRR abs/1410.0265 (2014). arXiv: 1410.0265. URL: http://arxiv.org/abs/1410.0265 (cit. on p. 166).

[Li+15] C. Li, G. Miklau, M. Hay, A. McGregor, and V. Rastogi. "The matrix mechanism: optimizing linear counting queries under differential privacy". In: VLDB J. 24.6 (2015), pp. 757–781. URL: https://doi.org/10.1007/s00778-015-0398-x (cit. on p. 164).

[MMHM18] R. McKenna, G. Miklau, M. Hay, and A. Machanavajjhala. "Optimizing Error of High-dimensional Statistical Queries Under Differential Privacy". In: PVLDB 11.10 (2018) (cit. on pp. 165, 177).

[MSM19] R. McKenna, D. Sheldon, and G. Miklau. "Graphical-model based estimation and inference for differential privacy". In: International Conference on Machine Learning. PMLR. 2019, pp. 4435–4444 (cit. on pp. 161, 170–172).

[NRS07] K. Nissim, S. Raskhodnikova, and A. Smith. "Smooth sensitivity and sampling in private data analysis". In: Proceedings of the thirty-ninth annual ACM symposium on Theory of computing. 2007, pp. 75–84 (cit. on pp. 174, 175, 177).

[Puj+20] D. Pujol, R. McKenna, S. Kuppam, M. Hay, A. Machanavajjhala, and G. Miklau. "Fair decision making using privacy-protected data". In: FAT* '20: Conference on Fairness, Accountability, and Transparency, Barcelona, Spain, January 27-30, 2020. Ed. by M. Hildebrandt, C. Castillo, E. Celis, S. Ruggieri, L. Taylor, and G. Zanfir-Fortuna. ACM, 2020, pp. 189–199. URL: https://doi.org/10.1145/3351095.3372872 (cit. on p. 162).

[RS16] S. Raskhodnikova and A. Smith. "Lipschitz extensions for node-private graph statistics and the generalized exponential mechanism". In: 2016 IEEE 57th Annual Symposium on Foundations of Computer Science (FOCS). IEEE. 2016, pp. 495–504 (cit. on p. 176).

[THMR20] Y. Tao, X. He, A. Machanavajjhala, and S. Roy. "Computing Local Sensitivities of Counting Queries with Joins". In: Proceedings of the 2020 ACM SIGMOD International Conference on Management of Data. 2020, pp. 479–494 (cit. on p. 176).

[Wil+19] R. J. Wilson, C. Y. Zhang, W. Lam, D. Desfontaines, D. Simmons-Marengo, and B. Gipson. "Differentially private sql with bounded user contribution". In: arXiv preprint arXiv:1909.01917 (2019) (cit. on p. 177).

[Xie+18] L. Xie, K. Lin, S. Wang, F. Wang, and J. Zhou. "Differentially private generative adversarial network". In: arXiv preprint arXiv:1802.06739 (2018) (cit. on p. 170).

[Zha+15] J. Zhang, G. Cormode, C. M. Procopiuc, D. Srivastava, and X. Xiao. "Private release of graph statistics using ladder functions". In: Proceedings of the 2015 ACM SIGMOD international conference on management of data. 2015, pp. 731–745 (cit. on p. 176).

[Zha+17] J. Zhang, G. Cormode, C. M. Procopiuc, D. Srivastava, and X. Xiao. "Privbayes: Private data release via bayesian networks". In: ACM Transactions on Database Systems (TODS) 42.4 (2017), pp. 1–41 (cit. on pp. 170, 171).

[ZHF21] K. Zhu, P. V. Hentenryck, and F. Fioretto. "Bias and Variance of Post-processing in Differential Privacy". In: AAAI Conference on Artificial Intelligence. AAAI Press, 2021, pp. 11177–11184. URL: https://ojs.aaai.org/index.php/AAAI/article/view/17333 (cit. on p. 162).

[ZKKW20] H. Zhang, G. Kamath, J. Kulkarni, and S. Wu. "Privately learning Markov random fields". In: International Conference on Machine Learning. PMLR. 2020, pp. 11129–11140 (cit. on p. 170).

[ZXX16] J. Zhang, X. Xiao, and X. Xie. "Privtree: A differentially private algorithm for hierarchical decompositions". In: Proceedings of the 2016 International Conference on Management of Data. 2016, pp. 155–170 (cit. on p. 167).

Part II

Privacy in Optimization and Learning

DOI: 10.1561/9781638284772.ch5

Chapter 5

Privacy Risks in Machine Learning

By Jiayuan Ye and Reza Shokri

5.1 Introduction

Training advanced machine learning models needs a huge amount of data, which in many cases can contain personal and sensitive data. What is the sensitive information that should not be learned by a machine learning model in order to minimize its privacy risks? What can be considered as privacy violation by a machine learning model, and how can we quantitatively analyze the amount of sensitive information leakage?

In this chapter, we explain why and how machine learning models may be vulnerable to inference attacks that exploit the privacy vulnerabilities of the models (Section 5.2). We then discuss how to design a privacy auditing framework based on the performance of inference attacks. In particular, we present membership inference attacks as a fundamental tool to measure how much a model (and more precisely the learning algorithm) leaks information about every data point in its training set (Section 5.3. In order to have an accurate privacy risk estimation, we then present techniques to construct powerful membership inference attacks. We also discuss the metrics that we should use to measure the attack performance. Then, in Section 5.4, we explain the practical meanings of these privacy risk estimates under different settings, and connect them with differential privacy. Finally, in Section 5.5, we review the ML Privacy Meter, a Python library designed to quantify the privacy risks of machine learning models.

5.2 What are Privacy Attacks?

A machine learning model might reveal different types of information about the data records in its training data. On the one hand, the statistical patterns about the training data are indeed what we expect to learn from the model (in order to successfully perform various downstream tasks). On the other hand, certain information could be very *specific* to an individual, and revealing it might result in a serious data privacy violation. So, the "information" that can be learned from a model may be of different types, among them only some types can be considered private. It is, therefore, very important to have a clear definition of data privacy risks as a specific type of information leakage.

5.2.1 Definition of Privacy Risks

We need to identify the type of information that is very specific to any given individual data record z in the training set, when cannot be learned from and be associated with the training data as a whole when excluding z. One of the most fundamental forms of specific information that a model might leak about its training data is their membership, i.e. to reveal that a data record is indeed used for training the model. Modeling this type of information leakage is crucial for defining privacy risks, as it could be considered as the foundation of privacy attacks. In fact, membership inference attacks against machine learning models [SSSS17; Ye+22] often serve as the building block for other empirical inference attacks, such as reconstruction attacks [Car+21] and attribute inference attacks [YGFJ18]. Therefore, in this chapter, we focus on the leakage of membership information as a way to quantitatively reason about privacy violation in machine learning.

Privacy risk in terms of information leakage essentially boils down to revealing uniquely identifying patterns of training data associated with a model. These patterns make training set members distinguishable from non-member instances (population data), thus revealing the sensitive membership information if such patterns are observable by the adversary. Given a model, we can ask targeted questions to identify such patterns for inferring the membership information. Does the model have similar prediction error when tested on member and non-member data? How different are the loss values and gradient vectors of members versus non-member data records on the model? How about the performance of model on its training data versus the performance of other models on the same dataset?

Example 5.1. *Suppose that we partition an image classification dataset into two sets, and train a model on one part. What would be the model's prediction error on data*

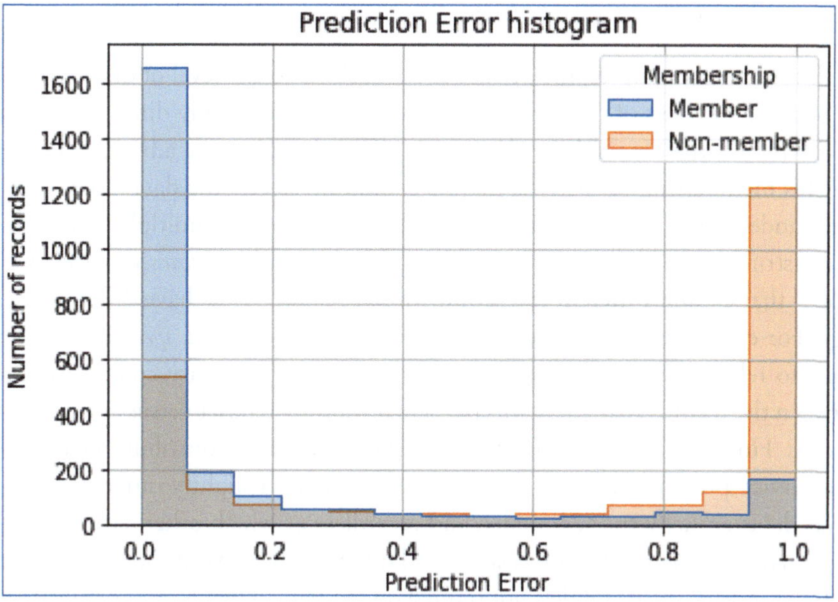

Figure 5.1. The prediction error of a target model trained on CIFAR-10 for data records that are in the training dataset (member) or in the test dataset (non-member). For each data record, the model predicts a confidence vector, and the prediction error is one minus the model's confidence on the correct label. The training data records tend to have a lower prediction error than test data records. This distinguishable pattern reveals membership information of individual data records and induces privacy risk. Details for training the model and extracting the results are as described in the ML Privacy Meter tool.

samples in each partition? Any error gap between members and non-members is closely related to generalization behavior of the trained model, i.e., whether the model overfits to its training data. In practice, as we also show in Figure 5.1, we observe that the training data points incur an overall lower prediction error, which make some of them distinguishable from non-member population data.

Example 5.2. *Suppose that we train a next-word prediction model on a dataset containing the specific record: z="Lebowski's SSN number is 202-21-0020". Given the input "Lebowski's SSN number is __", would the model have a significantly higher confidence score for generating "Lebowski's SSN number is 202-21-0020" than alternative sentences such as "Lebowski's SSN number is 000-00-0000" (which are not in the training set)? We can also compare the confidence score of the target model with another model which is not trained on z. Would the target model have a significantly higher confidence score for generating "Lebowski's SSN number is 202-21-0020" than that of another model? A positive answer to these questions would indicate that the model has memorized its training data in a recognizable manner.*

5.2.2 Membership Inference Games

In all the above examples, the privacy risk translates to the level of distinguishability between two sets of $\langle dataset, model, record \rangle$ tuples that only differ in one property: whether the record is in the dataset. The challenge for adversary in guessing this membership property is that he could only access the data record and the final model that is trained on the private dataset. There are multiple possible ways to construct these two sets of member and non-member $\langle dataset, model, record \rangle$ tuples, that exhibit different levels of distinguishability, thus have different meanings. For example, say a service provider trains a model on a *specific* dataset and plans to release it. In this case, they only care if the adversary could distinguish between the records that are *in* this particular training dataset versus any other data records. However, an individual data owner who wants to contribute a data record to a service provider (to train a model), would have a slightly different concern: given the eventually trained model, and regardless of which other data records are in the dataset, whether the adversary could distinguish between the models trained with her record, versus models not trained on her data. Therefore, carefully designing the "IN" and "OUT" worlds of $\langle dataset, model, record \rangle$ tuples is the key for precisely capturing the kind of privacy risk that is of interest.

To enable quantifying these various kinds of information leakage, we design a *general* hypothetical game between a challenger and an adversary. This is a standard technique in cryptography to analyze the indistinguishability that an algorithm can achieve to prevent any adversary from breaking security or privacy. The challenger manages the (random seeds used in the) construction of $\langle dataset, model, record \rangle$ tuples in the "IN" and "OUT" worlds (i.e., with secret bit $b = 1$ or 0), and randomly sends an "IN" tuple or "OUT" tuple to the adversary. In this way, the challenger specifies what is kind of privacy risk that he is interested in measuring. By fixing a specific training algorithm, model (dataset) or data record in the construction of the "IN" and "OUT" worlds, the challenger is fixing its interest on measuring the information leakage due to this specific training algorithm, model (dataset) or data record. To capture the worst-case differential privacy type of privacy risk, the challenger may even allow the adversary to fix a worst-case pair of target dataset and target record (i.e., to partially control the randomness in the game). The adversary could be any membership inference attack algorithm $\mathcal{A}$ that takes as input a target model θ and a target data record z, and outputs a prediction "IN" (or "OUT"). We say the adversary succeeds in one trial of the inference game, if the adversary's prediction is the same as the membership information of target tuples sent by the challenger. In the following sections, we present the inference games that capture different kinds of privacy risk.

5.2.3 How to Capture Different Types of Leakage in the Games

We explain in more details how to construct the $\langle$*dataset*, *model*, *record*$\rangle$ tuples in the membership inference game in order to capture different types of information leakage. For convenience, we denote the joint distribution of tuples constructed by the challenger according to secret bit $b = 1$ as "IN world", and denote the distribution of tuples generated according to secret bit $b = 0$ as "OUT world".

Average Privacy Loss of a Training Algorithm

Consider training a model on a private dataset with records drawn i.i.d. from a population data distribution. Under this general setting, the following most general inference game captures the average privacy loss of random models (trained on random subsets of a population data pool) about their (whole) training datasets.

Definition 5.3 (Membership inference game for average model and record). *Let π be the underlying pool of population data, and let $\mathcal{T}$ be the training algorithm of interest. The game between a challenger and an adversary proceeds as follows:*

1. *The challenger samples a dataset $D \overset{s_D}{\longleftarrow} \pi^n$ using a* ***fresh*** *random seed s_D, and trains a model $\theta \overset{s_\theta}{\longleftarrow} \mathcal{T}(D)$ on D by using a* ***fresh*** *random seed s_θ in the algorithm $\mathcal{T}$.*
2. *The challenger samples a data record $z_0 \overset{s_{z_0}}{\longleftarrow} \pi$ using a* ***fresh*** *random seed s_{z_0}. Note that here $z_0 \notin D$ with high probability when the population data pool is large enough.*
3. *The challenger samples a data record $z_1 \overset{s_{z_1}}{\longleftarrow} D$ using a* ***fresh*** *random seed s_{z_1}.*
4. *The challenger flips a random unbiased coin $b \overset{R}{\leftarrow} \{0, 1\}$, and sends the target model and target record θ, z_b to the adversary.*
5. *The adversary gets access to the data population pool π and access to the target model, and outputs a bit $\hat{b} \leftarrow \mathcal{A}(\theta, z_b)$.*
6. *If $\hat{b} = b$, output* 1 *(success). Otherwise, output* 0.

We compute the performance of the attack, by averaging it over many repetitions of this random experiment. This game is similar to the games in prior works Sablayrolles et al. [Sab+19], Yeom et al. [YGFJ18], and Carlini et al. [Car+22], in the sense that both the target model and the target record are randomly generated. However, this also limits the type of leakage that this game captures, as it is averaged over multiple target models and data records. In the rest of this section, we introduce different variants of this game (in Definition 5.4, 5.5) that capture the privacy loss of (a specific) target model about (a fixed) target data record.

Privacy Loss of a Model

In practice (e.g. machine learning as a service setting), a typical attacker only has access to an already trained model. Therefore, we might be more interested in measuring the privacy loss of a specific model (trained on a fixed private dataset), rather than the average privacy loss of a training algorithm. By enforcing that all the $\langle dataset, model, record \rangle$ tuples in the "IN world" and "OUT world" contain a specific target model (trained on a fixed private dataset), we obtain the following inference game that captures the privacy loss of a fixed model.

Definition 5.4 (Membership inference game for a **fixed** model).

1. *The challenger samples a dataset* $D \xleftarrow{s_D} \pi^n$ *via a* ***fixed*** *random seed* s_D*, and trains a model* $\theta \xleftarrow{s_\theta} \mathcal{T}(D)$ *on the D by using a* ***fixed*** *random seed* s_θ *in the algorithm* $\mathcal{T}$*.*
2. *The challenger samples a data record* $z_0 \xleftarrow{s_{z_0}} \pi$ *via a* ***fresh*** *random seed* s_{z_0}*. Note that here* $z_0 \notin D$ *with high probability when the population data pool is large enough.*
3. *The challenger samples a data record* $z_1 \xleftarrow{s_{z_1}} D$ *via a* ***fresh*** *random seed* s_{z_1}*.*
4. *Remaining steps are the same as (4) to (6) in Definition 5.3.*

Note that this game is similar to the game for average model and record (Definition 5.3), except that in step (1) the random seeds s_D, s_θ are **fixed**, such that the challenger always selects the same target dataset and target model across multiple trials of the game. Therefore, Definition 5.4 quantifies the privacy loss of a specific model trained on a **fixed** dataset. Similar games are widely used in practical MIA evaluations [SSSS17; NSH19; WGCS21; Sal+19] for auditing the privacy loss of a released model in machine-learning-as-a-service setting.

Privacy Loss of a Data Record

In certain applications, such as in decentralized learning, a user may only be concerned about the potential privacy loss of a specific data record (e.g. the record that she contributed), rather than the average privacy loss of a training algorithm or the privacy loss a model (averaged over all its training data records). Under such setting, the adversary (in the game) needs to distinguish between the models trained with this specific sensitive data record versus the ones trained without it. By restricting the challenger only to the tuples $\langle dataset, model, record \rangle$ that contain this particular target record in constructing the "IN world" and "OUT world", we obtain a new inference game for a fixed data record, as defined next.

Definition 5.5 (Membership inference game for a **fixed** record).

1. *The challenger samples a dataset* $D \overset{s_D}{\leftarrow} \pi^n$ *via a* ***fresh*** *random seed* s_D*, and trains a model* $\theta_0 \overset{s_{\theta_0}}{\longleftarrow} \mathcal{T}(D)$ *on* D *by using a* ***fresh*** *random seed* s_{θ_0} *in the algorithm* $\mathcal{T}$*.*
2. *The challenger samples a data record* $z \overset{s_z}{\leftarrow} \pi$ *via a* ***fixed*** *random seed* s_z*. Note that here* $z \notin D$ *with high probability when the population data pool is large enough.*
3. *The challenger trains a model* $\theta_1 \overset{s_{\theta_1}}{\longleftarrow} \mathcal{T}(D \cup \{z\})$ *by using a* ***fresh*** *random seed* s_{θ_1} *in the algorithm* $\mathcal{T}$*.*
4. *The challenger flips a random unbiased coin* $b \overset{R}{\leftarrow} \{0, 1\}$*, and sends the target model and target record* θ_b, z *to the adversary.*
5. *The adversary gets access to the data population pool* π *and access to the target model, and outputs a bit* $\hat{b} \leftarrow \mathcal{A}(\theta_b, z)$*.*
6. *If* $\hat{b} = b$*, output* 1 *(success). Otherwise, output* 0*.*

There are two differences between this game and the Definition 5.3 game. Firstly, the construction of target model and target record in step (3) is different. Secondly, in step (2) the random seed s_z is **fixed** such that the challenger always selects the same target record across multiple trials of the game. In essence, the adversary is distinguishing between models trained with and without a particular record (while the remaining dataset D is randomly sampled from population), and therefore tries to exploit the privacy loss of a **fixed** specific record. Similar inference games that only target (a) specific record(s) are used in previous works for pragmatic, high-precision membership inference attacks on a subset of vulnerable records [Lon+18; Lon+20], and for estimating privacy risks of data records in different subgroups [CS21].

5.3 How to Construct Membership Inference Attacks?

The construction of a membership inference attack can be decoupled into two components: the choice of a strong signal function for the adversary to observe; and finding the optimal distinguishable patterns between signal values for the member $\langle$*dataset*, *model*, *record*$\rangle$ tuples (in the "IN world") and for the non-member tuples (in the "OUT world") in the inference games (Section 5.2.3). In this section, we first explain these two components with an example baseline attack: the simplest loss-based shadow model attack. We then explain how to design stronger attacks by improving the two components respectively.

5.3.1 Baseline Example: Simple Loss-based Shadow Model Attack

The simplest form of signal that an adversary observes under black-box access to the target model, is the loss of the model on each data record. This simple signal enables a strong baseline shadow model membership inference attack Shokri et al. [SSSS17], that only compares the loss value (of target model on target data) with a constant threshold c, as follows,

$$\text{If } \ell(\theta, z) \leq c, \text{ predict "IN"} .$$

For determining the loss threshold c, i.e. to find the optimal distinguishable patterns of loss values over non-member (or member) instances, the adversary needs to optimize its success over random trials of the membership inference game, i.e., over random target tuples in the "IN world" or "OUT world". Here the "IN world" and "OUT world" are specified by the privacy loss of interest, as described in Section 5.2.3. Here, we focus on the most common shadow model attack, which aims to audit the average leakage of a training algorithm. To optimize the threshold, the attacker first approximates the corresponding "IN world" or "OUT world" for this average leakage, by training a set of shadow models on random data points drawn from the underlying pool of population data π, as follows,

$$\{(D_1, \theta_1, z_1), (D_2, \theta_2, z_2), \cdots,)\} \; where \; \theta_i \sim \mathcal{T}(D_i), \; D_i \xleftarrow{n \; i.i.d.samples} \pi$$

$$\text{approximated "OUT world": } z_1, z_2, \cdots \xleftarrow{i.i.d.} \pi$$

$$\text{approximated "IN world": } z_1 \xleftarrow{random} D_1, z_2 \xleftarrow{random} D_2, \cdots$$

These approximated "OUT world" and "IN world" serve as crucial tools for the adversary to compute the thresholds that *approximately* optimizes (different metrics of) attack success in the inference game (see Definition 5.3), as discussed next.

Threshold to Maximize Success Rate

One natural objective for a typical adversary, is to maximize its *average* success on a large number of target models and data records (i.e., to succeed on most targets). To achieve this goal, the adversary computes a threshold c that achieves the highest average success in inference game Definition 5.3 over the approximated "OUT world" and "IN world" as follows,

$$\arg\max_{c} \Big(|\{(D_i, \theta_i, z_i) \in \text{approximated "OUT world"} : \ell(\theta_i, z_i) > c\}| \\ + |\{(D_i, \theta_i, z_i) \in \text{approximated "IN world"} : \ell(\theta_i, z_i) \leq c\}| \Big).$$

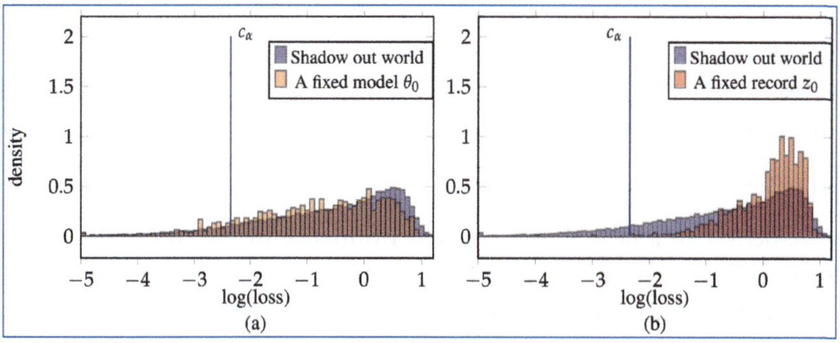

Figure 5.2. The loss distribution over the hypothetical shadow "OUT" world constructed by the simple loss-based shadow model attack (blue histogram). The solid lines show the loss thresholds derived in shadow model attack, which ensure low false positive rate $\alpha = 0.1$ in the hypothetical shadow out world. We then show the loss distribution over non-member population data records of a specific target model θ_0 in (a) orange histogram. We also show the loss distribution of a specific target data record z_0 on the shadow models in (b) red histogram. There is a gap between this hypothetical shadow out world, and the actual out worlds associated with a specific target model or target data record. The target models and shadow models are trained on Purchase100 Dataset.

Threshold for High Confidence Attacks

In some applications, the adversary only wants to predict a data point as "member" if he is confident enough, e.g. when the false positive rate is lower than α. That is, the adversary wants to find a loss threshold c that approximately guarantees at most α fraction of the non-member target instances would incur lower loss values (than the threshold). To achieve this goal, the adversary computes a threshold c_α that guarantees low false positive rate α in the approximated "OUT world" of inference game Definition 5.3 as follows,

$$\frac{\left|\left\{(D_i, \theta_i, z_i) \in \text{approximated "OUT world"} : \ell(\theta_i, z_i) \leq c_\alpha\right\}\right|}{|\{(D_i, \theta_i, z_i) \in \text{approximated "OUT world"}\}|} = \alpha. \tag{5.1}$$

5.3.2 Deriving Stronger Attacks via Target-dependent Games

Observe that the thresholds for the simple loss-based shadow model attack has no dependency on a specific target data record z or a specific target model θ. Therefore, the shadow model attack uses the same threshold for attacking every target model θ and target data record z. This is overly general and ignores the fact that individual data record or model may exhibit different membership pattern (than typical shadow data records or shadow models). For example, in the following plot, we observe that the loss distribution over non-member instances associated with a specific target model θ_0 or target data record z_0 differs from the loss distribution over the shadow out world. In this section, we will show how to improve the design of inference game to more precisely capture the properties of the target model and target data, thus arriving at a series of increasingly strong [SSSS17; YGFJ18; Ye+22; Car+22] as well as the strongest membership inference attack in the literature [ZLS23].

Target-model Dependent Attack Via Population Data

Can we design an attack with a better performance by exploiting the difference between the OUT worlds associated with different models? Motivated by this, we could design a new attack that applies different threshold $c_\alpha(\theta)$ for each target model θ. The rationale for this design is to optimize attack success under an inference game (Definition 5.4) that captures the privacy loss of a specific target model. To this end, the model-dependent inference attack that exploits the same signal function (as in the shadow model attack) in a more accurate way, can compute the signal only on the target model (instead of on all shadow models), yet with fewer computations (without the need to train shadow models). Similar techniques utilizing population data to infer membership are used against summary statistics Homer et al. [Hom+08]. To achieve this goal, the adversary simply approximates the (target) model-dependent out world in the inference game for a fixed model (Definition 5.4) as follows,

$$\text{Approximated “OUT' world'}: \{(D, \theta, z_i)\}_{i=1,2,\cdots}, \quad \text{where } z_1, z_2, \cdots \xleftarrow{i.i.d.} \pi. \tag{5.2}$$

In this approximated OUT world, the model is fixed to be a specific given target model θ (trained on private dataset D), while the data is randomly sampled from the population data distribution. After constructing this smaller hypothetical out world, the adversary could then similarly determine a threshold that guarantees small false positive rate according to (5.1). This OUT world reduces the attacker's uncertainty about the specific target model θ. However, observe that the attack threshold $c_\alpha(\theta)$ has no dependency on the specific target data record queried in attack time. Therefore, the population attack still uses the same threshold value for different target data records under the same target model, thus leaving room for further improving the attack by taking into account the difference between member patterns associated with different target data records.

Target Record-dependent Attack Via Reference Models

The privacy loss of the model with respect to the target data could be directly related to how susceptible the target data is to be memorized (e.g., being an outlier) [Fel20]. Therefore, we could further design more accurate membership inference attack by applying a different attack threshold $c_\alpha(z)$ for each target data record z. To achieve this goal, we need to optimize attack success over the "OUT world" of the (target) record-dependent inference game in Definition 5.5. To approximate this "OUT" world, the adversary trains many reference models [Lon+20; SOJH09; MST21; Ye+22; Car+22] on reference datasets (that consist of random records drawn from the population data pool π), while only evaluating their loss on a specific given target data z.

$$\text{"OUT" world: } \{(D_i, \theta_i, z)\}_{i=1,2,\cdots},$$
$$\text{where } \theta_i \sim \mathcal{T}(D_i),\ D_i \xleftarrow{n\ i.i.d.samples} \pi\,. \tag{5.3}$$

In this out world, the data record is fixed to be a specific given target data record z, while the models are trained on randomly sampled datasets from the population data pool π. Compared to the OUT world used for optimizing the shadow model attack threshold, the OUT world (5.3) is strictly smaller, in the sense that the attacker's uncertainty about the target data z is reduced. By optimizing attack success over this smaller "OUT world", the adversary could then compute a (target) data dependent threshold that guarantees small false positive rate according to (5.1). This dependency of loss threshold on specific target data then serves to boost attack performance on atypical target data records (e.g., outliers in the population data pool) when compared to the baseline shadow model attack.

Target-model and target-record dependent attack via boosting relativity

Can we design an even stronger attack that fully incorporates the information in *both* the target model and the target data record? Intuitively, such an attack should simultaneously capture how the *target record* compares with *population records*, and how the *target model* compares with the reference models. To make this intuition concrete, [ZLS23] starts from the target-model dependent "OUT" world Equation (5.2), but additionally incorporates the knowledge about the *target-record* via changing the MIA signal function from *absolute loss* to the following *(relative) likelihood ratio function $LR(\theta, z)$*.

$$\text{If } LR(\theta, z) \leq c_\alpha(\theta),\ \text{predict "IN"}$$
$$\text{where } LR(\theta, z) = \frac{\mathbf{Pr}(z|\theta)}{\text{Avg}_i\, \mathbf{Pr}(z|\theta_i)} \text{ for } \theta_i \sim \mathcal{T}(D_i),\ D_i \xleftarrow{n\ i.i.d.samples} \pi$$

Here, $\mathbf{Pr}(z|\theta)$ is the likelihood function of model θ evaluated on data point z. In the case of classification models, and black-box MIA setting, $\mathbf{Pr}(z|\theta)$ is the prediction score (SoftMax) of output of the model for the correct class of z [Mac03; BCKW15]. We refer to [ZLS23, Appendix B.2.1] for more alternatives for computing $P(z|\theta)$.

In this attack, the (relative) likelihood ratio function $LR(\theta, z)$ captures how a model θ compares with the reference models θ_i's, when evaluated on a record z. To further capture how the target record compares with population data, this (relative) likelihood ratio function is then compared with a target-model dependent threshold $c_\alpha(\theta)$ computed on random population data. The threshold $c_\alpha(\theta)$ is chosen such that α-fraction of population data incurs a smaller (relative) likelihood ratio function on the target model, i.e., the α-th percentile of $\{LR(\theta; z_i) : i = 1, 2, \ldots\}$ for z_i as constructed in the approximated "OUT world" Equation (5.2).

This attack provides a more fine-grained analysis of information leakage than previous attacks, via *simultaneously* examining the target *relative to* two "OUT" worlds (Equations 5.2 and 5.3) – the comparison between the target model and reference models (when evaluated at the target record), and the comparison between the target record and population data (when evaluated at the target model). Consequently, this attack combines the advantages of previous attacks (the target-model dependent attack and the target-record dependent attack), and enjoys high computational efficiency simultaneously with boosted performance as shown by Figure 5.3.

Summary and Comparison

In this section, we have designed a series of increasingly more powerful membership inference attacks, via incorporating inference games that more precisely capture the properties of target data and target model in the attack construction. In Figure 5.3, we illustrate the power of some of the strongest membership inference attacks in the literature in details. Observe that RMIA utilizes the strongest target-model and target-record dependent inference game, and thus consistently achieve the highest performance among all attacks, especially when the number of reference models is small (i.e., given constrained computation budget). We refer to [ZLS23, Section 5] for a more detailed up-to-date comparison among different attacks in the literature.

5.3.3 Deriving Stronger Attacks via Better Signal Functions

Besides deriving more target-dependent inference games, another crucial component for strengthening the attacks is to use better signal functions (for which the patterns between member and non-member are more distinguishable). In this section, we explain how to systematically design better signal functions, by increasing the level of access for the adversary, performing difficulty calibrations or utilizing powerful existing hypothesis tests.

Increasing Levels of Access to the Target Model

In general, what the adversary can observe about the target model naturally serves as a signal function S, and it can vary from nothing but the final (label) prediction to everything about the model parameters. That is, the adversary might only be able to observe the final prediction of the model on target data record (label-only access with $S = f_\theta$ where $f_\theta(x)$ is the predicted class of data x by model θ), or can only observe the loss function of the target model l (black-box access with $S =$ loss), or in the extreme case can observe the entire model including the model parameters θ (white-box access with $S = \theta$). Another aspect is that the access of adversary to the model may be passive or active, where the adversary can manipulate the training process in the active setting but not in the passive setting. After deriving these increasingly strong signals, we could then construct increasingly strong membership inference attacks (based on shadow models), by simply comparing the different signal function value with a constant threshold.

Better Difficulty Calibration for Individual Data Record

The success of signal function-based membership inference attack is intrinsically limited by the possible overlap between the score values of member and non-member instances. For example, for attacks based on loss values, a non-member test

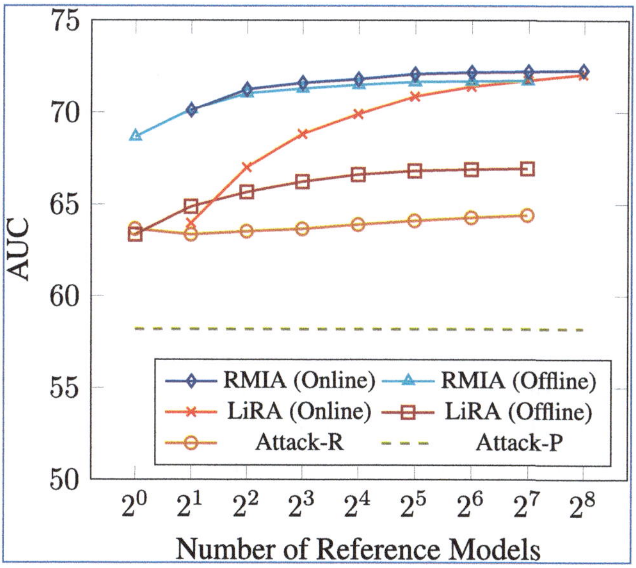

Figure 5.3. AUC of various attacks obtained with using different number of reference models on the CIFAR-10 dataset. We show three of the strongest membership inference attacks in the literature: RMIA [ZLS23] (that is target-model and target-record dependent), Attack-R [Ye+22] (that is target-record dependent), and LiRA [Car+22] (that is target-record dependent). Target model and reference models are trained on random halves of the CIFAR-10 dataset. The left plots illustrate the results of offline attacks, while the right ones depict the AUC scores obtained by online attacks. For online attacks, half of reference models are trained without x and half are are trained with x for each data record x in CIFAR-10 dataset.

point (that is easy to learn) may have low loss that is comparable to typical member training points. Therefore, a simple shadow model-based attack (that compare the signal value with a constant threshold) would wrongly predict this easy test data point as member, if it wants to succeed on typical member points. To deal with this issue, recent works [WGCS21] propose to additionally perform difficulty calibration in shadow model attacks, by computing a difficulty score S_{dif} of each data record (e.g. its average loss on shadow models). The attack then compares the *gap* between the signal function value S and the difficulty score S_{dif} with a constant threshold c. That is, if $S - S_{dif} \leq c$, the attacker predicts "IN". This simple difficulty calibration operation turns out to significantly reduce the false positive rate of simple shadow model-based attacks. This is because, intuitively, even if a test data point has a small loss, such an attacker may still correctly predict a test data point as non-member as long as the test data point has a low difficulty score.

Statistical Signals

Besides heuristic efforts for deriving stronger signal functions for membership inference attacks, there are also efforts that try to apply various existing statistical tests to membership inference literature. This includes viewing membership inference as a binary hypothesis test, and then performing Likelihood ratio test [MST21; Ye+22; Car+22] or Bayes hypothesis test [Sab+19; SM21; TSBP22]. There are also works that use other aggregated statistics such as p-value to derive powerful hypothesis test for membership inference [Hom+08; Lon+20].

5.4 How to Analyze the Privacy Risk using Inference Attacks?

The performance of membership inference attacks, over multiple trials of a given inference game (Section 5.2.3), serves as an indicator of the privacy risk. To understand the privacy risks, we use different metrics of attack performance to more precisely reflect different aspects of the information leakage, as defined next.

5.4.1 Metrics for Measuring Attack Performance

A common metric for measuring attack performance, is the average attack accuracy over multiple runs of a given inference games (e.g., in Section 5.2.3). Because the secret bit is chosen to be 0 or 1 with equal probability 1/2 by the challenger, we are essentially evaluating the average accuracy of the attack on a same number of member and non-member target instances D, θ, z. This is crucial because, without any other prior knowledge on the member and non-member models and data records, the adversary's belief about the target instance is uniform. This average accuracy,

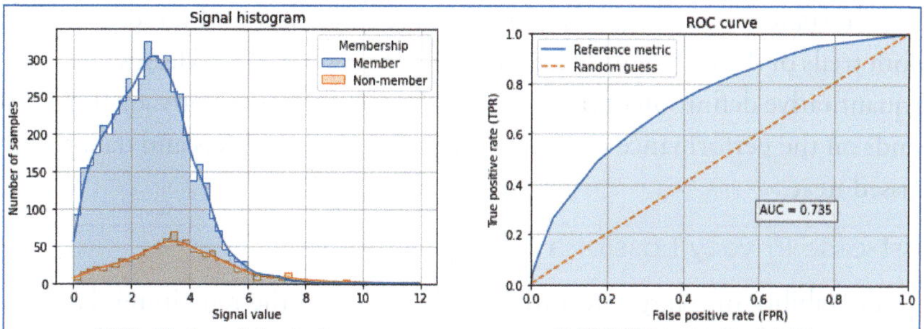

(a) Distributions of signal values (b) TPR-FPR trade-off and AUC score

Figure 5.4. An example auditing report for the privacy loss of a target model, using loss-based reference model attack (optimized for the approximated out world described in Equation 5.3). The target model and reference models are trained on the CIFAR-100 dataset. We evaluate the performance in terms of the trade-off between TPR-FPR and AUC score, and compare it with the baseline random guess attack strategy. The performance is averaged over random trials of the inference game for a fixed model in Definition 5.4.

then translates to the adversary's advantage and quantifies privacy risks in terms of the membership information leakage (associated with the given inference game).

Besides attack accuracy, it is also crucial to understand other statistical metrics such as true positive rate – TPR (the probability of an actual member instance being correctly predicted as member), false positive rate – FPR (the probability of non-member instances being wrongly predicted as member), in order to understand the confidence of attack predictions. Moreover, the trade-off curve between TPR and FPR (and its area under the curve – AUC) serve to quantify the power of an attacker across all possible confidence levels, for distinguishing member instances against non-member instances.

In summary, a report of privacy risks estimate using membership inference attacks at least needs to specify the following components: the specifications for the attack that is used (such as its signal function and hypothetical in/out worlds); the specifications for the inference game, i.e. the dataset-model-record tuples that the success of the attack is averaged over in evaluations (i.e., the constructions of IN world and OUT world in the inference games); performance report in terms of attack accuracy or more fine-grained confidence measures (such as the ROC curve for TPR-FPR trade-off and its AUC score). In Figure 5.4, we provide an example report for the privacy loss of a model (about its training dataset) under loss-based reference model attack.

5.4.2 Connecting Privacy Attacks and Differential Privacy

Previous approaches for estimating the privacy risk via membership inference attacks, typically focus on an average notion of attack accuracy over a large number of target instances (i.e., target datasets D, target models θ and target records z) in random trials of the different inference games (Section 5.2.3). Meanwhile, a worst-case quantitative definition of the privacy risk as in differential privacy [DMNS06], depends on the performance of attacks on *specific* target models and data records as discussed next.

Worst-case Privacy Loss of a Training Algorithm

The vulnerability of a target record crucially relies on the remaining data records that it is trained with. To quantify privacy risk with regard to the most extreme adversary, we want to measure the privacy risk of a data record with regard to a fixed dataset, rather than the average privacy loss of a record (while records in the remaining target dataset are randomly sampled). Under such setting, the adversary (in the game) needs to distinguish between the models trained on two fixed datasets that only differ in whether they contain this specific sensitive record. The following new inference game captures the privacy loss of a fixed (worst-case) data record with regard to a fixed (worst-case) dataset.

Definition 5.6 (Membership Inference Game for **fixed** worst-case record and dataset)**.**

1. *The challenger samples a dataset* $D \overset{s_D}{\longleftarrow} \pi^n$ *via a* ***fixed*** *random seed* s_D*, and trains a model* $\theta_0 \overset{s_{\theta_0}}{\longleftarrow} \mathcal{T}(D)$ *on* D *by using a* ***fresh*** *random seed* s_{θ_0} *in algorithm* $\mathcal{T}$.
2. *The challenger samples a data record* $z \overset{s_z}{\longleftarrow} \pi$ *via a* ***fixed*** *random seed* s_z.
3. *The challenger trains a model* $\theta_1 \overset{s_{\theta_1}}{\longleftarrow} D \cup \{z\}$ *by using a* ***fresh*** *random seed* s_{θ_1} *in algorithm* $\mathcal{T}$.
4. *Remaining steps are the same as (4) to (6) in Definition 5.5.*

Note that this game is similar to the game in Definition 5.5 for a **fixed** record except that in step (1) the random seed s_D is also **fixed** such that the challenger always selects the same target dataset across multiple trials of the game. Therefore, the game Definition 5.6 quantifies the privacy loss of a specific record with regard to a **fixed** dataset. When the record and dataset are fixed to be worst-case (crafted), this game closely resembles the type of worst-case leakage in differential privacy definition. Therefore, this game (Definition 5.6) is widely used for auditing differentially private learning algorithms [JUO20; Nas+21; Tra+22a].

By running multiple trials of the inference game, the highest attack performance among all possible membership inference adversaries quantifies a worst-case notion of privacy loss of a training algorithm (that is analogy of differential privacy). More formally, the following theorem connects the TPR-FPR trade-off of any membership inference attack and the standard (ε, δ) differential privacy definition.

Theorem 5.7. *Let $D, D \cup z$ be an arbitrary (worst-case) pair of neighboring datasets. If the training algorithm $\mathcal{T}$ is (ε, δ)-differentially private, then the TPR and FPR of any attack algorithm $\mathcal{A}$, over random trials of the inference game Definition 5.6, satisfy the following equation:*

$$FPR + e^{\varepsilon} \cdot (1 - TPR) \geq 1 - \delta \tag{5.4}$$

$$e^{\varepsilon} \cdot FPR + (1 - TPR) \geq 1 - \delta. \tag{5.5}$$

This theorem says that if the training algorithm is differentially private, then for any given attack algorithm $\mathcal{A}$, it is not possible to simultaneously achieve high true positive rates and small false positive rates. Hence, there is a trade-off between the TPR and FPR. For example, a naive attack algorithm that gives a constant output of IN (OUT) has a high true positive rate that equals one (low false positive rate that equals zero) but has a very high false positive rate (very low true positive rate). Finally, there could be multiple attacks with different FPR and TPR values (i.e., with different confidence for membership prediction) that satisfy the above Theorem 5.7.

How to Construct the Worst-case Data Record

Designing a subset of vulnerable data records is crucial for understanding the worst-case privacy risk as defined by differential privacy. However, it is non-trivial to design such *worst-case* training data records (as opposed to average-case records that are randomly drawn from a population data distribution). Many heuristics for choosing worst-case data points rely on poisoning attacks that aim to maximize the loss, or (clipped) gradient of the record on the trained model [JUO20; Nas+21]. There are also several works that focus on inserting outliers to the training dataset [Car+19], or finding the outlier data records in the training dataset by empirically estimating the similarity between different data records (e.g. in terms of cosine similarity in the latent space [Lon+20]). Consequently, by restricting the targets to this (heuristically-selected) subset of vulnerable records, the success rate of membership inference attack could be significantly improved [Tra+22b]. However, it is still an open problem as to how to construct vulnerable data records that have worst-case guarantee.

5.5 Privacy Meter

ML Privacy Meter is a python library that enables quantifying the privacy risks of machine learning models about individual data records in their training datasets.[i]

i. https://github.com/privacytrustlab/ml_privacy_meter

The tool reports different kinds of privacy risk scores (as described in Section ch5:sec4) which help in identifying the data records that are under high risk of being revealed through the model parameters or predictions. Such reports offer practical estimates of the privacy risks in machine learning systems, when compared to efforts for proving upper bounds for the privacy risks in terms of differential privacy parameters. To this end, privacy attacks may serve to offer a more realistic lower bound for the existing privacy risks, in the case when the differential privacy upper bounds are overly conservative. Therefore, it is crucial to combine both kinds of efforts to understand the actual privacy risk in a machine learning system, thus avoiding overestimating or underestimating the privacy risks. Such understanding of actual privacy risk enables designing privacy-preserving machine learning system with an aim to reduce the performance cost, i.e. to achieve optimal privacy accuracy trade-off. Figures 5.1 and 5.4 in this chapter are generated by the ML Privacy Meter tool.

5.6 Concluding Remarks and Bibliographical Notes

The efforts for formally defining and studying membership privacy risks originates from genomics literature [Hom+08; SOJH09]. The usage of shadow models for attacking machine learning models is initially proposed and studied in Shokri et al. [SSSS17]. Later works [YGFJ18; NSH19] further derived simper and stronger variants of the shadow model attack by exploiting other signals such as the loss and gradient norm. Following the inference game studied in shadow model attacks (that captures average privacy loss of a training algorithm), Sablayrolles et al. [Sab+19] and Murakonda et al. [MST21] further study the problem of optimal attack strategy for membership inference, from the perspective of deriving powerful hypothesis tests under certain assumptions about the training algorithm or the model. Recently, there are efforts for improving the shadow model-based membership inference attacks, via reducing the adversary's uncertainty about properties of a specific data record in the inference games, or via taking into account of difficulty of each data record, see Ye et al. [Ye+22], Carlini et al. [Car+22], and Watson et al. [WGCS21] for detailed discussions. Although these new attacks outperform attacks that are based on the behaviors of shadow models on population data by a large margin, they do not strictly dominate them on all membership inference queries (e.g., on out-of-distribution non-member queries), as observed in Zarifzadeh et al. [ZLS23]. Additionally, to achieve strong performance, these new attacks often require training many reference models for attacking each target data record, thus incurring high computation cost. Motivated by these limitations, the recent work of Zarifzadeh et al. [ZLS23] proposes to use a novel pair-wise inference game, so as to leverages both population data and reference models in attack construction. The resultant attack RMIA [ZLS23] was then shown to enjoy enhanced attack power and robustness against changes in adversary's background knowledge.

The problem of translating the performance of membership inference attack into meaningful reports for privacy risk estimates is increasingly studied in recent years. Yeom et al. [YGFJ18] and Jayaraman and Evans [JE19] focus on translating *overall* attack accuracy (on general targets) to differential privacy parameter estimate. Jagielski et al. [JUO20], Nasr et al. [Nas+21], and Zanella-Béguelin et al. [Zan+23] further translate the empirically measured FPR and TPR of the attacks (on *worst-case* poisoned data records) into statistical lower bound estimates for differential privacy. Following on these line of works, Steinke et al. [SNJ24] and Pillutla et al. [Pil+24] further translates *average-case* FPR and TPR of the attacks (on randomly sampled training data and test data) to statistical lower bound estimates for differential privacy, thus significantly reducing the required number of trained models for privacy auditing (to as few as one or two). These translations (such as Theorem 5.7) rely on variants of the binary hypothesis testing formulation of differential privacy [WZ10; KOV15], and bounds the error of an arbitrary test (i.e., a membership inference attack strategy) with the differential privacy parameters of the training algorithm. There are also connections between the TPR-FPR curve of membership inference attack and other more fine-grained variant of differential privacy definition, such as Gaussian differential privacy [DRS19]. See Murakonda et al. [MST21] for more discussions.

Recently, there are also increasing discussions about what the best metrics for measuring attack performance are, to more precisely capture the actual privacy risks in machine learning models. These metrics include precision [SSSS17; Lon+20; WGCS21], unbalanced attack accuracy [Sab+19; WGCS21], TPR-FPR curve [MST21; Ye+22; WGCS21; Car+22].

References

[BCKW15] C. Blundell, J. Cornebise, K. Kavukcuoglu, and D. Wierstra. "Weight uncertainty in neural network". In: International conference on machine learning. PMLR. 2015, pp. 1613–1622 (cit. on p. 195).

[Car+19] N. Carlini, C. Liu, Ú. Erlingsson, J. Kos, and D. Song. "The secret sharer: Evaluating and testing unintended memorization in neural networks". In: 28th {USENIX} Security Symposium ({USENIX} Security 19). 2019, pp. 267–284 (cit. on p. 201).

[Car+21] N. Carlini, F. Tramer, E. Wallace, M. Jagielski, A. Herbert-Voss, K. Lee, A. Roberts, T. Brown, D. Song, U. Erlingsson, et al. "Extracting training data from large language models". In: 30th USENIX Security Symposium (USENIX Security 21). 2021, pp. 2633–2650 (cit. on p. 186).

[Car+22] N. Carlini, S. Chien, M. Nasr, S. Song, A. Terzis, and F. Tramer. "Membership inference attacks from first principles". In: 2022 IEEE Symposium on Security and Privacy (SP). IEEE. 2022, pp. 1897–1914 (cit. on pp. 189, 194, 195, 197, 198, 202, 203).

[CS21] H. Chang and R. Shokri. "On the privacy risks of algorithmic fairness". In: 2021 IEEE European Symposium on Security and Privacy (EuroS&P). IEEE. 2021, pp. 292–303 (cit. on p. 191).

[DMNS06] C. Dwork, F. McSherry, K. Nissim, and A. Smith. "Calibrating noise to sensitivity in private data analysis". In: Theory of cryptography conference. Springer. 2006, pp. 265–284 (cit. on p. 200).

[DRS19] J. Dong, A. Roth, and W. J. Su. "Gaussian differential privacy". In: arXiv preprint arXiv:1905.02383 (2019) (cit. on p. 203).

[Fel20] V. Feldman. "Does learning require memorization? a short tale about a long tail". In: Proceedings of the 52nd Annual ACM SIGACT Symposium on Theory of Computing. 2020, pp. 954–959 (cit. on p. 194).

[Hom+08] N. Homer, S. Szelinger, M. Redman, D. Duggan, W. Tembe, J. Muehling, J. V. Pearson, D. A. Stephan, S. F. Nelson, and D. W. Craig. "Resolving individuals contributing trace amounts of DNA to highly complex mixtures using high-density SNP genotyping microarrays". In: PLoS genetics 4.8 (2008), e1000167 (cit. on pp. 194, 198, 202).

[JE19] B. Jayaraman and D. Evans. "Evaluating differentially private machine learning in practice". In: 28th {USENIX} Security Symposium ({USENIX} Security 19). 2019, pp. 1895–1912 (cit. on p. 203).

[JUO20] M. Jagielski, J. Ullman, and A. Oprea. "Auditing differentially private machine learning: How private is private sgd?" In: arXiv preprint arXiv:2006.07709 (2020) (cit. on pp. 200, 201, 203).

[KOV15] P. Kairouz, S. Oh, and P. Viswanath. "The composition theorem for differential privacy". In: International conference on machine learning. PMLR. 2015, pp. 1376–1385 (cit. on p. 203).

[Lon+18] Y. Long, V. Bindschaedler, L. Wang, D. Bu, X. Wang, H. Tang, C. A. Gunter, and K. Chen. "Understanding membership inferences on well-generalized learning models". In: arXiv preprint arXiv:1802.04889 (2018) (cit. on p. 191).

[Lon+20] Y. Long, L. Wang, D. Bu, V. Bindschaedler, X. Wang, H. Tang, C. A. Gunter, and K. Chen. "A Pragmatic Approach to Membership Inferences on Machine Learning Models". In: 2020 IEEE European Symposium on Security and Privacy (EuroS&P). IEEE. 2020, pp. 521–534 (cit. on pp. 191, 195, 198, 201, 203).

[Mac03] D. J. MacKay. Information theory, inference and learning algorithms. Cambridge university press, 2003 (cit. on p. 195).

[MST21] S. K. Murakonda, R. Shokri, and G. Theodorakopoulos. "Quantifying the Privacy Risks of Learning High-Dimensional Graphical Models". In: International Conference on Artificial Intelligence and Statistics. 2021, pp. 2287–2295 (cit. on pp. 195, 198, 202, 203).

[Nas+21] M. Nasr, S. Song, A. Thakurta, N. Papernot, and N. Carlini. "Adversary instantiation: Lower bounds for differentially private machine learning". In: arXiv preprint arXiv:2101.04535 (2021) (cit. on pp. 200, 201, 203).

[NSH19] M. Nasr, R. Shokri, and A. Houmansadr. "Comprehensive Privacy Analysis of Deep Learning: Passive and Active White-box Inference Attacks against Centralized and Federated Learning". In: IEEE Symposium on Security and Privacy (SP). 2019, pp. 1022–1036 (cit. on pp. 190, 202).

[Pil+24] K. Pillutla, G. Andrew, P. Kairouz, H. B. McMahan, A. Oprea, and S. Oh. "Unleashing the power of randomization in auditing differentially private ML". In: Advances in Neural Information Processing Systems 36 (2024) (cit. on p. 203).

[Sab+19] A. Sablayrolles, M. Douze, C. Schmid, Y. Ollivier, and H. Jégou. "White-box vs black-box: Bayes optimal strategies for membership inference". In: International Conference on Machine Learning. 2019, pp. 5558–5567 (cit. on pp. 189, 198, 202, 203).

[Sal+19] A. Salem, Y. Zhang, M. Humbert, M. Fritz, and M. Backes. "ML-Leaks: Model and Data Independent Membership Inference Attacks and Defenses on Machine Learning Models". In: Network and Distributed Systems Security Symposium 2019. Internet Society. 2019 (cit. on p. 190).

[SM21] L. Song and P. Mittal. "Systematic evaluation of privacy risks of machine learning models". In: 30th {USENIX} Security Symposium ({USENIX} Security 21). 2021 (cit. on p. 198).

[SNJ24] T. Steinke, M. Nasr, and M. Jagielski. "Privacy auditing with one (1) training run". In: Advances in Neural Information Processing Systems 36 (2024) (cit. on p. 203).

[SOJH09] S. Sankararaman, G. Obozinski, M. I. Jordan, and E. Halperin. "Genomic privacy and limits of individual detection in a pool". In: (2009), p. 965 (cit. on pp. 195, 202).

[SSSS17] R. Shokri, M. Stronati, C. Song, and V. Shmatikov. "Membership inference attacks against machine learning models". In: 2017 IEEE symposium on security and privacy (SP). IEEE. 2017, pp. 3–18 (cit. on pp. 186, 190, 192, 194, 202, 203).

[Tra+22a] F. Tramer, A. Terzis, T. Steinke, S. Song, M. Jagielski, and N. Carlini. "Debugging Differential Privacy: A Case Study for Privacy Auditing". In: arXiv preprint arXiv:2202.12219 (2022) (cit. on p. 200).

[Tra+22b] F. Tramèr, R. Shokri, A. S. Joaquin, H. Le, M. Jagielski, S. Hong, and N. Carlini. "Truth Serum: Poisoning Machine Learning Models to Reveal Their Secrets". In: arXiv preprint arXiv:2204.00032 (2022) (cit. on p. 201).

[TSBP22] A. Thudi, I. Shumailov, F. Boenisch, and N. Papernot. "Bounding Membership Inference". In: arXiv preprint arXiv:2202.12232 (2022) (cit. on p. 198).

[WGCS21] L. Watson, C. Guo, G. Cormode, and A. Sablayrolles. "On the Importance of Difficulty Calibration in Membership Inference Attacks". In: arXiv preprint arXiv:2111.08440 (2021) (cit. on pp. 190, 198, 202, 203).

[WZ10] L. Wasserman and S. Zhou. "A statistical framework for differential privacy". In: Journal of the American Statistical Association 105.489 (2010), pp. 375–389 (cit. on p. 203).

[Ye+22] J. Ye, A. Maddi, S. K. Murakonda, V. Bindschaedler, and R. Shokri. "Enhanced Membership Inference Attacks against Machine Learning Models". In: Proceedings of the 2022 ACM SIGSAC Conference on Computer and Communications Security. CCS '22. New York, NY, USA: Association for Computing Machinery, 2022, pp. 3093–3106 (cit. on pp. 186, 194, 195, 197, 198, 202, 203).

[YGFJ18] S. Yeom, I. Giacomelli, M. Fredrikson, and S. Jha. "Privacy risk in machine learning: Analyzing the connection to overfitting". In: 2018 IEEE 31st Computer Security Foundations Symposium (CSF). 2018, pp. 268–282 (cit. on pp. 186, 189, 194, 202, 203).

[Zan+23] S. Zanella-Béguelin, L. Wutschitz, S. Tople, A. Salem, V. Rühle, A. Paverd, M. Naseri, B. Köpf, and D. Jones. "Bayesian estimation of differential privacy". In: International Conference on Machine Learning. PMLR. 2023, pp. 40624–40636 (cit. on p. 203).

[ZLS23] S. Zarifzadeh, P. Liu, and R. Shokri. "Low-Cost High-Power Membership Inference by Boosting Relativity". In: arXiv preprint arXiv:2312.03262 (2023) (cit. on pp. 194–197, 202, 203).

DOI: 10.1561/9781638284772.ch6

Chapter 6

Private Optimization

By Abhradeep Thakurta

6.1 Introduction

Consider a data set $D = \{d_1, \ldots, d_n\}$ drawn from some domain $\mathcal{D}^*$, and a loss function $\mathcal{L}(\theta; D) = \sum_{i=1}^{n} \ell(\theta; d_i)$, where $\theta \in \mathbb{R}^p$ is the model, and $\ell : \mathbb{R}^p \times \mathcal{D}$ is the loss function on individual data samples. In this chapter, we will focus on algorithms for estimating (6.1) while preserving (ε, δ)-differential privacy, where $\mathcal{C} \subseteq \mathbb{R}^p$ is the constraint set

$$\theta^* \in \arg\min_{\theta \in \mathcal{C}} \mathcal{L}(\theta; D). \tag{6.1}$$

The above formulation is often called the Empirical Risk Minization (ERM), and is powerful enough to capture a large class of learning tasks. For example, i) in linear regression the data record is $d_i = (\mathbf{x}_i, y_i)$ (with $\mathbf{x}_i \in \mathbb{R}^d$ being the feature vector, and y_i being the response) and the loss function is $\ell(\theta; d_i) = (y_i - \langle \mathbf{x}_i, \theta \rangle)^2$, ii) in logistic regression the loss function is $\ell(\theta; d_i) = \ln\left(1 + e^{-y_i \langle \mathbf{x}_i, \theta \rangle}\right)$, and iii) in the case of deep networks with binary cross entropy, the loss function is $\ell(\theta; d_i) = \ln\left(1 + e^{-y_i \cdot h_\theta(\mathbf{x}_i)}\right)$, where $h_\theta(\cdot)$ is the network parameterized by the model weights θ. ERM frameworks also allow a direct a direct way of minimizing the population loss (a.k.a. true risk or the test accuracy), i.e,

$$\theta^*_{\text{pop}} \in \arg\min_{\theta \in \mathcal{C}} \mathbb{E}_{d \sim \mathcal{T}} \left[\ell(\theta; d)\right]. \tag{6.2}$$

In (6.2), $\mathcal{T}$ is a distribution over the domain $\mathcal{D}$. If the data set D is drawn i.i.d. from the distribution $\mathcal{T}$, it is then not hard to show by the so-called uniform convergence theorem [SSSS09] that the following holds for any $\theta \in \mathcal{C}$, with probability at least $1 - \beta$ over the randomness of D. In (6.3), L is the ℓ_2-Lipschitz constant (Defnition 6.1) on the individual loss functions $\ell(\cdot;\cdot)$ w.r.t. the first parameter, and $\|\mathcal{C}\|_2$ is the ℓ_2-diameter of the constraint set $\mathcal{C}$. Hence, if one can estimate θ^* well with differential privacy, then it immediately implies a strong bound on the true risk[i]. In this chapter, we will hence focus on solving the ERM problem (defined in (6.1)) with differential privacy.

$$\begin{aligned} &\underbrace{\mathbb{E}_{d \sim \mathcal{T}} \left[\ell(\theta; d)\right] - \mathbb{E}_{d \sim \mathcal{T}} \left[\ell(\theta^*_{\text{pop}}; d)\right]}_{\textbf{Excess true risk}} \\ &= \frac{1}{n} \left(\underbrace{\mathcal{L}(\theta; D) - \mathcal{L}(\theta^*; D)}_{\textbf{Excess empirical risk}} \right) \\ &+ O\left(L \|\mathcal{C}\|_2 \cdot \sqrt{\frac{p \cdot \ln(n) \cdot \ln(d/\beta)}{n}} \right). \end{aligned} \tag{6.3}$$

To begin with, we need the following properties of (convex) function that we will be using throughout the chapter. In each of the algorithms, and the corresponding analysis, we will explicitly state which properties of the function we are assuming.

Definition 6.1 (L-Lipschitz continuity). *A function $f : \mathcal{C} \to \mathbb{R}$ is L-Lipschitz w.r.t. the ℓ_q-norm if the following is true for any $\theta_1, \theta_2 \in \mathcal{C}$:*

$$\left|f(\theta_1) - f(\theta_2)\right| \leq L \cdot \|\theta_1 - \theta_2\|_q. \tag{6.4}$$

Unless mentioned explicitly, we will assume Lipschitzness w.r.t. the ℓ_2-norm.

Definition 6.2 (γ-Smoothness). *A function $f : \mathcal{C} \to \mathbb{R}$ is γ-smooth, if the following is true for any $\theta_1, \theta_2 \in \mathcal{C}$:*

$$f(\theta_2) \leq f(\theta_1) + \langle \nabla f(\theta_1), \theta_2 - \theta_1 \rangle + \frac{\gamma}{2} \|\theta_2 - \theta_1\|_2^2. \tag{6.5}$$

---

i. There are more sophisticated and tighter methods for converting from excess empirical risk to excess true risk [SSSS09; BFTT19], but they are beyond the scope of this chapter.

Definition 6.3 (Δ-Strong convexity). *A function $f : \mathcal{C} \rightarrow \mathbb{R}$ is Δ-strongly convex, if the following is true for any $\theta_1, \theta_2 \in \mathcal{C}$ and for any $\alpha \in (0, 1]$:*

$$f(\alpha \cdot \theta_1 + (1-\alpha) \cdot \theta_2) \leq \alpha \cdot f(\theta_1) + (1-\alpha) \cdot f(\theta_2) - \frac{\Delta \cdot \alpha(1-\alpha)}{2} \|\theta_2 - \theta_1\|_2^2. \tag{6.6}$$

If $\Delta = 0$, we say that the function f is convex. If f is differentiable, we can replace the condition in (6.6) *with,*

$$f(\theta_2) \geq f(\theta_1) + \langle \nabla f(\theta_1), \theta_2 - \theta_1 \rangle + \frac{\Delta}{2} \|\theta_2 - \theta_1\|_2^2. \tag{6.7}$$

Overview of the Chapter

The chapter is organized as follows. We will first discuss DP-ERM algorithms that satisfy pure ε-differential privacy. The specific algorithms we will discuss are i) Exponential mechanism [MT07; BST14], and ii) Objective perturbation [CMS11; KST12]. Then, we will move on to discuss DP-ERM algorithms that satisfy (ε, δ)-differential privacy. There, we will focus our attention on a couple of algorithms, namely, differentially private (stochastic) gradient descent (DP-SGD) [BST14; Aba+16; TTZ14a] and differentially private follow the regularized leader (DP-FTRL) [Kai+21b; ST13a; AS17]. We will then provide a (ε, δ)-differentially private algorithm for the high-dimensional setting where the dimensionality $p \gg n$. This algorithm is called the private Frank-Wolfe [TTZ15]. Finally, we will demonstrate how (and when) these algorithms provide optimal privacy/utility trade-offs by visiting some of the lower bounding techniques in DP-ERM.

Note: All the results in this section are in the add/remove model of differential privacy (see Section 1.4.1 of Chapter 1). They can be easily translated to the replacement model by paying a factor of two in the privacy parameters via standard methods [DR+14].

6.2 Empirical Risk Minimization with ε-DP

In this section, we provide algorithms for solving the ERM problem in (6.1) under ε-differential privacy.

6.2.1 Exponential Mechanism based Private ERM

The first algorithm we look at is based on the classic exponential mechanism [MT07]. Later we will see that this algorithm is indeed optimal for the case when for any data sample $d \in \mathcal{D}$, the loss function $\ell(\theta; d)$ is convex and L-Lipschitz in its first parameter, within the convex constraint set $\mathcal{C}$.

Algorithm 1 $\mathcal{A}_{\text{exp-samp}}$: Exponential mechanism based convex optimization

Require: Data set of size n: D, loss function: ℓ, constraint set: $\mathcal{C}$, ℓ_2-Lipschitz constant: L, privacy parameter: ε

$\mathcal{L}(\theta; D) \leftarrow \sum_{i=1}^{n} \ell(\theta; d_i)$.

Sample and **output** a point θ^{priv} from the constraint set $\mathcal{C}$ w.p. $\propto \exp\left(-\frac{\varepsilon}{2L\|\mathcal{C}\|_2} \cdot \mathcal{L}(\theta; D)\right)$.

First, we show that Algorithm $\mathcal{A}_{\text{exp-samp}}$ is ε-differentially private. The proof will go via fairly standard arguments used in analyzing exponential mechanism. A vanilla analysis of the sampling distribution in the algorithm would require the loss $\ell(\theta; \cdot)$ to be bounded in terms of its value. However, by using a fixed anchoring point θ_0, it suffices to operate with the Lipschitzness assumption.

Theorem 6.4. *Algorithm 1 is ε-differentially private.*

Proof. Consider the kernel $\mu(\theta; D) = \exp\left(-\frac{\varepsilon}{2L\|\mathcal{C}\|_2} \cdot \mathcal{L}(\theta; D)\right)$ of the probability distribution in Algorithm $\mathcal{A}_{\text{exp-samp}}$. Let $\theta_0 \in \mathcal{C}$ be any fixed model parameter. Now, notice that the sampling distribution generated by $\mu(\theta)$ is identical to the distribution generated by the following kernel: $\widehat{\mu}(\theta; D) = \exp\left(-\frac{\varepsilon}{2L\|\mathcal{C}\|_2} \cdot (\mathcal{L}(\theta; D) - \mathcal{L}(\theta_0; D))\right)$. Hence, in the rest of the proof we will only consider $\widehat{\mu}(\theta; D)$.

Consider any two neighboring data sets D and D'. Let d be the data record on which they differ. W.l.o.g., data set D has data record d, and D' does not. For any θ, θ_0, we have the following.

$$\left|(\mathcal{L}(\theta; D) - \mathcal{L}(\theta_0; D)) - \left(\mathcal{L}(\theta; D') - \mathcal{L}(\theta_0; D')\right)\right| = |\ell(\theta; d) - \ell(\theta_0; d)|$$
$$\leq L \cdot \|\theta - \theta_0\|_2 \leq L\,\|\mathcal{C}\|_2\,. \tag{6.8}$$

To ensure differential privacy we need to make sure that for any measurable set $S \subseteq \mathcal{C}$, the following is true.

$$e^{-\varepsilon} \leq \frac{\int_{\theta \in S} \mu\,(\theta; D)}{\int_{\theta \in \mathcal{C}} \mu\,(\theta; D)} \cdot \frac{\int_{\theta \in \mathcal{C}} \mu\,(\theta; D')}{\int_{\theta \in S} \mu\,(\theta; D')} \leq e^{\varepsilon}. \tag{6.9}$$

By (6.8), for any $\theta \in \mathcal{C}$, $e^{-\varepsilon/2} \leq \frac{\mu(\theta;D)}{\mu(\theta;D')} \leq e^{-\varepsilon/2}$. Hence, the condition in (6.9) is immediately satisfied. This completes the proof. □

In Theorem 6.5 we show that for Algorithm 1, the excess empirical risk is bounded by $O\left(\frac{pL\|C\|_2}{\varepsilon}\right)$. In the proof, we will heavily use convexity property of the loss function $\ell(\cdot;\cdot)$ to show this bound.

Note: The following simpler bound is easy to prove without relying on convexity: Let $\mathbb{B}$ be a unit ball centered at the origin. If $r\mathbb{B} \subseteq C$, then the excess empirical risk is bounded by $O\left(\frac{pL\|C\|_2}{\varepsilon} \cdot \ln\left(\frac{\varepsilon nL\|C\|_2}{r}\right)\right)$. We leave the proof of this statement as an exercise. This result is significant because it shows that one can obtain both DP guarantee, and strong excess empirical risk bounds just by assuming the loss function to be L-Lipschitz within the constraint set.

Theorem 6.5. *Let θ^{priv} be the output of Algorithm 1 above. Then, we have the following guarantee on the expected excess risk. (The expectation is over the randomness of the algorithm.)*

$$\mathbf{E}\left[\mathcal{L}(\theta^{\mathrm{priv}}; D) - \mathcal{L}(\theta^*; D)\right] = O\left(\frac{pL\,\|C\|_2}{\varepsilon}\right).$$

Here, $\theta^* \in \arg\min_{\theta \in C} \mathcal{L}(\theta; D)$.

Proof. Consider any differential cone Ω centered at θ^*. We will first bound the excess empirical risk, conditioned on $\theta^{\mathrm{priv}} \in \Omega$. Since the bound will be true for any Ω, by the law of total expectation, the guarantee in the theorem statement immediately follows.

Let $\Gamma \geq 0$ be a fixed parameter to be defined later. For the purpose of brevity, let $f(\theta) = \mathcal{L}(\theta; D) - \mathcal{L}(\theta^*; D)$. We first split Ω into different levels A_i's, where each A_i is defined as follows:

$$A_i = \left\{\theta \in \Omega \cap C : (i-1) \cdot \Gamma \leq f(\theta) \leq i \cdot \Gamma\right\}. \tag{6.10}$$

Notice that A_1 corresponds to the region, where the excess empirical risk $f(\theta) \leq \Gamma$. Instead of directly computing the probability of θ^{priv} lying outside A_1, we will individually compute the probability of θ^{priv} being in each of $A_i, i > 1$ individually, and then take an union bound over these probabilities. Typically, this line of argument is referred to as the "peeling argument".

Since Ω is a differential cone, and $f(\theta)$ is continuous on C, it follows that within $\Omega \cap C, f(\theta)$ only depends on $\|\theta - \theta^*\|_2$. Centered at θ^*, let $r_1, r_2, \ldots$ be the end boundaries for the sets $A_1, A_2, \ldots$ respectively. Hence, one can redefine (6.10) as follows.

$$A_i = \left\{\theta \in \Omega \cap C : r_{i-1} \leq f(\theta) \leq r_i\right\}, \tag{6.11}$$

In Claim 6.6 we show that due to convexity of $f(\theta)$, the gap between successive r_i's (i.e., $r_i - r_{i-1}$) is decreasing for $i \geq 3$.

Claim 6.6. *Convexity of $f(\theta)$ implies that $r_i - r_{i-1} \leq r_{i-1} - r_{i-2}$ for all $i \geq 3$.*

Proof. Since θ^* is the minimizer of $f(\theta)$ within the constraint set $\mathcal{C}$, and since $f(\theta)$ is convex, we have the following any two $\theta_1, \theta_2 \in \mathcal{C} \cap \Omega$ with $f(\theta_2) \geq f(\theta_1)$: $\|\theta_2 - \theta^*\|_2 \geq \|\theta_1 - \theta^*\|_2$. This immediately implies the claim.

Now, recall the volume of any of the A_i is given by $\text{Vol}(A_i) = \text{const} \cdot \int_{r_{i-1}}^{r_i} r^{p-1} dr$. Hence, we have the following:

$$\frac{\text{Vol}(A_i)}{\text{Vol}(A_2)} = \left(\frac{r_{i-1}}{r_1}\right)^p \cdot \frac{(r_i/r_{i-1})^p - 1}{(r_2/r_1)^p - 1} \leq \left(\frac{r_{i-1}}{r_1}\right)^p \leq (i-1)^p. \tag{6.12}$$

□

The last two inequalities in (6.12) follows directly from Claim 6.6. Recall the definition of Γ. Hence we have the following for the excess empirical risk $f(\theta^{\text{priv}}) \geq 4\Gamma$, conditioned on $\theta^{\text{priv}} \in \mathcal{C} \cap \Omega$. In the following, we remove the conditioning for brevity.

$$\mathbf{Pr}[f(\theta^{\text{priv}}) \geq 4\Gamma] \leq \frac{\mathbf{Pr}[\theta^{\text{priv}} \in \bigcup_{i=4}^{\infty}]}{\mathbf{Pr}[\theta^{\text{priv}} \in A_2]} \leq \sum_{i=4}^{\infty} \frac{\text{Vol}(A_i)}{\text{Vol}(A_2)} \cdot \exp\left(-\frac{\varepsilon(i-3)\Gamma}{2L\|\mathcal{C}\|_2}\right) \tag{6.13}$$

$$\leq \sum_{i=4}^{\infty} (i-1)^p \cdot \exp\left(-\frac{\varepsilon(i-3)\Gamma}{2L\|\mathcal{C}\|_2}\right)$$

$$\leq \frac{3^p \exp\left(-\frac{\varepsilon\Gamma}{2L\|\mathcal{C}\|_2}\right)}{1 - 2^p \exp\left(-\frac{\varepsilon\Gamma}{2L\|\mathcal{C}\|_2}\right)}. \tag{6.14}$$

The last inequality in (6.14) follows from the fact that $(i-1)^p \leq 3^p \cdot \left(2^{i-1}\right)^p$ for all $i \geq 4$. Hence for every $t > 0$, if we choose $\Gamma = \frac{2L\|\mathcal{C}\|_2}{\varepsilon} \cdot \left((p+1)\ln(3) + t\right)$, then we have the following.

$$\mathbf{Pr}\left[f(\theta^{\text{priv}}) \geq \frac{8L\|\mathcal{C}\|_2}{\varepsilon} \cdot \left((p+1)\ln(3) + t\right)\right] \leq e^{-t}. \tag{6.15}$$

Since (6.15) is true for all $t \geq 0$, we have the required bound as a corollary. □

Oracle Complexity

It is not obvious how to implement Algorithm 1 efficiently. Even before that we need to decide on how we measure computational complexity. In this section, and in the rest of the chapter, we will measure the complexity in terms of number of oracle calls to the gradients of individual loss function $\nabla \ell(\theta; d)$. This is consistent with the standard optimization literature [Bub15].

Since the loss functions $\ell(\cdot; \cdot)$ are convex in the first parameter, Step 2 of Algorithm 1 results in sampling from a log-concave distribution. Classic results from sampling theory [LV06] allows sampling efficiently from these distribution, albeit the convergence is usually in the total-variation-distance (TVD). In order to guarantee ε-differential privacy, it is necessary to have the sampling distribution to converge to the true distribution induced by Step 2 of Algorithm 1 in the ℓ_∞-distance. [BST14], which got improved by [MV21], provides algorithms with ℓ_∞-distance convergence and oracle complexity of $O\left(\frac{n}{\varepsilon}\text{poly}\left(p\right)\right)$.

Requirement of Convexity

While the utility analysis of Algorithm 1 heavily relies on convexity, the privacy analysis does not. The privacy analysis only assumes that $\ell(\theta; d)$ is L-Lipschitz w.r.t. the ℓ_2-norm. As it will be more obvious in the later parts of this chapter, such a property is rare in algorithms designed for DP optimization. However, the general philosophy regarding the design of DP optimization algorithms that the reader should keep in mind is that, it is always desirable that the privacy property of an algorithm should rely on minimal set of assumptions, which in particular should be enforceable/efficiently testable. It is okay to make stronger assumptions for the corresponding utility analysis. Convexity, unfortunately, is not an efficiently testable property in general.

Note on Optimality

The utility bound obtained in Theorem 6.5 is indeed optimal. One can use use standard machinery of the so-called "packing argument" [HT10; BST14] to achieve the lower bound.

6.2.2 Objective Perturbation for Private ERM

While Algorithm $\mathcal{A}_{\text{exp-samp}}$ is optimal for pure ε-DP (i.e., with $\delta = 0$), any natural extension of $\mathcal{A}_{\text{exp-samp}}$ is not known to be optimal in the case of (ε, δ)-DP. In this section we will see an algorithm that is simultaneously optimal for both ε-DP and (ε, δ)-DP. Additionally, this algorithm will be computationally efficient in regards to oracle complexity. The algorithm is called *objective perturbation* (Algorithm 2) [CMS11; KST12]. Along with the loss function $\ell(\theta; \cdot)$ being L-Lipschitz w.r.t. ℓ_2-norm, it requires two additional properties: i) $\ell(\theta; \cdot)$ should be twice continuously differentiable, ii) $\lambda_{\max}\left(\nabla_\theta^2 \ell(\theta; \cdot)\right) \leq \lambda_{\max}$, and iii) $\text{rank}\left(\nabla_\theta^2 \ell(\theta; \cdot)\right) \leq r$. Here $\lambda_{\max}(\cdot)$ corresponds to the maximum eigenvalue of a positive semidefinite (PSD) matrix.

Algorithm 2 $\mathcal{A}_{\text{obj-pert}}$: Objective Perturbation

Require: Data set of size n: D, loss function: ℓ, ℓ_2-Lipschitz constant: L, constraint set: $\mathcal{C}$, ℓ_2-regularization: Δ, noise multiplier: λ.

1: $\mathcal{L}(\theta; D) \leftarrow \sum_{i=1}^{n} \ell(\theta; d_i)$.

2: $\theta^{\text{priv}} \leftarrow \arg\min_{\theta \in \mathcal{C}} \mathcal{L}(\theta; D) + \frac{\Delta}{2} \|\theta\|_2^2 + \langle b, \theta \rangle$, where $b \sim \mathcal{G}(L \cdot \lambda)$ and $\mathcal{G}(\sigma) := \frac{\exp\left(-\frac{\|x\|_2}{\sigma}\right)}{\int_{x \in \mathbb{R}^d} \exp\left(-\frac{\|x\|_2}{\sigma}\right)}$.

3: **Output** θ^{priv}.

In Theorem 6.7 we provide the privacy guarantee for Algorithm 2. Notice that the regularization parameter Δ has to be lower bounded to ensure DP. As it will be clear later, this lower bound is much lower than that what one would set to get an optimal excess empirical risk bound. In Theorem 6.7, we only provide the privacy analysis for the setting where the constraint set $\mathcal{C} = \mathbb{R}^p$. While the privacy guarantee holds for any convex constraint set $\mathcal{C} \subseteq \mathbb{R}^p$, the proof is much more involved and requires measure theoretic arguments. We encourage curious readers to look at [KST12] for more details.

The proof of Theorem 6.7 will provide a curious connection to exponential mechanism, which was not known earlier, prior to this book chapter.

Theorem 6.7. *Let the loss function $\ell(\theta; d)$ be twice continuously differentiable for all $\theta \in \mathcal{C}$, and for all $d \in \mathcal{D}$. Furthermore, $\forall \theta \in \mathcal{C}, \forall d \in \mathcal{D} : \|\nabla \ell(\theta; d)\|_2 \leq L$, $\lambda_{\max}\left(\nabla^2 \ell(\theta; d)\right) \leq \lambda_{\max}$ and $\text{rank}\left(\nabla_\theta^2 \ell(\theta; d)\right) \leq r$. If we set the noise multiplier $\lambda = 2/\varepsilon$, and the regularization parameter $\Delta \geq \frac{r\lambda_{\max}}{1-\exp(-\varepsilon/2)}$, then Algorithm 2 (Algorithm $\mathcal{A}_{\text{obj-pert}}$) satisfies ε-differential privacy.*

Proof for the special case when $\mathcal{C} = \mathbb{R}^p$. Consider the regularized loss function $\mathcal{J}(\theta; D) = \mathcal{L}(\theta; D) + \frac{\Delta}{2} \|\theta\|_2^2$. Consider the following probability distribution:

$$\mu_D(\theta) \propto \exp\left(-\frac{\varepsilon}{2L} \cdot \|\nabla \mathcal{J}(\theta; D)\|_2\right) \cdot \frac{1}{\det\left(\nabla^2 \mathcal{J}(\theta; D)\right)}. \tag{6.16}$$

Additionally, let $b_D(\theta) = \nabla \mathcal{J}(\theta; D)$. Since, $\mathcal{J}(\theta; D)$ is a strictly convex function, the mapping is a bijection. Let $\nu_D(b)$ be the induced distribution on the random variable $b_D(\theta)$. By the Radon-Nikodym theorem [Bil08], we have the following:

$$\nu_D(b) \propto \exp\left(-\frac{\varepsilon}{2L} \cdot \|b\|_2\right) \cdot \frac{\det(\nabla^2 \mathcal{J}(\theta; D))}{\det(\nabla^2 \mathcal{J}(\theta; D))} = \exp\left(-\frac{\varepsilon}{2L} \cdot \|b\|_2\right). \tag{6.17}$$

Notice that the induced distribution $\nu_D(b)$ is independent of the data set D. Hence, from here on we will remove the subscript D in the rest of the proof, and refer the distribution as $\nu(b)$. Going back to (6.16), we want to understand the differential privacy property of $\mu_D(\theta)$. For two neighboring data sets D and D', and at a given θ, we have the following:

$$\frac{\mu_D(\theta)}{\mu_{D'}(\theta)} = \underbrace{\frac{\nu(b_D(\theta))}{\nu(b_{D'}(\theta))}}_{A} \cdot \underbrace{\frac{\det\left(\nabla^2 \mathcal{J}(\theta; D')\right)}{\det\left(\nabla^2 \mathcal{J}(\theta; D)\right)}}_{B}. \tag{6.18}$$

We can easily bound term A in (6.18) by the ℓ_2-Lipschitz property of the loss function $\ell(\cdot;\cdot)$. By definition of $b_D(\theta)$, we have the following:

$$\|b_D(\theta) - b_{D'}(\theta)\|_2 = \left\|\nabla \mathcal{J}(\theta; D) - \nabla \mathcal{J}(\theta; D')\right\|_2 \leq L. \tag{6.19}$$

Therefore, by triangle inequality, the term A in (6.18) is upper bounded by $\exp\left(\frac{\varepsilon}{2}\right)$. Next, we will bound term B in (6.18). For the purpose of brevity, let $W = \nabla^2 \mathcal{J}(\theta; D')$ and $W' = \nabla^2 \mathcal{J}(\theta; D')$. We prove the following claim.

Claim 6.8. *Under the assumptions of Theorem 6.7, we have* $\frac{\det(W')}{\det(W)} \leq \frac{\Delta}{\Delta - r\lambda_{\max}}$.

Proof. Since the rank of any $\nabla^2 \ell(\theta; d)$ is upper bounded by r, it follows that the matrix $E = W' - W$ has rank at most r. Let $\sigma_1 \geq \sigma_2 \geq \ldots \geq \sigma_p \geq \Delta$ be the eigenvalues of the matrix W, and $\sigma'_1 \geq \sigma'_2 \geq \ldots \geq \sigma'_p \geq \Delta$ correspondingly for W'. Recall that $\det(W) = \prod_{i=1}^{p} \sigma_i$. Therefore, we have the following.

$$\frac{\det\left(W'\right)}{\det\left(W\right)} = \prod_{i=1}^{p} \frac{\sigma'_i}{\sigma_i} = \prod_{i=1}^{p} \left(1 + \frac{\sigma'_i - \sigma_i}{\sigma_i}\right) \leq \prod_{i=1}^{p} \left(1 + \frac{|\sigma'_i - \sigma_i|}{\Delta}\right) \tag{6.20}$$

$$= 1 + \sum_{i=1}^{p} \frac{|\sigma'_i - \sigma_i|}{\Delta} + \sum_{i,j \in [p], i \neq j} \frac{\prod_{k \in \{i,j\}} |\sigma'_k - \sigma_k|}{\Delta^2} + \cdots \tag{6.21}$$

$$\leq 1 + \frac{r\lambda_{\max}}{\Delta} + \left(\frac{r\lambda_{\max}}{\Delta}\right)^2 + \cdots \leq \frac{\Delta}{\Delta - r\lambda_{\max}}. \tag{6.22}$$

The inequality in (6.20) follows from the fact that each of the eigenvalues are lower bounded by Δ. The first inequality in (6.22) follows from the fact that $\forall i \in [p], |\sigma'_i - \sigma_i| \leq r\lambda_{\max}$. The last inequality in (6.22) follows from fact that $\Delta \geq r\lambda_{\max}$. This completes the proof. ☐

Since by assumption $\Delta \geq \frac{r\lambda_{\max}}{1 - \exp(-\varepsilon/2)}$, term B in (6.18) is upper bounded by $\exp\left(\frac{\varepsilon}{2}\right)$. Hence, we have proved that the sampling distribution in (6.16) satisfies ε-differential privacy. In the rest of the proof we will show that the distribution of θ^{priv} in Algorithm $\mathcal{A}_{\text{obj-pert}}$ is identical to (6.16).

Since we are operating the in the unconstrained space, i.e., $\mathcal{C} = \mathbb{R}^d$, we have the following:

$$b = -\left(\nabla \mathcal{L}(\theta; D) + \Delta\theta\right) = -\left(\nabla \mathcal{J}(\theta; D)\right). \tag{6.23}$$

By using Radon-Nikodym theorem [Bil08], we have the following distribution on θ^{priv}:

$$\mu(\theta^{\mathsf{priv}}) = \nu(b) \cdot \frac{1}{\det(\nabla^2 \mathcal{J}(\theta; D))}. \tag{6.24}$$

Here, $\nu(b)$ is the is the pdf of the distribution on the random variable b, which is proportional to $\exp\left(-\frac{\varepsilon}{2L} \cdot \|b\|_2\right)$. This completes the proof. □

Analogous to Theorem 6.5, we provide the utility guarantee of Algorithm $\mathcal{A}_{\mathsf{obj-pert}}$ in Theorem 6.9.

Theorem 6.9. *Recall all the parameter choices in Theorem 6.7 for Algorithm 2 (Algorithm $\mathcal{A}_{\mathsf{obj-pert}}$). Additionally, assume $\frac{r\lambda_{\max}}{1-\exp(-\varepsilon/2)} \leq \frac{\sqrt{32}\cdot pL}{\varepsilon\|\mathcal{C}\|_2}$, where $\operatorname{rank}\left(\nabla^2_\theta \ell(\theta; d)\right) \leq r, \forall\theta \in \mathcal{C}, d \in \mathcal{D}$, and $0 \in \mathcal{C}$. Then, under appropriate choice of the regularization parameter Δ, the following is true:*

$$\mathbb{E}\left[\mathcal{L}(\theta^{\mathsf{priv}}, D) - \mathcal{L}(\theta^*; D)\right] = O\left(\frac{pL\,\|\mathcal{C}\|_2}{\varepsilon}\right).$$

Proof. Consider the regularized loss function $\mathcal{J}(\theta; D) = \mathcal{L}(\theta; D) + \frac{\Delta}{2}\|\theta\|_2^2$, and the noisy regularized loss function $\mathcal{J}_{\mathsf{noisy}}(\theta; D) = \mathcal{J}(\theta; D) + \langle b, \theta\rangle$. Let the following be the minimizers for each of the losses: $\theta^{\mathsf{priv}} = \arg\min_{\theta\in\mathcal{C}} \mathcal{J}_{\mathsf{noisy}}(\theta; D)$, $\widehat{\theta} = \arg\min_{\theta\in\mathcal{C}} \mathcal{J}(\theta; D)$, and $\theta^* =\in \arg\min_{\theta\in\mathcal{C}} \mathcal{L}(\theta; D)$.

By the strong convexity property of $\mathcal{J}_{\mathsf{noisy}}(\theta; D)$, the following is true:

$$\mathcal{J}_{\mathsf{noisy}}(\widehat{\theta}; D) \geq \mathcal{J}_{\mathsf{noisy}}(\theta^{\mathsf{priv}}; D) + \frac{\Delta}{2}\left\|\widehat{\theta} - \theta^{\mathsf{priv}}\right\|_2^2 \tag{6.25}$$

$$\Leftrightarrow \mathcal{J}(\widehat{\theta}; D) + \langle b, \widehat{\theta}\rangle \geq \mathcal{J}(\theta^{\mathsf{priv}}; D) + \langle b, \theta^{\mathsf{priv}}\rangle + \frac{\Delta}{2}\left\|\widehat{\theta} - \theta^{\mathsf{priv}}\right\|_2^2 \tag{6.26}$$

$$\Leftrightarrow \left(\mathcal{J}(\widehat{\theta}; D) - \mathcal{J}(\theta^{\mathsf{priv}}; D)\right) + \langle b, \widehat{\theta} - \theta^{\mathsf{priv}}\rangle \geq \frac{\Delta}{2}\left\|\widehat{\theta} - \theta^{\mathsf{priv}}\right\|_2^2 \tag{6.27}$$

$$\Rightarrow \|b\|_2 \left\|\widehat{\theta} - \theta^{\text{priv}}\right\|_2 \geq \langle b, \widehat{\theta} - \theta^{\text{priv}} \rangle \geq \frac{\Delta}{2} \left\|\widehat{\theta} - \theta^{\text{priv}}\right\|_2^2 \tag{6.28}$$

$$\Rightarrow \left\|\widehat{\theta} - \theta^{\text{priv}}\right\|_2 \leq \frac{2\|b\|_2}{\Delta}. \tag{6.29}$$

In the above (6.28) follows from the fact that $\left(\mathcal{J}(\widehat{\theta}; D) - \mathcal{J}(\theta^{\text{priv}}; D)\right) \leq 0$, and the inequality in (6.29) follows via Cauchy-Schwartz. Using (6.28) we immediately have the following inequality, which bounds the difference $\mathcal{J}(\theta^{\text{priv}}; D) - \mathcal{J}(\widehat{\theta}; D)$.

$$\mathcal{J}_{\text{noisy}}(\widehat{\theta}; D) \geq \mathcal{J}_{\text{noisy}}(\theta^{\text{priv}}; D) + \frac{\Delta}{2} \left\|\widehat{\theta} - \theta^{\text{priv}}\right\|_2^2 \tag{6.30}$$

$$\Leftrightarrow \mathcal{J}(\widehat{\theta}; D) + \langle b, \widehat{\theta} \rangle \geq \mathcal{J}(\theta^{\text{priv}}; D) + \langle b, \theta^{\text{priv}} \rangle + \frac{\Delta}{2} \left\|\widehat{\theta} - \theta^{\text{priv}}\right\|_2^2 \tag{6.31}$$

$$\Leftrightarrow \mathcal{J}(\theta^{\text{priv}}; D) - \mathcal{J}(\widehat{\theta}; D) \leq \langle b, \widehat{\theta} - \theta^{\text{priv}} \rangle - \frac{\Delta}{2} \left\|\widehat{\theta} - \theta^{\text{priv}}\right\|_2^2 \tag{6.32}$$

$$\Rightarrow \mathcal{J}(\theta^{\text{priv}}; D) - \mathcal{J}(\widehat{\theta}; D) \leq \|b\|_2 \cdot \left\|\widehat{\theta} - \theta^{\text{priv}}\right\|_2 \leq \frac{2\|b\|_2^2}{\Delta}. \tag{6.33}$$

Now, we finally bound $\mathcal{L}(\theta^{\text{priv}}; D) - \mathcal{L}(\theta^*; D)$ in terms of $\|b\|_2$. We have the following:

$$\begin{aligned}
\mathcal{L}(\theta^{\text{priv}}; D) - \mathcal{L}(\theta^*; D) &= \left(\mathcal{L}(\theta^{\text{priv}}; D) + \frac{\Delta}{2} \left\|\theta^{\text{priv}}\right\|_2^2\right) \\
&\quad - \left(\mathcal{L}(\theta^*; D) + \frac{\Delta}{2} \|\theta^*\|_2^2\right) \\
&\quad + \frac{\Delta}{2} \left(\|\theta^*\|_2^2 - \left\|\theta^{\text{priv}}\right\|_2^2\right) && (6.34) \\
&\leq \mathcal{J}(\theta^{\text{priv}}; D) - \mathcal{J}(\theta^*; D) + \frac{\Delta}{2} \|\theta^*\|_2^2 && (6.35) \\
&\leq \mathcal{J}(\theta^{\text{priv}}; D) - \mathcal{J}(\widehat{\theta}; D) + \frac{\Delta}{2} \|\theta^*\|_2^2 \\
&\leq \left(\frac{2\|b\|_2^2}{\Delta} + \frac{\Delta}{2} \|\theta^*\|_2^2\right). && (6.36)
\end{aligned}$$

The first inequality in (6.36) follows from the fact that $\mathcal{J}(\theta; D) \geq \mathcal{J}(\widehat{\theta}; D), \forall \theta \in \mathcal{C}$, and the second inequality follows from (6.33). Taking expectation on both sides of (6.36), and optimizing for $\Delta = \frac{2\cdot\sqrt{\mathbb{E}[\|b\|_2^2]}}{\|C\|_2}$, we have the following:

$$\mathbb{E}\left[\mathcal{L}(\theta^{\text{priv}}; D) - \mathcal{L}(\theta^*; D)\right] \le \frac{2\mathbb{E}\left[\|b\|_2^2\right]}{\Delta} + \frac{\Delta}{2}\|\theta^*\|_2^2 \le \frac{2\mathbb{E}\left[\|b\|_2^2\right]}{\Delta} + \frac{\Delta}{2}\|C\|_2^2$$
$$\le \|C\|_2 \cdot \sqrt{\mathbb{E}\left[\|b\|_2^2\right]}. \tag{6.37}$$

Given the distribution on b in Algorithm $\mathcal{A}_{\text{obj-pert}}$, it is not hard to observe that $\|b\|_2 \sim \text{Gamma}\left(p, \frac{\varepsilon}{2L}\right)$. Therefore, by standard properties of Gamma distribution, we have $\mathbb{E}\left[\|b\|_2^2\right] = \frac{4pL^2}{\varepsilon^2} + \frac{4p^2L^2}{\varepsilon^2} \le \frac{8p^2L^2}{\varepsilon^2}$. Plugging in this bound in (6.37) completes the proof. □

Requirement on Smoothness, and Bounded Rank Hessian, and Convexity

For the privacy analysis in Theorem 6.7, we made these assumptions, beyond just assuming that the loss function $\ell(\cdot;\cdot)$ is ℓ_2-Lipschitz bounded. In the following, we discuss the necessity of these assumptions.

Consider a simple problem where the data sample $d_i \in \mathbb{R}$, and the loss function $\ell(\theta; d_i) = |\theta - d_i|$, i.e., the ERM problem $\arg\min_{\theta\in\mathbb{R}} \sum_{i=1}^{n} |\theta - d_i|$ is estimating the median of the data set $D = \{d_1, \ldots, d_n\}$, with each d_i being unique. For brevity, assume n is odd, so there is a unique median. Clearly, the function is non-differentiable at $\theta \in \{d_1, \ldots, d_n\}$, and hence non-smooth at those points. We focus on the loss function $\mathcal{L}(\theta; D)$ at $\theta = d_{\text{med}}$. Notice that the slope of $\mathcal{L}(\theta; D)$ in the vicinity of d_{med} is either -1 or $+1$. Now, since $|b|$ exponentially distributed (as $p = 1$), we have $\mathbf{Pr}[|b| \le 1/2] = 1 - \exp(-\varepsilon/4)$. If the strong convexity term $\Delta = 0$ in Algorithm $\mathcal{A}_{\text{obj-pert}}$, then clearly, with probability at least $1-\exp(-\varepsilon/4)$, Algorithm $\mathcal{A}_{\text{obj-pert}}$ outputs $\theta^{\text{priv}} = d_{\text{med}}$. As d_{med} is a data point in the data set D, it is a direct violation of ε-DP. One might argue that non-zero value of strong convexity parameter Δ will improve the situation. To move the minimizer away from d_{med}, it is necessary that $\Delta \ge \frac{1}{2|d_{\text{med}}|}$ to ensure that the absolute value of the slope of the regularizer at d_{med} is at least $1/2$. Since, d_{med} can be arbitrary close to zero, Δ has to be potentially infinite, which in turn will destroy any utility of the algorithm. This argument shows that smoothness is a necessary condition of Algorithm $\mathcal{A}_{\text{obj-pert}}$ to ensure DP.

While convexity is a necessary condition for the proof of privacy in Algorithm $\mathcal{A}_{\text{obj-pert}}$, it is possible that one may be able to design variants of $\mathcal{A}_{\text{obj-pert}}$ that does not rely on convexity for privacy. Curiously, if one observes the sampling distribution of θ^{priv} in (6.16), then it would be obvious that removing the scaling term with $\det\left(\nabla^2 \mathcal{J}(\theta; D)\right)$ with result in a sampling distribution that can proven to ensure ε-DP without relying on convexity, or even smoothness. (The proof will be a direct extension of the privacy theorem for Algorithm $\mathcal{A}_{\text{exp-samp}}$, i.e., Theorem 6.4.) It is an active area of research to design variants of Objective perturbation to be amenable to non-convex losses [NRVW20]. There is not much of an intuition there whether the condition on the regularization parameter Δ should necessarily depend on the rank of the Hessian (r). It may be a slack in the analysis of Theorem 6.7.

Computational Efficiency

While Algorithm $\mathcal{A}_{\text{obj-pert}}$ is a mathematically well-defined object, it is unclear how to implement it in practice. In particular, for arbitrary convex losses, any reasonable optimization procedure will not reach the true minimizer θ^{priv} with finite oracle complexity. Given a pre-specified parameter γ, there are optimization methods [Bub15] that will be ensure that they will output a model $\theta^\dagger$ s.t. $\left\|\nabla \mathcal{J}_{\text{noisy}}(\theta^\dagger; D)\right\|_2 \leq \gamma$ with $O\left(n/\text{poly}(\gamma)\right)$ oracle complexity. (Here $\mathcal{J}_{\text{noisy}}(\theta; D) = \mathcal{L}(\theta; D) + \frac{\Delta}{2}\|\theta\|_2^2 + \langle b, \theta\rangle$.) In the unconstrained setting $\mathcal{C} = \mathbb{R}^p$, because of Δ-strong convexity of $\mathcal{J}_{\text{noisy}}$, it implies $\left\|\theta^\dagger - \theta^{\text{priv}}\right\|_2 = O\left(\frac{\gamma}{\Delta}\right)$. Therefore, one can add an additional DP-friendly noise with standard deviation $O\left(\frac{\gamma}{\Delta\varepsilon}\right)$, to cover for $\left\|\theta^\dagger - \theta^{\text{priv}}\right\|_2$. For the constrained setting, one can first perform the above procedure on the unconstrained problem, and then project onto the constraint set $\mathcal{C}$. For a detailed discussion on this approach, see [Iye+19; BFTT19].

Excess Empirical Risk for Strongly Convex Functions

Theorem 6.9 is stated for just Lipschitz convex functions. However, the proof essentially goes via bounding the excess empirical risk for the strongly convex objective $\mathcal{J}(\theta; D) = \mathcal{L}(\theta; D) + \frac{\Delta}{2}\|\theta\|_2^2$ (see (6.33)). Using this machinery, one can obtain an excess empirical risk of $O\left(\frac{L^2p^2}{\Delta n\varepsilon^2}\right)$, if each of the individual loss function $\ell(\theta; d)$ is assumed to be Δ-strongly convex. Notice that this bound is tight [BST14]. While Algorithm $\mathcal{A}_{\text{obj-pert}}$ requires assumptions like smoothness for the privacy proof, a variant of the exponential mechanism $\mathcal{A}_{\text{exp-samp}}$ can also achieve a similar bound, albeit a more complicated analysis. (See Section 4 of [BST14] for more details.)

Extension to (ε, δ)-DP Variant

We will discuss algorithms that are specifically designed to obtain strong privacy/utility trade-offs in the (ε, δ)-DP setting. But it is worth mentioning that Algorithm $\mathcal{A}_{\text{obj-pert}}$ can be shown to provide strong privacy/utility trade-offs in the (ε, δ)-DP setting too. The only change that is needed is the following: Change the noise distribution of b to $\mathcal{N}\left(0, O\left(\frac{L\sqrt{\ln(1/\delta)}}{\varepsilon}\right)^2 \cdot \mathbb{I}_p\right)$. Since Gaussian distribution has a tighter concentration, the excess empirical risk becomes

$O\left(\frac{L\|C\|_2\cdot\sqrt{p\ln(1/\delta)}}{\varepsilon}\right)$. This bound is also known to be tight [BST14]. In Section 6.3 we will study algorithms that achieve similar bounds, however, do not require assumptions like smoothness, or bounded rank of the Hessian. Also, the privacy guarantee of these algorithms will not depend on the convexity of the loss function.

6.3 Empirical Risk Minimization with (ε, δ)-DP

In this section we will look at algorithms that achieve optimal privacy/utility trade-offs under (ε, δ)-DP, while assuming the loss function $\ell(\theta; d)$ being L-Lipschitz in θ, w.r.t. ℓ_2-norm. As we discussed earlier $\mathcal{A}_{\text{obj-pert}}$ achieves similar bounds, but require additional assumptions like smoothness, and bounded rank of the Hessian. Algorithmically, the main difference from Algorithms 1 or Algorithm 2 is that we will not argue privacy for the final model θ^{priv}. Rather, the privacy guarantee will hold for the complete optimization path (i.e., the intermediate models that will get generated. This eventually will imply the (ε, δ)-DP guarantee of the final model θ^{priv}. Since we "privatize" the complete optimization path, as opposed to arguing privacy for the final model θ^{priv}, the resulting algorithms operate under weaker privacy assumptions.

6.3.1 Differentially Private (Stochastic) Gradient Descent (DP-SGD)

DP-SGD [SCS13; BST14; Aba+16] is currently the most widely-used differentially private learning algorithm in practice, with at least two large-scale open source implementations TensorFlow-Privacy [Aba+15], and Opacus [You+21]. Along with its practical success, it also provides optimal privacy/utility trade-offs analytically. While there are various variants of DP-SGD in the literature [SSTT21], the one we will primarily focus on in this chapter is the full-gradient descent version. The presentation of the algorithm (Algorithm 3) will be primarily based on [SSTT21].

There are a few distinctive properties of the algorithm. First, notice the term *clipping norm.* Unlike Algorithms $\mathcal{A}_{\text{exp-samp}}$ and $\mathcal{A}_{\text{obj-pert}}$ above, Algorithm $\mathcal{A}_{\text{DP-SGD}}$ does not assume that the loss function $\ell(\theta; d)$ is ℓ_2-Lipschitz. Rather via the clipping norm bound, in Step 3, it enforces that the ℓ_2-norm of the gradient[ii] of any individual $\ell(\theta; d_i)$ is bounded by L. Second, as we mentioned earlier,

ii. All the results for Algorithm $\mathcal{A}_{\text{DP-SGD}}$ holds if the gradient is replaced by subgradient. So, differentiability is not a necessary condition.

Algorithm 3 $\mathcal{A}_{\text{DP-SGD}}$: Differentially private stochastic gradient descent (DP-SGD)

Require: Data set $D = \{d_1, \cdots, d_n\}$, loss function: $\ell : \mathbf{R}^p \times \mathcal{D} \rightarrow \mathbf{R}$, clipping norm: L, constraint set: $\mathcal{C} \subseteq \mathbf{R}^p$, number of iterations: T, noise multiplier: λ, learning rate: η.

1: $\theta_0 \leftarrow 0$.

2: **for** $t = 0, \ldots, T-1$ **do**

3: $\quad g_t = \sum_{i=1}^{n} \text{clip}\left(\nabla \ell(\theta_t; d_i)\right)$, where $\text{clip}(v) = v \cdot \min\left\{1, \frac{L}{\|v\|_2}\right\}$.

4: $\quad \theta_{t+1} \leftarrow \Pi_{\mathcal{C}}\left(\theta_t - \eta\left(g_t + \mathcal{N}\left(0, \sigma^2\right)\right)\right)$, where $\Pi_{\mathcal{C}}(\mathrm{v}) = \arg\min_{\theta \in \mathcal{C}} \|v - \theta\|_2$ and $\sigma = L \cdot \lambda$.

5: **end for**

6: **return** $\theta^{\text{priv}} = \frac{1}{T} \sum_{t=1}^{T} \theta_t$.

---

we will show that the entire optimization path $\{\theta_0, \ldots, \theta_T\}$ is (ε, δ)-DP. Third, in Step 6 we output the average of all the models. One can provide similar utility/privacy trade-off for the last iterate too, i.e., θ_T [BST14]. We chose the average model purely for the simplicity of analysis. Fourth, unlike traditional SGD (stochastic gradient descent) [Bub15], where each g_t is computed on a minibatch of examples from the training set D, in Algorithm $\mathcal{A}_{\text{DP-SGD}}$ we use the complete gradient. As we will discuss later, the privacy/utility trade-off that we will obtain for Algorithm $\mathcal{A}_{\text{DP-SGD}}$ can also be obtained via using a minibatch of size one in each step $t \in [T]$, drawn i.i.d. from D. For the purpose of brevity, we will provide the main analysis in the context of full-batch gradient.

In the following, we first provide the privacy guarantee for Algorithm $\mathcal{A}_{\text{DP-SGD}}$.

Theorem 6.10. *If we choose the noise multiplier* $\lambda = \frac{\sqrt{2T(\ln(1/\delta)+\varepsilon)}}{\varepsilon}$, *then Algorithm* $\mathcal{A}_{\text{DP-SGD}}$ *(Algorithm 3) satisfies* (ε, δ)*-differential privacy.*

Proof. Consider the estimation of any g_t in Step 3 of Algorithm $\mathcal{A}_{\text{DP-SGD}}$, given θ_t. Let D and D' be two neighboring data sets, and g_t and g_t' be the corresponding gradient estimates at θ_t. Due to the clip$(\cdot)$ function, we have the following: $\left\|g_t - g_t'\right\|_2 \leq L$. Therefore, we can think $g_t : t \in [T]$ to be a set of T adaptively chosen queries on the data set D, with each query having ℓ_2-sensitivity of L. By standard composition property of Gaussian mechanism (described in Part I of the book), if we choose the noise scale to be $\lambda = \frac{\sqrt{2T(\ln(1/\delta)+\varepsilon)}}{\varepsilon}$, then the set of $\{\theta_1, \ldots, \theta_t\}$ satisfies (ε, δ)-differential privacy. □

Next, we move on to prove the utility guarantee of Algorithm $\mathcal{A}_{\text{DP-SGD}}$. We show the following:

Theorem 6.11. *Assume that* $\|\nabla\ell(\theta;d)\|_2 \leq L$ *for all* $d \in \mathcal{D}$ *and* $\theta \in \mathcal{C}$, *and* $0 \in \mathcal{C}$ *Under appropriate choice of the learning rate* η, *and setting the number of steps* $T = \frac{n^2\varepsilon^2}{p}$ *and the noise multiplier* $\lambda = \frac{\sqrt{2T(\ln(1/\delta)+\varepsilon)}}{\varepsilon}$, *we have the following:*

$$\mathbb{E}\left[\mathcal{L}(\theta^{\mathsf{priv}}, D) - \mathcal{L}(\theta^*; D)\right] = O\left(\frac{L\,\|\mathcal{C}\|_2}{\varepsilon}\sqrt{p(\ln(1/\delta)+\varepsilon)}\right).$$

Proof. We prove the theorem via the standard template for analyzing SGD methods [Bub15]. Recall $\theta^{\mathsf{priv}} = \frac{1}{T}\sum_{t=1}^{T}\theta_t$, where $\{\theta_1,\ldots,\theta_T\}$ are the models in each iterate of DP-GD. By convexity, and the standard linearization trick in convex optimization [Bub15], we have:

$$\mathcal{L}\left(\theta^{\mathsf{priv}}; D\right) - \mathcal{L}\left(\theta^*; D\right) \leq \frac{1}{T}\sum_{t=1}^{T}\langle\nabla\mathcal{L}(\theta_t; D), \theta_t - \theta^*\rangle. \tag{6.38}$$

Let b_t is the Gaussian noise vector added at time step t To bound the error in (6.38), we will use a potential argument w.r.t. the potential function

$$\Psi_t(\theta) = \mathbb{E}_{b_1,\ldots,b_t}\left[\left\|\theta - \theta^*\right\|_2^2\right] = \mathbb{E}_{b_1,\ldots,b_{t-1}}\left[\mathbb{E}_{b_t}\left[\left.\left\|\theta - \theta^*\right\|_2^2\right| b_1,\ldots,b_{t-1}\right]\right].$$

Recall the update step in Algorithm $\mathcal{A}_{\mathrm{DP-SGD}}$: $\theta_{t+1} \leftarrow \Pi_{\mathcal{C}}(\theta_t - \eta(\nabla\mathcal{L}(\theta_t; D) + b_t))$. Since, by assumption the loss function $\ell(\theta; d)$ is ℓ_2-Lipschitz bounded, clip$(\cdot)$ does not have any effect. We get the following by simple algebraic manipulation:

$$\begin{aligned}
\Psi_t(\theta_{t+1}) &= \mathbb{E}_{b_1,\ldots,b_t}\left[\left\|\Pi_{\mathcal{C}}\left(\theta_t - \eta(\nabla\mathcal{L}(\theta_t; D) + b_t)\right) - \theta^*\right\|_2^2\right] && (6.39)\\
&\leq \mathbb{E}_{b_1,\ldots,b_t}\left[\left\|\left(\theta_t - \theta^*\right) - \eta(\nabla\mathcal{L}(\theta_t; D) + b_t)\right\|_2^2\right] && (6.40)\\
&= \Psi_t(\theta_t) - 2\eta\mathbb{E}_{b_1,\ldots,b_t}\left[\langle\nabla\mathcal{L}(\theta_t; D) + b_t, \theta_t - \theta^*\rangle\right]\\
&\quad + \eta^2\mathbb{E}_{b_1,\ldots,b_t}\left[\|\nabla\mathcal{L}(\theta_t; D) + b_t\|_2^2\right] && (6.41)\\
&\leq \Psi_t(\theta_t) - 2\eta\mathbb{E}_{b_1,\ldots,b_t}\left[\langle\nabla\mathcal{L}(\theta_t; D), \theta_t - \theta^*\rangle\right]\\
&\quad + \eta^2\left(n^2L^2 + \mathbb{E}_{b_t}\left[\|b_t\|_2^2\right]\right) && (6.42)\\
&= \Psi_{t-1}(\theta_t) - 2\eta\mathbb{E}_{b_1,\ldots,b_t}\left[\langle\nabla\mathcal{L}(\theta_t; D), \theta_t - \theta^*\rangle\right]\\
&\quad + \eta^2L^2\left(n^2 + p\cdot\lambda^2\right), && (6.43)
\end{aligned}$$

where (6.40) follows from the fact that ℓ_2-projection onto a convex constraint set $\mathcal{C}$ always reduces the ℓ_2-distance, and (6.43) follows because $b_t \sim \mathcal{N}(0, L^2\lambda^2)^p$ and thus $\mathbb{E}_{b_t}\left[\|b_t\|_2^2\right] = p\cdot L^2\lambda^2$. Rearranging the terms in (6.43), we have the following,

$$\mathbb{E}\left[\langle \nabla \mathcal{L}(\theta_t; D), \theta_t - \theta^* \rangle\right] \leq \frac{1}{2\eta}\left(\Psi_{t-1}(\theta_t) - \Psi_t(\theta_{t+1})\right) + \frac{\eta L^2}{2}\left(n^2 + p \cdot \lambda^2\right). \tag{6.44}$$

Summing up (6.44) for all $t \in [T]$, averaging over the T iterations, and combining with (6.38), we get:

$$\mathbb{E}\left[\mathcal{L}\left(\theta^{\text{priv}}; D\right)\right] - \mathcal{L}\left(\theta^*; D\right) \leq \frac{1}{2T\eta}\Psi(0) + \frac{\eta L^2}{2}\left(n^2 + p \cdot \lambda^2\right),$$
$$\text{where } \Psi(\theta) = \left\|\theta - \theta^*\right\|_2^2 \tag{6.45}$$

Setting η to minimize the RHS, we have

$$\mathbb{E}\left[\mathcal{L}\left(\theta^{\text{priv}}; D\right)\right] - \mathcal{L}\left(\theta^*; D\right) \leq L\left\|\mathcal{C}\right\|_2 \cdot \sqrt{\frac{n^2 + p \cdot \lambda^2}{T}} \tag{6.46}$$
$$= L\left\|\mathcal{C}\right\|_2 \sqrt{\frac{n^2}{T} + \frac{2p \cdot (\ln(1/\delta) + \varepsilon)}{\varepsilon^2}}, \tag{6.47}$$

where the equality in (6.47) follows by plugging in $\lambda = \frac{\sqrt{2T(\ln(1/\delta)+\varepsilon)}}{\varepsilon}$. Now, setting $T = \frac{n^2\varepsilon^2}{p}$, we have

$$\mathbb{E}\left[\mathcal{L}\left(\theta^{\text{priv}}; D\right)\right] - \mathcal{L}\left(\theta^*; D\right) \leq \frac{L\left\|\mathcal{C}\right\|_2 \sqrt{3p \cdot (\ln(1/\delta) + \varepsilon)}}{\varepsilon}. \tag{6.48}$$

This completes the proof. □

Oracle Complexity

Notice, Algorithm $\mathcal{A}_{\text{DP-SGD}}$ reaches an *average* excess empirical risk of $\widetilde{O}\left(\frac{\sqrt{p}}{\varepsilon n}\right)$ in $T = \frac{n^2\varepsilon^2}{p}$ steps. For non-smooth, and non-strongly convex losses, this rate of convergence is tight for SGD based methods (up to dependence on dimensionality), i.e., in $\Theta(1/\alpha^2)$ steps, one can get to an error of α. This demonstrates an important phenomenon. DP does not slow down the rate of convergence in comparison to a non-private SGD method up to the error allowed under privacy constraints. Furthermore, even if we set $T \to \infty$, under appropriate choice of the learning rate η, the excess empirical risk remains the same. This implies, Algorithm $\mathcal{A}_{\text{DP-SGD}}$ does not need the number of steps T to tuned for optimal privacy/utility trade-off as long as $T \geq \frac{n^2\varepsilon^2}{p}$. This property is not true in general for iterative DP optimization methods.

The oracle complexity of Algorithm $\mathcal{A}_{\text{DP-SGD}}$ (for achieving the excess empirical risk in Theorem 6.11) is $\frac{n^3\varepsilon^2}{p}$. This because in each of the T steps, Algorithm $\mathcal{A}_{\text{DP-SGD}}$ performs n gradient evaluations.

Improving Oracle Complexity with Privacy Amplification by Sampling

One can improve the oracle complexity of Algorithm $\mathcal{A}_{\text{DP-SGD}}$ via special tool in the DP literature called, privacy amplification by sampling [Kas+08]. Informally, privacy amplification by sampling says that if an algorithm $\mathcal{A}$ is $\varepsilon_0 \leq \frac{1}{2}$-DP on a data set D, then on a data set D_{samp}, where each entry of D is sampled with probability q, $\mathcal{A}(D_{\text{samp}})$ satisfies $O(q \cdot \varepsilon_0)$-DP. One can use this tool to show that essentially at the same level of noise as in Step 4 of Algorithm $\mathcal{A}_{\text{DP-SGD}}$, one can use $g_t = n \cdot \text{clip}\left(\nabla \ell(\theta_t; d)\right)$ (in Step 3) with d sampled uniformly at random from the data D, independently at each time step T. Since, modulo clipping, the new g_t is an unbiased estimator of the gradient $\nabla \mathcal{L}(\theta_t; D)$, the utility guarantee in Theorem 6.11 remain unchanged. This reduces the oracle complexity by a factor of n for Algorithm $\mathcal{A}_{\text{DP-SGD}}$. For a focused analysis of privacy amplification via sampling, the reader is referred to Chapter 3.6.

Excess ERM Bound for Strongly Convex Losses

In Theorem 6.11 we provided the guarantee only for ℓ_2-Lipschitz convex losses. One can use the same Algorithm $\mathcal{A}_{\text{DP-SGD}}$, with appropriate learning rate η, to obtain optimal privacy/utility trade-off when the loss function $\ell(\theta; d)$ satisfies Δ-strong convexity, along with L-Lipschitzness. The excess empirical risk bound in that case is $O\left(\frac{Lp\ln^3(n/\delta)}{\Delta n\varepsilon^2}\right)$ [BST14]. As we will discuss later, this bound is tight.

Dimension Independent Excess ERM Bounds

In all the results we saw so far there is an explicit polynomial dependence of the dimensionality

(p) on the error. For of generalized linear models (e.g., logistic regression), one can completely avoid this dependence when $\mathcal{C} = R^p$ and achieve an excess empirical risk of $O\left(\frac{L\|\theta^*\|_2\sqrt{n\ln(1/\delta)}}{\varepsilon}\right)$. Algorithm $\mathcal{A}_{\text{DP-SGD}}$, with appropriate choice of the learning rate η is capable of achieving this bound. (See [STT20] for more details.)

6.3.2 Differentially Private Follow-the-regularized-leader (DP-FTRL)

Till now we assumed that the complete data set D is at the disposal of the optimization algorithm. However, there are problem settings where the data arrives in the form of a stream. Non-privately, the algorithms that are designed in that space are typically called online convex optimization (OCO) algorithms [Sha+11]. More formally, suppose we have a stream of data samples $D = [d_1, \ldots, d_n] \in \mathcal{D}^n$, where $\mathcal{D}$ is the domain of data samples, and a loss function $\ell : \mathcal{C} \times \mathcal{D} \rightarrow \mathbb{R}$, where $\mathcal{C} \in \mathbb{R}^p$ is the space of all models. We consider the setting of regret minimization.

Regret Minimization

At every time step $t \in [n]$, while observing samples $\{d_1, \ldots, d_{t-1}\}$, the algorithm $\mathcal{A}$ outputs a model $\theta_t \in \mathcal{C}$ which is used to predict on example d_t provided by an adversary after observing $\{\theta_1, \ldots, \theta_t\}$. The performance of $\mathcal{A}$ is measured in terms of regret against an arbitrary post-hoc comparator $\theta^* \in \mathcal{C}$, maximized over the choice of $[d_1, \ldots, d_n]$ by the adversary, where d_t is a function of $\{d_1, \ldots, d_{t-1}\}$ and $\{\theta_1, \ldots, \theta_t\}$:

$$R_D(\mathcal{A}; \theta^*) = \left[\sum_{t=1}^{n} \ell(\theta_t; d_t) - \sum_{t=1}^{n} \ell(\theta^*; d_t) \right]. \tag{6.49}$$

We consider the algorithm $\mathcal{A}$ low-regret if $R(\mathcal{A}; \theta^*) = o(n)$. To ensure a low-regret algorithm, we will assume $\|\nabla \ell(\theta; d)\|_2 \leq L$ for any data sample d, and any models $\theta \in \mathcal{C}$. The quantity $R_D(\mathcal{A}; \theta^*)$ is also called the *adversarial regret* [Haz19; Sha+11]. One can also look at a related quantity *stochastic regret* [HK14], where the data samples in D are drawn i.i.d. from some distribution τ. In this chapter, we will only focus on adversarial regret.

In (6.54), we show that the regret is an upper bound on the excess empirical risk in (6.3). Hence, for the remainder of this section, we will only focus on bounding $R(\mathcal{A}; \theta^*)$. Although we have not discussed the DP-FTRL algorithm ($\mathcal{A}_{\mathrm{FTRL}}$), we want to highlight a specific attribute of the algorithm $\mathcal{A}_{\mathrm{FTRL}}$ in order to connect the regret to the excess empirical risk. At any time step t, to estimate θ_{t+1}, $\mathcal{A}_{\mathrm{FTRL}}$ only uses DP estimates (via Gaussian mechanism) for a set of queries of the form $\sum_{i=\tau_1}^{\tau_2} \nabla \ell(\theta_i; d_i)$, where $0 \leq \tau_1, \tau_2 \leq t$.

Now, given the data set D, consider another data set $\widehat{D}$ with n data samples with each entry of $\widehat{D} = \{\widehat{d}_1, \ldots, \widehat{d}_n\}$ is sampled i.i.d. with replacement from D. First notice that with probability at least $1 - \delta$, no data sample in D appears more that $O(\ln(n/\delta))$ number of times. This follows from the standard use of Chernoff bound. Because of the way $\mathcal{A}_{\mathrm{FTRL}}$ operates, this would increase the ℓ_2-sensitivity of any query that $\mathcal{A}_{\mathrm{FTRL}}$ considers from L to $L \cdot \ln(n/\delta)$, with probability $1 - \delta$. This in-turn means if adding $\mathcal{L}(0, L^2\lambda^2)$ to each query that $\mathcal{A}_{\mathrm{FTRL}}(D)$ considers satisfies (ε, δ)-DP, then adding $\mathcal{N}(0, O(L^2 \ln^2(n/\delta)\lambda^2))$ satisfies (ε, δ)-DP for $\mathcal{A}_{\mathrm{FTRL}}$ when operating on data set $\widehat{D}$. This calculation says that if $\mathcal{A}_{\mathrm{FTRL}}$ operates on $\widehat{D}$ instead of D, then the error due to noise will only go up by a factor of polylog (n/δ).

Next we relate $\mathcal{L}(\theta; D)$ with $\mathcal{L}(\theta; \widehat{D})$, to ensure that one can use $\widehat{D}$ as a proxy for the data set D. Let $\{\theta_1, \ldots, \theta_n\}$ be the models output by $\mathcal{A}_{\text{FTRL}}$ on data set $\widehat{D}$. We have the following in (6.54).

$$\mathcal{L}\left(\frac{1}{n}\sum_{t=1}^{n}\theta_t; D\right) - \min_{\theta\in\mathcal{C}}\mathcal{L}(\theta; D) \leq \frac{1}{n}\left(\sum_{t=1}^{n}\mathcal{L}\left(\theta_t; D\right)\right) - \min_{\theta\in\mathcal{C}}\mathcal{L}(\theta; D) \quad (6.50)$$

$$= \sum_{t=1}^{n}\left(\frac{1}{n}\sum_{i=1}^{n}\ell\left(\theta_t; d_i\right)\right) - \min_{\theta\in\mathcal{C}}\mathcal{L}(\theta; D) \quad (6.51)$$

$$= \sum_{t=1}^{n}\mathbb{E}_{\widehat{d}_t}\left[\ell\left(\theta_t; \widehat{d}_t\right)\right] - \min_{\theta\in\mathcal{C}}\mathcal{L}(\theta; D) \quad (6.52)$$

$$= \mathbb{E}_{\widehat{D}}\left[\sum_{t=1}^{n}\ell\left(\theta_t; \widehat{d}_t\right)\right] - \min_{\theta\in\mathcal{C}}\mathbb{E}_{\widehat{D}}\left[\mathcal{L}(\theta; \widehat{D})\right] \quad (6.53)$$

$$\leq \mathbb{E}_{\widehat{D}}\left[\sum_{t=1}^{n}\ell\left(\theta_t; \widehat{d}_t\right) - \min_{\theta\in\mathcal{C}}\mathcal{L}(\theta; \widehat{D})\right] \quad (6.54)$$

$$\leq \mathbb{E}_{\widehat{D}}\left[R_D\left(\mathcal{A}_{\text{FTRL}}; \arg\min_{\theta\in\mathcal{C}}\mathcal{L}\left(\theta; \widehat{D}\right)\right)\right]. \quad (6.55)$$

Equation (6.50) follows from Jensen's inequality, and the equality in (6.52) follows from the fact that θ_t is independent of $\widehat{d}_t$. By (6.54) it follows that the regret of $\mathcal{A}_{\text{FTRL}}$ on data set $\widehat{D}$ is an upper bound on the excess empirical risk of $\theta^{\text{priv}} = \frac{1}{n}\sum_{t=1}^{n}\theta_t$ on the data set D.

Notion of Privacy

Since we are in the add/remove model of differential privacy, in the streaming setting removing one data sample can change time of arrival of all other data samples appearing after it. To ensure that such a thing does not happen, we operate with a notion of differential privacy, that preserves the length of the stream, even in the add/remove variant.

Definition 6.12 (Differential privacy). *Let $\mathcal{D}$ be the domain of data records, $\perp \notin \mathcal{D}$ be a special element, and let $\widehat{\mathcal{D}} = \mathcal{D} \cup \{\perp\}$ be the extended domain. A randomized algorithm $\mathcal{A} : \widehat{\mathcal{D}}^n \to \mathcal{S}$ is (ε, δ)-differentially private if for any data set $D \in \widehat{\mathcal{D}}^n$ and any neighbor $D' \in \widehat{\mathcal{D}}^n$ (formed from D by replacing one record with $\perp$), and for any* *event $S \in \mathcal{S}$, we have*

$$\mathbf{Pr}[\mathcal{A}(D) \in S] \leq e^{\varepsilon} \cdot \mathbf{Pr}[\mathcal{A}(D') \in S] + \delta, \quad \textit{and}$$
$$\mathbf{Pr}[\mathcal{A}(D') \in S] \leq e^{\varepsilon} \cdot \mathbf{Pr}[\mathcal{A}(D) \in S] + \delta,$$

where the probability is over the randomness of $\mathcal{A}$.

In Algorithm $\mathcal{A}_{\text{FTRL}}$ (Differentially Private Follow-the-regularized-leader (DP-FTRL)), we treat $\perp$ specially, namely assuming it always produces a zero gradient.

Interlude on Estimating Prefix-sum with (ε, δ)-DP

Before we present the description of Algorithm $\mathcal{A}_{\text{FTRL}}$, we will take an interlude to a seemingly unrelated problem of estimating prefix sums: Consider a sequence of vectors $X = \{x_1, \ldots, x_n\}$, with each $x_i \in \mathbb{R}^p$ and $\|x_i\|_2 \leq L$.

The objective it design a differentially private algorithm that outputs an approximation to $\{s_1, \ldots, s_t\}$, where each $s_t = \sum_{i=1}^{t} x_i$. We allow x_{t+1} to be *adaptively* chosen based on the outputs $\{s_1, \ldots, s_t\}$. [DNPR10; CSS11] studies this problem in the context of *privacy under continual observation*. Here, we provide the algorithm from [DNPR10] based on a binary tree data structure.

A naïve solution to the problem would be the following: $\forall t \in [n]$, output $s_t^{\text{priv}} \leftarrow s_t + \mathcal{N}\left(0, L^2\lambda^2\right)$, where $\lambda = \frac{\sqrt{2n(\ln(1/\delta)+\varepsilon)}}{\varepsilon}$. By standard properties of Gaussian mechanism described earlier in the book, this algorithm is (ε, δ)-differentially private. However, the error in each of the estimate s_t^{priv}, i.e., $\mathbb{E}\left[\left\|s_t - s_t^{\text{priv}}\right\|_2\right]$, is $\Omega\left(\frac{\sqrt{np\ln(1/\delta)}}{\varepsilon}\right)$. Based on an algorithm by [DNPR10; CSS11], we provide an algorithm that reduces the error to $\Omega\left(\frac{\sqrt{n\ln^2(n)\cdot\ln(1/\delta)}}{\varepsilon}\right)$. In the following we describe the algorithm.

There are three main functions in the algorithm, namely, InitializeTree, AddToTree, GetSum. At a high-level, InitializeTree initializes the tree data structure $\mathcal{T}$ with $2^{\lceil \lg(n) \rceil}$ leaf nodes, AddToTree allows adding a new vector x_t to $\mathcal{T}$, and GetSum returns the prefix sum $\sum_{i=1}^{t} x_i$ privately. It follows from [ST13a] that for a sequence of (adaptively chosen) vectors $\{x_t\}_{t=1}^{n}$, if we perform AddToTree $(\mathcal{T}, t, x_t)$ for each $t \in [n]$, then we can write GetSum $(\mathcal{T}, t) = \sum_{i=1}^{t} x_i + b_t$ where b_t is normally distributed with mean zero, and $\forall t \in [n], \mathbb{E}\left[\|b_t\|_2\right] \leq L\lambda\sqrt{p\lceil \lg(n) \rceil}$. Now, since any data sample in the data set X affects only $\lceil \lg(n) \rceil$ nodes in the binary tree $\mathcal{T}$, hence setting $\lambda = \frac{\sqrt{2\lceil \lg(n) \rceil(\ln(1/\delta)+\varepsilon)}}{\varepsilon}$ would ensure that the algorithm is (ε, δ)-differentially private. The formal description of the algorithm is given below.

1. InitializeTree (n, λ^2, L): Initialize a complete binary tree $\mathcal{T}$ with $2^{\lceil \lg(n) \rceil}$ leaf nodes, with each node being sampled i.i.d. from $\mathcal{N}(0, L^2\lambda^2 \cdot \mathbb{I}_{p \times p})$.

2. AddToTree $(\mathcal{T}, t, v)$: Add v to all the nodes along the path to the root of $\mathcal{T}$, starting from t-th leaf node.
3. GetSum $(\mathcal{T}, t)$: Let $[\mathsf{node}_1, \ldots, \mathsf{node}_h]$ be the list of nodes from the root of $\mathcal{T}$ to the t-th leaf node, with node_1 being the root node and node_h being the leaf node.
   (a) Initialize $s \leftarrow \mathbf{0}^p$ and convert t to binary in h bit representation $[b_1, \ldots, b_h]$, with b_1 being the most significant bit.
   (b) For each $j \in [h]$, if $b_j = 1$, then add the value in left sibling of node_j to s. Here if node_j is the left child, then it is treated as its own left sibling.
   (c) Return s.

We have the following theorem to formally quantify the privacy/utility trade-off for the tree aggregation algorithm.

Theorem 6.13 (Follows from [ST13a]). *Let $X = \{x_1, \ldots, x_n\}$ be a sequence of adaptively chosen data vectors with $\forall u \in [n]$, $\|x_i\|_2 \leq L, x_i \in \mathbb{R}^p$. The tree aggregation algorithm described above is (ε, δ)-differentially private with noise multiplier $\lambda = \frac{\sqrt{2\lceil \lg(n) \rceil (\ln(1/\delta)+\varepsilon)}}{\varepsilon}$. Furthermore, the outputs s_t^{priv} that approximates $s_t = \sum_{i=1}^{t} x_t$ has the following property:*

$$\mathbb{E}\left[\left\| s_t^{\text{priv}} - s_t \right\|_2\right] \leq L\lambda\sqrt{p\lceil \lg(n) \rceil}.$$

Algorithmic Description of DP-FTRL ($\mathcal{A}_{\text{FTRL}}$)

The main idea of DP-FTRL [Kai+21b; ST13a; AS17] is based on three observations: i) For online convex optimization, to bound the regret, for a given loss function $\ell(\theta; d_t)$ (i.e., the loss at time step t), it suffices for the algorithm to operate on a linearization of the loss at θ_t (the model output at time step t): $\tilde{\ell}(\theta; d_t) = \langle \nabla_\theta \ell(\theta_t; d_t), \theta - \theta_t \rangle$, ii) Under appropriate choice of λ, optimizing for $\theta_{t+1} = \arg\min_{\theta \in \mathcal{C}} \sum_{i=1}^{t} \tilde{\ell}(\theta; d_t) + \frac{\lambda}{2} \|\theta\|_2^2$ over $\theta \in \mathcal{C}$ gives a good model at step $t+1$, and iii) For all $t \in [n]$, one can privately keep track of $\sum_{i=1}^{t} \tilde{\ell}(\theta; d_t)$ using the *tree aggregation protocol* [DNPR10; CSS11] described above.

In Theorem 6.14, we provide the privacy guarantee for Algorithm 4. The proof is immediate from Theorem 6.13.

Theorem 6.14 (Privacy guarantee). *If the noise multiplier $\lambda = \frac{\sqrt{2\lceil \lg(n) \rceil (\ln(1/\delta)+\varepsilon)}}{\varepsilon}$, then Algorithm 4 (Algorithm $\mathcal{A}_{\text{FTRL}}$) guarantees (ε, δ)-differential privacy.*

The theorem here gives a regret guarantee for Algorithm 4 against a *fully adaptive* [Sha+11] adversary who chooses the loss function $\ell(\theta; d_t)$ based on $[\theta_1, \ldots, \theta_t]$, but without knowing the internal randomness of the algorithm.

Algorithm 4 $\mathcal{A}_{\text{FTRL}}$: Differentially Private Follow-The-Regularized-Leader (DP-FTRL)

Require: Data set: $D = \{d_1, \cdots, d_n\}$ arriving in a stream, in an arbitrary order; constraint set: $\mathcal{C}$, noise multiplier: λ, regularization parameter: Δ, clipping norm: L.

$\theta_1 \leftarrow \arg\min_{\theta \in \mathcal{C}} \frac{\Delta}{2} \|\theta\|_2^2$. **Output** θ_1.
$\mathcal{T} \leftarrow \mathsf{InitializeTree}\,(n, \sigma^2, L)$.
for $t \in [n]$ **do**
  Let $\nabla_t \leftarrow \text{clip}\,(\nabla_\theta \ell(\theta_t; d_t), L)$, where $\text{clip}\,(v, L) = v \cdot \min\left\{\frac{L}{\|v\|_2}, 1\right\}$, taking $\nabla_\theta \ell(\theta; \bot) = \mathbf{0}$.
  $\mathcal{T} \leftarrow \mathsf{AddToTree}\,(\mathcal{T}, t, \nabla_t)$.
  $s_t \leftarrow \mathsf{GetSum}\,(\mathcal{T}, t)$, i.e., estimate $\sum_{i=1}^{t} \nabla_i$ via tree-aggregation protocol.
  $\theta_{t+1} \leftarrow \arg\min_{\theta \in \mathcal{C}} \langle s_t, \theta \rangle + \frac{\Delta}{2} \|\theta\|_2^2$. **Output** θ_{t+1}.
end for

Theorem 6.15 (Regret guarantee). *Let $\{\theta_1, \ldots, \theta_n\}$ be the outputs of Algorithm $\mathcal{A}_{\text{FTRL}}$ (Algorithm 4), and L be a bound on the ℓ_2-Lipschitz constant of the loss functions. W.p. at least $1 - \beta$ over the randomness of $\mathcal{A}_{\text{FTRL}}$, the following is true for any $\theta^* \in \mathcal{C}$.*

$$\frac{1}{n}\sum_{t=1}^{n} \ell(\theta_t; d_t) - \frac{1}{n}\sum_{t=1}^{n} \ell(\theta^*; d_t) \leq \frac{L\lambda\sqrt{p\lceil \lg n \rceil \ln(n/\beta)} + L^2}{\Delta} + \frac{\Delta}{2}\left(\|\theta^*\|_2^2 - \|\theta_1\|_2^2\right).$$

Setting Δ optimally and plugging in the noise multiplier λ from Theorem 6.14 to ensure (ε, δ)-differential privacy, we have

$$R_D(\mathcal{A}_{\text{FTRL}}; \theta^*) = O\left(L\left\|\theta^*\right\|_2 \sqrt{n} \cdot \left(1 + \sqrt{\frac{p^{1/2}(\ln^2(1/\delta) + \varepsilon)\ln(1/\beta)}{\varepsilon}}\right)\right).$$

Proof. Recall that by Algorithm $\mathcal{A}_{\text{FTRL}}$, $\theta_{t+1} \leftarrow \arg\min_{\theta \in \mathcal{C}} \underbrace{\sum_{i=1}^{t} \langle \nabla_i, \theta \rangle + \frac{\Delta}{2} \|\theta\|_2^2 + \langle b_t, \theta \rangle}_{J_t^{\text{priv}}(\theta)}$, where the Gaussian noise $b_t = s_t - \sum_{i=1}^{t} \nabla_i$ for s_t being the output of $\mathsf{GetSum}\,(\mathcal{T}, t)$. By standard concentration of spherical Gaussians, w.p. at least $1 - \beta$, $\forall t \in [n]$, $\|b_t\|_2 \leq L\lambda\sqrt{p\lceil \lg(n) \rceil \ln(n/\beta)}$. We will use this bound to control the error introduced due to privacy. Now, consider the optimizer of the non-private objective:

$$\widetilde{\theta}_{t+1} \leftarrow \arg\min_{\theta \in \mathcal{C}} \underbrace{\sum_{i=1}^{t} \langle \nabla_i, \theta \rangle + \frac{\Delta}{2} \|\theta\|_2^2}_{J_t^{\text{np}}(\theta)}, \qquad \text{where } \nabla_t = \nabla \ell(\theta_t; d_t).$$

That is, post-hoc we consider the hypothetical application of non-private FTRL to the same sequence of *linearized* loss functions $f_t(\widetilde{\theta}) = \langle \nabla_t, \widetilde{\theta} \rangle = \langle \nabla \ell(\theta_t; d_t), \widetilde{\theta} \rangle$ seen in the private training run. In the following, we will first bound how much the models output by $\mathcal{A}_{\text{FTRL}}$ deviate from models output by the hypothetical non-private FTRL discussed above. Then, we invoke standard regret bound for FTRL, while accounting for the deviation of the models output by $\mathcal{A}_{\text{FTRL}}$. By the same calculation as in (6.29) in Section 6.2.2, we obtain

$$\left\|\widetilde{\theta}_{t+1} - \theta_{t+1}\right\|_2 \leq \frac{\|b_t\|_2}{\Delta}. \tag{6.56}$$

We can now easily bound the regret. By standard linear approximation "trick" from the online learning literature [Sha12; Haz19], we have the following. For $\nabla_t = \nabla_\theta \ell(\theta_t; d_t)$,

$$\begin{aligned}
\sum_{t=1}^{n} \ell(\theta_t; d_t) - \sum_{t=1}^{n} \ell(\theta^*; d_t) &\leq \sum_{t=1}^{n} \langle \nabla_t, \theta_t - \theta^* \rangle \\
&= \sum_{t=1}^{n} \langle \nabla_t, \theta_t - \widetilde{\theta}_t + \widetilde{\theta}_t - \theta^* \rangle \\
&= \underbrace{\sum_{t=1}^{n} \langle \nabla_t, \widetilde{\theta}_t - \theta^* \rangle}_{A} + \underbrace{\sum_{t=1}^{n} \langle \nabla_t, \theta_t - \widetilde{\theta}_t \rangle}_{B}.
\end{aligned} \tag{6.57}$$

One can bound the term A in (6.57) by Theorem 5.2 of [Haz19] and get $A \leq \left(\frac{L^2 n}{\Delta} + \frac{\Delta}{2}\left(\|\theta^*\|_2^2 - \|\theta_1\|_2^2\right)\right)$. As for term B, using (6.56) and the concentration on b_t mentioned earlier, we have, w.p. at least $1 - \beta$,

$$B \leq \sum_{t=1}^{n} \|\nabla_t\|_2 \cdot \left\|\widetilde{\theta}_t - \theta_t\right\|_2 \leq \sum_{t=1}^{n} L \cdot \left\|\widetilde{\theta}_t - \theta_t\right\|_2 \leq \frac{2L\lambda\sqrt{p\lceil \lg n \rceil \ln(n/\beta)}}{\Delta}. \tag{6.58}$$

Combining (6.57) and (6.58), we immediately have the first part of the theorem. To prove the second part, we just optimize for the regularization parameter Δ and plug in the noise multiplier λ from Theorem 6.14. □

Translating Theorem 6.15 Into Excess Empirical Risk

As we saw in (6.54), one can interpret the regret guarantee as a bound on the excess empirical risk. This essentially means the excess empirical risk one can obtain by using Algorithm $\mathcal{A}_{\mathrm{FTRL}}$ is $O\left(\frac{p^{1/4}\sqrt{n}\ln^2(1/\delta)}{\sqrt{\varepsilon}} \cdot \mathrm{polylog}\,(n)\right)$. While this bound is strictly worse than the one we obtained for Algorithm $\mathcal{A}_{\mathrm{DP-SGD}}$ via Theorem 6.11, the oracle complexity of $\mathcal{A}_{\mathrm{FTRL}}$ is better by a factor of n. A natural question that arises is whether, we can have $\mathcal{A}_{\mathrm{FTRL}}$ achieve similar utility guarantee as $\mathcal{A}_{\mathrm{DP-SGD}}$ under similar oracle complexity. This is still an open question for research.

Practical Extensions

One of the major advantages of DP-FTRL over DP-SGD is that it can operate over a stream of data samples, while still providing strong privacy/utility trade-offs. This makes it an attractive choice for settings like federated learning (FL), where there isn't a single static data set in a centralized location. However, extending DP-FTRL to settings require a much more involved privacy analysis as one user can contribute multiple training examples, during the training process. See [Kai+21a] for a detailed discussion.

6.4 DP Empirical Risk Minimization with ℓ_1/ℓ_∞-geometry

The algorithms presented till now best work when the objective function is Lipschitz with respect to ℓ_2-norm. But in many machine learning tasks, especially those with sparsity constraint, the objective function is often Lipschitz with respect to ℓ_1-norm. For example, in the high-dimensional linear regression setting e.g. the classical LASSO algorithm [Tib96], we would like to compute $\arg\min_{\|\theta\|_1 \le s} \|X\theta - y\|_2^2$. In the usual case of $|x_{ij}| = O(1), |y_i| = O(s)$, the loss function $\ell(\theta; (x_i, y_i)) = \|y_i - \langle x_i, \theta\rangle\|_2^2$ is $O(s)$-Lipschitz with respect to ℓ_1-norm but is $O(s\sqrt{p})$-Lipschitz with respect to ℓ_2-norm within the constraint set $\|\theta\|_1 \le s$. Here x_i correspond to the i-th row of the design matrix X, and y_i corresponds to the i-th coordinate of the response vector y.

Let us consider the data set $D = \{(x_1, y_1), \ldots, (x_n, y_n)\}$, the loss function $\mathcal{L}(\theta; D) = \sum_{i=1}^{n} (y_i - \langle x_i, \theta\rangle)^2$, and the constraint set $\mathcal{C}$ to be $\|\theta\|_1 \le s$. Then applying any of the algorithms mentioned earlier on the corresponding ERM problem would result in an excess empirical risk of $\widetilde{O}_{\varepsilon,\delta}\left(s^2\sqrt{p}\right)$. For the interesting high-dimensional parameter regime, where $s \ll n \ll p$, this bound is vacuous. We would ideally want an excess empirical risk of the form $O_{\varepsilon,\delta}\left(\text{poly}\left(s, \ln(p)\right)\right)$. Here, $\widetilde{O}_{\varepsilon,\delta}(\cdot)$ hides the privacy parameters ε and δ.

In this section, we will show that in the high-dimensional setting it is more effective to use the private version of the classical Frank-Wolfe algorithm [FW56]. In particular, we show that for LASSO, such algorithm achieves the nearly optimal privacy risk of $\Theta_{\varepsilon,\delta}(s^2 \cdot \text{polylog}\,(p) \cdot n^{1/3})$.

6.4.1 Frank-Wolfe Algorithm

We present the algorithm in this section as a purely optimization procedure that minimizes a convex function $f : \mathcal{C} \to \mathbb{R}$. The Frank-Wolfe algorithm [FW56] can be regarded as a "greedy" algorithm which moves towards the optimum solution in the first order approximation (see Algorithm 5 for the description). How fast Frank-Wolfe algorithm converges depends f's "curvature", defined as follows according to [Cla10; Jag13]. We remark that a γ-smooth function on $\mathcal{C}$ has curvature constant bounded by $\gamma\ \|\mathcal{C}\|_2^2$.

Definition 6.16 (Curvature constant). *For $f : \mathcal{C} \to \mathbb{R}$, define Γ_f as below.*

$$\Gamma_f := \sup_{\theta_1,\theta_2,\in\mathcal{C},\gamma\in(0,1],\theta_3=\theta_1+\gamma(\theta_2-\theta_1)} \frac{2}{\gamma^2}\left(f(\theta_3) - f(\theta_1) - \langle \theta_3 - \theta_1, \nabla f(\theta_1)\rangle\right).$$

Remark 6.17. *One can show ([Cla10; Jag13]) that for any $q, r \geq 1$ such that $q^{-1} + r^{-1} = 1$, Γ_f is upper bounded by $\lambda\|\mathcal{C}\|_q^2$, where $\lambda = \max_{\theta\in\mathcal{C},\|v\|_q=1} \|\nabla^2 f(\theta)\cdot v\|_r$.*

Remark 6.18. *One useful bound is for the quadratic programming $f(\theta) = \theta^\top X^T X\theta + \langle b, \theta\rangle$. In this case, by [Cla10], $\Gamma_f \leq \max_{a,b\in X\cdot\mathcal{C}} \|a - b\|_2^2$. When $\mathcal{C}$ is centrally symmetric, we have the bound $\Gamma_f \leq 4\max_{\theta\in\mathcal{C}} \|X\theta\|_2^2$.*

Algorithm 5 Frank-Wolfe algorithm

Require: $\mathcal{C} \subseteq \mathbb{R}^p, f : \mathcal{C} \to \mathbb{R}, \mu$

Choose an arbitrary θ_1 from $\mathcal{C}$;

for $t = 1$ to $T - 1$ **do**

  Compute $\widehat{\theta}_t = \arg\min_{\theta\in\mathcal{C}}\langle \nabla f(\theta_t), \theta - \theta_t\rangle$;

  Set $\theta_{t+1} = \theta_t + \mu(\widehat{\theta}_t - \theta_t)$;

end for

return θ_T.

Define $\theta^* = \arg\min_{\theta\in\mathcal{C}} f(\theta)$. The following theorem shows the convergence of Frank-Wolfe algorithm.

Theorem 6.19 ([Cla10; Jag13]). *If we set* $\mu = 1/T$, *then* $f(\theta_T) - f(\theta^*) = O(\Gamma_f/T)$.

While the Frank-Wolfe algorithm does not necessarily provide faster convergence compared to the gradient-descent based method, it has two major advantages. First, on Line 3, it reduces the problem to solving a minimization of linear function. When $\mathcal{C}$ is defined by small number of vertices, e.g. when $\mathcal{C}$ is an ℓ_1-ball, the minimization can be done by checking $\langle \nabla f(\theta_t), x\rangle$ for each vertex x of $\mathcal{C}$. This can be done efficiently. Secondly, each step in Frank-Wolfe takes a convex combination of θ_t and $\widehat{\theta}_t$, which is on the boundary of $\mathcal{C}$. Hence each intermediate solution is always inside $\mathcal{C}$ (sometimes called *projection free*), and the final outcome θ_T is the convex combination of up to T points on the boundary of $\mathcal{C}$ (or vertices of $\mathcal{C}$ when $\mathcal{C}$ is a polytope). Such outcome might be desired, for example when $\mathcal{C}$ is a polytope, as it corresponds to a sparse solution. Due to these reasons Frank-Wolfe algorithm has found many applications in machine learning [SSZ10; HK12; Cla10]. As we shall see below, these properties are also useful for obtaining low risk bounds for their private version.

6.4.2 Private Frank-Wolfe Algorithm

There are different ways to make Algorithm 5 private, dependent on the geometry of $\mathcal{C}$. Here we focus on the important case where $\mathcal{C}$ is a polytope, corresponding to the LASSO problem. In this case, we apply the exponential mechanism [MT07] to achieve privacy. We now present a private version of the Frank-Wolfe algorithm. We can achieve privacy by replacing Line 3 in Algorithm 5 with its private version in one of two ways. In the first variant, we can apply exponential mechanism [MT07] to guarantee privacy; and in the second variant, we can apply objective perturbation (Algorithm $\mathcal{A}_{\text{obj-pert}}$) or DP-SGD (Algorithm $\mathcal{A}_{\text{DP-SGD}}$) or DP-FTRL (Algorithm $\mathcal{A}_{\text{FTRL}}$). The first variant works especially well when $\mathcal{C}$ is a polytope defined by polynomially many vertices. In this case, we show that the error depends on the ℓ_1-Lipschitz constant, which can be much smaller than the ℓ_2-Lipschitz constant. In particular, the private Frank-Wolfe algorithm is nearly optimal for the important high-dimensional sparse linear regression (or compressive sensing) problem. For the details on the second variant, see [TTZ15].

Algorithm 6 describes the private version of Frank-Wolfe algorithm for the polytope case, i.e. when $\mathcal{C}$ is a convex hull of a finite set S of vertices (or corners). In this case, we know that any linear function is minimized at one point of S per the following basic fact.

Fact 6.20. *Let* $\mathcal{C} \subseteq \mathbb{R}^p$ *be the convex hull of a compact set* $S \subseteq \mathbb{R}^p$. *For any vector* $v \in \mathbb{R}^p$, $\arg\min_{\theta \in \mathcal{C}} \langle \theta, v\rangle \cap S \neq \emptyset$.

Since θ_{t+1} can be selected as one of $|S|$ vertices, by applying the exponential mechanism [MT07], we obtain differentially private algorithm with risk logarithmically dependent on $|S|$. When $|S|$ is polynomial in p, it leads to an error bound with $\ln p$ dependence. While the exponential mechanism can be applied to the general $\mathcal{C}$ as well, its error would depend on the size of a cover of the boundary of $\mathcal{C}$, which can be exponential in p, leading to an error bound with polynomial dependence on p.

Algorithm 6 $\mathcal{A}_{\text{Noise-FW(polytope)}}$: Differentially Private Frank-Wolfe Algorithm (Polytope Case)

Require: Data set: $D = \{d_1, \cdots, d_n\}$, loss function: $\mathcal{L}(\theta; D) = \sum_{i=1}^{n} \mathcal{L}(\theta; d_i)$ (with ℓ_1-Lipschitz constant L_1 for ℓ), privacy parameters: (ε, δ), convex set: $\mathcal{C} = conv(S)$ with $\|\mathcal{C}\|_1$ denoting $\max_{s\in S} \|s\|_1$ and S being the set of corners.

Choose an arbitrary θ_1 from $\mathcal{C}$;
for $t = 1$ to $T - 1$ **do**
 $\forall s \in S, \alpha_s \leftarrow \langle s, \nabla\mathcal{L}(\theta_t; D)\rangle + \text{Lap}\left(\frac{L_1\|\mathcal{C}\|_1\sqrt{8T\ln(1/\delta)}}{n\varepsilon}\right)$, where $\text{Lap}(\lambda) \sim \frac{1}{2\lambda}e^{-|x|/\lambda}$.
 $\widehat{\theta_t} \leftarrow \arg\min_{s\in S} \alpha_s$.
 $\theta_{t+1} \leftarrow (1-\mu)\theta_t + \mu\widehat{\theta_t}$, where $\mu = \frac{1}{T+2}$.
end for
Output $\theta^{\text{priv}} = \theta_T$.

Theorem 6.21 (Privacy guarantee). *Algorithm 6 (Algorithm $\mathcal{A}_{\text{Noise-FW(polytope)}}$) is (ε, δ)-differentially private.*

The proof of privacy follows from a straight forward use of exponential mechanism [MT07; BLST10] (the noisy maximum version from [BLST10], Theorem 5) and the advanced composition theorem discussed earlier in the book. In Theorem 6.22 we prove the utility guarantee for the private Frank-Wolfe algorithm for the convex polytope case. Define $\Gamma_\ell = \max_{d\in\mathcal{D}} C_\ell(d)$ over all the possible data sets in the domain.

Theorem 6.22 (Utility guarantee). *Let L_1,S and $\|\mathcal{C}\|_1$ be defined as in Algorithms 6 (Algorithm $\mathcal{A}_{\text{Noise-FW(polytope)}}$). Let Γ_ℓ be an upper bound on the curvature constant (defined in Definition 6.16) for the loss function $\ell(\cdot; d)$ that holds for all $d \in \mathcal{D}$. In Algorithm $\mathcal{A}_{\text{Noise-FW(polytope)}}$, if we set $T = \frac{\Gamma_\ell^{2/3}(n\varepsilon)^{2/3}}{(L_1\|\mathcal{C}\|_1)^{2/3}}$, then*

$$\mathbf{E}\left[\mathcal{L}(\theta^{priv}; D)\right] - \min_{\theta\in\mathcal{C}} \mathcal{L}(\theta; D)$$

$$= O\left(\frac{\Gamma_\ell{}^{1/3}\,(L_1\,\|C\|_1)^{2/3}\,n^{1/3}\ln(n|S|)\sqrt{\ln(1/\delta)}}{\varepsilon^{2/3}}\right).$$

Here the expectation is over the randomness of the algorithm.

Proof. For ease of notation we hide the dependence of $\mathcal{L}$ on the data set D and represent it simply as $\mathcal{L}(\theta)$. In order to prove the utility guarantee we first invoke the utility guarantee of the non-private noisy Frank-Wolfe algorithm from [Jag13] (Theorem 1).

Theorem 6.23 (Non-private utility guarantee [Jag13]). *Assume the conditions in Theorem 6.22 and let $\gamma > 0$ be fixed. Recall that $\mu = 1/(T+2)$ and let $\phi_1 \in C$. Suppose that $\langle s_1, \cdots, s_T\rangle$ is a sequence of vectors from C, with $\phi_{t+1} = (1-\mu)\phi_t + \mu s_t$ such that for all $t \in [T]$,*

$$\langle s_t, \nabla\mathcal{L}(\phi_t)\rangle \le \min_{s\in C}\langle s, \nabla\mathcal{L}(\phi_t)\rangle + \frac{1}{2}\gamma\,\mu(n\cdot\Gamma_\ell).$$

Then,

$$\mathcal{L}(\phi_T) - \min_{\theta\in C}\mathcal{L}(\theta) \le \frac{2n\cdot\Gamma_\ell}{T+2}(1+\gamma).$$

Since the convex set C is a polytope with corners in S, if s_t in Theorem 6.23 corresponds to $\widehat{\theta}_t$ in Algorithm $\mathcal{A}_{\text{Noise-FW(polytope)}}$, and ϕ_t corresponds to θ_t in $\mathcal{A}_{\text{Noise-FW(polytope)}}$, then using the tail properties of Laplace distribution and Fact 6.20 one can show that with probability at least $1-\beta$, the term γ in Theorem 6.23 is at most $O\left(\frac{L_1\|C\|_1\sqrt{8T\ln(1/\delta)}\ln(|S|T/\beta)}{\mu\varepsilon(n\cdot\Gamma_\ell)}\right)$. Plugging in this bound in Theorem 6.23, we immediately get that with probability at least $1-\beta$,

$$\mathcal{L}(\theta_T) - \min_{\theta\in C}\mathcal{L}(\theta) = O\left(\frac{\Gamma_{\mathcal{L}}}{T} + \frac{L_1\,\|C\|_1\sqrt{8T\ln(1/\delta)}\ln(|S|T/\zeta)}{\varepsilon}\right). \quad (6.59)$$

From, (6.59) we can conclude the following in expectation.

$$\mathbf{E}\left[\mathcal{L}(\theta_T) - \min_{\theta\in C}\mathcal{L}(\theta)\right]$$

$$= O\left(\frac{n\cdot\Gamma_\ell}{T} + \frac{L_1\,\|C\|_1\sqrt{8T\ln(1/\delta)}\ln(TL_1\,\|C\|_1\cdot|S|)}{\varepsilon}\right). \quad (6.60)$$

Setting $T = \frac{\Gamma_\ell{}^{2/3}(n\varepsilon)^{2/3}}{(L_1\|C\|_1)^{2/3}}$ results in the claimed utility guarantee. □

6.4.3 Nearly Optimal Private LASSO

We now apply the private Frank-Wolfe algorithm $\mathcal{A}_{\text{Noise-FW(polytope)}}$ to the important case of the sparse linear regression (or LASSO) problem. We show that the private Frank-Wolfe algorithm leads to a nearly tight $O_{\varepsilon,\delta}(n^{1/3} \cdot \text{polylog}(p))$ bound. $O_{\varepsilon,\delta}(\cdot)$ hides terms in the privacy parameters.

Problem Definition

Given a data set $D = \{(x_1, y_1), \cdots, (x_n, y_n)\}$ of n-samples from the domain $\mathcal{D} = \{(x, y) : x \in \mathbb{R}^p, y \in [-1, 1], \|x\|_\infty \leq 1\}$, and the convex set $\mathcal{C} = \ell_1^p$. Define the squared loss,

$$\mathcal{L}(\theta; D) = \frac{1}{2} \sum_{i \in [n]} (\langle x_i, \theta \rangle - y_i)^2 . \tag{6.61}$$

The objective is to compute $\theta^{\text{priv}} \in \mathcal{C}$ to minimize $\mathcal{L}(\theta; D)$ while preserving privacy with respect to add/removal of individual (x_i, y_i) pair. The non-private setting of the above problem is a variant of the least squares problem with ℓ_1 regularization, which was started by the work of LASSO [Tib96; Tib+97] and intensively studied in the past years [HTF01; DJ04; CT05; Don06; CT07; BRT09; BM12; RWY09; Zha13]. One important reason for using ℓ_1 regularization is to induce sparse solutions, i.e. θ with small number of non-zero coordinates. This is especially interesting for the so called "high-dimensional" setting where $p \gg n$. Indeed, via a long line of work [DJ04; CT05; Don06; Wai06; CT07; BRT09], it has been shown that under suitable condition of X, using ℓ_1 regularization can indeed produce a nearly optimal sparse solution, providing theoretical support to the empirical success of LASSO.

Since the ℓ_1 ball is the convex hull of $2p$ vertices, we can apply the private Frank-Wolfe algorithm $\mathcal{A}_{\text{Noise-FW(polytope)}}$. For the above setting, it is easy to check that the ℓ_1-Lipschitz constant is bounded by $O(1)$. Further, by applying the bound on quadratic programming Remark 6.18, we have that $C_\ell \leq 4 \max_{\theta \in \mathcal{C}, \|x\|_\infty \leq 1} \langle x, \theta \rangle^2 = O(1)$ since $\mathcal{C}$ is the unit ℓ_1 ball, and $|x_{ij}| \leq 1$. Hence $\Gamma_\ell = O(1)$. Now applying Theorem 6.22, we have

Corollary 6.24. *Let $D = \{(x_1, y_1), \cdots, (x_n, y_n)\}$ of n samples from the domain $\mathcal{D} = \{(x, y) : \|x\|_\infty \leq 1, |y| \leq 1\}$, and the convex set $\mathcal{C}$ equal to the ℓ_1-ball. The output θ^{priv} of Algorithm $\mathcal{A}_{\text{Noise-FW(polytope)}}$ ensures the following.*

$$\mathbf{E}\left[\mathcal{L}(\theta^{priv}; D)\right] - \min_{\theta \in \mathcal{C}} \mathcal{L}(\theta; D) = O\left(\frac{n^{1/3} \ln(np/\delta)}{\varepsilon^{2/3}}\right).$$

Comparison to Algorithms for Private Sparse Support Selection

For a high-dimensional linear regression problem of the form $y = \langle x, \theta^* \rangle +$ noise with $\|\theta^*\|_0 = O(1)$, Algorithms in [KST12; ST13b] allow one to identify the non-zero coordinates of $]\theta^*$ exactly under (ε, δ)-DP. It is not hard to observe that this is a much tighter guarantee as opposed to Corollary 6.24. However, the algorithms in [KST12; ST13b] operate under much stronger assumptions like *restricted strong convexity* or *mutual incoherence* [Wai06]. These assumptions are known to be necessary even for non-private support selection, and may be too hard to satisfy in practice [Was12].

Note on the Lower Bound

As mentioned earlier, the bound obtained via Corollary 6.24 is essentially tight. The proof of the lower bound follows the standard template of fingerprinting codes, use to prove lower bounds for (ε, δ)-DP [Vad17; TTZ15].

Oracle Complexity

Algorithm $\mathcal{A}_{\text{Noise}-\text{FW(polytope)}}$ essentially makes $O(T \cdot n)$ oracle calls to obtain the tight privacy/utility trade-off. Compared to non-private Frank-Wolfe, the oracle complexity remain unchanged up to terms depending on the privacy parameters (ε, δ), and additional poly-logarithmic factors. This is a common theme we saw in all the algorithms in this chapter. Differential privacy tends not hurt the rate of convergence. However, it only allows convergence to a specific error level allowed by the privacy constraints.

6.5 Lower Bounds, and Algorithms not Considered

6.5.1 Lower Bounds on Private Constrained Optimization

In this section, we discuss at a high-level some of the standard lower bounding techniques used for proving optimality of DP optimization algorithms. The lower bounds for the algorithms considered in this chapter are in some form dependent on the lower bound for estimating one-way marginals with DP (Theorem 6.25 below.)

Theorem 6.25 (Lower bounds for 1-way marginals)**.**

1. ***ε-differential private algorithms:*** *Let $n, p \in \mathbb{N}$ and $\varepsilon > 0$. There is a number $M = \Omega\left(\min\left(n, p/\varepsilon\right)\right)$ such that for every ε-differentially private algorithm $\mathcal{A}$, there is a dataset $D = \{d_1, \ldots, d_n\} \subseteq \left\{-\frac{1}{\sqrt{p}}, \frac{1}{\sqrt{p}}\right\}^p$ with $\left\|\sum_{i=1}^n d_i\right\|_2 \in [M-1, M+1]$ such that, with probability at least $1/2$ (taken over the algorithm*

random coins), we have

$$\left\|\mathcal{A}(D) - q(D)\right\|_2 = \Omega\left(\min\left(1, \frac{p}{\varepsilon n}\right)\right),$$

where $q(D) = \frac{1}{n}\sum_{i=1}^{n} d_i$.

2. (ε, δ)***-differential private algorithms:*** *Let* $n, p \in \mathbb{N}$, $\varepsilon > 0$, *and* $\delta = o(\frac{1}{n})$. *There is a number* $M = \Omega\left(\min\left(n, \sqrt{p}/\varepsilon\right)\right)$ *such that for every* (ε, δ)*-differentially private algorithm* $\mathcal{A}$, *there is a dataset* $D = \{d_1, \ldots, d_n\} \subseteq \left\{-\frac{1}{\sqrt{p}}, \frac{1}{\sqrt{p}}\right\}^p$ *with* $\left\|\sum_{i=1}^{n} d_i\right\|_2 \in [M-1, M+1]$ *such that, with probability at least* $1/3$ *(taken over the algorithm random coins), we have*

$$l\left\|\mathcal{A}(D) - q(D)\right\|_2 = \Omega\left(\min\left(1, \frac{\sqrt{p}}{\varepsilon n}\right)\right),$$

where $q(D) = \frac{1}{n}\sum_{i=1}^{n} d_i$.

Now define a dataset $D = \{d_1, \ldots, d_n\}$ with data points drawn from $\left\{-\frac{1}{\sqrt{p}}, \frac{1}{\sqrt{p}}\right\}^p$, and any $\theta \in \mathbb{B}$, define $\mathcal{L}(\theta; D) = -\langle\theta, \sum_{i=1}^{n} d_i\rangle$. Clearly, $\mathcal{L}$ is linear and, hence, Lipschitz and convex. Note that, whenever $\left\|\sum_{i=1}^{n} d_i\right\|_2 > 0$, $\theta^* = \frac{\sum_{i=1}^{n} d_i}{\|\sum_{i=1}^{n} d_i\|_2}$ is the minimizer of $\mathcal{L}(\theta; D)$ over $\mathbb{B}$. Next, we show lower bounds on the excess empirical risk incurred by any ε and (ε, δ) differentially private algorithm with output $\theta^{\text{priv}} \in \mathbb{B}$.

Theorem 6.26 (Lower bound for ε-differentially private algorithms)**.** *Let* $n, p \in \mathbb{N}$ *and* $\varepsilon > 0$. *For every* ε*-differentially private algorithm (whose output is denoted by* θ^{priv}*), there is a dataset* $D = \{d_1, \ldots, d_n\} \subseteq \left\{-\frac{1}{\sqrt{p}}, \frac{1}{\sqrt{p}}\right\}^p$ *such that, with probability at least* $1/2$ *(over the algorithm random coins), we must have*

$$\mathcal{L}(\theta; D) - \mathcal{L}(\theta^*; D) = \Omega\left(\min\left(n, p/\varepsilon\right)\right),$$

where $\theta^* = \frac{\sum_{i=1}^{n} d_i}{\|\sum_{i=1}^{n} d_i\|_2}$ *is the minimizer of* $\mathcal{L}(\theta; D)$ *over* $\mathbb{B}$ *and* $\mathcal{L}$ *is defined above.*

Proof. Let $\mathcal{A}$ be an ε-differentially private algorithm for minimizing $\mathcal{L}$ and let θ^{priv} denote its output. First, observe that for any $\theta \in \mathbb{B}$ and dataset D, $\mathcal{L}(\theta; D) - \mathcal{L}(\theta^*; D) = \left\|\sum_{i=1}^{n} d_i\right\|_2 (1 - \langle\theta, \theta^*\rangle)$. Hence, we have $\mathcal{L}(\theta; D) - \mathcal{L}(\theta^*; D) \geq \frac{1}{2}\left\|\sum_{i=1}^{n} d_i\right\|_2 \|\theta - \theta^*\|_2^2$. This is due to the fact that $\|\theta - \theta^*\|_2^2 = \|\theta^*\|_2^2 + \|\theta\|_2^2 - 2\langle\theta, \theta^*\rangle$ and the fact that $\theta^*, \theta \in \mathbb{B}$.

Let $M = \Omega\left(\min\left(n, p/\varepsilon\right)\right)$ be as in Part 1 of Theorem 6.25. Suppose, for the sake of a contradiction, that for every dataset $D \subseteq \left\{-\frac{1}{\sqrt{p}}, \frac{1}{\sqrt{p}}\right\}^p$ with $\left\|\sum_{i=1}^{n} d_i\right\|_2 \in [M-1, M+1]$, with probability more than $1/2$, we have

$\left\|\theta^{\mathsf{priv}} - \theta^*\right\|_2 \neq \Omega(1)$. Let $\tilde{\mathcal{A}}$ be an ε-DP algorithm that first runs $\mathcal{A}$ on the data and then outputs $\frac{M}{n}\theta^{\mathsf{priv}}$. Note that this implies that for every data set $D \subseteq \left\{-\frac{1}{\sqrt{p}}, \frac{1}{\sqrt{p}}\right\}^p$ with $\left\|\sum_{i=1}^n d_i\right\|_2 \in [M-1, M+1]$, with probability more than $1/2$, $\left\|\tilde{\mathcal{A}}(D) - q(D)\right\|_2 \neq \Omega\left(\min\left(1, \frac{p}{\varepsilon n}\right)\right)$ which contradicts Part 1 of Theorem 6.25. Thus, there must exist a dataset $D \subseteq \left\{-\frac{1}{\sqrt{p}}, \frac{1}{\sqrt{p}}\right\}^p$ with $\left\|\sum_{i=1}^n d_i\right\|_2 = \Omega\left(\min\left(n, p/\varepsilon\right)\right)$ such that with probability at least $1/2$, we have $\left\|\theta^{\mathsf{priv}} - \theta^*\right\|_2 = \Omega(1)$. Therefore, from the observation we made in the previous paragraph, we have, with probability at least $1/2$, $\mathcal{L}(\theta^{\mathsf{priv}}; D) - \mathcal{L}(\theta^*; D) = \Omega\left(\min\left(n, p/\varepsilon\right)\right)$. □

The lower bound for the (ε, δ)-DP case follows by the same argument as in Theorem 6.26, but reducing the problem instance to Part 2 in Theorem 6.25. The lower bound for the setting in Section 6.4 follows from a slightly complicated variant of Theorem 6.25. We encourage the readers to read [TTZ15] for more details.

6.5.2 Algorithms not Considered

In the exposition of this chapter, we left out quite a few important algorithms, primarily for the ease of presentation. In this section, we highlight some of them, and encourage interested readers to explore more.

Additional Assumptions on the Loss Function

In this chapter, we primarily focused on obtaining excess empirical risk bounds for Lipschitz convex convex functions. For the ℓ_2-Lipschitz setting, if we additionally allow the loss functions to be Δ-strongly convex, then the excess empirical risk for the pure ε-case improves to $O\left(\frac{L^2 p^2 \log(n)}{n\Delta\varepsilon^2}\right)$. The algorithm is a two stage-algorithm, with a first localization step to identify a small set where the true minimizer lies, and then running Algorithm $\mathcal{A}_{\mathrm{exp-samp}}$ on that set [BST14]. In the (ε, δ)-case, the corresponding excess empirical risk becomes $O\left(\frac{L^2 p \cdot \mathrm{polylog}(n/\delta)}{n\Delta\varepsilon^2}\right)$. The algorithms that achieve this bound are mild variants of Algorithms $\mathcal{A}_{\mathrm{DP-SGD}}$ and $\mathcal{A}_{\mathrm{obj-pert}}$. Assuming smoothness however, does not improve the excess empirical risk. However, it improves the rate of convergence/oracle complexity to achieve the same error.

Algorithms for Optimal Population Risk

As mentioned in the beginning of the chapter that we would focus only on excess empirical risk, and for estimating the excess true/population risk we would use (6.3). While this is a natural way to translate from excess empirical risk to excess population risk, this translation does not result in optimal excess population risk. For ℓ_2-Lipschitz convex functions (with Lipschitz constant $O(1)$, and for a constraint set with $\|\mathcal{C}\|_2 = O(1)$) the optimal population risk is $O\left(\left(\frac{1}{\sqrt{n}} + \frac{\sqrt{p \cdot \ln(1/\delta)}}{\varepsilon n}\right) \cdot \text{polylog}\,(n)\right)$, and for 1-strongly convex functions it is $O\left(\left(\frac{1}{n} + \frac{p \cdot \ln(1/\delta)}{\varepsilon^2 n^2}\right) \cdot \text{polylog}\,(n)\right)$. Notice that in both these cases, the lower-order term in n only depends on the privacy parameter, as opposed to the one obtained via (6.3). The algorithms that achieve these bounds are variants of Algorithm $\mathcal{A}_{\text{DP-SGD}}$ or Algorithm $\mathcal{A}_{\text{obj-pert}}$, with substantially more involved utility analysis, using tools from algorithmic stability. For a detailed discussion on these techniques, see [BFGT20]. When the geometry is ℓ_1/ℓ_∞ (as in Section 6.4), the corresponding optimal excess population risk of $O\left(\sqrt{\frac{\ln(p)}{n}} + \frac{\sqrt{\ln(p)\ln(1/\delta)}}{(n\varepsilon)^{2/3}}\right)$ is obtained a variant of Algorithm $\mathcal{A}_{\text{Noise-FW(polytope)}}$. This bound assumes all the assumptions in Corollary 6.24. For a detailed exposition to this result see [AFKT21].

Other Algorithms not Discussed

For the purposes of brevity, we left out the discussion of a number of algorithms. In particular, we did not mention any algorithm which are optimal under local differential privacy [STU17]. We also did not discuss algorithms like *private cutting plane methods* [STU17], *output perturbation* [CMS11], *bolt-on privacy* [Wu+17], *private mirror descent* [TTZ14b], *privacy amplification by iteration* [FMTT18]. Many of these algorithms have advantages over the algorithms mentioned in this chapter, under specific problem settings. We encourage the readers to explore these algorithms, and their impact on the broader space of private constrained optimization.

In this chapter, we focused only on convex loss functions. As mentioned earlier algorithms like $\mathcal{A}_{\text{FTRL}}$, $\mathcal{A}_{\text{DP-SGD}}$, and $\mathcal{A}_{\text{Noise-FW(polytope)}}$ are applicable to non-convex losses too, as their privacy do not depend on convexity. While there are restricted utility analyses for non-convex losses [STT20; WCX19], it is still an active area of research. Additionally, there are better algorithms known specific to problems like linear regression [STU17; She19], or principal component analysis [DTTZ14; LMV21]. We did not explore these problems in this chapter.

Acknowledgements

Most of the presentation in this chapter is based off prior work, unless mentioned explicitly. The privacy/utility analysis of Algorithms $\mathcal{A}_{\text{exp-samp}}$ and $\mathcal{A}_{\text{DP-SGD}}$ are based on [BST14], Algorithm $\mathcal{A}_{\text{obj-pert}}$ is based on [KST12], Algorithm $\mathcal{A}_{\text{FTRL}}$ is based on [Kai+21b], and Algorithm $\mathcal{A}_{\text{Noise-FW(polytope)}}$ is based on [TTZ15]. We sincerely apologize for unintentional omission of any related results in this space.

References

[Aba+15] M. Abadi et al. TensorFlow: Large-Scale Machine Learning on Heterogeneous Systems. Software available from tensorflow.org. 2015. URL: https://www.tensorflow.org/ (cit. on p. 222).

[Aba+16] M. Abadi, A. Chu, I. J. Goodfellow, H. B. McMahan, I. Mironov, K. Talwar, and L. Zhang. "Deep Learning with Differential Privacy". In: Proc. of the 2016 ACM SIGSAC Conf. on Computer and Communications Security (CCS'16). 2016, pp. 308–318 (cit. on pp. 211, 222).

[AFKT21] H. Asi, V. Feldman, T. Koren, and K. Talwar. "Private Stochastic Convex Optimization: Optimal Rates in L1 Geometry". In: Proceedings of the 38th International Conference on Machine Learning. 2021, pp. 393–403 (cit. on p. 242).

[AS17] N. Agarwal and K. Singh. "The price of differential privacy for online learning". In: International Conference on Machine Learning. PMLR. 2017, pp. 32–40 (cit. on pp. 211, 230).

[BFGT20] R. Bassily, V. Feldman, C. Guzmán, and K. Talwar. "Stability of Stochastic Gradient Descent on Nonsmooth Convex Losses". In: Advances in Neural Information Processing Systems 33 (2020) (cit. on p. 242).

[BFTT19] R. Bassily, V. Feldman, K. Talwar, and A. Thakurta. "Private stochastic convex optimization with optimal rates". In: Advances in Neural Information Processing Systems. 2019, pp. 11279–11288 (cit. on pp. 210, 221).

[Bil08] P. Billingsley. Probability and measure. John Wiley & Sons, 2008 (cit. on pp. 216, 218).

[BLST10] R. Bhaskar, S. Laxman, A. Smith, and A. Thakurta. "Discovering frequent patterns in sensitive data". In: KDD. New York, NY, USA, 2010 (cit. on p. 236).

[BM12] M. Bayati and A. Montanari. "The LASSO risk for gaussian matrices". In: IEEE Transactions on Information Theory (2012) (cit. on p. 238).

[BRT09] P. J. Bickel, Y. Ritov, and A. B. Tsybakov. "Simultaneous analysis of Lasso and Dantzig selector". In: The Annals of Statistics (2009), pp. 1705–1732 (cit. on p. 238).

[BST14] R. Bassily, A. Smith, and A. Thakurta. "Private Empirical Risk Minimization: Efficient Algorithms and Tight Error Bounds". In: Proc. of the 2014 IEEE 55th Annual Symp. on Foundations of Computer Science (FOCS). 2014, pp. 464–473 (cit. on pp. 211, 215, 221–223, 226, 241, 242).

[Bub15] S. Bubeck. "Convex optimization: Algorithms and complexity". In: Foundations and Trends® in Machine Learning 8.3-4 (2015), pp. 231–357 (cit. on pp. 215, 221, 223, 224).

[Cla10] K. L. Clarkson. "Coresets, sparse greedy approximation, and the Frank-Wolfe algorithm". In: ACM Transations on Algorithms (2010) (cit. on pp. 234, 235).

[CMS11] K. Chaudhuri, C. Monteleoni, and A. D. Sarwate. "Differentially private empirical risk minimization". In: Journal of Machine Learning Research 12.Mar (2011), pp. 1069–1109 (cit. on pp. 211, 215, 242).

[CSS11] T.-H. H. Chan, E. Shi, and D. Song. "Private and Continual Release of Statistics". In: ACM Trans. on Information Systems Security 14.3 (Nov. 2011), 26:1–26:24 (cit. on pp. 229, 230).

[CT05] E. Candes and T. Tao. "Decoding by linear programming". In: IEEE Transactions on Information Theory 51 (2005) (cit. on p. 238).

[CT07] E. Candes and T. Tao. "The Dantzig selector: Statistical estimation when p is much larger than n". In: The Annals of Statistics (2007), pp. 2313–2351 (cit. on p. 238).

[DJ04] D. Donoho and J. Jin. "Higher criticism for detecting sparse heterogeneous mixtures". In: Annals of Statistics (2004), pp. 962–994 (cit. on p. 238).

[DNPR10] C. Dwork, M. Naor, T. Pitassi, and G. N. Rothblum. "Differential Privacy Under Continual Observation". In: Proc. of the Forty-Second ACM Symp. on Theory of Computing (STOC'10). 2010, pp. 715–724 (cit. on pp. 229, 230).

[Don06] D. L. Donoho. "Compressed sensing". In: IEEE Transactions on Information Theory (2006) (cit. on p. 238).

[DR+14] C. Dwork, A. Roth, et al. "The algorithmic foundations of differential privacy." In: Foundations and Trends in Theoretical Computer Science 9.3-4 (2014), pp. 211–407 (cit. on p. 211).

[DTTZ14] C. Dwork, K. Talwar, A. Thakurta, and L. Zhang. "Analyze gauss: optimal bounds for privacy-preserving principal component analysis". In: Proceedings of the forty-sixth annual ACM symposium on Theory of computing. 2014, pp. 11–20 (cit. on p. 242).

[FMTT18] V. Feldman, I. Mironov, K. Talwar, and A. Thakurta. "Privacy Amplification by Iteration". In: 59th Annual IEEE Symp. on Foundations of Computer Science (FOCS). 2018, pp. 521–532 (cit. on p. 242).

[FW56] M. Frank and P. Wolfe. "An algorithm for quadratic programming". In: Naval research logistics quarterly 3.1-2 (1956), pp. 95–110 (cit. on p. 234).

[Haz19] E. Hazan. "Introduction to online convex optimization". In: arXiv preprint arXiv:1909.05207 (2019) (cit. on pp. 227, 232).

[HK12] E. Hazan and S. Kale. "Projection-free Online Learning". In: ICML. 2012 (cit. on p. 235).

[HK14] E. Hazan and S. Kale. "Beyond the regret minimization barrier: optimal algorithms for stochastic strongly-convex optimization". In: The Journal of Machine Learning Research 15.1 (2014), pp. 2489–2512 (cit. on p. 227).

[HT10] M. Hardt and K. Talwar. "On the geometry of differential privacy". In: Proceedings of the forty-second ACM symposium on Theory of computing. 2010, pp. 705–714 (cit. on p. 215).

[HTF01] T. Hastie, R. Tibshirani, and J. Friedman. The Elements of Statistical Learning. Springer Series in Statistics. Springer New York Inc., 2001 (cit. on p. 238).

[Iye+19] R. Iyengar, J. P. Near, D. Song, O. Thakkar, A. Thakurta, and L. Wang. "Towards practical differentially private convex optimization". In: 2019 IEEE Symposium on Security and Privacy (SP). 2019 (cit. on p. 221).

[Jag13] M. Jaggi. "Revisiting {Frank-Wolfe}: Projection-free sparse convex optimization". In: ICML. 2013 (cit. on pp. 234, 235, 237).

[Kai+21a] P. Kairouz, B. McMahan, S. Song, O. Thakkar, A. Thakurta, and Z. Xu. "Practical and Private (Deep) Learning without Sampling or Shuffling". In: CoRR abs/2103.00039 (2021). URL: https://arxiv.org/abs/2103.00039 (cit. on p. 233).

[Kai+21b] P. Kairouz, B. Mcmahan, S. Song, O. Thakkar, A. Thakurta, and Z. Xu. "Practical and Private (Deep) Learning Without Sampling or Shuffling". In: Proceedings of the 38th International Conference on Machine Learning. 2021, pp. 5213–5225 (cit. on pp. 211, 230, 243).

[Kas+08] S. P. Kasiviswanathan, H. K. Lee, K. Nissim, S. Raskhodnikova, and A. D. Smith. "What Can We Learn Privately?" In: 49th Annual IEEE Symp. on Foundations of Computer Science (FOCS). 2008, pp. 531–540 (cit. on p. 226).

[KST12] D. Kifer, A. Smith, and A. Thakurta. "Private convex empirical risk minimization and high-dimensional regression". In: Conference on Learning Theory. 2012, pp. 25–1 (cit. on pp. 211, 215, 216, 239, 242).

[LMV21] J. Leake, C. McSwiggen, and N. K. Vishnoi. "Sampling matrices from Harish-Chandra–Itzykson–Zuber densities with applications to Quantum inference and differential privacy". In: Proceedings of the 53rd Annual ACM SIGACT Symposium on Theory of Computing. 2021, pp. 1384–1397 (cit. on p. 242).

[LV06] L. Lovász and S. Vempala. "Fast algorithms for logconcave functions: Sampling, rounding, integration and optimization". In: 2006 47th Annual IEEE Symposium on Foundations of Computer Science (FOCS'06). IEEE. 2006, pp. 57–68 (cit. on p. 215).

[MT07] F. McSherry and K. Talwar. "Mechanism design via differential privacy". In: 48th Annual IEEE Symposium on Foundations of Computer Science (FOCS'07). IEEE. 2007, pp. 94–103 (cit. on pp. 211, 235, 236).

[MV21] O. Mangoubi and N. K. Vishnoi. "Sampling from Log-Concave Distributions with Infinity-Distance Guarantees and Applications to Differentially Private Optimization". In: arXiv preprint arXiv:2111.04089 (2021) (cit. on p. 215).

[NRVW20] S. Neel, A. Roth, G. Vietri, and S. Wu. "Oracle efficient private non-convex optimization". In: International Conference on Machine Learning. PMLR. 2020, pp. 7243–7252 (cit. on p. 221).

[RWY09] G. Raskutti, M. J. Wainwright, and B. Yu. "Minimax rates of estimation for high-dimensional linear regression over ℓ_q-balls". In: ArXiv e-prints (Oct. 2009). arXiv: 0910 . 2042 [math.ST] (cit. on p. 238).

[SCS13] S. Song, K. Chaudhuri, and A. D. Sarwate. "Stochastic gradient descent with differentially private updates". In: 2013 IEEE Global Conference on Signal and Information Processing. IEEE. 2013, pp. 245–248 (cit. on p. 222).

[Sha+11] S. Shalev-Shwartz et al. "Online learning and online convex optimization". In: Foundations and trends in Machine Learning 4.2 (2011), pp. 107–194 (cit. on pp. 227, 230).

[Sha12] S. Shalev-Shwartz. "Online learning and online convex optimization". In: Foundations and Trends in Machine Learning 4.2 (2012), pp. 107–194 (cit. on p. 232).

[She19] O. Sheffet. "Old techniques in differentially private linear regression". In: Algorithmic Learning Theory. PMLR. 2019, pp. 789–827 (cit. on p. 242).

[SSSS09] S. Shalev-Shwartz, O. Shamir, N. Srebro, and K. Sridharan. "Stochastic Convex Optimization". In: COLT 2009 - The 22nd Conference on Learning Theory, Montreal, Quebec, Canada, June 18-21, 2009. 2009 (cit. on p. 210).

[SSTT21] S. Song, T. Steinke, O. Thakkar, and A. Thakurta. "Evading the Curse of Dimensionality in Unconstrained Private GLMs". In: Proceedings of The 24th International Conference on Artificial Intelligence and Statistics. Vol. 130. 2021, pp. 2638–2646 (cit. on p. 222).

[SSZ10] S. Shalev-Shwartz, N. Srebro, and T. Zhang. "Trading accuracy for sparsity in optimization problems with sparsity constraints". In: SIAM Journal on Optimization (2010) (cit. on p. 235).

[ST13a] A. Smith and A. Thakurta. "(Nearly) optimal algorithms for private online learning in full-information and bandit settings". In: Advances in Neural Information Processing Systems. 2013, pp. 2733–2741 (cit. on pp. 211, 229, 230).

[ST13b] A. Smith and A. Thakurta. "Differentially Private Feature Selection via Stability Arguments, and the Robustness of the Lasso". In: COLT. 2013 (cit. on p. 239).

[STT20] S. Song, O. Thakkar, and A. Thakurta. "Characterizing Private Clipped Gradient Descent on Convex Generalized Linear Problems". In: arXiv preprint arXiv:2006.06783 (2020) (cit. on pp. 226, 242).

[STU17] A. Smith, A. Thakurta, and J. Upadhyay. "Is interaction necessary for distributed private learning?" In: 2017 IEEE Symposium on Security and Privacy (SP). IEEE. 2017, pp. 58–77 (cit. on p. 242).

[Tib+97] R. Tibshirani et al. "The lasso method for variable selection in the Cox model". In: Statistics in medicine 16.4 (1997), pp. 385–395 (cit. on p. 238).

[Tib96] R. Tibshirani. "Regression shrinkage and selection via the lasso". In: Journal of the Royal Statistical Society. Series B (Methodological) (1996) (cit. on pp. 233, 238).

[TTZ14a] K. Talwar, A. Thakurta, and L. Zhang. "Private Empirical Risk Minimization Beyond the Worst Case: The Effect of the Constraint Set Geometry". In: CoRR abs/1411.5417 (2014) (cit. on p. 211).

[TTZ14b] K. Talwar, A. Thakurta, and L. Zhang. "Private empirical risk minimization beyond the worst case: The effect of the constraint set geometry". In: arXiv preprint arXiv:1411.5417 (2014) (cit. on p. 242).

[TTZ15] K. Talwar, A. Thakurta, and L. Zhang. "Nearly optimal private lasso". In: Advances in Neural Information Processing Systems 28 (2015) (cit. on pp. 211, 235, 239, 241, 243).

[Vad17] S. Vadhan. "The complexity of differential privacy". In: Tutorials on the Foundations of Cryptography. Springer, 2017, pp. 347–450 (cit. on p. 239).

[Wai06] M. J. Wainwright. "Sharp Thresholds for High-Dimensional and Noisy Recovery of Sparsity Using ℓ_1-Constrained Quadratic Programs". In: IEEE Transactions on Information Theory. 2006 (cit. on pp. 238, 239).

[Was12] L. Wasserman. "Restricted Isometry Property, Rest In Peace". In: Blog-post (2012). URL: http://normaldeviate.wordpress.com/2012/08/07/rip-rip-restricted-isometry-property-rest-in-peace/ (cit. on p. 239).

[WCX19] D. Wang, C. Chen, and J. Xu. "Differentially Private Empirical Risk Minimization with Non-convex Loss Functions". In: Proceedings of the 36th International Conference on Machine Learning. 2019, pp. 6526–6535 (cit. on p. 242).

[Wu+17] X. Wu, F. Li, A. Kumar, K. Chaudhuri, S. Jha, and J. Naughton. "Bolt-on differential privacy for scalable stochastic gradient descent-based analytics". In: Proceedings of the 2017 ACM International Conference on Management of Data. 2017, pp. 1307–1322 (cit. on p. 242).

[You+21] A. Yousefpour, I. Shilov, A. Sablayrolles, D. Testuggine, K. Prasad, M. Malek, J. Nguyen, S. Ghosh, A. Bharadwaj, J. Zhao, G. Cormode, and I. Mironov. "Opacus: User-Friendly Differential Privacy Library in PyTorch". In: arXiv preprint arXiv:2109.12298 (2021) (cit. on p. 222).

[Zha13] L. Zhang. "Nearly optimal minimax estimator for high dimensional sparse linear regression". In: Annals of Statistics (2013) (cit. on p. 238).

DOI: 10.1561/9781638284772.ch7

Chapter 7

Private Deep Learning

By Nicolas Papernot

Because they learn features from data directly, rather than rely on human engineering, deep neural networks and the associated *deep learning* algorithms continue to see increased adoption from machine learning practitioners. This creates new information flows involving data analyzed in systems deploying deep learning in particular when this data is used to train the neural networks. This data is often about individuals and can be sensitive in nature in application domains like healthcare or language modeling. To prevent models from leaking private information included in their training data, it is thus important to develop deep learning algorithms that are respectful of their training data's privacy.

In this chapter, we introduce two classes of approaches to train deep neural networks with differential privacy, an established framework to reason about the privacy of algorithms. The first is a variant of a popular learning algorithm—stochastic gradient descent. The second does not require any modifications of the learning algorithm and instead obtains privacy through postprocessing of the model's outputs. We conclude with a discussion of practical aspects of deploying deep learning with differential privacy as well as current research problems.

7.1 Introduction

The intuition behind deep learning is to learn hierarchical representations of data [LBH15]. Deep learning algorithms rely on deep neural networks to model data, where a deep neural network is obtained by stacking multiple layers of neurons—each layer representing one abstraction of the data. Classical approaches to machine learning typically rely heavily on the features chosen to represent the data at the input of the model in order to extract a mapping between the input features and the output. For instance, the scale-invariant feature transform [Low99] was used in several areas of computer vision to represent images at the input of a model while encoding priors such as the fact that feature extraction should be invariant to translation or rotation of the image. Instead, deep learning promises to alleviate any human feature engineering and instead extract useful representations directly from the data, in conjunction to learning the mapping between inputs and outputs [LBH15; GBCB16]. These representations are learned by a deep neural network's different layers. Intuitively, one expects representations to be increasingly more abstract as one goes through the model's hierarchy of layers: eventually, we'd like the representation to be sufficiently abstract that it disentangles the different factors of variation so that we can predict the desired output. For instance, in a classification problem we would like the last representation output by a model to linearly separate the different classes of the problem. Deep learning makes representation learning easier by sequentially composing representations: the model starts by learning a first representation from its inputs, this first representation is then itself used as an input to learn a second representation, and so on, until we obtain the model's last representation which is used to infer the model output.

Deep learning enabled many promising developments in the machine learning community. The first successes of deep learning saw applications to computer vision, and in particular object recognition [KSH12]. Since then, these techniques have been applied to other vision problems including in healthcare to diagnose certain conditions from xray images of human chests [Irv+19; CHBB20]. Another domain is the one of language modeling, with the ability to translate between natural languages being a prominent application [BCB14].

Because of the sensitive nature of data analyzed in these applications, it is important to reason about the privacy of deep learning algorithms. Take the example of a machine learning model trained to predict whether a patient was readmitted to a hospital shortly after being dismissed. Being part of the training set for such a model is itself private information: individuals may wish to keep secret the fact that they were hospitalized. In this chapter, we present research which demonstrates that an adversary can use the model's prediction to infer whether a particular patient record's was included to train the model (see Section 7.2.1 on membership inference). This jeopardizes the privacy of individuals who contributed their medical records to the model's training set and could decrease their willingness to consent the sharing of their medical record in the future. In another example, imagine that a machine learning model is trained to model the English language on a corpus of private correspondence. Such a model could for instance be used to predict the next words being typed by a user on a smartphone keyboard. If a user types "My address is", we would like to ensure that the model does not complete the sentence with the address of a different user. These two examples surface the need for an approach to deep learning which provides strong guarantees of privacy for the training data. Here, we focus on the framework of differential privacy to reason about such guarantees because it is the most established framework for this purpose. Differential privacy allows us to quantify the degree of privacy protection provided by an algorithm on the underlying (sensitive) data set it operates on. The reader is referred to Chapter 1 for a review of the notion of differential privacy and its properties. That said, differential privacy is not a silver bullet for all privacy-related questions. We discuss these other aspects of privacy that fall outside the scope of differential privacy in Section 7.6

Overview of the Chapter

In this chapter, we introduce two approaches for deep learning with differential privacy: differentially private stochastic gradient descent (see Section 7.4) and the private aggregation of teacher ensembles (see Section 7.5). Before we do so, we first cover attacks against the privacy of training data used to train deep neural networks (Section 7.2). For clarity of exposition, we focus on deep learning approaches for classification in a supervised setting. In other words, the outputs of our models are always chosen among a discrete set of *classes* (e.g., a set of objects for object classification in computer vision).

7.2 Privacy Attacks against Deep Learning

It is often wrongly assumed that a model that generalizes well preserves privacy. One of the reasons this is not true is that generalization guarantees are average-case whereas privacy needs to be provided for everyone, thus it is a worst-case guarantee. The best way to illustrate this is with attacks that show how deep learning algorithms can leak private information contained in their training set, especially so when the dataset contains outlier that deviate from distributional assumptions made about the data.

The canonical privacy attack against deep learning is membership inference (see Chapter 5). In this attack, the goal of the adversary is simply to infer whether a given data point was included in the model's training set or not [SSSS17]. This may be seen as a weak attack against the private data used to train the model—given that it requires that the adversary already know the data point and its attributes prior to the attack—but recall that certain applications of deep learning include healthcare.

Imagine a model is trained on data obtained from patients who all had a certain medical condition, e.g., cancer, to predict their reaction to certain drugs based on morphological information. In this case, being part of the dataset is itself a sensitive attribute which an individual may not wish to reveal.

Furthermore, the membership inference adversary is also very much in line with the definition of differential privacy, which as we will see in greater detail later in this chapter, asks that the output of a differentially private learning algorithm not significantly change when a single training record is added, modified, or deleted [DMNS06]. This makes membership inference an interesting adversary to have in mind if one wishes to evaluate the strength of the privacy guarantees provided by an algorithm that claims to be privacy-preserving. Indeed, stronger guarantees of differential privacy (as evidenced by analytically proving a smaller upper bound on the privacy leakage ε) imply a lower success rate of membership inference. We will discuss work in this vein later in Section 7.7.2, after we have introduced algorithms for deep learning with differential privacy in Sections 7.4 and 7.5.

More sophisticated attacks will seek to recover missing attributes of a data record already partially known to the adversary. For instance, an adversary may already know the name, age, and zip code for an individual but would like to recover another attribute, e.g., the individual's blood type, included in the record analyzed by the machine learning model. Ultimately, an adversary would like to extract entire training points from the deep learning model. We will detail how such an attack was mounted on a language model.

7.2.1 Membership Inference

Membership inference attacks were covered in details in Chapter 5, we review them here within the notation considered in this chapter for completeness.

In membership inference, the adversary is given the capability of querying the model for predictions on any input of their choice. Shokri et al. introduce the first approach for membership inference against deep learning [SSSS17]. Let us write x the input which the adversary would like to know whether it was in the training set or not to train a model h. The authors propose that the adversary train a model to solve the membership inference task. The adversary will train this second machine learning model m to take in as its input the predictions $h(x)$ of the first model, that is the victim model, on the input x of interest to the adversary and output a binary label $m(h(x)) \in \{0, 1\}$ indicating whether or not x was used to train h. Note that membership inference attacks were initially introduced with the assumption that the adversary can not only observe the victim model's predictions but also its confidence on these predictions. Put another way, the victim prediction $h(x)$ is a confidence vector indicating the likelihood that the input x belongs to each of the classes of the task.

Of course, the adversary is unable to access the data used to train h. As a consequence, they cannot directly collect a set of prediction vectors on inputs in and out of the victim model's training set to train the binary membership inference classifier m from this set. Instead, the adversary will first seek to produce a collection of shadow models h_i whose training set is known to the adversary. In Shokri et al., the authors train shadow models from the same distribution than the one used to sample training data for the victim model.[i] However, it was later shown that this data only needs be from the same domain as the victim model's training data [Sal+18]. These shadow models h_i can then be used to train the membership inference classifier m because the adversary has access to their training set and can thus collect a dataset of prediction vectors $h_i(x)$ for inputs x which are both *in* and *out* of the dataset used to train h_i.

Why is training the membership inference classifier m possible? Intuitively, this is because the confidence scores output by the shadow models—and later the victim model—vary from training to non-training points. In fact, this difference can be so important that Shalem et al. [Sal+18] show that simply thresholding the confidence score for the label predicted by the victim model is sufficient for the adversary to have better than random chance at inferring membership: the adversary simply predicts that a point was in the training set when the prediction is associated with a high confidence score, and conversely points with low confidence predictions are predicted to be outside the training set. In the limit, the adversary could further simplify the attack to predict that a point is a member of the training set if and only if it is correctly classified [YGFJ18]. Put another way, the membership inference classifier m of Shokri et al. can be though of as calibrating this confidence threshold automatically by observing a collection of predictions made on points in and out of the training set. Training a membership inference classifier also has the added benefit that this classifier can learn from any privacy leakage induced by the confidence scores associated with the other classes of the problem which do not end up being predicted—as opposed to the approach of Shalem et al., which focuses on the label receiving the largest score.

More recently, Choquette-Choo et al. [CTCP20] innovate over the initial work of Shokri et al. to propose an attack strategy that does *not* require that the adversary have access to the confidence scores output by a model. To obtain additional private leakage to what was obtained previously by simply guessing that correctly-classified inputs were members of the training data (see supra

i. This is simulated in their experiments by splitting the training set in multiple disjoint sets.

on [YGFJ18]), Choquette-Choo et al. make *multiple* queries to the victim model to infer membership inference of a *single* input. These queries are crafted to approximate the confidence of the victim model; the adversary compares the perturbation magnitude a point can sustain before it is classified by the victim model with a different label. The larger that perturbation, the more confident the victim model is in predicting on this input. In turn, the more likely this input is to be a member of the training set. Perturbations introduced to measure this proxy of confidence can vary from domain to domain. The authors first consider data augmentations typically used to regularize training in the machine learning literature, such as translations and rotations in the image domain. When little is known about the domain, the adversary may proceed by inserting isotropic Gaussian noise to inputs but also perturbations computed through gradient descent to approximate as closely as possible the distance to the victim model's decision boundary—as would be done to find an adversarial example.[ii] Intuitively, this attack exploits the fact that training points are further away from the victim model's decision boundaries. While attacks described above exploited confidence scores to measure this distance in the output domain of the victim model, Choquette-Choo et al. thus measured this distance directly in the input domain by comparing the victim model's predicted class on multiple inputs between the point of interest (for membership inference) and the model's decision boundary. Thus, the resulting strategy is a *label-only* membership inference attack, but it comes at the expense of (possibly significantly) higher query complexity.

We refer the reader to Chapter 5 for a more in-depth discussion of membership inference attacks, including refinements over these initial attack methodologies.

7.2.2 Attribute Inference and Training Data Extraction

Membership inference is not equally successful on all training points. Certain points may be more susceptible to membership inference because they are outlier to the training distribution; Yeom et al. analyze the connection between membership inference and overfitting [YGFJ18]. They report that overfitting is sufficient but not necessary for membership inference, as we will discuss in more details later in Section 7.2.3. This difference in the worst-case and average-case perspectives can lead to further privacy leakage where signal from the model can be exploited not

ii. Adversarial examples are inputs crafted by an adversary to force a model to misclassify. Most algorithms craft adversarial examples by performing a form of gradient descent from an originally correctly classified input towards one of the model's decision boundaries surrounding it [Big+13; Sze+13]. When instead the adversary operates without access to the model, in a black-box setting, this requires that the adversary either obtain a copy of the victim model [Pap+17], playing a similar role to the shadow models of Shokri et al. in the context of membership inference, or that the adversary make multiple queries to perform zero-order optimization [Che+17] and recover gradients through finite differences.

only to perform membership inference, but also to recover information about the training data which was initially unknown to the adversary: e.g., missing attributes of a training point or even the training point itself altogether. Next, we describe one approach for each of these two adversarial goals. Both approaches have in common that they reduce the problem or recovering information unknown to the adversary to the problem of membership inference.

Attribute Inference

Whereas membership inference assumes the adversary already has access to the data point they are interested in testing the membership of, attribute inference instead assumes the adversary only has partial access to this data point. The adversary desires to recover missing attributed from this data point.

For instance, Yeom et al. mention the problem of an adversary with partial access to a medical record who wishes to recover some of the missing attributes of this patient's record [YGFJ18]. The authors introduce an approach which reduces the problem of attribute inference to membership inference. The adversary randomly guesses a value for the missing attribute and performs membership inference on the resulting data point. If the point is accepted as a member of the training set, the adversary assumes that their random guess for the value of the missing attribute was correct. Otherwise, the adversary makes a new guess and repeats the membership inference test. Yeom et al. note that the adversary will be further advantaged should they have any knowledge of the distribution of attribute values which would help them improve their guessing strategy. This observation is also exploited by the work we describe next below.

Extracting Training Data

Indeed, Carlini et al. [Car+20] further extend Yeom et al.'s attack strategy to perform training data extraction from a large language model known as GPT-2 [Rad+19]. The attack strategy is also an extension of the membership inference attacks described previously; it further assumes that the adversary has access to a generative model, that is a model which can be used to sample data points from the underlying data distribution. Carlini et al. use the victim model itself since it is a generative language model. The attack strategy is as follows: the adversary first randomly generates a large pool of data points from the input domain of the victim model, then these inputs are ranked by decreasing likelihood with or without the help of the language model, finally membership inference is done on inputs ranked highest with the victim model this time. Similar to Yeom et al., the crux of the attack is thus for the adversary to sample points—using the language model—that are more likely to be training points, which then reduces training data extraction to the problem of membership inference. Generating such points may require significant adversarial knowledge. Here, this is evidenced by the adversary's access to the victim model itself and to knowledge about its training data collection process. Nevertheless, the authors show how this simple attack strategy is able to extract personal information about one individual from GPT-2's training set, which is a large corpus of data crawled from the Internet.

7.2.3 Take-aways from the Attacks

Research on attacks is motivated by the need to inform defenses. The different attacks we presented above all point to an intricate relationship between overfitting and privacy leakage.

Membership Inference and Overfitting

Recall that membership inference is not equally successful on all training points. Does that mean that overfitting is necessary to obtain a membership inference signal? Although the initial work of Shokri et al suggested that this was the case [SSSS17], later the analysis of Yeom et al. shows that overfitting is sufficient but not necessary [YGFJ18]. Yeom et al. obtain this result by formalizing the gain an adversary obtains from membership inference on stable classifiers which provably do not overfit. We note however that this adversary remains largely an analytical tool and that instantiating it in practice may not always be possible because it is assumed that the adversary colludes with the learning algorithm to obtain a model on which membership inference is successful despite the lack of overfitting. It is also possible for overfitting to facilitate white-box membership inference, that is attacks that inspect a model's parameters. For instance, Leino and Fredrikson [LF20] leverage the idiosyncratic use of features by a model to improve membership inference success. Taking a step back, these results imply that points who are outlier to the training data distribution but are still included in the training set are more susceptible to membership inference—because the model will have overfitted to memorize the correct prediction for these outliers [Lon+18]—but that no point is safe from the privacy leakage associated with membership inference.

The Need for Differential Privacy

Perhaps the single most important take-away from these attacks on the privacy of training data in deep learning, and in particular from results on membership inference, is that simple defense mechanisms such as obfuscating the model's confidence [SSSS17] or regularizing training through an ℓ_2 objective penalty [SSSS17; NSH18; Jia+19] or dropout [Jia+19] are not sufficient to prevent leakage of private information. Furthermore, attacks vary greatly in the assumptions they make about the adversary's knowledge and capabilities, suggesting that it is difficult for the defender to foresee the (auxiliary) knowledge which an adversary will exploit to leak private information from the model [NS08]. Results we have presented thus far hence point to the need for a worst-case framework to reason about the privacy of training algorithm. This is precisely what differential privacy promises. Thus, we next turn to two approaches which can train deep neural networks while providing differential privacy guarantees that bound how much private information leaks from the training data.

7.3 How to Obtain Differential Privacy in Deep Learning?

Training deep neural networks with differential privacy is challenging because the loss function minimized during learning is non-convex. This rules out approaches like objective perturbation [CMS11; KST12] introduced in the convex setting. The two approaches to deep learning with differential privacy we present in this Chapter follow the same design principle.[iii] First, the learning procedure is approximated by a sequential composition of computations whose sensitivity is known. Second, noise is added to these computations. Finally, the total privacy loss of the resulting learning procedure is analyzed to determine the differential privacy guarantees it provides. While we present the two approaches in the context of training deep neural networks, they can also be used for convex learners and can sometimes outperform approaches tailored to the convex setting [Iye+19].

As discussed in Section 1.4.1 of Chapter 1, an essential step to design a differentially private algorithm is to estimate its sensitivity to neighboring input datasets. This is a prerequisite to calibrate noise which is added to the algorithm's computations. Measuring sensitivity of learning algorithms used to train deep neural networks is not an easy task given that the model's architecture yields a non-convex optimization problem to set the model's parameter values.

In the following two Sections, we describe two approaches which differ in the way that they control the sensitivity of the learning algorithm. The first approach named DP-SGD (see Section 7.4) proposes to modify the model updates computed by stochastic gradient descent, in order to achieve a differentially private stochastic gradient descent. At a high level, modifications are two-fold: the gradients are first clipped to control sensitivity, and then they are noised to obtain differential privacy. The second approach named PATE (see Section 7.5) instead proposes to have an ensemble of models trained without privacy predict with differential

iii. Note that the first approach injects noise within the algorithm's computations while the second approach injects noise to the algorithm's outputs. Differential privacy can also be obtained by injecting noise to the algorithm's inputs, but this class of approaches is out of scope here because it is not specific to deep learning.

privacy by having these models predict in aggregate rather than revealing their individual predictions. Because each model only contributes part of the final prediction, the sensitivity of the inference procedure can be controlled and differential privacy obtained.

In the remainder of this Section, we establish terminology and concepts which will be instrumental in understanding the privacy analysis of both DP-SGD in Section 7.4 and PATE in Section 7.5. These concepts allow us to reason about the privacy loss of each computation performed by the learning algorithm, as well as accounting required throughout learning to derive privacy guarantees post hoc.

7.3.1 Reasoning about the Privacy Loss

When developing the analysis of randomized algorithms to prove that they are differentially private, it can be useful to observe that it is equivalent to show that a randomized algorithm is differentially private and that a tail bound can be established on the randomized algorithm's privacy loss. Here, the privacy loss of a randomized algorithm $\mathcal{M}$ is a random variable defined as:

Definition 7.1 (Privacy Loss). *Let $d, d' \in \mathcal{D}^n$ be neighboring datasets. For an auxiliary input aux and outcome $o \in \mathcal{R}$, we define the privacy loss of the randomized mechanism $\mathcal{M}$ at o to be:*

$$c(o, \mathcal{M}, aux, d, d') = \log \frac{Pr[\mathcal{M}(aux, d) = o]}{Pr[\mathcal{M}(aux, d') = o]}$$

In the context of deep learning, where the randomized algorithm is the training procedure, this allows us to reason about the privacy of one access to the training data. To capture multiple accesses to the training data (e.g., each step of a stochastic gradient descent), it is necessary to compose the privacy loss incurred at each data access. Coming back to the attacks we described in Section 7.2, this is intuitive because a model trained for longer is given more opportunities to memorize private information contained in its training set. Unfortunately, directly composing tail bounds on the privacy loss can significantly loosen the overall bound thus resulting in meaningless guarantees of differential privacy for learning. Thus, several modern approaches including Abadi et al. [Aba+16] propose to instead analyze the moments of the privacy loss random variable.

7.3.2 The Moments Accountant

Key to the privacy analysis of both DP-SGD and PATE (which we will present in Sections 7.4 and 7.5 respectively) is the moments accountant, a stronger accounting method to accumulate the privacy loss expended by the learning algorithm each time it accesses the training data. Different from tail bounds on the privacy loss, bounds on the log moments of the privacy loss compose *linearly.* Reasoning over moments of the privacy loss random variable enables the moments accountant to yield a much tighter analysis of the privacy guarantees of learning algorithms which are composed of a sequence of differentially private mechanism applications.

Abadi et al. define the λth moment as the log of moment generating function evaluated at the value λ.

Definition 7.2 (λ^{th} moment). *The λth moment for the privacy loss of the randomized mechanism $\mathcal{M}$ is:*

$$\alpha_{\mathcal{M}}(\lambda, aux, d, d') = \log \mathbb{E}_{o \sim \mathcal{M}(aux,d)}[\exp(\lambda \cdot c(o, \mathcal{M}, aux, d, d'))].$$

Because a data-independent differential privacy guarantee should hold for all possible pairs of neighboring datasets, the analyses of DP-SGD and PATE look at bounding all possible λ^{th} moments for a given mechanism $\mathcal{M}$, regardless of the auxiliary input *aux* or the pair of datasets d, d'. This yields the following variable α of interest:

$$\alpha_{\mathcal{M}}(\lambda) = \max_{aux,d,d'} \alpha_{\mathcal{M}}(\lambda, aux, d, d'). \tag{7.1}$$

Abadi et al. prove two properties of α which are instrumental in the moments accountant ability to offer a tighter privacy analysis of DP-SGD and PATE. First, they show that the log moments of the privacy loss random variable composes linearly. This is useful to analyze randomized algorithms like DP-SGD and PATE which—as we will explain later—can be viewed as a sequential application of k differentially private mechanisms $\mathcal{M}_i$. In the differential privacy literature, such a sequential application is referred to as adaptive composition: the auxiliary input *aux* of the kth mechanism $\mathcal{M}_k$ is the output of all the previous mechanisms.

Theorem 7.3 (Composability of α). *] If a mechanism $\mathcal{M}$ consists of a sequence of adaptive mechanisms $\mathcal{M}_1, \mathcal{M}_2, ..., \mathcal{M}_k$ where $\mathcal{M}_i : \prod_{j=1}^{i-1} \mathcal{R}_j \times \mathcal{D} \rightarrow \mathcal{R}_i$, then for any λ:*

$$\alpha_{\mathcal{M}}(\lambda) \leq \sum_{i=1}^{k} \alpha_{\mathcal{M}_i}(\lambda). \tag{7.2}$$

We will later see how in the case of both DP-SGD and PATE, this composability property is used to bound the moment of the total privacy loss incurred by the learning algorithm across all of its accesses to the training data. Once this accounting is complete, a value of ε for the differential privacy is derived from the bound on α through an application of the following tail bound.

Theorem 7.4 (Tail bound on α). *] For any ε, the mechanism $\mathcal{M}$ is (ε, δ)-differentially private for:*

$$\delta = \min_{\lambda} exp(\alpha_{\mathcal{M}}(\lambda) - \lambda\varepsilon). \tag{7.3}$$

7.4 Differentially Private Stochastic Gradient Descent (DP-SGD)

The work of Abadi et al. [Aba+16] on DP-SGD builds on a line of work [SCS13; BST14], which was itself initiated by the pioneering work of Chaudhuri et al. [CMS11]. One of its key innovations is the introduction of the novel analysis technique known as the moments accountant (see Section 7.3) to improve the privacy guarantee which one can prove after training a deep neural network with DP-SGD. We first introduce DP-SGD in its most modern form, and then outline a sketch for the analysis of its privacy guarantees in Section 7.4.2.

7.4.1 The DP-SGD Algorithm

Let us first describe a typical *non-private* stochastic gradient descent. To begin, one samples a minibatches of training data, that is randomly draw a small number[iv] of training examples (X, Y) from the training set where X are the inputs and Y the labels associated with these examples. One then computes the loss $l(\theta, X, Y)$ of the model h, averaged over all examples contained in the minibatch. The loss measures the error between the model's predictions and the labels we expected it to produce. A common choice for multi-class classification problems is the cross-entropy, which computes for a single training example (x_i, y_i):

$$l(\theta, x_i, y_i) = -\sum_j y_{ij} \log h_j(x_i),$$

where j indexes the classes of the classification problem, and i indexes the different examples included in the minibatch such that $(X, Y) = \{(x_i, y_i)\}_i$. Next, one computes the gradient of the average loss across the minibatch with respect to the model's parameters. Such a gradient can be computed because deep neural networks

iv. This number of training examples included in a minibatch, i.e., its *size*, is chosen first and foremost to accommodate the hardware computing gradient descent. For instance, if the machine is equipped with an accelerator for matrix algebra, e.g., a GPU, it is generally-speaking beneficial to use the largest minibatch size which will fit in the accelerator's memory. However, other factors may be relevant in the choice of minimatch size and may commend a smaller size; smaller minibatches were for example observed to introduce a regularization effect in learning although this effect is not consistently obtained [Sha+18]. Thus, in practice one treats the minibatch size as a hyperparameter of stochastic gradient descent.

are differentiable, and this computation is made more efficient by the backpropagation algorithm [RHW86]. This gradient is multiplied by a constant α called the learning rate before it is subtracted to the current model parameter θ to obtain a step of gradient descent:

$$\theta \leftarrow \theta - \alpha \frac{\partial \frac{1}{N} \sum_i l(\theta, x_i, y_i)}{\partial \theta}, \tag{7.4}$$

where N is the size of the minibatch. The learning rate is a hyperparameter controlling the size of each step of gradient descent. To bootstrap this procedure, one initializes the model parameters θ to a random value. The steps described above are then applies repeatedly until the deep neural network's parameters are deemed to have converged. Ideally, one would like the model to converge to the global minimum of the loss function it is trained to minimize. However, deep neural networks being non-convex learners, one must be satisfied with one of the local minima that approximates the global minimal loss value. In practice, the stopping criterion is typically decided by evaluating the performance of the model on a holdout set of data known as the validation set. This validation accuracy should generally increase as steps of gradient descent are taken. Once this validation accuracy plateaus or starts to decrease (indicating overfitting [Zha+16]), gradient descent is interrupted.

The modifications made by Abadi et al. [Aba+16] to obtain a differentially private stochastic gradient descent algorithm are three fold. First, all operations within the minibatch are performed on a *per-example* basis. This means that the loss is no longer averaged across examples included in the minibatch. Instead, the loss $l(\theta, x_i, y_i)$ of each training example (x_i, y_i) is computed individually. The same holds for gradients of the loss with respect to the model parameters:

$$g_i = \frac{\partial l(\theta, x_i, y_i)}{\partial \theta}.$$

The second key modification made is to clip each of these per example gradients to have a maximum ℓ_2 norm C:

$$g_i \leftarrow g_i \cdot \min\left(1, \frac{C}{\|g_i\|_2}\right). \tag{7.5}$$

Intuitively, this bounds the influence of each training example on learning, and more important this bound is known to be C. We can thus derive the sensitivity of the learning algorithm from the value C of this bound. This is essential to the third, and last, modification introduced to obtain differential privacy: Gaussian noise whose standard deviation is calibrated to be linearly proportional to C

is added to each of these clipped gradients.[v] The rest of the procedure is unmodified: the average of noisy clipped gradients is multiplied by the learning rate and subtracted to the model parameters to update the model. Abadi et al. thus obtain the following gradient descent step:

$$\theta \leftarrow \theta - \alpha \frac{1}{N} \sum_i \left(\frac{\partial l(\theta, x_i, y_i)}{\partial \theta} \cdot \min\left(1, \frac{C}{\|g_i\|_2}\right) + N(0, \sigma^2 C^2) \right), \quad (7.6)$$

where σ is a hyperparameter of the differentially private stochastic gradient descent. Generally speaking, the larger the value of σ is, the tighter the resulting differential privacy guarantee is (i.e., one can prove a smaller bound on the privacy loss ε).

7.4.2 Privacy Analysis of DP-SGD

The analysis of DP-SGD relies on composition theorems to accumulate the privacy budget spent by gradient descent across multiple steps; each step is accounted for and further increases the privacy cost of learning. In addition to the application of advanced composition theorems to compute the overall privacy budget, one can also refine the analysis of DP-SGD by reasoning about its guarantees with definitions like zero-concentrated differential privacy [BS16] or Renyi differential privacy [Mir17]. For simplicity, we expose here the analysis provided by Abadi et al. [Aba+16]. It derives the differential privacy guarantees obtained by training with DP-SGD from an application of the moments accountant.

We begin by analyzing the λth moment for the privacy loss of an *individual* step of gradient descent. Recall that each step of DP-SGD noises the clipped gradient computed over a minibatch J of examples chosen independently at random with probability q. Thus a step of DP-SGD can be written as $\mathcal{M}(d) = \sum_{i \in J} f(x_i, y_i) + N(0, \sigma^2)$ where $f(x_i, y_i)$ computes the clipped gradient for example (x_i, y_i) and σ here incorporates the clipping norm C for simplicity of presentation. The authors show that under certain conditions (see the paper), the following upper bound holds:

$$\alpha_{\mathcal{M}}(\lambda) \leq \frac{q^2 \lambda(\lambda + 1)}{(1 - q)\sigma^2} + O(q^3 \lambda^3 / \sigma^3).$$

v. Note that adding noise to gradients is commonly done in deep learning to regularize learning [Nee+15]. Here, it is however crucial to first clip gradients before they are noised, and then to calibrate the standard deviation of noise added to the clipping bound. Otherwise, one would be unable to prove that the resulting procedure is differentially private.

They then leverage the composability of a sequence of adaptive mechanisms (the individual steps of gradient descent) to obtain the λth moment $\alpha(\lambda)$ for the privacy loss of the *complete* gradient descent. If we denote by T the total number of steps of gradient descent completed, the following is derived by an application of Equation 7.2:

$$\alpha(\lambda) \leq \frac{Tq^2\lambda^2}{\sigma^2}.$$

Through an application of the tail bound on the moments for the privacy loss (see Equation 7.3) gives the main result of Abadi et al., which is that DP-SGD is (ε, δ)-differentially private for any $\varepsilon < c_1 q^2 T$ and $\delta > 0$ if we choose:

$$\sigma \geq c_2 \frac{q\sqrt{T \log(1/\delta)}}{\varepsilon}, \tag{7.7}$$

for some constants c_1 and c_2.

In practice, it is interesting to note that interpreting this analysis and the guarantees it provides can be non-trivial. First, the analysis assumes that each minibatch is obtained by *independently* uniformly sampling training examples. Instead, many practical implementation of stochastic gradient descent only analyze *permutations* of the training set at each epoch so they must be carefully extended to obtain an valid implementation of DP-SGD. Second, the analysis leverages randomness in the sampling of each minibatch to guarantee differential privacy. This result is known as privacy amplification by subsampling in the literature [BBG18]. However, this requires that the randomness is of cryptographic strength, which again is not always the case in all practical implementations. We come back to additional practical considerations for implementing DP-SGD in Section 7.6.

7.5 Private Aggregation of Teacher Ensembles (PATE)

DP-SGD obtains differential privacy by modifying the learning procedure itself to bound its sensitivity and randomize it accordingly. This means that any deviations from the learning procedure captured by the existing theoretical analysis requires new efforts to bound the privacy leakage. This may limit the ability of DP-SGD to new developments in the machine learning community (although it has proven itself remarkably amenable to a wide range of learning tasks beyond classification and variants of SGD like the widely-used Adam [KB14] optimizer). A good example is the one of batch normalization, now a prevalent technique in modern deep learning [IS15], thanks to its ability to regularize the norm of internal model activations which can help prevent overfitting and improve convergence of the optimization procedure. However, batch normalization involves the computation of statistics across all examples included in a minibatch. This means that it cannot be used in conjunction with DP-SGD because privacy guarantees rely on the gradient computation being performed on a per-example basis. This motivates the need for another privacy-preserving approach to deep learning which does not limit how the model is trained.

Papernot et al. [Pap+16; Pap+17] introduce such an approach with the private aggregation of teacher ensembles (PATE). Rather than modify the learning algorithm used to train a model, PATE introduces changes to how data is fed to the learning procedure and how model predictions are revealed.

7.5.1 The PATE Approach

In PATE, one starts by splitting the training set whose privacy needs to be protected in k partitions. These are partitions in the mathematical sense, so one point from the original training set is included in exactly one of the partitions (which are non-overlapping and do not repeat any of the points). From each of these partitions, one trains a machine learning model. There are no restrictions on how each of the models are trained. This means we can for instance use techniques such as batch normalization, whose privacy would be difficult to analyze if we wanted to take an approach in the vein of DP-SGD. In PATE, each model could even be trained with different techniques (e.g., deep learning, decision tree, etc.). Because one trains a model on each of the k partitions, we obtain an ensemble of k models trained independently but all solving the same task. We give the name of *teacher* to each of these k models. Next, PATE deploys this ensemble of teachers to predict on test inputs while bounding leakage of private information from the training data.

PATE obtains privacy by having these teachers predict collectively and revealing their aggregate prediction rather than their individual predictions. Specifically, each teacher is given the input[vi] x that we would like to predict on and commits a vote for one of the labels of the problem. One then builds a histogram of these votes, where each bar $n_j(x)$ of the histogram corresponds to a label j of the problem and indicates how many teachers voted for this label j. The label predicted by PATE is the one which received the most number of votes, i.e., the argmax of this histogram:

$$\arg\max_j n_j(x).$$

vi. To avoid ambiguity, let us stress that all teachers simultaneously predict on the same input here.

Such a mechanism is common in machine learning, even when one does not seek to provide guarantee, because bagging predictors is an instance of ensemble learning which commonly improves generalization [Bre96].

Intuitively, it can be seen that when most teachers agree on the label to be predicted, revealing the most frequent label does not leak much private information in the sense that this prediction was made independently by many teachers. Given that each of these teachers learned from a different set of data, a single training record contained in the original training set (prior to partitioning) could have only influenced one of the teachers, and as a consequence had a negligible impact on the computation of the most frequent label. That said, this voting mechanism is not sufficient to obtain differential privacy because there still exists certain edge cases where a single training point can change the outcome of voting. To see why, observe that if we have an ensemble of k teachers such that k is an odd integer and that $n_a(x) = \frac{k-1}{2} + 1$ teachers voted for label a while the remaining $n_b(x) = \frac{k-1}{2}$ teachers voted for another label b when they are presented with a test input, then a single teacher changing its prediction from label a to b can result in the voting mechanism outputting b rather than a as would have been the case initially.

This shows that in the worst case one teacher alone is able to change the outcome of the voting mechanism. Because each teacher is trained without any form of privacy, we thus have to assume that changing one of the training examples (in the original set before it is partitioned) can change the predictions of the teacher trained on the partition containing this example. Put altogether, this implies that the sensitivity of the mechanism is such that each training record can in the worst case affect at most 2 of histogram bars by $+/-1$ votes. This allows us to calibrate the noise that we need to add to the histogram before we obtain a differentially private prediction. In fact, privately releasing the argmax of a histogram is a well-known problem in the differential privacy literature and the properties of such *histogram queries* are well understood [DR+14]. Specifically, the resulting voting mechanism for PATE computes the following:

$$\arg\max_j \left\{ n_j(x) + Lap\left(\frac{2}{\gamma}\right) \right\}, \tag{7.8}$$

where $Lap(b)$ is the Laplacian distribution with location 0 and scale b.

7.5.2 Privacy Analysis of PATE

A first privacy analysis of the variant of PATE we presented in Section 7.5.1 can be derived from the differential privacy of the Laplace mechanism for histogram queries. Indeed, consider a single prediction made by PATE. This prediction is a histogram query, which is known to be (γ, δ)-differentially private [DR+14]. Next, we turn to the analysis of a sequence of T predictions made by PATE. Given that each of these predictions is differentially private, we can compose their privacy guarantee to obtain the privacy guarantee achieved overall when making the T predictions. If we naively compose, this results in the T predictions being $(T\gamma, T\delta)$-differentially private. This however yields poor utility when computing Equation 7.8 for most practical values of γ and T. Thus, we turn to the moments accountant we introduced in Section 7.3.2.

Applying the Moments Accountant

Recall that the moments accountant instead proposes to reason in the log space of the moment generating function of the privacy loss. For PATE with the Laplace mechanism, we have that the privacy loss is equal to the noise parameter of the Laplace distribution itself [DR+14]: $c(o, \mathcal{M}, aux, d, d') = \gamma$. From Equation 7.1, we then have that:

$$\alpha_{\mathcal{M}}(\lambda, aux, d, d') = \log \mathbb{E}_{o \sim \mathcal{M}(aux,d)}[\exp(\lambda\gamma)] = \lambda\gamma .$$

We compute these for several integer values of $\lambda \geq 1$. We can then use the tail bound from Definition 7.4 to derive the (ε, δ)-differential privacy guarantee achieved:

$$\varepsilon = \frac{\min_\lambda \alpha_{\mathcal{M}}(\lambda) - \log \delta}{\lambda}. \tag{7.9}$$

Still, this may result in poor utility for practical values of γ and T. There are several ways one can improve the utility-privacy trade-off of PATE. Of course, one can obtain better bounds on the log moments of the privacy loss. For instance, Bun and Steinke [BS16] allow us to show that we also have $\alpha_{\mathcal{M}}(\lambda) \leq \frac{1}{2}\gamma^2\lambda(\lambda+1)$. We can thus retain the best of the two bounds for each of our log moment computations:

$$\alpha_{\mathcal{M}}(\lambda) = \min\{2\lambda\gamma, \frac{1}{2}\gamma^2\lambda(\lambda+1)\}.$$

Data-dependent Analysis

Up to now, our analysis of PATE has been data-independent; that is, our privacy analysis does not depend on the particular dataset which the learning algorithm takes as an input. This is made clear by the maximum operator over aux, d, d' when computing $\alpha_{\mathcal{M}}$ in Equation 7.1. However, in many cases the teachers in the ensemble exhibit a strong consensus on the label they predict: that is one of the labels is assigned most of the votes in the histogram computing by the voting mechanism in PATE. When this is the case, the privacy cost is much smaller than what is suggested by the data-independent analysis.

To obtain such a data-dependent privacy analysis of PATE, Papernot et al. [Pap+16] prove a bound of the log moment of the privacy loss which depends on the probability q that the noisy argmax mechanism will output the wrong label after noising the votes originally cast by teachers:

$$\alpha_{\mathcal{M}}^{dd} = \log\left((1-q)\left(\frac{1-q}{1-e^{\gamma}q}\right)^{\lambda} + qe^{\gamma\lambda} \right). \tag{7.10}$$

The probability q can be derived from the votes cast by teachers as follows:

$$q \leq \sum_{j \neq j^*} \frac{2 + \frac{\gamma}{2}(n_{j^*} - n_j)}{4exp(\frac{\gamma}{2}(n_{j^*} - n_j))}. \tag{7.11}$$

The rest of the privacy analysis is identical to its data-independent counterpart.

In practice, the data-dependent analysis may not always be superior to the data-independent analysis. This is however not a drawback given that we can combine the two effectively at the level of the log moment computation. Indeed, one can compute $\alpha_{\mathcal{M}}$ as follows:

$$\alpha_{\mathcal{M}}(\lambda) = \min\{2\lambda\gamma, \frac{1}{2}\gamma^2\lambda(\lambda+1), \alpha_{\mathcal{M}}^{dd}\}. \tag{7.12}$$

To summarize, the combined data-independent and data-dependent analysis is as follows:

1. Compute the probability q that the noisy argmax will output a prediction that is not the most frequent vote cast by teachers.
2. Compute the three bounds (two data-independent, and one data-dependent based on the value of q) on the log moments of the privacy loss.
3. Retain the minimum bound as in Equation 7.12 for each moment.
4. Derive the (ε, δ)-differential privacy guarantee from the tail bound property of the log moment, as in Equation 7.9.

With data-dependent analysis, we are able to prove a tighter bound on the privacy loss and thus the same mechanism (with constant utility) became "more" private. This however should be interpreted carefully because the guarantee now depends on the dataset which the algorithm is operating on (rather than holding for any possible dataset) and releasing the value of ε now leaks private information. Thus, it is possible to noise the value of data-dependent ε estimates to prevent any additional private information leakage (see Papernot et al. [Pap+16] for a detailed discussion and an example approach for doing so based on the smooth analysis of Nissim et al. [NRS07]).

Training a Student Model

Even with the data-dependent analysis, the privacy budget increases every time a query is answered by PATE. That is, the privacy leakage induced by responding to each query is bounded but non-zero. Thus, the mechanism will either be able to answer a small number of queries only or provide little utility (because the noise injected will have to be larger to decrease the per-query cost of a larger number of queries to be answered). To alleviate this limitation, the privacy-preserving labels predicted by the teacher ensemble can be use to train a student model. This student model can query teachers with unlabeled *public* data. The student will then learn from the labels predicted by the teachers. Once the student is trained, the total privacy budget expended is fixed and the teachers can be discarded. The student can then answer as many queries as it wants, this will not impact the bound. To further improve the utility-privacy tradeoff, the student can also be trained with a semi-supervised learning approach [Sal+16; Ber+19].

7.6 Practical Considerations for Private Deep Learning

Having introduced two approaches to deep learning with differential privacy, DP-SGD and PATE, we now outline a few practical considerations and observations stemming from experience implementing both of these approaches.

7.6.1 Tuning Hyperparameters and the Utility-Privacy Tradeoff

The first obstacle is the accuracy of privacy-preserving models. Datasets are often sampled from a distribution with heavy tails (see Chapter 10). For instance, in a medical application, there are typically (and fortunately) fewer patients with a given medical condition than patients without that condition. This means that there are fewer training examples for patients with each medical condition to learn from. Because differential privacy prevents us from learning patterns which are not found generally across the training data, it limits our ability to learn from these patients for which we have very few examples of [SPGG21]. More generally, there is often a trade-off between the accuracy of a model and the strength of the differential privacy guarantee it was trained with: the smaller the privacy budget is, the larger the impact on accuracy typically is. That said, this tension is not always inevitable and there are instances where privacy and accuracy are synergistic because differential privacy implies generalization (but not vice versa) [Dwo+15]. When there is a tradeoff, it can be partially mitigated by carefully setting the hyperparameters that control both approaches.

As far as DP-SGD is concerned, clipping and noising are common regularizer in machine learning so the fact that DP-SGD may be potentially harmful to performance can be counter-intuitive. That said, there are key differences in how clipping and noising are used to obtain DP-SGD. First, clipping is typically done on the *average* gradient computed over an entire minibatch. Instead, DP-SGD applies clipping on a *per-example* basis. Work has began understanding the effect this has on learning [STT20], but it remains an open problem to mitigate its impact on the accuracy [Pap+20] of training. Similarly, the impact of noising on DP-SGD remains to be understood. Another important hyperparameter in DP-SGD is the size of the minibatch. Practical experience shows that larger minibatches often yield better tradeoffs between utility and privacy [De+22]. That said, possible values for the size of the minibatch are often limited by hardware constraining the computational feasibility of calculating gradients for a large number of training examples simultaneously. Finally, given that the privacy guarantee of DP-SGD is proportional to the number T of gradient descent steps (recall Equation 7.7), it is important to tune this number and adjust accordingly the learning rate to compensate for a smaller number of steps being taken.

In the case of PATE, the key hyperparameter to be tuned is the number of teachers k to use. Increasing the number of teachers generally improves the privacy guarantee. Because more votes are being aggregated, it is easier to introduce more noise in the aggregation without affecting the outcome of the aggregation (i.e., degrading utility). However, increasing the number of teachers generally has diminishing returns beyond a certain point because each teacher receive so little data to learn from that it becomes a *weak learner*. Thus, there is often in practice an optimal number of teachers to be picked by training teachers with a partition of data whose size varies.

7.6.2 System Perspective on Privacy

Abadi et al. [Aba+17] remark that the privacy of training data may depend on other stages of the data life cycle. Here, we have not discussed techniques for sanitizing the data. These often take the form of removing data attributes which may identify an individual, a class of technique known as data anonymization. We chose not to discuss these approaches because their limitations are well-understood in the privacy community. Fundamentally, anonymization assumes the data owner can anticipate which information the adversary will have access to so that they can deduce with attributes may identify an individual. In other words, anonymization is highly context-dependent and does not provide nearly as strong guarantees as those expressed in the framework of differential privacy. Anonymization may however be beneficial at the data collection stage in certain settings, in particular to minimize the amount of data that is retained about an individual. Indeed, this may be beneficial in settings where proper access control is not enforced when accessing the training data or its byproducts like machine learning models. We discuss this further in Section 7.6.4. Finally, Abadi et al. note the importance of mechanisms for data deletion and data retention policies. This has been put forward in several legislative frameworks, most prominently in the European Union's General Data Protection Regulation [Man13]. Deleting training data raises the question of what should be done to machine learning models trained on this data. Indeed, even if these models were trained with differential privacy, they would still be influenced by the training data which was deleted (although if the model was trained with differential privacy, this influence would be bounded). Consequently, research has began towards enabling machine unlearning, that is the process of deleting any influence a training point may have had on the machine learning model's parameters. Research on machine unlearning initially focused on learning algorithms which can be expressed in the statistical query learning framework [CY15]. However, this approach does not apply to deep learning because deep neural networks are trained using adaptive statistical query algorithms, which make queries that depend on all queries previously made. Instead, work by Bourtoule et al. [Bou+21] proposes an approach for machine unlearning that is applicable to any model trained with stochastic gradient descent—thus including deep learning.

7.6.3 Public Data

It is interesting to note that the utility of both DP-SGD and PATE can be improved with the availability of public data. We already covered in Section 7.5 how public data is required to train a student model in PATE. Without such public data, the privacy budget of PATE would be unbounded over time (i.e., it would increase each time the teachers answer an additional query). This would of course lead to a disadvantageous tradeoff between utility and privacy. Instead, with public data it is easier to improve this tradeoff because the student can learn with very little supervision from the teachers. The less supervision required, the stronger the privacy guarantee achieved. Here, it is interesting to note that any progress made in the machine learning community towards learning with less supervision can be directly applied to improve the utility-privacy tradeoff in PATE, as demonstrated with the invention of MixMatch [Ber+19].

Models trained with DP-SGD can also be improved with public data: for instance, models can be pre-trained or fine-tuned with public data. Pre-training is now a common practice in machine learning with privacy [LTLH21; De+22]. Fine-tuning is an alternative to pre-training. Intuitively, fine-tuning has the advantage that the private model was already trained so one can exploit this information to select the public data which will most help alleviate the deficiencies of the private model [Zha+19].

We will come back to the issue of data complexity in Section 7.7.1, where we will see that the benefits of public data are a symptom for a more fundamental question in private deep learning around the (im)possibility of learning features from limited data with privacy.

7.6.4 Confidentiality vs. Privacy

In computer security, confidentiality is achieved when information is only accessible to parties who are authorized to access it [Bis02]. In the context of data involved in deep learning algorithms, this means that the training and test data should only be visible to authorized users. This is a guarantee which is orthogonal to the one of differential privacy, where we instead want to prevent inferences about the data (even inferences that can be made without direct access to the data).

To provide confidentiality, one must apply cryptographic primitives so as to encrypt the data and require a key to decrypt the corresponding plaintext. To enable applications of deep learning to encrypted data, some proposed homomorphic machine learning techniques [Gil+16]. These are however difficult to scale to deep neural networks because of the non-linear activation functions they include [TB18]. These techniques can be leveraged to train the model without decrypting data (i.e., perform gradient descent over encrypted data). Cryptography can also be used to make predictions over encrypted test inputs. This is useful when one wants to offload compute associated with the model (e.g. to a cloud provider) without revealing the test inputs (e.g., patient records collected by a hospital).

It is important to note that confidentiality does not imply privacy, or vice versa. This confusion arises frequently, in particular in the context of distributed learning. For instance, federated learning [Kon+16] is an approach for distributed learning with confidentiality but it does not provide any privacy guarantee (in the sense of differential privacy) unless it is combined with an optimizer like DP-SGD. If DP-SGD is not employed, federated learning may leak private information more so than a centralized learning algorithm because it exposes the intermediate model updates [MSDS19; Boe+23b; Boe+23a]. To obtain both confidentiality and privacy, one can also combine cryptographic primitives with the PATE approach from Section 7.5. This yields a form of collaborative learning where the different teachers can be distributed [Cho+21].

7.7 Research Issues

In the rest of this chapter, we present some of the questions currently being investigated by the research community. This is done to give the reader a sense of the limitations of current approaches, at a more abstract level than the practical considerations of Section 7.6. The list of questions covered here is by no means meant to be comprehensive.

7.7.1 Is Representation Learning possible with Privacy?

Representation learning is fundamental to deep learning. In essence, the intuition behind training neural networks with multiple hidden layers is precisely to have each of these layers extract a representation of the data. The last layer of a deep neural network can be thought as a linear model taking in as its input a representation whose features were learned by composing all of the previous layers of the deep neural network. This alleviates the need for human feature engineering, as demonstrated by the successful application of deep learning to raw images or audio. That said, the trade-off empirically observed between model utility and privacy raises the question of whether current approaches to deep learning can indeed learn representations while satisfying the constraints of differential privacy.

A Feature Perspective

Put another way, is the deep learning promise of not having to human engineer features compatible with the constrains of privacy. Indeed, Tramèr and Boneh [TB20] remark that private deep learning often falls short, in terms of *prediction accuracy*, to shallow models trained without privacy. Building on this observation, they compare the performance of private deep learning with private *shallow* learning combined with human-engineered features. They for instance find that it is possible to simultaneously outperform the accuracy and privacy of private deep learning on CIFAR10 by training a linear model whose features are human engineered. In their experiment, they extract these features with a scaterring network [OM15] which is a non-learned feature extractor. They find that one of the roadblocks preventing DP-SGD from achieving representation learning that outperforms shallow learning from human-engineered features is that the privacy guarantees require that each training point be only involved in a small number of updates. This is a roadblock to deep learning of representations with differential privacy, because deep learning often involves long training procedures taking multiple passes through the dataset (i.e., epochs) to uncover the features which project data on a representation that mostly[vii] linearly separates the data. Tramèr and Boneh then outline the increased data complexity of private deep learning, surfacing the need for larger datasets to

vii. Not all datasets will be linearly separable, and here we are referring to the split in deep neural network architectures described above: the last layer can be interpreted as a linear model taking in as input the features learned by the rest of the architecture.

enable representation learning with privacy. The reader may recall our related discussion in Section 7.6 on public data. This observation is also consistent with a prior successful application of DP-SGD to language modeling in a setting where the data collected spans billions of users [MRTZ17]. Alternatively, Tramèr and Boneh propose to tackle this increased data complexity through transfer learning, as previously studied in the non-private setting [KSL19].

An Architecture Perspective

Having discussed the role that features play in private deep learning, it is natural to consider next the role played by the model's architecture. Deep neural networks are often the fruit of an extensive empirical architectural design phase, combined with the necessary hyperparameter tuning. This is done empirically and involves a large number of runs. It is thus tempting to reuse existing architectures known to perform well and train them, with privacy this time, on datasets that are sensitive. This avoids the cost of hyperparameter tuning with privacy guarantees, which would involve composing the cost of the training run associated with each hyperparameter value that was considered [PS21]. However, Papernot et al. [Pap+20] show how reusing hyperparameter values that were optimal for the non-private setting to now train with a private optimizer can lead to suboptimal architectural choices because the deep neural network is designed for optimal convergence with a non-private optimizer like SGD rather than with a private optimizer such as DP-SGD.

7.7.2 Is the Analysis of DP-SGD (or PATE) Tight?

In the following, we focus on DP-SGD for clarity of exposition, but the discussion is also relevant to PATE. Because the framework of differential privacy involves a rather strict definition of what it means for an algorithm to be private, and in particular that this definition is *worst-case*, it is legitimate to ask whether the guarantees obtained by training with DP-SGD are sufficiently strong, even if the bound on the privacy cost ε is too large to be meaningful in terms to probabilities. Indeed, in theory any value of ε above 1 is not meaningful because the value of ε is used to create an interval between two probabilities (which naturally take values between 0 and 1). This is an important issue in practice because practitioners are faced with the fact that they need to calibrate the standard deviation of Gaussian noise added to gradient descent in DP-SGD with the desired strength of differential privacy guarantee. Recall that increasing the linear factor σ generally leads to smaller values of ε. While it is easy to say that a model is more private than another model by comparing the values of ε we are able to prove (assuming both models are trained using an algorithm whose privacy analysis is tight), it is more difficult to provide an absolute threshold after which we consider an algorithm to be "private". This is of course an important issue which merits attention from legislative bodies interested in creating new privacy regulations based on the framework of differential privacy.

There are two ways in which one could improve the trade-off between utility and differential privacy in the context of deep learning. First, one could realize that the privacy analysis of DP-SGD is loose, leading to an overestimate of the worst-case privacy leakage. This would mean that efforts towards improving our theoretical understanding of DP-SGD could lead to tighter analysis of its privacy guarantees, and as a by-product to improved trade-offs between utility and differential privacy. Such refined analysis could also require that one make additional assumptions restraining the adversary's capabilities. Second, it is possible that we could invent novel algorithms for learning with differential privacy that afford between utility-privacy trade-offs. These algorithms could be improved variants of DP-SGD or completely new approaches for learning with differential privacy.

It is thus tempting to evaluate the performance of differentially private models in the face of adversaries mounting attacks such as the ones presented in Section 7.2. This would help assess how "far" the analytical guarantees one can prove are from the empirical guarantees of privacy. One should of course be careful about making such an evaluation because the conclusion one makes are very different from the conclusions derived from the analysis of differential privacy guarantees. Put simply, differential privacy guarantees provide an upper bound on the privacy leakage, whereas mounting an attack provides a lower bound on this privacy leakage. Indeed, the adversary is only able to demonstrate that they can extract at least as much private information as they could under that specific attack and threat model. Nothing prevents a more sophisticated adversary from extracting more private information if they are able to gain additional knowledge in the future or discover a new attack strategy. Instead, the guarantees provided by a specific analysis technique for differential privacy hold regardless of the knowledge and capabilities available to the adversary as long as these comply with the definition of differential privacy. Furthermore, this also means that in practice while the analytical bound obtained is fixed given a specific analysis technique, the results of an empirical evaluation of the success of a privacy attack or of the model utility may vary greatly. As a consequence, one should take great care when comparing the privacy-utility tradeoff obtained through analytical guarantees and the privacy-utility tradeoff measured through an empirical evaluation of attack success [EMRS19].

With all of these caveats stated clearly, let us now turn our attention to studies that have recently evaluated the robustness of models trained with differential privacy in the face of attacks targeting the privacy of training data. While these attacks cannot replace the analytical bounds discussed above, they can nevertheless inform theoretical research on these bounds. Jagielski et al. [JUO20] take a first step towards such an evaluation by instantiating a poisoning adversary to audit the guarantees provided by DP-SGD. They observe that if a model is ε-differentially private, an adversary should have bounded success of at most $\frac{e^{k\varepsilon}}{1+e^{\varepsilon}}$ in telling whether a model was trained on a dataset D or a second dataset $D \cup S$ where S is a set of k poisoning points. To help the adversary succeed as closely as possible as tolerated by the differential privacy guarantee, Jagielski et al. propose a novel attack which minimizes the variance of model parameters when crafting poisoning points.

Building on these results, Nasr et al. [Nas+21] introduce a spectrum of adversaries ranging from the black-box adversary of Jagielski et al. to a more sophisticated (and perhaps unrealistic) adversaries. This enables Nasr et al. to obtain stronger lower bounds on the privacy leakage. This also has the added benefit of singling out the adversarial capabilities needed to match the maximal privacy leakage tolerated by the analytical upper bound on privacy.

7.7.3 Connection Between Privacy and Robustness

Because differential privacy is a worst-case guarantee that implies a form of generalization, it is natural to ask whether learning with differential privacy also nurtures a form of robustness. Machine learning algorithms are indeed known to be vulnerable to both training and test time manipulation of data, the former being referred to as a poisoning [BNL12] attack while the latter is known as an adversarial example [Big+13; Sze+13]. We should be careful when drawing connections between privacy and robustness because results from the differential privacy literature show improvement in average-case generalization whereas robustness requires worst-case guarantees: an adversary will always choose the attack that is the most effective.

We have already outlined the connection between differentially private learning and poisoning in Section 7.7.2. This connection has led Ma et al. to study how differential privacy can be used to defend against poisoning attacks against ridge and logistic regressions [MZH19].

Now take the case of adversarial examples. They are crafted by exploiting the excessive sensitivity of machine learning models to input-domain perturbations. Such perturbations can be found by gradient descent, using the same techniques and tools than those required to train the model (e.g., backpropagation for gradient descent). Song et al. have first noted that improving robustness of models to adversarial examples may lead to additional leakage of private information [SSM19]. This can be understood intuitively with the example of adversarial training, a common technique to improve a model's robustness to adversarial examples: it encourages the model to be a more constant predictor around its training inputs. This means in turn that a membership inference attack is easier to mount because training points are characterized by smoother regions of the loss surface. Research has also investigated whether techniques from the adversarial example literature can be leveraged to contain privacy leakage from a model [NSH18; Jia+19], but these generally provide empirical guarantees which do not have the properties that make differential privacy attractive (e.g., it is agnostic to adversarial knowledge or capabilities).

7.8 Concluding Remarks

In this Chapter, we first motivated the need for privacy-preserving approaches to deep learning. In addition to needs for privacy inherent to fostering user trust and complying with regulation in place, attacks leaking private information from the training data of machine learning models demonstrate that learning algorithms retain information specific to individual training points. We then presented two approaches for privacy-preserving deep learning, DP-SGD and PATE. While DP-SGD is currently the de facto approach for private deep learning, PATE has potential to shine when it comes to training large model architectures or when predicting in distributed settings from a collection of models. In the rest of the Chapter, we presented challenges that practitioners will likely face but also more fundamental questions that researchers are currently tackling to improve our understanding of how to learn with privacy. While deep learning has enabled key innovations in the past years, deep learning with privacy is still in its infancy. Addressing its current limitations will be key to enable responsible applications of artificial intelligence in areas like healthcare where the potential benefits to society are immense but the risks are commensurately important. Achieving privacy-preserving deep learning by design, rather than attempting to retrofit existing algorithms with privacy considerations is perhaps one of the most promising avenues for future work in this area.

Acknowledgments

The author would like to thank Abhradeep Guha Thakurta for helpful discussions and co-authoring a blog post on a similar topic which helped preparing the exposition of ideas presented here.

References

[Aba+16] M. Abadi, A. Chu, I. Goodfellow, H. B. McMahan, I. Mironov, K. Talwar, and L. Zhang. “Deep Learning with Differential Privacy”. In: Proceedings of the 2016 ACM SIGSAC Conference on

Computer and Communications Security. CCS '16. Vienna, Austria: Association for Computing Machinery, 2016, pp. 308–318. ISBN: 9781450341394. URL: https://doi.org/10.1145/2976749.2978318 (cit. on pp. 260, 262–264).

[Aba+17] M. Abadi, U. Erlingsson, I. Goodfellow, H. B. McMahan, I. Mironov, N. Papernot, K. Talwar, and L. Zhang. "On the protection of private information in machine learning systems: Two recent approches". In: 2017 IEEE 30th Computer Security Foundations Symposium (CSF). IEEE. 2017, pp. 1–6 (cit. on p. 271).

[BBG18] B. Balle, G. Barthe, and M. Gaboardi. "Privacy amplification by subsampling: Tight analyses via couplings and divergences". In: arXiv preprint arXiv:1807.01647 (2018) (cit. on p. 265).

[BCB14] D. Bahdanau, K. Cho, and Y. Bengio. "Neural machine translation by jointly learning to align and translate". In: arXiv preprint arXiv:1409.0473 (2014) (cit. on p. 252).

[Ber+19] D. Berthelot, N. Carlini, I. Goodfellow, N. Papernot, A. Oliver, and C. Raffel. "Mixmatch: A holistic approach to semi-supervised learning". In: arXiv preprint arXiv:1905.02249 (2019) (cit. on pp. 270, 272).

[Big+13] B. Biggio, I. Corona, D. Maiorca, B. Nelson, N. Šrndić, P. Laskov, G. Giacinto, and F. Roli. "Evasion attacks against machine learning at test time". In: Joint European conference on machine learning and knowledge discovery in databases. Springer. 2013, pp. 387–402 (cit. on pp. 256, 277).

[Bis02] M. A. Bishop. The art and science of computer security. 2002 (cit. on p. 273).

[BNL12] B. Biggio, B. Nelson, and P. Laskov. "Poisoning attacks against support vector machines". In: arXiv preprint arXiv:1206.6389 (2012) (cit. on p. 277).

[Boe+23a] F. Boenisch, A. Dziedzic, R. Schuster, A. S. Shamsabadi, I. Shumailov, and N. Papernot. "Reconstructing Individual Data Points in Federated Learning Hardened with Differential Privacy and Secure Aggregation". In: 2023 IEEE 8th European Symposium on Security and Privacy (EuroS&P). IEEE. 2023, pp. 241–257 (cit. on p. 273).

[Boe+23b] F. Boenisch, A. Dziedzic, R. Schuster, A. S. Shamsabadi, I. Shumailov, and N. Papernot. "When the curious abandon honesty: Federated learning is not private". In: 2023 IEEE 8th European Symposium on Security and Privacy (EuroS&P). IEEE. 2023, pp. 175–199 (cit. on p. 273).

[Bou+21] L. Bourtoule, V. Chandrasekaran, C. A. Choquette-Choo, H. Jia, A. Travers, B. Zhang, D. Lie, and N. Papernot. "Machine unlearning". In: Proceedings of the 42nd IEEE Symposium on Security and Privacy, San Francisco, CA. 2021 (cit. on p. 272).

[Bre96] L. Breiman. "Bagging predictors". In: Machine learning 24.2 (1996), pp. 123–140 (cit. on p. 267).

[BS16] M. Bun and T. Steinke. "Concentrated differential privacy: Simplifications, extensions, and lower bounds". In: Theory of Cryptography Conference. Springer. 2016, pp. 635–658. URL: https://arxiv.org/abs/1605.02065 (cit. on pp. 264, 268).

[BST14] R. Bassily, A. Smith, and A. Thakurta. "Private empirical risk minimization: Efficient algorithms and tight error bounds". In: 2014 IEEE 55th annual symposium on foundations of computer science. IEEE. 2014, pp. 464–473 (cit. on p. 262).

[Car+20] N. Carlini, F. Tramer, E. Wallace, M. Jagielski, A. Herbert-Voss, K. Lee, A. Roberts, T. Brown, D. Song, U. Erlingsson, et al. "Extracting training data from large language models". In: arXiv preprint arXiv:2012.07805 (2020) (cit. on p. 257).

[CHBB20] J. P. Cohen, M. Hashir, R. Brooks, and H. Bertrand. "On the limits of cross-domain generalization in automated X-ray prediction". In: Medical Imaging with Deep Learning. PMLR. 2020, pp. 136–155 (cit. on p. 252).

[Che+17] P.-Y. Chen, H. Zhang, Y. Sharma, J. Yi, and C.-J. Hsieh. "Zoo: Zeroth order optimization based black-box attacks to deep neural networks without training substitute models". In: Proceedings of the 10th ACM workshop on artificial intelligence and security. 2017, pp. 15–26 (cit. on p. 256).

[Cho+21] C. A. Choquette-Choo, N. Dullerud, A. Dziedzic, Y. Zhang, S. Jha, N. Papernot, and X. Wang. "CaPC Learning: Confidential and Private Collaborative Learning". In: arXiv preprint arXiv:2102.05188 (2021) (cit. on p. 273).

[CMS11] K. Chaudhuri, C. Monteleoni, and A. D. Sarwate. "Differentially private empirical risk minimization". In: Journal of Machine Learning Research 12.Mar (2011), pp. 1069–1109 (cit. on pp. 259, 262).

[CTCP20] C. A. C. Choo, F. Tramer, N. Carlini, and N. Papernot. "Label-only membership inference attacks". In: arXiv preprint arXiv:2007.14321 (2020) (cit. on p. 255).

[CY15] Y. Cao and J. Yang. "Towards making systems forget with machine unlearning". In: 2015 IEEE Symposium on Security and Privacy. IEEE. 2015, pp. 463–480 (cit. on p. 272).

[De+22] S. De, L. Berrada, J. Hayes, S. L. Smith, and B. Balle. "Unlocking high-accuracy differentially private image classification through scale". In: arXiv preprint arXiv:2204.13650 (2022) (cit. on pp. 271, 272).

[DMNS06] C. Dwork, F. McSherry, K. Nissim, and A. Smith. "Calibrating noise to sensitivity in private data analysis". In: Theory of cryptography conference. Springer. 2006, pp. 265–284 (cit. on p. 254).

[DR+14] C. Dwork, A. Roth, et al. "The algorithmic foundations of differential privacy." In: Foundations and Trends in Theoretical Computer Science 9.3-4 (2014), pp. 211–407 (cit. on pp. 267, 268).

[Dwo+15] C. Dwork, V. Feldman, M. Hardt, T. Pitassi, O. Reingold, and A. Roth. "Generalization in adaptive data analysis and holdout reuse". In: arXiv preprint arXiv:1506.02629 (2015) (cit. on p. 270).

[EMRS19] Ú. Erlingsson, I. Mironov, A. Raghunathan, and S. Song. "That which we call private". In: arXiv preprint arXiv:1908.03566 (2019) (cit. on p. 276).

[GBCB16] I. Goodfellow, Y. Bengio, A. Courville, and Y. Bengio. Deep learning. Vol. 1. MIT Press, 2016 (cit. on p. 252).

[Gil+16] R. Gilad-Bachrach, N. Dowlin, K. Laine, K. Lauter, M. Naehrig, and J. Wernsing. "Cryptonets: Applying neural networks to encrypted data with high throughput and accuracy". In: International conference on machine learning. PMLR. 2016, pp. 201–210 (cit. on p. 273).

[Irv+19] J. Irvin, P. Rajpurkar, M. Ko, Y. Yu, S. Ciurea-Ilcus, C. Chute, H. Marklund, B. Haghgoo, R. Ball, K. Shpanskaya, et al. "Chexpert: A large chest radiograph dataset with uncertainty labels and expert comparison". In: Proceedings of the AAAI Conference on Artificial Intelligence. Vol. 33. 01. 2019, pp. 590–597 (cit. on p. 252).

[IS15] S. Ioffe and C. Szegedy. "Batch normalization: Accelerating deep network training by reducing internal covariate shift". In: International conference on machine learning. PMLR. 2015, pp. 448–456 (cit. on p. 266).

[Iye+19] R. Iyengar, J. P. Near, D. Song, O. Thakkar, A. Thakurta, and L. Wang. "Towards practical differentially private convex optimization". In: 2019 IEEE Symposium on Security and Privacy (SP). 2019 (cit. on p. 259).

[Jia+19] J. Jia, A. Salem, M. Backes, Y. Zhang, and N. Z. Gong. "Memguard: Defending against black-box membership inference attacks via adversarial examples". In: Proceedings of the 2019 ACM SIGSAC Conference on Computer and Communications Security. 2019, pp. 259–274 (cit. on pp. 258, 278).

[JUO20] M. Jagielski, J. Ullman, and A. Oprea. "Auditing differentially private machine learning: How private is private sgd?" In: arXiv preprint arXiv:2006.07709 (2020) (cit. on p. 276).

[KB14] D. P. Kingma and J. Ba. "Adam: A method for stochastic optimization". In: arXiv preprint arXiv:1412.6980 (2014) (cit. on p. 265).

[Kon+16] J. Konečný, H. B. McMahan, F. X. Yu, P. Richtárik, A. T. Suresh, and D. Bacon. "Federated learning: Strategies for improving communication efficiency". In: arXiv preprint arXiv:1610.05492 (2016) (cit. on p. 273).

[KSH12] A. Krizhevsky, I. Sutskever, and G. E. Hinton. "Imagenet classification with deep convolutional neural networks". In: Advances in neural information processing systems 25 (2012), pp. 1097–1105 (cit. on p. 252).

[KSL19] S. Kornblith, J. Shlens, and Q. V. Le. "Do better imagenet models transfer better?" In: Proceedings of the IEEE/CVF Conference on Computer Vision and Pattern Recognition. 2019, pp. 2661–2671 (cit. on p. 275).

[KST12] D. Kifer, A. Smith, and A. Thakurta. "Private convex empirical risk minimization and high-dimensional regression". In: Conference on Learning Theory. 2012, pp. 25–1 (cit. on p. 259).

[LBH15] Y. LeCun, Y. Bengio, and G. Hinton. "Deep learning". In: nature 521.7553 (2015), pp. 436–444 (cit. on pp. 251, 252).

[LF20] K. Leino and M. Fredrikson. "Stolen memories: Leveraging model memorization for calibrated white-box membership inference". In: 29th {USENIX} Security Symposium ({USENIX} Security 20). 2020, pp. 1605–1622 (cit. on p. 258).

[Lon+18] Y. Long, V. Bindschaedler, L. Wang, D. Bu, X. Wang, H. Tang, C. A. Gunter, and K. Chen. "Understanding membership inferences on well-generalized learning models". In: arXiv preprint arXiv:1802.04889 (2018) (cit. on p. 258).

[Low99] D. G. Lowe. "Object recognition from local scale-invariant features". In: Proceedings of the seventh IEEE international conference on computer vision. Vol. 2. Ieee. 1999, pp. 1150–1157 (cit. on p. 252).

[LTLH21] X. Li, F. Tramer, P. Liang, and T. Hashimoto. "Large language models can be strong differentially private learners". In: arXiv preprint arXiv:2110.05679 (2021) (cit. on p. 272).

[Man13] A. Mantelero. "The EU Proposal for a General Data Protection Regulation and the roots of the 'right to be forgotten'". In: Computer Law & Security Review 29.3 (2013), pp. 229–235 (cit. on p. 272).

[Mir17] I. Mironov. "Rényi differential privacy". In: 2017 IEEE 30th computer security foundations symposium (CSF). IEEE. 2017, pp. 263–275 (cit. on p. 264).

[MRTZ17] H. B. McMahan, D. Ramage, K. Talwar, and L. Zhang. "Learning differentially private recurrent language models". In: arXiv preprint arXiv:1710.06963 (2017) (cit. on p. 275).

[MSDS19] L. Melis, C. Song, E. De Cristofaro, and V. Shmatikov. "Exploiting unintended feature leakage in collaborative learning". In: 2019 IEEE Symposium on Security and Privacy (SP). 2019, pp. 691–706 (cit. on p. 273).

[MZH19] Y. Ma, X. Zhu, and J. Hsu. "Data poisoning against differentially-private learners: Attacks and defenses". In: arXiv preprint arXiv:1903.09860 (2019) (cit. on p. 277).

[Nas+21] M. Nasr, S. Song, A. Thakurta, N. Papernot, and N. Carlini. "Adversary instantiation: Lower bounds for differentially private machine learning". In: arXiv preprint arXiv:2101.04535 (2021) (cit. on p. 277).

[Nee+15] A. Neelakantan, L. Vilnis, Q. V. Le, I. Sutskever, L. Kaiser, K. Kurach, and J. Martens. "Adding gradient noise improves learning for very deep networks". In: arXiv preprint arXiv:1511.06807 (2015) (cit. on p. 264).

[NRS07] K. Nissim, S. Raskhodnikova, and A. Smith. "Smooth sensitivity and sampling in private data analysis". In: Proceedings of the thirty-ninth annual ACM symposium on Theory of computing. 2007, pp. 75–84 (cit. on p. 269).

[NS08] A. Narayanan and V. Shmatikov. "Robust de-anonymization of large sparse datasets". In: 2008 IEEE Symposium on Security and Privacy (sp 2008). IEEE. 2008, pp. 111–125 (cit. on p. 259).

[NSH18] M. Nasr, R. Shokri, and A. Houmansadr. "Machine Learning with Membership Privacy using Adversarial Regularization". In: Proceedings of the 2018 ACM SIGSAC Conference on Computer and Communications Security. 2018, pp. 634–646 (cit. on pp. 258, 278).

[OM15] E. Oyallon and S. Mallat. "Deep roto-translation scattering for object classification". In: Proceedings of the IEEE Conference on Computer Vision and Pattern Recognition. 2015, pp. 2865–2873 (cit. on p. 274).

[Pap+16] N. Papernot, M. Abadi, U. Erlingsson, I. Goodfellow, and K. Talwar. "Semi-supervised knowledge transfer for deep learning from private training data". In: arXiv preprint arXiv:1610.05755 (2016) (cit. on pp. 266, 269).

[Pap+17] N. Papernot, P. McDaniel, I. Goodfellow, S. Jha, Z. B. Celik, and A. Swami. "Practical black-box attacks against machine learning". In: Proceedings of the 2017 ACM on Asia conference on computer and communications security. 2017, pp. 506–519 (cit. on pp. 256, 266).

[Pap+20] N. Papernot, A. Thakurta, S. Song, S. Chien, and Ú. Erlingsson. "Tempered sigmoid activations for deep learning with differential privacy". In: arXiv preprint arXiv:2007.14191 (2020) (cit. on pp. 271, 275).

[PS21] N. Papernot and T. Steinke. “Hyperparameter tuning with renyi differential privacy”. In: arXiv preprint arXiv:2110.03620 (2021) (cit. on p. 275).

[Rad+19] A. Radford, J. Wu, R. Child, D. Luan, D. Amodei, I. Sutskever, et al. “Language models are unsupervised multitask learners”. In: OpenAI blog 1.8 (2019), p. 9 (cit. on p. 257).

[RHW86] D. E. Rumelhart, G. E. Hinton, and R. J. Williams. “Learning representations by back-propagating errors”. In: nature 323.6088 (1986), pp. 533–536 (cit. on p. 263).

[Sal+16] T. Salimans, I. Goodfellow, W. Zaremba, V. Cheung, A. Radford, and X. Chen. “Improved techniques for training gans”. In: Advances in neural information processing systems 29 (2016), pp. 2234–2242 (cit. on p. 270).

[Sal+18] A. Salem, Y. Zhang, M. Humbert, P. Berrang, M. Fritz, and M. Backes. “Ml-leaks: Model and data independent membership inference attacks and defenses on machine learning models”. In: arXiv preprint arXiv:1806.01246 (2018) (cit. on p. 255).

[SCS13] S. Song, K. Chaudhuri, and A. D. Sarwate. “Stochastic gradient descent with differentially private updates”. In: 2013 IEEE Global Conference on Signal and Information Processing. IEEE. 2013, pp. 245–248 (cit. on p. 262).

[Sha+18] C. J. Shallue, J. Lee, J. Antognini, J. Sohl-Dickstein, R. Frostig, and G. E. Dahl. “Measuring the effects of data parallelism on neural network training”. In: arXiv preprint arXiv:1811.03600 (2018) (cit. on p. 262).

[SPGG21] V. M. Suriyakumar, N. Papernot, A. Goldenberg, and M. Ghassemi. “Chasing Your Long Tails: Differentially Private Prediction in Health Care Settings”. In: Proceedings of the 2021 ACM Conference on Fairness, Accountability, and Transparency. 2021, pp. 723–734 (cit. on p. 270).

[SSM19] L. Song, R. Shokri, and P. Mittal. “Privacy risks of securing machine learning models against adversarial examples”. In: Proceedings of the 2019 ACM SIGSAC Conference on Computer and Communications Security. 2019, pp. 241–257 (cit. on p. 277).

[SSSS17] R. Shokri, M. Stronati, C. Song, and V. Shmatikov. "Membership inference attacks against machine learning models". In: 2017 IEEE symposium on security and privacy (SP). IEEE. 2017, pp. 3–18 (cit. on pp. 253, 254, 258).

[STT20] S. Song, O. Thakkar, and A. Thakurta. "Characterizing Private Clipped Gradient Descent on Convex Generalized Linear Problems". In: arXiv preprint arXiv:2006.06783 (2020) (cit. on p. 271).

[Sze+13] C. Szegedy, W. Zaremba, I. Sutskever, J. Bruna, D. Erhan, I. Goodfellow, and R. Fergus. "Intriguing properties of neural networks". In: arXiv preprint arXiv:1312.6199 (2013) (cit. on pp. 256, 277).

[TB18] F. Tramer and D. Boneh. "Slalom: Fast, verifiable and private execution of neural networks in trusted hardware". In: arXiv preprint arXiv:1806.03287 (2018) (cit. on p. 273).

[TB20] F. Tramèr and D. Boneh. "Differentially Private Learning Needs Better Features (or Much More Data)". In: arXiv preprint arXiv:2011.11660 (2020) (cit. on p. 274).

[YGFJ18] S. Yeom, I. Giacomelli, M. Fredrikson, and S. Jha. "Privacy risk in machine learning: Analyzing the connection to overfitting". In: 2018 IEEE 31st Computer Security Foundations Symposium (CSF). 2018, pp. 268–282 (cit. on pp. 255–258).

[Zha+16] C. Zhang, S. Bengio, M. Hardt, B. Recht, and O. Vinyals. "Understanding deep learning requires rethinking generalization". In: arXiv preprint arXiv:1611.03530 (2016) (cit. on p. 263).

[Zha+19] Z. Zhao, N. Papernot, S. Singh, N. Polyzotis, and A. Odena. "Improving differentially private models with active learning". In: arXiv preprint arXiv:1910.01177 (2019) (cit. on p. 272).

DOI: 10.1561/9781638284772.ch8

Chapter 8

Private Federated Learning

By Kallista Bonawitz, Peter Kairouz, Brendan McMahan and Daniel Ramage

8.1 Introduction

Machine learning and data science are key tools in science, public policy, and the design of products and services thanks to the increasing affordability of collecting, storing, and processing large quantities of data. But centralized collection can expose individuals to privacy risks and organizations to legal risks if data is not properly managed. Starting with early work in 2016 [McM+17; MR17], an expanding community of researchers has explored how data ownership and provenance can be made first-class concepts in systems for learning and analytics in areas now known as FL (federated learning) and FA (federated analytics). With this expanding community, interest has broadened from the initial work on federations of mobile devices to include FL across organizational silos, IoT (Internet of Things) devices, and more. In light of this, Kairouz et al. [Kai+19] proposed a broader definition that emphasized data locality. Since this definition was proposed, the field has continued to mature, revealing new challenges related to scalability, verifiability, and operational complexity. These challenges, particularly in the age of very large foundation models, have motivated a renewed focus on the core privacy properties of a system rather than the specific location of computation. To better capture these evolving principles and aspirations, a new definition has been proposed in [Dal+24]:

> ***Federated learning (FL)*** *is a machine learning setting where multiple entities (clients) collaborate in solving a machine learning problem, under the coordination of a service provider. A complete FL system should enable clients to maintain full control over their data, the set of workloads allowed to access their data, and the anonymization properties of those workloads. FL systems should provide appropriate transparency and control to the users whose data is managed by FL clients.*

This updated perspective emphasizes that claims about a system's privacy require a nuanced description of how it addresses a multifaceted set of principles, a topic we will explore throughout this chapter.

An approach very similar in both philosophy and implementation, recently termed federated analytics [RM20], can be taken to allow data scientists to generate analytical insight from the combined information in decentralized datasets. While the focus here is on FL, much of the discussion on technology and privacy applies equally well to FA use cases.

Overview of the Chapter

This chapter provides a brief introduction to key concepts in federated learning and analytics with an emphasis on how privacy technologies may be combined in real-world systems and how their use charts a path toward societal benefit from aggregate statistics in new domains and with minimized risk to the individuals and the organizations who are custodians of the data. After defining FL and contrasting it with traditional centralized learning, we will discuss privacy in federated technologies, examining data minimization techniques (Section 8.2) and data anonymization methods using differential privacy (Section 8.3). We will also track the practical evolution of these technologies, highlighting key production deployments. Finally, the chapter discusses Federated Analytics, which broadens FL for performing data science tasks on decentralized data (Section 8.4), and concludes by examining the open challenges and future directions for the field.

8.1.1 Privacy Principals for Federated Learning and Analytics

To ground a more detailed discussion of FL, let us begin by clarifying the relevant notions of privacy. Privacy is an inherently multifaceted concept, even when restricted to the realm of the products and services offered by a technology company, which is the focus here. Four key components of privacy are highlighted in this context: (1) transparency and consent, (2) data minimization, (3) anonymization of released aggregates, and (4) verifiability.

Transparency and consent are foundational to privacy: they are how users of the product/service both understand and approve of the ways in which their data will be used. Privacy technology cannot replace transparency and consent, but data-stewardship approaches based on strong privacy technologies make it easier for all parties involved to reason about which types of data usage might be possible (and which are ruled out by design), thereby enabling clearer privacy statements that are simpler to understand, verify, and enforce.

The role of privacy technology becomes more clear when considering specific goals that can be advanced by computation on privacy-sensitive user data; for example, improving a mobile keyboard suggestions based on user input to the virtual keyboard. How can the keyboard be improved in as minimally invasive a manner as possible? The computation goals are primarily the training of ML (machine-learning) models (federated learning) and the calculation of metrics or other aggregate statistics on user data (federated analytics). As we will see, both analytics and (perhaps less obviously) machine learning can be accomplished via appropriately chosen aggregations over (possibly preprocessed) user data. In this context, specializations of three of the above-mentioned broad privacy principles apply:

- *The principle of data minimization*, as applied to aggregations, includes the objective to collect only the data needed for the specific computation (focused collection), to limit access to data at all stages, to process individuals' data as early as possible (early aggregation), and to discard both collected and processed data as soon as possible (minimal retention). That is, data minimization implies restricting access to all data to the smallest set of people possible, often accomplished via security mechanisms, such as encryption at rest and on the wire, access-control lists, and also more nascent technologies such as secure multiparty computation and trusted execution environments, to be discussed later.
- *The principle of data anonymization* captures the objective that the final released output of the computation does not reveal anything unique to an individual. When this principle is specialized to anonymous aggregation, the goal is that data contributed by any individual user to the computation has only a small (limited, measured, and/or mitigated) influence on the final aggregate output. For example, aggregate statistics including model parameters, when released to an engineer—or beyond—should not vary significantly based on whether any particular user's data was included in the aggregation. The XKCD comic shown in Figure 8.1 illustrates a humorous example where this principle is not respected, but this memorization phenomenon has been shown to be a real issue for modern deep networks [Car+19; Car+20].
- *The principle of verifiability* asserts that privacy claims should be verifiable, ideally by users, external auditors, and the service provider itself. Mechanisms supporting verification can include open sourcing relevant code and

Figure 8.1. Randall Munroe humorously captured the risks of allowing one user's data too much influence on the final model in xkcd.com/2169/.

systems designs, public ledgers, trusted execution environment hardware, secure multi-party computation protocols, and alike.

The practical application of these privacy principles in production systems has evolved significantly since the inception of FL. Table 8.1 summarizes this progression, contrasting how core privacy guarantees were implemented in early FL systems (circa 2017–2020) with more recent practices (2021–2024), and it outlines an emerging state for the field, which we will discuss more in Section 8.3.2. The table illustrates a clear trajectory towards stronger, more comprehensive, and externally verifiable privacy protections.

By design, FL structurally embodies data minimization. Figure 8.2 compares the federated approach to more standard centralized techniques. Critically, the federated approach is architecturally designed to prevent the service provider from accessing raw, unaggregated client data. In its classic implementation, this is achieved by making data collection and aggregation inseparable: purpose-specific transformations of client data are computed on-device and sent only for the purpose of immediate aggregation. In newer paradigms that use confidential computing, this same principle is upheld through cryptography, where encrypted client

Table 8.1. A summary of how different privacy principles are addressed under the FL 2017-2020 practice, the FL 2021-2024 practice, and an updated 2025+ goal-state based on the new FL definition we propose. Adapted from [Dal+24].

Privacy Principles	FL 2017–2020	FL 2021–2024	FL 2025–?
Data minimization	Data remain on devices; focused updates and immediate aggregation for model training.	Trusted and cryptographic aggregation methods can additionally guarantee unaggregated updates invisible to the service provider.	Secured data on device or cloud with access verifiably limited to specific workloads and immediately revocable (or within a short TTL).
Data anonymization	No formal anonymization, but messages are collected for the purpose of immediate aggregation.	Distributed DP can provide acceptable utility for some tasks, and protection from an honest-but-curious service provider; central DP can provide better utility, and strong DP protection for the model released to end users but assumes a trusted aggregator.	Achieve the utility of current Central DP approaches, while also offering strong protection against even a malicious service provider; users can verify that only anonymized results are released, and can enforce their privacy preferences.
Transparency and control	Users can choose whether to participate in training, and potentially inspect the on-device binaries and network usage.	Users can additionally inspect the source code of *some* FL instances such as Private Compute Core [Mar+22], while others remain closed source and proprietary.	Users can view a human-readable summary of the purpose and (privacy) properties of any computation their data participated in, and those properties can be verified. Users can make fine-grained choices about which FL workloads to run, or delegate that power to an organization of their choice.
Verifiability and auditability	Where code is open-sourced, it can be inspected; verifying the identity of the code running on devices is possible but difficult.	Same as FL 2017–2020	Client and server-side code verify each others' integrity via remote attestation. Clients can verify the data minimization and anonymization properties of server-side computation. Clients and servers verify each others' authenticity via (ideally independent) Public Key Infrastructure (PKI).

contributions are processed only within a verifiable, trusted execution environment. In either architecture, analysts have no access to per-client messages. Federated learning and federated analytics are instances of a general federated computation schema that embodies these data-minimization practices. This contrasts sharply with the typical approach of centralized processing, which replaces on-device preprocessing and aggregation with bulk data collection, with the primary minimization happening on the server only after the raw data has been logged.

The ML and analytics goals considered here are compatible with the objective of anonymous aggregation. With ML, the goal is to train a model that generalizes well to all users, without overfitting or memorizing the specifics of any individual's data. Similarly, with statistical queries, the goal is to estimate population-level statistics that are not significantly influenced by any single contribution. However, achieving this is a non-trivial challenge, as modern deep learning models have been shown to be prone to memorizing rare or unique training examples, necessitating the use of explicit privacy-enhancing technologies.

The federated paradigm strengthens its guarantees by combining its architectural design with other techniques—particularly differential privacy (DP) and empirical privacy auditing, which are treated in more depth later—to ensure released aggregates are formally anonymous. This creates a system with built-in, technologically enforced protections. This situation contrasts sharply with the privacy relationship you might have with a bank or health-care provider, where the data anonymization principle may not apply. In those interactions, trust in the provider to use sensitive data only for its intended purpose remains the fundamental tenet.

A third foundational principle, which has grown in importance as FL has matured, is verifiability. While data minimization and anonymization provide strong theoretical protections, they historically required users to trust that the service provider was correctly implementing the protocols. Verifiability addresses this trust gap by enabling users and external auditors to cryptographically confirm that the system is performing computations as promised. This principle became central as technologies like trusted execution environments made it practical to remotely attest to the code running on a server, ensuring that only approved, privacy-preserving operations are ever performed on client data. This shifts the model from simply trusting the provider's policies to relying on verifiable, mathematical guarantees.

8.1.2 Federated Learning Settings and Applications

As indicated earlier, the defining characteristics of FL include keeping raw data decentralized and learning via aggregation. This assumption of locally generated data—often heterogeneous in distribution and quantity—distinguishes FL from more typical data center-based distributed learning settings, where data can be arbitrarily distributed and shuffled, and any worker node in the computation can access any of the data.

The role of a central orchestrator is practically useful and often necessary, as in the case of mobile devices that lack fixed IP addresses and require a central server to mediate device-to-device communication. It further constrains the space of relevant algorithms, and helps to distinguish FL from more general forms of decentralized

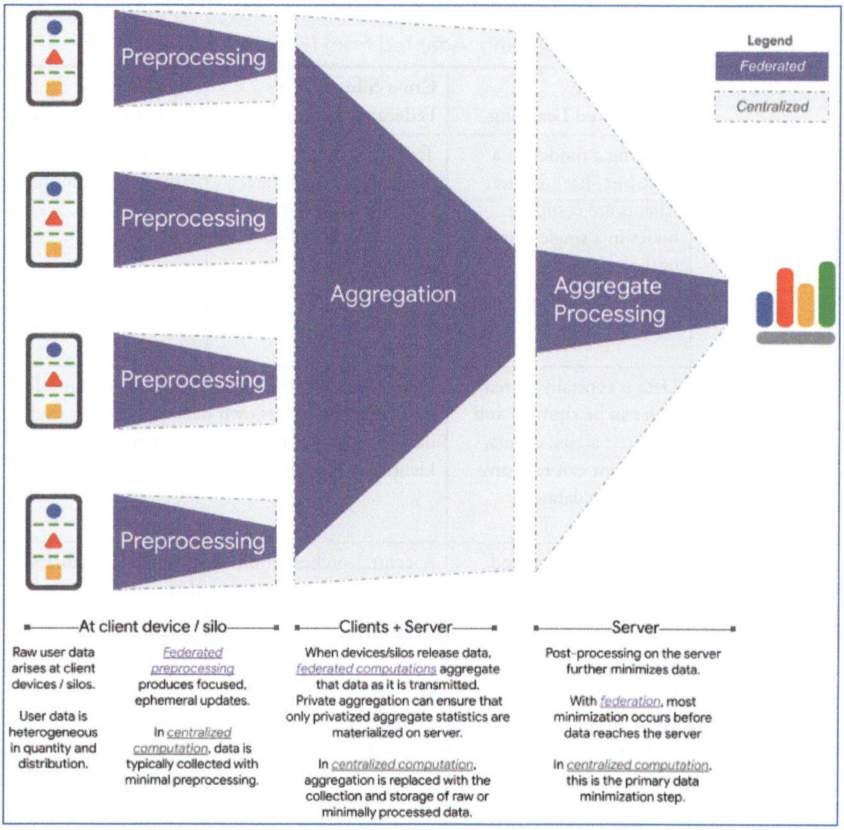

Figure 8.2. Federated learning and federated analytics are instances of a general federated computation schema that embodies data minimization practices. The more typical approach of centralized processing replaces on-device preprocessing and aggregation with data collection, with the primary minimization happening on the server during the processing of the logged data.

learning, including peer-to-peer approaches. From the basic definition, two FL settings have received particular attention:

- Cross-device FL, where the clients are large numbers of mobile or IoT devices.
- Cross-silo FL, where the clients are a typically smaller number of organizations, institutions, or other data silos.

Table 8.2, adapted from Kairouz et al. [Kai+19], summarizes the key characteristics of the FL settings, highlights some of the key differences between the cross-device and cross-silo settings, as well as contrasting with data center distributed learning.

Cross-device FL is now used by both Google [Bon+19] and Apple [Pau+21] for Android and iOS phones, respectively, for many applications such as mobile keyboard prediction; cross-device FA is being explored for problems such as health

Table 8.2. Typical characteristics of federated learning settings in contrast to traditional single-data center distributed learning. Adapted from [Kai+19].

	Data-center Distributed Learning	Cross-Silo Federated Learning	Cross-Device Federated Learning
Setting	Training a model on a large but "flat" dataset. Clients are compute nodes in a single cluster or data center.	Training a model on siloed data. Clients are different organizations (e.g., medical or financial) or data centers in different geographical regions.	The clients are a very large number of mobile or IoT devices.
Data Distribution	Data is centrally stored, so it can be shuffled and balanced across clients. Any client can read any part of the dataset.	Data is generated locally and remains decentralized. Each client stores its own data and cannot read the data of other clients. Data is not independently or identically distributed.	
Orchestration	Centrally orchestrated.	A central orchestration server/service organizes the training, but never sees raw data.	
Distribution Scale	Typically 1 – 1000 clients.	Typically 2 – 100 clients.	Up to 10^{10} clients.
Client Properties	Clients are reliable and almost always available to participate in computations. Clients may be directly addressed, and can maintain state across computation rounds.		Clients are often unavailable and can only be accessed by random sampling from available devices. For large populations a single client will typically only participate once in a given computation.

research (e.g., Google Health Studies). Since these early systems were described, the deployment of FL in production has accelerated significantly. At Google, FL powers numerous features in the Gboard mobile keyboard, including next-word prediction, smart compose, and emoji suggestions [Har+18; Xu+23]. Further applications include keyword spotting for virtual assistants [Har+22], smart text selection in Android [HK23], and smart reply in Android Messages [Goo20b]. Apple uses federated learning for features like scene identification in Photos [App23] and understanding aggregate trends for Apple Intelligence [App25], while Meta has developed systems for applications such as Ad prediction [Hub+22; Sto+22].

Cross-silo FL has received considerable attention as well. Health and medical applications are a primary motivation, with significant investments from Nvidia, IBM, and Intel, as well as numerous startups. Another application that is on the rise is finance, with investments from WeBank, Credit Suisse, Intel, and others.

8.1.3 Algorithms for Cross-device Federated Learning

Modern ML approaches, particularly deep learning, are generally data hungry and compute intensive, and so the feasibility of the federated training of production-quality models was far from a foregone conclusion. Much of our early work, particularly [McM+17] focused on establishing a proof of concept. This work introduced the federated averaging algorithm, which continues to see widespread use, though many variations and improvements have been subsequently proposed.

The core idea builds on the classic SGD (stochastic gradient descent) algorithm, which is widely used for the training of ML models in more traditional settings. The model is given as a function from training examples to predictions, parameterized by a vector of model weights, and a loss function that measures the error between the prediction and the true output (label). SGD proceeds by sampling a batch of training examples (typically from 10s to 1000s), computing the average gradient of the loss function with respect to the model weights, and then adjusting the model weights in the opposite direction of the gradient. By appropriately tuning the size of the steps taken on each iteration, SGD can be shown to have desirable convergence properties, even for nonconvex functions.

The simplest extension of SGD to the federated setting would be to broadcast the current model weights to a random set of clients, have them each compute the gradient of the loss on their local data, average these gradients across clients at the server, and then update the global model weights. SGD, however, often requires 10^5 or more iterations to produce a high-accuracy model. Back-of-the-envelope calculations suggest a single iteration might take minutes in the federated setting, implying federated training might take between a month and a year—outside the realm of practicality.

The key idea of federated averaging is intuitive: Decrease communication and startup costs by taking multiple steps of SGD locally on each device, and then average the resulting models (or model updates) less frequently. If models are averaged after each local step, this reduces to SGD (and is probably too slow); if models are averaged too infrequently, they might diverge and averaging could produce a worse model. Is there a sweet spot in between? Empirically, the 2017 paper [McM+17] showed that the answer is yes, demonstrating that moderate-sized language models (e.g., for next-word prediction) and image-classification models could be trained in fewer than 1,000 communication rounds. This reduces the expected training time to a few days—still much slower than would be possible with a high-performance compute cluster on centralized data, but within the realm of feasibility for real-world production use.

This algorithm also demonstrates the key privacy point mentioned earlier—that model training can be reduced to the (repeated) application of a federated aggregation (the averaging of model gradients or updates), as in Figure 8.2.

In practice, FedAvg and its variants fit into a generalized two-stage optimization framework where clients perform local updates using a client optimizer, and the server applies the aggregated update using a server optimizer. This flexible structure allows FL systems to incorporate advances from centralized training. For example, adaptive optimizers like Adam or Yogi can be used on the server to significantly improve performance, particularly for language tasks. This framework is also compatible with the integration of privacy technologies like differential privacy, as we will see in Section 8.3.

8.1.4 Workflows and Systems for Cross-device Federated Learning

Having a feasible algorithm for FL is a necessary starting point, but making cross-device FL a productive approach for ML-driven product teams requires much more. Based on Google's experience deploying cross-device FL across multiple Google products, the typical workflow often includes the following steps:

1. **Identifying a problem well suited for FL.** Typically this means a moderately sized (1-50 MB) on-device model is desired; training data potentially available on-device is richer or more representative than data available in the data center; there are privacy or other reasons to prefer not to centralize the data; and the feedback signal (labels) necessary to train the model are readily available on-device (for example, a model for next-word prediction can naturally be trained based on what users type if they ignore predicted next words; an image-classification model would be harder to train unless interaction with the app naturally led to labeled images).
2. **Model development and evaluation.** As with any ML task, choosing the right model architecture and hyperparameters (learning rates, batch sizes, regularization) is critical to success in FL. The challenge can be bigger in the federated setting, which introduces a number of new hyperparameters (e.g., number of clients participating in each round, how many local steps to take before averaging). Often the starting point is to do coarse model selection and tuning using a simulation of FL based on proxy data available in the data center. Final tuning and evaluation must be conducted using federated training on real devices, however, as the differences in data distribution, real-world device fleet characteristics, and many other factors are impossible to capture fully in simulation. Evaluation must also be conducted in a federated manner: independent from the training process, the candidate global model

is sent to (held-out) devices so that accuracy metrics can be computed on these devices' local datasets and aggregated by the server (both simple averages and histograms over per-client performance are important). Taken together, these needs give rise to two key infrastructure requirements: (1) providing high-performance FL simulation infrastructure that allows a smooth transition to running on real devices; (2) a cross-device infrastructure that makes it easy to manage multiple simultaneous training and evaluation tasks.

3. **Deployment.** Once a high-quality candidate model is selected in step 2, the deployment of that model (e.g., making user-visible next-word predictions in a mobile keyboard) typically follows the same procedures that are used for a data center-trained model: additional validation and testing (potentially including manual quality assurance), live A/B testing to compare to the previous production model, and a staged rollout to the full device fleet (potentially several-orders-of-magnitude more devices than actually participated in the training of the model).

It is worth emphasizing that all the work in step 2 has no impact on the user experience of the devices participating in training and evaluation; models being trained with FL do not make predictions visible to the user unless they go through the deployment step. Ensuring this processing does not otherwise negatively impact the device is a key infrastructure challenge. For example, heavyweight computation might execute only when the devices are idle, plugged in, and on an unmetered Wi-Fi network.

Figure 8.3 illustrates the model development and deployment workflows. Building a scalable infrastructure and compelling developer APIs for these workflows is a significant challenge. A paper by Bonawitz et al. [Bon+19] provides an overview of Google's production system as of 2019. Since then, other large-scale systems have been described by companies like Apple [Pau+21] and Meta [Hub+22], and a new system for "confidential federated computations" was recently introduced by Google [Eic+24; Dal+24]. These systems face common challenges related to scale, client heterogeneity, and availability, but they have adopted different strategies to manage them. For instance, while Google's early system was designed around synchronous rounds (with over-selection of clients to mitigate dropouts), Meta's system uses an asynchronous approach to improve robustness and efficiency.

8.1.5 Privacy for Federated Technologies

FL provides a variety of privacy advantages out of the box. In the spirit of data minimization, the raw data stays on the device, updates sent to the server are focused for a particular purpose, ephemeral, and aggregated as soon as possible. In particular, no non-aggregated data is persisted on the server; end-to-end encryption protects

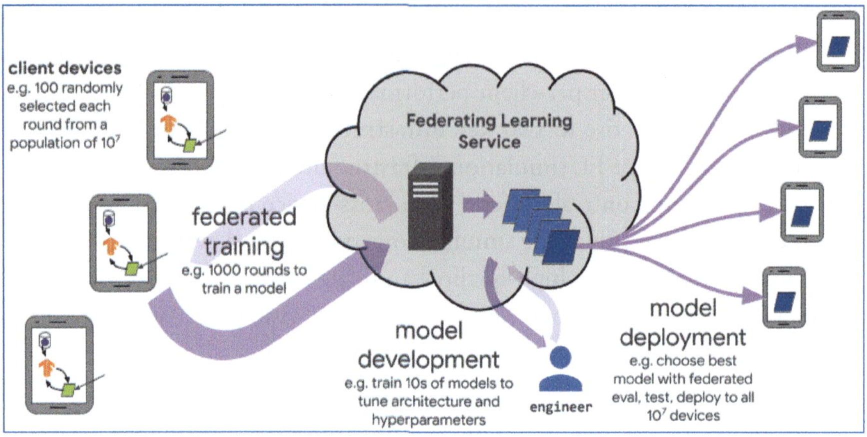

Figure 8.3. Components and phases of a cross-device FL system.

data in transit, and both the decryption keys and decrypted values are held only ephemerally in RAM. ML engineers and analysts interacting with the system can access only aggregated data. The fundamental role of aggregates in the federated approach makes it natural to limit the influence of any individual client on the output, but algorithms need to be carefully designed if the goal is to provide more formal guarantees such as differential privacy.

Researchers at Google and beyond are strengthening the privacy guarantees that an FL system can make. While the basic FL approach has proven feasible and gained substantial adoption, its combination with other techniques described in this section is still far from "on by default for most uses of FL." Even as the state of the art advances, inherent tensions with other objectives (including fairness, accuracy, development velocity, and computational cost) will likely prevent a one-size-fits-all approach to data minimization and anonymization. Thus, practitioners benefit from continued advancement of research ideas and software implementations for composable privacy enhancing techniques. Ultimately, decisions about privacy technology deployment are made by product or service teams in consultation with domain-specific privacy, policy, and legal experts. As privacy technologists, our obligation is two-fold: to enable products to offer more privacy through usable FL systems and, perhaps more importantly, to help policy experts strengthen privacy definitions and requirements over time.

In analyzing the privacy properties of a federated system, it is useful to consider access points and threat models. Building on Figure 8.3, one can ask what private information might an actor learn with access to various parts of the system. With access to the physical device or network? With root or physical access to the servers providing the FL service? To the models and metrics released to the ML engineer? To the final deployed model?

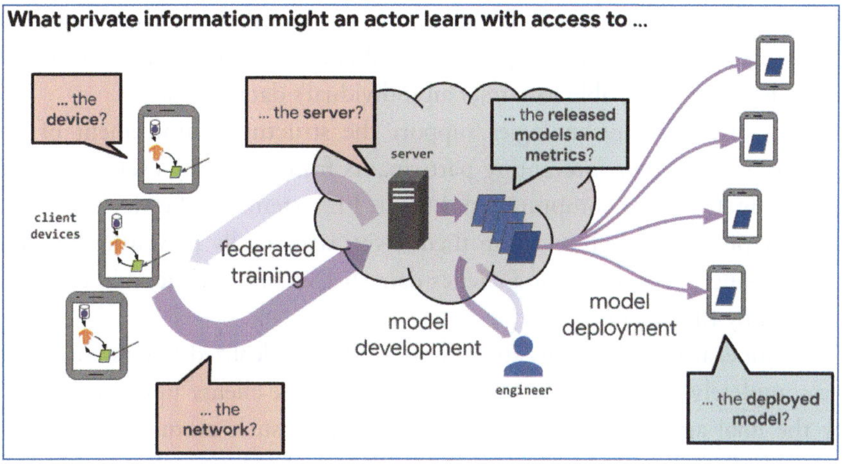

Figure 8.4. Threat models for an end-to-end federated learning system. The goal of the system is to release some models and metrics to the model engineer, and eventually deploy a model to production. Thus, anonymous aggregation is essential for these released outputs of the computation. Data minimization approaches can address potential threats to the device, network, and server, e.g. improving security and minimizing the retention of data and intermediate results.

The number of potentially-malicious parties varies dramatically as information flows through this system. A very small number of parties should have physical or root access to the coordinating server, for example, but nearly anyone might be able to access the final model shipped out to a large fleet of smartphones.

Privacy claims must therefore be assessed for a complete end-to-end system. A guarantee that the final deployed model has not memorized user data may not matter if suitable security precautions are not taken to protect the raw data on device or an intermediate computation state in transit. Other techniques can provide even stronger guarantees.

Figure 8.4 shows threat models for an end-to-end FL system and the role of data minimization and anonymous aggregation. Data minimization addresses potential threats to the device, network, and server by, e.g., improving security and minimizing the retention of data and intermediate results. When models and metrics are released to the model engineer or deployed to production, anonymous aggregation protects individuals' data from parties with access to these released outputs.

8.2 Data Minimization for Federated Aggregation

At several points in a federated computation, the participants expect one another to take the appropriate actions, and only those actions. For example, the server expects the clients to execute their preprocessing step accurately; the clients expect the server to keep their individual updates a secret until they have been aggregated; both the clients and the server expect that neither the data analyst nor the deployed ML model user will be able to extract an individual's data; and so on.

Privacy-preserving technologies support the structural enforcement of these interparty expectations, preventing participants from deviating even if they happen to be malicious or compromised. In fact, FL systems can be viewed as a kind of privacy-preserving technology in themselves, structurally preventing the server from accessing anything about a client's data that was not included in the update submitted by that client.

Take, for example, the aggregation phase of FL. An idealized system might imagine a completely trusted third party who aggregates the clients' updates and reveals only the final aggregate to the server. In reality, no such mutually trusted third party typically exists to play this role, but various technologies allow an FL system to simulate such a third party under a wide range of conditions.

For example, a server could run the aggregation procedure within a secure enclave—a specially constructed piece of hardware that can not only prove to the clients what code it is running, but also ensure that no one (not even the hardware's owner) can observe or tamper with the execution of that code. Currently, however, the availability of secure enclaves is limited, both in the cloud and on consumer devices, and available enclaves may implement only some of the desired enclave properties (secure measurement, confidentiality, and integrity [Sub+17]). Moreover, even when available and full-featured, secure enclaves may come with additional limitations, including very limited memory or speed; vulnerability to data exposure via side channels (e.g., cache-timing attacks); difficult-to-verify correctness (because of proprietary implementation details); dependence on manufacturer-provided attestation services (and key secrecy); etc.

Distributed cryptographic protocols for secure multiparty computation can be used collaboratively to simulate a trusted third party without the need for specialized hardware, so long as a sufficiently large number of the participants behave honestly. While secure multiparty computation for arbitrary functions remains computationally prohibitive in most cases, specialized secure aggregation algorithms for vector summation in the federated setting have been developed that provably preserve privacy even against an adversary that observes the server and controls a significant fraction of the clients, while maintaining robustness against clients dropping out of the computation [Bon+17]. Such algorithms are both:

- Communication efficient - $O(\log n + l)$ communication per client, where n is the number of users and l is the vector length, with small constants yielding less than twice the communication of aggregation in the clear for a wide range of practical settings; and

- Computation efficient - $O(\log(2n) + l \log n)$ computation per client [Bel+20].

Cryptographic secure aggregation protocols have been deployed in commercial federated computing systems for years [Bon+19; RM20]. The development of highly efficient algorithms [Bel+20] has been critical for this, enabling the aggregation of updates for models with millions of parameters from thousands of clients per round. This technology is now used in production to train Gboard language models and Android smart selection models [Xu+23; Zha+23; HK23].

Beyond private aggregation, privacy-preserving technologies can be used to secure other parts of an FL system. For example, either secure enclaves or cryptographic techniques (e.g., zero knowledge proofs) can ensure that the server may trust that clients have preprocessed faithfully. Even the model broadcast stage can benefit: For many learning tasks, an individual client may have data relevant to only a small portion of the model; in this case, the client can privately retrieve just that segment of the model for training, again using either secure enclaves or cryptographic techniques (e.g., private information retrieval) to ensure that the server learns nothing about the segment of the model for which the client has relevant training data.

8.3 Data Anonymization for Federated Aggregation

While secure enclaves and private aggregation techniques can strengthen data minimization, they are not designed specifically to produce anonymous aggregates—for example, limiting the influence of a user on the model being trained. Indeed, a growing body of research suggests that the learned model can (in some cases) leak sensitive information [Car+19; Car+20].

The gold-standard approach to data anonymization is DP (differential privacy) [DMNS06]. For a generic procedure that aggregates records in a database, DP requires bounding any record's contribution to the aggregate and then adding an appropriately scaled random perturbation. For example, as discussed in Section 7.4 of Chapter 7, in DP-SGD (differentially private stochastic gradient descent) you clip the ℓ_2 norm of the gradients, aggregate the clipped gradients, and add Gaussian noise in each training round [SCS13; BST14; Aba+16].

Differentially private algorithms are necessarily randomized, and hence you can consider the distribution of models produced by an algorithm on a particular dataset. Intuitively, differential privacy says this distribution over models is similar when the algorithm is run on input datasets that differ by a single record. Formally, DP is commonly quantified by privacy loss parameters (ε, δ), where a smaller (ε, δ) pair corresponds to increased privacy. A randomized algorithm A is (ε, δ)-differentially private if for all possible outputs (e.g., models) m, and for all datasets D and D' that differ in at most one record:

$$\Pr\left(A(D) = m\right) \leq e^{\varepsilon} \Pr\left(A(D') = m\right) + \delta. \tag{8.1}$$

This goes beyond simply bounding the sensitivity of the model to each record by adding noise proportional to any record's influence, therefore ensuring sufficient randomness to mask any one record's contribution to the output. For a review of Differential Privacy and its properties, please see Chapter 1.

8.3.1 Privacy Units

In the context of cross-device FL, a record is typically defined as all the training examples of a single user/client [MRTZ18]. This notion of DP is referred to as user-level DP and is stronger than example-level DP where a record corresponds to a single training example, because in general one user may contribute many training examples. Even in centralized settings, FL algorithms are well suited for training with user-level DP guarantees, because they compute a single update to the model from all of a user's data, making it much easier to bound each user's total influence on the model update (and hence final model).

In the context of cross-silo FL, the unit of privacy can take on a different meaning. For example, it is possible to define a record as all the examples on a data silo if the participating institutions want to ensure that an adversary who has access to the model iterates or final model cannot determine whether or not a particular institution's dataset was used in the training of that model. User-level DP can still be meaningful in cross-silo settings where each silo holds data for multiple users. Enforcing user-level privacy, however, may be more challenging if multiple institutions have records from the same user.

8.3.2 The Differentially Private Federated Averaging (DP-FedAvg) Algorithm

The easiest way to train federated models with user-level DP is to extend the Federated Averaging (FedAvg) algorithm in the following ways:

- When on-device training is completed, the model update is clipped to bound the ℓ_2 sensitivity of the update.
- Once the server has aggregated all the clipped model updates, it adds Gaussian noise.

Algorithm 7 A Single Round of Differentially Private Federated Averaging (DP-FedAvg)

Parameters: Model update x_i for each client i; ℓ_2 clip norm $c > 0$; Target noise variance $\sigma^2 > 0$

function ClientProcedure(x_i, c)
  return $\hat{x}_i = \min(1, c/\|x_i\|_2) \cdot x_i$ ▷ Clip model update locally
end function

function ServerProcedure($\hat{x}_1, \cdots, \hat{x}_n, \sigma^2$)
  return $\bar{x} = \frac{1}{n}\sum_i \hat{x}_i + \mathcal{N}(0, \sigma^2 I)$ ▷ Add Gaussian noise on the server
end function

This is shown in Algorithm 7. We note that Algorithm 7 uses a fixed ℓ_2 clip norm of c. Observe that for a fixed target ε, σ (the noise's standard deviation) has to scale linearly with c. On the one hand, choosing a small c implies a smaller σ but leads to (potentially) higher bias as it may lead to more frequently clipping of model updates. On the other hand, choosing a large c implies a larger σ, increasing the variance of per-round gradient estimate. Thus, there is no good a priori setting of the clipping norm across tasks and learning settings: the model update norm distribution depends on the model architecture and loss, the amount of data on each device, the client learning rate, and possibly various other parameters.

To resolve this issue, [ATMR21] proposes a method wherein instead of a fixed clipping norm, one clips to a value at a specified quantile of the model update norm distribution, where the value at the quantile is itself estimated online, with differential privacy. The method tracks the quantile closely, uses a negligible amount of privacy budget, is compatible with other federated learning technologies such as compression and secure aggregation, and has a straightforward joint DP analysis with DP-FedAvg. Experiments demonstrate that adaptive clipping to the median update norm works well across a range of realistic federated learning tasks, sometimes outperforming even the best fixed clip chosen in hindsight, and without the need to tune any clipping hyperparameter. The implementation details can be found in Algorithm 1 of [ATMR21].

8.3.3 Formal Privacy Guarantees for Cross-Device FL

While it is easy to add DP to the FedAvg algorithm, providing a formal (ε, δ) is more complex and requires mathematical care. Providing formal (ε, δ) guarantees in the context of cross-device FL systems can be particularly challenging because the set of all eligible users is dynamic and not known in advance, and the participating users may drop out at any point in the protocol [Bon+19; Bal+20]. To address this challenge, Kairouz et al. [Kai+21] propose a concrete approach to overcome these challenges based on the DP-FTRL ("DP-Follow-The-Regularized-Leader") algorithm, described in detail in Section 6.3.2. This method was recently used to train and launch a federated language model with a rigorous DP guarantee [MT21]. In fact, this approach, assuming an honest server for noise addition, has been used to train and launch over thirty Gboard language models with meaningful, formal (ε, δ)-DP guarantees, with ε values in the range of $[0.994, 13.69]$ for $\delta = 10^{-10}$ [Xu+23].

The primary difference between DP-FTRL and DP-SGD methods is that DP-FTRL uses correlated noise instead of independent noise in each training round. For an in-depth treatment of this topic, we direct the review to the comprehensive monograph by Pillutla et al. [Pil+25].

8.3.4 Distributing Trust in Differentially Private Federated Learning

Over the past decade, an extensive set of techniques has been developed for differentially private data analysis, particularly for the central or trusted-aggregator setting, where the raw (or minimized) data is collected by a trusted service provider that implements the DP algorithm. Another area of significant interest is the local model of DP [Kas+08], where the data is perturbed on the client side before it is collected by a service provider (see also Chapter 2 of this book for an extensive discussion about Local DP). Local DP avoids the need for a fully trusted aggregator, but it is now well established that local DP leads to a steep hit in accuracy.

To recover the utility of central DP without having to rely on a fully trusted central server, a set of approaches, often referred to as distributed DP, can be used [Bit+17; KLS21; AKL21]. The goal is to render the output differentially private before it becomes visible (in plaintext) to the server. Under distributed DP, clients first compute minimal application-specific reports, perturb these slightly with random noise, and then execute a private aggregation protocol. The server then has access only to the output of the private aggregation protocol. The noise added by individual clients is typically insufficient for a meaningful local DP guarantee on its own. After private aggregation, however, the output of the private aggregation protocol provides a stronger DP guarantee based on the total sum of noise added across all clients. This applies even to someone with access to the server under the security assumptions necessary for the private aggregation protocol. This approach has been used in production to train smart text selection models in Android [HK23], although achieving strong formal DP guarantees can be challenging in practice due to difficulties with techniques like privacy amplification via sampling in large-scale cross-device federated systems. A very nascent line of work explores how to physically distribute DP-FTRL based algorithms across participating devices (see [Bal+24]), but more work is needed to make these approaches feasible in practice at scale.

For the sake of completeness, we briefly summarize a distributed DP via secure aggregation protocol based on the distributed discrete Gaussian mechanism in Algorithm 8. The implementation details can be found in [KLS21].

Algorithm 8 A single round of the Distributed Discrete Gaussian Mechanism

Parameters: Model update $x_i \in \mathbb{R}^d$ for each client i; ℓ_2 clip norm $c > 0$; Target noise variance $\sigma^2 > 0$; Secure Aggregation's modulus $M \in \mathbb{N}$; A random rotation matrix U_{rotate}; A large scaling parameter s

function ClientProcedure($x_i, c, M, \sigma^2, U_{\text{rotate}}, s$)
  Clip and scale x_i so that $||x_i'||_2 < s \cdot c$
  Randomly rotate vector: $x_i'' = U_{\text{rotate}} \cdot x_i'$
  Stochastically round x_i'' to obtain $x_i''' \in \mathbb{Z}^d$
  Compute $Z_i = x_i''' + \mathcal{N}_{\mathbb{Z}}(0, \sigma^2) \mod M$, where $\mathcal{N}_{\mathbb{Z}}$ is the discrete Gaussian noise
  return $Z_i \in \mathbb{Z}_M^d$
end function

$S = \sum_i Z_i \mod M$: the output of the Secure Aggregation protocol

function ServerProcedure(S, U_{rotate}, s)
  return $(1/s)\, U_{\text{rotate}}^T S$ ▷ Unscale and unrotate the output of Secure Aggregation
end function

Significant practical challenges arise when physically distributing the DP mechanism and employing private aggregation to limit an honest-but-curious server's view to a DP aggregate in each round. First, the required multi-round cryptographic communications are computationally intensive and introduce high network overhead, which can account for the vast majority of training time. Further, these systems are fragile and highly susceptible to client dropouts, a common occurrence in real-world federated settings. When a client drops out, its noise contribution is lost, which can compromise the formal DP guarantee by making the final aggregate less noisy than required by the privacy budget. Second, the approach presented in Algorithm 8 distributes DP mechanisms that add independent Gaussian noise in every round (e.g DP-FedAvg), but it is not capable of distributing DP mechanisms that add correlated Gaussian noise across training rounds (e.g. DP-FTRL), which is necessary for achieving formal DP guarantees in the context of cross-device FL. Third, this approach is susceptible to Sibyl attacks since a malicious could (in theory) control all but one of the devices participating in a training round, reducing the privacy guarantee substantially.

To address these challenges, a new approach, called Confidential Federated Computations (CFC), was recently introduced [Eic+24; VR25]. CFC leverages hardware-based Trusted Execution Environments (TEEs), which create a secure, isolated enclave on the server where data can be processed in a confidential and tamper-proof manner, inaccessible even to the server operator. This architecture makes it possible to deploy high-utility DP algorithms that use correlated noise across training rounds without the need for a trusted server, closing the utility gap while providing strong, verifiable privacy.

The framework's verifiability is built on a "chain of trust" that begins on the user's device. Before uploading, data is encrypted and cryptographically bound to a specific, publicly auditable "Access Policy" that dictates exactly which computations are permitted to process it. A TEE-hosted service called the "Ledger" acts as a keymaster, only releasing decryption keys to other TEEs that use cryptographic attestation to prove they are running an authorized, open-source computation from the policy.

A primary early application of this system is Confidential Federated Analytics, which was deployed to improve Google Keyboard (Gboard). In particular, it was used to discover new, frequently typed out-of-vocabulary Indonesian words. In the past, this task relied on locally DP protocols like TrieHH [Zhu+20], which struggled to detect rare words or work well in low-volume languages due to high noise. With CFC, user devices submit encrypted local data to a server-side TEE that runs a verified DP histogram algorithm, enabling Google to extract useful aggregate insights with far lower noise and tighter privacy guarantees ($\varepsilon = \ln 3$ per week, per device). The system successfully uncovered 3,600 missing words in just two days, showcasing both improved utility and user trust through verifiability and hardware-enforced privacy. The application of CFC in the context of training a model on federated data is widely believed to be possible but has not happened yet.

8.3.5 Complementary Privacy Auditing Empirical Techniques

For an algorithm to provide a formal user-level DP guarantee, it must not only bound the sensitivity of the model to each user's data, but also add noise proportional to that sensitivity. While the addition of sufficient random noise is required to ensure a small enough ε for the DP definition itself to offer a strong guarantee, empirically it has been observed that limiting sensitivity even with small amounts of noise (or no noise at all) can significantly reduce memorization [Ram+20]. This gap is to be expected, as DP assumes a "worst-case adversary" with infinite computation and access to arbitrary side information. These assumptions are often unrealistic in practice. Thus, there are substantial advantages to training using a DP algorithm that limits each user's influence, even if the explicit random noise introduced into the training process is not enough to ensure a small ε formally. Nevertheless, designing practical FL and FA algorithms that achieve small ε guarantees is an important area of ongoing research.

Model auditing techniques can be used to further quantify the advantages of training with DP [Car+19; Car+20; Ram+20]. These techniques are empirical in nature and can be applied during or after training. They broadly include techniques that quantify how much a model overlearns (or memorizes) unique or rare training examples and techniques that quantify to what extent it is possible to infer whether or not a user's examples were used during training. These auditing techniques are useful even when a large ε is used, as they can quantify the gap between DP's worst-case adversaries and realistic ones with limited computational power and side information. They can also serve as a complementary technology for pressure-testing DP implementations: unlike the formal mathematical statements of DP, these auditing techniques are applied to complete end-to-end systems, potentially catching software bugs or mis-chosen parameters.

Some additional discussion regarding auditing the information leakage of a system is presented in Chapter 16.

8.4 Federated Analytics

The focus of this chapter so far has primarily been on FL. Beyond learning ML models, data analysts are often interested in applying data science methods to the analysis of raw data that is stored locally on users' devices. For example, analysts may be interested in learning aggregate model metrics, popular trends and activities, or geospatial location heatmaps. All of this can be done using FA [RM20]. Similar to FL, FA works by running local computations over each device's data and making only the aggregated results available to product engineers. Unlike FL, however, FA aims to support basic data science needs, such as counts, averages, histograms, quantiles, and other SQL-like queries. Two prominent examples of FA in practice are: (1) its use in Google Health Studies to power privacy-preserving health research [Goo20a], and (2) its use for environmental studies to provide cities with critical information about transportation-related greenhouse gas emissions, derived from aggregated and anonymized Google Maps Timeline [Bia+24].

Consider an application where an analyst wants to use FA to learn the 10 most frequently played songs in a music library shared by many users. The federated and privacy techniques discussed above can be used to perform this task. For example, clients can encode which songs they have listened to into a binary vector of length equal to the size of the library and use distributed DP to ensure that the server sees only a differentially private sum of these vectors, giving a DP histogram of how many users have played each song. As this example illustrates, however, FA tasks can differ from FL ones in several ways:

1. FA algorithms are often noninteractive and involve rounds with a large number of clients. In other words, unlike FL applications, there are no diminishing returns from having more clients in a round. Therefore, applying DP is less challenging in FA since each round can contain a large number of clients, and fewer rounds are needed.
2. There is no need for the same clients to participate again in later rounds. In fact, clients that participate again may bias the results of the algorithm. Therefore an FA task is best served by an infrastructure that limits the number of times any individual can participate.
3. FA tasks are typically sparse, making efficient private sparse aggregation a particularly important topic; many open research questions exist in this space.

It is worth noting that while limiting client participation and sparse aggregation are particularly relevant to FA, they have applications for FL problems as well.

8.5 Concluding Remarks

We are optimistic that FL will continue to expand, both as a research field and as a set of practical tools and software systems that allow applications by more people to more types of data and problem domains.

Despite this progress, significant challenges remain. The first is scaling to the enormous size of modern foundation models, whose multi-billion parameter counts are orders of magnitude larger than what current cross-device FL systems can handle due to on-device compute, memory, and network constraints. Second, providing strong, externally verifiable privacy guarantees for server-side computations remains a difficult open problem, particularly in defending against a malicious service provider. Finally, the operational complexity of coordinating training across millions of heterogeneous and unreliable devices creates persistent system-level hurdles that can hinder broader adoption.

A promising path forward, which embodies the updated, property-centric definition of FL, involves leveraging confidential cloud computing. Recent proposals outline a paradigm of Confidential Federated Computations [Eic+24], where clients encrypt their data before upload. This data can then only be processed inside a server-side Trusted Execution Environment (TEE) running a verifiably open-source workload. A trusted ledger service ensures that decryption keys are only released to approved, privacy-preserving workloads (e.g., a workload that provably implements a DP aggregation algorithm). This approach could resolve the scalability bottleneck by moving heavy computation off-device, enabling federated training of large models, while simultaneously strengthening privacy by providing verifiable, end-to-end guarantees about how data is processed, regardless of its location. This evolution represents an exciting next chapter for the field, aiming to achieve stronger privacy with greater flexibility and scale.

For those interested in learning more about active research directions, the recent vision paper "Federated Learning in Practice: Reflections and Projections" discusses the evolution of FL, latest advances and deployments, lingering and emerging challenges, and the future of federated technologies [Dal+24]. The relatively established monograph "Advances and Open Problems in Federated Learning" provides a broad survey, with coverage of important topics not covered in this chapter, including personalization, robustness, fairness, and systems challenges [Kai+19]. If you are interested in a more hands-on introduction to FL, such as trying out algorithms in a simulation environment on either your own data or standard data sets, the Google Parfait GitHub library is a great place to start. It contains many examples that can be executed and modified on the fly in the browser using Google Colab.

Acknowledgements

The authors would like to thank Alex Ingerman and Marco Gruteser for helpful feedback on earlier drafts of this chapter, as well as the many people at Google who have helped develop these ideas and bring them to practice.

References

[Aba+16] M. Abadi, A. Chu, I. Goodfellow, H. B. McMahan, I. Mironov, K. Talwar, and L. Zhang. "Deep Learning with Differential Privacy". In: Proceedings of the 2016 ACM SIGSAC Conference on Computer and Communications Security. CCS '16. Vienna, Austria: Association for Computing Machinery, 2016, pp. 308–318. ISBN: 9781450341394. URL: https://doi.org/10.1145/2976749.2978318 (cit. on p. 301).

[AKL21] N. Agarwal, P. Kairouz, and Z. Liu. "The skellam mechanism for differentially private federated learning". In: Advances in Neural Information Processing Systems 34 (2021) (cit. on p. 304).

[App23] Apple. Learning Iconic Scenes with Differential Privacy. https://machinelearning.apple.com/research/scenes-differential-privacy. 2023 (cit. on p. 294).

[App25] Apple. Understanding Aggregate Trends for Apple Intelligence Using Differential Privacy. https://machinelearning.apple.com/research/differential-privacy-aggregate-trends. 2025 (cit. on p. 294).

[ATMR21] G. Andrew, O. Thakkar, B. McMahan, and S. Ramaswamy. "Differentially private learning with adaptive clipping". In: Advances in Neural Information Processing Systems 34 (2021) (cit. on p. 303).

[Bal+20] B. Balle, P. Kairouz, H. B. McMahan, O. Thakkar, and A. Thakurta. "Privacy amplification via random check-ins". In: NeurIPS. 2020 (cit. on p. 304).

[Bal+24] M. Ball, J. Bell-Clark, A. Gascon, P. Kairouz, S. Oh, and Z. Xie. "Secure Stateful Aggregation: A Practical Protocol with Applications in Differentially-Private Federated Learning". In: arXiv preprint arXiv:2410.11368 (2024) (cit. on p. 305).

[Bel+20] J. H. Bell, K. A. Bonawitz, A. Gascón, T. Lepoint, and M. Raykova. "Secure single-server aggregation with (poly) logarithmic overhead". In: Proceedings of the 2020 ACM SIGSAC Conference on Computer and Communications Security. 2020, pp. 1253–1269 (cit. on p. 301).

[Bia+24] C. Bian, A. Cheu, S. Chiknavaryan, Z. Gong, M. Gruteser, O. Guinan, Y. Guzman, P. Kairouz, A. Lagzdin, R. McKenna, et al. "Mayfly: Private Aggregate Insights from Ephemeral Streams of On-Device User Data". In: arXiv preprint arXiv:2412.07962 (2024) (cit. on p. 307).

[Bit+17] A. Bittau, Ú. Erlingsson, P. Maniatis, I. Mironov, A. Raghunathan, D. Lie, M. Rudominer, U. Kode, J. Tinnes, and B. Seefeld. "Prochlo: Strong Privacy for Analytics in the Crowd". In: Proceedings of the Symposium on Operating Systems Principles (SOSP). 2017, pp. 441–459. URL: https://arxiv.org/abs/1710.00901 (cit. on p. 304).

[Bon+17] K. Bonawitz, V. Ivanov, B. Kreuter, A. Marcedone, H. B. McMahan, S. Patel, D. Ramage, A. Segal, and K. Seth. "Practical secure aggregation for privacy-preserving machine learning". In: proceedings of the 2017 ACM SIGSAC Conference on Computer and Communications Security. 2017, pp. 1175–1191 (cit. on p. 300).

[Bon+19] K. Bonawitz, H. Eichner, W. Grieskamp, D. Huba, A. Ingerman, V. Ivanov, C. Kiddon, J. Konecny, S. Mazzocchi, H. B. McMahan, et al. "Towards federated learning at scale: System design". In: arXiv preprint arXiv:1902.01046 (2019) (cit. on pp. 293, 297, 301, 304).

[BST14] R. Bassily, A. Smith, and A. Thakurta. "Private Empirical Risk Minimization: Efficient Algorithms and Tight Error Bounds". In: Proc. of the 2014 IEEE 55th Annual Symp. on Foundations of Computer Science (FOCS). 2014, pp. 464–473 (cit. on p. 301).

[Car+19] N. Carlini, C. Liu, Ú. Erlingsson, J. Kos, and D. Song. "The secret sharer: Evaluating and testing unintended memorization in neural networks". In: 28th {USENIX} Security Symposium ({USENIX} Security 19). 2019, pp. 267–284 (cit. on pp. 289, 301, 307).

[Car+20] N. Carlini, F. Tramer, E. Wallace, M. Jagielski, A. Herbert-Voss, K. Lee, A. Roberts, T. Brown, D. Song, U. Erlingsson, et al. "Extracting training data from large language models". In: arXiv preprint arXiv:2012.07805 (2020) (cit. on pp. 289, 301, 307).

[Dal+24] K. Daly, H. Eichner, P. Kairouz, H. B. McMahan, D. Ramage, and Z. Xu. "Federated learning in practice: reflections and projections". In: 2024 IEEE 6th International Conference on Trust, Privacy and Security in Intelligent Systems, and Applications (TPS-ISA). IEEE. 2024, pp. 148–156 (cit. on pp. 287, 291, 297, 309).

[DMNS06] C. Dwork, F. McSherry, K. Nissim, and A. D. Smith. "Calibrating Noise to Sensitivity in Private Data Analysis". In: IACR Theory of Cryptography Conference (TCC), New York, New York. Vol. 3876. Lecture Notes in Computer Science. Springer-Verlag, 2006, pp. 265–284 (cit. on p. 301).

[Eic+24] H. Eichner, D. Ramage, K. Bonawitz, D. Huba, T. Santoro, B. McLarnon, T. Van Overveldt, N. Fallen, P. Kairouz, A. Cheu, et al. "Confidential Federated Computations". In: arXiv preprint arXiv:2404.10764 (2024) (cit. on pp. 297, 306, 308).

[Goo20a] Google. Advancing health research with Google Health Studies. https://blog.google/technology/health/google-health-studies-app/. 2020 (cit. on p. 307).

[Goo20b] Google. Your chats stay private while Messages improves suggestions. https://support.google.com/messages/answer/9327902. 2020 (cit. on p. 294).

[Har+18] A. Hard, K. Rao, R. Mathews, S. Ramaswamy, F. Beaufays, S. Augenstein, H. Eichner, C. Kiddon, and D. Ramage. "Federated learning for mobile keyboard prediction". In: arXiv preprint arXiv:1811.03604 (2018) (cit. on p. 294).

[Har+22] A. Hard, K. Partridge, N. Chen, S. Augenstein, A. Shah, H. J. Park, A. Park, S. Ng, J. Nguyen, I. L. Moreno, et al. "Production federated keyword spotting via distillation, filtering, and joint federated-centralized training". In: arXiv preprint arXiv:2204.06322 (2022) (cit. on p. 294).

[HK23] F. Hartmann and P. Kairouz. Distributed differential privacy for federated learning. https://research.google/blog/distributed-differential-privacy-for-federated-learning. 2023 (cit. on pp. 294, 301, 304).

[Hub+22] D. Huba, J. Nguyen, K. Malik, R. Zhu, M. Rabbat, A. Yousefpour, C.-J. Wu, H. Zhan, P. Ustinov, H. Srinivas, et al. "Papaya: Practical, private, and scalable federated learning". In: Proceedings of Machine Learning and Systems 4 (2022), pp. 814–832 (cit. on pp. 294, 297).

[Kai+19] P. Kairouz, H. B. McMahan, B. Avent, A. Bellet, M. Bennis, A. N. Bhagoji, K. Bonawitz, Z. Charles, G. Cormode, R. Cummings, et al. "Advances and open problems in federated learning". In: arXiv preprint arXiv:1912.04977 (2019) (cit. on pp. 287, 293, 294, 309).

[Kai+21] P. Kairouz, B. Mcmahan, S. Song, O. Thakkar, A. Thakurta, and Z. Xu. "Practical and Private (Deep) Learning Without Sampling or Shuffling". In: Proceedings of the 38th International Conference on Machine Learning. 2021, pp. 5213–5225 (cit. on p. 304).

[Kas+08] S. P. Kasiviswanathan, H. K. Lee, K. Nissim, S. Raskhodnikova, and A. D. Smith. "What Can We Learn Privately?" In: 49th Annual IEEE Symposium on Foundations of Computer Science, FOCS 2008. IEEE Computer Society, 2008, pp. 531–540. URL: https://doi.org/10.1109/FOCS.2008.27 (cit. on p. 304).

[KLS21] P. Kairouz, Z. Liu, and T. Steinke. "The distributed discrete gaussian mechanism for federated learning with secure aggregation". In: arXiv preprint arXiv:2102.06387 (2021) (cit. on pp. 304, 305).

[Mar+22] E. Marchiori, S. de Haas, S. Volnov, R. Falcon, R. Pinto, and M. Zamarato. "Android Private Compute Core Architecture". In: arXiv preprint arXiv:2209.10317 (2022) (cit. on p. 291).

[McM+17] B. McMahan, E. Moore, D. Ramage, S. Hampson, and B. A. y Arcas. "Communication-efficient learning of deep networks from decentralized data". In: Artificial intelligence and statistics. PMLR. 2017, pp. 1273–1282 (cit. on pp. 287, 295).

[MR17] B. McMahan and D. Ramage. Federated Learning: Collaborative Machine Learning without Centralized Training Data. https://ai.googleblog.com/2017/04/federated-learning-collaborative.html. 2017 (cit. on p. 287).

[MRTZ18] H. B. McMahan, D. Ramage, K. Talwar, and L. Zhang. "Learning Differentially Private Recurrent Language Models". In: International Conference on Learning Representations (ICLR). 2018 (cit. on p. 302).

[MT21] B. McMahan and A. Thakurta. Federated Learning with Formal Differential Privacy Guarantees. https://ai.googleblog.com/2022/02/federated-learning-with-formal.html. 2021 (cit. on p. 304).

[Pau+21] M. Paulik, M. Seigel, H. Mason, D. Telaar, J. Kluivers, R. van Dalen, C. W. Lau, L. Carlson, F. Granqvist, C. Vandevelde, et al. "Federated Evaluation and Tuning for On-Device Personalization: System Design & Applications". In: arXiv preprint arXiv:2102.08503 (2021) (cit. on pp. 293, 297).

[Pil+25] K. Pillutla, J. Upadhyay, C. A. Choquette-Choo, K. Dvijotham, A. Ganesh, M. Henzinger, J. Katz, R. McKenna, H. B. McMahan, K. Rush, et al. "Correlated Noise Mechanisms for Differentially Private Learning". In: arXiv preprint arXiv:2506.08201 (2025) (cit. on p. 304).

[Ram+20] S. Ramaswamy, O. Thakkar, R. Mathews, G. Andrew, H. B. McMahan, and F. Beaufays. "Training production language models without memorizing user data". In: arXiv preprint arXiv:2009.10031 (2020) (cit. on pp. 306, 307).

[RM20] D. Ramage and S. Mazzocchi. Federated Analytics: Collaborative Data Science without Data Collection. https://ai.googleblog.com/2020/05/federated-analytics-collaborative-data.html. 2020 (cit. on pp. 288, 301, 307).

[SCS13] S. Song, K. Chaudhuri, and A. D. Sarwate. "Stochastic gradient descent with differentially private updates". In: 2013 IEEE Global Conference on Signal and Information Processing. IEEE. 2013, pp. 245–248 (cit. on p. 301).

[Sto+22] B. Stojkovic, J. Woodbridge, Z. Fang, J. Cai, A. Petrov, S. Iyer, D. Huang, P. Yau, A. S. Kumar, H. Jawa, et al. "Applied federated learning: Architectural design for robust and efficient learning in privacy aware settings". In: arXiv preprint arXiv:2206.00807 (2022) (cit. on p. 294).

[Sub+17] P. Subramanyan, R. Sinha, I. Lebedev, S. Devadas, and S. A. Seshia. "A formal foundation for secure remote execution of enclaves". In: Proceedings of the 2017 ACM SIGSAC Conference on Computer and Communications Security. 2017, pp. 2435–2450 (cit. on p. 300).

[VR25] T. Van Overveldt and D. Ramage. Discovering new words with confidential federated analytics. https://research.google/blog/discovering-new-words-with-confidential-federated-analytics. 2025 (cit. on p. 306).

[Xu+23] Z. Xu, Y. Zhang, G. Andrew, C. Choquette, P. Kairouz, B. McMahan, J. Rosenstock, and Y. Zhang. Federated Learning of Gboard Language Models with Differential Privacy. 2023 (cit. on pp. 294, 301, 304).

[Zha+23] Y. Zhang, D. Ramage, Z. Xu, Y. Zhang, S. Zhai, and P. Kairouz. "Private Federated Learning in Gboard". In: arXiv preprint arXiv:2306.14793 (2023) (cit. on p. 301).

[Zhu+20] W. Zhu, P. Kairouz, B. McMahan, H. Sun, and W. Li. "Federated heavy hitters discovery with differential privacy". In: International Conference on Artificial Intelligence and Statistics. PMLR. 2020, pp. 3837–3847 (cit. on p. 306).

Part III

Application Areas

DOI: 10.1561/9781638284772.ch9

Chapter 9

Differential Privacy and Medical Data Analysis

By Vinith M. Suriyakumar, Nicolas Papernot and Anna Goldenberg

9.1 Introduction

Medical data analysis is crucial to advancing our understanding of human health and biology. Analyzing electronic health records (EHR) has helped provide insights into disease trajectories [Raj+18], lab and test efficacy [Gha+17], racial disparities [CSG19], and hospital operations [Wan+19]. Medical image analysis for x-rays, magnetic resonance images (MRIs), computed tomography (CTs), positron emission tomography (PET) have provided improved understanding of disease [SLMG20] and potential improvements to screening protocols to help detect disease earlier [TBL17]. Finally, analyzing *omics* data such as genomics, proteomics, and metabolomics have given us a much deeper of understanding of the biological mechanisms that underly disease progression [Mob+18], disease inheritance, and drug efficacy [Hon+18].

Medical data is incredibly personal and sensitive thus it requires strong privacy protections. Regulations around the world help govern the mechanisms used to protect the privacy of medical data. These regulations set the different levels of privacy required depending on who is accessing the data and the purpose of the data access. The current standard practice amongst most regulations is anonymization. However, this mechanism for protecting data privacy is not robust to a number of attacks such as reconstruction attacks, differential attacks, and linkage attacks. The reader is referred to Chapters 1 and 5 for more details on privacy issues arising in statistical data release and machine learning systems, respectively.

In this chapter, we discuss regulations that govern the privacy of medical data for a variety of countries around the world and examples of medical data privacy breaches. We discuss why differential privacy is a promising framework for the next gold standard in medical data privacy. Finally, we discuss conducting both statistical analyses and machine learning on medical data with guarantees of differential privacy.

We survey a number of different case studies for different important statistical tasks in medicine. These include survival analysis, cohort identification, variant lookup, and genome-wide association studies. We present custom differentially private algorithms developed by researchers for these tasks, some of which provide optimal privacy-utility tradeoffs.

For machine learning, we present case studies of prediction and data synthesis across across different data modalities including electronic health records, medical images, and genomics data. We discuss some studies that show extreme loss of utility when incorporating differential privacy and others that have found minimal loss in utility. We contrast these studies to show some of the fundamental technical challenges that need work to help move differentially private machine learning to deployment in medicine. Given the global scale of medical research and the siloed nature of medical data we discuss applications of differentially private federated learning to medical data. It is clear that as research progresses, DP distributed learning will help learn higher utility models by allowing hospitals around the world to privately collaborate on model training.

Finally, we discuss the current challenges of applying differential privacy to medical data analysis and future opportunities for advancing applications of differential privacy in medical data analysis. This discussion will focus on methodological, ethical and interdisciplinary directions that could be explored to help differential privacy become the next standard practice for privacy in medical data analysis.

9.2 Data Privacy in Medicine

Medical data captures a historical view of chronic disease status, past procedures, lab values, imaging, genetics, and much more. Breaches of privacy in medicine can negatively impact an individual's dignity and cause them harm. An example is if a patient seeking mental health care or with positive HIV status experiences a privacy breach. They may face judgement and stigma from friends and family members. To prevent these harms, there are laws and regulations around the world that govern how medical data privacy is protected. In contrast, there is a burgeoning need for medical data to be made publicly available to improve health research and general clinical knowledge. In many settings, the lack of such publicly available data for legitimate academic use can slow progress. We offer DP as a technical framework with many strong use cases in medical data and discuss when it is most appropriate given these contrasting needs.

9.2.1 Medical Data Privacy Laws Around the World

In the U.S., the Health Insurance Portability and Accountability Act (HIPAA) [Act96] governs individual rights for medical data privacy. The medical data that is protected under this law includes: information in electronic health records (EHRs), conversations between doctors and nurses often held in clinical notes, information about you that your health insurer stores, and billing information from interactions with the healthcare system [Offa]. There are different levels of access to medical data each with their own levels of privacy protections. Patients, healthcare providers, and any authorized family members or friends have full access to individual medical data. When this data is used for research or public health purposes it typically goes through a process called *anonymization*. This process removes certain pieces of data and adds noise to others to *de-identify* the data. We will discuss these two terms and the pitfalls of this process later on.

In Canada, since the healthcare system is managed provincially many provinces have their own variant of the Personal Information Protection and Electronic Documents Act (PIPEDA) which governs the privacy laws for medical data [Offb]. Broadly, the medical data protected under these laws includes: all information collected during interactions with the healthcare system (i.e. information inputted by doctors and nurses) and information collected by health insurance companies (e.g. prescriptions for medications). Similar to the U.S. there are varying levels of access and privacy protections.

In Europe, the General Data Protection Regulation (GDPR) governs the medical data privacy laws [Com18]. The medical data that is protected under the law is more broad than the previous regulations discussed: it covers all data generated from interactions with the healthcare system, data collected from wearable devices, data collected by health insurers, and health data that might be inferred from app usage. The levels of access and necessary permissions also differ from the previous regulations. Oftentimes, *explicit consent* is required for the processing of medical data.

In Asia, the regulations protecting medical data privacy differ between countries. China recently passed a set of regulations called the Personal Information Protection Law (PIPL) [Hor21] which took effect November 1, 2021. Similar to GDPR, these regulations protect medical data such as: data collected during interactions with the healthcare system, data collected from wearables, and data collected from apps that can be used to infer health. Additionally, explicit consent is required to process health data. India does not currently have any explicit regulations which protect the privacy of medical data but is covered under the regulations for sensitive data from the Information Technology (Reasonable Security Practices and Procedures and Sensitive Personal Data or Information) Rules 2011 [GKN21]. The data protected by these laws is similar to GDPR. Explicit consent is not required for the analysis of health data according to these regulations.

Similar to Asia, the regulations protecting medical data privacy vary widely between countries in Africa. This ranges from no explicit data privacy laws to having similar laws to GDPR [Uni]. For example, in South Africa, the National Health Act governs the medical data privacy laws. These regulations protect medical data including: data collected from your doctors and nurses during your interactions and conversations between your health care providers. Processing of this data is governed by the Protection of Personal Information Act (POPIA) which states that only healthcare institutions, social services, insurance companies, schools, and anyone authorized by the individual whose healthcare is being processed.

As we can see, the regulations governing medical data privacy are similar in many ways around the world but there are differences. The kind of data covered and the levels of access allowed for secondary analysis of medical data (e.g. research purposes) are not the same across the regulations discussed. One common protection across many of these regulations is the use of anonymization to protect individual privacy for secondary analyses of medical data. The regulations above and anonymization are often considered strong methods for protecting patient privacy especially for public data releases. Next, we will discuss instances of medical data privacy breaches that have occurred despite the use of anonymization.

9.2.2 Medical Data Privacy Breaches

Despite the protections in place from the regulations discussed, medical data privacy breaches have and continue to happen. First, we discuss how often breaches occur and common reasons for these breaches. We end with examples of medical data privacy breaches in the research literature but also real-world data breaches. These breaches often correspond to a failure of anonymization. These breaches span public releases of medical data, medical data stored by hospitals, and more recently medical data collected by wearables and smart devices. In the U.S. from 2009-2020 as documented in the HIPAA Journals, there have been over 2705 privacy breaches of 500 records or more [Ald21]. This has resulted in the exposure of 268 189 693 medical records in the U.S. which equates to 81.72% of the population over 11 years. The common sources of the largest breaches during this time period included: hacking, loss, theft, and unauthorized access / disclosure. A combination of security issues and privacy issues resulted in these breaches. They are evidence that we can help prevent some of them with stronger privacy protections but breaches due to security failing cannot be prevented with improved privacy protections.

A seminal example of such a breach in the research is that of Latanya Sweeney. Sweeney's research on re-identifying anonymized health data demonstrated that using only sex, zip code, and birth date that a large percentage of individuals are uniquely identifiable [Swe]. Sweeney demonstrated this using auxiliary data in what is known as a *linkage attack*. The study was able to uniquely link individuals in the Illinois Health Care Cost Containment Council data and the 1990 US Census using sex, zip code, and birth date with 87% accuracy. This study is a seminal example of the pitfalls of using anonymization for protecting medical data. See also Section 1.2 in Chapter 1 for additional discussion on why data anonymization fails to protect privacy.

In 2010, researchers showed that even genomic data could be re-identified using a combination of diagnostic codes, ethnicity, year of birth, and gender. The researchers in this study started from an anonymized sample of 1 174 793 patients from the Vanderbilt University Medical Center. In addition to this sample, they had a subset of 2762 of these patients who had been chosen for a genome wide association study (GWAS) on heart health. Their linkage attack leverages the fact that many of the people in the EHR are most likely to be candidates for the GWAS since most healthy individuals would not be in the EHR data.

In 2019, The Australian Department of Health released anonymized health data from 10% of the population (approx. 2.9 million people) which was re-identified six weeks later [CRT17]. To anonymize the data before release, an encrypted ID was used to represent each patient and all dates including date of birth were randomized to a day in a two week window. The researchers show that the anonymization and randomization procedures were not as protective of data privacy as originally thought. First, this was demonstrated using publicly available one-off information about individuals such as birth date, gender, and childbirth histories for women. Second, they demonstrate the efficacy of these attacks if there is access to a much larger dataset similar to Sweeney.

While the breaches we've presented so far have primarily been on statistical databases, similar attacks have been successful on machine learning models trained using medical data. Researchers have used membership inference attacks on large language models such as BERT [DCLT18] finetuned with clinical notes to identify whether a specific patient was in the training data [JRY21]. They show that these large clinical language models were susceptible to leaking up to 7% of the original training data. While this percentage is low, training data extraction is still a nascent field of research. So we can expect that these attacks will likely improve and more data will be leaked without protections.

All of these breaches are concerned with anonymized datasets that have been publicly released thus the intention of the users is not understood. For research purposes, the intent of researchers are well understood and defined. Still the appropriate security measures (such as trusted computing environments) are required to prevent any adversarial users from gaining unauthorized access to these systems. In these specific settings, the risk of breaches with anonymized data and access defined by the law is often lower. This is because it is assumed that researchers are not adversarial users who will attempt to re-identify individuals and the computing systems are secured. Once the data is meant to be made publicly available then DP is crucial to protecting patient privacy.

9.2.3 Differential Privacy as the New Gold Standard

The breaches and attacks presented are clear examples for why stronger privacy protections are needed for medical data analysis. Differential privacy is a prime candidate as the new gold standard because it is a framework for measuring and bounding the privacy leakage of running an algorithm on data without making assumptions about how an adversarial user tries to gain access and what the access already knows about the users in the data. In the rest of the chapter, we will present a series of case studies on analyzing medical data with differential privacy and training models with differential privacy for medical machine learning tasks.

9.3 Statistical Analysis

Statistical analysis of medical data is the cornerstone of the secondary use of medical data. These analyses have far reaching impacts including: improving hospital operations, treatment recommendations, understanding of chronic diseases, policy recommendations, and understanding of global pandemics. The most commonly analyzed sources of medical data include: electronic health records, randomized control trials, and genomics. There are different types of statistical analyses performed on these types of data as well. We will survey different types of differentially private statistical analyses on these types of data. Some of these algorithms will be extensions of those presented in previous chapters.

9.3.1 Electronic Health Records

Cohort Identification

Identifying cohorts of patients for clinical trials is an important use of electronic health record data. Most studies require a minimum number of patients to be enrolled. This starts with researchers identifying the total number of individuals eligible for the study. This question is a counting query. As discussed previously in Chapter 4, there have been many methods developed over time for privately answering counting queries. Methods that have been developed specifically for cohort identification typically allow analysts to leverage domain knowledge to improve the utility of the algorithms. This was first done using the exponential mechanism with a utility function defined by a set of user-defined parameters such as the expected upper and lower bounds for the counts [VSB12].

Their method was improved upon using a truncated geometric mechanism and post-processing to achieve optimal privacy-utility tradeoffs [CSKB20]. The mechanism differs from the original exponential mechanism in the noise distribution that is used and that it is optimal for asymmetric utility functions. First, the analyst defines the count query $q : \mathcal{R}^d \rightarrow \{0, 1\}$ (e.g. "How many individuals have Type 1 Diabetes?") and the associated privacy budget ε. Additionally, the analyst has a prior belief $\pi(c)$ (typically based on knowledge of disease prevalence) over the true count. Both the count query and the privacy budget are sent to a trusted data curator. Next, the data curator computes the true count c for the query posed by the analyst. After this, noise z is sampled from a truncated geometric distribution, defined as

$$
\begin{aligned}
Pr[Y = y] &= \frac{1-\alpha}{1+\alpha}\alpha^{|y|} \\
z &= \min\{\max(0, y), n\},
\end{aligned}
\tag{9.1}
$$

where $\alpha = \frac{1}{\varepsilon}$), and is added to the true count. This produces the noised count $\hat{c}$ (i.e. $\hat{c} = c + z$). The accuracy of the mechanism is evaluated using a loss function $\ell(c, \hat{c})$ that evaluates the error between the true count and the noisy count, A post-processing step is applied to $\hat{c}$ to maximize the utility of the final noised count. This was inspired by the user-specific post-processing step in [GRS12]. This step consists of minimizing the expected loss under the posterior belief of the true count c conditioned on the noisy count $\hat{c}$. The conditional output distribution is defined as $q_{TGM}(z|x; \alpha, n)$ n is the size of the database. The posterior belief over the true count c is then expressed as:

$$
q(c|\hat{c}; \pi, \alpha, n) \propto \pi(c) q_{TGM}(\hat{c}|c; \alpha, n). \tag{9.2}
$$

Finally, a post-processing map of $\hat{c}$ is defined by $T : [n] \rightarrow [n]$:

$$
T(\hat{c}|\pi, \ell, \alpha, n) = \arg\min_{y} \sum_{x} q(c|\hat{c}; \pi, \alpha, n)\ell(c, \hat{c}). \tag{9.3}
$$

This optimization problem is solved using the fast Fourier transform based convolution algorithms where the loss function is the difference between the true and noised count expressed as $\ell(c, \hat{c}) = (\hat{c} - c)$. This algorithm allows analysts to incorporate their beliefs about the true counts using knowledge of prevalence in general populations which is important for maximizing the utility in cohort identification. For example, if the query is about individuals with a rare disease then the analyst can reasonably believe the counts to be quite low. Knowing that the counts are low improves the utility by choosing a prior which places high probability on low counts. Thus ensuring that the noised counts do not diverge too far away from lower counts after the post-processing step.

This algorithm was evaluated on identifying a cohort for a study conducted on the effectiveness of genetic risk score in improving health outcomes associated with coronary heart disease (CHD) [Kul+16]. The study was looking to recruit participants in the Mayo Clinic Biobank with the following criteria: "age 45-65 years, non-Hispanic White ethnicity, no itory of atherosclerotic cardiovascular disease, not on statins, at intermediate risk for CHD (10 year CHD risk 5%-20%), and residents of Olmsted County Minnesota." 2026 subjects in the Biobank were eligible for the study, from which 216 subjects were enrolled. Focusing on queries of similar size, the authors of the above counting query algorithm aimed to estimate the number of eligible subjects in the Biobank. They demonstrate that for large counts ($c = 2000$) such as the query in [Kul+16] their algorithm returns 1998 at $\varepsilon = 0.05$ which is highly accurate. For smaller counts ($c = 100$) which require more noise to maintain the same level of privacy ($\varepsilon = 0.05$) the counts are still quite accurate at 88. These results show the efficacy of custom private counting query algorithms for cohort identification.

Survival Analysis

Survival analysis is concerned with predicting the time until death or an event of interest in a variety of situations in medicine (e.g. time to death after an organ transplant). Researchers developed a differentially private version of the nonparametric Kaplan-Meier survival model [BJO20] that provides minimal drops in utility. Survival analyses use event data up to time t to estimate the survival probability at time t. The algorithm they developed was inspired by work on continual release in differential privacy. They consider an event stream $S = (e_1, e_2, ..., e_t)$ where each event is defined as $e_i = (c_i, u_i, t_i)$ where c_i defines whether censoring occurred, u_i defines whether an event is uncensored, r_i denotes the patients remaining at time t and t_i is the time. To start we describe the K-M survival model without differential privacy and describe the changes made by the researchers to guarantee differential privacy. The Kaplan-Meier model uses the estimator defined as

$$S(t) = \prod_{i:t_i \leq t} (1 - \frac{u_i}{r_i}). \tag{9.4}$$

This estimator determines the probability of survival up to time t. Typically, the notion of adjacent data in DP is defined as two databases differing in one example. This notion does not apply directly to survival analyses. Thus, the study defines a new notion of neighboring streams as follows for DP survival analyses:

Definition 9.1. *Two streams S_t and S'_t are neighboring if at most one time $t_i \in \{1...t\}$ we find $|c_i - c'_i| + |u_i - u'_i| \leq 1$.*

The original definition of differential privacy is then used based on this definition of neighboring streams. The differentially private algorithm is composed of three parts: data partitioning, the survival curve computation, and post-processing. For data partitioning, the original stream S is separated into different groups that are made up of multiple events. This is necessary to organize the events by each of the individuals instead of treating each event as a separate piece of data. Each event e_i in S is processed individually into a group until $\Theta - 1$ events are processed. Both the number of events and the threshold θ are perturbed with noise to protect the privacy of the counts and size of each partition. A privacy budget of ε_1 is allocated to this procedure. These steps are required to ensure the proceeding steps in survival analysis are differentially private.

As described in Equation 9.4 the survival probability at each time is computed using the number of uncensored u_i and censored c_i events in a partition. The algorithm computes both of these quantities in a differentially private manner to compute $S(t)$. This is done using the binary tree mechanism for aggregating counts in an online fashion [CSS11; DNPR10]. This ensures that the noise added to the inputs only grows logarithmically instead of linearly. The new estimator is defined in Equation 9.5:

$$S(t) = S(t-1) \cdot \frac{N - \hat{u}_i - \hat{c}_{i-1}}{N - \hat{u}_{i-1} - \hat{c}_{i-1}}, \tag{9.5}$$

where $\hat{u}_i$ and $\hat{c}_i$ are the total number of uncensored and censored events up to partition i.

Finally, the post-processing step occurs as the addition of noise might violate some of the required properties of survival curves. The values of the curve must be monotonically decreasing as $t \to \infty$ and $S(t) \in [0, 1]$. First, another survival curve which respects these constraints $s^*(t)$ is computed that best matches the original differentially private curve $s(t)$. This is formulated as an optimization problem similar to previous work [HRMS09; BB72] and solved as an isotonic regression problem. A privacy budget of ε_2 is allocated for this computation. This method was tested on time to death of breast cancer patients in the Surveillance Epidemiology and End Results (SEER) dataset [HRE99]. The mean absolute error for the algorithm with a privacy budget of $\varepsilon = 1$ is no greater than 0.1 when the size of the dataset is 10000. They also demonstrate using the Komolgorov-Smirnov test that the differentially private curves are not statistically different. Again, by developing a custom DP algorithm based on the needs of survival analysis of medical data there isn't too much loss in utility.

9.3.2 Clinical Trials

Randomized control trials are the gold standard for testing new medications, vaccines, treatments and confirming findings in previous studies. After these trials are conducted, meta-analyses are conducted to determine actionable changes for practice and policy. Thus, there has been an effort to make the data from clinical trials more transparent. Currently, ClinicalTrials.gov [TWZ09; HC15] is the largest registry in the world containing data from more than 393 097 studies. At the core of analyzing this data is hypothesis testing. Scientists are interested in understanding for example whether a new cancer treatment A performs better than the existing cancer treatment B. One question that is often answered using clinical trials is an association between a disease and a drug [DDB11]. Many of these studies use contingency tables to represent the results of the trial, lending them to use the performing Pearson's χ^2 test to test independence. A concern with conducting these tests is the power of the test, partly determined by the sample size. Thus an important task for clinical trials is determining the necessary sample size for a specific amount of statistical power and confidence. An algorithm for determining the sample size with differential privacy was developed [VS09]. This algorithm is one of the only ones inspired by statistical tasks for analyzing clinical trial data. This is an important area of research in differentially private statistics and medical data.

Determining Sample Size

We start with the problem of proving that a drug is effective for treating a disease. Typically a certain confidence is required (e.g. $\alpha = 0.05$) for FDA approval. We setup a simple example from the study for when the outcome is binary (e.g. success or failure of a drug dosage in lowering blood pressure) [VS09]. We define our null hypothesis and alternative hypothesis below. For notation, the true sample size calculated without privacy is N while the sample size calculated with differential privacy is $\hat{N}$.

Consider a sample $x_1, x_2, ..., x_N \sim$ Bernoulli(p) and the test statistic of interest be the mean $\hat{\mu} = \frac{1}{N}\sum_{i=1}^{N} x_i$. Our hypothesis test is formulated as follows:

$$H_0 : \mu = \mu_0 \quad \text{v.s.} \quad H_a : \mu = \mu_0 + \delta,$$

where in our example $\hat{\mu}$ represents the proportion of people who responded to the drug treatment. To guarantee differential privacy, the study uses the the addition of Laplace noise $Z \sim L(\frac{\sqrt{2}}{\varepsilon N})$. The sampling distribution of $\hat{\mu}$ with this noise addition under the null hypothesis is approximated by $\mathcal{N}(\mu_0, \frac{\sigma^2}{N} + Z)$. Under the the alternate hypothesis it is approximated by $\mathcal{N}(\mu_0 + \delta, \frac{\sigma^2}{N} + Z)$. $\sigma^2 = \bar{\mu}(1 - \bar{\mu})$ where $\bar{\mu} = \mu_0 + \frac{\delta}{2}$. To calculate the true sample size N for confidence $1 - \alpha$ and power $1 - \beta$ the following equation must be solved:

$$\mu_0 + z_{1-\frac{\alpha}{2}}\sqrt{\frac{\sigma^2}{N} + \frac{2}{\varepsilon^2 N^2}} = \mu_0 + z_{1-\beta}\sqrt{\frac{\sigma^2}{N} + \frac{2}{\varepsilon^2 N^2}}, \tag{9.6}$$

which results in the following expression for the non-private sample size:

$$N = \frac{(z_{1-\frac{\alpha}{2}} + z_{1-\beta})^2 \sigma^2}{\delta^2}. \tag{9.7}$$

Using these two results, they derive the the expression for the private sample size N' is:

$$N' = N \cdot (\frac{1}{2} + \frac{1}{2}\sqrt{1 + \frac{8\delta^2}{\varepsilon^2 (z_{1-\frac{alpha}{2}} + z_{1-\beta})^2 \sigma^4}}). \tag{9.8}$$

Finally, to compute the exact sample size correction factor (i.e. the factor to multiply the true sample size to get the private sample size) numerical methods are used. Instead of noise from a Laplace distribution, the Normal Laplace is used such that: $X_1 \sim NL(\mu_0, \frac{\sigma^2}{N'}, \varepsilon N', \varepsilon N', 1)$ and $X_2 \sim NL(\mu_0 + \delta, \frac{\sigma^2}{N'}, \varepsilon N', \varepsilon N', 1)$. The exact private sample size N' is calculated by using a unique root-finder for the equation $F_{X_1}^{-1}(1-\frac{\alpha}{2}) = F_{X_2}^{-1}(1-\beta)$. The exact sample correction factor is found by $K = \frac{N'}{N}$. The authors evaluate the algorithm on synthetic tasks and for the Pearson χ^2 test of independence, demonstrating promising utility with the DP estimator. Further research should explore the utility of this method on real clinical trial data and the implications of using such a differentially private sample size calculation on the efficacy of trials.

9.3.3 Genomics

As biotechnology for genomic analysis has advanced, the utility of data analysis on genetic data has become incredibly apparent. Analysis of genomic data is broadly concerned with understanding the information contained in DNA and making predictions based on this data. Genomic data is important in advancing understanding of human disease and the underlying biological processes of these diseases. Given that genomic data is so unique to each individual any analysis of such data must provide strong privacy protections. Recent studies have shown the susceptibility of anonymized genomics data to reidentification [BHO20; AAC21; Goo09], suggesting a need for strong privacy protections. As discussed previously, the broad protections DP provides against any type of adversarial entity and auxiliary information make it well-suited for genomic data privacy. We present two examples of differentially private algorithms for the analysis of genomic data in two settings: looking up variants and genome-wide association studies.

Variant Lookup

In biomedicine, *beacons* are web services that scientists query for information about specific alleles. The development of beacons has been championed by The Beacon Project, an initiative from the Global Alliance for Genomics and health. Their goal is to enable better genomic and clinical data sharing. The queries posed by users of Beacons can be formulated as membership queries (discussed in Chapter 5). In this setting, scientists are interested in understanding if a variant of interest is included in a database. Both the exponential and the Laplace mechanism would suffice for these queries, but a mechanism with optimal privacy-utility tradeoffs based on the truncated geometric mechanism was developed [CSKB20]. We revisit the algorithm and problem setup described in Section 9.3.1. In this setting $c \in \{0, 1\}$ represents the true membership answer and $\hat{c}$ represents the membership answer returned from the truncated geometric mechanism. The user's prior belief over c is defined as $\pi(c)$.

The loss function in this setting is defined in Equation 9.9:

$$\ell(c, \hat{c}) = \begin{cases} \ell(c, 0) & \text{if } \hat{c} = 0, \\ \ell(c, 1) & \text{if } \hat{c} > 0 \end{cases}. \tag{9.9}$$

The post-processing step is formulated as the exact same optimization problem defined in Equation 9.3 which we restate below:

$$T(\hat{c}|\pi, \ell, \alpha, n) = \arg\min_{y} \sum_{x} q(c|\hat{c}; \pi, \alpha, n)\ell(c, \hat{c}). \tag{9.10}$$

This optimization problem is also solved using fast Fourier transform based convolution algorithms since c and $\hat{c}$ are discrete and the loss function for cohort identification is typically $\ell(c, \hat{c}) = (\hat{c} - c)$. The authors evaluated this algorithm on identifying the top variants of autism spectrum disorder (ASD) studied by [Vel+19] in the ClinVar database [Lan+20]. The mechanism was able to correctly answer 11 out of 17 membership queries at $\varepsilon = 0.2$. This is compared to the Laplace mechanism which produces comparable results and the exponential mechanism which produces much worse results. As expected, when the number of occurrences of the variant in the clinical database is larger the mechanism has a higher probability of answering correctly.

Genome-Wide Association Studies

Genome-wide association studies (GWAS) are used by scientists to capture associations between specific genetic markers and particular diseases [Uff+21]. These studies involve scanning the genomes of many different people to find genetic markers that are predictive of the presence of a disease. These findings are crucial to inform new prevention and treatment strategies. The cornerstone of these studies is performing statistical tests to measure the importance of a genetic marker for the presence of a disease. One of the challenges in performing differentially private GWAS is that the genome is extremely high dimensional. Thus the loss in utility incurred is high [USF13]. A promising algorithm called the neighbor method [JS13] was improved giving the current state of the art algorithm in identifying the top-k most significant genetic markers [SB16].

In GWAS, an allelic test statistic is used to test for associations between a genetic marker and disease status. Going forward we will refer to the genetic marker as a single nucleotide polymorphism (SNP). SNPs represent a variation at a single position in a DNA sequence for an individual. First, access to a case control cohort is assumed. For a given SNP, s_0, s_1 and s_2 are defined to be the number of individuals with 0, 1, or 2 copies of the minor allele in the control. We define r_0, r_1 and r_2 to be the same counts in the case cohort. Finally, n_0, n_1 and n_2 are the same quantities over the entire study population. R, N, S are the total number of case, study, and control participants. The allele test statistic used [SB16] is defined as:

$$Y(x, y) = \frac{2N(xS - yR)^2}{RS(x + y)(2N - x - y)}, \tag{9.11}$$

where $x = 2r_0 + r_1$ and $y = 2s_0 + s_1$.

The original neighbor method starts with a user defined threshold γ and selects all the SNPs where the allelic test statistic is higher than the threshold. To operationalize this, a notion of a neighbor distance is needed. For picking top k SNPs, the distance is defined as minimum number of individuals whose genotypes have to have be different for the SNP to be determined as significant. The algorithm uses this distance as presented in Algorithm 2. This distance works well for SNPs because it closely resembles the allele test statistic defined above. The major drawback of the original neighbor method is that the distance chosen sometimes gives different orderings than if we were to use the allelic test statistic.

To improve upon this issue, Next, we describe the improved neighbor method for picking the top k SNPs. The method starts with a user defined threshold γ. Significant SNPs are those with an allelic test statistic greater than this threshold (i.e. $Y(D)_i > \gamma$ where $Y(D)_i$ represents the allelic test statistic for the ith SNP in the study cohort D). Next a neighbor distance is defined as the minimum number of individuals whose genomes need to change in the database for SNP i to become significant. This translates to minimum Hamming distance. The neighbor method leverages the intuition that the test statistic and the neighbor distance are closely related. If the SNP has a strong association with the disease than it will take many more changes to make the allele not insignificant. We present the modified neighbor algorithm in Algorithm 1.

Algorithm 1 Neighbor Method for Picking Top k SNPs [SB16]

Require: Study D, number of SNPs to return k, privacy budgets ε_1 and ε_2
Ensure: List of k SNPs that is $\varepsilon_1 + \varepsilon_2$ differentially private
  Let γ be the mean score of the kth and $k+1$th highest scoring SNP.
  Let $\gamma_{private}$ be a private estimate of γ using the Laplacian mechanism and privacy budget ε_1
  Return list of SNPs from subroutine Algorithm 2 with privacy budget ε_2 and threshold value $\gamma_{private}$

Algorithm 1 runs in constant time the details of which can be found in [SB16]. The last step of the algorithm is to return the allelic test estimates for the chosen top k SNPs. Instead of using output perturbation, the authors use input perturbation before computing the test statistic which guarantees differential privacy via post-processing. The only difference in Equation 9.11 is that noise sampled from $Lap(\frac{2}{\varepsilon})$ is added to both x and y. This algorithm is evaluated on a rheumatoid arthritis dataset, NARAC-1 [Ple+07]. The dataset contains 893 cases and 1244 controls, with a total of 62 441 SNPs. The method performs significantly better than the traditional Laplacian mechanism in terms of accuracy (i.e. percentage of SNPs correctly identified). When $k = 3, \varepsilon = 0.5$ the accuracy of the method is 80%. For a larger number of SNPs (i.e. $k = 15$), the method achieves 80% accuracy at $\varepsilon = 5.0$.

In this section, we presented custom differentially private algorithms for common types of statistical analyses in medicine. This included: cohort identification, survival analyses, determining sample size for clinical trials, variant lookup, and performing genome-wide association studies. We discuss how the utility of standard differentially private algorithms can be improved significantly by incorporating medical domain knowledge into the algorithm design. This is a common theme throughout applying differential privacy to medical data analysis. An important and upcoming area of research is developing differentially private algorithms to analyze data generated from wearable devices. Analyzing this type of data is becoming an important part of understanding human health with lots of opportunities for interesting DP algorithm development beyond what has initially been done [KJY18; Lin+16; Wu+20; Ren+16; Sal+16; UJM19].

Algorithm 2 Subroutine for Picking Top k SNPs [JS13]

Require: Study D, number of SNPs to return k, privacy budgets ε, threshold γ
Ensure: List of k SNPs that is ε differentially private
  for i = 0, ..., m **do**
    if $Y(D)_i > \gamma$ **then**
      $d_i = \min_{D'}(\{|D - D'| : Y(D')_i < \gamma, |D'| = |D|\})$
    else
      $d_i = 1 - \min_{D'}(\{|D - D'| : Y(D')_i > \gamma, |D'| = |D|\})$
    end if
  end for
  $\gamma_i = \exp(\frac{\varepsilon}{2k}d)_i$ for all i
  Without replacement, choose k SNPs where $Pr(\text{SNP}_i) \propto \gamma_i$
  Return the list of chosen SNPs

Many of the problems we discussed in this section are focused on membership in a database or counting the number of events in a database. Recently, there has been surging interest in developing diagnostic and prognostic models for different diseases or adverse events. This is motivated by the broad use of electronic health records and rapid success in developing high performing machine learning models for different modalities (i.e. time series, images, and natural language). The algorithms presented above are not designed for making predictions about disease presence or risk of developing a disease from labs, vitals, images, and clinical notes. Thus, we need to use more complex algorithms from machine learning to support creating models for diagnosis and risk prediction. In the next section, we discuss the application of DP to machine learning for medical data.

9.4 Machine Learning

Machine learning has demonstrated great potential to learn clinically relevant patterns from medical data across a wide variety of tasks. These tasks include disease / acuity prediction (e.g. mortality, breast cancer, kidney failure) [Tom+19; Gul+16; Wu+19; Raj+18; Gha+15], improvements to hospital operations (length of stay) [Wan+19], drug response prediction [Ram+19; Kue+20], and tumor segmentations [Hav+17; Koh+18]. However, as discussed in Chapter 5, machine learning models are susceptible to privacy attacks such as membership inference and attribute inference [JRY21]. The potential for these attacks to occur is especially concerning when analyzing medical data. Without the use of differential privacy, sensitive health information such as HIV status of patients included in training data may be leaked. In this section, we will review different applications of differentially private machine learning (discussed in Chapters 7 and 8) for analyzing medical data. We will focus on: prediction and generating synthetic data.

9.4.1 Prediction

There have been various applications of DP machine learning and deep learning to different types of medical data such as: electronic health records, medical images, and genomics data. This subsection will focus on differentially private prediction in the central setting.

Electronic Health Records

A follow up study [SPGG21], examined the impact of applying DP machine learning to these prediction tasks. To train these models with differential privacy, the study uses differentially private stochastic gradient descent (DP-SGD) . The main changes to standard SGD are the addition of clipping individual gradients and adding Gaussian noise to these gradients. Further details are presented in Chapter 7. They demonstrate for tasks such as mortality where only 7% of patients passed away for both linear models and deep learning the drop in area under the curve (AUC) is quite high (22% and 26% respectively) for privacy budget $\varepsilon = 3.54, \delta = 10^{-5}$. These drops in utility are too high for the models to be useful in practice. This work demonstrates the need for more research on DP machine learning for high-dimensional multivariate time series medical data.

Another important prediction task from EHR data is 30-day readmission. Differentially private deep learning was applied to this prediction task [Cho+18] showing more promise for differentially private deep learning than the previous study. The authors use a dataset [Str+14] from the UCI Machine Learning Respository that contains 101 000 medical records over 10 years with information such as demographics, potential risk factors such as diabetes, and the readmission label. The major difference between this dataset and the one in the previous study is that it is larger and lower dimensional. Both of these factors are important for reducing the utility loss from private training. The model trained is a small neural network with one hidden layer of size 32 and one output layer. They fix the privacy parameters as $\varepsilon = 1.0$ and $\delta = 10^{-5}$. The non-private model gives an AUC of 0.67 while the private one gives an AUC of 0.63. This is a much more reasonable drop in utility. Thus, algorithms such as DP-SGD are showing promise on predicting important tasks from electronic health record data when the dataset is larger and lower dimensional. This is expected given the known tradeoffs between utility and data dimension for DP-SGD.

These are the two main studies that have applied differentially private machine learning and deep learning to prediction from EHR data. Both studies show the settings that DP-SGD is currently performing well and ones where more work is necessary. This is an active area of research that we hope readers will take an interest in.

Imaging

Next, we focus on applications of differentially private deep learning for disease prediction from medical images such as chest x-rays, magnetic resonance images (MRIs) and computed tomography (CTs) images. Similar to EHR data there are a limited number of studies on the application of current methods. Chest x-rays are often used by radiologists to diagnose issues such as pneumonia, collapsed lungs, pleural effusion, and the presence of tumors in the chest cavity and lungs. Pretrained DenseNet-121 models finetuned on chest x-ray datasets have shown promise in multi-label disease prediction achieving an AUC of 0.86 [SLMG20]. Following a similar procedure using differentially private fine-tuning, extreme drops in utility were observed (AUC = 0.50) at all privacy levels [SPGG21]. The authors cite the large dimensionality of the model and the long tailedness of the label distribution as reasons for such a large drop in utility. Work towards making the error DP learning algorithms independent of dimensionality will surely help improve the utility of DP deep learning models for medical imaging. This seems quite difficult in full generality but there have been several works [MMZ22; ZWB20; KDRT21] that have proven dimension independence or near dimension independence. This is essential for medical data broadly due to its high dimensionality across different modalities such as multivariate time series, images, and genomics.

Another study showed great success in predicting pneumonia from chest x-rays and semantic segmentation of liver CT [Zil+21]. The chest x-ray dataset used is from the Pediatric Pneumonia dataset [Ker+18] which contains 5232 images. 3883 of these images depicted pneumonia while the other 1349 were normal. The entire dataset was split into 85% for training and 15% for testing. Given the class imbalance the loss was reweighted as $w_i = \frac{c_i}{n_i}$ where i represents the class and n_i represents the total dataset size and c_i represents the number of samples of class i. The authors trained a VGG-11 [SZ14] model on images of size 224 × 224. The Gaussian Differential Privacy (GDP) accountant [BDLS20] was used for privacy accounting which differs from the Renyi DP Accountant [Aba+16; MTZ19] that is typically used. Their results show a modest drop in AUC of 11.2% at a privacy budget of $\varepsilon = 0.52$.

For semantic segmentation, they use the Medical Segmentation Decathlon Liver Segmentation Dataset [Sim+19]. The prediction task of importance is tumor segmentation which is incredibly important for treatment planning in oncology. The dataset consisted of 5184 training samples. A U-Net using VGG-11 was trained for this semantic segmentation task. This task was evaluated using the dice score which measures the similarity between the predicted segmentation map and the ground-truth segmentation (performed by radiologists). For $\varepsilon = 0.35$ they find that the drop in the dice score between the private and non-private model is minimal at 0.007. Both of these results show a lot of promise in applying differentially private deep learning to medical image segmentation.

Finally, we discuss an application of DP-SGD to a well-studied medical imaging deep learning problem which is prediction of diabetic retinopathy from fundus photography [SSKT20]. The authors study the privacy-utility tradeoffs of training residual networks with DP-SGD on this task. The dataset used is the APTOS 2019 Blindness Detection Dataset [KMD19] which contains 3600 training images which are labeled on a scale from 0 to 4 where 0 is no diabetic retinopathy and 4 is proliferative diabetic retinopathy (i.e severe disease). The models that were trained are pretrained 18 layer residual networks that were finetuned on the fundus images. This study notes similar drops in performance seen in [SPGG21] where the accuracy of models are around 50% or below. Thus differential privacy results in the models no longer being useful. The differences in these results are a direct product of issues such as dimensionality which are fundamental technical challenges that the differential privacy research community is addressing currently.

Genomics

Personalization of drug recommendations is important because individuals often have very different reactions to the same drug. Gene expression data has become an important source of data for predicting personalized drug sensitivity. The application of differentially private machine learning to this task has been studied in two related studies on drug sensitivity prediction [NHHK19; Hon+18]. This is the main example of DP machine learning applied to genomic data in the current literature. The authors focus on DREAM-NCI drug sensitivity prediction challenge [Cos+14]. This challenge focuses on identifying the best treatments based on genomic data for breast cancer cell lines. After pre-processing the gene expression data the dimensionality of the data is reduced to $d = 64$. The non-private algorithm for predicting drug sensitivity on this task is Bayesian linear regression. This study produces a differentially private version of Bayesian linear regression which experiences only modest drops of about 2–4% in accuracy from the non-private model.

9.4.2 Data Synthesis and Sharing

Making medical data publicly available is vital to advancing medical discoveries, helping improve transparency in medical research, and to making the research community more inclusive. Publicly releasing medical data while maintaining patient privacy is incredibly difficult. In Section 9.2, we discussed failures of publicly releasing medical data. An upcoming area of research for being able to publicly release medical data is differentially private data synthesis. This area of research has become especially promising due to the large amount of positive results from deep generative models such as diffusion models, GANs, and VAEs. In this section, we will discuss some of the recent successes in synthesizing medical data with differential privacy, some of the failures in doing so, and what the ongoing challenges are.

One recent success has been in simulating patients from the SPRINT (Systolic Blood Pressure Trial) Data Analysis Change held by the *New England Journal of Medicine* [BM17]. The SPRINT clinical trial examined the effect of intensive lowering of systolic blood pressure (< 120 mmHg) instead of aiming for a standard systolic blood pressure (< 140 mmHg). Researchers used this tabular data of 6000 patients to train an auxiliary classifier GAN (AC-GAN) with differential privacy to generate synthetic data similar to the original SPRINT data [Bea+19]. They compare the synthetic data generated with and without privacy guarantees quantitatively and qualitatively. The quantitative evaluation examined variable correlation structure and whether models trained on the synthetic achieved similar performance. The qualitative evaluation consisted of visualizing blood pressure trajectories and having clinicians attempt to differentiate between real and synthetic data. The visual inspection of the blood pressure trajectories showed very minimal differences for both intensive and standard patients between the private and non-private synthetic data. The accuracy of the four different models (logistic regression, random forest, nearest neighbors, and SVMs) dropped slightly more than 10% in the worst scenario. This is only a modest drop performance for differential privacy signalling that the private synthetic data still maintains a large amount of utility. It should be noted that the success of this study is promising but limited since the dataset was much simpler and lower dimensional than what we see in other domains such as medical imaging and genomics. In these higher dimensional settings, DP synthetic data generation is much more difficult. One key contribution of this study is a set of guidelines for evaluating the utility of private synthetic medical data. We summarize the guidelines below:

Quantitative

- Measure how similar the variable correlations are between the real data and the the private synthetic data

- Measure the performance of a classifier trained on the private synthetic data vs trained on real data and tested on real data
- Measure whether features have the same importance level between the classifiers trained on real and private synthetic data

Qualitative

- Visualize differences between real and private synthetic data (method will depend on data type)
- Have clinical experts attempt to differentiate between real and private synthetic data samples

Another study focused on generating synthetic EHR data (i.e. high dimensional multivariate time series) using dual adversarial autoencoders [Lee+20]. This study used the MIMIC-III [Joh+16] and the UT Physicians Clinical databases. The dual adversarial autoencoder (DAAE) contains three components: a sequence-to-sequence autoencoder (seq2seq AE), an inner GAN, and an outer GAN. The seq2seq AE is responsible for learning the latent space the encodes semantic features of target sequences and the temporal dynamics of these sequences. The inner GAN aims to match the learned space and the outer GAN aims to distinguish the real samples from the ones generated using the seq2seq AE. All of these different model components are trained using DP-SGD to guarantee differential privacy. The two evaluation components similar to the ones described above are evaluating the performance of models trained on the real vs synthetic data and having clinicians evaluate the plausibility of the synthetic sequences. The prediction task of interest is predicting top-k diagnosis codes. On this task the DAAE method is only marginally worse (0.1 on average) than the model trained on the real data across recall and precision at 10,20,30 on the MIMIC-III dataset. This study shows promise for training accurate prediction models on DP synthetic data for this specific task. It is unclear from the study though whether correlations in the original data are maintained and if feature importance remained consistent. Both of these are important evaluations for understanding if this method can be of use more broadly for other datasets and tasks.

Finally, we discuss an area where more research is needed to realize the potential of differentially private synthetic medical data which is medical images. Generating high quality synthetic medical images such as chest x-rays or dermatological images (e.g. pictures of skin lesions) has proven to be incredibly difficult [Che+21]. In this study, deep convolutional GANs trained with DP-SGD generate images of both quantitative and qualitative quality. Additionally, the classifiers trained on these images face significant drops in utility. This study demonstrates the additional work needed from the differential privacy community to demonstrate the promise of private synthetic medical images.

9.5 Federated Learning

The majority of medical data remains in private silos around the world. This inhibits the advancement of health research and the potential for developing high utility predictive models. Privacy is the paramount concern when sharing data across hospitals in an attempt to learn a predictive model that is better than each hospital using their individual data. Federated learning, is a technique that learns a central model and series of local models that keeps data in each of their respective silos. The technique alone is not private, requiring differentially private versions of FL algorithms (further details in Chapter 8) to protect privacy of the data even though it does not leave the silos. Here we discuss a couple of applications of DP federated learning to common medical machine learning tasks.

Similar to the work in the centralized setting [SPGG21], another study analyzed the efficacy of predicting prolonged length of stay and in hospital mortality from electronic records using DP federated learning [PDH19]. This study used the eICU database which contains EHR data from 52 different hospitals across the U.S. For both prolonged length of stay and mortality prediction DP federated averaging performs quite poorly unfortunately, especially in the class imbalanced mortality tasks. Many of the AUC values for each local hospital are below 0.5 at reasonable privacy budgets such as $\varepsilon < 10$. While these results are discouraging especially given the high number of hospitals in the dataset, other studies have shown more promise. It is unclear from this study what the different sources of utility loss were. For example, heterogeneity between the different hospitals may be a significant issue that leads to large utility loss for applying DP FL to larger cohorts of hospitals.

Another study developed a variant of DP-SGD that incorporates cyclical weight transfer to train neural networks with differential privacy in a distributed setting [BYFW18]. The algorithm used in this study differed from the traditional DP FL algorithm used in the prior study by using cyclical weight transfer. This means that the central weights are transferred to each institution after the aggregation of local steps. This study also focused on in hospital mortality for the eICU dataset and on classifying two different subtypes of breast cancer from gene expression data found in The Cancer Genome Atlas (TCGA) [Can+13]. At a privacy budget of $\varepsilon = 3.84$ and $\delta = 10^{-5}$ the drop in AUC between the non-private and private distributed model was 0.9% when the number of collaborating institutions was 5 and was a drop of 6% when only two institutions were collaborating. This is promising as it incentivizes more institutions to collaborate since it will help improve the utility at a specific privacy budget for all. For the subtype prediction task, for a privacy budget of $\varepsilon = 6.11$ and $\delta = 10^{-5}$ the drop in AUC went from 0.7% to 1.7% when going from one to three sites collaborating. The success suggests that cyclical weight transfer may be promising for reducing utility loss in DP FL. Although, it is hard to compare the two studies because of the differences in scale. The first study we discussed was across 52 different hospitals whereas this second study was across 5 at most. As mentioned previously, as the heterogeneity increases due to larger cohorts it might be that it is much more difficult to prevent drops in utility even for algorithms that use cyclical weight transfer.

Finally, we summarize an extensive study demonstrating the effectiveness of differentially private federated averaging at the individual patient level and at the hospital level [Sad+21]. They choose both logistic regression and neural networks across a variety of tasks including: survival prediction from heart failure, diabetes prediction, mortality prediction, SARS-CoV-2 positivity prediction, and adverse event prediction in individuals treated with Azithromycin. Across these tasks they demonstrate minimal drops in performance when using DP-FedAvg but that this also outperforms its centralized counterpart. Applications of differentially private federated learning to medical data are a new and active area of research that has the opportunity to help change the way hospitals collaborate around the world. There are still open problems to be addressed before wide-scale use such as large heterogeneity amongst hospitals.

In the previous two sections, we provided case studies on the successes and failures of differentially private machine learning and federated learning applied to medical data analysis. These studies provide guidance on fruitful technical directions for researchers to help make these technologies more widely applicable. Differentially private machine learning has the potential to help advance health research by making public sharing of data and models safer and easier. As discussed at the beginning of this chapter, anonymization for data release are susceptible to attacks. Currently, model sharing / publishing is rare due to privacy concerns. We end this chapter by outlining some of the challenges not yet mentioned and opportunities for helping realize differentially private statistics and machine learning into practice for medical data analysis.

9.6 Considerations for Deployment in Medicine

All of the case studies that we presented have been done in research settings. There has yet to be a large-scale deployment of differential privacy in a medical setting.

Here we discuss some of the hesitations that exist and areas of research that may be fruitful to help support the first large-scale deployment of DP for medical data analysis.

9.6.1 Health Inequities

There are many inequities in the healthcare system that have resulted in marginalized communities such as women and Black individuals receiving poor quality of care. Examples of this include: women suffering higher mortality rates from heart attacks [GCH18], Black patients receiving worse care for kidney disease [VEJ20], and Black women being 3× more likely to die during pregnancy than white women [Cre+14]. While medical machine learning is showing promise it is important for it to not exacerbate existing inequities. It could even potentially help be part of existing efforts to remove these inequities [CSG19]. Currently, differential privacy has a negative impact on fairness in medical machine learning [SPGG21]. There are potential solutions that may help alleviate these tradeoffs such as using publicly available data during differentially private training.

9.6.2 Robustness to Distribution Shift

Another important consideration especially for differentially private machine learning is the non-stationarity of medical data. Often times the underlying data distribution is changing due to different populations over time, policy changes, and new treatment recommendations. This means that the data distribution a model was trained on will differ from the test distribution. If models are not robust to distributional shifts then they will silently fail when deployed in practice [Nes+19; SSS18]. While it is well understood that differential privacy provides out-of-sample generalization, the connection to distributional robustness is not well understood. An initial study [Kul+] has proven that differential privacy guarantees distributional robustness but empirical understanding is still limited. Research which empirically explores the current impact of differential privacy on distributional robustness and develops algorithms to maintain both will be important for deploying differentially private machine learning in medical settings.

9.6.3 Education, Audits, and Policy

An incredibly important and underresearched topic in helping deploy differential privacy for medical data analysis is education and policy. Many individuals such as IT professionals, legal experts, data analysts, bioethicists, doctors, nurses, and patients do not know what differential privacy really means and what they should expect from it. For many individuals it is unclear what are the exact privacy protections that differential privacy does and does not provide for their medical data. This is incredibly important as misinterpretations of these protections can undermine the need for differential privacy over the current standard of anonymization. Data analysts are unsure of how implementing differential privacy would impact their current workflow for performing research and interacting with medical data. Legal and policy experts are unsure of what an acceptable level for the privacy budget ε is and what this means for the probability of an attack being successful. This leads to broader questions in medical data analysis which are also important in other contexts of how should one tradeoff between utility and a smaller privacy budget? Studies to understand the gap between expectations of differential privacy and the realities in medicine are needed similar to this [CKR21]. Research auditing differentially private statistics and machine learning [JUO20; Kif+20] is vital to providing legal and policy experts in medicine better understanding of the technology.

9.7 Concluding Remarks

In this chapter, we presented a broad overview of differentially private statistics and machine learning applied to medical data analysis. We discussed the need for differential privacy as the new gold standard for privacy in medicine. This was highlighted by the overwhelming amount of privacy breaches and re-identification of anonymized data that has occurred. We presented a series of case studies on differentially private statistical analyses applied to medical data. These case studies demonstrated that often times custom algorithms are needed for medical data analysis to achieve reasonable privacy-utility tradeoffs. These case studies covered important statistical tasks including cohort identification, survival analysis, variant lookup, and GWAS. We then examined applications of differentially private machine learning and deep learning to prediction and data synthesis. Given the global scale of medical research we discussed the promise of differentially private distributed learning for learning higher utility models and allowing hospitals to share data without comprising privacy. Finally, we discuss important research directions and issues to address for supporting large scale deployments of differential privacy for medical data analysis. As research progresses and more interdisciplinary work with the healthcare system takes place, deployments will start to occur, helping to provide better privacy protections for patient data.

References

[AAC21] K. Ayoz, E. Ayday, and A. E. Cicek. “Genome reconstruction attacks against genomic data-sharing beacons”. In: Proceedings on Privacy Enhancing Technologies. Privacy Enhancing Technologies Symposium. Vol. 2021. 3. NIH Public Access. 2021, p. 28 (cit. on p. 328).

[Aba+16] M. Abadi, A. Chu, I. Goodfellow, H. B. McMahan, I. Mironov, K. Talwar, and L. Zhang. “Deep Learning with Differential Privacy”. In: Proceedings of the 2016 ACM SIGSAC Conference on Computer and Communications Security. CCS ’16. Vienna, Austria: ACM, 2016, pp. 308–318 (cit. on p. 333).

[Act96] A. Act. “Health insurance portability and accountability act of 1996”. In: Public law 104 (1996), p. 191 (cit. on p. 319).

[Ald21] S. Alder. Healthcare Data Breach Statistics. en. https://www.hipaajournal.com/healthcare-data-breach-statistics/. Accessed: 2021-10-23. Jan. 2021 (cit. on p. 320).

[BB72] R. E. Barlow and H. D. Brunk. “The isotonic regression problem and its dual”. In: Journal of the American Statistical Association 67.337 (1972), pp. 140–147 (cit. on p. 325).

[BDLS20] Z. Bu, J. Dong, Q. Long, and W. J. Su. “Deep learning with Gaussian differential privacy”. In: Harvard data science review 2020.23 (2020) (cit. on p. 333).

[Bea+19] B. K. Beaulieu-Jones, Z. S. Wu, C. Williams, R. Lee, S. P. Bhavnani, J. B. Byrd, and C. S. Greene. “Privacy-preserving generative deep neural networks support clinical data sharing”. In: Circulation: Cardiovascular Quality and Outcomes 12.7 (2019), e005122 (cit. on p. 335).

[BHO20] L. Bonomi, Y. Huang, and L. Ohno-Machado. “Privacy challenges and research opportunities for genomic data sharing”. In: Nature genetics 52.7 (2020), pp. 646–654 (cit. on p. 328).

[BJO20] L. Bonomi, X. Jiang, and L. Ohno-Machado. “Protecting patient privacy in survival analyses”. In: Journal of the American Medical Informatics Association 27.3 (2020), pp. 366–375 (cit. on p. 324).

[BM17] N. S. Burns and P. W. Miller. “Learning what we didn’t know—the SPRINT data analysis challenge”. In: New England Journal of Medicine 376.23 (2017), pp. 2205–2207 (cit. on p. 335).

[BYFW18] B. K. Beaulieu-Jones, W. Yuan, S. G. Finlayson, and Z. S. Wu. "Privacy-preserving distributed deep learning for clinical data". In: arXiv preprint arXiv:1812.01484 (2018) (cit. on p. 337).

[Can+13] Cancer Genome Atlas Research Network, J. N. Weinstein, E. A. Collisson, G. B. Mills, K. R. M. Shaw, B. A. Ozenberger, K. Ellrott, I. Shmulevich, C. Sander, and J. M. Stuart. "The Cancer Genome Atlas Pan-Cancer analysis project". en. In: Nat. Genet. 45.10 (Oct. 2013), pp. 1113–1120 (cit. on p. 337).

[Che+21] V. Cheng, V. M. Suriyakumar, N. Dullerud, S. Joshi, and M. Ghassemi. "Can You Fake It Until You Make It? Impacts of Differentially Private Synthetic Data on Downstream Classification Fairness". In: Proceedings of the 2021 ACM Conference on Fairness, Accountability, and Transparency. 2021, pp. 149–160 (cit. on p. 336).

[Cho+18] E. Chou, T. Nguyen, J. Beal, A. Haque, and L. Fei-Fei. "A fully private pipeline for deep learning on electronic health records". In: arXiv preprint arXiv:1811.09951 (2018) (cit. on p. 332).

[CKR21] R. Cummings, G. Kaptchuk, and E. M. Redmiles. "" I need a better description": An Investigation Into User Expectations For Differential Privacy". In: arXiv preprint arXiv:2110.06452 (2021) (cit. on p. 340).

[Com18] E. Commission. 2018 reform of EU data protection rules. May 25, 2018. URL: https://ec.europa.eu/commission/sites/beta-political/files/data-protection-factsheet-changes_en.pdf (visited on 06/17/2019) (cit. on p. 319).

[Cos+14] J. C. Costello, L. M. Heiser, E. Georgii, M. Gönen, M. P. Menden, N. J. Wang, M. Bansal, P. Hintsanen, S. A. Khan, J.-P. Mpindi, et al. "A community effort to assess and improve drug sensitivity prediction algorithms". In: Nature biotechnology 32.12 (2014), pp. 1202–1212 (cit. on p. 334).

[Cre+14] A. A. Creanga, C. J. Berg, J. Y. Ko, S. L. Farr, V. T. Tong, F. C. Bruce, and W. M. Callaghan. "Maternal mortality and morbidity in the United States: where are we now?" In: Journal of women's health 23.1 (2014), pp. 3–9 (cit. on p. 339).

[CRT17] C. Culnane, B. I. P. Rubinstein, and V. Teague. "Health Data in an Open World". In: (Dec. 2017). arXiv: 1712.05627 [cs.CY] (cit. on p. 321).

[CSG19] I. Y. Chen, P. Szolovits, and M. Ghassemi. "Can AI Help Reduce Disparities in General Medical and Mental Health Care?" In: AMA Journal of Ethics 21.2 (2019), pp. 167–179 (cit. on pp. 317, 339).

[CSKB20] H. Cho, S. Simmons, R. Kim, and B. Berger. "Privacy-preserving biomedical database queries with optimal privacy-utility trade-offs". In: Cell systems 10.5 (2020), pp. 408–416 (cit. on pp. 323, 328).

[CSS11] T.-H. H. Chan, E. Shi, and D. Song. "Private and continual release of statistics". In: ACM Transactions on Information and System Security (TISSEC) 14.3 (2011), pp. 1–24 (cit. on p. 325).

[DCLT18] J. Devlin, M.-W. Chang, K. Lee, and K. Toutanova. "BERT: Pre-training of Deep Bidirectional Transformers for Language Understanding". In: arXiv:1810.04805 [cs] (2018). arXiv: 1810.04805. URL: http://arxiv.org/abs/1810.04805 (visited on 05/22/2019) (cit. on p. 321).

[DDB11] J. T. Dudley, T. Deshpande, and A. J. Butte. "Exploiting drug–disease relationships for computational drug repositioning". In: Briefings in bioinformatics 12.4 (2011), pp. 303–311 (cit. on p. 326).

[DNPR10] C. Dwork, M. Naor, T. Pitassi, and G. N. Rothblum. "Differential privacy under continual observation". In: Proceedings of the forty-second ACM symposium on Theory of computing. 2010, pp. 715–724 (cit. on p. 325).

[GCH18] B. N. Greenwood, S. Carnahan, and L. Huang. "Patient–physician gender concordance and increased mortality among female heart attack patients". In: Proceedings of the National Academy of Sciences 115.34 (2018), pp. 8569–8574 (cit. on p. 339).

[Gha+15] M. Ghassemi, M. A. F. Pimentel, T. Naumann, T. Brennan, D. A. Clifton, P. Szolovits, and M. Feng. "A Multivariate Timeseries Modeling Approach to Severity of Illness Assessment and Forecasting in ICU with Sparse, Heterogeneous Clinical Data". en. In: Twenty-Ninth AAAI Conference on Artificial Intelligence. Feb. 2015. URL: https://www.aaai.org/ocs/index.php/AAAI/AAAI15/paper/view/9393 (visited on 05/21/2019) (cit. on p. 331).

[Gha+17] M. Ghassemi, M. Wu, M. C. Hughes, P. Szolovits, and F. Doshi-Velez. "Predicting intervention onset in the ICU with switching state space models". In: AMIA Summits on Translational Science Proceedings 2017 (2017), p. 82 (cit. on p. 317).

[GKN21] N. Gandhi, S. Kapoor, and S. Nailwal. At a glance: data protection and management of health data in India. https://www.lexology.com/library/detail.aspx?g=0fdcef36-61a8-4e00-9bed-8abcf6866c96. Accessed: 2021-10-23. Jan. 2021 (cit. on p. 320).

[Goo09] M. T. Goodrich. "The mastermind attack on genomic data". In: 2009 30th IEEE Symposium on Security and Privacy. IEEE. 2009, pp. 204–218 (cit. on p. 328).

[GRS12] A. Ghosh, T. Roughgarden, and M. Sundararajan. "Universally utility-maximizing privacy mechanisms". In: SIAM Journal on Computing 41.6 (2012), pp. 1673–1693 (cit. on p. 323).

[Gul+16] V. Gulshan, L. Peng, M. Coram, M. C. Stumpe, D. Wu, A. Narayanaswamy, S. Venugopalan, K. Widner, T. Madams, J. Cuadros, R. Kim, R. Raman, P. C. Nelson, J. L. Mega, and D. R. Webster. "Development and Validation of a Deep Learning Algorithm for Detection of Diabetic Retinopathy in Retinal Fundus Photographs". en. In: JAMA 316.22 (2016), pp. 2402–2410 (cit. on p. 331).

[Hav+17] M. Havaei, A. Davy, D. Warde-Farley, A. Biard, A. Courville, Y. Bengio, C. Pal, P.-M. Jodoin, and H. Larochelle. "Brain tumor segmentation with deep neural networks". In: Medical image analysis 35 (2017), pp. 18–31 (cit. on p. 331).

[HC15] K. L. Hudson and F. S. Collins. "Sharing and reporting the results of clinical trials". In: Jama 313.4 (2015), pp. 355–356 (cit. on p. 326).

[Hon+18] A. Honkela, M. Das, A. Nieminen, O. Dikmen, and S. Kaski. "Efficient differentially private learning improves drug sensitivity prediction". In: Biology direct 13.1 (2018), pp. 1–12 (cit. on pp. 317, 334).

[Hor21] J. Horwitz. "China passes new personal data privacy law, to take effect Nov. 1". In: Reuters (Aug. 2021) (cit. on p. 319).

[HRE99] B. F. Hankey, L. A. Ries, and B. K. Edwards. "The surveillance, epidemiology, and end results program: a national resource". In: Cancer Epidemiology and Prevention Biomarkers 8.12 (1999), pp. 1117–1121 (cit. on p. 325).

[HRMS09] M. Hay, V. Rastogi, G. Miklau, and D. Suciu. "Boosting the accuracy of differentially-private histograms through consistency". In: arXiv preprint arXiv:0904.0942 (2009) (cit. on p. 325).

[Joh+16] A. E. W. Johnson, T. J. Pollard, L. Shen, L.-w. H. Lehman, M. Feng, M. Ghassemi, B. Moody, P. Szolovits, L. A. Celi, and R. G. Mark. "MIMIC-III, a freely accessible critical care database". en. In: Scientific Data 3.1 (May 2016), pp. 1–9. ISSN: 2052-4463. URL: https://www.nature.com/articles/sdata201635 (visited on 11/04/2019) (cit. on p. 336).

[JRY21] A. Jagannatha, B. P. S. Rawat, and H. Yu. "Membership Inference Attack Susceptibility of Clinical Language Models". In: arXiv preprint arXiv:2104.08305 (2021) (cit. on pp. 321, 332).

[JS13] A. Johnson and V. Shmatikov. "Privacy-preserving data exploration in genome-wide association studies". In: Proceedings of the 19th ACM SIGKDD international conference on Knowledge discovery and data mining. 2013, pp. 1079–1087 (cit. on pp. 329, 331).

[JUO20] M. Jagielski, J. Ullman, and A. Oprea. "Auditing differentially private machine learning: How private is private sgd?" In: arXiv preprint arXiv:2006.07709 (2020) (cit. on p. 340).

[KDRT21] P. Kairouz, M. R. Diaz, K. Rush, and A. Thakurta. "(Nearly) Dimension Independent Private ERM with AdaGrad Rates via Publicly Estimated Subspaces". In: Conference on Learning Theory. PMLR. 2021, pp. 2717–2746 (cit. on p. 333).

[Ker+18] D. S. Kermany, M. Goldbaum, W. Cai, C. C. Valentim, H. Liang, S. L. Baxter, A. McKeown, G. Yang, X. Wu, F. Yan, et al. "Identifying medical diagnoses and treatable diseases by image-based deep learning". In: Cell 172.5 (2018), pp. 1122–1131 (cit. on p. 333).

[Kif+20] D. Kifer, S. Messing, A. Roth, A. Thakurta, and D. Zhang. "Guidelines for implementing and auditing differentially private systems". In: arXiv preprint arXiv:2002.04049 (2020) (cit. on p. 340).

[KJY18] J. W. Kim, B. Jang, and H. Yoo. "Privacy-preserving aggregation of personal health data streams". In: PloS one 13.11 (2018), e0207639 (cit. on p. 331).

[KMD19] Karthik, Maggie, and S. Dane. APTOS 2019 Blindness Detection. https://kaggle.com/competitions/aptos2019-blindness-detection. Kaggle. 2019 (cit. on p. 334).

[Koh+18] S. A. Kohl, B. Romera-Paredes, C. Meyer, J. De Fauw, J. R. Ledsam, K. H. Maier-Hein, S. Eslami, D. J. Rezende, and O. Ronneberger. "A probabilistic u-net for segmentation of ambiguous images". In: arXiv preprint arXiv:1806.05034 (2018) (cit. on p. 331).

[Kue+20] B. M. Kuenzi, J. Park, S. H. Fong, K. S. Sanchez, J. Lee, J. F. Kreisberg, J. Ma, and T. Ideker. "Predicting drug response and synergy using a deep learning model of human cancer cells". In: Cancer cell 38.5 (2020), pp. 672–684 (cit. on p. 331).

[Kul+] B. Kulynych, Y.-Y. Yang, Y. Yu, J. Błasiok, and P. Nakkiran. "What you see is what you get: Distributional generalization for algorithm design in deep learning". In: () (cit. on p. 339).

[Kul+16] I. J. Kullo, H. Jouni, E. E. Austin, S.-A. Brown, T. M. Kruisselbrink, I. N. Isseh, R. A. Haddad, T. S. Marroush, K. Shameer, J. E. Olson, et al. "Incorporating a genetic risk score into coronary heart disease risk estimates: effect on low-density lipoprotein cholesterol levels (the MI-GENES clinical trial)". In: Circulation 133.12 (2016), pp. 1181–1188 (cit. on p. 324).

[Lan+20] M. J. Landrum, S. Chitipiralla, G. R. Brown, C. Chen, B. Gu, J. Hart, D. Hoffman, W. Jang, K. Kaur, C. Liu, et al. "ClinVar: improvements to accessing data". In: Nucleic acids research 48.D1 (2020), pp. D835–D844 (cit. on p. 328).

[Lee+20] D. Lee, H. Yu, X. Jiang, D. Rogith, M. Gudala, M. Tejani, Q. Zhang, and L. Xiong. "Generating sequential electronic health records using dual adversarial autoencoder". In: Journal of the American Medical Informatics Association 27.9 (2020), pp. 1411–1419 (cit. on p. 336).

[Lin+16] C. Lin, Z. Song, H. Song, Y. Zhou, Y. Wang, and G. Wu. "Differential privacy preserving in big data analytics for connected health". In: Journal of medical systems 40.4 (2016), p. 97 (cit. on p. 331).

[MMZ22] Y.-A. Ma, T. V. Marinov, and T. Zhang. "Dimension independent generalization of dp-sgd for overparameterized smooth convex optimization". In: arXiv preprint arXiv:2206.01836 (2022) (cit. on p. 333).

[Mob+18] P. Mobadersany, S. Yousefi, M. Amgad, D. A. Gutman, J. S. Barnholtz-Sloan, J. E. V. Vega, D. J. Brat, and L. A. Cooper. "Predicting cancer outcomes from histology and genomics using convolutional networks". In: Proceedings of the National Academy of Sciences 115.13 (2018), E2970–E2979 (cit. on p. 317).

[MTZ19] I. Mironov, K. Talwar, and L. Zhang. "R\'enyi differential privacy of the sampled gaussian mechanism". In: arXiv preprint arXiv:1908.10530 (2019) (cit. on p. 333).

[Nes+19] B. Nestor, M. B. A. McDermott, W. Boag, G. Berner, T. Naumann, M. C. Hughes, A. Goldenberg, and M. Ghassemi. Feature Robustness in Non-stationary Health Records: Caveats to Deployable Model Performance in Common Clinical Machine Learning Tasks. 2019 (cit. on p. 339).

[NHHK19] T. Niinimäki, M. A. Heikkilä, A. Honkela, and S. Kaski. "Representation transfer for differentially private drug sensitivity prediction". In: Bioinformatics 35.14 (2019), pp. i218–i224 (cit. on p. 334).

[Offa] Office for Civil Rights (OCR). Your Rights Under HIPAA. https://www.hhs.gov/hipaa/for-individuals/guidance-materials-for-consumers/index.html. Accessed: 2021-10-23 (cit. on p. 319).

[Offb] Office of the Privacy Commissioner of Canada. Provincial laws that may apply instead of PIPEDA. https://www.priv.gc.ca/en/privacy-topics/privacy-laws-in-canada/the-personal-information-protection-and-electronic-documents-act-pipeda/r_o_p/prov-pipeda/. Accessed: 2021-10-23 (cit. on p. 319).

[PDH19] S. R. Pfohl, A. M. Dai, and K. Heller. "Federated and Differentially Private Learning for Electronic Health Records". In: arXiv preprint arXiv:1911.05861 (2019) (cit. on p. 337).

[Ple+07] R. M. Plenge, M. Seielstad, L. Padyukov, A. T. Lee, E. F. Remmers, B. Ding, A. Liew, H. Khalili, A. Chandrasekaran, L. R. Davies, et al. "TRAF1–C5 as a risk locus for rheumatoid arthritis—a genomewide study". In: New England Journal of Medicine 357.12 (2007), pp. 1199–1209 (cit. on p. 330).

[Raj+18] A. Rajkomar, E. Oren, K. Chen, A. M. Dai, N. Hajaj, M. Hardt, P. J. Liu, X. Liu, J. Marcus, M. Sun, et al. "Scalable and accurate deep learning with electronic health records". In: NPJ Digital Medicine 1.1 (2018), p. 18 (cit. on pp. 317, 331).

[Ram+19] L. Rampášek, D. Hidru, P. Smirnov, B. Haibe-Kains, and A. Goldenberg. “Dr. VAE: improving drug response prediction via modeling of drug perturbation effects”. In: Bioinformatics 35.19 (2019), pp. 3743–3751 (cit. on p. 331).

[Ren+16] H. Ren, H. Li, X. Liang, S. He, Y. Dai, and L. Zhao. “Privacy-enhanced and multifunctional health data aggregation under differential privacy guarantees”. In: Sensors 16.9 (2016), p. 1463 (cit. on p. 331).

[Sad+21] A. Sadilek, L. Liu, D. Nguyen, M. Kamruzzaman, S. Serghiou, B. Rader, A. Ingerman, S. Mellem, P. Kairouz, E. O. Nsoesie, et al. “Privacy-first health research with federated learning”. In: NPJ digital medicine 4.1 (2021), pp. 1–8 (cit. on p. 338).

[Sal+16] N. Saleheen, S. Chakraborty, N. Ali, M. M. Rahman, S. M. Hossain, R. Bari, E. Buder, M. Srivastava, and S. Kumar. “mSieve: differential behavioral privacy in time series of mobile sensor data”. In: Proceedings of the 2016 ACM International Joint Conference on Pervasive and Ubiquitous Computing. 2016, pp. 706–717 (cit. on p. 331).

[SB16] S. Simmons and B. Berger. “Realizing privacy preserving genome-wide association studies”. In: Bioinformatics 32.9 (2016), pp. 1293–1300 (cit. on pp. 329, 330).

[Sim+19] A. L. Simpson, M. Antonelli, S. Bakas, M. Bilello, K. Farahani, B. Van Ginneken, A. Kopp-Schneider, B. A. Landman, G. Litjens, B. Menze, et al. “A large annotated medical image dataset for the development and evaluation of segmentation algorithms”. In: arXiv preprint arXiv:1902.09063 (2019) (cit. on p. 334).

[SLMG20] L. Seyyed-Kalantari, G. Liu, M. McDermott, and M. Ghassemi. “CheXclusion: Fairness gaps in deep chest X-ray classifiers”. In: arXiv preprint arXiv:2003.00827 (2020) (cit. on pp. 317, 333).

[SPGG21] V. M. Suriyakumar, N. Papernot, A. Goldenberg, and M. Ghassemi. “Chasing Your Long Tails: Differentially Private Prediction in Health Care Settings”. In: Proceedings of the 2021 ACM Conference on Fairness, Accountability, and Transparency. 2021, pp. 723–734 (cit. on pp. 332–334, 337, 339).

[SSKT20] S. Singh, H. Sikka, S. Kotti, and A. Trask. “Benchmarking differentially private residual networks for medical imagery”. In: arXiv preprint arXiv:2005.13099 (2020) (cit. on p. 334).

[SSS18] A. Subbaswamy, P. Schulam, and S. Saria. "Preventing failures due to dataset shift: Learning predictive models that transport". In: arXiv preprint arXiv:1812.04597 (2018) (cit. on p. 339).

[Str+14] B. Strack, J. P. DeShazo, C. Gennings, J. L. Olmo, S. Ventura, K. J. Cios, and J. N. Clore. "Impact of HbA1c measurement on hospital readmission rates: analysis of 70,000 clinical database patient records". In: BioMed research international 2014 (2014) (cit. on p. 332).

[Swe] L. Sweeney. Simple demographics often identify people uniquely. https://dataprivacylab.org/projects/identifiability/paper1.pdf. Accessed: 2021-10-23 (cit. on p. 321).

[SZ14] K. Simonyan and A. Zisserman. "Very deep convolutional networks for large-scale image recognition". In: arXiv preprint arXiv:1409.1556 (2014) (cit. on p. 333).

[TBL17] A. D. Trister, D. S. Buist, and C. I. Lee. "Will machine learning tip the balance in breast cancer screening?" In: JAMA oncology 3.11 (2017), pp. 1463–1464 (cit. on p. 317).

[Tom+19] N. Tomašev, X. Glorot, J. W. Rae, M. Zielinski, H. Askham, A. Saraiva, A. Mottram, C. Meyer, S. Ravuri, I. Protsyuk, A. Connell, C. O. Hughes, A. Karthikesalingam, J. Cornebise, H. Montgomery, G. Rees, C. Laing, C. R. Baker, K. Peterson, R. Reeves, D. Hassabis, D. King, M. Suleyman, T. Back, C. Nielson, J. R. Ledsam, and S. Mohamed. "A clinically applicable approach to continuous prediction of future acute kidney injury". en. In: Nature 572.7767 (Aug. 2019), pp. 116–119 (cit. on p. 331).

[TWZ09] T. Tse, R. J. Williams, and D. A. Zarin. "Reporting "basic results" in ClinicalTrials. gov". In: Chest 136.1 (2009), pp. 295–303 (cit. on p. 326).

[Uff+21] E. Uffelmann, Q. Q. Huang, N. S. Munung, J. de Vries, Y. Okada, A. R. Martin, H. C. Martin, T. Lappalainen, and D. Posthuma. "Genome-wide association studies". In: Nature Reviews Methods Primers 1.1 (2021), p. 59. URL: https://doi.org/10.1038/s43586-021-00056-9 (cit. on p. 329).

[UJM19] A. Ukil, A. J. Jara, and L. Marin. "Data-driven automated cardiac health management with robust edge analytics and de-risking". In: Sensors 19.12 (2019), p. 2733 (cit. on p. 331).

[Uni] United Nations. "COVID-19 and Human Rights: We Are All in This Together". In: () (cit. on p. 320).

[USF13] C. Uhlerop, A. Slavković, and S. E. Fienberg. "Privacy-preserving data sharing for genome-wide association studies". In: The Journal of privacy and confidentiality 5.1 (2013), p. 137 (cit. on p. 329).

[VEJ20] D. A. Vyas, L. G. Eisenstein, and D. S. Jones. Hidden in Plain Sight—Reconsidering the Use of Race Correction in Clinical Algorithms. 2020 (cit. on p. 339).

[Vel+19] D. Velmeshev, L. Schirmer, D. Jung, M. Haeussler, Y. Perez, S. Mayer, A. Bhaduri, N. Goyal, D. H. Rowitch, and A. R. Kriegstein. "Single-cell genomics identifies cell type–specific molecular changes in autism". In: Science 364.6441 (2019), pp. 685–689 (cit. on p. 328).

[VS09] D. Vu and A. Slavkovic. "Differential privacy for clinical trial data: Preliminary evaluations". In: 2009 IEEE International Conference on Data Mining Workshops. IEEE. 2009, pp. 138–143 (cit. on p. 326).

[VSB12] S. A. Vinterbo, A. D. Sarwate, and A. A. Boxwala. "Protecting count queries in study design". In: Journal of the American Medical Informatics Association 19.5 (2012), pp. 750–757 (cit. on p. 323).

[Wan+19] S. Wang, M. B. A. McDermott, G. Chauhan, M. C. Hughes, T. Naumann, and M. Ghassemi. "MIMIC-Extract: A Data Extraction, Preprocessing, and Representation Pipeline for MIMIC-III". In: arXiv:1907.08322 [cs, stat] (July 2019). arXiv: 1907.08322. URL: http://arxiv.org/abs/1907.08322 (visited on 11/04/2019) (cit. on pp. 317, 331).

[Wu+19] D. Wu, H. Kobayashi, C. Ding, L. Cheng, and K. G. M. Ghassemi. "Modeling the Biological Pathology Continuum with HSIC-regularized Wasserstein Auto-encoders". In: arXiv:1901.06618 [cs, stat] (2019). arXiv: 1901.06618. URL: http://arxiv.org/abs/1901.06618 (visited on 05/22/2019) (cit. on p. 331).

[Wu+20] X. Wu, M. R. Khosravi, L. Qi, G. Ji, W. Dou, and X. Xu. "Locally private frequency estimation of physical symptoms for infectious disease analysis in internet of medical things". In: Computer Communications 162 (2020), pp. 139–151 (cit. on p. 331).

[Zil+21] A. Ziller, D. Usynin, R. Braren, M. Makowski, D. Rueckert, and G. Kaissis. "Medical imaging deep learning with differential privacy". In: Scientific Reports 11.1 (2021), pp. 1–8 (cit. on p. 333).

[ZWB20] Y. Zhou, Z. S. Wu, and A. Banerjee. "Bypassing the Ambient Dimension: Private SGD with Gradient Subspace Identification". In: arXiv preprint arXiv:2007.03813 (2020) (cit. on p. 333).

DOI: 10.1561/9781638284772.ch10

Chapter 10

Differential Privacy in Energy Systems

By James Anderson, Fengyu Zhou and Steven H. Low

10.1 Introduction

The electricity network is one of the two largest infrastructures mankind has ever built, the other being the telephone network (now the Internet), both came into being around 130 years ago. This vast electricity network comprises high-voltage transmission lines that span long distances, forming the backbone of electricity distribution, and lower-voltage distribution networks that deliver electricity over shorter distances to consumers. In the United States alone, the grid connects more than 23,000 generators to countless loads such as buildings, machinery, and appliances. As of 2019, these generators have a total nameplate capacity of 1.2 terawatts and produced approximately 4 trillion kilowatt-hours of electricity, with close to 60% generated from fossil fuels.

The evolution of this network into a "smart grid" has ushered in an era where electricity generation, distribution, and consumption are more efficient and responsive than ever before. Smart grids leverage advanced communication technologies and data analytics to balance supply and demand dynamically, integrate renewable energy sources, and empower consumers with real-time information. However, this increased reliance on data introduces significant privacy concerns. Detailed energy consumption data, if mishandled, can reveal sensitive information about individuals and businesses.

For example, consider smart meters installed in homes that record electricity usage at fine-grained intervals. While this data helps utility companies optimize grid operations and offer personalized services, it can also expose intimate details about a household's daily routines. An unauthorized party accessing this data could determine when residents are away, what appliances they use, or even infer lifestyle habits. Such privacy breaches not only threaten individual security but also erode trust in smart grid technologies.

How can we protect privacy in such a complex infrastructure network? In this chapter, we explore the intersection of energy systems and privacy, focusing on how differential privacy can be applied to protect sensitive data used as input to complex optimization problems adopted in power systems operations. In particular, we focus on optimal power flow (OPF) problems, which are essential for determining the most efficient way to distribute electricity across a network, and how differential privacy can enable the release of useful data sets that protect sensitive load information at specific locations.

Overview of the Chapter

We begin by introducing the fundamentals of electric grid operation in Section 10.2), to set the stage for understanding the complexities and data requirements of modern power systems. Next, we review the privacy challenges inherent in energy systems (Section 10.3) and discuss how the proliferation of advanced metering infrastructure raises concerns about unintended information disclosure. We then provide a mathematical model of power grids, in Section 10.4, which is essential for formulating optimal power flow problems. In Section 10.5, we focus on private DC optimal power flow data sets. We discuss the application of differential privacy to the DC-OPF problem, examining how to balance the need for data utility with the requirement to protect sensitive load information. Finally, we provide some remarks on the current state of research and future directions in integrating differential privacy into energy systems (Section 10.6). Our goal is to highlight the potential of differential privacy to enable secure and efficient operation of smart grids, encouraging further exploration and application of these techniques in the energy sector.

10.2 Electric Grid Operation

An electricity network consists of high-voltage long-distance backbone networks, called transmission networks, that connect to many low-voltage short-distance networks, called distribution networks. Different parts of the grid have their own nominal voltages, and voltages at all points of the network must be stabilized to within a few percent of their nominal values at all times.

The challenge of grid operation is to match supply with demand without violating voltage and transmission line limits. Secure operation refers to the grid's ability to withstand and survive disturbances. There are two main types of disturbances. The first type consists of generation and transmission outages. The second type is due to non-dispatchable and volatile generations and demands. Secure operation is achieved through analyzing credible contingencies offline that may lead to voltage or line limit violations, reserving capacities in advance when scheduling generations, monitoring system state in real time, and taking corrective actions when a contingency occurs. Traditionally, resources for control are mostly bulk generators and, occasionally, a small number of industrial loads. In the future, flexible loads will also be included at scale.

The control architecture consists of three mechanisms operating at different timescales, from seconds to tens of minutes to 24 hours. Rapid small random load or generation fluctuations are handled by generators that can increase or decrease their outputs quickly and continuously. They are equipped with their own governors with droop control and provide *regulation services*, usually under automatic generation control, and on a minute-by-minute basis. Slower fluctuations at a timescale up to a real-time dispatch period, e.g., 5-60 minutes, are handled by generation units connected to the grid and provide *load-following services*. While load-following patterns of customers are highly correlated and often predictable, e.g., because loads often depend heavily on weather, regulation patterns tend to be smaller, more rapid and random fluctuations with zero mean. Both regulation and load-following services require continuous actions by participating units but these actions are typically small or predictable. They have been sufficient for dealing with the second type of disturbances traditionally, though they may become inadequate as volatility increases in the future.

In contrast, the imbalance due to the outage of a bulk generator or a major transmission line that imports power can be large and unpredictable, and can threaten system stability. Disturbances of this type are handled by *reserve services* and are scheduled a day in advance. This is called unit commitment. When a generator fails and is disconnected, supply and demand become unbalanced and frequency starts to drop. The power imbalance must be made up by other generators or reduction in load, in addition, the system frequency must be restored to its nominal value. If generation reserve capacity is insufficient to meet demand, frequency will continue to drop which can disconnect other generators to protect them from damage, potentially leading to involuntary load shedding and even system collapse. When a transmission line or transformer is disconnected, power flows in the network will redistribute and line limits can be violated, potentially leading to cascading line outages.

Over the last century the operation of the transmission network has been largely centralized, open-loop, deterministic and worst-case preventive; demands are forecast, and generations are centrally scheduled based on the forecast. Typically an operating point of the network is chosen so that the network can survive the outage of any single generator or transmission unit. This strategy has performed extremely well, since aggregate loads are fairly predictable, generators are fully controllable (dispatchable), the grid is often over provisioned, and large outages are relatively rare.

10.2.1 Need Control Paradigm

We are, however, at a cusp of historic transformation, driven by sustainability, to become more distributed, dynamic, open and complex. Renewable sources such as wind and solar will continue to replace traditional bulk generators, greatly increasing generation uncertainty and reducing traditional control resources. Distributed energy resources, such as small-scale wind and solar generators, electric vehicles, smart buildings, small appliances, and smart electronics, will proliferate, many equipped with the ability to measure, compute, communicate and actuate in real time. Unlike the large majority of endpoints today that are merely passive loads, these distributed energy resources are active endpoints that can introduce large, frequent, and random fluctuations in supply, demand, voltage and frequency. Their connected intelligence, however, offers a new paradigm to manage the future grid based on real-time communication, computation, and control. The continual increase in generation and demand volatility makes it necessary to close the loop and actively control these distributed energy resources at scale based on timely data.

Data are being collected by distributed energy resources behind the meters as well as by high resolution and synchronized phasor measurement units that are being deployed inside the infrastructure. These different types of data may be collected by different organizations at different parts of the network. They can all be useful for real-time control of the future grid, provided a standardized platform for data sharing can be developed that provides right incentives and preserve necessary privacy. In addition to the physical control of the network, there is an energy market, i.e., a commodity market for incentivizing a competitive energy supply industry. Although we won't go into much detail here, there are three types of short-run markets in practice, a day-ahead market, a real-time market, and an ancillary services market. They are typically operated by an independent system operator at timescales ranging from minutes to a day. Traditionally these markets transact electricity produced by generators to meet inelastic demand. It the future they will also trade demand response from flexible loads. Data privacy issues will clearly need to be introduced into a market platform when this becomes possible. The focus of this chapter will be on releasing data sets that contain sensitive load data, i.e., power demands across a network, such that *optimal power flow* problems (a key element in grid management that matches power demand with production).

10.2.2 Markets

There are three types of short-run markets in practice, a day-ahead market, a real-time market, and an ancillary services market. They are typically operated by an independent system operator at timescales ranging from minutes to a day. Traditionally these markets transact electricity produced by generators to meet inelastic demand. It the future they will also trade demand response from flexible loads.

Day-ahead Market

Bulk generators such as nuclear, coal and gas generators still generate the majority of electricity today, e.g., they generate approximately two thirds of electricity as of 2020 in the US. They often need a nontrivial amount of time and cost to start up and shut down, e.g., the startup time for a nuclear plant can be on the order of hours. This motivates the day-ahead market which usually closes 12–36 hours in advance of energy delivery and determines which generators will be online and their output levels for each hour or half hour over a 24-hour horizon. The day-ahead market also computes consumption schedules, electricity prices, as well as capacity reserves based on the production offers and demand bids submitted by market participants. This is the problem of *unit commitment.*

Real-time Market

A *real-time market,* also called a *spot market* or a *balancing* market, operates at a timescale of minutes, e.g., 5–15 minutes. It computes adjustment to generation and consumption levels as well as prices and reserves at delivery time as uncertainty in generation, consumption or network state is resolved. This is the problem of *economic dispatch* and discussed in Section 10.5.2.

Ancillary Services Market

Finally markets for ancillary services are emerging, driven by reliability requirements in the presence of increasing uncertainty due to renewable or distributed generations such as wind and solar power as well as increasing ability to coordinate flexible loads such as smart buildings, electric vehicles, and other appliances to provide energy services. These services include reserve capacities for generator or transmission contingencies, or demand response for frequency regulation. Reserve capacities may be spinning reserve where a generation unit that is online may generate at only 80% of its capacity with the unused capacity reserved for contingency operation. They may also be non-spinning reserve where a more expensive fast-acting unit remains offline but is ready to be turned on within minutes of a contingency.

10.3 Energy Systems and Privacy

In this section we provide a brief overview of the different application areas within energy networks that have been studied from a privacy perspective. In some areas, differential privacy has already been applied, in others, its potential use is clear. We end this section with an application of the classical Laplacian and exponential mechanisms of differential privacy (see Chapter 1 for a review on these mechanisms) implemented on real data taken from an electric vehicle charging network in Pasadena, California.

10.3.1 Overview

The new distributed and dynamic architecture of the power network, in combination with intelligent sensing and metering is frequently referred to as the *smart grid*. In contrast to the traditional power networks, information flow in a smart grid is bi-directional. Individual users (consumers) can actively manage their energy use, simultaneously, energy producers can more effectively reduce ceiling capacity and better control usage via smart pricing. Smart grids will also make it possible for consumers to become energy producers. However, to make this a reality, vast amounts of time-series data is required from participating entities, and with this come many security and privacy concerns [MM09; ZPAB13; HRC19]. Smart meters (devices that monitor home power usage and can be used to switch appliances on and off automatically) are an obvious focal point for privacy concerns. It has been well known since the early nineties that non-intrusive appliance load monitoring i.e., passive measurements at the point of a traditional energy meter, can be used to identify exactly which appliances are being use in a home, and when [Har92]. Likewise, smart meters can also be used to infer home occupancy states [AR13]. Differential privacy is clearly a methodology that has great potential to resolve some of these concerns. We refer the reader to the following papers to get a sense of how differential privacy is applied; [Zha+15; MMA11; ZJWL14; GFDK19; GGP17; EE17; BBA16].

Beyond smart metering, differential privacy is finding application in several areas related to power and energy. In particular; the cost of introducing "noise" into the system and it's effect on pricing in energy markets is considered in [BKJB13]. Within the context of electricity and gas markets [FMV20] examines differential privacy into Stackelberg games. Private data sharing for better renewable energy forecasting is considered in [GBP21], and electric load forecasting in [Eib+18]. Unintended information disclosure is highlighted as a security issue for electric vehicle (EV) charging in [ADPK20]. In the next section we provide a simple case study of differential privacy applied to an EV charging station's data set.

10.3.2 Numerical Example: Electrical Vehicle Charging

In this subsection, we are going to show two examples where classic mechanisms are applied to data collected from an electric vehicle (EV) charging system; specifically the Adaptive Charging Network (ACN) based at Caltech in Pasadena, California. ACN was first deployed on the Caltech campus in early 2016 and the system uses smart scheduling algorithms to charge EVs for both Caltech and non-Caltech users.

As of 2020, ACN includes 126 level-2 EV charging stations (EVSEs) and 5 DC fast chargers (DCFCs) across three Caltech garages [Lee+20]. ACN is also operated at NASA's Jet Propulsion Laboratory (JPL) as well as at over 100 other sites across the US. The charging data, including user demand, parking time, delivered energy, etc., are collected for every charging session from the Caltech and JPL sites, and the data are published through the ACN Research Portal, available at *ev.caltech.edu*. Currently detailed information of over 60,000 charging sessions is available. We use this data as a toy example to demonstrate how classic mechanisms such as Laplace mechanism and exponential mechanism can be used to preserve differential privacy for different energy system applications.

For this demonstration, we use the data from November 1st to November 30th, 2019 at the Caltech site. In the first example, we are interested in the distribution of user demand for each charging session. We set the query as the histogram of the user-requested energy (in kWh) for each session, and the ground-truth histogram is given in Figure 10.1 (blue bars). In November 2019, there were in total 611 charging sessions, and from the histogram we can see that though the highest single-session demand was over 100 kWh, the majority of sessions requested less than 50 kWh. Roughly, 50kWh corresponds to a 200 mile driving range assuming the vehicle's MPGe is around 136. Over half of the sessions requested less than 20 kWh.

To preserve differential privacy for a histogram query, a commonly used mechanism is the Laplace mechanism, which we will review in Section 10.5.2. Note that we use slightly non-standard notation and use ϱ-differential privacy instead of ε-differential privacy (c.f. Definition 10.2). The Laplace mechanism injects an additive term drawn from a Laplacian distribution to the ground-truth data. The variance of the distribution is chosen according to the query sensitivity

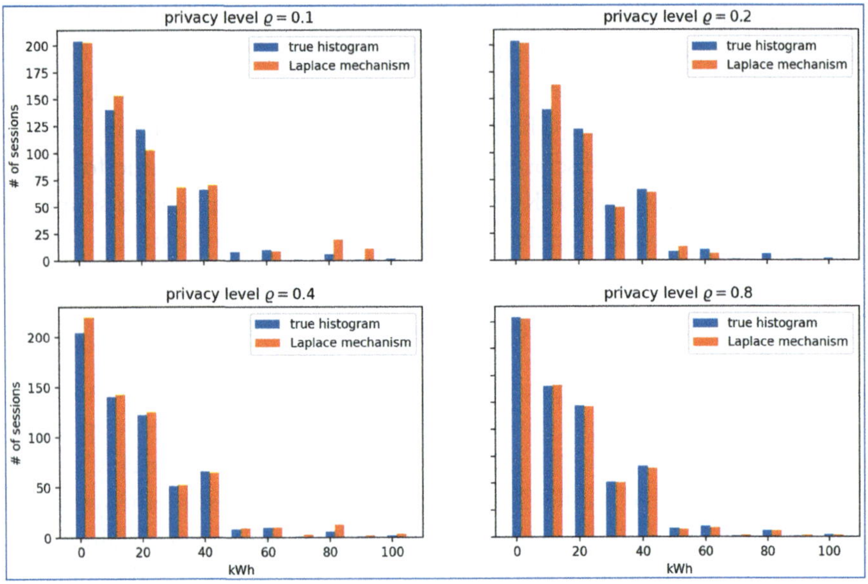

Figure 10.1. Apply Laplace mechanism when the query is the histogram of requested kWh per session.

and user-specified privacy level. The sensitivity of histogram query is 1, so the mechanism simply adds noise following Laplace distribution $\mathscr{L}(1/\varrho)$ where ϱ is the desired privacy level. Figure 10.1 displays the mechanism output for $\varrho = 0.1, 0.2, 0.4, 0.8$. By Theorem 3.6 in [DR+14], the noisy histogram (orange bars) in each subplot in Figure 10.1 is guaranteed to preserve ϱ-differential privacy for the corresponding value of ϱ and can be released publicly. As the value of ϱ increases, the public histogram gets closer to the ground truth, and less privacy is preserved. On the other hand, the public histogram can still characterize the high-level statistical pattern of the private histogram. In this example, readers could easily learn from the public data that almost all the charging sessions in November 2019 requested less than 50 kWh and over half of them requested between 0 and 20 kWh.

In the second example we focus on the categorical query. We want to know which day has the highest daily total demand (i.e., the summation of all the energy demanded during that day). Red bars in Figure 10.2 illustrates the total daily demand over the 30-day period. From the plot together with a 2019 calendar, we could easily see the weekly pattern that the demand is typically high during weekdays and drops over the weekend. Note that November 28th in 2019 is the Thanksgiving holiday, so the demand is also low on and after that day. Two days with the highest demand are Nov 8th and 12th, when the daily demands are as high as 771 kWh. As we query the date with the highest daily demand, we expect

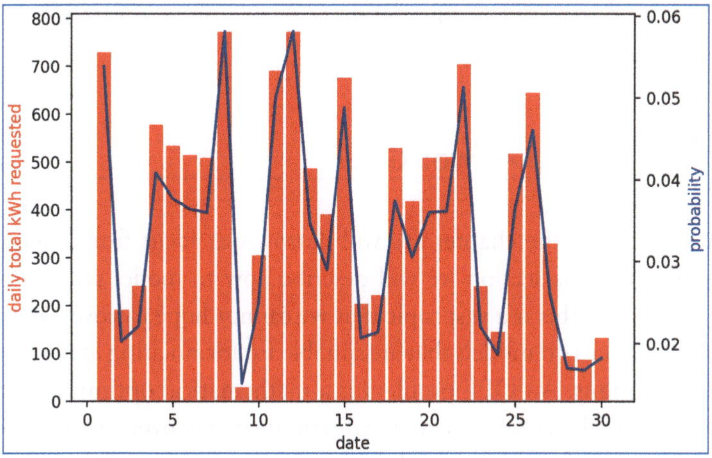

Figure 10.2. Application of the exponential mechanism to the query "what is the date with the highest load demand?".

the mechanism to output Nov 8th or Nov 12th (or other dates with high demand) with high probability.

In this case, Laplace mechanism may not be an appropriate choice for two reasons. First, the Laplace mechanism always outputs floating point data, which makes no sense for categorical queries such as the date. Second, if we view the date as numerical data and compute its worst-case sensitivity, the sensitivity value could be larger than necessary. For example, it is possible that the date with the highest demand will change from Nov 1st to Nov 30th after we insert a new session record which increases the demand on Nov 30th, and it implies that the worst-case sensitivity is 29 if we view the date as numerical data. However, a more appropriate mechanism to process worst-case is the exponential mechanism. We refer to [DR+14; LLSY16] for the detailed derivation, and here we only present the high-level idea and illustrate the results on ACN data. To apply the exponential mechanism, we first choose a utility function $u(\mathbf{d}, o)$ where $\mathbf{d}$ is the dataset and o stands for the output (the date in our example). We let $u(\mathbf{d}, o)$ return the total daily demand on date o for dataset $\mathbf{d}$, so we want the mechanism to return the date with large utility value. By the exponential mechanism, we output each candidate o with probability proportional to $\exp(\frac{\varrho u(\mathbf{d},o)}{\Delta u})$,[i] where Δu is the sensitivity of utility function u. The probability distribution to output each date has been shown in Figure 10.2 (blue curve). We can see that the probability distribution tracks the quality function well, so there is a fair chance for the mechanism to output the date

i. Here we use the fact that the utility function is monotone with respect to o. In a more general setting, the probability should be proportional to $\exp(\frac{\varrho u(\mathbf{d},o)}{2\Delta u})$.

with very high energy demand, though the true maximum may still be missed for privacy consideration.

10.4 Modelling a Power Grid

For the remainder of the chapter, we will narrow our focus from energy systems to power grids. In this section we will describe how to model power flow over a network. Of course, this is a vast topic that we cannot hope to cover in its entirety. Instead, we will focus on models that are suitable for formulating *optimal power flow* (OPF) optimizations. An OPF problem is a mathematical optimization problem, the solution of which determines how to distribute power over a network subject to physical an operational constraints. In subsequent sections of this chapter we will turn our attention to privacy preservation of data sets obtained from solutions to OPF problems. Our intention is to convey how tools from differential privacy can be applied in this setting, thus we have mostly opt for simplicity over realism. In many cases, the more realistic results don't exist yet, in others, the realism simply clouds the results by introducing unnecessary notation and more equations.

10.4.1 Network Model

We begin by describing how the physical power network can be described mathematically. The starting point is to view a power network as a collection of nodes (where a node may correspond to a power source, sink, or both) end edges (transmission or distribution lines) which connect nodes. In power engineering, nodes are typically referred to *buses*. We will use the two interchangeably.

The most natural way to model such a system is via a graph $\mathcal{G}(\mathcal{V}, \mathcal{E})$ where $\mathcal{V}$ is the set of all buses in the network and $\mathcal{E}$ denotes the set of edges connecting the buses. To reduce the notional overhead we will often omit the arguments $(\mathcal{V}, \mathcal{E})$ and simply refer to a graph as $\mathcal{G}$. The set $\mathcal{V}$ can be decomposed into two sets according to whether a bus is a power source (referred to as a generator bus, or simply a generator), i.e., a point at which power is produced and injected into a network, or, a power sink (referred to as a load bus, or simply a load), i.e., a point where power is consumed and removed from the network. The set $\mathcal{V}$ can thus be decomposed as $\mathcal{V} = \mathcal{V}_{\mathrm{G}} \cup \mathcal{V}_{\mathrm{L}}$. In real networks it is common for a bus to consist of both generators and loads. Our representation $\mathcal{V}$ does not preclude this, however, we will make the assumption that all buses in our networks are either generators or loads and not both. This assumption is not restrictive (in the DC power flow model) as we can always model a power system in this manner, it does however simplify notation and analysis. We denote the number of generator and load buses in the network by N_{G} and N_{L} respectively and denote $N = N_{\mathrm{G}} + N_{\mathrm{L}}$. For notational convenience, we assume the nodes are ordered as $\mathcal{V}_{\mathrm{G}} = \{1, \ldots, N_{\mathrm{G}}\}$ and $\mathcal{V}_{\mathrm{L}} = \{N_{\mathrm{G}} + 1, \ldots, N_{\mathrm{G}} + N_{\mathrm{L}}\}$. Buses are connected via the edge set $\mathcal{E} \subseteq \mathcal{V} \times \mathcal{V}$, we label the edge set $\mathcal{E} = \{e_1, \ldots, e_E\}$. When $\mathcal{G}$ is undirected, $(l, m) \in \mathcal{E}$ if and only if $(m, l) \in \mathcal{E}$. For directed graphs, if $e_i(l, m) \in \mathcal{E}$ we say that l is the *source* and m is the *target* denoted by $s(e_i) = l$ and $t(e_i) = m$ respectively.

It will often be convenient to represent a $\mathcal{G}$ via matrices. In particular the incidence matrix $\mathbf{C} \in \mathbb{R}^{N \times E}$ describes how edges connect to vertices. When $\mathcal{G}$ is undirected, a direction is arbitrarily assigned to each edge. The matrix $\mathbf{C}$ is then defined as

$$\mathbf{C}_{ij} = \begin{cases} +1 & \text{if } s(e_j) = i, \\ -1 & \text{if } t(e_j) = i, \\ 0 & \text{otherwise.} \end{cases}$$

As we will see in subsequent sections, it will often be useful to overload our graph model to take into account weights on edges. These weights will be related to certain electrical properties of transmission and distribution lines. To accommodate this, we introduce a diagonal matrix $\mathbf{W} \in \mathbb{C}^{E \times E}$. Together with the incidence matrix, we can form the weighted $N \times N$ Laplacian matrix $\mathbf{L} = \mathbf{CWC}^T$.

10.4.2 Power Flow Model

A power flow model provides a mathematical description of how quantities such as current, voltage, and power relate to each other at points over a network. Our goal here is to provide some intuition into how electrical engineers model these networks. The material covered is standard, some excellent references include [MLBB20; Bie15; Mom17]. However, the remainder of this chapter can still be understood purely from a mathematical perspective with no knowledge of the underlying physics needed!

In power engineering, we typically express such quantities as complex numbers. Consider a sinusoidal voltage function $v(t) = V_{\max} \cos(\omega t + \theta_V)$, using Euler's identity we see that

$$v(t) = \Re[V_{\max} e^{j\theta_V} e^{j\omega t}],$$

where $j = \sqrt{-1}$ and $\Re$ denotes the real part of a complex number. Define the *effective phasor* $V = \frac{(V_{\max} e^{j\theta_V})}{\sqrt{2}}$, then the voltage function can be expressed as

$$v(t) = \Re[\sqrt{2} V e^{j\omega t}].$$

Current and power can also be expressed as phasors in an analogous manner. The instantaneous power is defined as $p(t) = v(t)i(t)$. Assume the voltage and current both have angular frequency ω, then the average power over the period $T = \frac{2\pi}{\omega}$ is

$$P = \frac{1}{T}\int_0^T p(t)\mathrm{d}t = \frac{1}{2}V_{\max}I_{\max}\cos(\theta_V - \theta_I).$$

It is not difficult to see that $P = \Re\,[VI^*]$. However, this is only part of the story. Define the complex power as $S = VI^*$ and the *reactive power* $Q = \Im[VI^*]$ where $\Im$ denotes the imaging part of a complex number, then

$$S = VI^* = P + jQ, \tag{10.1}$$

where superscript $*$ denotes complex conjugation. When designing power systems, it is important to consider not just the average power P, but also reactive power, Q. For example, from the definition of S, it is clear that for fixed P and $|V|$, the magnitude of the current increases with $|Q|$ to which there are associated thermal costs that should not be ignored. Finally, voltage and current are related to each other via $I = YV$, where Y is a complex number known as the admittance which we define as $Y = G - jB$ (the reciprocal of admittance is *impedance* and is commonly denoted by Z, i.e., $V = ZI$). We are now ready to describe a model for how power flows over a network.

We begin by taking the graph that models the power network and labeling one of the buses as the *slack bus* for which we assume $|V| = 1$ and its phase is 0°. Without loss of generality we label the slack bus as bus 1. As we move to the network setting we will use bold-faced upper-case characters to denote vectors of voltages, currents, and power flow for the whole network.

Every transmission line (edge) in the network is modeled by the Π-model. Consider the line (j,k): In the Π-model, the line is described by the tuple of admittances $(y^s_{jk}, y^m_{jk}, y^m_{kj})$ corresponding the series admittance and two (not necessarily equal) shunt admittances at each end of the line, respectively. Note that there is only one series admittance for each line and so $y^s_{jk} = y^s_{kj}$. Let I_{jk} denote the branch current from bus j (equivalently node j in $\mathcal{V}$) to bus k (equivalently node $k \in \mathcal{V}$), and I_{kj} the current from bus k to j. The presence of the shunt elements means that summation of these two quantities is not necessarily zero. We now proceed to develop a set of equations that relates all the current injections $I_1, I_2, \ldots$ in the network to the voltages $V_1, V_2, \ldots$. Collecting the quantities in a the complex vectors $\mathbf{I}$ and $\mathbf{V}$ and applying Kirchhoff's current law at each bus in the network we have

$$\mathbf{I} = \mathbf{YV}, \quad \text{where for } i \neq j$$

$$\mathbf{Y}_{ij} = \begin{cases} -y^s_{ij} & \text{if } (i,j) \in \mathcal{E} \\ 0 & \text{otherwise} \end{cases}, \quad \text{and} \quad \mathbf{Y}_{jj} = y^m_{jj} + \sum_{(j,k)\in\mathcal{E}} y^s_{jk},$$

where $y^m_{jj} = \sum_{(j,k)\in\mathcal{E}} y^s_{jk}$.

The complex $N \times N$ matrix $\mathbf{Y}$ is called the *admittance* matrix. Finally, combining the relationship between current and voltage through the network with complex power balance as defined by (10.1), we obtain

$$\mathbf{S}_j = \sum_{(j,k)\in\mathcal{E}} (y^s_{jk})^*(|\mathbf{V}_j|^2 - \mathbf{V}_j\mathbf{V}_k^*) + (y^m_{jj})^*|\mathbf{V}_j|^2, \quad \text{for all } j \in \mathcal{V}, \tag{10.2}$$

the *net power injection* at bus j. Including the slack bus, there are N equations in (10.2) in $2N$ complex variables $\mathbf{S}_j, \mathbf{V}_j$. The system of equations (10.2) can equivalently be written in polar form with $4N$ real variables $\mathbf{P}_j$, $\mathbf{Q}_j$, $|\mathbf{V}_j|$, and $\boldsymbol{\theta}_j$, where $\mathbf{V}_j = |\mathbf{V}_j|e^{j\boldsymbol{\theta}_j}$ and $\mathbf{S}_j = \mathbf{P}_j + j\mathbf{Q}_j$. To simplify notation, we denote $y^m_{jj} = \mathbf{G}_{jj} - j\mathbf{B}_{jj}$ and $y^s_{jk} = \mathbf{G}_{jk} - j\mathbf{B}_{jk}$. When $j = k$ (shunt admittances at bus j) we have that $\mathbf{G}_{jj} \geq 0, \mathbf{B}_{jj} \leq 0$, and for $j \neq k$ (line (j,k) series admittance), $\mathbf{G}_{jj} \geq 0, \mathbf{B}_{jj} \geq 0$. It follows that for each $j \in \mathcal{V}$,(10.2) becomes

$$\begin{aligned} \mathbf{P}_j &= \left(\sum_k \mathbf{G}_{jk}\right)|\mathbf{V}_j|^2 - \sum_{k\neq j} |\mathbf{V}_j||\mathbf{V}_k|(\mathbf{G}_{jk}\cos\boldsymbol{\theta}_{jk} - \mathbf{B}_{jk}\sin\boldsymbol{\theta}_{jk}), \\ \mathbf{Q}_j &= \left(\sum_k \mathbf{B}_{jk}\right)|\mathbf{V}_j|^2 - \sum_{k\neq j} |\mathbf{V}_j||\mathbf{V}_k|(\mathbf{B}_{jk}\cos\boldsymbol{\theta}_{jk} + \mathbf{G}_{jk}\sin\boldsymbol{\theta}_{jk}), \end{aligned} \tag{10.3}$$

where $\boldsymbol{\theta}_{jk} := \boldsymbol{\theta}_j - \boldsymbol{\theta}_k$ is the voltage phase angle difference for line $(j,k) \in \mathcal{E}$.

Obtaining solutions to either (10.2) or (10.3) is known as a *power flow problem.* Typically, half the variables will be specified and the remaining variables must be solved for. The power flow equations are nonlinear and so iterative methods are often required to obtain solutions.

The reason for wanting to solve power flow problems in the first place is to determine how power will flow when parameters such as voltage requirements, generation demand and production are specified at each bus. Note that earlier we defined $\mathbf{S}_j$ to be the *net* complex power injection at bus j. The implication is that at each bus power may be produced and removed. So, formally $\mathbf{S}_j = \mathbf{S}^g_j - \mathbf{S}^d_j = (\mathbf{P}^g_j - \mathbf{P}^d_j) + j(\mathbf{Q}^g_j - \mathbf{Q}^d_j)$, where superscripts g and d refer to generate and demand respectively. Buses in the network are typically classified as into three types; PV buses, PQ buses, and slack buses. This classification is somewhat synthetic, but useful for our purposes. Determining which variables in the problem are fixed, and which are specified, depends on the bus classification. See Table 10.1 for specific details. PV buses are typically generator buses, PQ buses are typically buses with a constant power load. The slack bus is required to ensure a solution exists and that power balance is achieved.

The focus of the remainder of this chapter is *optimal power flow problems* (OPFs). An OPF is an optimization problem where power flow equations (10.2) or (10.3)

Table 10.1. Power flow equation data categorized by bus type.

Bus type \ Data	Specified	Solve for
PV	$P_j^g, P_j^d, \lvert V_j \rvert$	Q_j^g, θ_j
PQ	P_j^d, Q_j^d	$\lvert V_j \rvert, \theta_j$
Slack	$V_1 = \lvert V_1 \rvert \angle 0°$	P_1, Q_1

appear as constraints. In the next section we concentrate on a specific form of an OPF, and discuss where privacy issues arise and how differential privacy can be used to allow for the public release of OPF problem data.

10.5 Private DC Optimal Power Flow Data Sets

Optimal power flow problems seek to minimize (or maximize) a function, typically generation cost, user disutility, or power loss, subject to the physics of power flow (10.2), and network operational constraints such as line capacity, and voltage magnitude constraints. The OPF problem was first formulated by Carpentier in the 60's [Car62] and it remains an active area of research today. OPF problems arise in many aspects of power engineering including unit commitment (determining which generators will participate in power production), economic dispatch (determine the power output of participating generators), $N - K$ safety (ensuring network stability should K line failures occur), state estimation, and demand response, to name a few. The literature on OPF problems is vast and we will only cover OPF problem formulation at a very high level. For a detailed view of the OPF landscape we refer the reader to the following surveys [FSR12; HG91] and the tutorial [FR16].

10.5.1 Optimal Power Flow

Beyond their importance to power network operation, OPF problems receive so much attention because the power flow equations (10.2) are nonlinear (quadratic) functions. As such, the resulting optimization problems (in which the power flow equations are constraints) are quadratically constrained and non-convex. Such problems are NP-complete in general, and so heuristics are needed to provide solutions. Convex relaxations based on semidefinite programming is a popular approach for solving OPF problems, and in many cases such methods come with strong theoretical guarantees, see [Low14a; Low14b] for an overview of this type of approach and [Zoh+20] for general conic optimization formulations. We will now describe the most general form of an OPF problem and then restrict our attention to a more manageable special case.

We stack all complex powers injections into the vector $\mathbf{S} = \mathbf{P} + j\mathbf{Q}$, an alternating current (AC) OPF problem takes the form:

$$\begin{aligned} \underset{\mathbf{V},\mathbf{S}}{\text{minimize}} \quad & f(\mathbf{P}^g) \\ \text{subject to} \quad & \mathbf{V}_{\min} \leq |\mathbf{V}|^2 \leq \mathbf{V}_{\max}, \\ & \mathbf{S}^j_{\min} \leq \sum_{(j,k)\in\mathcal{E}} (y^s_{jk})^* \mathbf{V}_j (\mathbf{V}^*_j - \mathbf{V}^*_k) \leq \mathbf{S}^j_{\max}, \quad \text{for } j = 1, \ldots, N, \end{aligned} \tag{10.4}$$

where $\mathbf{P}^g$ is the vector of real power generation. Here we have assumed no shunt devices, i.e., $y^m_{jj} = 0$ for all j. The objective function f is quadratic and assumed to be separable across all generators. Generically, it takes the form:

$$f(\mathbf{P}^g) = \sum_{i=1}^{N_G} f_i(\mathbf{P}^g_l), \quad \text{with} \quad f_i(\mathbf{P}^g_i) = c_{i2}(\mathbf{P}^g_i)^2 + c_{i1}\mathbf{P}^g_i + c_i.$$

The vectors $\mathbf{V}_{\min}$ and $\mathbf{V}_{\max}$ contain non-negative lower and upper limits for the squared voltage magnitudes. The voltage magnitude vector inequalities are taken element-wise. With slight abuse of notation, the constrains on $\mathbf{S}$ should be read as two sets of constraints, one on the real part and one on the imaginary part. The OPF formulation (10.4) is sufficiently general so as to allow:

- Unbounded load or generation at bus i: $\mathbf{S}^j_{\min} = -\infty - j\infty$, $\mathbf{S}^j_{\max} = \infty + j\infty$.
- Arbitrary slack bus values: $\mathbf{V}^0_{\min} = \mathbf{V}^0_{\max} = c$, with corresponding net power injection unbounded.
- Fixed net power injection: $\mathbf{S}^j_{\min} = \mathbf{S}^j_{\max}$.

As mentioned above, solving (10.4) is theoretically and numerically challenging. Given that solving OPF problems in the general form of (10.4) is not straight forward, we will primarily work with a restricted version of (10.4) known as the DC-OPF, where DC stands for direct current. The DC-OPF model is convex (and hence global solutions can be found), furthermore it is formulated as a *linear program* (LP) which is perhaps the best understood convex programming class, and many efficient solvers exist allowing us to solve them at scale. With respect to differential privacy, the DC-OPF problem is more fully understood. We will describe work on privacy preserving mechanism for the full OPF problem towards the end of the end chapter.

10.5.2 DC Optimal Power Flow

We now turn our attention to DC OPF problems [SA74; PMVB05; CV14]. Although DC-OPF problems are more restrictive than their AC counterparts [OCS04], the simplicity of dealing with a linear program allows us to focus more on data privacy and less on the intricacies of non-convex optimization. The following assumptions bring about the DC power flow model (which then become constraints in an optimization problem):

1. Voltage angle differences across a line are assumed to be small. For a line $(i,j) \in \mathcal{E}$, use the small angle approximation $\sin(\boldsymbol{\theta}_i - \boldsymbol{\theta}_j) \approx \boldsymbol{\theta}_i - \boldsymbol{\theta}_j$ where angle are measured in radians.
2. Voltage magnitudes, $|\mathbf{V}_i|$ are assumed to be constants.
3. All lines are lossless, i.e. $\mathbf{G}_{ik} = 0$, and so $\mathbf{Y}_{ik} = j\mathbf{B}_{ik}$ for all $(i,k) \in \mathcal{E}$.

Under normal operating conditions, the voltage magnitude constants are approximately one. Applying the above three points to the expression for real power at bus j in (10.3) gives:

$$\mathbf{P}_j = \sum_{(j,k)\in\mathcal{E}} \mathbf{B}_{jk}(\boldsymbol{\theta}_j - \boldsymbol{\theta}_k). \tag{10.5}$$

In the DC model, reactive power is ignored and so $\mathbf{P}_j$ completely characterizes the power flow. Of use to us is the fact that (10.5) is linear in the decision variables $\boldsymbol{\theta}_j, \boldsymbol{\theta}_k$, and $\mathbf{P}_j$. As a consequence of (10.5) (equivalently, by definition of a lossless line) it follows that $\sum_j \mathbf{P}_j = 0$, i.e., active power is conserved across the network. Active power conservation does not hold when dealing with the AC power flow equations where the loss on a given line is proportional to the inverse of the magnitude of the line impedance multiplied by magnitude of the voltage difference squared. The final assumption made is to replace the quadratic cost function f in (10.4) with a linear cost function $\sum_i c_i \mathbf{P}_i^g$. Recalling the definition of the Laplacian matrix from Section 10.4.1, we arrive at the DC-OPF problem:

$$\begin{aligned} \underset{\mathbf{P}^g,\boldsymbol{\theta}}{\text{minimize}} \quad & \sum_{i=1}^{N_G} c_i \mathbf{P}_i^g \\ \text{subject to} \quad & \mathbf{CBC}^T\boldsymbol{\theta} = \mathbf{P}, \quad \boldsymbol{\theta}_1 = 0, \\ & \mathbf{p}_{\min} \le \mathbf{BC}^T\boldsymbol{\theta} \le \mathbf{p}_{\max}, \\ & \mathbf{P}^g_{\min} \le \mathbf{P}^g \le \mathbf{P}^g_{\max}, \end{aligned} \tag{10.6}$$

which is a linear program. The vector $\mathbf{P} \in \mathbb{R}^N$ is the vector of net power injections with each element assigned to be a generator or load. The subset that correspond to generators are denoted $\mathbf{P}^g$. The matrix $\mathbf{C}$ is the graph incidence matrix, and $\mathbf{B}$ is a diagonal matrix containing the (positive) susceptances. The susceptances are obtained from the elements $\mathbf{B}_{jk}$, i.e., the complex part of the admittance matrix.

Definition 10.1. *We refer to the vectors* $\mathbf{P}^g_{\max}, \mathbf{P}^g_{\min}, \mathbf{p}_{\max}$, *and* $\mathbf{p}_{\min}$ *as the network parameters and define the network parameter vector* $\xi := [(\mathbf{P}^g_{\max})^T, (\mathbf{P}^g_{\min})^T, (\mathbf{p}_{\max})^T, (\mathbf{p}_{\min})^T]^T$.

With a tractable model for power flow optimization in hand, we turn our attention to the issue of privacy. The natural questions to consider are; i) what data is it that needs to be kept private (we will also motivate this with the qualifier "and why")? and, ii) is it possible to use differential privacy in this setting. The answer to part ii) should come as no surprise given the title of this monograph and the length of this chapter – yes, but with significant modifications. To answer the first question, we must consider the DC-OPF problem (10.6) (from now on referred to simply as the/an OPF problem) and note that it encodes the network model and the power flow equations. It may be surprising to many that it is the demand at the load buses that grid operators are most keen to keep private. Network topology can mostly be inferred by inspection (it's difficult to hide above-ground power lines, power plants, and substations). Generation data is often publicly available (often in aggregate form) and the various constraint values need not often be known precisely. We thus focus on the problem of keeping load data private as we address the following three points:

1. The data that we would like to publicly release as $(\mathbf{P}^g, \mathbf{P}^l)$. The net power at every bus in the network is $\mathbf{P}_i$ which we have decomposed into $\mathbf{P}^g_i$ and $\mathbf{P}^d_i$ for $i = 1, \ldots N$. The main concern is that $\mathbf{P}^g$ is dependent upon $\mathbf{P}^d$, specifically it is related through the deterministic optimization problem (10.6). This dependence needs to be accounted for, else information about $\mathbf{P}^l$ may be inferred from $\mathbf{P}^g$ (and the publicly available aggregate statistics for $\mathbf{P}^g$).
2. The OPF (10.6) encodes the physical structure of the power network $\mathcal{G}(\mathcal{V}, \mathcal{E})$. A fundamental question here is how the network structure affects achievable privacy levels. Put another way, is the data generated by some power network "easier" to keep private simply because of the network topology? To what extent can this be quantified?
3. Similarly, how do the OPF constraints affect privacy guarantees?

At this point it is important to make two points. There exists a wide body of work on differential privacy and linear programming (and optimization more generally). The goal of this work is *not* to privately solve a linear program. Our goal is to be able to publicly release the data set $(\mathbf{P}^g, \mathbf{P}^l)$ with a differential privacy guarantee along the lines of "changes in generation data will not disclose sensitive load data".

The second point we wish to make is that we are releasing the data so that data users can analyze the data and run their own OPF algorithms on. As such, we provide no guarantees that the the released data will be the solution to any OPF problem. We do not believe this to be restrictive as the OPF cost function and exact constraints are likely not available anyway. Users of the data will have accurate load demand data that (satisfies a differential privacy guarantee) to work with. Load data is typically the most important part of the data set – and most difficult to obtain. In later sections we describe work work where the data released does satisfy an AC optimal power flow problem.

Recalling that we assume the slack bus is bus 1, we also make explicit the partition on the Laplacian equality constraint;

$$\theta_1 = 0, \quad \mathbf{CBC}^T\boldsymbol{\theta} = \begin{bmatrix} \mathbf{P}^g \\ \mathbf{P}^l \end{bmatrix} =: \mathbf{L},$$

and assume that (10.6) is well-posed, i.e. upper-bound constraints are greater than or equal to lower-bound constraints. For simplicity we focus on the Laplace mechanism which relies on the Laplace distribution $\mathscr{L}(\cdot)$. For a random variable $X \sim \mathscr{L}(b)$, the probability density function is given by

$$f_X(x \mid b) = \frac{1}{2b} \exp\left(\frac{-|x|}{b}\right),$$

the variance is given by $\sigma^2 = 2b^2$. Intuitively an increase in b corresponds to the distribution flattening out and spreading about the origin. For the purposes of establishing notation we now state some well known results that we will build from.

Suppose that $\mathcal{D}^n$ is the data space for n users. A *query* is a function $\tilde{\mathcal{M}} : \mathcal{D}^n \to \mathbb{R}^r$.In many cases, statistical queries correspond to $r = 1$. A *mechanism*, $\mathcal{M}$, is a randomized function of $\mathbf{d} \subseteq \mathcal{D}^n$. In this work we shall consider additive mechanisms of the form $\mathcal{M}(\mathbf{d}) := \tilde{\mathcal{M}} + \mathbf{Y}$ where $\mathbf{Y}$ is an appropriately defined vector of random variables.

Definition 10.2 (ϱ-Differential privacy). *The mechanism $\mathcal{M}$ preserves ϱ-differential privacy if and only if for all $\mathbf{d}, \mathbf{d}' \in \mathcal{D}^n$ such that $\|\mathbf{d} - \mathbf{d}'\|_0 \leq 1$ and all $\mathcal{W} \subseteq \mathbb{R}^r$, we have*

$$\mathbf{Pr}\{\mathcal{M}(\mathbf{d}) \in \mathcal{W}\} \leq \exp(\varrho)\, \mathbf{Pr}\{\mathcal{M}(\mathbf{d}') \in \mathcal{W}\}.$$

An intuitive way to understand this definition is to rearrange it and use the approximation $\exp(\varrho) \approx 1 + \varrho$ for small positive ϱ, thus

$$\frac{\mathbf{Pr}\{\mathcal{M}(\mathbf{d}) \in \mathcal{W}\}}{\mathbf{Pr}\{\mathcal{M}(\mathbf{d}') \in \mathcal{W}\}} \leq 1 + \varrho.$$

From this we see that when $\mathbf{d}$ and $\mathbf{d}'$ differ by a single element, the probability density of the corresponding mechanisms are similar. The similarity is characterized by ϱ which is referred to as the the *privacy budget.*

Theorem 10.3 (Differentially private Laplace mechanism)**.** *The Laplace mechanism* $\tilde{\mathcal{M}}(\mathbf{d}) + \mathbf{Y}$ *with* $\mathbf{Y}_i \sim \mathscr{L}(\frac{\Delta}{\varrho})$ *for* $i = 1, \ldots, r$*, where*

$$\Delta := \underset{\|\mathbf{d}-\mathbf{d}'\|_0 \leq 1}{\text{maximize}} \quad \|\tilde{\mathcal{M}}(\mathbf{d}) - \tilde{\mathcal{M}}(\mathbf{d}')\|_1, \tag{10.7}$$

provides ϱ*-differential privacy.*

The non-negative scalar Δ is the ℓ_1 sensitivity of the query $\tilde{\mathcal{M}}$. Theorem 10.3 clearly shows us that the variance of the distribution depends on the sensitivity of the query and the level of privacy required. The more sensitive a query is, the "more" noise that must be added to attain a fixed privacy level. Similarly, when less privacy is required, the variance of the distribution decreases.

In the case of optimal power flow data, $\mathbf{d} = (\mathbf{P}^{g\star}, \mathbf{P}^l)$. To emphasize the relationship between the load demand and power generation, we introduce the "OPF operator". Informally, the OPF operator is a nonlinear operator that maps the vector of power loads $\mathbf{P}^l$, solves an OPF problem, and returns the optimal vector[ii] of power generation $\mathbf{P}^{g\star}$. We express this operation as $\mathbf{P}^{g\star} = \mathcal{OPF}(\mathbf{P}^l)$. From this point on, we drop the $\star$ from our notation. It should be implicitly understood that $\mathcal{OPF}$ returns an optimal solution. It will also always be clear from context which OPF problem is being solved. Using this notation, we can now express the problem data as $\mathbf{d} = (\mathcal{OPF}(\mathbf{P}^l), \mathbf{P}^l)$, which leads to the ℓ_1 sensitivity function

$$\underset{\|(\mathcal{OPF}(\mathbf{P}^l),\mathbf{P}^l)-(\mathcal{OPF}(\mathbf{P}^l),\mathbf{P}^l)'\|_0 \leq 1}{\text{maximize}} \quad \|\tilde{\mathcal{M}}(\mathcal{OPF}(\mathbf{P}^l), \mathbf{P}^l) - \tilde{\mathcal{M}}(\{\mathcal{OPF}(\mathbf{P}^l), \mathbf{P}^l\}')\|_1, \tag{10.8}$$

which because of the complex dependencies between load and optimal generation, is a significantly more complicated object than (10.7). Indeed, characterizing the sensitivity function (10.8) is the central to developing an understanding of how differential privacy can be applied to optimal power flow data. As "defined" so far, the OPF operator is applicable to both AC and DC OPF problems. However, at the time of writing, little is known about the behavior of $\mathcal{OPF}$ when the associated OPF problem is anything other than a DC problem. It is also important to note that $\mathcal{OPF}$ is specific to the way the an OPF problem is modeled. In the AC setting, the same power flows can be modeled in different (but equivalent) ways which leads to different OPF problems – the AC OPF Problem 10.4 is just one realization, a

ii. Here we assume that the optimal solution is unique, and this assumption will be further discussed in the next subsection.

different realization will induce a different $\mathcal{OPF}$. We will now focus out attention on the DC OPF operator.

10.5.3 The DC OPF Operator

The OPF operator has been studied in detail in [ZAL20; AZL20] in the DC setting. In this section we will provide a summary of the key results regarding the sensitivity function. In subsequent sections these results will be leveraged to help us understand how network structure and OPF problem data (constraint limits, cost function) determine variance of Laplace distribution required to provide ϱ-differential privacy guarantees.

The first issue we address is when does $\mathcal{OPF}$ return a unique solution? Even although (10.6) is a linear program with a polyhedral constraint set, there is no guarantee that there is a unique solution. In this case $\mathcal{OPF}$ will return the set of all optimal generation vectors. Working with set-valued operators is not trivial and we would like to avoid such a situation. Fortunately, this is straight forward. In [ZAL20] the precise conditions for uniqueness of solution were provided. The exact conditions are somewhat involved and would require several new sets to be defined, which for this chapter would clutter the presentation. Instead, we shall use the fact that the necessary sets are dense with respect to larger, easy to specify sets. The consequence of this is that should the specific problem instance under study fail to meet these conditions, then with probability one, a perturbation to the problem description will satisfy the criteria. For this reason we make the following assumptions:

Assumption 10.4. *The OPF operator maps to a singleton, i.e.,* $\mathcal{OPF} : \mathbb{R}_+^{N_\mathrm{L}} \to \mathbb{R}^{N_\mathrm{G}}$. *The mapping is continuous everywhere and differentiable almost everywhere. Furthermore, all points in the image space of* $\mathcal{OPF}$ *are optimal solutions of* (10.6).

Remark 10.5. *Loosely speaking, the assumptions above are valid when the coefficients* $\mathbf{c}_i$ *for* $i = 1, \ldots, N_\mathrm{G}$ *are all non-negative. The parameters that define OPF* (10.6), $\{\mathbf{p}_{\min}, \mathbf{p}_{\max}, \mathbf{P}^g_{\min}, \mathbf{P}^g_{\max}\}$, *are chosen such that a feasible solution exists, and the feasible solution has* $N_\mathrm{G} - 1$ *active inequalities. Full details are available in [ZAL20].*

The OPF operator is now used to define the concept of "monotonicity" for power networks. Recall that a function $f : \mathbb{R}^n \to \mathbb{R}$ is said to be monotonic (sometimes referred to as "order preserving"), if for all $\mathbf{x}, \mathbf{y} \in \mathbb{R}^n$ we have that

$$\mathbf{x} \geq \mathbf{y} \quad \Rightarrow \quad f(\mathbf{x}) \geq f(\mathbf{y}),$$

where the inequality on the left hand side is taken element-wise. In order to reconcile monotonicity with differential privacy, we will consider the case where f above is replaced by $\mathcal{OPF}$ and $\mathbf{x}$ and $\mathbf{y}$ are constrained to differ in exactly one element.

Definition 10.6 (Monotonicity). *A power system is said to be monotone if for all* $\mathbf{x}, \mathbf{y} \in \mathbb{R}^{N_G}$ *such that* $\mathbf{x} \geq \mathbf{y}$ *and with* $\mathbf{x}$ *and* $\mathbf{y}$ *being feasible load profiles, we have that* $\mathcal{OPF}(\mathbf{x}) \geq \mathcal{OPF}(\mathbf{y})$.

In words, a power system is monotone if, given a vector of power demands (loads) and corresponding optimal generations, a load increase will not cause a decrease in power generated at any bus in the network.

Monotonicity, as per Definition 10.6 attempts to characterize how the optimal power generation reacts to a change in load. Clearly, monotonicity is related to the ℓ_1 sensitivity function (10.8). Unfortunately, Definition 10.6 only provides a partial characterization of the load–generation relationship. In order to provide a complete characterization, we introduce the the notion of (δ, ε)-monotonicity.

Definition 10.7 ((δ, ε)-monotonicity). *For* $\delta > 0$, *and* $\varepsilon \geq 0$, *a power system is said to be* (δ, ε)*-monotone if for all* $\mathbf{x}, \mathbf{y} \in \mathbb{R}^{N_L}$ *such that* $\mathbf{y} + \delta\mathbf{1} \geq \mathbf{x} \geq \mathbf{y}$ *and* $\|\mathbf{x} - \mathbf{y}\|_0 = 1$, *we have that*

$$\sum_{i=1}^{N_G} [\mathcal{OPF}_i(\mathbf{x}) - \mathcal{OPF}_i(\mathbf{y})]^- \geq -\varepsilon,$$

where for $[z]^- := \min\{0, z\}$ *for* $z \in \mathbb{R}$.

In the definition above, the parameter ε covers for the fact that power generation is allowed to decrease, and δ describes the "spread" of the load $\mathbf{y}$. Clearly, any system which is monotone according to Definition 10.6 is $(\delta, 0)$-monotone for any choice of positive δ. Note that any value of ε that satisfies the inequality in Definition 10.7 is valid, however, when we make use of monotonicity in the context of privacy later on, the smaller ε is, the better. Determining the (δ, ε) parameters is in general a difficult task. For certain classes of networks we can provide analytic expressions.

IEEE 9-bus Network

We first consider a simple test network with 9 buses. The network consists of 3 generator and 6 load buses. The IEEE 9-bus network is perhaps the simplest and most commonly used network for studying optimal power flow problems. Here we use it to illustrate the fact that monotonicity can be too stringent a requirement for even simple networks. We then use it to provide some intuition about (δ, ε)-monotonicity. The network is depicted in Figure 10.3. At each of the generator buses and two of the load buses, we have included a graph which shows how various loads and generations change.

We first consider bus 9 (lower left corner of Figure 10.3). The graph associated with bus 9 shows that the load, i.e., power demanded at this bus increases with time. It is assumed that all other loads remain constant. Note that although the

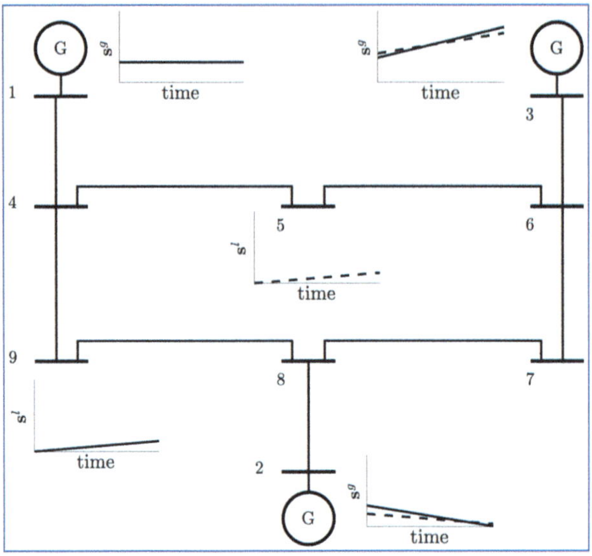

Figure 10.3. IEEE 9-bus network. The 'G' nodes denote generators, and the numbered lines are transmission lines.

line looks continuous, in reality this is a set of discrete loads. For every value of the load, we solve (10.6), or equivalently calculate $\mathbf{P}^g = \mathcal{OPF}(\mathbf{P}^l)$ and plot the resulting generations for each of the three generators on their respective graphs. If the network (for this particular choice of network parameters) was monotone, then graphs at each of the 3 generator buses would all be non-decreasing. At bus 1, the graph is non-decreasing. In fact, it is constant. This is likely because the generator is at its maximum capacity. At bus 3, an increase in power generation is observed. Surprisingly, at bus 2, the generator decreases its power output. From this we conclude that the system in not monotonic. This simulation highlights the complexity optimal power flow problems – despite bus 2 being closer to bus 9 (in a graph theoretical distance sense) it is bus 3 that provides the additional power required. In Figure 10.3 we also consider the case where the load at bus 5 is varied (with all other loads kept constant) and see similar results (dashed lines). We state the following theorem without proof.

Remark 10.8. *The IEEE 9-bus network is* $(\delta, 2.01\delta)$*-monotone. This parameterization is invariant to changes in the cost function and* ξ.

The implication of this is that the optimal generation at any bus in the network will not decrease by more than 2.01 times the increase in the load.

In addition to monotonicity, we will also discuss derivatives of $\mathcal{OPF}$. Combined with monotonicity, this will provide an almost complete understanding of the sensitivity of the problem. As with monotonicity, the exact details for when derivatives can be taken are described in [ZAL20]. For now we rely on Assumption 10.4 and assume everything is well defined. Of interest to us is the how the optimal power generation at each generator changes as a function of changes in the load. We denote the vector of derivatives of $\mathcal{OPF}$ with respect to the loads by $\partial_{\mathbf{P}^l}\mathcal{OPF}(\mathbf{P}^l)$.

Theorem 10.9. *When Assumption 10.4 holds, the local derivative $\partial_{\mathbf{P}^l}\mathcal{OPF}(\mathbf{P}^l)$ exists and the set of binding constraints in* (10.6) *remains unchanged.*

The second part of the statement in Theorem 10.9 is useful because it also tells us about the behavior of the optimal power flow problem. It tells us that for almost all the problem instances, when the load changes, any constraints that have hit their upper or lower limits will remain at those limits and no new constraints will reach capacity. We can actually go one stage further and write down an explicit algebraic relationship between the load and the optimal generation and voltage angle. To proceed, we need to define two sets that account for binding inequalities in (10.6).

Definition 10.10. *Consider the DC OPF problem* (10.6) *and the graph $\mathcal{G}(\mathcal{V}, \mathcal{E})$ associated with it. Assume that* (10.6) *has been solved. Define the set $\mathcal{S}_{\mathrm{G}} \subseteq \mathcal{V}_{\mathrm{G}}$ as the set of generators producing power at maximum or minimum capacity, i.e., equal to the corresponding value in $\mathbf{P}^g_{\max}$ or $\mathbf{P}^g_{\min}$. Likewise do the same for edges with power flows at maximum or minimum capacity corresponding to $\mathbf{p}_{\max}, \mathbf{p}_{\min}$. Denote this set as $\mathcal{S}_{\mathrm{B}}$.*

We will not prove this here, but it can be shown that the total number of active constraints is

$$|\mathcal{S}_{\mathrm{B}}| + |\mathcal{S}_{\mathrm{G}}| = N_{\mathrm{G}} - 1,$$

where $|\cdot|$ applied to a set denotes cardinality.

The Jacobian matrix defines the effect of all load changes on all optimal generations. Assume the network parameters are fixed, i.e., $\boldsymbol{\xi}$ is constant and that the coefficients in the cost function c_i are all positive. Formally, the Jacobian is

$$[\mathbf{J}(\mathbf{P}^l; \mathbf{c}, \boldsymbol{\xi})]_{i,j} := \frac{\partial(\mathbf{P}^g_i)^\star}{\partial \mathbf{P}^l_j} = \frac{\partial[\mathcal{OPF}(\mathbf{P}^l)]_i}{\partial \mathbf{P}^l_j}.$$

However, if one has access to the solution of (10.6) then the Jacobian can be stated explicitly as a function of $\boldsymbol{\xi}$ and $(\mathcal{S}_{\mathrm{G}}, \mathcal{S}_{\mathrm{B}})$. We briefly introduce the following notation; let $\mathbf{I}^N$ denote the $n \times n$ identity matrix. Given a set $\mathcal{S}$ let $\mathbf{I}^N_{\mathcal{S}}$ denotes the matrix formed by stacking the rows of $\mathbf{I}^N$ indexed by the elements of $\mathcal{S}$.

Theorem 10.11. *When Assumption 10.4 holds, and the set of binding constraints of* (10.6) *is known, the Jacobian $\mathbf{J}(\mathbf{P}^l; \mathbf{c}, \boldsymbol{\xi})$ can be explicitly written as*

$$\mathbf{J}(\mathcal{S}_{\mathrm{G}}, \mathcal{S}_{\mathrm{B}}) = \boldsymbol{\Psi} \cdot (\mathbf{I}^N_{[N_{\mathrm{L}}]})^T$$

where $\boldsymbol{\Psi} = -\mathbf{I}^N_{[N_L]}\mathbf{L}\mathbf{Z}(\mathcal{S}_G, \mathcal{S}_B)^T$, *where* $\mathbf{L} = \mathbf{C}\mathbf{B}\mathbf{C}^T$, *and*

$$\mathbf{Z}(\mathcal{S}_G, \mathcal{S}_B)^T = \begin{bmatrix} \mathbf{I}^N_{\mathcal{V}_L}\mathbf{L} \\ \mathbf{I}^N_{\mathcal{V}_G}\mathbf{L} \\ \mathbf{I}^E_{\mathcal{S}_B}\mathbf{B}\mathbf{C}^T \\ \mathbf{e}_1 \end{bmatrix}^{-1},$$

and the inverse always exists.

The Jacobian matrix is useful in its own right, it also serves two other purposes. It can be used to provide an upper-bound on the ℓ_1 sensitivity Δ – although we won't pursue that further here. The Jacobian also provides useful insight into how to gauge the (δ, ε)-monotonicity parameters.

Taken together, Definitions 10.7, 10.10, and Theorem 10.11 provide all the information about the sensitivity of $\mathcal{OPF}$ required in order to apply differential privacy to the data set $\mathbf{d} = (\mathbf{P}^{g\star}, \mathbf{P}^l)$. For details on how to compute sensitivity, the reader is referred to [ZAL20; AZL20]. Note that the Jacobian definition and the closed-form expression produce the same matrix. Unless a specific form the Jacobian is required, we drop the arguments and simply refer to it as $\mathbf{J}$.

10.5.4 Differential Privacy

We are now in a position to integrate the results from the previous section regarding sensitivity, with the classical ideas of differential privacy. For simplicity, we focus on the Laplacian mechanism. We make no claim about this mechanism being "perfect" for power system data sets. The goal is to demonstrate that potential for privacy methods in this application domain. Proofs of the main results can be found in [ZAL19]

To reiterate, our goal is to release data sets of the form $\mathbf{d} = (\mathbf{P}^{g\star}, \mathbf{P}^l)$ in order for users to i) run statistical queries on the load-demand data, and/or ii) solve optimal power flow problems using realistic load data. With regards to the second problem, network parameters $\boldsymbol{\xi}$, and the cost function may, or may not, be publicly available. We assume that the network graph is available.

The mechanism $\mathcal{M}$ acts on both vectors $\mathbf{P}^{g\star}$ and $\mathbf{P}^l$, for brevity, instead of writing $\mathcal{M}(\mathbf{P}^{g\star}, \mathbf{P}^l)$, we will instead simply write $\mathcal{M}(\mathbf{P}^l)$ and it is to be implicitly understood that the optimal generations are obtained by solving an appropriate DC optimal power flow problem.

We will now show that the task of designing a mechanism that hides individual load changes, follows the classical results closely. Indeed, most of the difficulty was in formulating how to measure query sensitivity when the query involves solving a linear program. The first step is to modify the definition of differential privacy.

Definition 10.12 ((Δ, ϱ)-differential privacy). *For $\Delta > 0$ and $\varrho > 0$, the mechanism $\mathcal{M}$ is said to preserve (Δ, ϱ)-differential privacy if and only if for all $(\mathbf{P}^l)'$ and $(\mathbf{P}^l)''$ such that*

$$\|(\mathbf{P}^l)' - (\mathbf{P}^l)''\|_0 \leq 1 \quad \textit{and} \quad \|(\mathbf{P}^l)' - (\mathbf{P}^l)''\|_1 \leq \Delta,$$

and for all $\mathcal{W} \subseteq \mathbb{R}^r$, we have

$$\mathbf{Pr}\{\mathcal{M}((\mathbf{P}^l)') \in \mathcal{W}\} \leq \exp(\varrho)\, \mathbf{Pr}\{\mathcal{M}((\mathbf{P}^l)'') \in \mathcal{W}\}.$$

Remark 10.13. *The notation used in Definition 10.12 should not be confused with the standard notion of (ε, δ)-differential privacy used outside of this chapter. We also reiterate that $\mathcal{M}(\mathbf{P}^l)$ is shorthand for $\mathcal{M}(\mathbf{P}^{g\star}, \mathbf{P}^l)$.*

A straight forward application of Theorem 10.3 can be applied to Definition 10.12.

Lemma 10.14. *Assume $\tilde{\mathcal{M}}(\mathbf{P}^{g\star}, P^l)$ is a deterministic query. The mechanism $\mathcal{M} = \tilde{\mathcal{M}} + \mathbf{Y}$ with $\mathbf{Y}_i \sim \mathscr{L}(\frac{\Delta_1}{\varrho})$ for $i = 1, \ldots, r$, preserves (Δ, ϱ)-differential privacy, if for any $(\mathbf{P}^l)'$ and $(\mathbf{P}^l)''$ such that $\|(\mathbf{P}^l)' - (\mathbf{P}^l)''\|_0 \leq 1$ and $\|(\mathbf{P}^l)' - (\mathbf{P}^l)''\|_1 \leq \Delta$, Δ_1 satisfies $\|\tilde{\mathcal{M}}((\mathbf{P}^l)') - \tilde{\mathcal{M}}((\mathbf{P}^l)'')\|_1 \leq \Delta_1$.*

This result doesn't transparently take into account the underlying properties of the network or the associated OPF problem. Before we present the most general and transparent result, we require one final definition. Denote by $\mathbf{J}_{\tilde{\mathcal{M}}}$ the Jacobian matrix of the query function, i.e., the matrix of partial derivatives of the query $\tilde{\mathcal{M}}$ with respect to changes in the load vector.

Theorem 10.15. *Suppose a power system is (Δ, ε)-monotone, and the magnitude of all the elements in the Jacobian matrix $\mathbf{J}_{\tilde{\mathcal{M}}}$ are upper bounded by τ. Then the mechanism $\mathcal{M} = \tilde{\mathcal{M}} + \mathbf{Y}$, with $\mathbf{Y}_i \sim \mathscr{L}(\frac{2\tau r(\Delta+\varepsilon)}{\varrho})$, provides (Δ, ϱ)-differential privacy.*

The theorem above makes it clear power system with associated optimal power problems that are far from monotone (large values of ε) require distributions with a significantly larger variance than their monotone counterparts. Note that Theorem 10.15 is only applicable for smooth and differential queries, and the Jacobian matrix $\mathbf{J}_{\tilde{\mathcal{M}}}$ is different from the Jacobian matrix $\mathbf{J}$ of $\mathcal{OPF}$ operator, which we defined earlier. One way to interpret Theorem 10.15 is that the query $\tilde{\mathcal{M}}(\mathcal{OPF}(\mathbf{P}^l), \mathbf{P}^l)$ can be viewed as the composition of functions $\tilde{\mathcal{M}}$ and $\mathcal{OPF}$. By the chain rule, its ℓ_1 sensitivity can also be decomposed as the sensitivity of $\tilde{\mathcal{M}}$ (characterized by τ) and the sensitivity of $\mathcal{OPF}$ (characterized by (Δ, ε)-monotonicity).

Corollary 10.16. *Let τ and $\mathcal{M}$ be defined as in Theorem 10.15. A monotone power system with $\mathbf{Y}_i \sim \mathscr{L}(\frac{2\tau r\Delta}{\varrho})$, ensures (Δ, ϱ)-differential privacy.*

One has to be careful when interpreting the Corollary 10.16. As any monotone system is $(\Delta, 0)$-monotone for any value of $\Delta > 0$, it is tempting to simply make Δ arbitrarily small in order to make $\frac{2\tau\Delta}{\varrho}$ arbitrarily small. However, Δ controls the privacy level as well, thus making it arbitrarily small will compromise more privacy of the power system data.

The final scenario we consider concerns aggregated data. It is often the case that power flow data is available in aggregate form. Most often, data from a geographical region is pooled, and summary statistics about the data set are released. We consider the following simple scenario (more complicated settings are easily accommodated for): Instead of the data owner releasing $\mathbf{d}(\mathbf{P}^{g\star}, \mathbf{P}^l)$, summary statistics for certain "regions" are released. A disaggregation algorithm then acts on this data to try and reverse engineer the original $\mathbf{d}(\mathbf{P}^{g\star}, \mathbf{P}^l)$. Of course, exact recovery is almost surely impossible, but generating estimates of the data that is consistent with the aggregated data is possible [AZL18]. Let's make things more concrete. Assume the power network and data set we care about has been split into m distinct regions $\mathcal{R}_1, \ldots, \mathcal{R}_m$, where $\mathcal{R}_i \subset \mathcal{V}$. For simplicity assume that $\mathcal{R}_i \cap \mathcal{R}_j = \emptyset$ for all i, j. The aggregation query for region i returns two quantities, the sum of the load and the sum of the generation:

$$\tilde{\mathcal{M}}_i^g = \sum_{j \in \mathcal{R}_i} \mathbf{P}_j^g, \quad \tilde{\mathcal{M}}_i^l = \sum_{j \in \mathcal{R}_i} \mathbf{P}_j^l,$$

where again we have dropped the $\star$ superscript from the generation vector. The data owner discloses corrupted versions of $\tilde{\mathcal{M}}_i^g$ and $\mathcal{M}_i^g$. we assume that these statistics are to be released using the Laplacian mechanism. In a more realistic scenario, the exponential mechanism would be used as this may prevent sign changes in the data. We pursue the Laplacian mechanism as it fits with the results presented so far. The Laplace mechanism adds iid Laplace random variables and is defined to be

$$\mathcal{M}^{\text{agg}}(\mathbf{P}^g, \mathbf{P}^l) = [\mathcal{M}_1^g, \ldots, \mathcal{M}_m^g, \mathcal{M}_1^l, \ldots, \mathcal{M}_m^l],$$

with $\mathcal{M}_i^g = \tilde{\mathcal{M}}_i^g + \mathbf{Y}_i$ and $\mathcal{M}_i^l = \tilde{\mathcal{M}}_i^l + \mathbf{Y}_i$. Using this definition of the aggregation mechanism we arrive at the following result:

Lemma 10.17. *Let the power system of interest be (Δ, ε)-monotone. The mechanism $\mathcal{M}^{\text{agg}}$ preserves (Δ, ϱ)-differential privacy when $\mathbf{Y}_i^g, \mathbf{Y}_i^l$ for $i = 1, \ldots, m$ are i.i.d. random variables drawn from $\mathscr{L}(\frac{2(\Delta+\varepsilon)}{\varrho})$.*

An important observation to make is that the variance of the Laplace distribution in Lemma 10.17 does not depend on the number of aggregated regions m, or the number of buses in a region. For the aggregation query, it is straight forward to show that the $\mathbf{J}_{\tilde{\mathcal{M}}}$ upper bound, τ in Theorem 10.15 is equal to one.

10.5.5 Beyond DC-OPF

The previous section outlined how differential privacy can be applied to data generated from DC OPF problems. There is however a body of work that applies differential privacy to OPF problems with the full AC power flow equations in various privacy scenarios: [FV18; MFV20b; MFV20a; Dvo+20]. We won't delve deeply into this topic, however we will illustrate the difficulties of dealing with AC optimal power flow problems and describe how the work in [MFV20a] addresses these problems.

The fundamental issue that arises when dealing with the AC-OPF Problem 10.4 and its variants, is that perturbations to the load profile may result in an infeasible optimization problem. Moreover, even when the perturbed problem is feasible, the magnitude of the difference between the true optimal solution and the perturbed solution may be large. The closeness of the two solutions is termed *fidelity*. In the DC setting, fidelity is quantified using the results characterizing the sensitivity of the $\mathcal{OPF}$ operator as described in Section 10.5.3. Unfortunately, there is no straight forward extension to the AC-OPF setting. However, the abstraction of $\mathcal{OPF}$ as a mapping from load to optimal generation is useful and used without the theoretical guarantees provided in the DC setting. In [MFV20a], algorithms are developed with two goals in mind:

1. *Privacy:* The vector of (complex) demands $\mathbf{S}^d$ and the perturbed loads $\hat{\mathbf{S}}^d$ should satisfy:
   (a) $|\mathbf{S}_i^d - \hat{\mathbf{S}}_i^d| \leq \alpha$ and $\mathbf{S}_j^d = \hat{\mathbf{S}}_j^d$ for all $j \neq i$, where $\alpha > 0$.
   (b) For $\mathbf{S}^d$ and $\hat{\mathbf{S}}^d$ satisfying the adjacency relationship above,

$$\mathbf{Pr}\{\mathcal{M}(\mathbf{S}^d) \in \mathcal{W}\} \leq \exp(\varrho)\,\mathbf{Pr}\{\mathcal{M}(\hat{\mathbf{S}}_j^d) \in \mathcal{W}\}$$

2. *Fidelity:* The obfuscated loads $\hat{\mathbf{S}}^d$ provide an objective value that is close to ground truth:

$$|f(\mathcal{OPF}(\hat{\mathbf{S}}^d)) - \mathcal{O}^\star| \leq \beta\mathcal{O}^\star,$$

   for $\beta > 0$, where $\mathcal{O}^\star = f(\mathcal{OPF}(\mathbf{S}^d))$ with f the cost function from (10.4). Note, here we have overloaded $\mathcal{OPF}$ to return a solution to an AC optimal power flow problem. No claims about uniqueness are made. When multiple optimal solutions exist, a single solution is chosen at random.

Here we highlight some of the subtleties and difficulties of dealing with AC power flow models. The first obstacle in out path is that the Laplacian mechanism now needs to be applied to a query which may return complex values. Inspired by the work from differential locational privacy [ABCP13], complex numbers are represented in a polar coordinate system (as opposed to a planar system) and the *polar Laplacian distribution* is used. A desirable property of the polar Laplacian pdf is that the the radius and angle (that define the random complex variable) can be drawn independently from each other. In contrast, using a multi-dimensional Laplacian distribution would require drawing both parameters together in order to achieve the correct scaling. As a result, drawing the random variable $z = r\exp(j\theta)$ is done by drawing θ uniformly at random from $[0, 2\pi)$. Obtaining r is a two step process: first, draw a scalar p uniformly at random from $[0, 1)$ and the set $r = C_\varepsilon^{-1}(p)$, where

$$C_\varepsilon^{-1}(p) = -\frac{1}{\varepsilon}(W_{-1}(\frac{p-1}{e}) + 1),$$

and W_{-1} is the (-1 branch of the) Lambert W function. The ε term is the measure of differential privacy required in the classical sense of ε-differential privacy. The output of the privacy stage is a load vector $\tilde{\mathbf{S}}^d$ that is additively corrupted by random variables from the polar Laplacian distribution. This intermediate vector will be the input to the fidelity phase.

The fidelity phase is more challenging. One way to view this phase is as post-processing the complex vector $\tilde{\mathbf{S}}^d$. Formally it takes the form of a bi-level (sometimes referred to as a multi-stage) optimization problem [Dem02]:

$$\begin{aligned} \underset{\mathbf{S}^g, \hat{\mathbf{S}}^d}{\text{minimize}} \quad & \|\hat{\mathbf{S}}^d - \tilde{\mathbf{S}}^d\|_2^2 \\ \text{subject to} \quad & |f(\mathbf{S}^g) - \mathcal{O}^\star| \leq \beta\mathcal{O}^\star \\ & \mathbf{S}^g = \mathcal{OPF}(\hat{\mathbf{S}}^d). \end{aligned} \tag{10.9}$$

We re-iterate that $\mathcal{OPF}$ here in notationally overloaded and it refers to a mapping of complex load demands to optimal complex power generations through the AC-OPF Problem 10.4. The interpretation of the fidelity post-processing stage is that of re-distributing the Laplacian noise that was introduced in the first step of the process. While the combination of the polar Laplacian distribution and the bi-level post-processing stage achieve the two goals set out at the beginning of the section, unfortunately, solving (10.9) is intractable. Indeed, bi-level programs are strongly NP-hard, moreover, verifying a solution of a such a problem is NP-hard [VSJ94]. The work in [MFV20a] proposes three relaxations to the fidelity stage, each of which satisfies the bound

$$\frac{\|\hat{\mathbf{S}}^d - \mathbf{S}^d\|_2}{\|\tilde{\mathbf{S}}^d - \mathbf{S}^d\|_2} \leq 2,$$

where $\tilde{\mathbf{S}}^d$ is the is the output of (10.9). Extensive numerical simulations assess the accuracy and typical behaviors of the three relaxations in addition to their computational run-times. It is shown that the methods proposed offer orders of magnitude better accuracy than naively applying the Laplacian mechanism to the load data.

10.6 Concluding Remarks

In this chapter we have provided a high level overview of modern energy systems, with a focus on the path from energy production to transmission and control. Our aim was to highlight the need for privacy in energy systems, and specifically examine how differential privacy can be applied in relation to optimal power flow data. The majority of the chapter examined the DC-OPF setting where convex (linear) programming is the algorithmic tool of choice. We concluded by dipping into the significantly harder problem of preserving privacy of AC-OPF data, where we tried to highlight some of the inherent challenges.

This is a new and rapidly evolving area of research, we hope this survey will attract more attention to research at the interface of energy and privacy.

References

[ABCP13] M. E. Andrés, N. E. Bordenabe, K. Chatzikokolakis, and C. Palamidessi. "Geo-indistinguishability: Differential privacy for location-based systems". In: Proceedings of the 2013 ACM SIGSAC conference on Computer & communications security. 2013, pp. 901–914 (cit. on p. 379).

[ADPK20] S. Acharya, Y. Dvorkin, H. Pandžić, and R. Karri. "Cybersecurity of Smart Electric Vehicle Charging: A Power Grid Perspective". In: IEEE Access 8 (2020), pp. 214434–214453 (cit. on p. 359).

[AR13] A. Albert and R. Rajagopal. "Smart meter driven segmentation: What your consumption says about you". In: IEEE Transactions on power systems 28.4 (2013), pp. 4019–4030 (cit. on p. 358).

[AZL18] J. Anderson, F. Zhou, and S. H. Low. "Disaggregation for networked power systems". In: 2018 Power Systems Computation Conference (PSCC). IEEE. 2018, pp. 1–7 (cit. on p. 378).

[AZL20] J. Anderson, F. Zhou, and S. H. Low. "Worst-case sensitivity of DC optimal power flow problems". In: 2020 American Control

Conference (ACC). IEEE. 2020, pp. 3156–3163 (cit. on pp. 372, 376).

[BBA16] P. Barbosa, A. Brito, and H. Almeida. "A technique to provide differential privacy for appliance usage in smart metering". In: Information Sciences 370 (2016), pp. 355–367 (cit. on p. 358).

[Bie15] D. Bienstock. Electrical transmission system cascades and vulnerability: an operations research viewpoint. SIAM, 2015 (cit. on p. 363).

[BKJB13] E. Buchmann, S. Kessler, P. Jochem, and K. Böhm. "The costs of privacy in local energy markets". In: 2013 IEEE 15th Conference on Business Informatics. IEEE. 2013, pp. 198–207 (cit. on p. 359).

[Car62] J. Carpentier. "Contribution to the economic dispatch problem". In: Bulletin de la Societe Francoise des Electriciens 3.8 (1962), pp. 431–447 (cit. on p. 366).

[CV14] C. Coffrin and P. Van Hentenryck. "A linear-programming approximation of AC power flows". In: INFORMS Journal on Computing 26.4 (2014), pp. 718–734 (cit. on p. 368).

[Dem02] S. Dempe. Foundations of bilevel programming. Springer Science & Business Media, 2002 (cit. on p. 380).

[DR+14] C. Dwork, A. Roth, et al. "The algorithmic foundations of differential privacy." In: Foundations and Trends in Theoretical Computer Science 9.3-4 (2014), pp. 211–407 (cit. on pp. 360, 361).

[Dvo+20] V. Dvorkin, F. Fioretto, P. Van Hentenryck, P. Pinson, and J. Kazempour. "Differentially Private Optimal Power Flow for Distribution Grids". In: IEEE Transactions on Power Systems (2020) (cit. on p. 379).

[EE17] G. Eibl and D. Engel. "Differential privacy for real smart metering data". In: Computer Science-Research and Development 32.1-2 (2017), pp. 173–182 (cit. on p. 358).

[Eib+18] G. Eibl, K. Bao, P.-W. Grassal, D. Bernau, and H. Schmeck. "The influence of differential privacy on short term electric load forecasting". In: Energy Informatics 1.1 (2018), pp. 93–113 (cit. on p. 359).

[FMV20] F. Fioretto, L. Mitridati, and P. Van Hentenryck. "Differential privacy for Stackelberg games". In: arXiv preprint arXiv:2002.00944 (2020) (cit. on p. 359).

[FR16] S. Frank and S. Rebennack. "An introduction to optimal power flow: Theory, formulation, and examples". In: IIE Transactions 48.12 (2016), pp. 1172–1197 (cit. on p. 366).

[FSR12] S. Frank, I. Steponavice, and S. Rebennack. "Optimal power flow: a bibliographic survey I". In: Energy systems 3.3 (2012), pp. 221–258 (cit. on p. 366).

[FV18] F. Fioretto and P. Van Hentenryck. "Constrained-based differential privacy: Releasing optimal power flow benchmarks privately". In: International Conference on the Integration of Constraint Programming, Artificial Intelligence, and Operations Research. Springer. 2018, pp. 215–231 (cit. on p. 379).

[GBP21] C. Goncalves, R. J. Bessa, and P. Pinson. "Privacy-preserving Distributed Learning for Renewable Energy Forecasting". In: IEEE Transactions on Sustainable Energy (2021) (cit. on p. 359).

[GFDK19] M. GhoddousiBoroujeni, D. Fay, C. Dimitrakakis, and M. Kamgarpour. "Privacy of real-time pricing in smart grid". In: 2019 IEEE 58th Conference on Decision and Control (CDC). IEEE. 2019, pp. 5162–5167 (cit. on p. 358).

[GGP17] G. Giaconi, D. Gündüz, and H. V. Poor. "Smart meter privacy with renewable energy and an energy storage device". In: IEEE Transactions on Information Forensics and Security 13.1 (2017), pp. 129–142 (cit. on p. 358).

[Har92] G. W. Hart. "Nonintrusive appliance load monitoring". In: Proceedings of the IEEE 80.12 (1992), pp. 1870–1891 (cit. on p. 358).

[HG91] M. Huneault and F. Galiana. "A survey of the optimal power flow literature". In: IEEE transactions on Power Systems 6.2 (1991), pp. 762–770 (cit. on p. 366).

[HRC19] M. U. Hassan, M. H. Rehmani, and J. Chen. "Differential privacy techniques for cyber physical systems: a survey". In: IEEE Communications Surveys & Tutorials 22.1 (2019), pp. 746–789 (cit. on p. 358).

[Lee+20] Z. J. Lee, G. Lee, T. Lee, C. Jin, R. Lee, Z. Low, D. Chang, C. Ortega, and S. H. Low. "Adaptive Charging Networks: A Framework for Smart Electric Vehicle Charging". In: arXiv preprint arXiv:2012.02636 (2020) (cit. on p. 359).

[LLSY16] N. Li, M. Lyu, D. Su, and W. Yang. "Differential privacy: From theory to practice". In: Synthesis Lectures on Information Security, Privacy, & Trust 8.4 (2016), pp. 1–138 (cit. on p. 361).

[Low14a] S. H. Low. "Convex relaxation of optimal power flow?Part I: Formulations and equivalence". In: IEEE Transactions on Control of Network Systems 1.1 (2014), pp. 15–27 (cit. on p. 366).

[Low14b] S. H. Low. "Convex relaxation of optimal power flow?Part II: Exactness". In: IEEE Transactions on Control of Network Systems 1.2 (2014), pp. 177–189 (cit. on p. 366).

[MFV20a] T. W. Mak, F. Fioretto, and P. Van Hentenryck. "Bilevel Optimization for Differentially Private Optimization in Energy Systems". In: arXiv e-prints (2020), arXiv–2001 (cit. on pp. 379, 380).

[MFV20b] T. W. Mak, F. Fioretto, and P. Van Hentenryck. "Privacy-preserving obfuscation for distributed power systems". In: Electric Power Systems Research 189 (2020), p. 106718 (cit. on p. 379).

[MLBB20] J. Machowski, Z. Lubosny, J. W. Bialek, and J. R. Bumby. Power system dynamics: stability and control. John Wiley & Sons, 2020 (cit. on p. 363).

[MM09] P. McDaniel and S. McLaughlin. "Security and privacy challenges in the smart grid". In: IEEE Security & Privacy 7.3 (2009), pp. 75–77 (cit. on p. 358).

[MMA11] S. McLaughlin, P. McDaniel, and W. Aiello. "Protecting consumer privacy from electric load monitoring". In: Proceedings of the 18th ACM conference on Computer and communications security. 2011, pp. 87–98 (cit. on p. 358).

[Mom17] J. A. Momoh. Electric power system applications of optimization. CRC press, 2017 (cit. on p. 363).

[OCS04] T. J. Overbye, X. Cheng, and Y. Sun. "A comparison of the AC and DC power flow models for LMP calculations". In: 37th Annual Hawaii International Conference on System Sciences, 2004. Proceedings of the. IEEE. 2004, 9–pp (cit. on p. 368).

[PMVB05] K. Purchala, L. Meeus, D. Van Dommelen, and R. Belmans. "Usefulness of DC power flow for active power flow analysis". In: IEEE Power Engineering Society General Meeting, 2005. IEEE. 2005, pp. 454–459 (cit. on p. 368).

[SA74] B. Stott and O. Alsac. "Fast decoupled load flow". In: IEEE transactions on power apparatus and systems 3 (1974), pp. 859–869 (cit. on p. 368).

[VSJ94] L. Vicente, G. Savard, and J. Júdice. "Descent approaches for quadratic bilevel programming". In: Journal of Optimization Theory and Applications 81.2 (1994), pp. 379–399 (cit. on p. 380).

[ZAL19] F. Zhou, J. Anderson, and S. H. Low. "Differential privacy of aggregated DC optimal power flow data". In: 2019 American Control Conference (ACC). IEEE. 2019, pp. 1307–1314 (cit. on p. 376).

[ZAL20] F. Zhou, J. Anderson, and S. H. Low. "The optimal power flow operator: Theory and computation". In: IEEE Transactions on Control of Network Systems (2020) (cit. on pp. 372, 375, 376).

[Zha+15] Z. Zhang, Z. Qin, L. Zhu, W. Jiang, C. Xu, and K. Ren. "Toward practical differential privacy in smart grid with capacity-limited rechargeable batteries". In: arXiv preprint arXiv:1507.03000 (2015) (cit. on p. 358).

[ZJWL14] J. Zhao, T. Jung, Y. Wang, and X. Li. "Achieving differential privacy of data disclosure in the smart grid". In: IEEE INFOCOM 2014-IEEE Conference on Computer Communications. IEEE. 2014, pp. 504–512 (cit. on p. 358).

[Zoh+20] F. Zohrizadeh, C. Josz, M. Jin, R. Madani, J. Lavaei, and S. Sojoudi. "A survey on conic relaxations of optimal power flow problem". In: European journal of operational research 287.2 (2020), pp. 391–409 (cit. on p. 367).

[ZPAB13] S. Zeadally, A.-S. K. Pathan, C. Alcaraz, and M. Badra. "Towards privacy protection in smart grid". In: Wireless personal communications 73.1 (2013), pp. 23–50 (cit. on p. 358).

DOI: 10.1561/9781638284772.ch11

Chapter 11

Image and Video Data Analysis

By Liyue Fan

11.1 Introduction

Image and video data have been increasingly generated and their analysis is ubiquitous in our daily life. The richness of visual data as well as recent technological advances in computer vision inflict great privacy concerns. Classic differential privacy, which originated in statistical databases, has been applied to generating aggregate statistics or training machine learning models, while protecting the privacy of input data. The rigorous nature of DP makes it desirable for protecting sensitive information that can be inferred from image and video data. As a recent research direction, this chapter discusses the role of differential privacy in image and video analysis, especially the developments in sanitizing image and video data. Specifically, we will look at DP notions that aim to quantify sensitive information in image and video data. Furthermore, we will introduce practical privacy and quality measures for evaluating DP methods. We realize that much of the image and video analysis is based on machine learning techniques, and thus direct interested readers to Part II for learning with differential privacy.

As a society, we collectively generate massive amounts of image and video data at a high speed. Studies show that photo-sharing is one of the most common activities of over two-thirds of American adults who now use social media [Dug15; Smi17].

(a) Blurred face of a survivor of human trafficking [UNO10].

(b) Mosaic faces in a police raid [Ait16].

Figure 11.1. Example news images where faces have been obfuscated for privacy (best when zoom).

Approximately 1,000 Terabytes of video data are generated every minute [Kno13] from social media sites to surveillance cameras. Applications that rely on image and video data are ubiquitous, from surveillance to tele-medicine, from facial recognition to eye tracking. In this chapter we will look at the application of differential privacy to image and video data and understand how DP methods intersect with image and video applications.

11.1.1 Perceptions and Expectations for Visual Privacy

Visual anonymity in images and videos is very important for communication research and modern journalism. By providing anonymity, individuals are able to speak more freely [Ano98; Mar01; Sco04], e.g., for conveying sensitive information, expressing marginalized views, and protecting them from retaliation or subsequent contact. Currently visual anonymity is often achieved by blurring or mosaicing faces in pictures and video clips. Figure 11.1 shows two examples where visual anonymity is necessary for those being photographed.

Furthermore, privacy is a significant concern in social media [SCB17] and digital surveillance [WR14]. Researchers have studied the human perceptions of sensitive visual content [LTKC18], shared privacy expectations for online images [Hoy+20], as well as the impact on the viewer's experience when transforming parts of images for enhanced privacy [Li+17; Has+18]. Examples of content categories commonly deemed sensitive in image and video data are identity, children, nudity, and medical condition (e.g., hospital stay).

Moreover, laws and regulations protect the privacy of image and video data. The HIPAA privacy rule requires that full-face photographs and any comparable images must be removed under the Safe Harbor Method. Photographs that can be linked to a patient are considered identifiable information, and therefore, they are subject to HIPAA requirements [NBB19]. The General Data Protection Regulation (GDPR), effective since 2018, aims to increase the privacy of the European Union's citizens and visitors. It is important for organizations and businesses to consider image and video data as "personal data" or "sensitive personal data" in GDPR terms, and implement and ensure privacy protection accordingly.

11.1.2 Existing Privacy Methods

Various privacy solutions have been proposed for image and video analysis. We categorize commonly adopted image and video privacy methods that do not depend on differential privacy in the following groups.

- **Standard obfuscation.** Popular image obfuscation techniques are *pixelization* (also referred to as mosaicing), *blurring*, and *masking*. The goal is to obscure the content such that it is no longer recognizable. Pixelization can be achieved by superposing a rectangular grid over the original image and averaging the color values of the pixels within each grid cell. On the other hand, blurring, i.e., Gaussian blur, removes details from an image by convolving the 2D Gaussian distribution function with the image. Social media platforms may provide their own implementations, e.g., YouTube face blur [SP17] for video uploads. Masking replaces sensitive content with uninformative pixel values, e.g., a solid rectangle of black pixels over a face.
- **Fusion and perturbation.** Image *fusion* and *perturbation* have also been adopted for visual privacy. For instance, Newton et al. [NSM05] proposed to achieve k-anonymity for a set of face images. Their method, named k-same, "averages" face data for a group of individuals, such that each face in the published dataset appears at least k times. In [OR15], a face "morphing" scheme was proposed where the input face image is mixed with another face image to suppress gender information. Recent works, such as [MRR18; RGRB19], show the promise of adversarial perturbations. In [MRR18], perturbed face images could confound gender classifiers, while preserving the accuracy of face matchers. In [RGRB19], adversarial images were created by using a fast flipping attribute technique, and were able to fool DNNs networks in predicting binary facial attributes.
- **Cryptography.** A number of cryptography-based solutions have been developed to utilize untrusted service providers for image storage, sharing, and analysis. For instance, P3 [RGO13] enables privacy-preserving image sharing by encrypting the significant DCT coefficients, and authorized recipients can decrypt and reconstruct the input image. Furthermore, several approaches have been proposed to perform analysis on encrypted image data, e.g., for privacy-preserving image retrieval [Xia+16], extracting features [HLP12], and learning models [BCCW19].

11.1.3 Privacy Risks

Here we review a range of privacy risks associated with sharing image and video data. An in-depth discussion on privacy inference attacks in machine learning models is available in Chapter 5.

Re-identification

Given obfuscated image data, re-identification attacks aim to predict the identity of individuals or the class label of objects. For example, McPherson et al. [MSS16] developed neural network-based models which could be trained to re-identify faces and hand-written digits, and to recognize objects, on images obfuscated with pixelization, YouTube face blur [SP17], and P3 [RGO13] image sharing system. The re-identification rate of faces is up to 98%, after performing pixelization with a relatively large window, e.g., 16 × 16 pixels. Similarly, Hill et al. [HZSS16] showed that text obfuscated by pixelization can be reconstructed with a large accuracy using hidden Markov models (HMM). Those attack results show that existing image obfuscation techniques may yield unrecognizable images by human users, but state-of-the-art image recognition algorithms, e.g., deep learning based techniques, can successfully recover sensitive information.

Attribute Inference

In biometric template matching, visual data is utilized for recognition. Attribute inference refers to the estimation of other personal attributes, such as gender, age, and facial expression. Dantcheva et al. [DER15] surveyed techniques to extract a range of soft biometrics, such as face, body, fingerprint, hand, and iris, from image and video data, and recent results on the accurate estimation of demographic attributes (e.g., age, gender, race and ethnicity) and medical attributes (e.g., health and body weight). Wang and Kosinski [WK18] showed that sexual orientation can be inferred from facial images, with an accuracy of around 83% to 91%.

Model Inversion

When machine learning models are shared, sensitive training data may be reconstructed via model inversion attacks. Image analysis models have been targeted in model inversion. Fredrikson et al. [FJR15] reconstructed face images from trained neural network models for facial recognition. Zhang et al. [Zha+20] proposed several techniques to reconstruct images with higher quality. As seen in Figure 11.2, the reconstructed image needs not be perfect in order for human or algorithms to recognize the identity information. It is reported that human users can identify the reconstructed faces with an average of 80% accuracy [FJR15], and using state-of-the-art classifiers the reconstructed faces can be identified with accuracy of up to 82% [Zha+20].

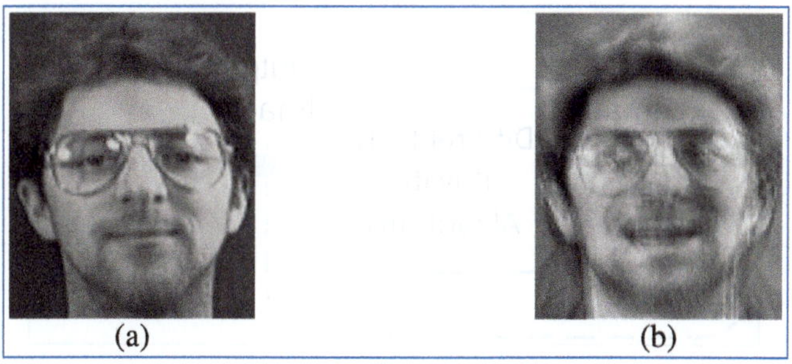

Figure 11.2. Example training image (a) and reconstructed image (b) given an identity label and a trained facial recognition model [FJR15].

Membership Inference

Membership inference tells whether a given record is present in the input dataset which is used to produce certain outputs, e.g., aggregate statistics, recommender systems, and machine learning models. Recent work studied membership inference attacks on image models [SSSS17; HRSF20]. An adversary is able to learn whether an image is part of the training set that produced a given model, by exploiting overfitting artifacts on training data.

11.1.4 Application of Differential Privacy

Differential privacy (DP) has become the state-of-the-art privacy paradigm for statistical databases. As introduced in Chapter 1, in *central* DP model, a trusted server is responsible for data aggregation and analysis, and the presence of any record in the input is protected. In the *local* DP model (see Chapter 2), the server is no longer trusted, and the exact value of each input record is protected. There are two general approaches for applying DP to image and video analysis as follows.

- **Training Machine Learning Models.** In image and video analysis, DP can be applied to training models while protecting the presence of each training sample. For instance, Abadi et al. [Aba+16] proposed differentially private stochastic gradient descent (DP-SGD) for deep learning and the moment accountant (MA) technique to account for differential privacy across training epochs. With training data are distributed at different sites, DP can be achieved in a federated learning setup [Li+19], or via private aggregation of teacher ensembles [Pap+16]. Recently, DP has also been applied to train generative adversarial networks to produce synthetic images [Xie+18; TKP19].
- **Sanitizing Image and Video Data.** A different approach is to apply DP to sanitizing sensitive information in image and video data, and the sanitized data can be shared with untrusted parties for further analysis. Figure 11.3

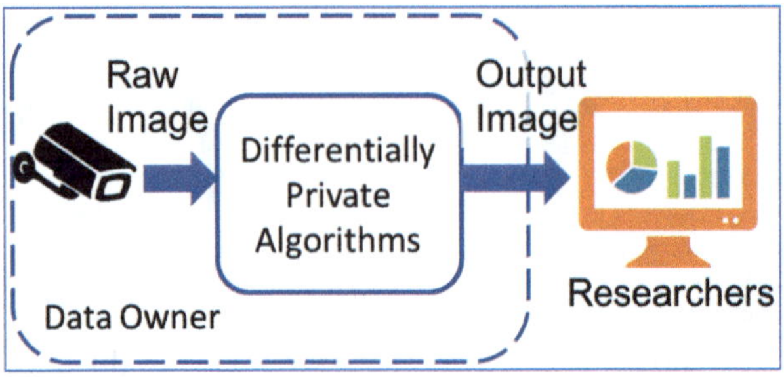

Figure 11.3. Differential Privacy Setting for Sanitizing Image and Video Data. Note that a video is a sequence of images, also known as video frames.

depicts such a setting where a data owner wishes to share image or video data with untrusted recipients, e.g., researchers, servers, or the greater public. The data owner must sanitize the data prior to its publication, in order to guarantee DP. Thanks to the resistance to post-processing [DR+14], any analysis performed on the sanitized data would not inflict additional DP cost.

In-depth analysis of DP for machine learning, including its applications and challenges, is conducted in other chapters of the book. Therefore, in this chapter we primarily discuss the second approach, where DP is applied to *sanitizing image and video data*. We identify two main advantages of the sanitization approach: (1) it offers resistance to post-processing, as mentioned above; (2) it is compatible with personalized privacy, e.g., user-specified ε and δ values for DP guarantees. Those properties would make DP highly desirable for conducting privacy-preserving analysis and for meeting users' privacy needs.

Overview of the Chapter

In the rest of the chapter, we will introduce challenges of applying DP to image and video data sanitization and review the progress of the research community to this date (Section 11.2). In addition to theories, in Section 11.3 we will also introduce important practical privacy protections and utility measures that methods with DP guarantees should keep in mind. Finally, in Section 11.4, we will discuss challenges should be addressed in collaboration with other communities, such as understanding the user perceptions and the deployment in real systems.

11.2 Sanitizing Image and Video Data with DP

In this section, we introduce challenges of applying DP to image and video data sanitization and review the progress made by the research community. Recall our problem setting in Figure 11.3. The sanitization algorithm operates on image or video data, such that the output does not allow an adversary (e.g., researchers or the greater public) to infer much about sensitive information in the input data.

The key question to address by DP methods in image and video settings is: *what information is protected by DP?* Not surprisingly, this question also helps us categorize and comparatively analyze recent developments in DP for image/video data made by the research community. With this question in mind, we introduce challenges and solutions for sanitizing image and video data with DP. Recall that a video is a sequence of images, i.e., video frames. We will start our discussion with image sanitization, i.e., obfuscation.

11.2.1 Pixel-Level Privacy for Images

For simplicity, let's consider inputs to DP algorithms are grey-scale images. A grey-scale image is a matrix and elements in the matrix are integer pixel values between 0 and 255 (i.e., 0 is black and 255 is white).

Protecting a Single Pixel

In order to adapt differential privacy to image data, a straight-forward idea is to consider pixels as "records" of a database. Therefore, a DP algorithm should protect the values of individual pixels. In a recent study [Joh+20], the following notion was proposed to protect each pixel.

Definition 11.1. [Pixel-DP] Let s denote a randomized algorithm and S be any subset of the image space of s. Then, we say s is (ε, δ)-differentially private if for any S and any pair of neighboring inputs x and x',

$$\Pr[s(x) \in S] \leq e^{\varepsilon}\Pr[s(x') \in S] + \delta \tag{11.1}$$

where neighboring inputs x and x' correspond to two images that differ by at most one pixel.

As can be seen, the above definition is very similar to the classic (ε, δ)-DP [DR+14]. Two input images are *neighbors* if they differ by at most one pixel. The authors of [Joh+20] adopted a randomized mechanism for each pixel such that either the real pixel or a default value, e.g., 127, is reported with a coin flip. Applied to images taken by eye tracking devices, the authors argued that per pixel randomization is more suitable for pupil tracking applications, compared to blur-based obfuscations.

Protecting Multiple Pixels Simultaneously

An immediate concern regarding Definition 11.1 is that hiding the presence of one pixel in the input image may not provide strong privacy, i.e., hiding sensitive information in the input image. Let's look at some images based on widely used PETS

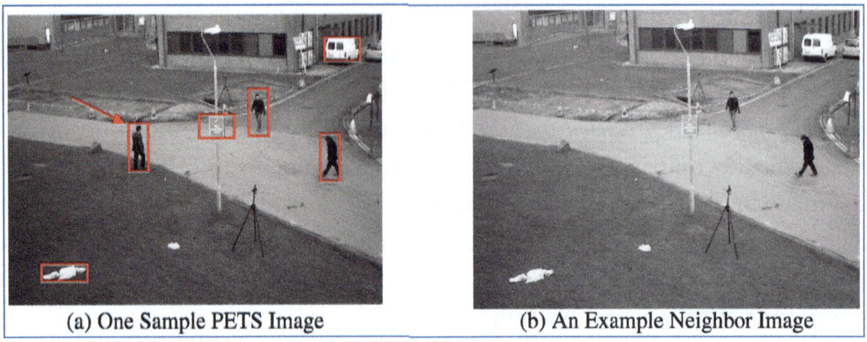

Figure 11.4. (a): sample image from PETS dataset where each red rectangle represents some sensitive information and contains $\sim$ 360 pixels. (b): an example neighboring image for (a) by removing the leftmost pedestrian. [Fan18]

dataset [Lea+15] as an example. This dataset contains video frame sequences widely used in Multiple Object Tracking studies. Each red rectangle in Figure 11.4(a) illustrates one type of sensitive information, such as a pedestrian, a van, an object on grass, and a signage; and each rectangle contains $\sim$ 360 pixels, i.e., much higher than one.

We are thus motivated to consider a stronger privacy model, in which sensitive information represented by *multiple* pixels should be protected. [Fan18] proposed a customizable notion for neighboring images.

Definition 11.2. [m-Neighborhood] Two images I_1 and I_2 are m-neighboring images if they have the same dimension and differ by at most m pixels.

As can be seen, Definition 11.2 is a generalization of the 1-pixel neighborhood discussed above. In comparison, Definition 11.2 provides *stronger* privacy: allowing up to m pixels to differ enables us to protect the presence or absence of any sensitive information which can be represented by those pixels in an image. Recall object, text, or person in Figure 11.4. The following is a strict ε-DP definition for m-neighboring images proposed in [Fan18].

Definition 11.3. [Image-DP] A randomized mechanism $\mathcal{A}$ gives ε-differential privacy if for any m-neighboring inputs I_1 and I_2, and for any possible output $\widetilde{I} \in Range(\mathcal{A})$,

$$\Pr[\mathcal{A}(I_1) = \widetilde{I}] \leq e^{\varepsilon} \Pr[\mathcal{A}(I_2) = \widetilde{I}] \tag{11.2}$$

where the probability is taken over the randomness of $\mathcal{A}$.

With Image-DP, an adversary cannot distinguish between any pair of neighboring images by observing the output image. The privacy of the pedestrian, and any other sensitive information represented by at most m pixels, can thus be protected.

Table 11.1. Qualitative Comparisons for Differentially Private Image Obfuscation: each column represents one obfuscation method; each row lists the obfuscation outcomes for the same input image from the *AT&T* faces dataset. We observe that DP obfuscations inflict only a small quality loss, compared to non-private obfuscations.

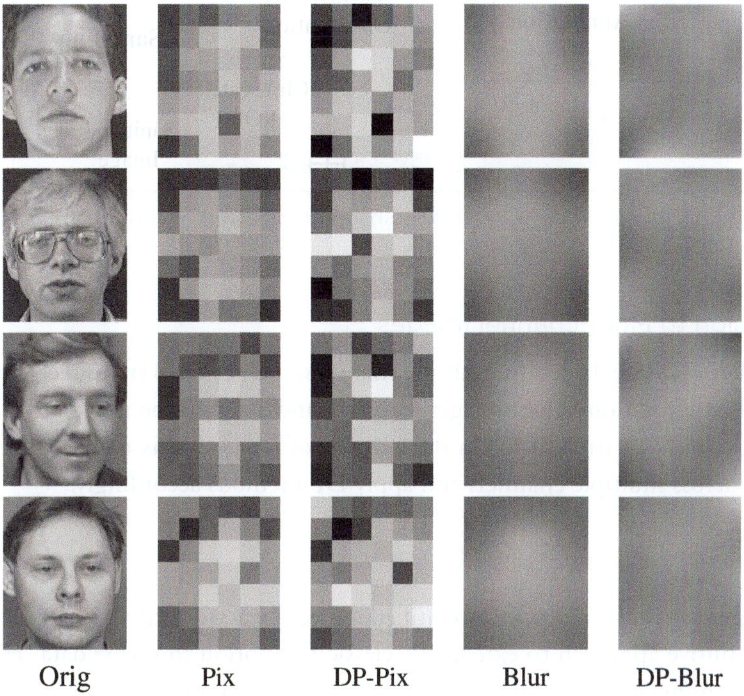

When adopting the definitions above, a data owner can choose an appropriate m value in order to customize the level of privacy protection, i.e., achieving indistinguishability in a smaller or larger range of neighboring images. Note that it is assumed that removing those pixels is sufficient to protect the privacy of the underlying information, by definition of differential privacy [DR+14].

Applied to Standard Obfuscation

Differentially private obfuscation mechanisms for *pixelization* and *Gaussian blur* were proposed in [Fan18; Fan19a]. Sample *AT&T* images are provided in Table 11.1. For pixelization (Pix and DP-Pix), the block size is set to 16×16; for Gaussian blur (Blur and DP-Blur), the kernel size is set to 99×99. The image DP parameters are set as $m = 16$ and $\varepsilon = 0.5$ for both pixelization and Gaussian blur. Applied to image obfuscation, Image DP inflicts a small quality Loss, compared to non-private obfuscations. Quantitative quality as well as privacy can be measured for DP image obfuscations, which are discussed in depth in the next section.

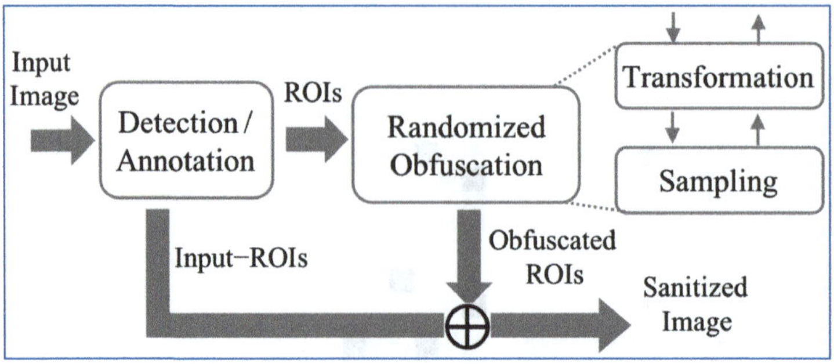

Figure 11.5. A Privacy-Preserving Image Sharing Framework with Perceptual Obfuscation [Fan19b].

Extension to Multi-channel Images

Considering image data with multiple channels, such as RGB (red-green-blue) and HSV (hue-saturation-value) images, each channel may not be independent of the other channels. A straight-forward extension of image DP is to split the privacy budget across multiple channels and apply DP methods accordingly.

11.2.2 Perceptual Image Privacy

In the previous subsection, we quantified image privacy directly with pixels, which is an intuitive approach to extend the classic DP notion to image data. However, the way an image conveys its content is unique and complex. Therefore, we argue that it could be beneficial to first quantify the perceived information from an input image and then apply rigorous privacy. In fact, certain image modifications that inflict pixel value changes may not significantly affect the human perception of image content, for instance, after JPEG image compression [PM92] or adding a small constant to every pixel. The *challenge* is thus to effectively model what can be perceived in an image, despite the aforementioned modifications, and to develop DP methods to protect the perceived information.

Singular Value Decomposition

In [Fan19b], Singular Value Decomposition (SVD) was considered to capture the perceptual information in input images. It is known that SVD can extract most of the geometric structure and characteristics of the image data. Prior work on perceptual image hashing methods [KVM04] based on SVD have been shown to robustly hash visually similar images, such as after compression, rotation, and cropping. The intuition of SVD is that any real or complex matrix A can be decomposed into a product of three matrices, i.e., $A = U\Sigma V^T$, where U and V are left and right singular vector matrices, Σ is a non-negative diagonal matrix, consisting of the singular values. Intuitively, the singular vectors in U and V, capture the geometric *features* in an image, while the singular values in Σ can be interpreted as the *magnitudes* of the features.

Privacy in High-dimensional Spaces

As a strong attack model, we can assume an adversary who may have approximate knowledge about an input image. Specifically, the adversary knows the set of images that are visually similar to a given image (including the image itself), e.g., with the same singular matrices i.e., U and V, but different singular values, i.e., Σ. The adversarial goal is to infer the exact input image by observing the obfuscated image. To protect the private singular values, the study of [Fan19b] adopted a variant of differential privacy [CABP13] for up to k singular values, as follows.

Definition 11.4. [$\varepsilon \cdot d_k$-privacy] Suppose domains $\mathcal{X}, \mathcal{Z} \subset \mathbb{R}^k$ and d_k denotes the Euclidean metric in $\mathbb{R}^k$. A mechanism $K : \mathcal{X} \rightarrow \mathcal{Z}$ satisfies $\varepsilon \cdot d_k$-privacy, if and only if $\forall x, x' \in \mathcal{X}$,

$$K(x)(Z) \leq e^{\varepsilon \cdot d_k(x,x')} K(x')(Z) \quad \forall Z \in \mathcal{Z}. \tag{11.3}$$

This definition shows that the output of a mechanism should be "indistinguishable" to protect privacy, and the level of indistinguishability is proportional to the distance $d_k(x, x')$ between two inputs x and x'. For an adversary who observes the certain output Z, i.e., privacy-enhanced singular values, it is challenging to infer the exact input to the mechanism, i.e., real singular values. A sampling-based mechanism K in $\mathbb{R}^k$ was designed in [Fan19b] to satisfy Definition 11.4.

SVD-based Obfuscation (DP-SVD)

Figure 11.5 depicts the proposed framework for privacy-preserving image data sharing. An image often contains one or more regions-of-interest (ROIs), such as faces, objects, text, etc., where obfuscation is needed to protect privacy. Such ROIs can be detected automatically or annotated by data owners. The randomized obfuscation will be applied to the ROIs. The obfuscation step involves two components: transformation and sampling. A ROI will first be *transformed* to obtain the feature vector, i.e., singular values, and the vector will be truncated and go through the *sampling* step to achieve differential privacy guarantees; the sampled vector will be used in the *inverse* transform, resulting in the obfuscated ROI image.

Similar to standard obfuscations, applying DP-SVD incurs distortions in the image data. As can be seen in Figure 11.6, shapes in the image are distorted but high-level information is still perceptible after obfuscation. The intuition is that values close to the real singular values are sampled with higher probabilities, thanks to the relaxation of differential privacy (Definition 11.4). Evaluations that quantify the perceptual similarity between images will be discussed in the next section.

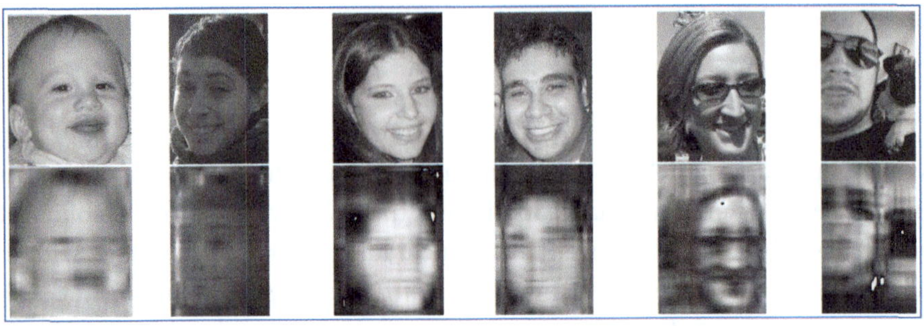

Figure 11.6. Example Images from the PIPA Dataset: row 1 - original images ; row 2 - images in Row 1 obfuscated by DP-SVD with $k = 4$ and $\varepsilon = 0.5$ [Fan19b].

11.2.3 Privacy in Videos

Essentially, a video consists of a sequence of frames, where each frame itself is an image. An natural extension of a DP definition for images in Sections 11.2.1 and 11.2.2 is to apply DP to every frame. However, it could be computationally expensive, especially given high "frames-per-second" (FPS) rates for current video cameras; furthermore, it results in a large privacy cost, i.e., the privacy guarantee degrades as the number of frames increases. It is thus important to quantify privacy for sensitive content, such as pedestrians and objects, which may appear in multiple frames in a video sequence.

Privacy for Input Videos

A recent work [WXH20] consider two videos as neighbors if they differ in at most one visual element, considering the element's appearance throughout the video sequence.

Definition 11.5. [Neighboring Videos] To protect sensitive visual elements in the video, two input videos V and V' that differ in any visual element γ in all frames are considered as two neighboring inputs. Note that V and V' have identical number of frames and background scene.

As can be seen, Definition 11.5 extends image DP to 3D, considering pixels belonging to a specific visual element (e.g., person or object) in all frames of the video. Based on the neighbor definition, the (ε, δ)-DP notion can be extended to videos.

Definition 11.6. [(ε, δ)-DP for Videos] A randomization algorithm $\mathcal{A}$ satisfies (ε, δ)-differential privacy if for every video V, we can divide the output space $range(\mathcal{A})$ into two sets Ω_1 and Ω_2 such that, (1) $\Pr[\mathcal{A}(V) \in \Omega_1] \leq \delta$, and (2) for any of V's neighboring video V' and for all output $O \in \Omega_2$, $e^{-\varepsilon} \leq \frac{\Pr[\mathcal{A}(V)=O]}{\Pr[\mathcal{A}(V')=O]} \leq e^{\varepsilon}$.

Figure 11.7. Example Sanitized Video Frames using MOT [Mil+16] Dataset: (a) video frame via pixel sampling [WXH20]; (b) video frame via synthesis [WHKV20].

The relaxation in Definition 11.6 is needed to account for the unique information contributed by a visual element in the input video. For instance, consider a mechanism $\mathcal{A}$ that randomly selects pixels from an input video. Furthermore, let y be a vehicle in video V but not in V', i.e., $V' = V \setminus y$. Observing any pixels of y in $\mathcal{A}$'s output would allow an adversary to infer the presence of the vehicle in the input, as the probability of observing those pixels in $\mathcal{A}(V')$ is 0. The analysis of δ remains open in [WXH20]. A video frame produced by pixel sampling is shown in Figure 11.7(a). It can be seen that with weaker DP guarantees, visual elements, e.g., pedestrians with distinctive outfits, may still be identified.

Privacy for Occurrences

As illustrated in Figure 11.7(a), it is quite challenging to protect the presence of visual elements in videos. The privacy model may be relaxed to protecting the *occurrences* of each visual element. In other words, assume the presence of an visual element in the video is public (as in the *local DP* setting); the secret is which frames the visual element appears in. [WHKV20] proposed the following notion to achieve indistinguishability for the occurrences of visual elements (i.e., objects).

Definition 11.7. [ε-Object Indistinguishably] Suppose video V contains M frames and each object O_i is represented by a bit vector $B_i = \{b_i^k | k = 1, \cdots, M\}$, where b_i^k is set to 1 if O_i appears in the k-th frame and 0 otherwise. A randomization algorithm $\mathcal{A}$ satisfies ε-object indistinguishability if and only if for any two input objects $O_i, O_j \in \mathcal{O}$ in the input video V, and for any output object of $\mathcal{A}$ in the synthetic video V^* (denoted as y), we have

$$Pr[\mathcal{A}(O_i) = y] \leq e^{\varepsilon} Pr[\mathcal{A}(O_j) = y] \tag{11.4}$$

Based on Definition 11.7, it is intuitive that we can apply randomized response mechanisms, such as RAPPOR [EPK14], to the bit vectors of objects in order to satisfy Equation 11.4.

(a) Non-private Gaze Heatmap. (b) Private Gaze Heatmap.

Figure 11.8. Eye Gaze Heatmaps of an Individual User on a Web Page [LCFK21]: (a) raw data; (b) differentially private heatmap (ε=3).

Video Synthesis

Video frames can be sanitized by applying the privacy models in Definition 11.6 or Definition 11.7, and the mechanisms respectively. Figure 11.7 presents two sample output frames obtained respectively. As can be seen, sampling pixels allows for subsequent tasks, such as pedestrian detection. Video synthesis is less ambiguous, e.g., in terms of pedestrian counting, and does not disclosing identifying information by replacing pedestrians with icons. A natural question is: how do we evaluate the quality of output video frames? We will discuss that in the next section.

11.2.4 Adaptations to Eye Tracking

Eye-tracking applications capture large amounts of image and video data via webcams, wearable glasses, or mixed reality headsets. Eye gaze positions in a scene are used by eye-tracking applications to estimate what the user is viewing in order to prefetch contents or trigger events. An example gaze heatmap of a user on a web page is depicted in Figure 11.8(a). As can be seen, eye gaze data are essentially 2D positions in a given scene. It is thus intuitive that the geo-indistinguishability framework [ABCP13] may be adopted for eye-tracking applications [LCFK21].

Definition 11.8. [(ε, r)-geo-indistinguishability] A mechanism $\mathcal{M} : X \to Z$ is defined to be (ε, r)-geo-indistinguishable if and only if for all pairs of inputs $(x, x') \in X \times X$ such that $d(x, x') \leq r$,

$$\Pr[\mathcal{M}(x) \in S] \leq e^{\varepsilon \cdot d(x,x')} \Pr[\mathcal{M}(x') \in S], \forall S \subset Z \tag{11.5}$$

where $d(\cdot, \cdot)$ denotes the Euclidean metric.

Input x and x' give the corresponding eye gaze positions and the pair (x, x') can be considered as r-Euclidean neighbors if $d(x, x') \leq r$. As eye gaze streams are collected from each user, the authors of [LCFK21] adopted the w-event privacy model to achieve a privacy-utility tradeoff. A private heatmap with $\varepsilon = 3$ is depicted in Figure 11.8(b).

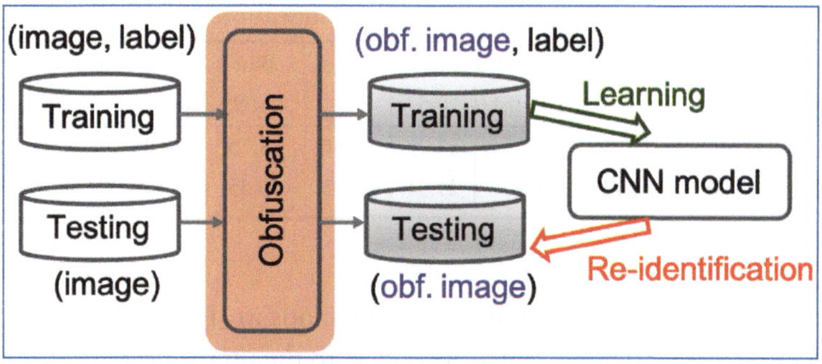

Figure 11.9. Adaptive Re-identification Evaluation for Image Obfuscation Methods: step 1 - both training and testing partitions go through the same type of obfuscation; step 2 - a CNN model is trained to predict identity labels on the training set; step 3 - the trained CNN model infers the identity labels of the test set.

11.3 Practical Considerations for DP Methods

In this section, we will discuss practical considerations for applying DP to image and video data. Specifically, we will look at measures of effective privacy protection and quantitative measures for output quality, which are important evaluation metrics for DP methods.

11.3.1 Effective Privacy Protection

The privacy guarantees of DP are well grounded theoretically. To facilitate the adoption of DP methods, it is important to understand the privacy protection achieved in practice, e.g., whether empirical privacy risks are mitigated by DP methods. Here we primarily illustrate how re-identification risks can be measured in practice and discuss adaptations for other risk measures.

Re-identification Risks

An important risk for visual data is that inference attacks can be launched against the sanitized data, despite the application of any obfuscation methods. To evaluate differentially private image obfuscation, we can carry out such inference attacks to understand the mitigation effects of DP. A CNN based re-identification attack was first proposed in [MSS16]. We adopt a similar attack below to evaluate the re-identification risks for DP-Pix and DP-Blur on two commonly used datasets.

Adaptive Re-identification Evaluation

An adaptive re-identification attack can be carried out to understand how much can be learned about a given obfuscation method, e.g., pixelization. The attack

Table 11.2. Accuracy (in %) of CNN Re-Identification Attacks [Fan19a].

Dataset	Random	Pix	DP-Pix ($b = 16$)			Blur	DP-Blur ($k = 99$)		
	–	$b = 16$	$\varepsilon = 0.1$	0.5	1	$k = 99$	$\varepsilon = 0.1$	0.5	1
AT&T	2.50	96.25	3.75	43.75	77.50	88.75	**1.25**	7.50	17.50
MNIST	**10.00**	52.13	16.41	21.51	22.95	76.35	11.35	11.75	13.43

was carried out to evaluate DP obfuscation methods in [Fan18; Fan19a], which is depicted in Figure 11.9. Here, "identity" refers to the user ID for a facial image, or the class label for hand-writings and objects. As can be seen, the same obfuscation method will be applied to image data in both training and testing partitions. In the context of DP obfuscation, we maintain the same privacy level (e.g., m and ε as in Definition 11.3) as well as other hyper-parameters (e.g., b for pixelization and k for Gaussian blur) when obfuscating training and testing images. That helps simulate a powerful attacker, who possesses knowledge about the obfuscation method. Subsequently, the obfuscated training set, which includes images and their labels, will be used to train a CNN-based deep model to predict labels. Note that the architecture of the CNN model could be adapted to each dataset. At the inference phase, the trained CNN model predicts labels for the obfuscated testing images. The accuracy of the prediction indicates the level of re-identification risks for the dataset and the obfuscation method.

Evaluation results for DP-Pix and DP-Blur are shown in Table 11.2, using the AT&T face database and the MNIST dataset. The "Random" column indicates the re-identification risks incurred by randomly guessing the label for each image. This column was populated according to the total number of classes in each dataset. Every other column shows the accuracy of re-identification for the corresponding obfuscation method as described above. As can be seen, the standard obfuscation methods, i.e., pixelization and Gaussian blur, will still allow an adversary to effectively learn to associate an obfuscated image with its label. The re-identification accuracy of faces is up to 96.25% and up to 76.35% for hand-written digits. These results may be surprising to some readers, especially when combined with the example images in Table 11.1. Again this showcases that images unrecognizable to human users may not be effectively *private*.

By introducing DP to image obfuscation, we can observe a reduction in re-identification accuracy, while the reduction depends on the parameters as well as the dataset. DP methods reduce face re-identification to as low as 1.25%, which is lower than random guessing, and MNIST re-identification to 11.35%. These results indicate that DP obfuscations provide stronger empirical privacy protection than standard obfuscation methods.

Re-identification for Eye Images and Videos

Similarly, features can be extracted from **videos** for re-identification evaluations. In [LCFK21], aggregate statistics of fixation/saccade features over several gaze video sessions were used to predict user's identity. The authors adopted a discriminant analysis classifier where the training and testing video sets correspond to the same privacy configuration. Re-identification for eye images requires specific methods, e.g., segmentation-based iris recognition [Gan+16]. Specifically, privacy-enhanced eye images will be compared to reference images and correct recognition rates [Joh+20] indicate the level of privacy risks. We refer interested readers to [RF21] for a comparative evaluation of DP methods on iris recognition risk mitigation.

Other Risk Measures

Attribute Inference Risks

Attributes of the person or object in image data are also subject to inference attacks. It is thus important to evaluate DP methods in mitigating attribute inference. For instance, multiple attributes, such as gender and smiling, can be inferred from facial images [CSVG18]. In [SHHB19], eye movement features were extracted to predict gender and to perform document type classification. [LCFK21] argued that scanpath features extracted from video gaze streams may distinguish users' psychophysiological traits. The framework in Figure 11.9 can be adapted for evaluating attribute inference risks. For instance, the choice of the model must correspond to the specific inference tasks. Another consideration is the nature of the dataset: the attack model can be either trained with clean data or DP-enhanced data.

Participation Inference Risks

Machine learning models trained with image data also leak information about the underlying training data. Although an adversary may not have direct access to the training images, membership inference (e.g., [SSSS17]) and model inversion (e.g., [FJR15]) can be carried out to predict whether an individual participates in the training set. A privacy researcher may adopt those attacks to evaluate the mitigation effects of DP methods in machine learning. An individual often contributes more than one image samples in the training set, e.g., in facial recognition applications (recall Figure 11.2). Therefore, model inversion may be applied to infer individual participation, with human users or machine classifiers to perform re-identification.

11.3.2 Quality Measures

It is also important to study the usefulness of DP methods in image and video analysis, in order to advance current research. Two types of measures are often adopted to evaluate the output of DP methods: *task-based* measures for specific applications built on the DP outputs and *generic* measures that do not depend on any applications.

Generic Quality Measures

Absolute Errors and Perceptual Quality

The quality of privacy-enhanced images was measured by Mean Squared Error (MSE) and Structural Similarity (SSIM) in [Fan18]. In addition, we may also consider the peak signal-to-noise ratio (PSNR) measure, which represents the ratio between the maximum pixel value and the MSE. The quality of privacy-enhanced videos can be measured by adapting single image quality measures to video frames. MSE, PSNR, and SSIM measure the difference between the input image and the sanitized image, thus applicable in a wide of range settings. Among them, SSIM [WBSS04] is a widely used perceptual quality measure, which considers the perceived similarity in structural information in addition to luminance and contrast. One advantage of SSIM over absolute error based quality measures, is that an image derived by subtracting a certain value from every pixel in the input image would preserve high structural similarity, despite significant absolute errors. As an example, in Figure 11.10, we show that subtracting a constant pixel value leads to MSE=210 and almost perfect structural similarity, i.e., SSIM = 99%. Deep learning based image quality measures have been proposed recently, such as LPIPS [Zha+18] and SIFID [SDM19], which may also be applied to evaluate the DP obfuscated images.

Statistical Measures

Image and video data are often represented as color histograms, i.e., distributions of pixels across all possible colors. Therefore, distributional similarity measures can

(a) Original Image (b) Mean-shifted Image

Figure 11.10. Comparison of "Boat" images: (a): original image; (b): mean-shifted image with MSE = 210 and SSIM = 99%. [WBSS04]

be adopted to compare the privacy-enhanced data with the input. For instance, [WXH20] adopted the Kullback–Leibler divergence for RGB pixel distributions between the input video and sanitized video. As another example, correlation coefficients were adopted to compare noisy gaze heatmaps to clean heatmaps [Liu+19]. When a set of images is generated with DP methods, e.g., in data synthesis [Fan20], measures are often adopted to quantify the realism and diversity of the generated dataset, e.g., via the Jensen-Shannon divergence and Inception Score.

Task-based Quality Measures

Specific tasks can be performed on the image and video data produced by DP methods. Performance measures for those tasks are thus suitable for evaluating the quality of DP outputs.

Image Analysis

Current DP methods aim to protect individual participation or identity while allowing for analysis tasks to be performed on the privacy-enhanced image data. For example, using the sanitized eye images, landmark detection and gaze estimation [PZBH18] can be performed. In addition, pupil detection was also evaluated on privacy-enhanced images in [Joh+20]. For facial images, we may consider attribute prediction tasks such as for gender and age, while protecting the identities. However, ensuring strong privacy and high utility for a single image may be challenging for DP based methods. We will discuss utility evaluation for machine learning based analysis shortly.

Video Analysis

In surveillance applications, video data is often analyzed to detect human [DT05] and objects [Yan+16]. Precision and recall measures can be adopted for detection tasks in privacy-enhanced video data. Furthermore, counting the total number of pedestrians or vehicles in a frame is important for anomaly detection applications [CZV08]. Such counting errors resulted from DP methods can be measured, e.g., using Mean Absolute Error. Moreover, tracking the appearance of a person or object in a video may also be of interest. For instance, [WXH20] measured the stay time of each pedestrian/vehicle, i.e., the number of video frames containing the pedestrian/vehicle; [WHKV20] measured how the trajectory of a pedestrian in the sanitized video frame sequence deviates from that of the original video.

Machine Learning

The performance of image models, such as for classification and segmentation, can be evaluated for DP-based machine learning methods, e.g., deep learning [Aba+16] and federated learning [Li+19]. Similarly, image models can be trained on privacy-enhanced image data, e.g., obtained via DP obfuscation or DP synthesis, and the performance of those models may indicate the quality of the training data. For instance, in [TKP19], multiple classifiers for hand-written digits were trained using synthetic data generated by DP generative models; those classifiers were tested on real image data. Compared to the same classifiers trained on real data, close performance indicates that DP generative models could capture the real data distribution.

11.4 Concluding Remarks

So far, we have talked about how DP can be applied to protecting sensitive information in image and video data. We have also shown how to evaluate whether DP methods are successful, e.g., in achieving practical privacy protection and producing usefulness results. But the story does not stop there. The richness and complexity of image and video data, as well as the ubiquity of their applications, require collaborative research with experts beyond the DP community to address the privacy concerns.

User Perceptions of Privacy and Utility

The visual nature of images and videos dictates that privacy and utility are not only defined by mathematical equations, but also inseparable from end user perceptions in specific contexts. Recent studies [Li+17; Has+18] measured the viewer perceived privacy and utility for photos shared in the context of online social networks. Survey participants were asked to recognize persons, objects, and properties in obscured photos. For evaluating utility, participants were asked to rate the obscured photos in satisfaction, information sufficiency, visual appeals, etc. Users have been involved to evaluate privacy-preserving eye tracking via web cams [LCFK21]. Utility was quantified by scores users achieved in a game as well as self-reported enjoyment measures.

Deployment of DP Methods

As the local privacy mode is adopted in many image and video privacy methods, it is important to consider the feasibility to deploy those methods on user-owned devices. One consideration is the *computational overhead*. While DP methods based on aggregation (e.g., pixelization and blurring, gaze heatmaps) may not inflict significant overhead [SRF22], some problems/settings may be more challenging, e.g., private sampling in high-dimensional spaces and sanitizing videos with a large number of frames. Another consideration is the *integration* with devices and exiting platforms. We may need to consider the compatibility of DP methods with different cameras, imaging systems, and image and video analysis applications.

Acknowledgements

Liyue Fan is an Assistant Professor of Computer Science at UNC Charlotte. This work is supported in part by the National Science Foundation CNS-1949217, CNS-1951430, CNS-2144684, and the University of North Carolina. Any opinions, findings, and conclusions or recommendations expressed in this material are those of the author(s) and do not necessarily reflect the views of the sponsors, such as the National Science Foundation.

References

[Aba+16] M. Abadi, A. Chu, I. Goodfellow, H. B. McMahan, I. Mironov, K. Talwar, and L. Zhang. "Deep learning with differential privacy". In: Proceedings of the 2016 ACM SIGSAC Conference on Computer and Communications Security. ACM. 2016, pp. 308–318 (cit. on pp. 391, 405).

[ABCP13] M. E. Andrés, N. E. Bordenabe, K. Chatzikokolakis, and C. Palamidessi. "Geo-indistinguishability: Differential privacy for location-based systems". In: Proceedings of the 2013 ACM SIGSAC conference on Computer & communications security. 2013, pp. 901–914 (cit. on p. 400).

[Ano98] Anonymous. "To Reveal or Not to Reveal: A Theoretical Model of Anonymous Communication". In: Communication Theory 8.4 (1998), pp. 381–407. eprint: https://onlinelibrary.wiley.com/doi/pdf/10.1111/j.1468-2885.1998.tb00226.x. URL: https://onlinelibrary.wiley.com/doi/abs/10.1111/j.1468-2885.1998.tb00226.x (cit. on p. 388).

[BCCW19] F. Boemer, A. Costache, R. Cammarota, and C. Wierzynski. "NGraph-HE2: A High-Throughput Framework for Neural Network Inference on Encrypted Data". In: Proceedings of the 7th ACM Workshop on Encrypted Computing Applied Homomorphic Cryptography. WAHC-19. London, United Kingdom: Association for Computing Machinery, 2019, pp. 45–56. ISBN: 9781450368292. URL: https://doi.org/10.1145/3338469.3358944 (cit. on p. 389).

[CABP13] K. Chatzikokolakis, M. E. Andrés, N. E. Bordenabe, and C. Palamidessi. "Broadening the Scope of Differential Privacy Using Metrics". In: Privacy Enhancing Technologies. Ed. by E. De

Cristofaro and M. Wright. Berlin, Heidelberg: Springer Berlin Heidelberg, 2013, pp. 82–102. ISBN: 978-3-642-39077-7 (cit. on p. 397).

[CSVG18] S. Chhabra, R. Singh, M. Vatsa, and G. Gupta. “Anonymizing k-facial attributes via adversarial perturbations”. In: arXiv preprint arXiv:1805.09380 (2018) (cit. on p. 403).

[CZV08] A. B. Chan, Zhang-Sheng John Liang, and N. Vasconcelos. “Privacy preserving crowd monitoring: Counting people without people models or tracking”. In: 2008 IEEE Conference on Computer Vision and Pattern Recognition. 2008, pp. 1–7 (cit. on p. 405).

[DER15] A. Dantcheva, P. Elia, and A. Ross. “What else does your biometric data reveal? A survey on soft biometrics”. In: IEEE Transactions on Information Forensics and Security 11.3 (2015), pp. 441–467 (cit. on p. 390).

[DR+14] C. Dwork, A. Roth, et al. “The algorithmic foundations of differential privacy.” In: Foundations and Trends in Theoretical Computer Science 9.3-4 (2014), pp. 211–407 (cit. on pp. 392, 393, 395).

[DT05] N. Dalal and B. Triggs. “Histograms of oriented gradients for human detection”. In: 2005 IEEE computer society conference on computer vision and pattern recognition (CVPR’05). Vol. 1. Ieee. 2005, pp. 886–893 (cit. on p. 405).

[Dug15] M. Duggan. “Mobile Messaging and Social Media – 2015”. In: Pew Research Center (Aug. 2015) (cit. on p. 387).

[EPK14] Ú. Erlingsson, V. Pihur, and A. Korolova. “RAPPOR: Randomized Aggregatable Privacy-Preserving Ordinal Response”. In: Proceedings of the 2014 ACM SIGSAC Conference on Computer and Communications Security. CCS ’14. Scottsdale, Arizona, USA: Association for Computing Machinery, 2014, pp. 1054–1067. ISBN: 9781450329576. URL: https://doi.org/10.1145/2660267.2660348 (cit. on p. 399).

[Fan18] L. Fan. “Image pixelization with differential privacy”. In: IFIP Annual Conference on Data and Applications Security and Privacy. Springer. 2018, pp. 148–162 (cit. on pp. 394, 395, 402, 404).

[Fan19a] L. Fan. “Differential Privacy for Image Publication”. In: Theory and Practice of Differential Privacy Workshop. 2019 (cit. on pp. 395, 402).

[Fan19b] L. Fan. "Practical Image Obfuscation with Provable Privacy". In: 2019 IEEE International Conference on Multimedia and Expo (ICME). 2019, pp. 784–789 (cit. on pp. 396–398).

[Fan20] L. Fan. "A survey of differentially private generative adversarial networks". In: The AAAI Workshop on Privacy-Preserving Artificial Intelligence. 2020 (cit. on p. 405).

[FJR15] M. Fredrikson, S. Jha, and T. Ristenpart. "Model inversion attacks that exploit confidence information and basic countermeasures". In: Proceedings of the 22nd ACM SIGSAC Conference on Computer and Communications Security. 2015, pp. 1322–1333 (cit. on pp. 390, 391, 403).

[Gan+16] A. Gangwar, A. Joshi, A. Singh, F. Alonso-Fernandez, and J. Bigun. "IrisSeg: A fast and robust iris segmentation framework for non-ideal iris images". In: 2016 International Conference on Biometrics (ICB). 2016, pp. 1–8 (cit. on p. 403).

[Has+18] R. Hasan, E. Hassan, Y. Li, K. Caine, D. J. Crandall, R. Hoyle, and A. Kapadia. "Viewer experience of obscuring scene elements in photos to enhance privacy". In: Proceedings of the 2018 CHI Conference on Human Factors in Computing Systems. 2018, pp. 1–13 (cit. on pp. 388, 406).

[HLP12] C. Y. Hsu, C. S. Lu, and S. C. Pei. "Image Feature Extraction in Encrypted Domain With Privacy-Preserving SIFT". In: IEEE Transactions on Image Processing 21.11 (Nov. 2012), pp. 4593–4607. ISSN: 1057-7149 (cit. on p. 389).

[Hoy+20] R. Hoyle, L. Stark, Q. Ismail, D. Crandall, A. Kapadia, and D. Anthony. "Privacy norms and preferences for photos Posted Online". In: ACM Transactions on Computer-Human Interaction (TOCHI) 27.4 (2020), pp. 1–27 (cit. on p. 388).

[HRSF20] Y. He, S. Rahimian, B. Schiele, and M. Fritz. "Segmentations-leak: Membership inference attacks and defenses in semantic image segmentation". In: European Conference on Computer Vision. Springer. 2020, pp. 519–535 (cit. on p. 391).

[HZSS16] S. Hill, Z. Zhou, L. Saul, and H. Shacham. "On the (in) effectiveness of mosaicing and blurring as tools for document redaction". In: Proceedings on Privacy Enhancing Technologies 2016.4 (2016), pp. 403–417 (cit. on p. 390).

[Joh+20] B. John, A. Liu, L. Xia, S. Koppal, and E. Jain. "Let It Snow: Adding pixel noise to protect the user's identity". In: ACM Symposium on Eye Tracking Research and Applications. 2020, pp. 1–3 (cit. on pp. 393, 403, 405).

[Kno13] J. Knott. Video Surveillance Recordings Create 413 Petabytes of Data Every Day, http://www.cepro.com/article/video_surveillance_recordings_create_413_petabytes_of_data_every_day. 2013 (cit. on p. 388).

[KVM04] S. S. Kozat, R. Venkatesan, and M. K. Mihcak. "Robust perceptual image hashing via matrix invariants". In: Image Processing, 2004. ICIP '04. 2004 International Conference on. Vol. 5. Oct. 2004, 3443–3446 Vol. 5 (cit. on p. 396).

[LCFK21] J. Li, A. R. Chowdhury, K. Fawaz, and Y. Kim. "Kalεido: Real-Time Privacy Control for Eye-Tracking Systems". In: 30th USENIX Security Symposium (USENIX Security 21). Vancouver, B.C.: USENIX Association, Aug. 2021. URL: https://www.usenix.org/conference/usenixsecurity21/presentation/li-jingjie (cit. on pp. 400, 403, 406).

[Lea+15] L. Leal-Taixé, A. Milan, I. Reid, S. Roth, and K. Schindler. "Motchallenge 2015: Towards a benchmark for multi-target tracking". In: arXiv preprint arXiv:1504.01942 (2015) (cit. on p. 394).

[Li+17] Y. Li, N. Vishwamitra, B. P. Knijnenburg, H. Hu, and K. Caine. "Effectiveness and users' experience of obfuscation as a privacy-enhancing technology for sharing photos". In: Proceedings of the ACM on Human-Computer Interaction 1.CSCW (2017), pp. 1–24 (cit. on pp. 388, 406).

[Li+19] W. Li, F. Milletarì, D. Xu, N. Rieke, J. Hancox, W. Zhu, M. Baust, Y. Cheng, S. Ourselin, M. J. Cardoso, et al. "Privacy-preserving federated brain tumour segmentation". In: International Workshop on Machine Learning in Medical Imaging. Springer. 2019, pp. 133–141 (cit. on pp. 391, 405).

[Liu+19] A. Liu, L. Xia, A. Duchowski, R. Bailey, K. Holmqvist, and E. Jain. "Differential privacy for eye-tracking data". In: Proceedings of the 11th ACM Symposium on Eye Tracking Research & Applications. 2019, pp. 1–10 (cit. on p. 405).

[LTKC18] Y. Li, W. Troutman, B. P. Knijnenburg, and K. Caine. "Human perceptions of sensitive content in photos". In: Proceedings of the IEEE Conference on Computer Vision and Pattern Recognition Workshops. 2018, pp. 1590–1596 (cit. on p. 388).

[Mar01] G. Marx. Identity and anonymity: Some conceptual distinctions and issues for research. Princeton University Press, 2001 (cit. on p. 388).

[Mil+16] A. Milan, L. Leal-Taixé, I. D. Reid, S. Roth, and K. Schindler. "MOT16: A Benchmark for Multi-Object Tracking". In: CoRR abs/1603.00831 (2016). arXiv: 1603.00831. URL: http://arxiv.org/abs/1603.00831 (cit. on p. 399).

[MRR18] V. Mirjalili, S. Raschka, and A. Ross. "Gender Privacy: An Ensemble of Semi Adversarial Networks for Confounding Arbitrary Gender Classifiers". In: 2018 IEEE 9th International Conference on Biometrics Theory, Applications and Systems (BTAS). 2018, pp. 1–10 (cit. on p. 389).

[MSS16] R. McPherson, R. Shokri, and V. Shmatikov. "Defeating Image Obfuscation with Deep Learning". In: CoRR abs/1609.00408 (2016) (cit. on pp. 390, 401).

[NBB19] J. F. Nettrour, M. B. Burch, and B. S. Bal. "Patients, pictures, and privacy: managing clinical photographs in the smartphone era". In: Arthroplasty today 5.1 (2019), pp. 57–60 (cit. on p. 388).

[NSM05] E. M. Newton, L. Sweeney, and B. Malin. "Preserving privacy by de-identifying face images". In: IEEE transactions on Knowledge and Data Engineering 17.2 (2005), pp. 232–243 (cit. on p. 389).

[OR15] A. Othman and A. Ross. "Privacy of Facial Soft Biometrics: Suppressing Gender But Retaining Identity". In: Computer Vision - ECCV 2014 Workshops. Ed. by L. Agapito, M. M. Bronstein, and C. Rother. Cham: Springer International Publishing, 2015, pp. 682–696. ISBN: 978-3-319-16181-5 (cit. on p. 389).

[Pap+16] N. Papernot, M. Abadi, U. Erlingsson, I. Goodfellow, and K. Talwar. "Semi-supervised knowledge transfer for deep learning from private training data". In: arXiv preprint arXiv:1610.05755 (2016) (cit. on p. 391).

[PM92] W. Pennebaker and J. Mitchell. JPEG: Still Image Data Compression Standard. Chapman & Hall digital multimedia standards series. Springer US, 1992. ISBN: 9780442012724. URL: https://books.google.com/books?id=AepB%5C_PZ%5C_WMkC (cit. on p. 396).

[PZBH18] S. Park, X. Zhang, A. Bulling, and O. Hilliges. "Learning to Find Eye Region Landmarks for Remote Gaze Estimation in Unconstrained Settings". In: Proceedings of the 2018 ACM Symposium on Eye Tracking Research Applications. ETRA '18. Warsaw, Poland: Association for Computing Machinery, 2018. ISBN: 9781450357067. URL: https://doi.org/10.1145/3204493.3204545 (cit. on p. 405).

[RF21] D. Reilly and L. Fan. "A comparative evaluation of differentially private image obfuscation". In: 2021 Third IEEE International Conference on Trust, Privacy and Security in Intelligent Systems and Applications (TPS-ISA). IEEE. 2021, pp. 80–89 (cit. on p. 403).

[RGO13] M.-R. Ra, R. Govindan, and A. Ortega. "P3: Toward Privacy-Preserving Photo Sharing". In: Presented as part of the 10th USENIX Symposium on Networked Systems Design and Implementation (NSDI 13). Lombard, IL: USENIX, 2013, pp. 515–528. ISBN: 978-1-931971-00-3. URL: https://www.usenix.org/conference/nsdi13/technical-sessions/presentation/ra (cit. on pp. 389, 390).

[RGRB19] A. Rozsa, M. Ǵunther, E. M. Rudd, and T. E. Boult. "Facial attributes: Accuracy and adversarial robustness". In: Pattern Recognition Letters 124 (2019), pp. 100–108 (cit. on p. 389).

[SCB17] A. Squicciarini, C. Caragea, and R. Balakavi. "Toward automated online photo privacy". In: ACM Transactions on the Web (TWEB) 11.1 (2017), pp. 1–29 (cit. on p. 388).

[Sco04] C. R. Scott. "Benefits and drawbacks of anonymous online communication: Legal challenges and communicative recommendations". In: Free speech yearbook 41.1 (2004), pp. 127–141 (cit. on p. 388).

[SDM19] T. R. Shaham, T. Dekel, and T. Michaeli. "Singan: Learning a generative model from a single natural image". In: Proceedings of the IEEE/CVF international conference on computer vision. 2019, pp. 4570–4580 (cit. on p. 404).

[SHHB19] J. Steil, I. Hagestedt, M. X. Huang, and A. Bulling. "Privacy-aware eye tracking using differential privacy". In: Proceedings of the 11th ACM Symposium on Eye Tracking Research & Applications. 2019, pp. 1–9 (cit. on p. 403).

[Smi17] A. Smith. Record shares of Americans have smartphones, home broadband. https://www.pewresearch.org/fact-tank/2017/01/12/evolution-of-technology/. Accessed: 2021-02-28. Jan. 2017 (cit. on p. 387).

[SP17] R. Stevens and I. Pudney. Blur select faces with the updated Blur Faces tool. Ed. by youtube-eng.googleblog.com. [Online; posted 21-August-2017]. Aug. 2017. URL: https://youtube-eng.googleblog.com/2017/08/blur-select-faces-with-updated-blur.html (cit. on pp. 389, 390).

[SRF22] M. U. Saleem, D. Reilly, and L. Fan. "DP-Shield: Face Obfuscation with Differential Privacy". In: Proceedings of the 25th International Conference on Extending Database Technology, EDBT 2022, Edinburgh, UK, March 29 - April 1, 2022. Ed. by J. Stoyanovich, J. Teubner, P. Guagliardo, M. Nikolic, A. Pieris, J. M'uhlig, F. 'Ozcan, S. Schelter, H. V. Jagadish, and M. Zhang. OpenProceedings.org, 2022, 2:578–2:581. URL: https://doi.org/10.48786/edbt.2022.55 (cit. on p. 406).

[SSSS17] R. Shokri, M. Stronati, C. Song, and V. Shmatikov. "Membership inference attacks against machine learning models". In: 2017 IEEE symposium on security and privacy (SP). IEEE. 2017, pp. 3–18 (cit. on pp. 391, 403).

[TKP19] R. Torkzadehmahani, P. Kairouz, and B. Paten. "DP-CGAN: Differentially Private Synthetic Data and Label Generation". In: The IEEE Conference on Computer Vision and Pattern Recognition (CVPR) Workshops. June 2019 (cit. on pp. 391, 406).

[WBSS04] Z. Wang, A. C. Bovik, H. R. Sheikh, and E. P. Simoncelli. "Image quality assessment: from error visibility to structural similarity". In: IEEE Transactions on Image Processing 13.4 (Apr. 2004), pp. 600–612. ISSN: 1057-7149 (cit. on p. 404).

[WHKV20] H. Wang, Y. Hong, Y. Kong, and J. Vaidya. "Publishing video data with indistinguishable objects". In: 23rd International Conference on Extending Database Technology, EDBT 2020. OpenProceedings.org. 2020, pp. 323–334 (cit. on pp. 399, 405).

[WK18] Y. Wang and M. Kosinski. "Deep neural networks are more accurate than humans at detecting sexual orientation from facial images." In: Journal of personality and social psychology 114.2 (2018), p. 246 (cit. on p. 390).

[WR14] T. Winkler and B. Rinner. "Security and privacy protection in visual sensor networks: A survey". In: ACM Computing Surveys (CSUR) 47.1 (2014), pp. 1–42 (cit. on p. 388).

[WXH20] H. Wang, S. Xie, and Y. Hong. "VideoDP: A Flexible Platform for Video Analytics with Differential Privacy". In: Proceedings on Privacy Enhancing Technologies 2020.4 (2020), pp. 277–296 (cit. on pp. 398, 399, 405).

[Xia+16] Z. Xia, X. Wang, L. Zhang, Z. Qin, X. Sun, and K. Ren. "A Privacy-Preserving and Copy-Deterrence Content-Based Image Retrieval Scheme in Cloud Computing". In: IEEE Transactions on Information Forensics and Security 11.11 (Nov. 2016), pp. 2594–2608. ISSN: 1556-6013 (cit. on p. 389).

[Xie+18] L. Xie, K. Lin, S. Wang, F. Wang, and J. Zhou. "Differentially private generative adversarial network". In: arXiv preprint arXiv:1802.06739 (2018) (cit. on p. 391).

[Yan+16] J. Yang, B. Price, S. Cohen, H. Lee, and M.-H. Yang. "Object contour detection with a fully convolutional encoder-decoder network". In: Proceedings of the IEEE conference on computer vision and pattern recognition. 2016, pp. 193–202 (cit. on p. 405).

[Zha+18] R. Zhang, P. Isola, A. A. Efros, E. Shechtman, and O. Wang. "The unreasonable effectiveness of deep features as a perceptual metric". In: Proceedings of the IEEE conference on computer vision and pattern recognition. 2018, pp. 586–595 (cit. on p. 404).

[Zha+20] Y. Zhang, R. Jia, H. Pei, W. Wang, B. Li, and D. Song. "The Secret Revealer: Generative Model-Inversion Attacks Against Deep Neural Networks". In: Proceedings of the IEEE/CVF Conference on Computer Vision and Pattern Recognition (CVPR). June 2020 (cit. on p. 390).

Part IV

Tools and Testing

DOI: 10.1561/9781638284772.ch12

Chapter 12

Programming Frameworks for Differential Privacy

By Marco Gaboardi, Michael Hay and Salil Vadhan

Many programming frameworks have been introduced to support the development of differentially private software applications. In this chapter, we survey some of the conceptual ideas underlying these frameworks in a way that we hope will be helpful for both practitioners and researchers. For practitioners, the survey can provide a starting point for understanding what features may be valuable when selecting a programming framework. For researchers, it can help organize existing work in a unified way and provide context for understanding new features in future frameworks.

We do not attempt to be comprehensive in our coverage of the landscape of software tools for differential privacy (which is constantly growing) or in the issues relevant to implementation. In particular, we focus on programming frameworks for expressing and reasoning about differentially private statistical analyses, sometimes referred to as "queries." We refer readers interested in frameworks for large-scale machine learning pipelines to Chapter 7 and the references therein. Furthermore, there are a number of important issues in programming with differential privacy that we did not address, such as randomness generation, security, finite arithmetic, side channels, and scalability; discussions of these can be found in many of the papers we reference.

12.1 Introduction

One of the reasons for the popularity of Differential Privacy [DMNS06; DMNS16] is that it is based on a simple and elegant mathematical definition which enjoys several important properties. One of these properties is *composability*, which is captured by a number of composition theorems for differential privacy and its variants, as presented in Chapters 1 and 3. In essence, these composition theorems tell us that the privacy loss of a "combined" mechanism can be seen as a function of the privacy losses of the different components. This enables reasoning in terms of a *privacy-loss budget*, where a global limit on privacy loss is enforced by tracking the accumulated privacy losses of differentially private queries made by data analysts. In addition, it also tells us that different differentially private mechanisms can be put together to form a "combined" mechanism incurring a graceful degradation of the privacy loss. This property naturally leads to the idea of designing *programming frameworks* for differential privacy. In this chapter, we use the term "programming framework" in a rather broad and inclusive way to refer to those tools that have been designed to support the development of differentially private applications and which provide some building blocks in the form of basic mechanisms and methods to combine them.

Composability is not the only property that makes the design of programming frameworks possible. Another important property that differential privacy enjoys is *resilience to post-processing*, guaranteeing that manipulations of the result of a differentially private mechanism cannot compromise the privacy of the data (see Chapter 1 for a review on properties of Differential Privacy.) In addition, resilience to post-processing also guarantees that once the result of a mechanism is computed, we can forget about the method that was used to compute it. This property provides a sort of *modularity* that is akin to the one usually encountered in programming languages, where one can use library functions based on their specification, without knowing the details of their implementation. In particular, this property allows one to use differentially private components inside larger software projects without worrying about how the results computed by these components will be used. Composability and resilience to post-processing also permit one to solve a data analysis problem by first decomposing it into subproblems and then combining the results.

There are several reasons why using programming frameworks for designing differentially private applications is preferable to building differential privacy applications from scratch:

- **Increasing reliability.** Differential privacy is in its essence a probabilistic requirement on programs and reasoning about probabilistic guarantees can be challenging and error-prone, even for experts. (See, for example, [HPN11; Mir12; JMRO22; CSVW22; Han+22].) Errors in the design of differential privacy analyses, or bugs in their implementations, can compromise the privacy property of applications and undermine their goals. By providing a small set of programming primitives which can be thoroughly vetted, programming frameworks can help improve reliability and decrease errors in design and implementations of differentially private data analyses. In other words, programming frameworks can reduce the verification of the privacy properties of a program to the verification of the different components the frameworks provide.

- **Integration with familiar programming workflows.** Programming frameworks for differential privacy provide programming-level building blocks that can be used to implement differential privacy applications. These building blocks are usually presented as components of a library or of a domain-specific language. These libraries and domain-specific languages can be integrated in standard programming workflow. Hence, data analysts using these frameworks can combine general-purpose programming and domain-specific programming.
- **Focusing on functionality and utility.** When designing a differentially private data analysis for a specific statistical problem one has to ensure that the analysis both respects the probabilistic requirement of differential privacy and solves the intended statistical problem. Programming frameworks often provide ways of automatically ensuring that the differential privacy guarantee is met, without having to reason directly about the definition of differential privacy. So, by using these frameworks, a programmer or analyst can focus mainly on guaranteeing that the analysis solves the statistical problem at hand, which is the domain expertise of most end-user data scientists (who may not have expertise in differential privacy).
- **Supporting different computing environments.** Some programming frameworks are designed in a way that decouples the programming environment from the environment in which programs are actually executed, often called the *computing environment.* This separation allows a user to select a different computing environment based on their own requirements, which may relate to efficiency, security, and/or integration with existing data infrastructure.
- **Improving code reuse and helping build communities.** Another benefit of programming frameworks is that these frameworks can help the design of standardization processes and open-source initiatives incentivizing code reuse and better design practices. Programming frameworks can offer a common language that can be used by different contributors as a *lingua franca.* This in turn can help build communities of programmers and users around differential privacy.

There is by now a plethora of programming frameworks for differential privacy. A non-exhaustive list includes: *APEx* [GHIM19], *Adaptive Fuzz* [WHRP17], *Airavat* [Roy+10], *Chorus* [JNHS20], *DFuzz* [Gab+13] *Diffprivlib* [HBML19], *DPella* [LRG20], *Duet* [Nea+19], *Ektelo* [Zha+18], *Flex* [JNS18], *Fuzz* [RP10; HPN11] *Google SQL* [Wil+20], *Gupt* [Moh+12], *OpenDP* [GHV20], *PINQ* [McS09], *PrivateSQL* [Kot+19], and *PSI* [Gab+16], and *Tumult Analytics* [Ber+22].

Some of these are actively maintained open-source software tools, whereas others were only built as research prototypes. Moreover, the landscape is rapidly changing, with new tools emerging at a rapid pace. Thus we do not attempt to provide a comprehensive description of any specific tools in this survey. Instead, we identify some of the essential characteristics that cut across all of the tools, and only use the specific tools as exemplars of different design choices.

Overview of the Chapter

Chapter three key characteristics of programming frameworks for differential privacy: *privacy calculus*, which is how frameworks provide quantitative methods for bounding privacy loss without the need to compute probability distributions explicitly (Section 12.3), *composition and interactivity*, discussed in Section 12.4, which is how frameworks handle the cumulative privacy loss over multiple analyses, and *expressivity*, discussed in Section 12.5, refers to reviews the richness and variety of analyses that frameworks can express. In addition to these core characteristics, we discuss tools and techniques for the verification and testing of differential privacy implementations (Section 12.6).

12.2 Characteristics of DP Programming Frameworks

We organize our survey of differentially private programming frameworks around the following key characteristics.

1. **Privacy calculus.** A specific aspect of programming frameworks for differential privacy is that they provide some form of a quantitative calculus that allows one to bound the privacy loss of analyses written in the framework. These privacy calculi internalize different general techniques that have been identified in the differential privacy research literature. For example, several of the programming frameworks are based on privacy calculi designed around the concept of global sensitivity [DMNS16], and others around the sample-and-aggregate framework [NRS07]. In most of the cases, these calculi provide a form of *privacy specification* for different components that can be inspected

to guarantee differential privacy for an entire analysis built from those components.

2. **Composition and interactivity.** In addition to providing a privacy calculus to determine the privacy loss of a single analysis, programming frameworks for differential privacy often provide tools for tracking and controlling the cumulative privacy loss over multiple analyses via composition theorems for differential privacy. These tools range in their level of generality from supporting single, nonadaptive batches of queries to interactive systems where a human analyst can adaptively choose the next query based on the results of previous ones.
3. **Expressivity.** One key design aspect of any programming framework is *expressivity*. Programming frameworks for differential privacy are no exception. Differential privacy is often presented as a property of programs working on some data, but what exactly these programs are, and which statistical tasks they may be able to accomplish, may vary. For example, some programming frameworks are designed to support only programs representing a restricted class of queries, while others attempt to approximate arbitrary data analyses.

12.3 Privacy Calculus

Programming frameworks for differential privacy are usually based on some form of a *privacy calculus*, which is a principled way to guarantee that a data analysis is differentially private without explicitly computing the probability distributions of the data analysis on each pair of neighboring datasets. Generally, the privacy calculus specifies (a) how to determine whether an individual statistical computation is differentially private, and (b) how the privacy loss accumulates over multiple statistical computations. The latter is known as *composition* and is treated in the next section, along with interactivity. In this section, we focus on the former, how we determine that an individual computation is differentially private.

Most of the differential privacy programming frameworks use some form of reasoning based on *sensitivity*, or equivalently, *stability*.[i]

i. Historically, the terms sensitivity and stability have been used for related concepts in different settings in the differential privacy literature. From the paper that defined differential privacy [DMNS16], *sensitivity* has referred to functions mapping datasets to real numbers, vectors, or a general metric space, and measures how much the value of the function can change when one individual's data changes. Starting from PINQ [McS09], *stability* has referred to functions mapping datasets to datasets, measuring how much output datasets can differ per change in output datasets. As discussed below, both are special cases of more general notions bounding output "distances" as a function of input "distances" for mappings between arbitrary sets

We describe these concepts and some of their different incarnations below.

Differential Privacy and Global Stability

Recall from Chapter 1 that a mechanism M satisfies (pure) differentially privacy if for every two datasets x, x' that are *adjacent* (i.e. differ on one individual's data), the output distributions $M(x)$ and $M(x')$ are ε-close to each other (in the sense that for every set T of outputs, the probabilities of T under $M(x)$ and $M(x')$ are within a factor of e^{ε} of each other). More generally, by the group privacy property of pure differential privacy, if x and x' are at distance at most d (i.e, differ on at most d individuals' data), then the output distributions are $d\varepsilon$-close to each other. Thus, differential privacy can be viewed as a *stability* or *Lipschitz* property of randomized algorithms M, whereby close inputs map to close output distributions. We think of this as a *global* stability property because the stability constant ε provides a uniform bound over all pairs of datasets x and x'.

Thus, it is natural to use notions of global stability as the basis for the privacy calculus of a DP programming tool. Below we describe some of the variants of global stability that arise in existing frameworks, in increasing levels of generality.

Before proceeding, we remark that, even for simple tabular datasets, there are many ways to formalize the notion of *adjacent* datasets, and it is important to be careful and consistent about this choice when implementing differential privacy. In this chapter, except when explicitly stated otherwise, we model datasets as unordered multisets of records, and consider two datasets to be adjacent if we can obtain one from the other by adding or removing one individual's data. This formulation is often known as *unbounded DP* as it treats the number n of records as being unbounded and potentially private information. In contrast, *bounded DP* treats the number n of records as fixed, public information, and two datasets as adjacent if one can be obtained from the other by *changing* one individual's data.

Stable Dataset Transformations

The tool *PINQ* [McS09] supports *chaining* (pure) differentially private algorithms M with transformations T from datasets to datasets that are themselves stable. Specifically, we say that T is *c-stable* if for every two datasets x and x', the distance between the datasets $T(x)$ and $T(x')$ is at most a factor of c larger than the distance between x and x'. As a simple example, a "map" transformation

$$T_f(\{x_1, \ldots, x_n\}) = \{f(x_1), \ldots, f(x_n)\} \tag{12.1}$$

that have some notion of elements being "close" to each other. We choose "stability" as the terminology for the more general notion, mainly because it represents a feature we seek: functions that are most compatible with privacy are ones that remain "stable" or "*in*-sensitive" to small changes in their input.

is 1-stable, since record x_i of the input affects only one record $f(x_i)$ of the output.

Two key properties of stable transformations that make them useful for a privacy calculus are the following *Chaining Rules*:

1. if T is c-stable and M is ε-DP, then $M \circ T$ is $c\varepsilon$-DP, and
2. if T_1 is c_1-stable and T_2 is c_2-stable, then $T_1 \circ T_2$ is $c_1 c_2$-stable.

For example, using Chaining Rule 1 with T being a map function T_f as in Equation (12.1) and M being a differentially private noisy sum operator (which, say, clamps the values to $[0, 1]$, adds them up, and adds Laplace noise), we can estimate sums of arbitrary bounded functions f applied to records.

These two rules are the core of the privacy calculus of *PINQ* [McS09]. In addition, *PINQ* allows for reasoning about the stability of one-to-many transformations, which map a single dataset to several datasets (e.g. partitioning, which we will discuss below) and many-to-one transformations (e.g. database joins).

Special Cases of Stable Dataset Transformations

Some frameworks are based on specific families of stable transformations. For example, *Airavat* [Roy+10] allows stable transformations of the mapping kind T_f from Equation (12.1) as well as a k-stable generalization where each input record maps to k output records:

$$T_{f_1,\ldots,f_k}(\{x_1, \ldots, x_n\}) = \{f_j(x_i) : j = 1, \ldots, k, i = 1, \ldots, n\}.$$

This allows for efficient implementation in a map-reduce framework. These map transformations can be composed with a small family of differentially private reducers, like the noisy sum.

A different generalization of map transformations is used, for example, in the programming tool *GUPT* [Moh+12], which allows f to map a *set* of records (i.e. a dataset) to a single record. Then we can obtain a 1-stable transformation by specifying a (possibly random) partition $P = (P_1, \ldots, P_m)$ of the set of possible data records, and outputting

$$T_{P,f}(x) = \{f(x_{P_1}), \ldots, f(x_{P_m})\},$$

where x_{P_i} consists of the records of x in the partition piece P_i. This is a 1-stable transformation because each input record x_j affects at most one of the output records.[ii] We can then apply an arbitrary differentially private aggregator (such as a DP approximation of the average or median) to the output of $T_{P,f}(x)$ to obtain a

ii. However, if we worked with bounded DP, then the transformation would only be 2-stable, because changing one input record could move that record from one piece of the partition to another, thereby affecting two of the output records.

differentially private approximation of the estimator f, with the privacy justified by Chaining Rule 1. This realizes the "sample-and-aggregate" framework introduced in [NRS07]. The appeal of this framework is that f can be an arbitrary, *non-private* statistical analysis, and as long as f gives similar results on the different subsets of the dataset specified by P, then the aggregator should also give a similar result (with additional noise, to achieve privacy). The disadvantage is that dataset sizes often need to be quite large for sample-and-aggregate to be effective, since (a) each set P_i in the partition may need to be large in order for the $f(x_{P_i})$'s to well-approximate $f(x)$, and (b) the number m of sets on the partition may need to be large in order for the noise introduced by the DP aggregator to be small.

Stability on General Metric Spaces

Going beyond stable dataset-to-dataset transformations, *Fuzz* [RP10] can allow for reasoning about transformations between arbitrary metric spaces. Specifically, a transformation $T : \mathcal{X} \to \mathcal{Y}$ from metric space $(\mathcal{X}, d_{\mathcal{X}})$ to metric space $(\mathcal{Y}, d_{\mathcal{Y}})$ is *c-stable* (a.k.a. c-Lipschitz) if for all $x, x' \in \mathcal{X}$, we have

$$d_{\mathcal{Y}}(T(x), T(x')) \leq c \cdot d_{\mathcal{X}}(x, x').$$

For example, if $\mathcal{X}$ is the space of all datasets, $d_{\mathcal{X}}$ is the usual notion of distance on datasets discussed above, $\mathcal{Y} = \mathbb{R}$, and $d_{\mathcal{Y}}(y, y') = |y - y'|$, then a transformation T is c-stable if and only if T has *global sensitivity* at most c — the basis of the standard *Laplace mechanism* for differential privacy [DMNS16].

A benefit of this generalization is that it allows for breaking differentially private algorithms into smaller components, which in turn provides more modularity, code reuse, and easier verifiability. Let's consider the standard global sensitivity paradigm [DMNS16] for designing differentially private algorithms. Let T be a function from datasets to real numbers that has global sensitivity at most c, i.e. is c-stable as above. Then, as explained in Chapter 1, the mechanism

$$M(x) = T(x) + \text{Lap}(c/\varepsilon),$$

is an ε-differentially private algorithm. With reasoning about stability between arbitrary metric spaces, we can decompose the construction and analysis of M into two simpler, modular components. Specifically, note that $M = N \circ T$, where T is the function of global sensitivity at most c, and $N(z) = z + \text{Lap}(c/\varepsilon)$ adds noise to a single real number z. The noise-addition mechanism N has the property that two inputs z and z' that are close as real numbers (rather than as datasets) map to close output distributions. Specifically the distance between the distributions of $N(z)$ and $N(z')$ is at most a factor of (ε/c) times $|z - z'|$. Thus, by an appropriate generalization of Chaining Rule 1, the composition $N \circ T$ is $c \cdot (\varepsilon/c)$-DP; that is, it is ε-DP.

More generally, we call a (randomized) function like N where close inputs (with respect to any input metric) map to close output distributions (with respect to any metric on probability distributions) a *measurement*. In contrast, if we only allowed for reasoning about stable transformations and DP algorithms on datasets as above, then $M = T \circ N$ would have to be treated as an atomic function; now we can separate the components, and reuse the same noise-addition measurement N for different stable transformations T (and conversely).

Another benefit of this generalization is extending the privacy calculus to other input types, such as a database consisting of multiple tables. What distance metric is appropriate for a database is a nuanced question that depends on what data is being represented. Consider, for instance, a graph database consisting of a Node table and an Edge table. The right choice of metric would depend on whether one wants to protect a single edge, a node and all of its incident edges, or some other property of the data. Several programming frameworks support database inputs but vary in the distance metrics they support. For example, *Flex* [JNS18] measures distance in terms of number of rows (across all tables). On the graph database example, whether Flex offers node or edge-level protection would depend on the query being asked. *PrivateSQL* [Kot+19] uses distance metrics that incorporate integrity constraints that hold on the data. An example of such a constraint is as follows: if u is removed from the Node table, then all incident edges must be removed from the Edge table as well. This allows *PrivateSQL*, for instance, to capture node-level protection. *GoogleSQL* [Wil+20] is designed for databases where each row is "owned" by a user, each user may own several rows, and distances between two databases is measured in users rather than individual rows. This captures the notion of user-level protection that is desirable in applications where one user might "own" a large number of rows (e.g., in a database of credit card transactions). A limitation of this approach, however, is that it cannot be easily applied to graph data, because it cannot support scenarios where a data item can have multiple owners, which is the case for edges in this example.[iii]

Beyond Metric Spaces

The standard mathematical definition of a *metric* $d(x, x')$ is a real-valued function that satisfies requirements of nonnegativity, symmetry, and the triangle inequality. However, not all "closeness" notions that appear in the design of differentially private algorithms are convenient to express in terms of such metrics. For example, *approximate differential privacy* measures the closeness of distributions via two real

iii. For more information on differential privacy for databases, we recommend Near and He [NH21].

parameters ε and δ, whereas metrics are required to express distance via a single real number. Thus, the *OpenDP* Programming Framework [GHV20] allows for expressing more general stability notions whereby "d_{in}-close" inputs map to "d_{out}-close" outputs (or output distributions), for arbitrary, user-defined closeness relations that can be expressed in terms of parameters d_{in} and d_{out} of arbitrary type. In particular, *OpenDP* can support a variety of privacy measures, such as approximate DP [Dwo+06], concentrated DP [DR16; BS16], and f-DP [DRS22]. Also *Duet* [Nea+19] supports several privacy measures but it only supports stability notions over metric spaces. *Duet* combines two domain-specific languages: one is similar to *Fuzz* and supports only reasoning about transformations between arbitrary metric spaces, while the other supports instead reasoning about arbitrary measurements.

Local Stability

A difficulty with reasoning about global stability is that it can sometimes be overly conservative, in that the pair x, x' of datasets that maximize $d(T(x), T(x'))/d(x, x')$ may be artificial ones that are unlikely to arise in practice. Thus, it is attractive to try to reason using *local stability*, where we take x to be our actual, given dataset, and consider the quantity

$$\mathrm{LS}_T(x) = \max_{x':d(x,x')=1} d(T(x), T(x')).$$

Note that this is a data-dependent quantity, in contrast to global stability that does not depend on the given x.

Unfortunately, directly trying to substitute local stability for global stability in DP algorithms generally does not preserve privacy; the problem is that the stability itself (which ultimately controls the amount of noise introduced) can reveal sensitive information. Thus, there is a large body of work on how to approximate this idea (using variants of local stability) while obtaining algorithms that are genuinely differentially private. *Flex* [JNS18] is a tool whose design draws on this body of work to tackle the problem of privately answering database queries that involve joins. Whereas a join query can have large, possibly unbounded, *global* stability, its *local* stability can be much smaller. For instance, local sensitivity of a join between the Node and Edge tables representing a graph would be a function of the maximum node degree as opposed to the number of nodes. *Flex* leverages this property in its approach, called *elastic sensitivity*, which is a calculus for deriving an upper bound on the local stability of a complex database query expression. *Flex* combines its elastic sensitivity with techniques from prior work on appropriately calibrating noise to bounds on local stability.

12.4 Composition and Interactivity

In differential privacy, *composition* refers to reasoning about the privacy properties of an algorithm that is composed of one or more differentially private algorithms. The basic composition theorem for (pure) differential privacy says that if mechanisms M_1 and M_2 are ε_1-DP and ε_2-DP respectively, then the mechanism $M(x) = (M_1(x), M_2(x))$ that applies both mechanisms to the same dataset and outputs both results is $(\varepsilon_1 + \varepsilon_2)$-DP. Composition has two key applications in the context of programming frameworks. First, it allows for tracking the *cumulative* privacy loss that results from executing multiple statistical computations. Some programming frameworks help users manage the cumulative privacy loss by allowing them to impose a privacy loss "budget" and ensuring that the cumulative loss does not exceed the budget. Second, it is a useful tool in algorithm design as it facilitates the creation of new differentially private algorithms from existing components. Some programming frameworks facilitate the creation of new mechanisms in this way. Both of these applications of composition are enhanced by frameworks that support *interactivity*, where human analysts or programs can adaptively choose which mechanism M_2 to apply after receiving the result of a previous mechanism M_1.

While the composition rules for pure DP are fairly straightforward (epsilons add up), the composition rules for other variants of DP are less so, and this has been and continues to be an active area of research [KOV15; MV16; RRUV16; Aba+16; DR16; BS16; Mir17; DRS22; VW21; VZ22; Lyu22; WRRW22] (see Chapter 3 for more on composition.) We organize the rest of this section around the kinds of composition that are supported by programming frameworks for differential privacy.

No Composition

Some programming frameworks, such as *Flex* [JNS18] and *Diffprivlib* [HBML19], do not support composition or interactivity. That is, they enable one to control or calculate the privacy loss of an individual differentially private mechanism or query, but tracking the cumulative privacy loss is left to the user or an application built on top of the framework.

Non-adaptive Composition

Several programming frameworks allow the user to construct a program that evaluates a *batch* of statistical computations $M_1, \ldots, M_\ell$. The computations are *non-adaptive*, meaning that the sequence of computations is fixed: each M_i has fixed privacy loss parameters and its only input is the private dataset. An archetypal example is the released prototype of *PSI* [Gab+16] and its successor *DP Creator* [Ope22], which allows a data curator to choose a set of summary statistics (e.g., means, quantiles, histograms) to be released under a fixed privacy loss budget. Other frameworks that fall into this category include *Airavat* [Roy+10] and *PrivateSQL* [Kot+19].

Such frameworks are responsible for calculating the cumulative privacy loss of the program and typically ensuring it does not exceed a user-specified budget. Some employ the basic, pure DP composition theorem alluded to in the introduction to this section, but *PSI* uses (an approximation of) the optimal composition theorem for approximate DP [MV16]. However, these frameworks do not explicitly track the cumulative privacy loss across batches or support interaction with the user.[iv]

Adaptive Composition

Adaptive composition refers to the idea that subsequent mechanisms may depend on the results of evaluating earlier mechanisms (M_2 can depend on $M_1(x)$). In the most basic form of adaptive composition, one again has a fixed sequence of ℓ statistical computations, $M_1, \ldots, M_\ell$ where the privacy loss of each M_i is fixed, but each subsequent computation can depend on the results of previous computations—i.e., mechanism M_i is provided the results of earlier computations as auxiliary input. Formally, we compute the i'th result as $y_i = M_i(x; (y_1, y_2, \ldots, y_{i-1}))$, where x is the private dataset. With this kind of adaptivity, one can support iterative algorithms such as k-means clustering, an algorithm for grouping data into k clusters. Such an algorithm is inherently adaptive because it proceeds in rounds where the assignment to clusters in each round depends on a statistical summary produced in the previous round.

An example of a programming tool that supports this kind of composition is *Fuzz*. *Fuzz* uses a type system to statically analyze (at "compile time") the composition of a program. While *Fuzz* does support adaptive composition, it is limited to programs where the stability (or sensitivity, see Section 12.3) is a constant and therefore precludes supporting, say, a version of k-means where the number k of clusters or the number ℓ of iterations are user-specified inputs to the program. *DFuzz* [Gab+13] overcomes this limitation by extending the static type system approach to allow types to depend on input variables. Other more complex type systems have been studied, in order to go even farther in supporting the verification of differential privacy data analyses. We will discuss some of them briefly in Section 12.6.2.

iv. The paper describing the design of *PSI* [Gab+16] proposes a way to support interactivity with multiple batches, but the prototype implementation does not offer that functionality.

Fully Adaptive Composition and Interactivity

With the previously described programming frameworks, the entire statistical computation, even if adaptive, must be specified up front. While such frameworks can be useful for building complex algorithms, in many practical applications, it may be undesirable to bundle all computations into a single "one shot" algorithm. Instead, analysts may prefer to interactively query the data, receive (differentially private) responses, and adaptively choose the next query. In such a setting, the composition can be said to be fully adaptive because the number of rounds, the choice of mechanism, and its privacy parameters are all adaptively chosen by the analyst. Composition is more subtle in this setting [RRUV16].

The interactive setting can be modeled as an interactive protocol between two parties, an arbitrary adversarial strategy $\mathcal{A}$ (the analyst) and an interactive measurement $\mathcal{M}(x)$. The interaction proceeds in rounds where in round i, $\mathcal{A}$ selects a query q_i adaptively based on all previous answers $(a_1, \ldots, a_{i-1})$ and any randomness of $\mathcal{A}$. One can think of a query as a request to perform a differentially private computation with given privacy loss parameters. The query is sent to the interactive mechanism $\mathcal{M}$ which evaluates the query and returns answer a_i. Differential privacy is defined with respect the adversary's *view*, denoted $\text{View}(\mathcal{A} \leftrightarrow \mathcal{M}(x))$, of this interaction [VW21].

We highlight two programming frameworks in this setting. Both support a form of interaction known as a *privacy filter* [RRUV16], an interactive mechanism that takes a global privacy loss budget and admits adaptively selected computations provided that evaluating the computation would not cause the cumulative privacy loss to exceed a pre-specified budget. A variant is the concept of a *privacy odometer* [RRUV16], which tracks cumulative privacy loss but does not enforce a predetermined budget.

In the programming tool *PINQ*, the interactive mechanism is represented by a *PINQueryable*, a stateful object that encapsulates a private data source (a collection of records) and allows it to be queried within a given privacy-loss budget. Each *PINQueryable* exposes a set of pre-defined methods, which represent the available queries. An example method is NoisyAverage, which takes an ε and a function f and applies f to each tuple in the source, clamps the result to $[-1, 1]$, and returns a noisy average of the clamped results. The analyst $\mathcal{A}$ can be expressed as arbitrary code, written in the language C#; in particular, $\mathcal{A}$ can make fully adaptive queries to the *PINQueryable*, and the *PINQueryable* tracks the cumulative privacy loss and enforces the budget.

The programming tool *Adaptive Fuzz* [WHRP17] is built on top of *Fuzz*: it adds an outer "adaptive" layer that wraps around the static typechecker and runtime of *Fuzz*. Unlike *PINQ*, the available queries are not limited to a pre-defined set of methods, but rather a query can be any computation that the *Fuzz* typechecker can verify to be differentially private. An example of an application that *Adaptive Fuzz* can support is fitting a model using differentially private gradient descent with a data-dependent stopping criteria, such as the model error falling below a threshold. If the stopping criteria is reached before the budget is exhausted, any remaining budget can be applied to additional (adaptively chosen) computations.

Hierarchical (and Concurrent) Interactivity

While there are several frameworks that support interactivity, most operate like *Adaptive Fuzz* with a single "level" of interactivity: there is exactly one interactive mechanism that governs the adaptivity and any query to that mechanism must correspond to a *non-interactive* differentially private program. *Hierarchical interactivity* refers to the idea that an interactive mechanism could recursively spawn new interactive mechanisms.

Hierarchical interaction has many potential applications. It could be useful as a way of structuring programs that naturally have multiple layers of interactivity – for instance, the first layer of interactivity might be a privacy filter and the second layer of interactivity might include the execution of interactive primitives like Sparse Vector or Private Multiplicative Weights [DR+14]. Another application could be to allow a data curator to allow *multiple* analysts to operate concurrently on the data, each with their own privacy filter or odometer, such that the cumulative privacy loss is tracked appropriately. One could also imagine novel algorithms that involve asking interleaving queries to two or more instantiations of interactive mechanisms.

PINQ supports (a limited form of) hierarchical interactivity. Some of the methods available on a *PINQueryable* are capable of spawning new *PINQueryable* objects. For instance, the Partition method splits the dataset into multiple, disjoint datasets and returns a new *PINQueryable* for each one. Using such methods it is possible to start with an initial private data source and spawn a tree of related queryables.[v] Such a tree is illustrated in Figure 12.1.

Figure 12.1 also illustrates *PINQ*'s method for reasoning about the the composition of these multiple, related queryables. Each queryable internally has an agent which is responsible for managing requests to consume privacy budget through one of the measurement methods (like NoisyAverage). The agent associated with each new queryable has a reference to its parent queryable. The child is responsible for handling its request and translating it into an appropriate request to its parent. For instance suppose Q is a queryable with parent P and children $C_1, \ldots, C_k$ that are the result of calling Partition on Q. Because partition splits the data into disjoint

v. In fact, rather than a tree, the result structure can be a directed acyclic graph because *PINQ* also supports operators like Join that combines two queryables into one.

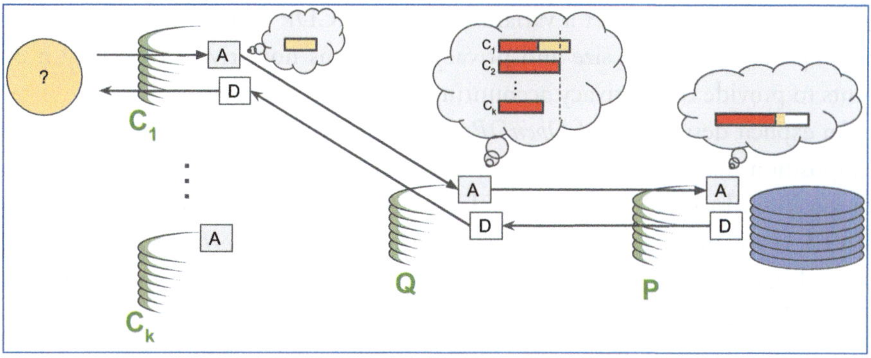

Figure 12.1. Illustration of hierarchical interactivity in *PINQ*. When a query (yellow circle) is submitted to *PINQueryable* C_1, its agent (A) forwards the budget request (yellow bar) to the agent of its parent, Q. In this case, because the children represent disjoint partitions of Q's data, the agent of Q keeps track of the cumulative privacy loss incurred at each child (red bars). When it receives the request from the child, it calculates how much this query would increase the maximum privacy loss and sends a request to the agent of its parent, P, who checks the residual cost against a budget. Since the request is under budget, response data (D) flows back to the *PINQueryable* where the query initiated.

subsets, interactions with the children satisfy *parallel composition* [McS09] and the cumulative privacy loss is the maximum of the loss incurred by any of the children.[vi] Therefore, when the agent of Q receives a request from its children, the amount of the request to its parent is only the *change* in the maximum (which might be zero).

Somewhat surprisingly, the more general concurrent composition of multiple interactive mechanisms has only recently been formally studied [VW21] and researchers have only recently presented proofs that other variants of DP such as f-DP [DRS22] and Renyi-DP [Mir17; BS16] satisfy concurrent composition theorems [VZ22; Lyu22; Han+23].

Extensibility

With both *PINQ* and *AdaptiveFuzz*, the composition is "baked in" to the programming framework itself. For example, the implementation of PINQ supports a specific definition of privacy (pure DP); its components exchange information using the parameters of that definition (ε) and the agents apply the composition rules of PureDP. Perhaps more fundamentally, it leans heavily on the fact that with group privacy under pure DP, the privacy loss grows linearly with the size of the group, which allows it to view an ε-DP measurement on a c-stable transformation of the dataset as equivalent to a $c\varepsilon$-DP measurement on the source (see Section 12.3.)

vi. This is similar to the stability analysis underlying the sample-and-aggregate framework and GUPT discussed above in Section 12.3.

Adapting PINQ to support a variant of DP like zCDP that has a non-linear relationship between group size and privacy loss seems non-trivial, especially if one wants to provide tight privacy accounting.

An explicit design goal of *OpenDP* is extensibility and its approach to handling composition makes it easy, in principle, to expand the library with new forms of composition. In the OpenDP formulation of a *measurement* (as discussed in Section 12.3), the privacy properties are explicitly encoded in a *privacy map* that transforms distances between input data(sets) to distances between output probability distributions, and the latter can be measured in any desired way.

To extend OpenDP with a new form of composition, one must simply define a new measurement operator that captures that composition operation. For example, basic non-adaptive composition is implemented as a measurement function that takes as input a list of measurement functions and applies them sequentially to the data. It can use the privacy maps of the measurements being combined plus the sequential composition theorem to determine its own privacy map.

12.5 Expressivity

Expressivity refers to the richness and variety of analyses that can be expressed in a given programming framework. These are naturally impacted by a framework's privacy calculus and support for composition. In particular, given that most analyses are expressed as a chaining of measurements and stable transformations, e.g. $M \circ T_k \circ T_{k-1} \circ \cdots T_1$, or compositions of such chainings, the expressivity of a programming framework is greatly impacted by which transformations, measurements, and composition procedures are supported. Thus, another relevant feature is *extensibility*, the support for adding new, user-defined building-block components such as transformations, measurements, and composition procedures, as just discussed. Following the same approach we used in previous sections we will not aim to have a general ranking between the frameworks in terms of expressivity, rather we will highlight some points with respect to expressivity in the design space of programming frameworks for differential privacy.

Allowing General-purpose Programming Together with DP

Several programming frameworks for differential privacy have been designed as libraries or domain-specific languages embedded inside general-purpose programming languages. This allows one to use the richness of the host language to enhance the expressivity of the programming framework. One of the earliest such examples is *PINQ* [McS09], which is designed as a domain-specific language integrated in the general-purpose language C#. Specifically, *PINQ* has been implemented as a

C# component built on top of the data-processing component LINQ. *PINQ* provides several basic transformations, mostly inspired by SQL such as filters, joins, groupby, map, etc and several basic measurements representing aggregation operations, such as count, sum, average, etc. In fact, most of the *PINQ* transformations and measurements consists of a thin layer of code encapsulating the corresponding LINQ transformations. This encapsulation mechanism is needed to guarantee differential privacy through a privacy calculus based on global sensitivity of the sort we discussed in Section 12.3.

Thanks to the integration with a general purpose programming language, *PINQ* supports general purpose programming that can be used to describe more complex data types, and to implement new transformation and mechanisms. Indeed, *PINQ*'s set of data types, transformations and measurements can be easily extended, in principle, by providing new implementations that match the same interface that primitive components have to match, and that respect the principles of the privacy calculus that *PINQ* implements. In fact this is a recipe for extensibility that several other programming frameworks for differential privacy have followed: new transformation and measurement primitives can be easily added to a programming framework by taking operations that are implemented in the underlying language and encapsulating them in order to guarantee their stability and sensitivity properties for their sound use in the corresponding privacy calculus.

As we discussed in Section 12.4, private data sources in *PINQ* are encapsulated in a *PINQueryable* object and can be accessed through chains of transformations followed by an aggregation. This chaining is one of the main principles for the interactions of *PINQueryable* objects with transformations and measurements. The encapsulation of data using queryables allows, in principle, extensions of *PINQ* that implement different forms of composition with different degrees of adaptivity and hierarchical and concurrent interactivity. Both chaining and composition are implemented in *PINQ* as C# routines that offer at the same time an interface for users and a component of the privacy calculus. Similarly to transformations and measurements, one could extend this family of chaining and composition components by providing new implementations in the underlying general-purpose language. However, while possible in principle, as discussed in the *PINQ* design document [McS09], these extensions are less straightforward than extensions of transformations and measurements, since they require redefining *PINQueryable* and its methods. More recent programming frameworks such as *OpenDP*, take a more explicit view on chaining and composition components: they are first class citizens, called *combinators*, with an explicit interface that can be used to interact with them, and explicit requirements for their privacy calculus properties. Thus, to add a new form of composition to *OpenDP* simply requires adding a new combinator capturing it.

In some situations, programming frameworks for differential privacy also allow [a] user to write and run arbitrary programs. Often these programs are required to be pure or "purified," i.e. without side effects that can potentially compromise privacy. Programming frameworks that work in synergy with a general-purpose programming language can use the resources of the host language in these situations. For example, as discussed in the *PINQ* design document [McS09], one can write C# programs using a set of methods which are side-effect free and which can be used in mapping operations. The distinction between methods that can have potential side effects and those that are side-effect-free is built into *PINQ*. Other approaches, such as the one implemented in DPella [LRG20], make this kind of distinction using types.

There is one additional benefit of using a general-purpose language that is worth discussing. General-purpose programming languages usually provide methods to access a variety of different kinds of data sources, e.g. relational databases, tabular data in various forms, streaming sources, etc. This allow programming frameworks for differential privacy to easily also support different kinds of data sources, and to process data independently from the way it is stored.

Support for a Specific Class of Queries

Most of the programming frameworks, instead of aiming to support the implementation of arbitrary differentially private data analyses, focus on a specific class of functions that are useful to implement a large class of analyses. For example, *PINQ* [McS09], *PrivateSQL* [Kot+19], *Flex* [JNS18], and others all aim at supporting SQL-like queries.

A different example is *Ektelo* [Zha+18]. Essentially, *Ektelo* is very similar to *PINQ* in many respects: it also provides transformations and measurements similar to the ones provided by *PINQ*, and a privacy calculus for them. However, instead of focusing on the components that are needed for SQL-like queries, it includes a large variety of basic transformations and measurements that allow one to construct numerous important differentially private algorithms for estimating workloads of *linear queries*. Linear queries are queries of a simplified form: they compute the average, or the sum, of the results obtained by mapping a given function (characterizing the specific linear query) on each record of a dataset. Despite their simplicity, when combined together in a workload, i.e. multiple queries together, linear queries allow one to solve many important statistical problems, such as histograms, cumulative distribution functions (CDFs), and contingency tables.

Ektelo's basic components include transformations and measurements, but also operations of three other families: 1) Operations that allow one to partition the data and to work on the individual partitions. For example, *Ektelo* provides a data-dependent operation `AHPpartition` which, given the data as an histogram, selects a partition of the data where the counts within a partition group are close. 2) Operations that allow one to manage a workload of queries by selecting queries that have different properties. For example, *Ektelo* supports an operation Worst-approx which returns a query, from a workload of queries, that has the property that on a synthetic dataset (or synthetic data distribution) deviates most from the true dataset. 3) Operations that perform some sort of inference as post-processing of the private answers. For example, *Ektelo* provides an operation MW which implements the Multiplicative Weights inference algorithm. All these operations can be combined to design more complex data analyses. For example, one can use basic transformations and measurements and operations of types 2) and 3) to implement the private data release algorithm MWEM [HLM12].

Despite the fact that its design focuses on the restricted class of linear queries, *Ektelo* is able to express in a concise way numerous differentially private algorithm that have been proposed for a variety of tasks. Moreover, thanks to its additional operations, *Ektelo* is also able to go beyond tasks that are usually considered as proper linear queries. For example, one can use *Ektelo* to privately select the structure of a Bayesian network.

Another programming framework using an approach similar to the one of *Ektelo* is *Chorus* [JNHS20]. Instead of focusing on linear queries, *Chorus* focuses on SQL queries and it provides several components to rewrite, analyze and post-process queries. These components allow *Chorus* to express in a concise way numerous complex differentially private algorithms such as MWEM, Sparse Vector, etc.

Support for a Specific Class of DP Algorithms

As we discussed in Section 12.3, there are several privacy calculi that one could use to guarantee differential privacy. Programming frameworks usually support one such privacy calculus, and the privacy calculus that a programming framework uses also affects its expressivity.

Programming frameworks that have been designed around the notion of global stability, such as *PINQ* and many others, allow one to implement a broad range of general differentially private data analyses. In contrast, programming frameworks that support other models, such as *GUPT* [Moh+12] for the sample and aggregate framework, or *Flex* [JNS18] for the local stability framework, are more limited in the class of data analyses that they can support.

The limitations of *GUPT*, and the sample and aggregate framework more generally, come from the fact that this framework only captures differentially private data analyses that can be implemented as a transformation that can be run independently on the pieces of a partition of the dataset, followed by one of a few pre-specified differentially private aggregators combining the obtained results. Most differentially private algorithms cannot be decomposed in this way.

The limitations of *Flex* and other local stability frameworks is that these frameworks are usually based on some approximation of the local stability that cannot in general be computed efficiently for every problem. This means that the programming framework using these approximation needs to be specialized to specific tasks. For example, *Flex*'s elastic sensitivity calculus is based on a careful case analysis of operators that appear in SQL expressions. It is not obvious how to extend this definition to arbitrary data analyses, and it is unclear whether such an extension would be tractable.

While these frameworks have limitations in terms of expressivity, they also have some benefit. For example, as we already mentioned in Section 12.3, the sample-and-aggregate framework allows one to take arbitrary non-private estimators that converge as the sample size grows and automatically construct differentially private analogues of them, albeit on larger datasets. Similarly, methods based on local stability can provide improved accuracy in certain situations.

Support for Reasoning About Accuracy

Most of the programming frameworks we discussed so far focus on providing support to users in order to write their differentially private data analyses and guarantee they are indeed private. However, another important aspect that users need to think about when designing differentially private analyses is *accuracy*. While there isn't one notion of accuracy that works in every situation, a notion of accuracy that is often considered in the differential privacy literature is based on probability bounds. As an example, (α, β)-*accuracy* expresses the following probability bound: if $\tilde{y}$ is the result of a differentially private analysis and y is the result one would achieve if one did the analysis without privacy constraints, then (α, β)-accuracy says that with probability at least $1 - \beta$, $\|y - \tilde{y}\| \leq \alpha$ where $\| \cdot \|$ is a suitable norm. For simple differentially private mechanisms, the α and β follow from the properties of the noise distributions they use.

Several programming frameworks have been conceived to also help users reason about the accuracy of their differentially private data analyses. One such example is *GUPT* [Moh+12], which provides its users with the possibility to select either the privacy budget or the (α, β)-accuracy they want for each data analysis. If users specify the accuracy level they are interested in, *GUPT* computes the corresponding privacy budget that is needed, and vice versa: if users specify the privacy budget they are interested in, *GUPT* computes the corresponding (α, β)-accuracy. A similar approach is also used by *PSI* [Gab+16], where users are provided with a budgeter interface that they can use to specify interactively either the privacy budget or the accuracy for the different queries. The usability of this budgeter interface has also been evaluated with users [MTKV18; Sar+22]. The approach used by *GUPT* and *PSI* is based on the accuracy bounds for the primitive noise distributions they use.

APEx [GHIM19] takes a further step and uses several specific analyses and linear programming to provide accuracy estimates for more complex algorithms, including some algorithms that have accuracy that depends on the data.

A different approach is proposed by *DPella* [LRG20], a programming framework which combines reasoning about privacy in the style of *PINQ*,[vii] with reasoning about (α, β)-accuracy. A user of *DPella* can write differentially private programs and obtain information about their privacy or accuracy. An interesting aspect of the *DPella* approach is that it allows for composing the accuracy of different mechanisms using the Union bound and Chernoff bounds in order to obtain accuracy properties for larger programs.

12.6 Tools for Verification and Testing

As we discussed above, an important motivation for the design of domain-specific programming frameworks for differential privacy comes from the difficulties that randomness, finite-precision arithmetic, budget accounting, etc. impose on differentially private program design. Programming frameworks can help improve the correctness and reliability of differentially private programs. However, as we discussed in Section 12.2, most of the programming frameworks allow one to assemble complex programs from basic primitives as building blocks that are considered trusted. This situation is less than ideal, since bugs in these primitives can affect the correctness of the overall data analyses. In order to help alleviate this problem, researchers have developed several verification and testing tools specifically designed to improve the correctness and reliability of differentially private primitives. In this section, we briefly review some of them, focusing on the techniques that they are based on. All these methods have to cope with the fact that black-box testing for differential privacy, as well as automated verification of differential privacy, are inherently difficult in the worst case [GM18; GNP20; BGG22].

12.6.1 Tools for Testing Differential Privacy Implementations

Testing is a powerful tool to improve the reliability and correctness of software. Following this intuition, several testing methods have been studied and implemented in order to increase confidence in claims of differential privacy for data analysis implementations. Early work on testing for differential privacy [JR11; DJRT13] reduced this problem to testing Lipchitz properties of functions, while subsequent work designed methods specific for differential privacy. *StatDP* [Din+18] provides

vii. Differently from what happen in *PINQ*, the privacy reasoning in DPella happens at compile time.

a testing framework based on hypothesis testing and counterexample generation to find violations in programs that claim to be differentially private. This testing framework considers programs as black box but also provides the option to use program analysis methods to estimate parameter values that can create violations. Following similar ideas, *GoogleSQL* [Wil+20] includes a stochastic tester in order to check whether some basic mechanism is differentially private. This tester is useful to analyze mechanisms of a restricted class, corresponding to aggregation functions, rather than end-to-end applications. *DP-Finder* [Bic+18] uses testing and numerical optimization techniques to prove lower bounds on the privacy parameters of specific programs. This method can be also used to find violations of differential privacy in implementations. *CheckDP* [WDKZ20] combines statistical testing with symbolic solving in order to guarantee that programs are differentially private; when the differential privacy guarantee is violated, this approach provides counterexamples. *DPCheck* [Zha+20] uses a combination of randomized testing and symbolic execution to identify violations of differential privacy in an automated way. *DP-Sniper* [BSBV21] uses machine-learning techniques to train a classifier to distinguish whether the result of a mechanism comes from a dataset or an adjacent one, and when possible to transform this classifier into a counterexample exhibiting a violation of differential privacy. *DP-Sniper* is also able to uncover violations due to floating-point arithmetic.

12.6.2 Tools for the Verification of Differential Privacy

Randomized testing as discussed above can help improve the reliability of differential privacy components. However, when the input space of these components is large, it is difficult for randomized testers to offer strong guarantees in terms of coverage, and the uncovered input space can still hide bugs in the design and implementations of these components. For this reason, several groups of researchers have also developed formal verification techniques, which can be used to mathematically prove the design and implementations of these components to be correct. An advantage of these approaches is that the verification can happen before the program is run, limiting the risks for the actual data.

A first approach in this line of work is based on the use of *program logics* and *interactive proof assistants*. These are formal tools that have been developed in order to formally verify properties of programs and their implementations. The idea behind these tools is that a user needs to provide a program, a specification that the program needs to satisfy, and a formal proof, in the form of a computer script, that the program meets the specification. The tool then checks that the formal proof is correct and that indeed the program respects the specification. In the case of differential privacy, the specification is that the program is differentially private. Several works have followed this approach [BKOB12; Bar+13; Bar+14; Bar+16b; Bar+16a; AH18] building on different program logics and proof assistants.

Another approach in this line of work is based on the use of advanced *type systems*, *symbolic execution* and *constraint solvers*. In this approach, a user needs to provide a program and its specification. The specification is usually in the form of a type specification in some rich language of types that also provides the guarantee that a program is differentially private. However, the user does not need to provide a formal proof connecting the program with its specification. Instead, this formal proof is synthesized by a type checker combined with constraint solving. In Section 12.3, we already discussed *Fuzz* [RP10], which was one of the first tools in this area. *Fuzz* is limited in expressivity: it can only type programs whose sensitivity is a constant. Several works have extended this approach [Gab+13; Bar+15; ZK17; Wan+19; WDKZ20; FCG21] and designed more and more expressive tools. The high level of confidence and formal guarantees that these tools provide goes beyond what can be usually achieved by code inspection and randomized testing. On the other hand, those tools are often difficult to use and often require expertise in formal verification or programming-language design, as well as differential privacy.

12.7 Concluding Remarks

Programming frameworks for differential privacy are instrumental in bridging the gap between the theoretical foundations of differential privacy and practical software applications. They provide robust privacy calculi, mechanisms for composition and interactivity, and varying levels of expressivity, enabling practitioners to design complex differentially private analyses more reliably and efficiently.

Throughout this chapter, we examined the foundational properties that make the design of these frameworks possible, including privacy calculus, composition, interactivity, and expressivity. The chapter also reviewed tools for verification and testing, which play a key role in ensuring the correctness and reliability of differentially private implementations.

As the field of differential privacy continues to evolve, so too will the programming frameworks and tools that support it. Future frameworks may offer enhanced expressivity, better integration with different computing environments, and improved methods for reasoning about accuracy and utility. Advances in verification and testing will further strengthen the reliability of differentially private software, addressing challenges related to randomness generation, security, and scalability.

Acknowledgements

Marco Gaboardi's work was partially supported by NSF through award # CNS-2040249. Salil Vadhan's work was supported by a grant from the Sloan Foundation and a Simons Investigator Award. Marco Gaboardi and Salil Vadhan's work was also partially supported by Cooperative Agreement CB20ADR0160001 with the U.S. Census Bureau. We thank Gary Benedetto, Mark Fleischer, Philip Leclerc, and Rolando Rodríguez from the Census Bureau for many helpful comments. The views expressed in this paper are those of the authors and not those of the U.S. Census Bureau, or any other sponsor.

References

[Aba+16] M. Abadi, A. Chu, I. Goodfellow, H. B. McMahan, I. Mironov, K. Talwar, and L. Zhang. "Deep Learning with Differential Privacy". In: Proceedings of the 2016 ACM SIGSAC Conference on Computer and Communications Security. CCS '16. Vienna, Austria: Association for Computing Machinery, 2016, pp. 308–318. ISBN: 9781450341394. URL: https://doi.org/10.1145/2976749.2978318 (cit. on p. 427).

[AH18] A. Albarghouthi and J. Hsu. "Synthesizing coupling proofs of differential privacy". In: Proc. ACM Program. Lang. 2.POPL (2018), 58:1–58:30. URL: https://doi.org/10.1145/3158146 (cit. on p. 439).

[Bar+13] G. Barthe, G. Danezis, B. Grégoire, C. Kunz, and S. Z. Béguelin. "Verified Computational Differential Privacy with Applications to Smart Metering". In: 2013 IEEE 26th Computer Security Foundations Symposium, New Orleans, LA, USA, June 26-28, 2013. IEEE Computer Society, 2013, pp. 287–301. URL: https://doi.org/10.1109/CSF.2013.26 (cit. on p. 439).

[Bar+14] G. Barthe, M. Gaboardi, E. J. G. Arias, J. Hsu, C. Kunz, and P. Strub. "Proving Differential Privacy in Hoare Logic". In: IEEE 27th Computer Security Foundations Symposium, CSF 2014, Vienna, Austria, 19-22 July, 2014. IEEE Computer Society, 2014, pp. 411–424. URL: https://doi.org/10.1109/CSF.2014.36 (cit. on p. 439).

[Bar+15] G. Barthe, M. Gaboardi, E. J. G. Arias, J. Hsu, A. Roth, and P. Strub. "Higher-Order Approximate Relational Refinement Types for Mechanism Design and Differential Privacy". In: Proceedings of the 42nd Annual ACM SIGPLAN-SIGACT Symposium on Principles of Programming Languages, POPL 2015, Mumbai, India, January 15-17, 2015. Ed. by S. K. Rajamani and D. Walker. ACM, 2015, pp. 55–68. URL: https://doi.org/10.1145/2676726.2677000 (cit. on p. 439).

[Bar+16a] G. Barthe, N. Fong, M. Gaboardi, B. Grégoire, J. Hsu, and P. Strub. "Advanced Probabilistic Couplings for Differential Privacy". In: Proceedings of the 2016 ACM SIGSAC Conference on Computer and Communications Security, Vienna, Austria, October 24-28, 2016. Ed. by E. R. Weippl, S. Katzenbeisser, C. Kruegel, A. C. Myers, and S. Halevi. ACM, 2016, pp. 55–67. URL: https://doi.org/10.1145/2976749.2978391 (cit. on p. 439).

[Bar+16b] G. Barthe, M. Gaboardi, B. Grégoire, J. Hsu, and P. Strub. "Proving Differential Privacy via Probabilistic Couplings". In: Proceedings of the 31st Annual ACM/IEEE Symposium on Logic in Computer Science, LICS '16, New York, NY, USA, July 5-8, 2016. Ed. by M. Grohe, E. Koskinen, and N. Shankar. ACM, 2016, pp. 749–758. URL: https://doi.org/10.1145/2933575.2934554 (cit. on p. 439).

[Ber+22] S. Berghel, P. Bohannon, D. Desfontaines, C. Estes, S. Haney, L. Hartman, M. Hay, A. Machanavajjhala, T. Magerlein, G. Miklau, A. Pai, W. Sexton, and R. Shrestha. "Tumult Analytics: a robust, easy-to-use, scalable, and expressive framework for differential privacy". In: arXiv preprint arXiv:2212.04133 (2022) (cit. on p. 420).

[BGG22] M. Bun, M. Gaboardi, and L. Glinskih. "The Complexity of Verifying Boolean Programs as Differentially Private". In: 2022 2022 IEEE 35th Computer Security Foundations Symposium (CSF) (CSF). Los Alamitos, CA, USA: IEEE Computer Society, Aug. 2022, pp. 380–395. URL: https://doi.ieeecomputersociety.org/10.1109/CSF54842.2022.00025 (cit. on p. 437).

[Bic+18] B. Bichsel, T. Gehr, D. Drachsler-Cohen, P. Tsankov, and M. T. Vechev. "DP-Finder: Finding Differential Privacy Violations by Sampling and Optimization". In: Proceedings of the 2018 ACM SIGSAC Conference on Computer and Communications Security, CCS 2018, Toronto, ON, Canada, October 15-19, 2018. Ed. by D. Lie, M. Mannan, M. Backes, and X. Wang. ACM, 2018, pp. 508–524. URL: https://doi.org/10.1145/3243734.3243863 (cit. on p. 438).

[BKOB12] G. Barthe, B. Köpf, F. Olmedo, and S. Z. Béguelin. "Probabilistic relational reasoning for differential privacy". In: Proceedings of the 39th ACM SIGPLAN-SIGACT Symposium on Principles of Programming Languages, POPL 2012, Philadelphia, Pennsylvania, USA, January 22-28, 2012. Ed. by J. Field and M. Hicks. ACM, 2012, pp. 97–110. URL: https://doi.org/10.1145/2103656.2103670 (cit. on p. 439).

[BS16] M. Bun and T. Steinke. "Concentrated Differential Privacy: Simplifications, Extensions, and Lower Bounds". In: Theory of Cryptography - 14th International Conference, TCC 2016-B, Beijing, China, October 31 - November 3, 2016, Proceedings, Part I. Ed. by M. Hirt and A. D. Smith. Vol. 9985. Lecture Notes in Computer Science. 2016, pp. 635–658. ISBN: 978-3-662-53640-7. URL: https://doi.org/10.1007/978-3-662-53641-4%5C_24 (cit. on pp. 426, 427, 431).

[BSBV21] B. Bichsel, S. Steffen, I. Bogunovic, and M. T. Vechev. "DP-Sniper: Black-Box Discovery of Differential Privacy Violations using Classifiers". In: 42nd IEEE Symposium on Security and Privacy, SP 2021, San Francisco, CA, USA, 24-27 May 2021. IEEE, 2021, pp. 391–409. URL: https://doi.org/10.1109/SP40001.2021.00081 (cit. on p. 438).

[CSVW22] S. Casacuberta, M. Shoemate, S. Vadhan, and C. Wagaman. "Widespread Underestimation of Sensitivity in Differentially Private Libraries and How to Fix It". In: Proceedings of the 29th ACM SIGSAC Conference on Computer and Communications Security (CCS '22). To appear. Preprint posted as arXiv:2207.10635 [cs.CR]. July 2022 (cit. on p. 418).

[Din+18] Z. Ding, Y. Wang, G. Wang, D. Zhang, and D. Kifer. "Detecting Violations of Differential Privacy". In: Proceedings of the 2018 ACM SIGSAC Conference on Computer and Communications Security, CCS 2018, Toronto, ON, Canada, October 15-19, 2018. Ed. by D. Lie, M. Mannan, M. Backes, and X. Wang. ACM, 2018, pp. 475–489. URL: https://doi.org/10.1145/3243734.3243818 (cit. on p. 437).

[DJRT13] K. Dixit, M. Jha, S. Raskhodnikova, and A. Thakurta. "Testing the Lipschitz Property over Product Distributions with Applications to Data Privacy". In: Theory of Cryptography - 10th Theory of Cryptography Conference, TCC 2013, Tokyo, Japan, March 3-6, 2013. Proceedings. Ed. by A. Sahai. Vol. 7785. Lecture Notes in Computer Science. Springer, 2013, pp. 418–436. URL: https://doi.org/10.1007/978-3-642-36594-2%5C_24 (cit. on p. 437).

[DMNS06] C. Dwork, F. McSherry, K. Nissim, and A. Smith. "Calibrating noise to sensitivity in private data analysis". In: Theory of cryptography conference. Springer. 2006, pp. 265–284 (cit. on p. 418).

[DMNS16] C. Dwork, F. McSherry, K. Nissim, and A. D. Smith. "Calibrating Noise to Sensitivity in Private Data Analysis". In: J. Priv. Confidentiality 7.3 (2016), pp. 17–51. URL: https://doi.org/10.29012/jpc.v7i3.405 (cit. on pp. 418, 420, 421, 424).

[DR+14] C. Dwork, A. Roth, et al. "The algorithmic foundations of differential privacy." In: Foundations and Trends in Theoretical Computer Science 9.3-4 (2014), pp. 211–407 (cit. on p. 430).

[DR16] C. Dwork and G. N. Rothblum. "Concentrated Differential Privacy". In: CoRR abs/1603.01887 (2016). arXiv: 1603.01887. URL: http://arxiv.org/abs/1603.01887 (cit. on pp. 426, 427).

[DRS22] J. Dong, A. Roth, and W. J. Su. "Gaussian differential privacy". In: Journal of the Royal Statistical Society: Series B (Statistical Methodology) 84.1 (2022), pp. 3–37. eprint: https://rss.onlinelibrary.wiley.com/doi/pdf/10.1111/rssb.12454. URL: https://rss.onlinelibrary.wiley.com/doi/abs/10.1111/rssb.12454 (cit. on pp. 426, 427, 431).

[Dwo+06] C. Dwork, K. Kenthapadi, F. McSherry, I. Mironov, and M. Naor. "Our data, ourselves: privacy via distributed noise generation". In: Advances in cryptology—EUROCRYPT 2006. Vol. 4004. Lecture Notes in Comput. Sci. Springer, Berlin, 2006, pp. 486–503. URL: http://dx.doi.org/10.1007/11761679_29 (cit. on p. 426).

[FCG21] G. P. Farina, S. Chong, and M. Gaboardi. "Coupled Relational Symbolic Execution for Differential Privacy". In: Programming Languages and Systems - 30th European Symposium on Programming, ESOP 2021, Held as Part of the European Joint Conferences on Theory and Practice of Software, ETAPS 2021, Luxembourg City, Luxembourg, March 27 - April 1, 2021, Proceedings. Ed. by N. Yoshida. Vol. 12648. Lecture Notes in Computer Science.

Springer, 2021, pp. 207–233. URL: https://doi.org/10.1007/978-3-030-72019-3%5C_8 (cit. on p. 439).

[Gab+13] M. Gaboardi, A. Haeberlen, J. Hsu, A. Narayan, and B. C. Pierce. "Linear dependent types for differential privacy". In: Proceedings of the 40th annual ACM SIGPLAN-SIGACT symposium on Principles of programming languages. 2013, pp. 357–370 (cit. on pp. 420, 428, 439).

[Gab+16] M. Gaboardi, J. Honaker, G. King, J. Murtagh, K. Nissim, J. Ullman, and S. Vadhan. "Psi ({\Psi}): a private data sharing interface". In: arXiv preprint arXiv:1609.04340 (2016) (cit. on pp. 420, 427, 428, 436).

[GHIM19] C. Ge, X. He, I. F. Ilyas, and A. Machanavajjhala. "Apex: Accuracy-aware differentially private data exploration". In: Proceedings of the 2019 International Conference on Management of Data. 2019, pp. 177–194 (cit. on pp. 420, 437).

[GHV20] M. Gaboardi, M. Hay, and S. Vadhan. "A programming framework for opendp". In: Manuscript, May (2020) (cit. on pp. 420, 426).

[GM18] A. C. Gilbert and A. McMillan. "Property testing for differential privacy". In: 2018 56th Annual Allerton Conference on Communication, Control, and Computing (Allerton). IEEE. 2018, pp. 249–258 (cit. on p. 437).

[GNP20] M. Gaboardi, K. Nissim, and D. Purser. "The Complexity of Verifying Loop-Free Programs as Differentially Private". In: 47th International Colloquium on Automata, Languages, and Programming, ICALP 2020, July 8-11, 2020, Saarbrücken, Germany (Virtual Conference). Ed. by A. Czumaj, A. Dawar, and E. Merelli. Vol. 168. LIPIcs. Schloss Dagstuhl - Leibniz-Zentrum für Informatik, 2020, 129:1–129:17. URL: https://doi.org/10.4230/LIPIcs.ICALP.2020.129 (cit. on p. 437).

[Han+22] S. Haney, D. Desfontaines, L. Hartman, R. Shrestha, and M. Hay. Precision-based attacks and interval refining: how to break, then fix, differential privacy on finite computers. 2022. URL: https://arxiv.org/abs/2207.13793 (cit. on p. 418).

[Han+23] S. Haney, M. Shoemate, G. Tian, S. Vadhan, A. Vyrros, V. Xu, and W. Zhang. "Concurrent Composition for Interactive Differential Privacy with Adaptive Privacy-Loss Parameters". In: Proceedings of the 2023 ACM SIGSAC Conference on Computer and Communications Security. 2023, pp. 1949–1963 (cit. on p. 431).

[HBML19] N. Holohan, S. Braghin, P. Mac Aonghusa, and K. Levacher. "Diffprivlib: the IBM differential privacy library". In: arXiv preprint arXiv:1907.02444 (2019) (cit. on pp. 420, 427).

[HLM12] M. Hardt, K. Ligett, and F. McSherry. "A simple and practical algorithm for differentially private data release". In: Advances in neural information processing systems 25 (2012) (cit. on p. 435).

[HPN11] A. Haeberlen, B. C. Pierce, and A. Narayan. "Differential Privacy Under Fire". In: 20th USENIX Security Symposium, San Francisco, CA, USA, August 8-12, 2011, Proceedings. USENIX Association, 2011. URL: http://static.usenix.org/events/sec11/tech/full%5C_papers/Haeberlen.pdf (cit. on pp. 418, 420).

[JMRO22] J. Jin, E. McMurtry, B. I. P. Rubinstein, and O. Ohrimenko. "Are We There Yet? Timing and Floating-Point Attacks on Differential Privacy Systems". In: 43rd IEEE Symposium on Security and Privacy, SP 2022, San Francisco, CA, USA, May 22-26, 2022. IEEE, 2022, pp. 473–488. URL: https://doi.org/10.1109/SP46214.2022.9833672 (cit. on p. 418).

[JNHS20] N. M. Johnson, J. P. Near, J. M. Hellerstein, and D. Song. "Chorus: a Programming Framework for Building Scalable Differential Privacy Mechanisms". In: IEEE European Symposium on Security and Privacy, EuroS&P 2020, Genoa, Italy, September 7-11, 2020. IEEE, 2020, pp. 535–551. URL: https://doi.org/10.1109/EuroSP48549.2020.00041 (cit. on pp. 420, 435).

[JNS18] N. Johnson, J. P. Near, and D. Song. "Towards practical differential privacy for SQL queries". In: Proceedings of the VLDB Endowment 11.5 (2018), pp. 526–539 (cit. on pp. 420, 425–427, 434, 435).

[JR11] M. Jha and S. Raskhodnikova. "Testing and Reconstruction of Lipschitz Functions with Applications to Data Privacy". In: IEEE 52nd Annual Symposium on Foundations of Computer Science, FOCS 2011, Palm Springs, CA, USA, October 22-25, 2011. Ed. by R. Ostrovsky. IEEE Computer Society, 2011, pp. 433–442. URL: https://doi.org/10.1109/FOCS.2011.13 (cit. on p. 437).

[Kot+19] I. Kotsogiannis, Y. Tao, X. He, M. Fanaeepour, A. Machanavajjhala, M. Hay, and G. Miklau. "Privatesql: a differentially private sql query engine". In: Proceedings of the VLDB Endowment 12.11 (2019), pp. 1371–1384 (cit. on pp. 420, 425, 428, 434).

[KOV15] P. Kairouz, S. Oh, and P. Viswanath. "The composition theorem for differential privacy". In: International conference on machine learning. PMLR. 2015, pp. 1376–1385 (cit. on p. 427).

[LRG20] E. Lobo-Vesga, A. Russo, and M. Gaboardi. "A programming framework for differential privacy with accuracy concentration bounds". In: 2020 IEEE Symposium on Security and Privacy (SP). IEEE. 2020, pp. 411–428 (cit. on pp. 420, 434, 437).

[Lyu22] X. Lyu. "Composition Theorems for Interactive Differential Privacy". In: arXiv preprint arXiv:2207.09397 (2022) (cit. on pp. 427, 431).

[McS09] F. D. McSherry. "Privacy integrated queries: an extensible platform for privacy-preserving data analysis". In: Proceedings of the 2009 ACM SIGMOD International Conference on Management of data. ACM. 2009, pp. 19–30 (cit. on pp. 420–423, 431–434).

[Mir12] I. Mironov. "On significance of the least significant bits for differential privacy". In: Proceedings of the 2012 ACM conference on Computer and communications security. 2012, pp. 650–661 (cit. on p. 418).

[Mir17] I. Mironov. "Rényi differential privacy". In: 2017 IEEE 30th computer security foundations symposium (CSF). IEEE. 2017, pp. 263–275 (cit. on pp. 427, 431).

[Moh+12] P. Mohan, A. Thakurta, E. Shi, D. Song, and D. E. Culler. "GUPT: privacy preserving data analysis made easy". In: Proceedings of the ACM SIGMOD International Conference on Management of Data, SIGMOD 2012, Scottsdale, AZ, USA, May 20-24, 2012. Ed. by K. S. Candan, Y. Chen, R. T. Snodgrass, L. Gravano, and A. Fuxman. ACM, 2012, pp. 349–360. URL: https://doi.org/10.1145/2213836.2213876 (cit. on pp. 420, 423, 435, 436).

[MTKV18] J. Murtagh, K. Taylor, G. Kellaris, and S. P. Vadhan. "Usable Differential Privacy: A Case Study with PSI". In: CoRR abs/1809.04103 (2018). arXiv: 1809.04103. URL: http://arxiv.org/abs/1809.04103 (cit. on p. 436).

[MV16] J. Murtagh and S. Vadhan. "The complexity of computing the optimal composition of differential privacy". In: Theory of Cryptography Conference. Springer. 2016, pp. 157–175 (cit. on pp. 427, 428).

[Nea+19] J. P. Near, D. Darais, C. Abuah, T. Stevens, P. Gaddamadugu, L. Wang, N. Somani, M. Zhang, N. Sharma, A. Shan, and D. Song. "Duet: an expressive higher-order language and linear type system for statically enforcing differential privacy". In: Proc. ACM Program. Lang. 3.OOPSLA (2019), 172:1–172:30. URL: https://doi.org/10.1145/3360598 (cit. on pp. 420, 426).

[NH21] J. P. Near and X. He. "Differential Privacy for Databases". In: Foundations and Trends® in Databases 11.2 (2021), pp. 109–225 (cit. on p. 425).

[NRS07] K. Nissim, S. Raskhodnikova, and A. D. Smith. "Smooth sensitivity and sampling in private data analysis". In: Proceedings of the 39th Annual ACM Symposium on Theory of Computing, San Diego, California, USA, June 11-13, 2007. Ed. by D. S. Johnson and U. Feige. ACM, 2007, pp. 75–84. URL: https://doi.org/10.1145/1250790.1250803 (cit. on pp. 420, 424).

[Ope22] OpenDP. DP Creator. https://github.com/opendp/dpcreator. Mar. 2022 (cit. on p. 427).

[Roy+10] I. Roy, S. T. V. Setty, A. Kilzer, V. Shmatikov, and E. Witchel. "Airavat: Security and Privacy for MapReduce". In: Proceedings of the 7th USENIX Symposium on Networked Systems Design and Implementation, NSDI 2010, April 28-30, 2010, San Jose, CA, USA. USENIX Association, 2010, pp. 297–312. URL: http://www.usenix.org/events/nsdi10/tech/full%5C_papers/roy.pdf (cit. on pp. 420, 423, 428).

[RP10] J. Reed and B. C. Pierce. "Distance makes the types grow stronger: a calculus for differential privacy". In: Proceeding of the 15th ACM SIGPLAN international conference on Functional programming, ICFP 2010, Baltimore, Maryland, USA, September 27-29, 2010. Ed. by P. Hudak and S. Weirich. ACM, 2010, pp. 157–168. ISBN: 978-1-60558-794-3. URL: https://doi.org/10.1145/1863543.1863568 (cit. on pp. 420, 424, 439).

[RRUV16] R. Rogers, A. Roth, J. Ullman, and S. Vadhan. "Privacy Odometers and Filters: Pay-as-you-Go Composition". In: Advances in Neural Information Processing Systems 29 (NIPS '16). Full version posted as arXiv:1605.08294 [cs.CR]. Dec. 2016, pp. 1921–1929 (cit. on pp. 427, 429).

[Sar+22] J. Sarathy, S. Song, A. Haque, T. Schlatter, and S. Vadhan. Don't Look at the Data! How Differential Privacy Reconfigures Practices of Data Science. Poster at the 8th Workshop on the Theory and Practice of Differential Privacy (TPDP '22). July 2022 (cit. on p. 436).

[VW21] S. Vadhan and T. Wang. "Concurrent Composition of Differential Privacy". In: Theory of Cryptography Conference. Springer. 2021, pp. 582–604 (cit. on pp. 427, 429, 431).

[VZ22] S. Vadhan and W. Zhang. "Concurrent Composition Theorems for all Standard Variants of Differential Privacy". In: arXiv preprint arXiv:2207.08335 (2022) (cit. on pp. 427, 431).

[Wan+19] Y. Wang, Z. Ding, G. Wang, D. Kifer, and D. Zhang. "Proving differential privacy with shadow execution". In: Proceedings of the 40th ACM SIGPLAN Conference on Programming Language Design and Implementation, PLDI 2019, Phoenix, AZ, USA, June 22-26, 2019. Ed. by K. S. McKinley and K. Fisher. ACM, 2019, pp. 655–669. URL: https://doi.org/10.1145/3314221.3314619 (cit. on p. 439).

[WDKZ20] Y. Wang, Z. Ding, D. Kifer, and D. Zhang. "CheckDP: An Automated and Integrated Approach for Proving Differential Privacy or Finding Precise Counterexamples". In: CCS '20: 2020 ACM SIGSAC Conference on Computer and Communications Security, Virtual Event, USA, November 9-13, 2020. Ed. by J. Ligatti, X. Ou, J. Katz, and G. Vigna. ACM, 2020, pp. 919–938. URL: https://doi.org/10.1145/3372297.3417282 (cit. on pp. 438, 439).

[WHRP17] D. Winograd-Cort, A. Haeberlen, A. Roth, and B. C. Pierce. "A framework for adaptive differential privacy". In: Proceedings of the ACM on Programming Languages 1.ICFP (2017), pp. 1–29 (cit. on pp. 420, 429).

[Wil+20] R. J. Wilson, C. Y. Zhang, W. Lam, D. Desfontaines, D. Simmons-Marengo, and B. Gipson. "Differentially Private SQL with Bounded User Contribution". In: Proc. Priv. Enhancing Technol. 2020.2 (2020), pp. 230–250. URL: https://doi.org/10.2478/popets-2020-0025 (cit. on pp. 420, 425, 438).

[WRRW22] J. Whitehouse, A. Ramdas, R. Rogers, and Z. S. Wu. "Fully adaptive composition in differential privacy". In: arXiv preprint arXiv:2203.05481 (2022) (cit. on p. 427).

[Zha+18] D. Zhang, R. McKenna, I. Kotsogiannis, M. Hay, A. Machanavajjhala, and G. Miklau. "Ektelo: A framework for defining differentially-private computations". In: Proceedings of the 2018 International Conference on Management of Data. ACM. 2018, pp. 115–130 (cit. on pp. 420, 434).

[Zha+20] H. Zhang, E. Roth, A. Haeberlen, B. C. Pierce, and A. Roth. "Testing differential privacy with dual interpreters". In: Proc. ACM Program. Lang. 4.OOPSLA (2020), 165:1–165:26. URL: https://doi.org/10.1145/3428233 (cit. on p. 438).

[ZK17] D. Zhang and D. Kifer. "LightDP: towards automating differential privacy proofs". In: Proceedings of the 44th ACM SIGPLAN Symposium on Principles of Programming Languages, POPL 2017, Paris, France, January 18-20, 2017. Ed. by G. Castagna and A. D. Gordon. ACM, 2017, pp. 888–901. URL: https://doi.org/10.1145/3009837.3009884 (cit. on p. 439).

DOI: 10.1561/9781638284772.ch13

Chapter 13

Machine Learning Tools

By Bryant Gipson, Andreas Terzis and Yurii Sushko

13.1 Introduction

For much of this book we have mostly concerned ourselves with the definitions, requirements and challenges in designing differentially private algorithms. In the previous chapter we also learned about the various general purpose tools available to developers, including those related to the analysis of databases. In this chapter, we will lean on all of the theory, caveats and gotchas learned so far, in addition to relying on the aforementioned tools in the pursuit of practical Differentially Private machine learning. Differential privacy offers a robust mathematical framework for preserving individual privacy in data analysis and machine learning. However, the practical implementation of differentially private machine learning models involves navigating a complex landscape of theoretical considerations, algorithmic challenges, and practical constraints. Successfully deploying such models requires careful planning, a deep understanding of the underlying principles, and thoughtful application of available tools and techniques.

Overview of the Chapter

The chapter begins by discussing the concept needed before embarking on such a task (Section 13.1.1), highlighting the importance of defining the unit of privacy, understanding the attack model, and setting accuracy requirements. We then delve into the methods and tools available for centralized training, examining their strengths, weaknesses, and practical considerations (Section 13.2). Therein, we also consider federated learning and discuss its methods, privacy implications, and the challenges it presents. Finally, in Section 13.4 we address the crucial aspect of privacy testing and evaluation and provide insights into potential vulnerabilities to help practitioners understand the effectiveness of their privacy-preserving strategies. The goal of this chapter is to equip practitioners and researchers with the knowledge and tools necessary to implement differentially private machine learning effectively, balancing privacy protection with utility and performance.

13.1.1 Preparing to Learn

In the French culinary world, before cooking there is *mise en place*. Literally "putting in place", or the process of preparing the space, tools, ingredients and state of mind required to prepare a meal. It is no less with differentially private machine learning which, as we learned in previous chapters, draws upon all knowledge and experience with differential privacy generally.

Regardless of the framework used, it is critical to outline the parameters and goals of what you want to achieve.

- **What is the unit of privacy?** A record, an individual, a business, a class of users? If you are training a spell-checker, the choice of whether one is protecting the fact that a user employed a specific word in an e-mail (e.g., "antiquarian") or, instead, the fact that they were included in training *at all* (e.g., some or all of Sarah's e-mails were used in training) may have material consequences on re-identifiability risk and model utility. Shorthand, these concepts are sometimes referred to as *record* or *example level privacy* [HDH17] or *user level privacy* [MRTZ18], and being explicit about this up front can greatly influence the choice and impact of parameters as well as the choice of frameworks.
- **What level of complexity do we need?** Machine Learning is an overloaded term and could mean anything from 2-dimensional least squares [Bjo96] to generative adversarial neural networks [Goo+14]. In many cases, when approaching a problem an individual may believe a Deep Neural Network [GBC16] is required when a simple `SELECT a,b,c GROUP BY x,y` may be all that's needed. In general, the more constrained the problem space, the more control one has over the units of privacy, privacy budget and the bounds on each.
- **What is the attack model?** It is not sufficient to "train with differential privacy" and be done with it. The following all have material consequences on

the privacy and utility of the outputs: the environment in which the training is performed, which intermediaries (e.g., servers, devices) have even transient access to the data, how much control an adversary has over inputs, how often training is performed and how the final model is to be accessed (e.g., are queries mediated or is the entire model, weights and all, exported to a public forum?).

- **What is the operational environment of training?** Very closely related to thinking about attack model, it's important to consider honest-but-curious and other forms of passive exposure that may occur from the environment in which training is performed. These might include everything from low-level server statistics, CPU profiling, crash logging, "aggregate" debugging information (e.g., not differentially private) to higher-level questions about model retention tracking (e.g., having access to more than one model trained on the same data has privacy budget implications), the model development cycle (are developers inspecting the results of models and retraining with new parameters?) or release frequency (are you accounting for budgeting across multiple pushes, etc.).
- **What data?** As with all methods guaranteeing differential privacy, machine learning tools cannot typically propose a privacy model, or parameters related to, the data they are being trained on. Retraining a model weekly on all historical data has very different privacy implications from training weekly on just the data from the past month. Regardless of the details of sampling, shuffling or other clever algorithmic schemes, making the most of the data you have allows one to make the strongest possible privacy statements that meet your needs.
- **What level of accuracy do you need?** Analysis of all data comes with built-in variance and uncertainty around results. The additional uncertainty added by differentially private methods may be negligible, or it may render any conclusions based on the output meaningless. Differential privacy allows one to make intentional choices about the trade-offs between risk and utility, and a rigorous analysis of the hard requirements of both can greatly aid in the use and scope of machine learning frameworks. An image classifier may need far less accuracy than a pharmacological dose recommendation system. Similarly, a distributed spell checker may have a marginal risk profile relative to a speech to text model that has been trained on doctor's notes. Understanding one's risk profile informs accuracy allowances, while knowing hard accuracy requirements guides expectations on user protection.

As with all Privacy & Security technologies, a holistic view of the privacy story you are providing is critical. A "mostly private" system can easily lull data stewards into a false sense of security, ironically increasing their risk of data exposure due to overconfidence in use or access.

All of the above considerations could apply to any system guaranteeing differential privacy, but machine learning in particular is a field with most frameworks providing control over only part of the full privacy story. Knowing their strengths and weaknesses is important; a chain is only as strong as its weakest link.

13.2 Practical Machine Learning

13.2.1 Preparation, cleaning and analysis

Much of data preparation borders on traditional statistics, database work and many good overviews on the subject exist online (e.g., [Sco21]). That said, a review of Chapter 13 on differentially private database analysis may help as well. In particular, one of the amazingly useful properties of differentially private guarantees is that all downstream consumers of DP data sets inherit and build on these guarantees.

Training on a DP data-set need not be DP itself at all under many circumstances. It may also allow a less restrictive privacy budget if upstream cleaning and preparation used some measure of DP protection.

Additionally, as noted above, rigorously defining the *unit of privacy* is critical to both preparation and the choice of the training method that follows. Typically this discussion breaks down into choice of record-level privacy or user-level privacy. As discussed in more detail in Chapter 1 (see, in particular, Section 1.4.2) and in Section 8.3.1 of Chapter 8 of this book, record-level privacy provides DP guarantees only for a single contribution from a user (e.g., a restaurant visit, a doctor's note, a photo) as opposed to a class of contributions from a user, denoted *group-level* privacy in Chapter 1 (all of their medical history, their web-browsing history, all of a hospital's payments to vendors, etc). Besides having privacy implications, this choice will affect data organization (are databases keyed by user id or something else) and must also be taken into account in cleaning and pre-aggregation steps to ensure no "cross-contamination" occurs across the unit of privacy. For example, it is common to perform statistical analysis on data prior to training. If the results of this analysis are subsequently used in the final ML design (e.g., in determining min/max or normalization bounds) they must also be computed in a differentially private manner or violate global guarantees.

Finally, this choice affects what *kind* of ML system to use. Private ML currently can be broadly categorized as centralized or federated, as reviewed in Chapter 1. Local DP is another flavor (see Chapter 2), though in the ML context it largely exists as a subset of federated learning, which this book discussed in Chapter 8.

Centralized training is faster and typically easier for developers to implement but mostly provides guarantees around record-level privacy (user-level can be constructed from components, though it must be done so explicitly). Moreover, the process of centralized training itself is only as private as the system it is performed on, requiring strong access controls and data governance. Federated training may require more data, has more moving parts and may be harder to debug and develop on but is safe from a larger range of attacks. Federated learning is also, almost by definition, a user-level protection scheme and so has additional benefits on this front. That said, federated algorithms distribute centralized intermediates (typically fully trained models) to the entire training fleet, allowing misconfigured systems to "perfectly" expose data to the entire world. Federated systems contain no guarantees around access to, or timely removal of, intermediate data and users are free to inspect them indefinitely, offline.

The next sections delve into the differences and tools available for both of these classes of training.

13.2.2 Centralized Training

In this section we consider a common use case. A data steward has full read access to a data-set containing user data that is keyed by some identifier (e.g., e-mail address, SSN, Business ID, Hospital Name) that represents the privacy unit. Ideally access and interaction to the primary data set is managed by rigorous access controls and privacy & security practices that are well beyond the scope of this book. A developer wants to perform some analysis across this data set, the results of which will be distributed to an audience beyond that of the primary developer.

While this setup may sound unremarkable, there are many layers of implicit trust here. The data collection methods, including transport and all intermediaries must be trusted or secure. The storage system must be similarly secure as is all communication between the primary training system and the back-end. Finally, all debugging, feedback and general developer interaction with training is similarly trusted. If this last assumption isn't realistic, e.g., if debugging statistics are shared externally, then these also need to be accounted for in privacy budget considerations.

Methods and Privacy

While differentially private database methods employ a large range of tools to ensure differentially private claims, machine learning employs only a few well-defined methods

Differentially private stochastic gradient descent (DP-SGD) is a modification of the standard stochastic gradient descent (SGD) algorithm in machine learning. For a review of the algorithm, the reader is referred to Section 6.3.1 of Chapter 6).

Models trained with DP-SGD have provable differential privacy (DP) guarantees, mitigating the risk of exposing sensitive training data. Intuitively, a model trained with differential privacy should not be affected by any single training example in its data set. DP-SGD techniques can also be used in federated learning to provide user-level differential privacy (any one user's data does should not affect the model).

Centralized training has a distinct advantage from the perspective of data governance and privacy: The privacy of the training process is as good as that of the environment in which it is performed. This is to say that a fully sand-boxed, air-gapped system, with tight access controls, would allow development time to focus almost exclusively on DP guarantees and parameters, rather than attack surface and data leakage. This is not true for federated learning.

There are Some Drawbacks to Well Developed Centralized Training

Because training has long-developed in service to applications on public data sets, most training systems have added privacy as augmentations or modules, rather than redesigning from a privacy standpoint. As a result, most systems assume a full permissions / full ownership model to training with debugging statistics, example records inspection and other access methods part of infrastructure. While a careful accounting of a privacy & security policy can mitigate these concerns, the possibility of accidental data leakage or differential privacy violation through published side-channels is increased because of this.

Additionally, because so much of centralized training relies on DP-SGD most differentially private training platforms provide record-level protections. This leaves the construction and reasoning about the broader contribution space (e.g., considering all of a patient's hospital records collectively) up to the developer. It is all-to-easy to naively assume "differential privacy" over a flat database, which is dominated by contributions from a few users, not realizing that guarantees do not hold for correlations or the membership of a user in a training set.

This being said, this remains the most common mode of machine learning and, as a result, is the best supported from the perspective of practical development.

Available Tools

The following is a list of available tools for implementing differential privacy ML models.

- **Opacus.** A library for training PyTorch models with differential privacy [TM20]. Opacus computes batched per-sample gradients which reduces training time compared to using microbatches. Moreover, it uses a cryptographically safe pseudo-random number generator for security-critical applications. Opacus keeps track of the privacy budget used during the training process, enabling early stopping and real-time monitoring.

- **TensorFlow Privacy.** TensorFlow Privacy (TF Privacy) [Mar+15] is an open-source library for differentially private training in TensorFlow. It works by defining differentially private subclasses of established optimizers. These differentially private optimizers can be used in conjunction with high-level APIs that use the Optimizer class, including TF.Estimator and Keras.
- **IBM Differential Privacy Library.** A Python library aimed at Differential Privacy generally, IBM's Differential Privacy Library or Diffprivlib [HBML19] contains a number of useful tools enabling Differentially Private training.

  In particular, besides common differential privacy patterns and tools, the library contains a budget accountant, useful for keeping track of privacy budget across multiple queries and data access. It is aimed at interactive training, allowing queries on remaining budget and context.
- **PATE.** As discussed in Section 7.5 of Chapter 7, the *Private Aggregation of Teacher Ensembles* (PATE) trains multiple *teacher models* on disjoint sensitive data (e.g., different users' data) and uses the teachers' aggregate consensus answers in a black-box fashion to supervise the training of a *student* model. By publishing only the student model (keeping the teachers private) and by adding carefully-calibrated noise to the aggregate answers used to train the student, the PATE work showed how to establish rigorous (ε, δ) differential-privacy guarantees [Pap+18].
- **OpenDP.** While, at the time of writing, not focused on ML, OpenDP [GHV20] is a rapidly growing group focused on differential privacy. An excellent resource for literature, codelabs and a burgeoning code base, it is expected that this group will continue to grow into machine learning in the long term. Additional details are provided in Chapter 13.

13.2.3 Federated Learning

As discussed in Chapter 8, Federated Learning is another form of differentially private learning that has rapidly grown in popularity over the last few years due to a number of attractive privacy properties and minimal assumptions about the safety of training pipelines. While this topic represents a broad field that touches on general distributed and private computing, it can also provide strong guarantees and has user-level privacy built into its foundational assumptions.

Methods and Privacy

Originally defined in [SS15], [McM+17] to address scalability and privacy issues inherent in collecting and training on mobile devices, Federated Learning (FL) has come to define a decentralized method for expressing distributed training in general.

Though details can vary, generally training is divided between a collection of devices which contain device specific data (photos, locations, etc.) and, depending on network details, a set of aggregator nodes that organize the overall training process.

Aggregator nodes distribute a state to clients which in turn perform some form of local training (this step is highly configurable and need not strictly represent deep networks) before returning updates to the aggregators. The flavor of update returned defines the mode of FL employed, typically Federated SGD [SS15] or Federated Averaging [McM+17].

Federated SGD is a generalization of SGD that computes gradient updates in a decentralized manner, which are aggregated into full SGD updates at the aggregator nodes. *Federated Averaging* takes Federated SGD one step further, training a model on a device for multiple rounds, returning a fully qualified set of model weights to the aggregator nodes, which then perform an average over the models. This algorithm and its differentially private counterpart are discussed in details in Chapter 8.

Communication between clients and servers typically uses a form of secure multi-party computation, e.g. [Bon+16], which protects data in transit but, importantly, *does not impact the differential privacy guarantees of the final model.* [i]

Differential privacy can be applied to the process at multiple layers; for maximal protection device updates can apply local differential privacy (e.g., randomized response [DR+14]), or at the aggregator nodes through a differentially private average (e.g., Algorithm 2.4 in [LLSY16]).

Regardless of the low-level details, federated learning has a number of attractive properties from the perspective of differential privacy: First, data, training and updates are all handled in an owner-centric setting. That is, all inputs to a model are naturally associated with a device id, user name or other identifier and allow differential privacy guarantees to be applied at the id level, across all of a user's contributions, rather than for a specific record. In the case of record-level guarantees (as is typical of centralized training) a person's pattern of location data, photos, word-choices, etc., might be individually protected at the feature level, but may be identifying in aggregate. Federated averaging allows the sum total contribution of a user/device/etc. to be contained within a single update, making issues such as privacy loss budget accounting and contribution bounding relatively straightforward. Second, sampling is a fundamental principle in federated learning for reasons of

i. While the details of how data is handled are critically important for a complete privacy story, it is the DP guarantees of the final aggregated model that have the strongest privacy implications.

performance as well as privacy. Importantly, sampling also has benefits in the calculation of the effective (ε, δ)-DP guarantees provided by the system [BST14].

Federated Learning has a Few Caveats

Similar to taking the median of medians or average of means, federated learning works very well for most applications where data is abundant and statistics are reasonably behaved across a set of users. For severely skewed distributions (e.g., number of videos uploaded per user), where a statistical feature is nearly unmeasurable for a single user or where "correlated sub-queries" are central to training (e.g., all users who are 2-σ above the average height), accuracy can be severely degraded. While these considerations can be mitigated with appropriate design (e.g., multiple models) they must be considered in planning. Finally, the attack surface for federated learning is considerably larger. Because federated algorithms distribute model state to every participant in training there is elevated risk of exposure of sensitive data.

In summary, while centralized training has a high risk of accidental leakage without a strong governance / privacy store for the enclosing system, it also benefits from a centralized attack surface that an adversary must intentionally overcome. Conversely, while federated learning builds strong governance and privacy into the design of the system itself, misconfigured systems can expose data to a broad audience who need only to be curious to view the results.

Available Tools

Unfortunately easy to use Open Source Federated Learning remains an incomplete story, mostly in the form of tools and code bases that a complete system could be built upon. We discuss a few of the options here, but for rigorous comparisons of utility and performance, the reader is referred to [Kho+21].

- **PySyft from OpenMined.** PySyft provides a highly configurable FL platform component with support for many platforms and languages, including Android, iOS and Web interfaces. PySyft is based on the OpenMined architecture which must be composed with other libraries to provide a fully federated offering. Differential privacy offerings in PySyft are based on Opacus and include a codelab suitable for research purposes. The platform has many industry partners and a healthy community and additional features are being continuously added.
- **Tensor Flow Federated (TFF).** TFF [IO19] is part of TensorFlow [Mar+15] and provides many of the concrete building blocks required for building an FL system. It is composed of client and server libraries required for local training and orchestrated Federated Averaging that a full-featured FL system would include. Included experimental datasets and codelabs are sufficient to

bootstrap FL in an experimental setting and could also form the basis of a production system.

TFF represents a framework for building distributed computations and differential privacy must be explicitly included from TF-Privacy or TFF components. An example DP Federated model based on [MRTZ17] is included within TFF documentation.

- **Federated AI Technology Enabler (FATE).** Developed by Webank's AI Department, FATE [Fed21] is based in part on Tensorflow and provides a number of different FL implementations depending on need. While highly configurable in distributed and training models, FATE focuses exclusively on Private Computing options (e.g., SecAgg and secure MPC) in its privacy story. While this protects all data in transit, Differential Privacy is required to protect against re-identification on the outputs and must rely on DP FedAvg [Kai+19] or TF-Privacy as above for DP guarantees.
- **Clara.** While limited license only, NVIDIA's Clara framework supports a number of machine learning tasks, including Federated Learning. Unsurprisingly, Clara provides excellent CUDA [NVF20] based GPU support for FL. Based on Tensorflow and AutoML, differential privacy must be constructed by the developer from available subroutines, as in other frameworks and only lists DP-SGD as a primary mechanism in documentation.
- **IBM Federated Learning.** A proprietary, limited license FL framework, with training based on Keras, PyTorch and Tensorflow, IBM FL [Lud+20] provides a DP Naive Bayes training system in addition to DP-SGD and FedAvg algorithms provided by dependent libraries.
- **Other entries in the space.** PFL [Bai21], a small, open-source FL framework from Baidu that relies on a less well-distributed FL platform called DL, PFL uses DP-SGD and FedAvg [Kai+19] to provide DP guarantees.

FL&DP [she21] is a small project from Sherpa.AI that provides the basics for Federated Learning, though with minimal documentation and insufficiently developed for production use-cases. It is worthy of note due to its focus on privacy offerings, including an adaptive Privacy Filter [Rod+20] based DP mechanism, in addition to FedAvg and a simple DP noising mechanism [DR+14] for binary data.

13.3 Management and Governance

Regardless of the method used above, the results of a single round of DP training should result in an (ε, δ)-private ML model, ready for use in applications or distribution to the public.

It is also worth calling out that this chapter is a work in progress from the perspective of the differential privacy community. At present, OpenDP's SmartNoise [GHV20] and IBM's DiffPrivLib [HBML19] are two standard frameworks that allow one to reason about privacy budget which, in many ways, is as important as the particulars of any given instance of machine learning.

The vast landscape of data set governance, sand-boxing and privacy in an end-to-end environment is sparsely populated. While private-by-design systems like Federated Learning can greatly help reason about and enforce a coherent privacy policy, much work remains to be done in order to make both training *and* the outputs of training fully private.

13.4 Privacy Testing and Evaluation

13.4.1 The Two Questions

A privacy-mindful ML practitioner might ask two complementary questions:

1. How does one *achieve* model privacy? Specifically, how does one produce a machine learning model while minimizing privacy risks related to the sensitive training data?
2. How does one *assess* model privacy? Specifically, how does one measure the risk of an adversary inferring something sensitive about the training data?

In theory, differential privacy provides great answers to both questions: privacy can be achieved by differentially private training (or even at earlier stages, by applying differential privacy to the training data) and can be assessed based on the spent privacy budget (i.e., the familiar ε and δ).

In practice, applying standard differential privacy with strong privacy guarantees can be challenging, i.e. because of reduced training speed, complexity (the training process involves techniques such as gradient clipping and adding noise which require additional parameter tuning), loss of utility (models trained with differential privacy can result in a significant decline in accuracy).

A few other ways to mitigate potential training data privacy risks include:

- Avoid over-fitting to ensure that the model is generalizing without (excessive) memorizing;
- Prefer small number of parameters to limit the model's ability to memorize;
- Ensure that each training sample is k-anonymous, that is it comes from at least k individuals to avoid unique or rare samples;
- Limit the effect of outliers (for example, by clipping gradient updates during training);

We emphasize that **none of these methods provide the same rigorous privacy guarantees as differential privacy**. Does this mean that these mitigations are useless in practice? Can we assess their effectiveness in a empirical manner? Let's figure it out.

13.4.2 Empirical Testing: Does Lack of Fever Mean a Healthy Patient?

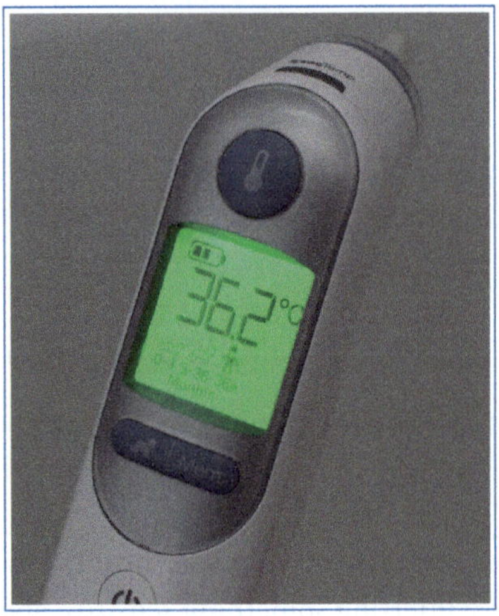

For a moment, let's appeal to a simple analogy. Measuring body temperature is one of the simplest and widely used tests in healthcare. High and sustained fever almost certainly signals a problem. High fever combined with other symptoms can justify performing more expensive, specific and accurate tests (e.g., a genomic PCR test).

Does lack of fever imply that a patient is healthy? Obviously, the answer is no. Does this make body temperature measurements useless? By no means. Measuring body temperature is, in a way, an effective empirical test for quickly detecting whether the patient may be unhealthy.

Coming back to machine learning and model privacy, we can apply a similar line of reasoning and leverage empirical tests to identify "health issues" (that is, privacy leaks), especially when applying differential privacy with strong parameters is infeasible or impractical.

These empirical tests can be designed to estimate the vulnerability of the model to various threats. Such tests can be very simple, for example: is the model significantly less accurate on the test set than on the training set? They can also be rather advanced, for example by building a sophisticated attacker that attempts to reconstruct the training set samples.

In brief, the differences between differential privacy and empirical tests can be summarized as follows:

Analysis	Properties
Differential privacy	Worst-case, principled analysis; Provides "upper bound" for the privacy risk
Empirical privacy tests	High specificity, but low sensitivity; Provides "lower bound" for the privacy risk

It is worth noting that the empirical tests **do not provide certainty that the model is safe**, similar to how normal body temperature does not mean that the patient is healthy. There can be false negatives. However, a comprehensive and broad set of tests that scrutinize model privacy from different angles can increase our level of confidence.

13.4.3 Examples

Privacy tests target a vast variety of threat models, the most common including:

Opaque- vs. transparent-box. depending on whether the attacker has access to the model internals or can only interact with the model from the outside.

Inference vs. reconstruction attacks. depending on whether the goal is to infer something sensitive about the training data or, much more ambitiously, partially of fully reconstruct training samples.

We do not intend to provide a comprehensive overview of existing privacy tests or formal definitions: there are excellent surveys out there [Liu+21; PMSW18]. Instead, we consider a few simple and well-researched test types.

Membership Inference Test

Membership inference aims to identify whether a particular sample was part of the training set [SSSS17]. This knowledge can be quite sensitive, e.g., in healthcare where being in the training set might imply presence of a particular medical condition. Even when this knowledge is not sensitive in itself, the ability to distinguish the training set samples by merely looking at the model or its predictions is an indicator for privacy risks.

The following is a simple recipe for converting this idea into an actionable privacy test.

1. *Train a classifier* that discriminates the training set samples based on model outputs. Such a classifier can be based on the prediction loss (the simpler setting) or the inner layers of a deep model (the more advanced setting).
2. *Use the accuracy of that classifier* as a proxy for privacy risks, e.g. area under the ROC (receiver operating characteristic) curve.

This setting assumes that the test is performed by an in-house privacy specialist who has access to the model, the training and test data and does not intend to attack the model, but to measure feasibility of such an attack. An actual attacker would need to do a bit more work and resort to an implicit analysis by first finding "similar" training data to build a "similar" model, which is often referred to as *shadow model* [SSSS17]. A comprehensive treatment of membership inference attacks is provided in Chapter 5.

Some of the utilities that support membership inference tests are:

- **ML Privacy Meter**, a library developed by the authors of the membership inference attack[MS20];
- **TensorFlow Privacy**, a library for training the differentially private models that also includes empirical tests such as membership inference or secret sharer [Goo18].

Both utilities support several membership inference tests, using different types of membership inference classifiers such as threshold-based classifiers or trained classifiers based on linear regressions, random forests, neural networks, etc.

Secret Sharer Test

Imagine the student is learning to add integer numbers by looking at examples, such as 1+1 = 2, 2+3 = 5, 2+4 = 6 and is provided with a wrong example...

$$1 + 2 = 12$$

Now, if the student to the question "what is 1+2" answers "12", they did not do a good job at learning addition and most likely simply memorized examples.

Memorizing is not great and not just for pedagogic reasons. Machine learning models memorizing training data introduce a privacy risk. The example with a student shows the key idea of the *secret sharer* attack [Car+19]. The key idea is to inject rogue, out-of-distribution examples ("secrets") into the training data and observe if the model is able to predict those. If it can do so, there is a potential privacy issue.

This secret sharer is conceptually simple and intuitive, however has some drawbacks. Such a test:

- **Requires re-training** of the model, which can be computationally expensive.

- **Is not fully generic**, as it needs a way to generate plausible out of distribution secrets (e.g., images or text sequences).

13.5 Concluding Remarks

When it comes to practical application at scale, ML privacy testing has a way to go. A few items on a wish list of ML practitioners:

- **Interpretability** is critical for decision making. For example, while the accuracy of the membership inference classifier is a good proxy for model memorization, there is no immediately obvious way to use this metric to claim the model is "reasonably safe". This is a fundamental limitation of this approach. *More tests* are needed. By their nature, privacy tests cannot with certainty guarantee that the model is "safe", similarly to how normal body temperature alone cannot make a doctor certain the patient is healthy. A doctor might decide to perform blood composition tests, measure blood pressure, perform a PCR test, and so on. We need a similar toolbox of tests that scrutinize the model tendency to memorize training data.
- **Scalability**. ML practitioners should have an easy way to perform such tests as part of their normal model training workflow, e.g. using TensorFlow, PyTorch, Opacus and so on. This requires the tests to be generic, fast and integrated into the most commonly used machine learning tools, e.g. PyTorch, Keras, TensorFlow, TorchServe, etc.

The future is exciting and the volume of new publications in the field is promising, but the progress will depend on collaboration of researchers, engineers and businesses. Bringing research to production in such cutting-edge area is a a hard and exciting challenge.

References

[Bai21] Baidu Research. Baidu PaddlePaddle Releases 21 New Capabilities to Accelerate Industry-Grade Model Development. http://research.baidu.com/Blog/index-view?id=126. 2021 (cit. on p. 460).

[Bjo96] A. Bjorck. Numerical Methods for Least Squares Problems. SIAM, 1996 (cit. on p. 452).

[Bon+16] K. A. Bonawitz, V. Ivanov, B. Kreuter, A. Marcedone, H. B. McMahan, S. Patel, D. Ramage, A. Segal, and K. Seth. "Practical

Secure Aggregation for Federated Learning on User-Held Data". In: NIPS Workshop on Private Multi-Party Machine Learning. 2016. URL: https://arxiv.org/abs/1611.04482 (cit. on p. 458).

[BST14] R. Bassily, A. Smith, and A. Thakurta. "Private empirical risk minimization: Efficient algorithms and tight error bounds". In: 2014 IEEE 55th annual symposium on foundations of computer science. IEEE. 2014, pp. 464–473 (cit. on p. 459).

[Car+19] N. Carlini, C. Liu, Ú. Erlingsson, J. Kos, and D. Song. "The secret sharer: Evaluating and testing unintended memorization in neural networks". In: 28th {USENIX} Security Symposium ({USENIX} Security 19). 2019, pp. 267–284 (cit. on p. 464).

[DR+14] C. Dwork, A. Roth, et al. "The algorithmic foundations of differential privacy." In: Foundations and Trends in Theoretical Computer Science 9.3-4 (2014), pp. 211–407 (cit. on pp. 458, 460).

[Fed21] FedAI Ecosystem. An Industrial Grade Federated Learning Framework. https://fate.fedai.org/. 2021 (cit. on p. 460).

[GBC16] I. Goodfellow, Y. Bengio, and A. Courville. Deep Learning. http://www.deeplearningbook.org. MIT Press, 2016 (cit. on p. 452).

[GHV20] M. Gaboardi, M. Hay, and S. Vadhan. "A programming framework for opendp". In: Manuscript, May (2020) (cit. on pp. 457, 461).

[Goo+14] I. J. Goodfellow, J. Pouget-Abadie, M. Mirza, B. Xu, D. Warde-Farley, S. Ozair, A. Courville, and Y. Bengio. "Generative Adversarial Nets". In: Proceedings of the 27th International Conference on Neural Information Processing Systems - Volume 2. NIPS'14. Montreal, Canada: MIT Press, 2014, pp. 2672–2680 (cit. on p. 452).

[Goo18] Google. TensorFlow Privacy Library. https://github.com/tensorflow/privacy & https://github.com/google/differential-privacy. 2018 (cit. on p. 464).

[HBML19] N. Holohan, S. Braghin, P. Mac Aonghusa, and K. Levacher. "Diffprivlib: the IBM differential privacy library". In: arXiv preprint arXiv:1907.02444 (2019) (cit. on pp. 457, 461).

[HDH17] D. Hofman, L. Duranti, and E. How. "Trust in the balance: Data protection laws as tools for privacy and security in the cloud". In: Algorithms 10.2 (2017), p. 47 (cit. on p. 452).

[IO19] A. Ingerman and K. Ostrowski. Introducing TensorFlow Federated. https://medium.com/tensorflow/introducing-tensorflow-federated-a4147aa20041. 2019 (cit. on p. 459).

[Kai+19] P. Kairouz, H. B. McMahan, B. Avent, A. Bellet, M. Bennis, A. N. Bhagoji, K. Bonawitz, Z. Charles, G. Cormode, R. Cummings, et al. "Advances and open problems in federated learning". In: arXiv preprint arXiv:1912.04977 (2019) (cit. on p. 460).

[Kho+21] I. Kholod, E. Yanaki, D. Fomichev, E. Shalugin, E. Novikova, E. Filippov, and M. Nordlund. "Open-Source Federated Learning Frameworks for IoT: A Comparative Review and Analysis". In: Sensors 21.1 (2021), p. 167 (cit. on p. 459).

[Liu+21] B. Liu, M. Ding, S. Shaham, W. Rahayu, F. Farokhi, and Z. Lin. "When Machine Learning Meets Privacy: A Survey and Outlook". In: ACM Comput. Surv. 54.2 (Mar. 2021). ISSN: 0360-0300. URL: https://doi.org/10.1145/3436755 (cit. on p. 463).

[LLSY16] N. Li, M. Lyu, D. Su, and W. Yang. "Differential privacy: From theory to practice". In: Synthesis Lectures on Information Security, Privacy, & Trust 8.4 (2016), pp. 1–138 (cit. on p. 458).

[Lud+20] H. Ludwig, N. Baracaldo, G. Thomas, Y. Zhou, A. Anwar, S. Rajamoni, Y. Ong, J. Radhakrishnan, A. Verma, M. Sinn, et al. "IBM Federated Learning: an Enterprise Framework White Paper V0. 1". In: arXiv preprint arXiv:2007.10987 (2020) (cit. on p. 460).

[Mar+15] Martín Abadi et al. TensorFlow: Large-Scale Machine Learning on Heterogeneous Systems. Software available from tensorflow.org. 2015. URL: http://tensorflow.org/ (cit. on pp. 457, 459).

[McM+17] B. McMahan, E. Moore, D. Ramage, S. Hampson, and B. A. y Arcas. "Communication-efficient learning of deep networks from decentralized data". In: Artificial intelligence and statistics. PMLR. 2017, pp. 1273–1282 (cit. on pp. 457, 458).

[MRTZ17] H. B. McMahan, D. Ramage, K. Talwar, and L. Zhang. "Learning Differentially Private Language Models Without Losing Accuracy". In: CoRR abs/1710.06963 (2017). arXiv: 1710.06963. URL: http://arxiv.org/abs/1710.06963 (cit. on p. 460).

[MRTZ18] H. B. McMahan, D. Ramage, K. Talwar, and L. Zhang. "Learning Differentially Private Recurrent Language Models". In: International Conference on Learning Representations. 2018. URL: https://openreview.net/forum?id=BJ0hF1Z0b (cit. on p. 452).

[MS20] S. K. Murakonda and R. Shokri. "ML Privacy Meter: Aiding regulatory compliance by quantifying the privacy risks of machine learning". In: arXiv preprint arXiv:2007.09339 (2020) (cit. on p. 464).

[NVF20] NVIDIA, P. Vingelmann, and F. H. Fitzek. CUDA, release: 10.2.89. 2020. URL: https://developer.nvidia.com/cuda-toolkit (cit. on p. 460).

[Pap+18] N. Papernot, S. Song, I. Mironov, A. Raghunathan, K. Talwar, and Ú. Erlingsson. "Scalable Private Learning with PATE". In: International Conference on Learning Representations (ICLR). 2018. URL: https://arxiv.org/abs/1802.08908 (cit. on p. 457).

[PMSW18] N. Papernot, P. McDaniel, A. Sinha, and M. P. Wellman. "SoK: Security and Privacy in Machine Learning". In: 2018 IEEE European Symposium on Security and Privacy (EuroSP). 2018, pp. 399–414 (cit. on p. 463).

[Rod+20] N. Rodríguez-Barroso, G. Stipcich, D. Jiménez-López, J. A. Ruiz-Millán, E. Martínez-Cámara, G. González-Seco, M. V. Luzón, M. A. Veganzones, and F. Herrera. "Federated Learning and Differential Privacy: Software tools analysis, the Sherpa.ai FL framework and methodological guidelines for preserving data privacy". In: Information Fusion 64 (2020), pp. 270–292 (cit. on p. 460).

[Sco21] L. Scott. Data Preparation for Machine Learning: The Ultimate Resource Guide. https://lionbridge.ai/articles/data-preparation-for-machine-learning-the-ultimate-resource-guide/. 2021 (cit. on p. 454).

[she21] sherpa.ai. We Research and Build Artificial Intelligence Technology and Services. https://sherpa.ai/. 2021 (cit. on p. 460).

[SS15] R. Shokri and V. Shmatikov. "Privacy-preserving deep learning". In: Proceedings of the 22nd ACM SIGSAC conference on computer and communications security. 2015, pp. 1310–1321 (cit. on pp. 457, 458).

[SSSS17] R. Shokri, M. Stronati, C. Song, and V. Shmatikov. "Membership inference attacks against machine learning models". In: 2017 IEEE symposium on security and privacy (SP). IEEE. 2017, pp. 3–18 (cit. on pp. 463, 464).

[TM20] D. Testuggine and I. Mironov. Introducing Opacus: A high-speed library for training PyTorch models with differential privacy. https://ai.facebook.com/blog/introducing-opacus-a-high-speed-library-for-training-pytorch-models-with-differential-privacy/. 2020 (cit. on p. 456).

DOI: 10.1561/9781638284772.ch14

Chapter 14

Challenges and Solutions to Deploying Differential Privacy

By Damien Desfontaines and Christine Task

So you have been put in charge of designing and deploying a differentially private mechanism for a practical use case. Congratulations!

If this is your first time working on a real-world deployment, you might be surprised at how much difference there is with academic work. Systems that never leave a research environment impact relatively few people, and have much simpler requirements. However, once a system has been deployed, it can impact many people, and entirely new ethical and practical challenges arise. These challenges are more complex than one can expect, but tackling them with care is essential. In this chapter, we discuss some of these challenges, and provide pointers on how to address them.

Overview of the Chapter

This chapter is organized as follows. First, in Section 14.1, we outline the process of listing, understanding, and communicating with your stakeholders: this step is essential to build a detailed and accurate understanding of the problem requirements. Second, in Section 14.2, we explain how you can gain an in-depth understanding your data, and underscore the need for development data. Third, in Section 14.3, we discuss success criteria: how to define your evaluation metrics, compute them, and communicate about them. Fourth, in Section 14.4, we focus on the engineering process, and provide a few pointers on how to build and maintain reliable, trustworthy software for privacy-critical applications. Finally, in Section 14.5, we address algorithmic tuning, and suggest a number of ways to improve the trade-off between privacy and utility for your differentially private mechanism.

14.1 Understanding Your Stakeholders

The first step to any design process is to understand the problem requirements. To do so, you must first understand who your system will impact, once deployed. These people are your *stakeholders*, and you need to be aware of who they are, and how to work with them. This is arguably the most important part of the deployment process, which we discuss in this first section.

There are four kinds of stakeholders.

- *Decision makers*, sometimes called *clients* or *project owners*, are the people ultimately responsible for the project. They make the final calls regarding its implementation. Different decision makers might have different levels of technical expertise. Some might heavily rely on your advice regarding all the details of the process, while others might want to be directly involved in important technical decisions.
- *Data users* are the people who will use the data you publish. Their goals and level of technical expertise can greatly vary depending on your project. Will you share data with trained statisticians who will want to publish rigorous research papers? Or are your data users public authorities, who mostly need simple visual representations of the data, and will not dive in the details of the data generation process? In either case, data users will be concerned with the accuracy of decisions and analyses made based on the privatized data.
- *Data subjects* are the people whose information is in the input data set. The goal of your differentially private process will be to publish statistical information that accurately represents your data subjects, while protecting their private data.
- *Impacted populations* are people who are affected by analyses and decisions that are based on the output of the differentially private system. Systems which have flaws regarding fairness, bias, or poor utility can negatively impact these individuals. However, systems which allow the safe sharing of high-quality information that was previously unavailable can have a significant positive impact.

It is important to keep all four groups in mind, and treat them with care and respect. This requires you to accurately understand their needs before you dive too deeply into the problem, and this is rarely as simple as asking for input. You need to allocate time and resources to engage with your stakeholders, and create active and ongoing collaborations with them. In the remainder of this section, we provide some guidance on typical issues that come with with various stakeholders.

14.1.1 Learning about the Problem

To understand what problem you are trying to solve, you need to be able to answer a number of questions. What are the decision makers' goals with the project? What will the data users want to do with the data? What are the privacy expectations of the data subjects, and what risks does the project bring them? Who might be affected by the data publication, even if they are not present in the initial data set? What impact might the project have on these people?

To answer these questions, start by having as many discussions with as many stakeholders as you can. When engaging with stakeholders, always keep an open mind. Let them explain their needs, the goals they have for the project, and the difficulties they anticipate. Don't push them to define only one workload or use case if that's not natural for them. Start by answering very basic questions about the problem first. Is this a prediction task or a data generation task? Are we trying to release a privatized version of the entire data set, or only a few key statistics? How sensitive is the data, what will it be used for? Then, narrow down the details to get a good picture of what you need to achieve. Initial discussions are particularly valuable: unlike future engagements, they are not yet influenced by the implementation work done so far. This makes it particularly important to collect as much valuable signal as possible at this stage.

A common pitfall at this stage is to redefine the problem to something easier, and then solve that simplified problem instead of the original one. This impulse is natural, especially for people with an academic background, but should be avoided. Especially in the initial stages of the project, you should be optimistic, and try to solve the *actual* problem with all its complexities. At some later point, you might need to make additional assumptions or simplify the problem. But trying to predict it in advance is doomed to failure. In addition, any change to the problem statement needs to be decided collaboratively with stakeholders, to ensure that what you produce will still have value for them.

14.1.2 Understanding the Policy Constraints

There is another important point that you should clarify at the very beginning: which policy constraints are you operating under, and who is in charge of defining those constraints? Differential privacy brings many policy choices that someone needs to make. What ε and δ parameters are we using? What is the *privacy unit*—are we protecting a single individual, or a single sensitive attribute, or a single individual during a fixed period of time? Where should the privacy boundary lie, and what should count towards the privacy budget computation?

The answers to these questions can simply be constraints given by the project's decision makers at the very beginning. This is simple, but rarely happens in practice: often, these stakeholders to want to make a decision based on a privacy vs. utility analysis, after an experimentation phase with various parameters. In any case, it is a good idea to discuss in advance about the way this choice will be made. It is also valuable to discuss possible failure modes in advance: what if future analyses reveal that only very loose privacy parameters allow acceptable utility? At which point do we consider privacy guarantees meaningless? Are there plans for alternative risk measurement methods, like trying to run reconstruction attacks on the data?

It can also happen that stakeholders simply rely on you for policy choices. When you're the privacy expert, people naturally expect you to be able to decide what is safe enough to publish. If that's the case, there are multiple approaches you can use to make these choices.

- To choose the privacy unit, you can reason about the possible goals of an attacker, and estimate how many correlations can be in the data of a single individual.
- For numerical parameters, some theoretical explanations of the impact of DP can help, like the interpretations of DP guarantees using Bayesian updating, or hypothesis testing.
- You can get inspiration from prior real-world examples of differentially private data publications [Des21].
- You can seek advice from other members of the differential privacy community. No standards have yet been widely adopted yet, but this might change over time, and open discussions among practitioners can only help.
- Finally, you should not be afraid to follow your best judgment. If someone needs to make a subjective decision, it might as well be the person with the most knowledge about differential privacy.

14.1.3 Communicating with Stakeholders

The people who will use your data are likely to be those with whom you will collaborate most closely. They will work with the data once published: they typically will have strong opinions about the strategy you will adopt. Data users can either be internal to your organization, or external. It is crucial to distinguish both situations, and interact with them differently.

Internal data users are best positioned to help you improve your approach over time: creating a good collaborative relationship with them is critical. They can provide you with invaluable feedback on every aspect of your deployment: defining your evaluation metrics, optimizing your data generation strategy, communicating about your results externally, and so on.

External data users are a different audience, and you should remember this when communicating with them. Since they are external to your organization, they do not have access to the raw data, but they might have previously had access to non-DP products from your organization. Their level of prior knowledge about DP might be low, and they have much less context than internal data users on why you made certain decisions. Communication with them can take multiple forms.

- Demonstration data products are the output trial runs of your algorithm on development data (see Section 14.2.2). They allow external folks to understand what kind of data is going to be produced by your algorithm, and possibly run validation experiments of their own.
- Evaluation metrics you developed internally can be shared with external data users, to give them a high-level idea of the level of error induced by the differentially private process.
- Presentations and press releases can be the opportunity to produce simple, understandable explanations of what is being done to the data, and how useful the output is going to be.

Different external stakeholders might have extremely different levels of expertise and motivations, so it is important to think about who your main audiences are, and adapt your communication to these different recipients. For example, demonstration data is mostly useful to data analysts and scientists who can dig in and come to their own conclusions. To provide transparency with the broader impacted population, it is worth partnering with public communication experts, who can produce simple material and organize outreach with media.

Communicating with external stakeholders before producing the final data is important for transparency, and allows you to collect valuable feedback. It is worth investing the time and effort to do this outreach with care and thoughtfulness: first impressions are important, so if the initial data you publish for demonstration purposes does not perform well at all, this might create panic and opposition to the project. Again, internal data users are your best allies to help you prevent such a scenario, by vetting your external communications before you publish them.

14.1.4 Dealing with Utility Concerns

When having conversations with stakeholders, especially those who are not yet familiar with differential privacy, it is frequent to encounter individuals who have serious concerns about the impact of DP on their use cases. Won't adding noise to the data destroy all and make all downstream analyses invalid?

These concerns are valid, and dismissing them can be disastrous for future collaborations. Instead, you need to address them with humility and helpfulness. Humility is crucial: data users know much better than you do how the output data will be used in practice. In all likelihood, they do not intend to do anything nefarious with the data, but might need to change their analyses in significant ways to take into account the effect of differential privacy. Their concerns are understandable and listening to them is important: take it as an opportunity to learn more about the concrete use cases of your data users, and improve your process accordingly.

To convince data users that the impact of differential privacy will be acceptable, use data: ask what kind of accuracy they care about, then measure and communicate the corresponding accuracy loss (see Section 14.3). Another complementary strategy is to create example runs on data they are already familiar with, so they can check for themselves (see Section 14.2.2).

As part of this process, it is possible that you will find out that the technology you are implementing does not quite succeed in overcoming the problems the data users are worried about. Be willing to admit it openly, and look at redefining the problem if needed (see Section 14.5.3).

14.1.5 Dealing with Undue Optimism

In early conversations with stakeholders, you may also encounter individuals who are overly confident about the applicability of differential privacy to their use case. You need to make sure that their expectations are properly calibrated, and that they are aware of the applicability limitations of differential privacy. Does their data set have fewer than a few hundred users? Do they want the output data to contain unstructured data like text or images? Does their use case needs exact precision? Do they need to preserve the ability to do user-level joins between data sets? In such cases, you need to be honest about what is and is not feasible. This is important both from an ethical standpoint and from a practical one: if the problem requires another privacy-enhancing technology, wasting time pursuing inadequate approaches does not benefit anyone.

It may not be immediately clear whether differential privacy is a good fit. One good litmus test is the question: will the use case lead to different outcomes if a single user changes their data? If so, in which conditions does this happen? Is this fundamental to the problem at hand, or is it possible to reformulate the problem in a way that is more robust to individual changes? If the problem seems to be a good fit for differential privacy, but you do not know of any existing approach for this problem, you also need to communicate this with your stakeholders. They cannot know a priori whether the problem requires only engineering and tweaking known methods, or entirely new scientific advances.

When differential privacy is impossible, it is also your responsibility to accurately explain the risks to your stakeholders. For example, suppose that your stakeholders say that they need to perform arbitrarily complex analyses, using every possible combination of features in high-dimensional data. Telling them that differential privacy cannot work for this use case is not enough: you also need to communicate the risks involved in such a data publication, for example by explaining them fundamental results about database reconstruction attacks. This way, they can then make an informed decision as to whether to limit some of the possible use cases, or re-scope the problem in a less ambitious way.

14.2 Understanding Your Data

Once you have a good understanding of the requirements of your application, it is time to start addressing the needs that you have identified. The first step of that process is understanding the data that you will be dealing with. You will have to decide what demonstration data you will use for developing, tuning and demonstrating your system. This data must have adequate complexity, and realistic distributional properties. This makes the data exploration stage particularly crucial to avoid incorrect assumptions: real-world data is much more complex and messy than you might initially think.

In this section, we list some questions that you will want to answer about your data, and we discuss how to choose development data.

14.2.1 Properties of Your Data

If you have access to the data, take a look at a sample to build an intuitive understanding of what you will be working with. For each of the fields that will be used in the algorithm, ask yourself the following questions. What is the type of the data? What is its precision? Are values missing? Is the data categorical or numerical? Does it contain time or location data? Are the features structured or unstructured; in the latter case, how can it be converted to a more structured format, and what information might be lost in the process? Are there structural constraints, like a field value being entirely determined by another?

Next, study the global characteristics of your data. Is your data sparse or dense, and how much of the important information exists in the sparser areas? Does each individual contribute a single record, or can multiple records contain information about the same person? Are the records independent, or do you need to deal with and preserve social network structures? Relationships between records are not always obvious: medical records can be correlated between members of the same family, and data in a record associated to a single person can sometimes reveal information about other people. Time or location data also frequently contains correlations, like trends over time, or similar activities happening on different locations.

It is also worth trying to understand which distributions approximate your data well. Most human data follows a skewed power law, with a long (and important) tail. Is this the case for the data you are working with? Be careful not to make spurious assumptions: actually look at each feature, and discover the correlations between pairs of features. Knowledge of correlations between features and between records is not only essential to understand the characteristics of your input data, it can also be leveraged later to build more useful algorithms (see Section 14.5.2).

Last but not least, are there particular subgroups or demographics in your data? Examples of such subgroups include racial groups, economic or geographic communities, or groups of people with a specific education level or immigration status. This is important to understand to ensure that you are providing fair accuracy for all subgroups, not just the majority population. Differential privacy only requires protecting single individuals, so relatively large subgroups (of hundreds or thousands of individuals) should be able to receive good accuracy even with privacy protections. However, your modeling approach itself may tend to overfit the majority group, and if your evaluation doesn't explicitly check for performance across subgroups, you may not realize that this happens [FTHZ22]. Don't forget: the people impacted by decisions made using your differentially private data are also one of your key stakeholders.

14.2.2 Choosing Development Data

Once you have built a good understanding of your data, you need to decide what you will use as input data for development and demonstration purposes. Without such development data, it is near-impossible to make believable promises about accuracy to your stakeholders. This data must be realistic, and must share the same properties than the data you will use for the final application. Thus, it is crucial to first gain a good understanding of your data: otherwise, your development data might differ in some important way from the production data, and your results might have unexpected problems. There are different ways of obtaining development data.

A first option is to generate a completely synthetic dataset manually, based on what you know about the data distribution. If this process is manual and based on a visual exploration of the original data, one can assume that the data generated this way is safe enough to be shared directly along with the results of experimentation.

This has an important advantage: it allows data users to run arbitrary analyses on this data, and provide in-depth feedback about the process. On the other hand, creating realistic synthetic data is often laborious and time-consuming. It is also very difficult to find out whether unexpected properties of the output come from the synthetic data itself, or from the process under test.

A second option is to split the data available to you in multiple parts: one will be used for development, and the other for the final product. This is particularly well-suited if some of the data is already public; for example, if some data was published without privacy protections in the past, and you are now trying to anonymize some more recent data. Then, it is likely that the distribution of the development data will be close to that of the final data, enabling reliable evaluations.

A third option, if you do not have access to such historical data, is to use all or part of your actual data for development purposes. Taking a sample allows you to mitigate the risks of overfitting the algorithm parameters to the data at hand, and limit potential exposure, though you also need to be mindful of how data size might influence the algorithm choice and evaluation metrics. Using the exact same data for development and final process can also be an option, which can be appropriate if all the evaluation is done with internal stakeholders. Otherwise, since the experimentation itself will necessarily leak some information about the development data, you would need to count this towards the final privacy budget.

14.3 Understanding Your Success Criteria

Once you understand your stakeholders needs and have selected your demonstration data, the next step is identify evaluation metrics. These will be used to communicate your system's performance to your team and your stakeholders.

It is very tempting to reduce the success of an engineering project to a single metric to optimize. Stakeholders want to understand how well you are doing, and simplicity makes communicating easier; in addition, optimizing a single score is much easier than having to control for a larger family of success criteria.

It is crucial to avoid this temptation. Your goal is to support your stakeholders, by producing high-quality results that will support good decision-making. This goal is very different from producing impressive accuracy numbers to convince academic reviewers that you are improving on the state of the art! A single score, like a mean-squared error number, can hide many problems: terrible performance on minority subgroups, overfitting, incorrect application of differential privacy... but those problems will still exist, and in a deployed system, they will impact real people.

The goal of a proper evaluation is to find, identify, understand, and if possible fix significant accuracy issues for the released data. Here are some things to keep in mind as you design this process.

14.3.1 Evaluation Approaches

Even complex evaluation suites are composed of a finite collection of metrics. The metrics will always provide an incomplete view of the impact of the differentially private algorithm on data utility: infinitely many analyses can be done on the output data, and our scores will only be able to capture a few. So how can you prioritize the right metric, and what should you be on the lookout for?

Collaborating with Stakeholders

Evaluation metrics should be designed in collaboration with your stakeholders, and more specifically the people who will use the data. Which analyses will they be doing? Are there a small number of specific analyses that are particularly crucial to get right? If so, can you reproduce them as part of the evaluation setup? Otherwise, can you find metrics that encapsulate a wide number of use cases for the published data?

To make sure that scoring well on your metrics will actually correspond to satisfying the needs of your stakeholders, one possible option is to ask them for suggestions. This might not be easy: people who are not used to dealing with uncertainty in their data analysis tasks might not know what kind of accuracy metric they care about. If that's the case, be proactive: try to come up with metrics that capture desired properties of the data, share these metrics with stakeholders, collect feedback, and iterate.

Considering Subgroups Explicitly

Impressive accuracy numbers can hide huge disparities within different subgroups. In particular, marginalized communities have a long history of having their needs ignored, and even with the best of intentions, you can inadvertently reproduce structural unfairness. It is crucial to be mindful of these risks, and address them explicitly.

At minimum, split your metrics by subgroups to check if algorithms perform worse for some communities. Simple tests for race, gender, age, etc., are a good start. They might not be enough, and might be difficult if your data does not contain explicit demographic information: you should be prepared to look further. What else might define communities and subgroups in your data: language, educational level, geographies? Media or entertainment engagement? Occupation? Religion?

This is another subject that you should discuss explicitly with your stakeholders. What complexities do they expect in the data? What problems do they foresee? If specific communities are more likely to be impacted by the use of data, they are a key stakeholder: involve them in the process of defining the problem, and seek their feedback on your evaluation metrics.

Separating the Impact of Different Processing Steps

Differentially private mechanisms often use multiple steps to achieve the desired privacy guarantees. For example, records are dropped to make sure that the contribution of each user is bounded, numerical values are clamped to bound their sensitivity, the privacy budget is split between multiple aggregations, noise is added at different stages, post-processing steps optimize accuracy, etc.

Try to quantify and isolate the effect of each step. How much data is lost due to record sampling? How much outlier data does clamping erase, and how does it bias the results? How much inaccuracies does the noise introduce compared to other factors? Does post-processing improve accuracy everywhere or only on average? Does it bias the data in some way?

Evaluating Differentially Private Synthetic Data

Most machine learning or data mining tasks have well-established accuracy metrics that can be used in evaluation processes. Differentially private synthetic data use cases are a little different. The goal is to create a new data set of synthetic records whose distributional properties mimic those of the original data. The entire point of synthetic data is to be suitable for yet-unknown use cases: this makes it much more difficult to define clear requirements. In fact, evaluation for synthetic data is itself an active area of research!

Good synthetic data must produce similar results to the original data for typical population-level analyses. At the very least, basic distributional properties like univariate distributions and correlations between features must be preserved. In addition, checking the performance of analyses of specific interest to your stakeholders is also worth doing, and should also be part of your approach. But you should keep in mind that these will only tell you part of the story: such evaluation metrics might fail to capture unexpected relationships between variables, or unknown use cases, and limit the utility and reliability of the data for exploration.

For a more comprehensive evaluation, several approaches are worth considering. We mentioned correlations between all pairs of features in the data set: this can naturally be extended to random k-marginals. For example, the NIST Differential Privacy Challenge [NIS20] computes the edit distance between real and synthetic data across a large number of randomly selected k-dimensional snapshots, after coarsening the data. Another option is to study how well a classifier can distinguish between real and synthetic records, which is implemented by the synthpop R library [Now+20].

These techniques provide more than an overall accuracy score: they also give you ability to dive deeper and identify where the algorithm performs poorly, either because of excessive divergence or bias. These will help guide your algorithm tuning, and provide a meaningful understanding of performance for your stakeholders.

14.3.2 Computing and Publishing Metrics

Defining your metrics is only part of the evaluation story: computing and communicating about your algorithm's performance is critical, and often far from trivial. In particular, running your algorithm only once and reporting the results as a raw list of scores is unhelpful. How can you ensure that the evaluation is reliable, and communicate its results in a way that fosters trust and maximizes the chance of getting useful feedback?

Generating Reliable Metrics

Your evaluation pipeline is part of the software system that you are designing and building. It should be written with the same care as the rest of your infrastructure (see Section 14.4): check the assumptions explicitly, and test the code thoroughly, including on ill-formed inputs. You want to ensure that edge cases get caught early, and do not impact your metrics in a subtle, undetectable way.

Since differential privacy pipelines output randomized data, you will probably need to run the evaluation many times to compute reliable numbers. This might be computationally expensive, so it is worth trying to see if some (or all) of these accuracy metrics can be computed on-the-fly: in simple cases, you might be able to know exactly what noise distribution will end up in the output, side-stepping the need for repeated pipeline runs. Sampling techniques or sketching algorithms might help. For more complex pipelines, you might have no other choice than running the pipeline many times until you can estimate the accuracy well enough; if possible, you can also return confidence intervals or significance measures for the evaluation metrics themselves.

Setting correct expectations when releasing the metrics is also crucial for reliability. No set of metrics can provide a comprehensive view of the output data: it is important to communicate about this fact, and be open about possible coverage gaps. Be proactive in communicating blind spots, and stay open to constructive criticism from stakeholders.

Visualizing Results

A graph is worth a thousand numbers. People can derive conclusions from a small handful of numbers, but not many more. But we saw how simplistic metrics will likely miss an important part of the accuracy story. The solution is clear: instead of drowning your audience in numbers, communicate your evaluation results in a visual way.

This can take multiple forms. Percentages (e.g. of partitions dropped) can be communicated visually, for example with stacked bar charts. When comparing accuracy metrics between subgroups, display the metrics side-by-side, and compare them to the global accuracy. If some of your data is hierarchical, visualize relative accuracy metrics at different levels of the hierarchy. Use a map to display results that vary across geographies. The impact of differential privacy often varies depending on the number of people in each partition: it can be very helpful to order (and possibly weigh) all partitions by size, and compare metrics along this axis. When the magnitude of the data differs wildly on different parts of the output space, logarithmic scales can be a helpful tool to make visualizations easier to grasp.

Differential privacy involves uncertainty, and it is likely that the evaluation metrics themselves are uncertain. To help stakeholders (and yourself!) build an intuitive understanding of this uncertainty, multiple tools are at your disposal. Confidence intervals are an obvious choice, and are particularly well-suited to understand the impact of differential privacy on statistical inference use cases. Quantile plots, or animations like hypothetical outcome plots, are good tools to use for this purpose as well.

Visualizations are great, but "interactive" visualizations are even better. Allowing your internal stakeholders to change various parameters on a slider and see the effect on evaluation metrics in near-real-time is very powerful. It is not always possible, but it is worth checking whether your use case would be compatible with building such a tool. Especially if the tool is only internal and specific to this use case, a spreadsheet can be good enough, and is typically faster to create than a more complex visualization dashboard. If you do create such a tool, be mindful about which defaults to set, and what parameters you include: starting from a very high privacy budget and allowing it to be unbounded can anchor the discussions around these potentially unsafe values.

Benchmark Scores

Of course, for any defensible value of ε, the output of your differentially private system will never exactly match the original data. The system will need to inject noise into the data, and this simple fact is often at the heart of controversies over deployments of differential privacy. How much noise is acceptable?

When communicating about your evaluation metrics, point out that adding randomization or noise to data is not a new idea. The data user community is already familiar with older processes that impact data quality to achieve some level of privacy protections, like subsampling or k-anonymity. It might be valuable to benchmark differential privacy's performance against these techniques: you may find that differential privacy offers better utility than these far less private approaches.

Statistical agencies and data owners have often used subsampling and de-identification to provide a form of informal privacy protection, allowing survey respondents to claim that their own data wasn't included in the published data. For example, the American Community Survey [US 21] publicly releases a 40% sample of their data. Subsampling, however, has two main issues. First, it is not an effective privacy-preserving technique, and does little to protect against reidentification attacks on rich data [RHD19]. Second, it typically has a significant impact on accuracy: discarding a lot of the data may have a larger impact on the data distribution than carefully adding sufficient noise to obfuscate the addition or removal of a single person. Thus, sampling error can be a good benchmark to explain the impact of differential privacy to stakeholders. The evaluation can be run on both the ground truth data and subsampled data, and then compared against the output of your differentially private system.

Another technique often used in public data releases is k-anonymity. The data is partitioned according to a set of quasi-identifiers, usually a combination of the demographic, geographic and sensitive variables, and any partition that contains fewer than k individuals is redacted. As discussed in Chapter 1, this approach does not provide robust privacy protection: individuals can often still be identified by features that were not part of the set of quasi-identifiers. Further, this approach also has a significant impact on accuracy, especially for diverse populations and minority groups. Relatively high values of k, such as $k = 25$, may require removing a significant amount of the complexity of the ground truth distribution. By contrast, differential privacy only requires obfuscating the addition or removal of a single individual, and carefully tuned algorithms are often better able to preserve that information. Similarly to above, evaluation metrics can be run on data redacted using k-anonymity, and compared against the output of the differentially private system.

14.4 Writing and Maintaining Software

The first three sections of this chapter were about defining the problem: who your stakeholders are, what does your data look like, and what your success criteria should be. The next step, of course, is to solve this problem. Chapter 4 presented a variety of techniques that can be used to generate useful differentially private data. But choosing an algorithm is only part of the story: implementing and deploying differential privacy in practice is also an engineering challenge. In this section, we provide generic advice on running software engineering projects, and specific recommendations for implementing differentially private algorithms.

14.4.1 Software Engineering for Production Use Cases

Software engineering is programming, integrated over time [WMW20]. Writing code that seems to work is the easy part. Team coordination, flexibility, documentation, scalability, robustness, etc.: these challenges are crucial aspects of the software engineering lifecycle, and ignoring them will lead to painful issues down the line.

Team Coordination

In all likelihood, the project will be a collaboration between multiple people. Team coordination tools and processes can help avoid duplicating efforts and improve the groups' overall productivity. Such tools and process include:

- Issue tracking software like Jira or GitLab Issues, to keep track of all the remaining tasks, of their status and of team member assignments;
- Revision tracking software like Git or Mercurial, to gracefully deal with concurrent modifications to the same code;
- Agile frameworks like Scrum can improve team productivity; even if one does not adopt a formal process framework, having regular discussions about the state of the project (e.g. daily standups) is often very valuable for team coordination.

The process that you are a part of impacts not only the team members working on the project, but your stakeholders as well. The team coordination tools and processes discussed above can also be used to communicate with your stakeholders about the state of the project, and collect feedback.

Modular Architectures and Configuration Files

Software engineering projects rarely follow a linear process where the requirements are first laid out then implemented, and the project ends. Requirements often change, and unexpected technical issues always come up: it is important to keep the design of the system modular, and try to ensure that changing one component will not require changing the entire code stack.

What does this mean in practice? Building modular software can be done by separating the different types of business logic into different interchangeable parts that communicate via clearly documented interfaces. For example, the input/output logic should be separate from the privacy logic: if the schema of the data changes, you want to be able to adapt only the data reading operation instead of having to change the whole pipeline.

Another type of separation is between the algorithm itself and its configuration: privacy parameters or hyperparameters for the mechanism should be specified in configuration files rather than in code, to avoid having to recompile the entire code to experiment with different values. To prevent unexpected results, avoid using default parameters, and instead, validate all parameters specified in configuration files.

Scaling

If you are dealing with data at a large scale—say, billions of values—or that might reach this size in the future, you need to consider scalability as a hard requirement from the very beginning. This typically adds constraints on which algorithms and tools you will be able to use.

On the theoretical front, pay attention to the time and memory complexity of the algorithms you're considering. On large data, only algorithms that are linear or near-linear in the size of their input might be acceptable, and constants hidden in the complexity analysis can be of great importance. As a general rule, if running the end-to-end pipeline takes more than a few hours, experimentation will be very painful, and this hinders team productivity. Eliminating classes of algorithms from the very start because they do not scale well will save time and effort.

On a practical level, some differential privacy libraries assume that all the data fits in RAM or on a single disk, and that the computation can be performed on a single machine. Meanwhile, others are well-suited for massively parallelizable computations, typically because they rely on existing large-scale data processing libraries. If you are not sure whether you need the latter, try running your algorithm on inputs of sufficient size to be an upper approximation of the possible size of your production inputs (including in the future). If the computation takes too long or fails to complete, you will know that it is not worth investing in making this tool work for your use case.

Experiment Harnesses

The first part of the project will likely be experimentation: different algorithms will be tried out and compared. It is tempting to simply write some experimental code, run it, and examine results without giving much thought as to where and how they are stored. Over time, a lot of experimental data will be generated and stored in a disorganized way, the link between experiment results and the corresponding code will be broken, and it will become difficult to compare newer runs to older results.

To prevent this, consider building an *experiment harness*. An experiment harness is a common piece of infrastructure that can implement some or all of the following features.

- Run a certain experiment multiple times and generate average metrics for this run. This is important, since randomized algorithms might perform very well or poorly on a single run, but have a different behavior on average.
- Automatically re-run a job if it fails, which is common when running many experiments at once, or performing experiments on very large data.
- Record the version of the code, its configuration, and its input data when running an experiment; annotate the output with this metadata.
- Run an experiment many times with a wide array of parameters (e.g. privacy parameters, or algorithm hyperparameters), and visualize the results to find out which performs best.
- Compare the results obtained between different runs.

Implementing such an experiment harness might seem like a significant investment, but is worth doing even for medium-scale projects: faster and easier experimentation leads to better outcomes.

14.4.2 Documentation and Long-term Maintenance

What will happen to your project in six months, two years, five years? If the pipeline you built will keep running continuously, who will monitor it, update its dependencies, and fix unexpected problems that might arise? Answering these questions early, possibly by involving the project stakeholders, is crucial to mitigate future problems.

In addition to having a long-term maintenance plan, you need to thoroughly document the system and its assumptions, to make sure that someone can take over and maintain it even if none of the original team members are still working on the project. Documenting this is not only useful for long-term maintenance: it also enables people to check that the implementation corresponds to the design, improving robustness and making it easier for new team members to quickly ramp up.

Finally, if your project is going to run many times over a long period, it is worth regularly revisiting the decisions that you made in the initial stages of the project. The data might have changed, some assumptions might no longer be true, or the relative importance of different use cases might have evolved. This makes it important to not only document which decisions you've taken (parameter choices, etc.), but also *why* you've taken them. This way, future maintainers can more easily know what might need to be revisited.

14.4.3 Implementing Differential Privacy

Similarly to cryptographic or other security-critical code, implementing differential privacy correctly is extremely difficult and error-prone. From floating-point subtleties to ill-formed inputs, from logic bugs to incorrect assumptions about the data, opportunities to introduce critical vulnerabilities are all too common. While Chapters 13 and 14 have, respectively, reviewed programming frameworks for differentially private data analysis and learning tasks, in this section, we outline how to avoid these pitfalls, and reduce the risk of having privacy-impacting bugs in your production pipeline.

Reusing or Contributing to Open-source Tools

The first mistake you can make is to write everything you need from scratch. A few organizations are building and publishing open-source libraries which you should use if you can [GHV21; Tea21b; Lab22]. They were written by experts, and some are already used for production use cases, so they have been more tested, peer-reviewed, and audited, than code you might write from scratch yourself.

Existing libraries typically operate at two different levels. Low-level primitives provide basic functionality like noise addition or common operations, and typically make assumptions about the data (e.g. a median algorithm that assumes that all elements come from distinct individuals). End-to-end libraries, by contrast, provide clear privacy guarantees as part of their interface, and avoid making many assumptions about the input data.

Whenever possible, you should use end-to-end tools: relying on fewer assumptions, and writing fewer code yourself, will lead to more robust software. Sometimes, you might think that the end-to-end tool cannot work for your use case, but it is worth double-checking: it might be possible to express your algorithm in a way that accommodates an existing tool, for example using pre-processing and post-processing. You can also contact the authors of existing tools to know if they would consider adding the feature you need to their software. If it is truly impossible, it is still worth using the lower-level libraries for more basic operations. Indeed, naively implementing even simple primitives like noise addition is likely to introduce vulnerabilities [Mir12], and fixing those is far from trivial. Don't reinvent the wheel if you can avoid it!

If you do not find the functionality you need, consider extending an existing open-source project rather than building something entirely on your own. Doing so has multiple advantages. Obviously, it allows other people to reuse your work, benefiting the entire community. In addition, existing maintainers might give you design guidance, and review your code, which also will lead to robustness improvements. Reach out to them as early as possible, so that you can get early feedback, and ensure that your proposed contributions fit the project goals and guidelines.

Robustness and Testing

Nobody can write bug-free software. The best you can do is use best practices to reduce the likelihood of introducing an issue impacting your system's privacy guarantees. Two such best practices are code reviewing and unit testing: all code that ends up in production should be reviewed by at least one person, and all logical branches should be covered by unit tests. Both steps are good opportunities to not only check that the implementation matches the design manually, but also to look for edge cases that might introduce vulnerabilities: extremely small or large floating-point values (both in parameters and in the data), missing/null values, NaN and infinity values, possible divisions by zero, integer overflows or underflows, rounding problems, hidden assumptions, etc.

For typical programs, unit testing checks that running a function on a given input returns the expected output. Of course, for code implementing differential privacy, the situation is more complicated: the core logic is randomized, so the output will differ between runs. The parts of the code that are not randomized can be tested as normal, but how to test the randomized logic? Multiple complementary approaches exist to tackle this problem.

- You can get rid of some of the randomness for testing purposes. This can be done e.g. by using extremely large privacy parameters which will result in no noise being added to the data. Alternatively, you can add flags to your software to use seeded random number generation, or skip the randomization entirely. If you do so, though, you must be careful not to allow regular users to use this functionality in production.
- Rather than checking that the output is exactly as expected, one can check that it lies between large bounds, calculated so that if the algorithm is correct, the output is almost certainly between these bounds.
- To test the DP property itself, which is a crucial part of ensuring the robustness of the implementation, multiple approaches can be taken; the simplest is to generate many samples, and check that the obtained distributions satisfy the expected closeness property [Bic+18; Din+18; Wil+19].

Finally, remember that the number of bugs in a program is generally proportional to its size and complexity. When making design or implementation decisions, you should consider simplicity as a feature, and try hard to keep the software as simple and understandable as possible, even it it comes at a small performance or utility cost.

Validation

How can you make sure that your system keeps behaving in a reasonable and predictable way over time? For pipelines that are run at regular intervals on newer data, significant changes are likely to happen at some point, so the input data might no longer match what is expected. Validating the input and output data is a good practice for any software engineering project, but is especially important for differentially private pipelines.

First, what happens if the schema changes? Don't wait to find out the hard way. Instead, implement input validation: before using the algorithm on the data, an initial stage should verify that the schema and data formatting conforms to the expectations, and fail gracefully if it doesn't. Second, what other assumptions did you make on the data, and what happens if they stop being true? The best way to deal with this potential issue is to turn assumptions into into properties of the data that are enforced as part of your pipeline. For example, rather than assuming the input data will always be between certain bounds, clamp all inputs to these bounds. Rather than assuming that each individual contributes fewer than k records, add logic to sample at most k records per person.

These input validation techniques are important, but they might not enough. Even software written according to best practices and run on well-formed data might sometimes fail in unexpected ways. How to make sure that your system never publishes wrong or nonsensical data? To protect against the unexpected, it is also a good practice to add soundness checks: logic that verifies that the output conforms to the expected format, has the expected size, and that the values are not completely off. When these soundness checks fail, hold off on data publication entirely until you debugged and fixed the issue, rather than publishing the portion of the data that looks good.

Even with soundness checks, mistakes can happen, and you might be forced to republish some data for which the initial publication was wrong in some subtle way. This will increase the total privacy budget cost, so it might be a good idea to save a portion of the privacy budget to correct possible future mistakes. There are also some techniques to minimize the privacy budget cost of such changes, for example the scaling factors method used in [Akt+20].

14.5 Algorithmic Tuning

So, you implemented the differentially private mechanism you had in mind, and the results are nowhere near your goals. The evaluation metrics show that the data isn't reliable enough for your stakeholders to feel safe using them. What next? Do not panic: this is a very common phenomenon. You simply reached an essential stage of the process of deploying differential privacy in practice: tuning.

This section outlines multiple approaches you can take to improve the utility of your data. We list them in the order that we recommend you follow when you need to improve your algorithm. First, start with the simplest approach: tweaking the parameters of your approach. This typically does not require too much work, and can lead to surprisingly large utility gains. Second, if this is not enough, try changing your approach. This can mean including more subtle optimizations in your pipeline, or exploring other kinds of algorithms altogether. Finally, if all else fails, you will likely need to revisit the problem definition entirely. This requires more collaboration with your stakeholders, but can unblock seemingly hopeless situations.

14.5.1 Tweak Parameters

Any differential privacy algorithm comes with parameters that you can tweak to optimize data utility. The overall privacy budget is obviously one of them, but is often not the only option at your disposal. For every configuration parameter that your algorithm uses, run experiments to see if changing its value leads to utility gains. Having a robust experiment harness and evaluation pipeline helps a lot in this process: the more you automate this process, the more efficiently you can explore the space of possible parameters.

This general approach applies to all kinds of parameters, but let us highlight specific examples, which we found to be particularly useful in practice.

Sampling Rates and Clamping Bounds

Differential privacy mechanisms are built on algorithms with bounded sensitivity: a single individual must contribute a bounded number of records, and each numerical value must be within a fixed range. The larger these values are, the more noise needs to be added to hide every individual's contribution.

It is tempting to use large values for these parameters. Dropping contributions or clamping outlier values erases some of your original data: it feels wrong, and might add significant bias in your data. This intuition is true in principle, but is still worth examining and quantifying. Does subsampling actually create bias, or is the effect virtually invisible? How much bias does clamping actually create, and can it be predicted or even corrected using post-processing? Can clamping outlier values be a desirable thing for data quality? Can bias be an acceptable trade-off to make in exchange for more accuracy? Surface these questions to your stakeholders, and use your evaluation metrics to convey trade-offs and outline possible options.

Privacy Budget Allocation

Complex mechanisms often require adding noise to distinct steps or queries, and the total privacy budget must be split across these. Changing the way you allocate the privacy budget can be valuable. For example, you can reduce the budget used for coarser aggregations, or queries that are less critical to the use cases of your stakeholders, and use the leftover budget to improve the accuracy of other queries. Again, this is an opportunity to ask data users for feedback about the relative priority of different use cases, and take it into account in your strategy.

Total Privacy Budget

Increasing the total privacy cost of your mechanism is an obvious way to boost utility. It is a good idea to keep this as a last resort in the parameter tweaking stage: this encourages you to find the optimal solution given a specific privacy budget, and you will end up with better privacy/utility trade-offs. Often, the gains obtained by increasing the privacy budget are somewhat underwhelming: a linear increase in the ε corresponds to an exponential degradation of privacy guarantees, but almost never an exponential improvement in utility. Nonetheless, giving your stakeholders information about what is feasible using different privacy budgets is part of your responsibilities.

This stage is also a good opportunity to check whether you could optimize the privacy budget accounting with minimal changes your algorithm. Using advanced composition theorems [KOV15], alternative definitions [Mir17; BS16], or privacy accounting software [Tea21a; WBZM21], might lead to significant gains. Changing some small details about the algorithm, like switching from Laplace noise to Gaussian noise, can greatly boost the impact of these advanced privacy accounting techniques.

How much should you feel comfortable increasing the total privacy budget? It depends on multiple factors: some of them are unsurprising, like the sensitivity of the input data, the level of exposure of the output data, or the potential risks for the people in the data. But the technical properties of your algorithm are also important. Differential privacy provides a lower bound on the level of privacy in the absolute worst case. In complex algorithms like training machine learning models, this lower bound might be a very pessimistic estimate. Many such mechanisms do not have a tight privacy analysis, or incorporate some other sources of uncertainty that are not taken into account in the privacy accounting. In this case, it might be worth complementing formal guarantees having large ε values with ad hoc, attack-based measures of privacy leakage. This is discussed in more detail in Chapters 5 and 16.

14.5.2 Change Your Approach

Tweaking parameters might not be enough to find a strategy that is acceptable for both utility and privacy. When this happens, it is the sign that you need to implement additional optimizations, or find an alternative approach entirely. Listing all possible approaches for given problems is beyond the scope of this book; instead, you can try reviewing the scientific literature, or asking other differential privacy experts. In this section, we focus on general principles of certain classes of optimizations, and smaller changes that can be implemented without replacing the entire approach.

Post-processing and Bias

Some differential privacy mechanisms rely on making noisy measurements, and then post-processing them to improve the utility or usability of the data [Abo+22].

If you are not doing any post-processing, it is worth checking whether you could. Additional constraints might exist in your data, and when you know about them, you can use them to correct the numbers and improve the overall accuracy without additional privacy cost. This happens with hierarchical categories: for example, when counts are released at multiple geographic levels or time periods, some counts must sum up to others along the hierarchy. This can also happen between features: for example, a feature corresponding to total income might be the sum of other features like wage, capital gains, and other income.

Another kind of post-processing uses publicly available facts about the output space. For example, with mobility data, you might know that the travel time between two neighborhoods is bounded between loose approximations of the minimum and maximum travel time. These kind of rules let you eliminate nonsensical query outcomes that the noise addition might create, and this can be a significant boost to accuracy. Having a solid understanding of your data, and a good working relationship with your internal stakeholders, is invaluable during this process.

Sometimes, the opposite is true. Post-processing might seem like an obvious good idea to make the results look better: for example, it is common to make sure that all noisy numbers are nonnegative by clamping them to 0 if they are negative. This makes sense, but can also create significant bias, especially if many of the original numbers are low [TFVY21; ZHF21; ZFH22]. For some statistical applications, getting rid of this post-processing, or releasing the data both before and after post-processing, can be the right choice. Furthermore, it you use other kinds of hard constraints to post-process your data, double-check that these assumptions do hold in the original data: you do not want the data to be "too clean" and introduce additional bias.

Using Hard Constraints

Post-processing is not the only way you can incorporate knowledge of hard constraints into your strategy. Modifying the strategy itself to avoid nonsensical outputs, rather than removing these outputs as post-processing, can often be equally or more efficient.

One way to put this idea in application is to avoid running certain queries for some records, and save privacy budget using parallel composition. For example, children cannot have college degrees or income: records below a certain age can be allocated more budget for other statistics, and skip over these irrelevant queries entirely.

Another way is to modify the queries to reflect these hard constraints. Consider, for example, mobility data containing the departure and arrival times of individual trips. Adding noise to aggregated departure and arrival times will likely lead to a situation where some departure times end up being later than arrival times, which is nonsensical. Instead, adding noise to departure time and to total trip duration will likely avoid this issue, leading to higher-quality data without post-processing.

Using Correlations

Hard rules and constraints that your data must satisfy are not the only kind of knowledge that you can use. Correlations in your data can also often be leveraged to improve the utility of your mechanism. These correlations can be either between features, or between individuals.

Knowing that pairs of features are heavily correlated might allow you to estimate more complex correlation relationships at a low privacy cost. Consider a data set with four features A, B, C, and D. If feature B is heavily correlated with feature C, then it might be beneficial to create a compound feature $B+C$, and query both the $(A, B+C)$ marginal and the $(B+C, D)$ marginal might be the best way to capture the 4-way marginal (A, B, C, D). More generally, knowing correlations between features of your data is a good way to detect which queries might be redundant, and can be removed or replaced to save privacy budget.

Correlations can also come from recurring patterns in the data: in temporal data, for example, the data might almost repeat itself every day, or every week. You can use this to smooth the data across days or weeks, and boost overall accuracy. Sometimes, recurring patterns are only present in part of the data: in mobility data, days from Monday to Thursday can look like each other, but weekends might see a lot of variation, e.g. depending on the weather. In that case, adapting privacy budget allocation or parallel partitioning to the day of the week might lead to accuracy gains.

Pre-processing

In some cases, pre-processing the data can also be helpful. This needs to be done carefully, of course: unlike post-processing, changing the data before applying a differentially private algorithm can change the sensitivity of the aggregations, and thus, have an impact on the privacy guarantees.

One form of pre-processing is feature grouping: the idea is to concatenate multiple categorical features together into a larger categorical feature. Changing the schema this way can reduce the number of queries and shrink the data space, without changing the underlying problem definition. It is particularly useful when many features are binary: rather than calculating each pair of marginals between binary values, you can generate a single histogram combining all possible combinations. Often, during this process, you will find that some combinations of values are impossible and can be omitted, providing an additional accuracy boost.

Another useful pre-processing technique is reweighting. When each record contributes to arbitrarily many records, one common option to limit the sensitivity is to subsample the data, to make sure that each record can only contribute to a fixed number of records. An alternative option is to weigh each contribution according to how many records are contributed to the same user: for example, if a user contributes a single record, it would count for 10 times more than contributions of a user with 10 records.

14.5.3 Change the Problem Definition

Sometimes, no matter how hard you try, you simply cannot reach an acceptable level of privacy and utility. The situation might seem hopeless, but one important option might still be open: revisiting the original problem statement.

It is typical for first attempts at generating differentially private data to mirror the original data publication strategy, and release the same set of statistics, only in a noisy way. This often leads to poor utility, especially in cases where each original query aggregates data in a fine-grained way, or where many queries are published. The problem is also common when the original data is high-dimensional or sparse.

Coarsening the aggregations is a good first step: if you increase the number of people in each individual statistic, it will reduce the relative impact of the noise. You can do this in multiple ways: group together individual age values into age ranges, calculate statistics over larger geographies or longer time periods, or generate statistics for individual dimensions rather than for the combination of many features. An middle ground option is to use adaptive algorithms, which select the level of granularity based on the sparsity of the data in different parts of the input space.

Minimizing the number of aggregations can also be a simple way of improving utility: the fewer queries you run on your data, the less you have to split the total privacy budget. Removing less important queries or dimensions might make the rest much more tractable.

Since these techniques will modify the schema of the output data, you cannot make these decisions on your own. You need to go back to your stakeholders, and negotiate your proposed changes to the problem definition. In these discussions, focus on use cases: what will the data be used for, and why does it need a given level of granularity, or a given statistic? Do so with empathy, listen to the needs of your stakeholders, and use initial evaluation metrics to convey the possible gains brought by changing the problem definition.

14.6 Concluding Remarks

The final and perhaps most important rule of the tuning process is to keep an open mind.

A lot of the features of real world problems remain to be explored formally. If your previous experience with differential privacy primarily comes from using simple error metrics on randomized or artificially generated data, you might have a lot of assumptions and expectations that won't apply to your concrete problem. Some things you expect to succeed will fail, and some fundamental performance limitations you believed held can actually be overcome. If you make sure your evaluation metrics are thorough, your engagement with your stakeholders is healthy and productive, and you foster creativity and persistence in the team experimenting with various approaches, you might be surprised by what you will find!

References

[Abo+22] J. Abowd, R. Ashmead, R. Cumings-Menon, S. Garfinkel, M. Heineck, C. Heiss, R. Johns, D. Kifer, P. Leclerc, A. Machanavajjhala, B. Moran, W. Sexton, M. Spence, and P. Zhuravlev. "The 2020 Census Disclosure Avoidance System TopDown Algorithm". In: Harvard Data Science Review Special Issue 2 (June 2022). https://hdsr.mitpress.mit.edu/pub/7evz361i (cit. on p. 493).

[Akt+20] A. Aktay, S. Bavadekar, G. Cossoul, J. Davis, D. Desfontaines, A. Fabrikant, E. Gabrilovich, K. Gadepalli, B. Gipson, M. Guevara, et al. "Google COVID-19 Community Mobility Reports: anonymization process description (version 1.1)". In: arXiv preprint arXiv:2004.04145 (2020) (cit. on p. 490).

[Bic+18] B. Bichsel, T. Gehr, D. Drachsler-Cohen, P. Tsankov, and M. Vechev. "Dp-finder: Finding differential privacy violations by sampling and optimization". In: Proceedings of the 2018 ACM SIGSAC Conference on Computer and Communications Security. 2018, pp. 508–524 (cit. on p. 489).

[BS16] M. Bun and T. Steinke. "Concentrated differential privacy: Simplifications, extensions, and lower bounds". In: Theory of Cryptography Conference. Springer. 2016, pp. 635–658. URL: https://arxiv.org/abs/1605.02065 (cit. on p. 492).

[Des21] D. Desfontaines. A list of real-world uses of differential privacy. https://desfontain.es/blog/real-world-differential-privacy.html. Ted is writing things (personal blog). Oct. 2021 (cit. on p. 474).

[Din+18] Z. Ding, Y. Wang, G. Wang, D. Zhang, and D. Kifer. "Detecting violations of differential privacy". In: Proceedings of the 2018 ACM SIGSAC Conference on Computer and Communications Security. 2018, pp. 475–489 (cit. on p. 489).

[FTHZ22] F. Fioretto, C. Tran, P. V. Hentenryck, and K. Zhu. "Differential Privacy and Fairness in Decisions and Learning Tasks: A Survey". In: International Joint Conference on Artificial Intelligence. ijcai.org, 2022, pp. 5470–5477. URL: https://doi.org/10.24963/ijcai.2022/766 (cit. on p. 478).

[GHV21] M. Gaboardi, M. Hay, and S. Vadhan. A Programming Framework for OpenDP. https://opendp.org/. Accessed: 2021-10-12. 2021 (cit. on p. 488).

[KOV15] P. Kairouz, S. Oh, and P. Viswanath. "The composition theorem for differential privacy". In: International conference on machine learning. PMLR. 2015, pp. 1376–1385 (cit. on p. 492).

[Lab22] T. Labs. Tumult Analytics. Version latest. Dec. 2022. URL: https://tmlt.dev (cit. on p. 488).

[Mir12] I. Mironov. "On significance of the least significant bits for differential privacy". In: Proceedings of the 2012 ACM conference on Computer and communications security. 2012, pp. 650–661 (cit. on p. 488).

[Mir17] I. Mironov. "Rényi differential privacy". In: 2017 IEEE 30th computer security foundations symposium (CSF). IEEE. 2017, pp. 263–275 (cit. on p. 492).

[NIS20] NIST. NIST 2020 Differential Privacy Temporal Map Challenge. Online https://www.nist.gov/ctl/pscr/open-innovation-prize-challenges/current-and-upcoming-prize-challenges/2020-differential. Accessed: 2021-10-11. 2020 (cit. on p. 481).

[Now+20] B. Nowok, G. M. Raab, C. Dibben, J. Snoke, and C. van Lissa. Generating Synthetic Versions of Sensitive Microdata for Statistical Disclosure Control. Online https://cran.r-project.org/package=synthpop. Accessed: 2021-10-11. 2020 (cit. on p. 482).

[RHD19] L. Rocher, J. M. Hendrickx, and Y.-A. De Montjoye. "Estimating the success of re-identifications in incomplete datasets using generative models". In: Nature communications 10.1 (2019), pp. 1–9 (cit. on p. 484).

[Tea21a] G. D. P. Team. dp-accounting – PyPI. https://pypi.org/project/dp-accounting/. Accessed: 2021-10-13. 2021 (cit. on p. 492).

[Tea21b] G. D. P. Team. Google's differential privacy libraries. https://github.com/google/differential-privacy. Accessed: 2021-10-12. 2021 (cit. on p. 488).

[TFVY21] C. Tran, F. Fioretto, P. Van Hentenryck, and Z. Yao. "Decision Making with Differential Privacy under a Fairness Lens". In: International Joint Conference on Artificial Intelligence. ijcai.org, 2021, pp. 560–566. URL: https://doi.org/10.24963/ijcai.2021/78 (cit. on p. 493).

[US 21] US Census Bureau. American Community Survey. Online https://www.census.gov/programs-surveys/acs. Accessed: 2021-10-12. 2021 (cit. on p. 484).

[WBZM21] Y.-X. Wang, B. Balle, Y. Zhu, and S. Mellem. autodp. https://github.com/yuxiangw/autodp. Accessed: 2021-10-13. 2021 (cit. on p. 492).

[Wil+19] R. J. Wilson, C. Y. Zhang, W. Lam, D. Desfontaines, D. Simmons-Marengo, and B. Gipson. "Differentially private sql with bounded user contribution". In: arXiv preprint arXiv:1909.01917 (2019) (cit. on p. 489).

[WMW20] T. Winters, T. Manshreck, and H. Wright. Software engineering at google: Lessons learned from programming over time. O'Reilly Media, 2020 (cit. on p. 485).

[ZFH22] K. Zhu, F. Fioretto, and P. V. Hentenryck. "Post-processing of Differentially Private Data: A Fairness Perspective". In: International Joint Conference on Artificial Intelligence. ijcai.org, 2022, pp. 4029–4035. URL: https://doi.org/10.24963/ijcai.2022/559 (cit. on p. 493).

[ZHF21] K. Zhu, P. V. Hentenryck, and F. Fioretto. "Bias and Variance of Post-processing in Differential Privacy". In: AAAI Conference on Artificial Intelligence. AAAI Press, 2021, pp. 11177–11184. URL: https://ojs.aaai.org/index.php/AAAI/article/view/17333 (cit. on p. 493).

DOI: 10.1561/9781638284772.ch15

Chapter 15

Testing Private Models

By Giovanni Cherubin, Konstantinos Chatzikokolakis and Catuscia Palamidessi

15.1 Introduction

Measuring the information leakage of a system is one of the founding pillars of security and privacy: quantifying how much sensitive information is leaked is crucial for the development of leakage-preventing methods that can be proved reliable in a strong mathematical sense. Therefore, establishing good measures of leakage and techniques to perform the measurement has been the focus of intensive research efforts in the areas of privacy and of quantitative information flow (QIF).

Until a decade ago, the most popular measure of leakage was Shannon mutual information (MI). However, in his seminal paper, [Smi09] showed that MI is not appropriate to represent a realistic attacker, and proposed a notion of leakage based on *Rényi min-entropy* (ME) instead. Meanwhile, [DMNS06] introduced the notion of *differential privacy*, which has become extremely popular. As we will see in Section 15.4, these two notions are related: Rényi min-entropy is (the logarithm of) the converse of the Bayes risk, and differential privacy has a Bayesian interpretation. Consequently, in this chapter we consider the general problem of estimating the Bayes risk of a system. We recall that the Bayes risk is the smallest error achievable by an adversary at predicting its inputs (secret information) given the outputs (observables). From the Bayes risk one can derive several leakage measures, including ME and the additive and multiplicative leakage [BCP09].

Most approaches in the literature are based on the white-box approach, which consists in calculating analytically the channel matrix of the system or privacy mechanism, constituted by the conditional probabilities of the outputs given the secrets, and then computing the desired leakage measures. For instance, the maximal log-likelihood ratio of differential privacy [DMNS06], mutual information [CHM05], min-entropy leakage [Smi09], and g-leakage [ACPS12]. However, while one typically has white-box access to the system they want to secure, determining a system's leakage analytically is often impractical, due to the size or complexity of its internals, or to the presence of unknown factors. These obstacles led to investigate methods for measuring a system's leakage in a black-box manner.

[CCG10] was the first work to propose a black-box approach, based on a *frequentist* paradigm. The idea is to run the system repeatedly on chosen inputs, and then count the relative frequencies of the inputs and respective outputs, so to estimate their joint probability distribution; from this distribution, it is then possible to compute estimates of the desired leakage measure. leakiEst [CG11; CKN13] and LeakWatch [CKN14; CKNP13] are applications of this principle.

Unfortunately, the frequentist approach does not always scale for real-world problems: as the number of possible input and output values of the channel matrix increases, the number of examples required for this method to converge becomes too large to gather. For example, LeakWatch requires a number of examples that is much larger than the product of the size of input and output space. For the same reason, this method cannot be used for systems with continuous outputs (unless we make strong assumptions about the output distribution).

Recently a more powerful and scalable approach was proposed, based on machine learning (ML). The idea is that the attack can be simulated by an ML classifier, that predicts the secret (label) from the observables (features). The accuracy of the model gives therefore an approximation of (the converse of) the Bayes risk, approximation that becomes more precise as the model approaches the ideal Bayes classifier. The *universally consistent* ML rules, that produce models converging to the Bayes classifier (as the size of the training set increases), can therefore be used to estimate with arbitrary precision the leakage of a system. The seminal work that introduced this principle, for estimating the Bayes risk of a traffic analysis adversary, was [Che17]. Subsequently, [CCP19] made more explicit the connections and applications of ML for leakage estimation in the context of QIF and differential privacy. These papers used the universally consistent Nearest Neighbor (NN) and k_n-NN rules. Afterwards, [RCPP20] investigated the application of this principle to estimate a more general notion of leakage (the g-leakage of [ACPS12]) using Neural Networks, which are also universally consistent.

In this chapter we focus on the nearest neighbor methods, because: (a) they are simple to reason about, and (b) we can identify the class of systems for which they will excel, which happens whenever the distribution is smooth with respect to a metric on the output, in the sense that it does not change too abruptly between two neighboring points. This is the case, for example, for time side channels, traffic analysis, and most mechanisms used for privacy.

In Sections 15.6 and 15.7 we provide a comparison of the nearest neighbors methods and of leakiEst. Most of the results are from [CCP19]: We show the evaluation of these estimators on synthetic data, where we know the true distributions and we can determine exactly when the estimates converge. Furthermore, we show the evaluation in a real dataset of users' locations (Gowalla, [CML11]), defended with three state-of-the-art privacy mechanisms: two geo-indistinguishability mechanisms (planar geometric and planar Laplace) [ABCP13], and the method by [OTP17], which we refer to as the Blahut-Arimoto mechanism. Note that geo-indistinguishability is an instance of d-privacy [CABP13], which is a local variant of differential privacy suited for metric domains. Crucially, the planar Laplace is real-valued, which k_n-NN methods can tackle out-of-the box, but the frequentist method cannot. The results confirm the intuition that the nearest neighbor methods give a strong advantage whenever there is a notion of metric in the output domain and the output distribution is smooth with respect to this metric.

The computations have been made via the tool F-BLEAU (Fast Black-box Leakage Estimation AUtomated), available at the URL https://github.com/gchers/fbleau.

15.2 Related Work

The most closely related works have been already discussed in the introduction. Here we discuss briefly some alternative approaches.

15.2.1 Auditing Differential Privacy in a Black-box Fashion

A recent line of research has proposed empirical methods for verifying whether a mechanism has a claimed level of differential privacy. The main idea is to use automated tools for finding witness inputs to the channel that give a lower bound on its true level of differential privacy.

DP-Sniper [BSBV21] trains a classifier to predict how likely an observed output was generated from one of two possible inputs, and then transforms this classifier into an attack, thus obtaining a lover bound on the degree of differential privacy. DP-Finder [Bic+18] samples the output, and then maximizes the likelihood ratio using gradient descent on the pair of candidate inputs. This requires differentiability of the noise generation, which is only possible for a limited class of mechanisms. For example, DP-Finder does not support arbitrary loops or hash functions such as those used in RAPPOR [EPK14]. StatDP [Din+18] tries to find a witness (pairs of inputs, output) for a fixed candidate likelihood ratio and reports a failure if it does not find such a witness.

15.2.2 Alternative Information-theoretic Measures for QIF and Differential Privacy

Shannon mutual information (MI) is the main alternative to the Bayes risk-based notions of leakage in the QIF literature. Although there is a relation between MI and Bayes risk [SV06], the corresponding models of attackers are very different: the first corresponds to an attacker who can try infinitely many times to guess the secret, while the second has only one try at his disposal [Smi09]. Consequently, MI and Bayes-risk measures, such as ME, can give very different results: [Smi09] shows two programs that have almost the same MI, but one has an ME several orders of magnitude larger than the other one; conversely, there are examples of two programs such that ME is 0 for both, while the MI is 0 in one case and strictly positive (several bits) in the other one.

There are various proposal for the black-box estimation of MI. For instance, leakiEst and LeakWatch use Kernel Density Estimation, which guarantees some degree of precision under smoothness assumptions on the distributions. On the other hand, the ML literature offered developments in this area: [Bel+18] proposed an MI lower bound estimator based on deep neural networks, and proved its consistency (i.e., it converges to the true MI value asymptotically). Similarly, other works constructed MI variational lower bounds [Che+16; CSWJ18].

Mutual information has also been used in the context of differential privacy. One of the most interesting works in this line of research was by [CY16]. They gave an equivalent definition of privacy using MI that reveal some of the subtleties of differential privacy. In contrast to previous works using unconditional mutual information, their paper demonstrated that differential privacy is fundamentally related to conditional mutual information, accompanied by a maximization over the database distribution.

15.3 Preliminaries

We define a system, and show that its leakage can be expressed in terms of the Bayes risk. We then introduce ML notions, which we will later use to estimate the Bayes risk.

Table 15.1. Notation adopted in this chapter.

Symbol	Description
$s \in \mathbb{S}$	A secret
$o \in \mathbb{O}$	An object/black-box output
$(s, o) \in \mathbb{S} \times \mathbb{O}$	An example
$(\pi, C_{s,o})$	A system, given a set of priors π and channel matrix C
μ	Distribution induced by a system on $\mathbb{S} \times \mathbb{O}$
$f : \mathbb{S} \mapsto \mathbb{O}$	A classifier
ℓ	Loss function w.r.t. which we evaluate a classifier
R^f	The expected misclassification error of a classifier f
R^*	The Bayes risk

15.3.1 Notation

We consider a system $(\pi, C_{s,o})$, that associates a secret input s to an observation (or object) o in a possibly randomized way. The system is defined by a set of prior probabilities $\pi(s) := P(s)$, $s \in \mathbb{S}$, and a channel matrix C of size $|\mathbb{S}| \times |\mathbb{O}|$, for which $C_{s,o} := P(o|s)$ for $s \in \mathbb{S}$ and $o \in \mathbb{O}$. We call $\mathbb{S} \times \mathbb{O}$ the example space. We assume the system does not change over time; for us, $\mathbb{S}$ is finite, and $\mathbb{O}$ is finite unless otherwise stated.

15.3.2 Differential Privacy (DP)

Next we briefly recall the notion of *differential privacy*, reformulating it in our channel-matrix formalism. We give a general definition, which encompasses both the notions of standard (central) differential privacy [DMNS06; Dwo06], and *local differential privacy* [Kas+08], see also Chapters 1 and 2 for additional details on these paradigms. Consider a system that takes inputs from a set $\mathbb{S}$, endowed with a symmetric *adjacency relation* $\sim \subseteq \mathbb{S} \times \mathbb{S}$ representing which pairs of inputs should be considered (almost) "indistinguishable". We say that s and s' are *adjacent* if $s \sim s'$. Intuitively a system (or mechanism) that takes inputs from $\mathbb{S}$ is differentially-private if the probability of its producing any output given input $s \in \mathbb{S}$ is roughly the same as the probability of its producing the same output given any other input $s' \in \mathbb{S}$ adjacent to s. Using the channel notation to represent a system/mechanism, this intuition is formalized as follows.

Definition 15.1 (ε-differential privacy[i]). *Let* $\varepsilon \geq 0$ *and* $\sim \subseteq \mathbb{S} \times \mathbb{S}$ *be an adjacency relation on secrets. A channel* $C : \mathbb{S} \times \mathbb{O} \to [0, 1]$ *provides* ε-differential privacy *if*

i. The definition we give here is for a discrete output space. In the continuous case, o should be replaced by a measurable set.

for any pair of values s, s′ s.t. s ∼ s′, and for any output value $o \in \mathbb{O}$,

$$C_{s,o} \leq e^{\varepsilon} C_{s',o}. \tag{15.1}$$

Note that our definition of differential privacy is in line with the influential Pufferfish framework by [KM14], in which the input domain can be arbitrary, and the adjacency relation can be customized to explicitly define what is considered to be indistinguishable. Traditional differential privacy is a particular instantiation of this definition in which the input space consists of datasets, and the adjacency relation is defined to reflect the usual distinction between the presence or absence of any single individual in a dataset. In the case of local differential privacy, the input space are the values of the attributes for a single individual, and the adjacency relation is that in which any two distinct values are adjacent.

Next, we introduce the main leakage measure used in QIF. In Section 15.4 we will show how it relates to differential privacy.

15.3.3 Leakage Measures

The state-of-the-art in QIF is represented by the leakage measures based on *g-vulnerability*, a family whose most representative member is min-vulnerability [Smi09], the complement of the Bayes risk. This chapter is concerned with finding tight estimates of the Bayes risk, which can then be used to estimate the appropriate leakage measure.

Bayes Risk

The Bayes risk, R^*, is the error of the optimal (idealized) classifier for the task of predicting a secret s given an observation o output by a system. It is defined with respect to a loss function $\ell : \mathbb{S} \times \mathbb{S} \mapsto \mathbb{R}_{\geq 0}$, where $\ell(s, s')$ is the risk of an adversary predicting s' for an observation o, when its actual secret is s. We focus on the 0-1 loss function, $\ell(s, s') := I(s \neq s')$, taking value 1 if $s \neq s'$, 0 otherwise. The Bayes risk of a system $(\pi, C_{s,o})$ is defined as:

$$R^* := 1 - \sum_{o \in \mathbb{O}} \max_{s \in \mathbb{S}} C_{s,o} \pi(s). \tag{15.2}$$

Random Guessing

A baseline for evaluating a system is the error committed by an idealized adversary who knows priors but has no access to the channel, and who's best strategy is to always output the secret with the highest prior. We call the error of this adversary random guessing error:

$$R^{\pi} := 1 - \max_{s \in \mathbb{S}} \pi(s). \tag{15.3}$$

15.3.4 Black-box Estimation of R^*

This chapter is concerned with estimating the Bayes risk given n examples sampled from the joint distribution μ on $\mathbb{S} \times \mathbb{O}$ generated by $(\pi, C_{s,o})$. By running the system n times on secrets $s_1, \ldots, s_n \in \mathbb{S}$, chosen according to π, we generate a sequence of corresponding outputs $o_1, \ldots, o_n$, thus forming a *training set*[ii] of examples $\{(o_1, s_1), \ldots, (o_n, s_n)\}$. From these data, we aim to make an estimate close to the real Bayes risk.

15.3.5 Learning Rules

We introduce ML rules (or, simply, *learning rules*), which are algorithms for producing a classifier given a set of training examples. We will use the error of some ML rules as an estimator of the Bayes risk.

Let $\mathcal{F} := \{f \mid f : \mathbb{O} \mapsto \mathbb{S}\}$ be a set of classifiers. A learning rule is a possibly randomized algorithm that, given a training set $\{(o_1, s_1), \ldots, (o_n, s_n)\}$, returns a classifier $f \in \mathcal{F}$, with the goal of minimizing the expected loss $\mathbb{E}\,\ell(f(o), s)$ for a new example (o, s) sampled from μ [Vap13]. In the case of the 0-1 loss function, the expected loss coincides with the *expected probability of error* (*expected error* for short), and if μ is generated by a system $(\pi, C_{s,o})$, then the expected error of a classifier $f : \mathbb{O} \mapsto \mathbb{S}$ is:

$$R^f = 1 - \sum_{o \in \mathbb{O}} C_{f(o),o}\pi(f(o)), \tag{15.4}$$

where $f(o)$ is the secret predicted for object o. If $\mathbb{O}$ is infinite (and μ is continuous) the summation is replaced by an integral.

15.3.6 Frequentist Estimate of R^*

The frequentist paradigm [CCG10] for measuring the leakage of a channel consists in estimating the probabilities $C_{s,o}$ by counting their frequency in the training data $(o_1, s_1), \ldots, (o_n, s_n)$:

$$P(o|s) \approx \hat{C}_{s,o} := \frac{|i : o_i = o, s_i = s|}{|i : s_i = s|}. \tag{15.5}$$

We can obtain the frequentist error from Equation (15.4):

$$R^{\text{Freq}} = 1 - \sum_{o} C_{f^{\text{Freq}}(o),o}\, \pi(f^{\text{Freq}}(o)), \tag{15.6}$$

---

ii. In line with the ML literature, we call the training or test "set" what is technically a multiset; also, we loosely use the set notation "{}" for both sets and multisets when the nature of the object is clear from the context.

where f^{Freq} is the frequentist classifier, namely:

$$f^{\mathrm{Freq}}(o) = \begin{cases} \arg\max_s (\hat{C}_{s,o}\, \hat{\pi}(s)) & \text{if } o \text{ in training data} \\ \arg\max_s \hat{\pi}(s) & \text{otherwise}, \end{cases} \tag{15.7}$$

where $\hat{\pi}$ is estimated from the examples: $\hat{\pi}(s) = {|i:s_i=s|}/{n}$.

Consider a finite example space $\mathbb{S} \times \mathbb{O}$. Provided with enough examples, the frequentist approach always converges: clearly, $\hat{C} \to C$ as $n \to \infty$, because events' frequencies converge to their probabilities by the Law of Large Numbers.

However, there is a fundamental issue with this approach. Given a training set $\{(o_1, s_1), \ldots, (o_n, s_n)\}$, the frequentist classifier can tell something meaningful (i.e., better than random guessing) for an object $o \in \mathbb{O}$, only as long as o appeared in the training set; but, for very large systems (e.g., those with a large object space), the probability of observing an example for each object classifier approaches *random guessing*. We study this matter further in Section subsec:random-system.

15.4 Relation between Differential Privacy and Bayes Risk

In this section we present the result of [Alv+15], which consists in a correspondence between bounds to the Bayes risk and bounds to differential privacy. Before going into that, however, we want to give the reader an intuition of the basic reason why there is such a correspondence, which is the fact that differential privacy can be interpreted in terms of Bayesian inference. We will explain this interpretation in detail because, although it has been reported in a number of papers [Alv+15; BK11; CABP13; DMNS06; KM14], it is not too well-known in the privacy community.

Here we present two alternative versions of the Bayesian interpretation. In the following, we consider a mechanism (or channel) C with input domain $\mathbb{S}$, and output domain $\mathbb{O}$, and an adjacency relation $\sim$ on $\mathbb{S}$. We will use the probability notation (rather than the channel notation) because we need to consider various probabilities distributions. Also, we will use S and O to denote the random variables associated to the distributions on $\mathbb{S}$ and $\mathbb{O}$, respectively.

Note that, given a prior distribution π on inputs to the mechanism, we can derive a joint distribution $P_{S,O}$ on $\mathbb{S} \times \mathbb{O}$, defined as:

$$P_{S,O}(s, o) := \pi(s)\; C_{s,o}, \tag{15.8}$$

and from the joint we can derive the marginal distribution P_O, as well as the conditional distribution $P_{S|O}$ for non-zero-probability values of $o \in \mathbb{O}$. Note that $P_{S|O}(s \mid o)$ is the posterior probability of s given the evidence o, in contrast to $\pi(s)$

which is the prior probability of s. Furthermore we have that $P_{O|S}$ coincides with C, and P_S coincides with π. When clear from the context, we omit subscripts on probability distributions, writing, e.g., $P(o)$, $P(s, o)$, and $P(s \mid o)$ for $P_O(o)$, $P_{S,O}(s, o)$, and $P_{S|O}(s \mid o)$, respectively.

Using this notation, the ε-differential privacy property of Definition 15.1 can be rewritten as:

$$\frac{P(o \mid s)}{P(o \mid s')} \leq e^{\varepsilon}, \qquad \text{for all } o \in \mathbb{O},\ s, s' \in \mathbb{S} \ \text{ s.t. } \ s \sim s'. \tag{15.9}$$

15.4.1 Interpretation of Differential Privacy in Terms of Hypothesis Testing

A first interpretation presents differential privacy in terms of a bound on the adversary's success in performing hypothesis testing on the secret value [CABP13; KM14]. More precisely, it expresses the property that the adversary's a priori capability of distinguishing between two adjacent secrets (e.g., two neighboring datasets differing only by the presence/absence of a single individual) does not change significantly after an observation of the mechanism's output (e.g., the answer to a query in that dataset). This guarantee (which, of course, depends on the value of the parameter ε) holds for every prior–and that is the reason DP is said to be *independent from the adversary's knowledge*. Formally:

Proposition 15.2. *ε-differential privacy (cf. Equation (15.9)) is equivalent to the following property:*

$$\frac{P(s \mid o)}{P(s' \mid o)} \leq e^{\varepsilon}\, \frac{P(s)}{P(s')}, \qquad \textit{for all } o \in \mathbb{O},\ s, s' \in \mathbb{S} \ \textit{s.t.} \ s \sim s', \ \textit{and all priors } P(\cdot) \textit{ on } \mathbb{S}. \tag{15.10}$$

Proof. The proof of the equivalence of Equations (15.9) and (15.10) follows immediately by the Bayes Theorem, which is the following equality:

$$P(s \mid o) = \frac{P(o \mid s)\, P(s)}{P(o)}. \tag{15.11}$$

Hence, we have:

$$\frac{P(s \mid o)}{P(s' \mid o)} = \frac{P(o \mid s)\, P(s)}{P(o)} \; \frac{P(o)}{(o \mid s')\, P(s')} = \frac{P(o \mid s)}{P(o \mid s')} \; \frac{P(s')}{P(s)}. \tag{15.12}$$

□

Note that in Equation (15.10), the ratio $P(s)/P(s')$ represents the adversary's capability of distinguishing between adjacent secrets s and s' a priori (i.e., before the output of the mechanism is observed), whereas the *likelihood ratio* $P(s|o)/P(s'|o)$ represents his capability of distinguishing between the same adjacent secrets after an output o of the mechanism is observed. Because of the universal quantification on all adjacent secret inputs s, s', outputs o, and prior distribution $P(\cdot)$ on inputs, Equation (15.10) exactly states differential privacy's guarantees against maximum distinguishability of two secrets.

15.4.2 Interpretation of Differential Privacy as Bound on the Increase of the Attacker's Knowledge

A second interpretation presents differential privacy in terms of a bound on the adversary's increase in information about the secret value [Alv+15; BK11; DMNS06]. In this case, however, the exact formulation depends on the nature of the adjacency relation $\sim$. We present here the examples of local differential privacy [Kas+08], and of the standard differential privacy on datasets [Dwo06; DMNS06].

Local Differential Privacy

In local differential privacy, the relation $\sim$ holds between every any pair of secrets values s and s' such that $s \neq s'$. The Bayesian interpretation is expressed in terms of a lower and upper bound on the ratio between the prior and posterior probabilistic knowledge of the secret:

$$e^{-\alpha} \leq \frac{P(s \mid o)}{P(s)} \leq e^{\alpha} \qquad \text{for all } o{\in}\mathbb{O},\ s{\in}\mathbb{S}, \text{ and all priors } P(\cdot) \text{ on } \mathbb{S}\,, \tag{15.13}$$

where α is a non-negative real number. Again, the fact that the prior is quantified universally means that this property does not depend on the prior knowledge of the adversary.

We now state precisely and prove the correspondence between DP and this Bayesian formulation.

Theorem 15.3. *Given a mechanism C:*

1. *If C satisfies inequality* (15.9), *then it satisfies inequality* (15.13) *with $\alpha = \varepsilon$.*
2. *If C satisfies inequality* (15.13), *then it satisfies inequality* (15.9) *with $\varepsilon = 2\,\alpha$.*

Proof. 1. Assume that (15.9) is satisfied. Then:

$$\frac{P(s \mid o)}{P(s)} = \frac{P(o \mid s)}{P(o)} \qquad \text{(by the Bayes theorem)}$$

$$
\begin{aligned}
&= \frac{P(o \mid s)}{\sum_{x \in \mathbb{S}} P(o, x)} && \text{(marginals)} \\
&= \frac{P(o \mid s)}{\sum_{x \in \mathbb{S}} P(o \mid x)\, P(x)} && \text{(chain rule)} \\
&\leq \frac{P(o \mid s)}{\sum_{x \in \mathbb{S}} e^{-\varepsilon} P(o \mid s)\, P(x)} && \text{(by (15.9))} \\
&= \frac{P(o \mid s)}{e^{-\varepsilon} P(o \mid s)} \\
&= e^{\varepsilon}.
\end{aligned}
$$

2. Assume that (15.13) is satisfied. Then:

$$
\begin{aligned}
\frac{P(o \mid s)}{P(o \mid s')} &= \frac{P(s \mid o)\, P(o)}{P(s)} \frac{P(s')}{P(s' \mid o) P(o)} && \text{(by the Bayes theorem)} \\
&= \frac{P(s \mid o)}{P(s)} \frac{P(s')}{P(s' \mid o)} \\
&\leq e^{\alpha}\, e^{\alpha} && \text{(by (15.13))} \\
&= e^{2\,\alpha}.
\end{aligned}
$$

□

Standard Differential Privacy on Datasets

Standard differential privacy is also called, nowadays, differential privacy in the central model. In this case, the relation $\sim$ holds between every two datasets that differ for the presence or absence of a single record. We will indicate by s the presence of the target record and by $\neg s$ its absence. We will indicate by d the rest of the dataset. By using this notation, the differential privacy property can be rewritten as:

$$
e^{-\varepsilon} \leq \frac{P(o \mid s, d)}{P(o \mid \neg s, d)} \leq e^{\varepsilon} \qquad \text{for all } o \in \mathbb{O}, s \in \mathbb{S}, \text{ and datasets } d\,. \tag{15.14}
$$

The Bayesian formulation is expressed by the following bounds, for some real number $\alpha \geq 0$:

$$
e^{-\alpha} \leq \frac{P(s \mid o, d)}{P(s \mid d)} \leq e^{\alpha} \qquad \text{for all } o \in \mathbb{O}, s \in \mathbb{S}, \text{ datasets } d, \text{ and all priors } P(\cdot) \text{ on } \mathbb{S}\,. \tag{15.15}
$$

and

$$e^{-\alpha} \leq \frac{P(\neg s \mid o, d)}{P(\neg s \mid d)} \leq e^{\alpha} \quad \text{for all } o \in \mathbb{O}, s \in \mathbb{S}, \text{ datasets } d, \text{ and all priors } P(\cdot) \text{ on } \mathbb{S}. \tag{15.16}$$

These inequality (15.15) and (15.16) mean that the prior and posterior probabilities (given the knowledge of the rest of the dataset[iii]) of the presence/absence of the target record do not differ too much. We now state precisely and prove the correspondence between DP and this Bayesian formulation.

Theorem 15.4. *Given a certain mechanism C:*

1. *If C satisfies inequality* (15.14), *then it satisfies inequalities* (15.15) *and* (15.16) *with* $\alpha = \varepsilon$.
2. *If C satisfies inequalities* (15.15) *and* (15.16), *then it satisfies inequality* (15.14) *with* $\varepsilon = 2\alpha$.

Proof. The proof is analogous to that of Theorem 15.3; we just need to add the conditioning on d on all probabilities measures. Furthermore, we need to use the fact that s and $\neg s$ are complementary events (also when conditioned on d), i.e., $P(s \mid d) + P(\neg s \mid d) = 1$. □

15.4.3 Bounds on Differential Privacy

In this section we show how to derive bounds on the level of differential privacy from bounds on the Bayes risk. We will use the results of [Alv+15], which establish a relation between the level of differential privacy of a mechanism C and and bounds on the ME (Rényi min-entropy leakage) induced by C.

Let us start with some terminology: for notational convenience we introduce the *minimum distinguishability level* of a mechanism C, denoted $MinDist(C)$, defined as follows:

$$MinDist(C) := \min\left\{\varepsilon \mid C_{s,o} \leq e^{\varepsilon}\, C_{s',o},\ s, s' \in \mathbb{S},\ s \sim s',\ o \in \mathbb{O}\right\}. \tag{15.17}$$

Obviously, we have that

$$MinDist(C) \leq \varepsilon \text{ if and only if } C \text{ is } \varepsilon\text{-differentially private.} \tag{15.18}$$

iii. The fact that the attacker knows the rest of the dataset is called *strong adversary assumption*. The Bayesian interpretation highlights that differential privacy makes this implicit assumption about the attacker.

Next, we recall the definition of Rényi min-entropy leakage [Smi09]. The Rényi min-entropy H_∞ is defined as follows:

$$\text{(Prior) Rényi min-entropy} \qquad H_\infty(S) := -\ln \max_{s\in\mathbb{S}} \pi(s) \tag{15.19}$$

$$\text{(Posterior) Rényi min-entropy} \qquad H_\infty(S \mid O) := -\ln \sum_{o\in\mathbb{O}} \max_{s\in\mathbb{S}}(\mathcal{C}_{s,o}\pi(s)), \tag{15.20}$$

where ln denotes the natural logarithm. The leakage for a mechanism C and a prior π, denoted by $\mathcal{L}_{C,\pi}$, is then defined as:

$$\begin{aligned} \mathcal{L}_{C,\pi} &:= H_\infty(S) - H_\infty(S \mid O) && (15.21) \\ &= \ln \frac{\sum_{o\in\mathbb{O}} \max_{s\in\mathbb{S}}(\mathcal{C}_{s,o}\pi(s))}{\max_{s\in\mathbb{S}} \pi(s)}. && (15.22) \end{aligned}$$

Note the correspondence with the Bayes risk (15.2): the random guessing risk (15.3)

$$\text{Bayes risk} \qquad R^* = 1 - e^{-H_\infty(S|O)} \tag{15.23}$$

$$\text{Random guessing risk} \qquad R^\pi = 1 - e^{-H_\infty(S)}. \tag{15.24}$$

It is also important to recall that the maximum leakage over all priors is given by the uniform prior $u(s) = 1/|\mathbb{S}|$ [BCP09], i.e.:

$$\max_\pi \mathcal{L}_{C,\pi} = \ln \mathcal{L}_{C,u} = \ln \frac{\sum_{o\in\mathbb{O}} \max_{s\in\mathbb{S}}(\mathcal{C}_{s,o}u(s)))}{\max_{s\in\mathbb{S}} u(s)} = \ln \sum_{o\in\mathbb{O}} \max_{s\in\mathbb{S}} \mathcal{C}_{s,o}. \tag{15.25}$$

Next, we note that $(\mathbb{S}, \sim)$ can be seen as an undirected graph, where the elements of $\mathbb{S}$ are the nodes and $s \sim s'$ represents an arc between s and s'. The distance between two secrets s and s' is the length of the minimum path between s and s'. We say that the graph $(\mathbb{S}, \sim)$ is vertex-transitive if for any pair s, s' there exists an automorphism σ such that $\sigma(s) = s'$. It is easy to see that, in a vertex-transitive graph, the cardinality of the set of nodes at distance d from a given node s is always the same independently from the choice of s. We will denote this number by n_d. The main result by [Alv+15] states an that differential privacy induces a bound from below on the posterior min-entropy. We reformulate it using our notation:

Theorem 15.5 (Theorem 12 in [Alv+15]). *If C is ε-differentially private, $(\mathbb{S}, \sim)$ is vertex-transitive, and the prior is uniform, then:*

$$H_\infty(S \mid O) \geq \ln \sum_d \frac{n_d}{e^{\varepsilon d}}. \tag{15.26}$$

We now show how this result applies to the particular cases of local differential privacy and of standard differential privacy on datasets.

Local Differential Privacy

From previous results we can obtain the following bound on the Bayes risk of a locally differentially private mechanism:

Theorem 15.6. *If C is a ε-locally differentially private mechanism, and the prior is uniform, then*

$$R^* \geq \frac{|\mathbb{S}| - 1}{e^{\varepsilon} + |\mathbb{S}| - 1}. \tag{15.27}$$

Proof. In the case of local differential privacy the graph $(\mathbb{S}, \sim)$ is a clique, namely there exists an arc between every pair of different nodes. It is easy to see that a clique is vertex-transitive. Furthermore the distance between s, s' is 0 if $s = s'$ and 1 otherwise. Hence:

$$n_d = \begin{cases} 1 & d = 0 \\ |\mathbb{S}| - 1 & d = 1 \end{cases} \tag{15.28}$$

Therefore, we have:

$$\begin{aligned}
R^* &= 1 - e^{-H_\infty(S|O)} && \text{(by (15.23))} && (15.29)\\
&\geq 1 - \frac{1}{\sum_d \frac{n_d}{e^{\varepsilon d}}} && \text{(by (15.26))} && (15.30)\\
&= 1 - \frac{1}{\frac{1}{e^{\varepsilon 0}} + \frac{|\mathbb{S}|-1}{e^{\varepsilon 1}}} && \text{(by (15.28))} && (15.31)\\
&= 1 - \frac{1}{1 + \frac{|\mathbb{S}|-1}{e^{\varepsilon}}} && && (15.32)\\
&= \frac{|\mathbb{S}| - 1}{e^{\varepsilon} + |\mathbb{S}| - 1}. && && (15.33)
\end{aligned}$$

□

Furthermore, we have that this bound is strict, namely there exist mechanisms C such that the inequality (15.27) is actually an equality. One such mechanism is the k-Randomized Response (k-RR) [KBR16], defined as the mechanism that returns the true s with probability $e^{\varepsilon}/e^{\varepsilon}+|\mathbb{S}|-1$, and returns any other s' with probability $1/e^{\varepsilon}+|\mathbb{S}|-1$, where ε is a parameter that regulates the level of privacy: k-RR with parameter ε, denoted as k-RR(ε), is ε-locally differentially private, and in fact ε is the minimum, i.e., MinDist(k-RR(ε)) $= \varepsilon$.

Proposition 15.7. *If C is the k-RR(ε) mechanism and the prior is uniform, then*

$$R^* = \frac{|\mathbb{S}| - 1}{e^{\mathcal{E}} + |\mathbb{S}| - 1}. \tag{15.34}$$

Proof.

$$\begin{aligned}
R^* &= 1 - e^{-H_\infty(S|O)} && \text{(by (15.23))} && (15.35)\\
&= 1 - e^{-u(s)\,\mathcal{L}_{C,u}} && \text{(by (15.21))} && (15.36)\\
&= 1 - \frac{1}{|\mathbb{S}|}\sum_{o\in\mathbb{O}} \max_{s\in\mathbb{S}} C_{s,o} && \text{(by (15.25))} && (15.37)\\
&= 1 - \frac{1}{|\mathbb{S}|}\sum_{s'\in\mathbb{S}} \max_{s\in\mathbb{S}} C_{s,s'} && (\mathbb{O} = \mathbb{S} \text{ in } k\text{-RR}) && (15.38)\\
&= 1 - \frac{1}{|\mathbb{S}|}\sum_{s'\in\mathbb{S}} \frac{e^{\mathcal{E}}}{e^{\mathcal{E}} + |\mathbb{S}| - 1} && \text{(by definition of } k\text{-RR)} && (15.39)\\
&= 1 - \frac{e^{\mathcal{E}}}{e^{\mathcal{E}} + |\mathbb{S}| - 1} && && (15.40)\\
&= \frac{|\mathbb{S}| - 1}{e^{\mathcal{E}} + |\mathbb{S}| - 1}. && && (15.41)
\end{aligned}$$

□

Theorem 15.6 allows to obtain a lower bound on differential privacy via an upper bound on the Bayes risk, which is in fact what we get with our machine learning method: our method provides an approximation from above of the Bayes classifier, (i.e., an upper bound) because the Bayes classifier is the optimal one: any other classifier has a higher risk.

Proposition 15.8 (Lower bound on local differential privacy). *Given a mechanism C, and uniform prior, we have:*

$$\text{if } R^* < b \text{ then } MinDist(C) > \ln\frac{(|\mathbb{S}| - 1)(1 - b)}{b}. \tag{15.42}$$

Proof. Assume, by contradiction, that $\text{MinDist}(C) \leq \ln\frac{(|\mathbb{S}|-1)(1-b)}{b}$. Then:

$$R^* \geq \frac{|\mathbb{S}| - 1}{\frac{(|\mathbb{S}|-1)(1-b)}{b} + |\mathbb{S}| - 1} \qquad \text{(by Theorem 15.6)} \tag{15.43}$$

$$= \frac{(|\mathbb{S}| - 1)\, b}{(|\mathbb{S}| - 1)(1 - b) + (|\mathbb{S}| - 1)\, b} \tag{15.44}$$

$$= b, \tag{15.45}$$

which contradicts the hypothesis that $R^* < b$. □

Proposition 15.8 provides a method to bound from below the ε-local differential privacy of a mechanism C: it is sufficient to generate a training set by applying C to a sequence of inputs sampled from the uniform distribution on $\mathbb{S}$, then construct a model f via machine learning, and measure its risk R^f, which is by definition an upper bound to R^* (i.e., set the b of Proposition 15.8 to be R^f). Note that, because of Proposition 15.7, the bound is strict, i.e., it is the best bound we can provide. The fact that by using an universally consistent rule we can approximate the Bayes risk arbitrarily well means that, at least for mechanisms for which Equation (15.34) holds, we can estimate the level of differential privacy at the desired level of precision.

We can also reverse the form of Proposition 15.8 to obtain a method to *audit* local differential privacy: to prove that C is not ε-locally differentially private, it is sufficient to construct a model f via machine learning as described above, and show that $R^f < \frac{|\mathbb{S}|-1}{e^{\varepsilon}+|\mathbb{S}|-1}$.

If we do not have any access to the mechanism C (so that we cannot generate the training set from the uniform prior) and we only have a collection of (*input*, *output*) pairs to form our training set (generated by applying the mechanism to existing data), then the following theorem allows us to still audit / derive a lower bound on ε-local differential privacy, at the price of estimating the prior distribution from the data.

Theorem 15.9. *Given a ε-locally differentially private mechanism C, and an arbitrary prior π, we have:*

$$R^* \geq 1 - (1 - R^{\pi}) \frac{|\mathbb{S}|\, e^{\varepsilon}}{e^{\varepsilon} + |\mathbb{S}| - 1}. \tag{15.46}$$

Proof. We start by observing that

$$\ln \frac{1 - R^*}{1 - R^{\pi}} = \mathcal{L}_{C,\pi} \leq \mathcal{L}_{C,u} = -\ln \frac{1}{|\mathbb{S}|} - H_{\infty}(S_u \mid O_u). \tag{15.47}$$

where S_u is the random variable associated to the uniform distribution on $\mathbb{S}$, and O_u is the random variable associated to the distribution on $\mathbb{O}$ generated by C and π.

The rest is similar to the proof of Theorem 15.6. Note also that Theorem 15.6 can be obtained as a particular case of Theorem 15.9. □

Hence, to prove that a mechanism is not ε-locally differentially private, it is sufficient to construct a model f via machine learning from the data at our disposal, estimate the prior π from the data, and show that $R^f < 1 - (1 - R^\pi)\frac{|\mathbb{S}|\, e^\varepsilon}{e^\varepsilon + |\mathbb{S}| - 1}$.

Standard Differential Privacy on Datasets

We consider now the case of the central model. We start by recalling the following result by [Alv+15], which is given for the bounded case, i.e., when there is an upper bound n to the possible number of records in the datasets. To be precise, [Alv+15] consider a notion of adjacency representing a change of value in exactly one of the records. Our notion of adjacency, instead, represents the presence or absence of exactly one of the records. To recast the result by [Alv+15] in our setting is sufficient to consider as domain of values a binary set standing for present/absent. Hence, the cardinality v of the set of possible values occurring in the formula of [Alv+15] is replaced in our case by 2.

Theorem 15.10 (Theorem 15 in [Alv+15], adapted to our setting)**.** *If a mechanism C is ε-differentially private, and the maximum number of possible records in the dataset is n, then*

$$\mathcal{L}_{C,u} \;\leq\; n \ln \frac{2\, e^\varepsilon}{1 + e^\varepsilon}. \tag{15.48}$$

The following theorem expresses the counterparts of Theorem 15.6 and Theorem 15.9.

Theorem 15.11. *If a mechanism C is ε-differentially private, the maximum number of possible records in the dataset is n, and π is the prior, then*

$$R^* \;\geq\; 1 - (1 - R^\pi)\left(\frac{2\, e^\varepsilon}{1 + e^\varepsilon}\right)^n. \tag{15.49}$$

Furthermore, if $\pi = u$ then

$$R^* \;\geq\; 1 - \left(\frac{e^\varepsilon}{1 + e^\varepsilon}\right)^n. \tag{15.50}$$

Proof. The proof is analogous to those of Theorem 15.6 and Theorem 15.9, using the bound on $\mathcal{L}_{C,u}$ expressed by Equation 15.48, and the fact that $u(s) = \frac{1}{2^n}$. □

As for local differential privacy, Theorem 15.10 allows to audit / derive a lower bound on ε-differential privacy.

15.5 Machine Learning Estimates of the Bayes Risk

In this section, we define the notion of a *universally consistent* learning rule, and show that the error of a classifier selected according to such a rule can be used for estimating the Bayes risk. Then, we introduce various universally consistent rules based on the nearest neighbor principle.

Throughout the section, we use interchangeably a system $(\pi, C_{s,o})$ and its corresponding joint distribution μ on $\mathbb{S} \times \mathbb{O}$. Note that there is a one-to-one correspondence between them.

15.5.1 Universally Consistent Rules

Consider a distribution μ and a learning rule A selecting a classifier $f_n \in \mathcal{F}$ according to n training examples sampled from μ. Intuitively, as the available training data increases, we would like the expected error of f_n for a new example (o, s) sampled from μ to be minimized (i.e., to get close the Bayes risk). The following definition captures this intuition.

Definition 15.12 (Consistent Learning Rule)**.** *Let μ be a distribution on $\mathbb{S} \times \mathbb{O}$ and let A be a learning rule. Let $f_n \in \mathcal{F}$ be a classifier selected by A using n training examples sampled from μ. Let $(\pi, C_{s,o})$ be the system corresponding to μ, and let R^{f_n} be the expected error of f_n, as defined by* (15.4)*. We say that A is consistent if $R^{f_n} \longrightarrow R^*$ as $n \longrightarrow \infty$.*

The next definition strengthens this property, by asking the rule to be consistent for all distributions:

Definition 15.13 (Universally Consistent (UC) Learning Rule)**.** *A learning rule is universally consistent if it is consistent for any distribution μ on $\mathbb{S} \times \mathbb{O}$.*

By this definition, the expected error of a classifier selected according to a universally consistent rule is also an estimator of the Bayes risk, since it converges to R^* as $n \longrightarrow \infty$.

In the rest of this section we introduce Bayes risk estimates based on universally consistent nearest neighbor rules; they are summarized in Table 15.2 together with their guarantees.

15.5.2 NN Estimate

The Nearest Neighbor (NN) is one of the simplest ML classifiers: given a training set and a new object o, it predicts the secret of its closest training observation (*nearest neighbor*). It is defined both for finite and infinite object spaces, although it is UC only in the first case.

We introduce a formulation of NN, which can be seen as an extension of the frequentist approach, that takes into account *ties* (i.e., neighbors that are equally close to the new object o), and which guarantees consistency when $\mathbb{O}$ is finite.

Consider a training set $\{(o_1, s_1), \ldots, (o_n, s_n)\}$, an object o, and a distance metric $d : \mathbb{O} \times \mathbb{O} \mapsto \mathbb{R}_{\geq 0}$. The NN classifier predicts a secret for o by taking a majority vote over the set of secrets whose objects have the smallest distance to o. Formally, let $I_{\min}(o) = \{i \mid d(o, o_i) = \min_{j=1\ldots n} d(o, o_j)\}$ and define:

$$\mathrm{NN}(o) = s_{h(o)}, \tag{15.51}$$

where

$$h(o) = \operatorname*{arg\,max}_{i \in I_{\min}(o)} |\{j \in I_{\min}(o) \mid s_j = s_i\}| \,. \tag{15.52}$$

We show that NN is universally consistent for finite $\mathbb{S} \times \mathbb{O}$.

Theorem 15.14 (Universal consistency of NN). *Consider a distribution on $\mathbb{S} \times \mathbb{O}$, where $\mathbb{S}$ and $\mathbb{O}$ are finite. Let R_n^{NN} be the expected error of the NN classifier for a new observation o. As the number of training examples $n \to \infty$:*

$$R_n^{\mathrm{NN}} \to R^*. \tag{15.53}$$

Sketch proof. For an observation o that appears in the training set, the NN classifier is equivalent to the frequentist approach. For a finite space $\mathbb{S} \times \mathbb{O}$, as $n \to \infty$, the probability that the training set contains all $o \in \mathbb{O}$ approaches 1. Thus, the NN rule is asymptotically (in n) equivalent to the frequentist approach, which means its error also converges to R^*. □

15.5.3 k_n-NN Estimate

Whilst NN guarantees universal consistency in finite example spaces, this does not hold for infinite $\mathbb{O}$. In this case, we can achieve universal consistency with the k-NN classifier, an extension of NN, for appropriate choices of the parameter k.

The k-NN classifier takes a majority vote among the secrets of its neighbors. Breaking ties in the k-NN definition requires more care than with NN. In the literature, this is generally done via strategies that add randomness or arbitrariness to the choice (e.g., if two neighbors have the same distance, select the one with the smallest index in the training data) [DGL13]. We use a novel tie-breaking strategy, which takes into account ties, but gives more importance to the closest neighbors. In early experiments, we observed this strategy had a faster convergence than standard approaches.

Consider a training set $\{(o_1, s_1), \ldots, (o_n, s_n)\}$, an object to predict o, and some metric $d : \mathbb{O} \times \mathbb{O} \mapsto \mathbb{R}_{\geq 0}$. Let $o_{(i)}$ denote the i-th closest object to o, and $s_{(i)}$ its respective secret. If ties do not occur after the k-th neighbor (i.e., if $d(o, o_{(k)}) \neq d(o, o_{(k+1)})$), then k-NN outputs the most frequent among the secrets of the first k neighbors:

$$k\text{-NN}(o) = s_{h(o)}, \tag{15.54}$$

where

$$h(o) = \arg\max_{i=1,\ldots,k} |\{j \in I_{\min}(o) \mid s_{(j)} = s_{(i)}\}|. \tag{15.55}$$

If ties exist after the k-th neighbor, that is, for $k' \leq k < k''$:

$$d(o, o_{(k')}) = \ldots = d(o, o_{(k)}) = \ldots = d(o, o_{(k'')}), \tag{15.56}$$

we proceed as follows. Let $\hat{s}$ be the most frequent secret in $\{s_{(k')}, \ldots, s_{(k'')}\}$; k-NN predicts the most frequent secret in the following multiset, truncated at the tail to have size k:

$$s_{(1)}, s_{(2)}, \ldots, s_{(k'-1)}, \hat{s}, \hat{s} \ldots, \hat{s}.$$

We now define k_n-NN, a universally consistent learning rule that selects a k-NN classifier for a training set of n examples by choosing k as a function of n.

Definition 15.15 (k_n-NN rule). *Given a training set of n examples, the k_n-NN rule selects a k-NN classifier, where k is chosen such that $k_n \to \infty$ and $k_n/n \to 0$ as $n \to \infty$.*

[Sto77] proved that k_n-NN is universally consistent:

Theorem 15.16 (Universal consistency of the k_n-NN rule). *Consider a probability distribution μ on the example space $\mathbb{S} \times \mathbb{O}$, where μ has a density. Select a distance metric d such that $(d, \mathbb{O})$ is separable[iv]. Then the expected error of the k_n-NN rule converges to R^* as $n \to \infty$.*

This holds for any distance metric. In our experiments, we will use the Euclidean distance, and we will evaluate k_n-NN rules for $k_n = \log n$ (natural logarithm) and $k_n = \log_{10} n$.

---

iv. A separable space is a space containing a countable dense subset; e.g., finite spaces and the space of q-dimensional vectors $\mathbb{R}^q$ with Euclidean metric.

Table 15.2. Estimates' guarantees as $n \to \infty$. Guarantees on infinite spaces also hold for finite space. Precise hyperparameter selection and assumptions for convergences are in [Che19].

Method	Guarantee	Space $\mathbb{O}$	Assumptions
Frequentist	$\to R^*$	finite	
NN	$\to R^*$	finite	
k_n-NN	$\to R^*$	infinite	
SVM (rbf)	$\to R^*$	infinite	$\mathbb{O}$ compact subset of $\mathbb{R}^m$
NN Bound	$\leq R^*$	infinite	$(d, \mathbb{O})$ separable

15.5.4 Additional Tools from ML

The family of UC rules is fairly large. An overview of them is by [DGL13], who, in addition to nearest neighbor methods, report histogram rules and kinds of neural networks; these are UC under requirements on their parameters. Steinwart proved that Support Vector Machine (SVM) is also UC for some parameter choices, in the case $|\mathbb{S}| = 2$ [Ste02]; to the best of our knowledge, attempts to construct an SVM that is UC when $|\mathbb{S}| > 2$ have failed so far (e.g., [Gla10]).

A more extensive list of UC methods applicable to leakage estimation, including a Bayes risk lower bound based on NN, is given by [Che19] and summarized in Table 15.2.

15.6 Evaluation on Synthetic Data

In this section we evaluate our estimates on several synthetic systems for which the channel matrix is known. For each system, we sample n examples from its distribution, and then compute the estimate on the whole object space as in Equation (15.4); this is possible because $\mathbb{O}$ is finite. Since for synthetic data we know the real Bayes risk, we can measure how many examples are required for the convergence of each estimate. We do this as follows: let R_n^f be an estimate of R^*, trained on a dataset of n examples. We say the estimate δ-converged to R^* after n examples if its relative change from R^* is smaller than δ:

$$\frac{\left|R_n^f - R^*\right|}{R^*} < \delta . \tag{15.57}$$

While relative change has the advantage of taking into account the magnitude of the compared values, it is not defined when the denominator is 0; therefore, when

Table 15.3. Synthetic systems.

Name	Privacy parameter	$\lvert\mathbb{S}\rvert$	$\lvert\mathbb{O}\rvert$	R^*
Geometric	1.0	100	10K	~ 0
Geometric	0.1	100	10K	0.007
Geometric	0.01	100	10K	0.600
Geometric	0.2	100	1K	0.364
Geometric	0.02	100	10K	0.364
Geometric	0.002	100	100K	0.364
Geometric	2	100K	100K	0.238
Geometric	2	100K	10K	0.924
Spiky	N/A	2	10K	0
Random	N/A	100	100	0.979

$R^* \approx 0$ (Table 15.3), we verify convergence with the absolute change:

$$\left| R_n^f - R^* \right| < \delta . \tag{15.58}$$

The systems used in our experiments are briefly discussed in this section, and summarized in Table 15.3. A uniform prior is assumed in all cases.

15.6.1 Geometric Systems

We first consider systems generated by adding geometric noise to the secret, one of the typical mechanisms used to implement differential privacy [Dwo06]. Their channel matrix has the following form:

$$C_{s,o} = P(o \mid s) = \lambda \exp\left(-\nu \lvert\, g(s) - o \,\rvert\right) , \tag{15.59}$$

where ν is a privacy parameter, λ a normalization factor, and g a function $\mathbb{S} \mapsto \mathbb{O}$.

We consider the following three parameters:

- the privacy parameter ν,
- the ratio $\lvert\mathbb{O}\rvert / \lvert\mathbb{S}\rvert$, and
- the size of the secret space $\lvert\mathbb{S}\rvert$.

We vary each of these parameters one at a time, to isolate their effect on the convergence rate.

Variation of the Privacy Parameter ν

We fix $\lvert\mathbb{S}\rvert = 100$, $\lvert\mathbb{O}\rvert = 10\text{K}$, and we consider three cases $\nu = 1.0$, $\nu = 0.1$ and $\nu = 0.01$. The results for the estimation of the Bayes risk and the convergence

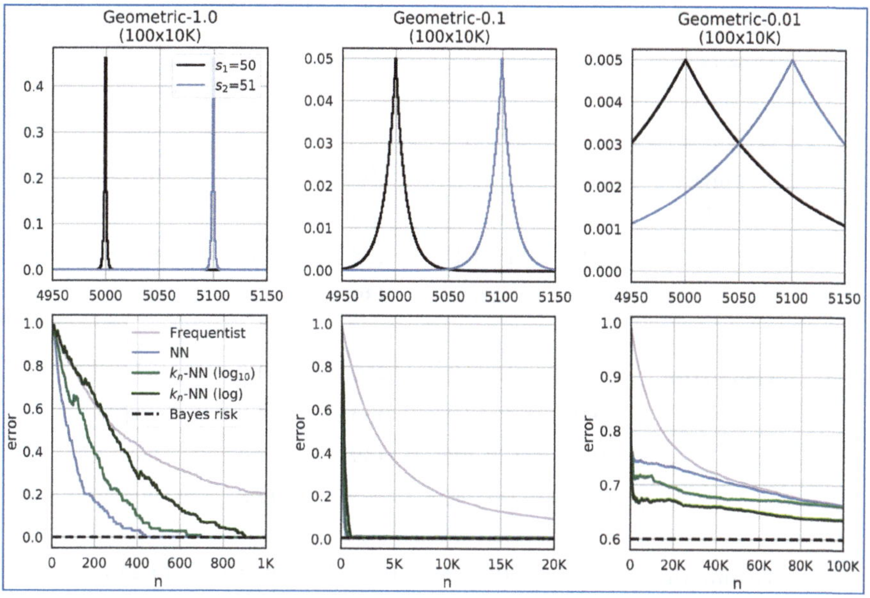

Figure 15.1. Estimates' convergence for geometric systems when varying their privacy parameter ν. The respective distributions are shown in the top figure for two adjacent secrets $s_1 \sim s_2$.

rate are illustrated in Figure 15.1 and Table 15.4 respectively. In the table, results are reported for convergence level $\delta \in \{0.1, 0.05, 0.01, 0.005\}$; an "X" means a particular estimate did not converge within 500K examples; a missing row for a certain δ means no estimate converged.

The results indicate that the nearest neighbor methods have a much faster convergence than the standard frequentist approach, particularly when dealing with large systems. The reason is that geometric systems have a regular behavior with respect to the Euclidean metric, which can be exploited by NN and k_n-NN to make good predictions for unseen objects.

Variation of the Ratio $|\mathbb{O}|/|\mathbb{S}|$

Now we fix $|\mathbb{S}| = 100$, and we consider three cases $|\mathbb{O}|/|\mathbb{S}| = 10$, $|\mathbb{O}|/|\mathbb{S}| = 100$, and $|\mathbb{O}|/|\mathbb{S}| = 1\text{K}$. (Note that we want to keep the ratio ν/Δ_g fixed. As a consequence ν has to vary: we set ν to 0.2, 0.02, and 0.002, respectively.) Results in Figure 15.2 and Table 15.5 show how the nearest neighbor methods become much better than the frequentist approach as $|\mathbb{O}|/|\mathbb{S}|$ increases. This is because the larger the object space, the larger the number of unseen objects at the moment of classification, and the more the frequentist approach has to rely on random guessing. The nearest neighbor methods are not that much affected because they can rely on the proximity to outputs already classified.

Table 15.4. Convergence of the estimates when varying ν, fixed $|\mathbb{S}| \times |\mathbb{O}| = 100 \times 10K$

System	δ	Freq.	NN	k_n-NN $\log_{10}$	k_n-NN log
Geometric ν = 1.0	0.1	1 994	**267**	396	679
	0.05	4 216	**325**	458	781
	0.01	19 828	**425**	633	899
	0.005	38 621	**439**	698	904
Geometric ν = 0.1	0.1	18 110	**269**	396	673
	0.05	35 016	**333**	458	768
	0.01	127 206	**439**	633	899
	0.005	211 742	4 844	**698**	904
Geometric ν = 0.01	0.1	105 453	103 357	99 852	**34 243**
	0.05	205 824	205 266	205 263	**199 604**

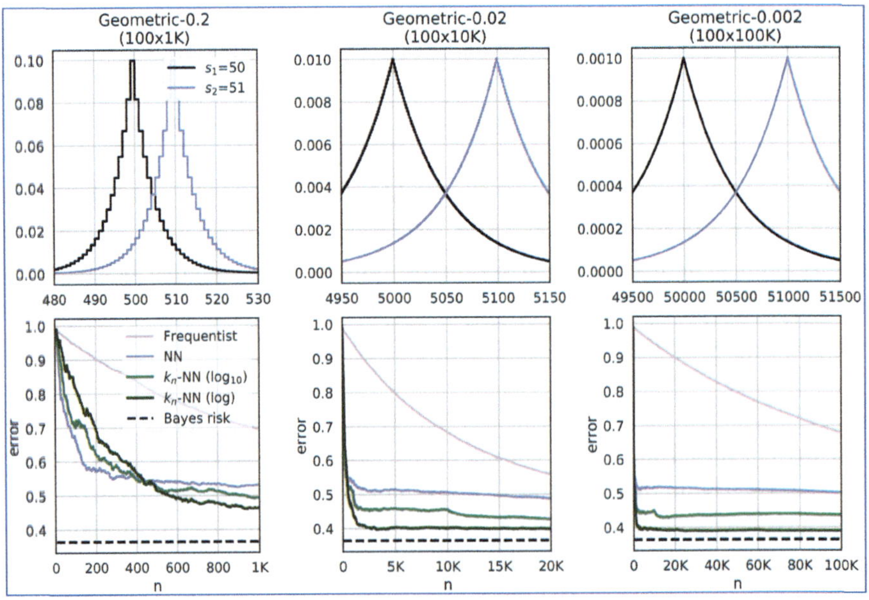

Figure 15.2. Estimates' convergence for geometric systems when varying the ratio $|\mathbb{O}|/|\mathbb{S}|$. The respective distributions are shown in the top figure for two adjacent secrets $s_1 \sim s_2$.

Table 15.5. Convergence of the estimates when varying $|\mathbb{O}|/|\mathbb{S}|$.

				k_n-NN	
System	δ	Freq.	NN	$\log_{10}$	log
Geometric 100x1K ν = 0.2	0.1	8 679	8 707	7 108	**2 505**
	0.05	14 823	14 853	14 853	**7 673**
	0.01	**51 694**	60 796	60 796	60 796
	0.005	**71 469**	**71 469**	**71 469**	**71 469**
Geometric 100x10K ν = 0.02	0.1	85 912	85 644	71 003	**11 197**
	0.05	152 904	152 698	151 153	**68 058**
Geometric 100x100K ν = 0.002	0.1	X	X	413 974	**2 967**

Case $|\mathbb{S}| \geq |\mathbb{O}|$

We fix $\nu = 2$, and we consider two cases: $|\mathbb{S}| = |\mathbb{O}|$ and $|\mathbb{S}| > |\mathbb{O}|$. It should be noted that the formulation of geometric systems prohibits the number of secrets to exceed the number of outputs; for this reason, in the system $|\mathbb{S}| > |\mathbb{O}|$ some secrets are associated with the same distribution over the output space.

The results in Figure 15.3 and Table 15.6 indicate that NN and frequentist are mostly equivalent: this is because they both need to observe at least one example for each secret. k_n-NN rules, on the other hand, show poor performances, due to the fact that they would need at least k_n examples for each secret. A natural extension of our work is to look at notions of metric also in the secret space for improving convergence.

15.6.2 Random System

In the previous sections, we have seen cases when our methods greatly outperform the frequentist approach, and a contrived system example for which they fail. We now consider a system generated randomly to evaluate their performances for a generic system.

System Description

We construct the channel matrix of a Random system by drawing its elements from the uniform distribution, $C_{s,o} \xleftarrow{\$} Uni(0, 1)$, and normalizing its rows.

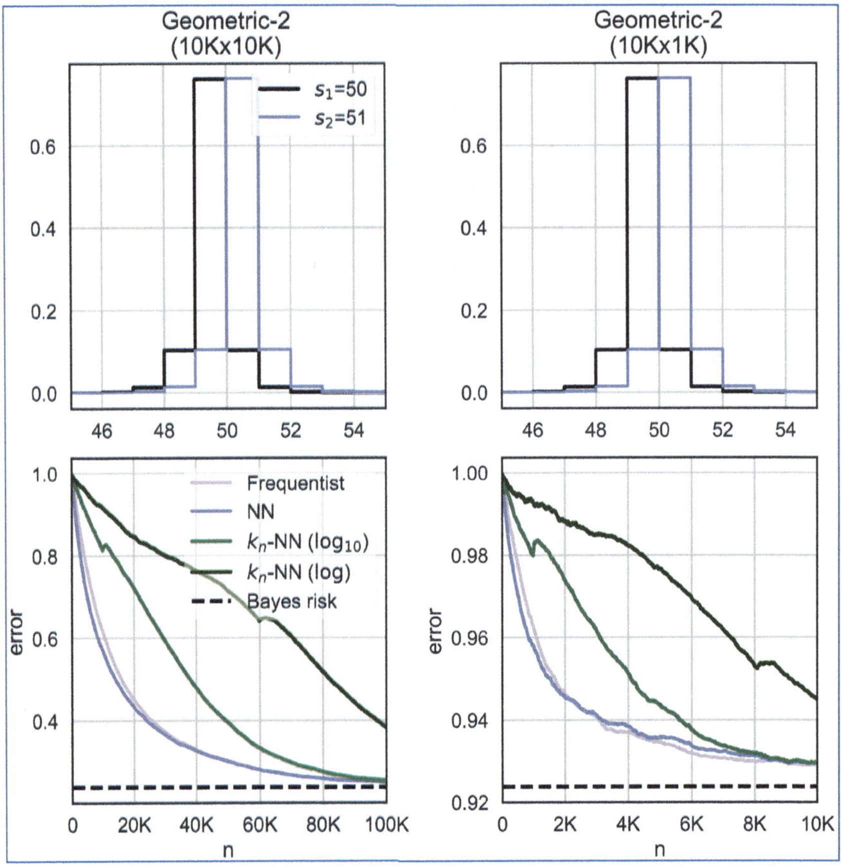

Figure 15.3. Estimates' convergence for geometric systems when $|\mathbb{S}| \geq |\mathbb{O}|$. The distributions are shown in the top figure for two adjacent secrets $s_1 \sim s_2$. In the case $|\mathbb{S}| > |\mathbb{O}|$ (right) there are $10 = 10K/1K$ identical distributions that coincide on s_1, and 10 identical distributions on s_2.

Evaluation

We consider a Random system with $|\mathbb{S}| = |\mathbb{O}| = 100$ and count the number of examples required for δ-convergence, for many δ's. Table 15.7 reports the results.

The frequentist estimate is slightly better than NN and k_n-NN for $\delta = 0.01$. However, for stricter convergence requirements ($\delta = 0.001$), all the methods require the same (large) number of examples. Figure 15.4 shows that indeed the methods begin to converge similarly already after 1K examples.

Discussion

Results showed that nearest neighbor estimates require significantly fewer examples than the frequentist approach when dealing with medium or large systems; however, they are generally equivalent to the frequentist approach in the case of small systems.

Table 15.6. Convergence of the estimates when $|\mathbb{S}| \geq |\mathbb{O}|$, $\nu = 2$.

System	δ	Freq.	NN	k_n-NN	
				$\log_{10}$	log
Geometric 10Kx10K	0.1	74 501	**73 085**	88 296	140 618
	0.05	95 500	**94 204**	107 707	155 403
	0.01	**137 099**	137 348	144 846	192 014
	0.005	**153 370**	**153 370**	159 075	203 363
Geometric 10Kx1K	0.1	**5**	**5**	**5**	**5**
	0.05	721	**514**	2 309	5 977
	0.01	**5 595**	6 171	7 330	12 354
	0.005	**10 770**	10 797	11 037	14 575

Table 15.7. Random: examples required for δ-convergence.

δ	Freq.	NN	k_n-NN	
			$\log_{10}$	log
0.05	**5**	**5**	**5**	**5**
0.01	**82**	139	202	500
0.005	**10 070**	**10 070**	**10 070**	**10 070**

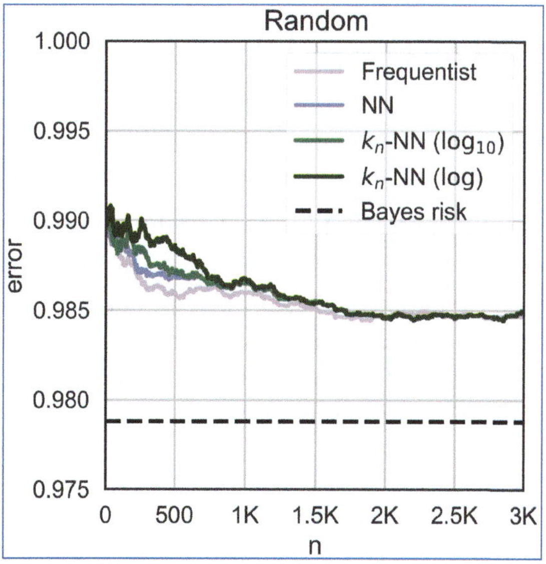

Figure 15.4. Estimates' convergence for a Random system (100 × 100).

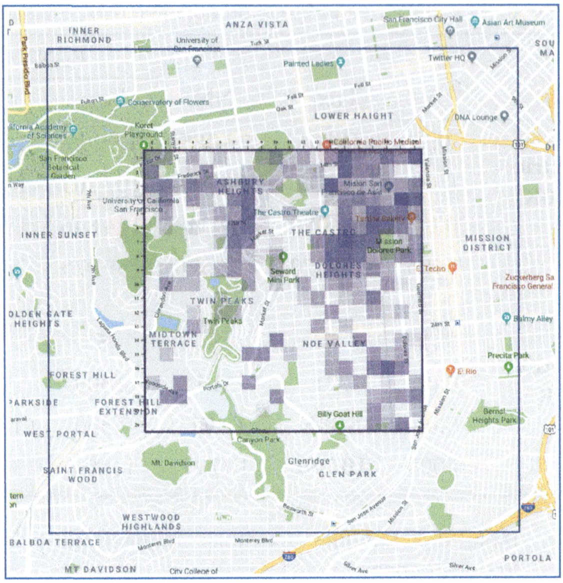

Figure 15.5. Area of San Francisco considered for the experiments. The input locations correspond to the inner square, the output locations to the outer one. The colored cells represent the distribution of the Gowalla checkins.

To better understand why this is the case, we provide a crude approximation of the frequentist Bayes risk estimate.

$$R_n^{\text{Freq}} \approx R^* \left(1 - \left(1 - \frac{1}{|\mathbb{O}|}\right)^n\right) + R^\pi \left(1 - \frac{1}{|\mathbb{O}|}\right)^n. \tag{15.60}$$

This approximation makes the very strong assumption that all objects are equally likely, i.e.: $P(o) = \frac{1}{|\mathbb{O}|}$. However, this is enough to give us an insight on the performance of the frequentist approach: $\left(1 - \frac{1}{|\mathbb{O}|}\right)^n$ is the probability that some object does not appear within a training set of size n. This weighs the value of the frequentist estimate between the optimal R^*, used when the object appears in the training data, and random guessing R^π: while the estimate converges asymptotically to the Bayes risk, the probability of observing an object – often related to the the size $|\mathbb{O}|$, has a major influence on its convergence rate.

15.7 Application to Location Privacy

We show that F-BLEAU can be successfully applied to estimate the degree of protection provided by mechanisms such as those used in location privacy. Since the purpose of this chapter is to evaluate the precision of F-BLEAU, we consider basic mechanisms for which the Bayes risk can also be computed directly. Of course, the intended applications of F-BLEAU are mechanisms or situations where the Bayes risk *cannot* be computed directly, either because this is too complicated, or because of the presence of unknown factors. Examples abound; for instance, the availability of additional information, like the presence of points of interest (e.g., shops, churches), or geographical characteristics of the area (e.g., roads, lakes) can affect the Bayes risk in ways that are impossible to evaluate formally.

We will consider the planar Laplacian and the planar geometric, which are the typical mechanisms used to obtain geo-indistinguishability [ABCP13], and one of the optimal mechanisms proposed by [OTP17] as a refinement of the optimal mechanism by [Sho+12]. The construction of the last relies on an algorithm that was proposed by Blahut and by Arimoto to solve the information theory problem of achieving an optimal trade-off between the minimization of the distortion rate and the the mutual information [CT06]. From now on, we shall refer to this as the Blahut-Arimoto mechanism. Note that the Laplacian is a continuous mechanism (i.e., its outputs are on a continuous plane); the other two are discrete.

In these experiments we also deploy the method that F-BLEAU uses in practice to compute the estimate of the Bayes risk: we first split the data into a training set and a hold-out set; then, for an increasing number of examples $n = 1, 2, \ldots$ we train the classifier on the first n examples on the training set, and then estimate its error on the hold-out set.

15.7.1 The Gowalla Dataset

We consider real location data from the Gowalla dataset [CML11], which contains users' checkins and their geographical location. We use a squared area in San Francisco, centered in the coordinates (37.755, -122.440), and extending for 1.5 Km in each direction. This input area corresponds to the inner (purple) square in Figure 15.5. We discretize the input using a grid of 20×20 cells of size 150×150 Sq m; the secret space $\mathbb{S}$ of the system thus consists of 400 locations. The prior distribution on the secrets is derived from the Gowalla checkins, and it is represented in Figure 15.5 by the different color intensities on the input grid. The output area is represented in Figure 15.5 by the outer (blue) square. It extends 1050 m (7 cells) more than the input square on every side. We consider a larger area for the output because the planar Laplacian and Geometric naturally expand outside the input square.[v] Since the planar Laplacian is continuous, its output domain $\mathbb{O}$ is constituted by all the points of the outer square. As for the planar Geometric and the

v. In fact these functions distribute the probability on the infinite plane, but on locations very distant from the origin the probability becomes negligible.

Blahut-Arimoto mechanisms, which are discrete, we divide the output square in a grid of 340×340 cells of size 15×15 Sq m; therefore, $|\mathbb{O}| = 340 \times 340 = 115,600$.

15.7.2 Defenses

The *planar Geometric* mechanism is characterized by a channel matrix $C_{s,o}$, representing the conditional probability of reporting the location o when the true location is s:

$$C_{s,o} = \lambda \exp\left(-\frac{\ln \nu}{100} d(s, o)\right), \tag{15.61}$$

where ν is a parameter controlling the level of noise, λ is a normalization factor, and d is the Euclidean distance.

The *planar Laplacian* is defined by the same equation, except that o belongs to a continuous domain, and the equation defines a probability density function.

As for the *Blahut-Arimoto*, it is obtained as the result of an iterative algorithm, whose definition can be found in [CT06].

15.7.3 Results

We evaluated the estimates' convergence as a function of the number of training examples n and for different values of the noise level: $\nu = \{2, 4, 8\}$. We randomly split the dataset ($100K$ examples) into training (75%) and hold-out (25%) sets, and then evaluated the convergence of the estimators on an increasing number of training examples, $5, 6, \ldots 75K$.

Results for the geometric noise (Figure 15.6) indicate faster convergence when ν is higher (which means less noise and lower Bayes risk), in line with the results for the synthetic systems of the previous section. In all cases, the nearest neighbor methods outperform the frequentist one, as we expected given the presence of a large number of outputs. Table 15.8 shows the number of examples required to achieve δ-convergence from the Bayes risk. The symbol "X" means we did not achieve a certain level of approximation with 75K examples.

The corresponding results for the Laplacian noise are shown in Figure 15.6 and in Table 15.9. In this case, the frequentist approach is not applicable, but the k_n-NN rule can still approximate the Bayes risk for some approximation levels.

The case of the Blahut-Arimoto mechanism is quite different: surprisingly, the output probability concentrates on a small number of locations. For instance, in the case $\nu = 2$, with 100K sampled pairs we obtained only 19 different output locations (which reduced to 14 after we mapped them on the 20×20 grid). Thanks to the small number of actual outputs, all the methods converge very fast. The results are shown in Figure 15.8 and in Table 15.10.

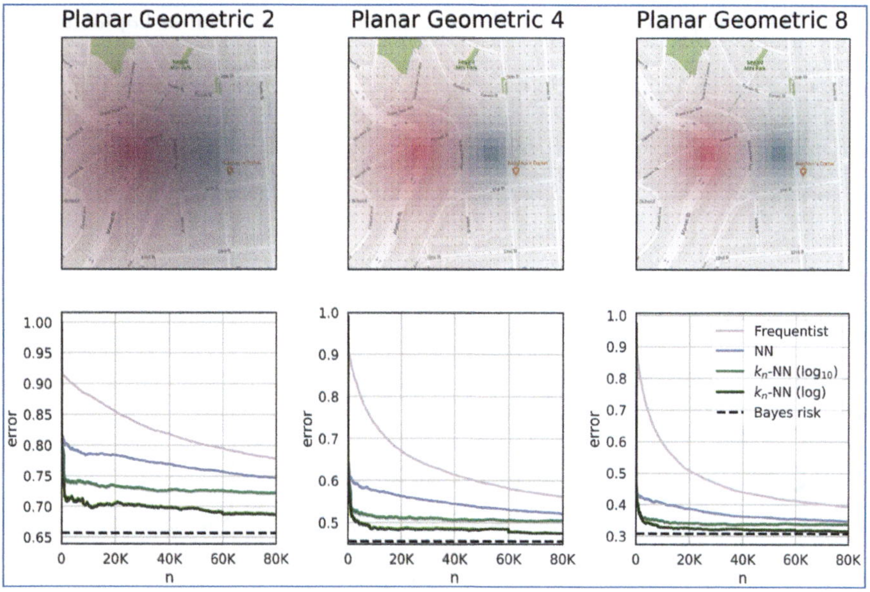

Figure 15.6. Estimates' convergence speed for the planar Geometric defense applied to the Gowalla dataset, for $\nu = 2$, $\nu = 4$ and $\nu = 8$, respectively. Above each graph is represented the distribution of the geometric noise for two adjacent input cells.

Table 15.8. Convergence for the Planar Geometric for various ν.

				k_n-NN	
ν	δ	frequentist	NN	log 10	log
2	0.1	X	X	25 795	**1 102**
	0.05	X	X	X	**55 480**
4	0.1	X	X	36 735	**2 820**
	0.05	X	X	X	**59 875**
8	0.1	X	X	15 253	**5 244**
	0.05	X	X	X	**19 948**

15.8 Practical Considerations on Leakage Estimation

15.8.1 The Limits of Black-box Leakage Estimation

No Free Lunch

One may wonder whether there is an "optimal" method; that is, a method that converges quicker than any other method across all the systems. It can be shown that no method is optimal in this sense. More precisely, for any two leakage estimators

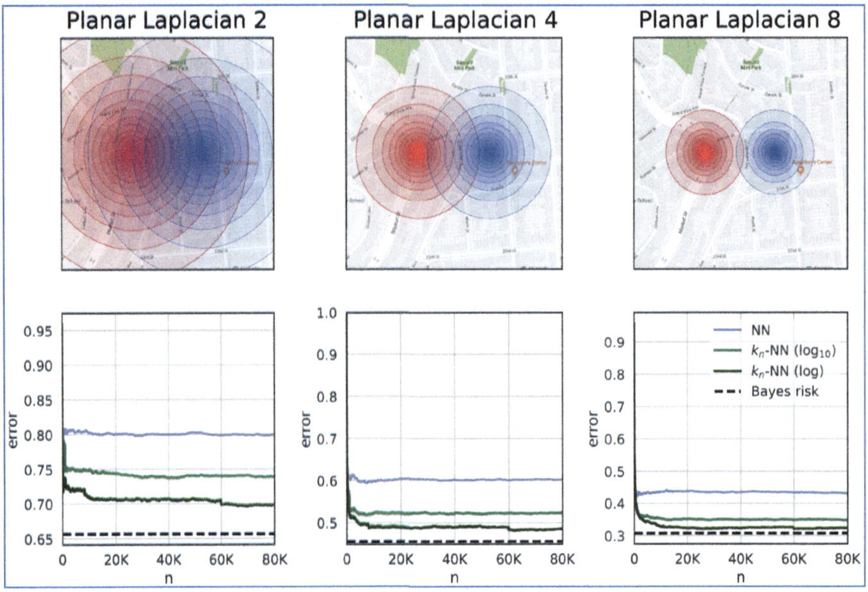

Figure 15.7. Estimates' convergence speed for the planar Laplacian defense applied to the Gowalla dataset, for $\nu = 2$, $\nu = 4$ and $\nu = 8$, respectively. Above each graph is represented the distribution of the geometric noise for two adjacent input cells.

Table 15.9. Convergence for the Planar Laplacian for various ν.

				k_n-NN	
ν	δ	frequentist	NN	log 10	log
2	0.1	N/A	X	X	**259**
4	0.1	N/A	X	X	**4 008**
8	0.1	N/A	X	X	**6 135**
	0.05	N/A	X	X	**19 961**

A and B, there are exactly as many systems (distributions) for which A will converge faster than B, and vice versa. This is a consequence of the No Free Lunch (NFL) theorem in machine learning [Wol96].

Note however that the NFL theorem is based on the assumption that all the systems (distributions) are equally likely in practice. In our experiments we observed that, for various real-world problems, ML-based methods are preferable to the frequentist approach. In addition, the frequentist approach cannot be used if the observables are continuous.

From the practical perspective of black-box security, the NFL demonstrates that we should always test several estimators and select the one that converges faster.

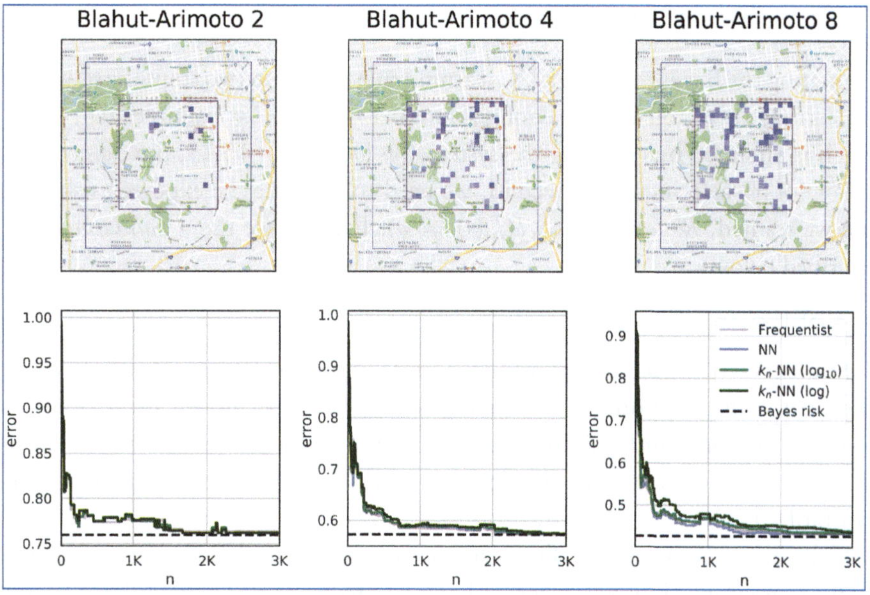

Figure 15.8. Estimates' convergence speed for the Blahut-Arimoto defense applied to the Gowalla dataset, for $\nu = 2$, $\nu = 4$ and $\nu = 8$, respectively. Above each graph is represented the distribution of the output probability as produced by the mechanism. All the outputs with non-null probability turn out to be inside the input square. The outputs are points on the 340×340 grid, but here are mapped on the coarser 20×20 grid for the sake of visual clarity.

Table 15.10. Convergence for the Blahut-Arimoto for various ν.

				k_n-NN	
ν	δ	frequentist	NN	log 10	log
2	0.1	**37**	**37**	**37**	**37**
	0.05	**135**	**135**	**135**	**135**
	0.01	1 671	1 664	**1 408**	**1 408**
	0.005	6 179	6 179	**1 671**	**1 671**
4	0.1	**220**	**220**	**220**	257
	0.05	503	**502**	509	703
	0.01	2 029	**1 986**	2 055	2 404
	0.005	2 197	**2 055**	2 280	2 658
8	0.1	**345**	401	553	1 285
	0.05	1 285	**1 170**	1 343	1 679
	0.01	2 104	**2 017**	2 495	4 190
	0.005	**2 231**	**2 231**	3 881	6 121

15.8.2 Estimating the Bayes Risk in Practice

Estimating the Bayes risk with a UC learning rule is done in two steps. First, we train the learning rule f_n on a "large enough" number n of *training* examples $\{(s_i, o_i)\}_{i=1}^n$, which is obtained by querying the system. By Definition 15.13, the expected risk of $R^{f_n} \to R^*$ as n increases. Second, we need to estimate the expected risk of the rule we trained, $R^{f_n} = \mathbb{E}_{(s,o)\sim\mu} I(f_n(s) \neq o)$. For this we use a *validation* set, as described below.

Size of the Training Set

If the observation space $\mathbb{O}$ is continuous, and without making any further assumption on the distribution μ, no convergence rate can be proven for a Bayes risk estimate. In other words, for any estimator of the Bayes risk (whether based or not on a UC rule), there exists a distribution μ which makes the estimator converge arbitrarily slowly.

If the observation space is finite, it may be possible to derive convergence rates for the estimators. However, in general, it is best to use as many examples as possible for training the learning rule.

Size of the Validation Set

There are several methods for estimating the expected risk of an ML algorithm. For simplicity, we focus on the *validation set* idea: we sample m examples $\{(s_i, o_i)\}_{i=1}^m$ by querying the system, and compute the empirical risk as $\hat{R}^{f_n} = {}^1\!/_m \sum_{i=1}^m I(f_n(s) \neq o)$.

Given a desired confidence interval for this estimate, we can determine precisely what its size m should be. For a validation set $\{(s_i, o_i)\}_{i=1}^m$ sampled from μ, let $E_i = I(f_n(o_i) \neq s_i)$, $i = 1, \ldots, m$ be the errors of the classifier f_n on the set. $E_1, \ldots, E_m$ are independent Bernoulli random variables with parameter $p = \mathbf{Pr}_{(s,o)\sim\mu}(f_n(o) \neq s) = R^{f_n}$. Let $\hat{R}^{f_n} = {}^1\!/_n \sum_{i=1}^m E_i$. By Hoeffding's inequality, we get the following:

$$\mathbf{Pr}(|\hat{R}^{f_n} - R^{f_n}| \geq t) \leq 2e^{-2mt^2},$$

for some parameter $t \in [0, 1]$.

Suppose we want our estimate $\hat{R}^{f_n}$ to differ not more than t from R^{f_n} in absolute terms with significance level $\alpha \in [0, 1]$. From the above expression, we derive that we should collect at least m examples, where m is:

$$m \geq \frac{\log({}^2\!/_\alpha)}{2t^2}.$$

For example, if we want to be $(1-\alpha)=0.95$ confident that our estimate does not differ more than $t=0.05$, we need at least $m=737$ validation examples.

15.9 Concluding Remarks

We showed that the black-box leakage of a system, measured until now with classical statistics paradigms (*frequentist* approach), can be effectively estimated via ML techniques. We considered a set of such techniques based on the nearest neighbor principle (i.e., close observations should be assigned the same secret), and evaluated them thoroughly on synthetic and real-world data. This allows to tackle problems that were impractical until now; furthermore, it sets a new paradigm in black-box security: thanks to an equivalence between ML and black-box leakage estimation, many results from the ML theory can be now imported into this practice (and vice versa).

Empirical evidence shows that the nearest neighbor techniques excel whenever there is a notion of metric they can exploit in the output space: whereas for unseen observations the frequentist approach needs to take a guess, nearest neighbor methods can use the information of neighboring observations. We also observe that whenever the output distribution is irregular, they are equivalent to the frequentist approach, but for maliciously crafted systems they can be misled. Even in those cases, however, we remark that asymptotically they are equivalent to the frequentist approach, thanks to their universal consistency property.

A crucial advantage of the ML formulation, as opposed to the frequentist approach, is that it gives immediate guarantees for systems with a continuous output space. Future work may extend this to systems with continuous secret space, which in ML terms would be formalized as regression (as opposed to the classification setting we considered here); work in this direction was done by Cherubin [Che19].

A current limitation of our methods is that they do not provide confidence intervals. We leave this as an open problem. We remark, however, that for continuous systems it is not possible to provide confidence intervals (or to prove convergence rates) under our weak assumptions [DGL13]; this constraint applies to any leakage estimation method.

Acknowledgement

The work of Catuscia Palamidessi was supported by the ERC grant HYPATIA under the European Union Horizon 2020 research and innovation programme, grant agreement n. 835294.

References

[ABCP13] M. E. Andrés, N. E. Bordenabe, K. Chatzikokolakis, and C. Palamidessi. "Geo-indistinguishability: Differential privacy for location-based systems". In: Proceedings of the 2013 ACM SIGSAC conference on Computer & communications security. 2013, pp. 901–914 (cit. on pp. 503, 529).

[ACPS12] M. S. Alvim, K. Chatzikokolakis, C. Palamidessi, and G. Smith. "Measuring Information Leakage Using Generalized Gain Functions". In: Proceedings of the 25th IEEE Computer Security Foundations Symposium (CSF). 2012, pp. 265–279. URL: http://hal.inria.fr/hal-00734044/en (cit. on p. 502).

[Alv+15] M. S. Alvim, M. E. Andrés, K. Chatzikokolakis, P. Degano, and C. Palamidessi. "On the information leakage of differentially-private mechanisms". In: Journal of Computer Security 23.4 (2015), pp. 427–469. URL: https://doi.org/10.3233/JCS-150528 (cit. on pp. 508, 510, 512, 513, 517).

[BCP09] C. Braun, K. Chatzikokolakis, and C. Palamidessi. "Quantitative Notions of Leakage for One-try Attacks". In: Proceedings of the 25th Conf. on Mathematical Foundations of Programming Semantics. Vol. 249. Electronic Notes in Theoretical Computer Science. Elsevier B.V., 2009, pp. 75–91. URL: http://hal.archives-ouvertes.fr/inria-00424852/en/ (cit. on pp. 502, 513).

[Bel+18] I. Belghazi, S. Rajeswar, A. Baratin, R. D. Hjelm, and A. Courville. "MINE: mutual information neural estimation". In: arXiv preprint arXiv:1801.04062 (2018) (cit. on p. 504).

[Bic+18] B. Bichsel, T. Gehr, D. Drachsler-Cohen, P. Tsankov, and M. T. Vechev. "DP-Finder: Finding Differential Privacy Violations by Sampling and Optimization". In: Proceedings of the 2018 ACM SIGSAC Conference on Computer and Communications Security, CCS 2018, Toronto, ON, Canada, October 15-19, 2018. Ed. by D. Lie, M. Mannan, M. Backes, and X. Wang. ACM, 2018, pp. 508–524. URL: https://doi.org/10.1145/3243734.3243863 (cit. on p. 503).

[BK11] G. Barthe and B. K'opf. "Information-theoretic Bounds for Differentially Private Mechanisms". In: Proceedings of the 24th IEEE Computer Security Foundations Symposium (CSF).

IEEE Computer Society, 2011, pp. 191–204 (cit. on pp. 508, 510).

[BSBV21] B. Bichsel, S. Steffen, I. Bogunovic, and M. Vechev. "DP-Sniper: Black-Box Discovery of Differential Privacy Violations using Classifiers". In: Proceedings of the 42nd IEEE Symposium on Security and Privacy. IEEE, 2021 (cit. on p. 503).

[CABP13] K. Chatzikokolakis, M. E. Andrés, N. E. Bordenabe, and C. Palamidessi. "Broadening the scope of Differential Privacy using metrics". In: Proceedings of the 13th International Symposium on Privacy Enhancing Technologies (PETS 2013). Ed. by E. De Cristofaro and M. Wright. Vol. 7981. Lecture Notes in Computer Science. Springer, 2013, pp. 82–102 (cit. on pp. 503, 508, 509).

[CCG10] K. Chatzikokolakis, T. Chothia, and A. Guha. "Statistical measurement of information leakage". In: Tools and Algorithms for the Construction and Analysis of Systems (2010), pp. 390–404 (cit. on pp. 502, 507).

[CCP19] G. Cherubin, K. Chatzikokolakis, and C. Palamidessi. "F-BLEAU: Fast Black-Box Leakage Estimation". In: 2019 IEEE Symposium on Security and Privacy, (SP). IEEE, 2019, pp. 835–852. URL: https://doi.org/10.1109/SP.2019.00073 (cit. on pp. 502, 503).

[CG11] T. Chothia and A. Guha. "A Statistical Test for Information Leaks Using Continuous Mutual Information". In: Proceedings of the 24th IEEE Computer Security Foundations Symposium, CSF 2011, Cernay-la-Ville, France, 27-29 June, 2011. IEEE Computer Society, 2011, pp. 177–190. URL: https://doi.org/10.1109/CSF.2011.19 (cit. on p. 502).

[Che+16] X. Chen, Y. Duan, R. Houthooft, J. Schulman, I. Sutskever, and P. Abbeel. "Infogan: Interpretable representation learning by information maximizing generative adversarial nets". In: Advances in neural information processing systems. 2016, pp. 2172–2180 (cit. on p. 504).

[Che17] G. Cherubin. "Bayes, not Na´ıve: Security Bounds on Website Fingerprinting Defenses". In: Proceedings on Privacy Enhancing Technologies 2017.4 (2017), pp. 215–231 (cit. on p. 502).

[Che19] G. Cherubin. "Black-box security: measuring black-box information leakage via machine learning". Royal Holloway, University of London, 2019 (cit. on pp. 521, 535).

[CHM05] D. Clark, S. Hunt, and P. Malacaria. "Quantitative Information Flow, Relations and Polymorphic Types". In: J. of Logic and Computation 18.2 (2005), pp. 181–199 (cit. on p. 502).

[CKN13] T. Chothia, Y. Kawamoto, and C. Novakovic. "A tool for estimating information leakage". In: International Conference on Computer Aided Verification (CAV). Springer. 2013, pp. 690–695 (cit. on p. 502).

[CKN14] T. Chothia, Y. Kawamoto, and C. Novakovic. "LeakWatch: Estimating Information Leakage from Java Programs". In: Proc. of ESORICS 2014 Part II. 2014, pp. 219–236 (cit. on p. 502).

[CKNP13] T. Chothia, Y. Kawamoto, C. Novakovic, and D. Parker. "Probabilistic point-to-point information leakage". In: Computer Security Foundations Symposium (CSF), 2013 IEEE 26th. IEEE. 2013, pp. 193–205 (cit. on p. 502).

[CML11] E. Cho, S. A. Myers, and J. Leskovec. "Friendship and Mobility: User Movement in Location-based Social Networks". In: Proceedings of the 17th ACM SIGKDD International Conference on Knowledge Discovery and Data Mining. KDD '11. San Diego, California, USA: ACM, 2011, pp. 1082–1090. ISBN: 978-1-4503-0813-7. URL: http://doi.acm.org/10.1145/2020408.2020579 (cit. on pp. 503, 529).

[CSWJ18] J. Chen, L. Song, M. J. Wainwright, and M. I. Jordan. "Learning to Explain: An Information-Theoretic Perspective on Model Interpretation". In: arXiv preprint arXiv:1802.07814 (2018) (cit. on p. 504).

[CT06] T. M. Cover and J. A. Thomas. Elements of Information Theory. Second. John Wiley & Sons, Inc., 2006 (cit. on pp. 529, 530).

[CY16] P. Cuff and L. Yu. "Differential Privacy As a Mutual Information Constraint". In: Proceedings of the 2016 ACM SIGSAC Conference on Computer and Communications Security (CCS). CCS '16. Vienna, Austria: ACM, 2016, pp. 43–54. ISBN: 978-1-4503-4139-4. URL: http://doi.acm.org/10.1145/2976749.2978308 (cit. on p. 504).

[DGL13] L. Devroye, L. Gy̋orfi, and G. Lugosi. A probabilistic theory of pattern recognition. Vol. 31. Springer Science & Business Media, 2013 (cit. on pp. 519, 521, 535).

[Din+18] Z. Ding, Y. Wang, G. Wang, D. Zhang, and D. Kifer. “Detecting Violations of Differential Privacy”. In: Proceedings of the 2018 ACM SIGSAC Conference on Computer and Communications Security. CCS ’18. Toronto, Canada: Association for Computing Machinery, 2018, pp. 475–489. ISBN: 9781450356930. URL: https://doi.org/10.1145/3243734.3243818 (cit. on p. 504).

[DMNS06] C. Dwork, F. Mcsherry, K. Nissim, and A. Smith. “Calibrating noise to sensitivity in private data analysis”. In: In Proceedings of the Third Theory of Cryptography Conference (TCC). Ed. by S. Halevi and T. Rabin. Vol. 3876. Lecture Notes in Computer Science. Springer, 2006, pp. 265–284 (cit. on pp. 501, 502, 505, 508, 510).

[Dwo06] C. Dwork. “Differential Privacy”. In: 33rd International Colloquium on Automata, Languages and Programming (ICALP 2006). Ed. by M. Bugliesi, B. Preneel, V. Sassone, and I. Wegener. Vol. 4052. Lecture Notes in Computer Science. Springer, 2006, pp. 1–12. ISBN: 3-540-35907-9. URL: http://dx.doi.org/10.1007/11787006_1 (cit. on pp. 505, 510, 522).

[EPK14] Ú. Erlingsson, V. Pihur, and A. Korolova. “RAPPOR: Randomized Aggregatable Privacy-Preserving Ordinal Response”. In: Proceedings of the 2014 ACM SIGSAC Conference on Computer and Communications Security (CCS). Ed. by G. Ahn, M. Yung, and N. Li. ACM, 2014, pp. 1054–1067. URL: http://doi.acm.org/10.1145/2660267.2660348 (cit. on p. 504).

[Gla10] T. Glasmachers. “Universal consistency of multi-class support vector classification”. In: Advances in Neural Information Processing Systems. 2010, pp. 739–747 (cit. on p. 521).

[Kas+08] S. P. Kasiviswanathan, H. K. Lee, K. Nissim, S. Raskhodnikova, and A. D. Smith. “What Can We Learn Privately?” In: 49th Annual IEEE Symposium on Foundations of Computer Science, FOCS 2008. IEEE Computer Society, 2008, pp. 531–540. URL: https://doi.org/10.1109/FOCS.2008.27 (cit. on pp. 505, 510).

[KBR16] P. Kairouz, K. Bonawitz, and D. Ramage. "Discrete Distribution Estimation under Local Privacy". In: Proceedings of The 33rd International Conference on Machine Learning. Ed. by M. F. Balcan and K. Q. Weinberger. Vol. 48. Proceedings of Machine Learning Research. New York, New York, USA: PMLR, June 2016, pp. 2436–2444. URL: https://proceedings.mlr.press/v48/kairouz16.html (cit. on p. 514).

[KM14] D. Kifer and A. Machanavajjhala. "Pufferfish: A framework for mathematical privacy definitions". In: ACM Transactions on Database Systems 39.1 (2014), 3:1–3:36. URL: https://doi.org/10.1145/2514689 (cit. on pp. 506, 508, 509).

[OTP17] S. Oya, C. Troncoso, and F. Pérez-González. "Back to the Drawing Board: Revisiting the Design of Optimal Location Privacy-preserving Mechanisms". In: Proceedings of the 2017 ACM SIGSAC Conference on Computer and Communications Security. CCS '17. Dallas, Texas, USA: ACM, 2017, pp. 1959–1972. ISBN: 978-1-4503-4946-8. URL: http://doi.acm.org/10.1145/3133956.3134004 (cit. on pp. 503, 529).

[RCPP20] M. Romanelli, K. Chatzikokolakis, C. Palamidessi, and P. Piantanida. "Estimating G-Leakage via Machine Learning". In: Proceedings of the ACM SIGSAC Conference on Computer and Communications Security (CCS). CCS '20. Virtual Event, USA: Association for Computing Machinery, 2020, pp. 697–716. ISBN: 9781450370899. URL: https://doi.org/10.1145/3372297.3423363 (cit. on p. 502).

[Sho+12] R. Shokri, G. Theodorakopoulos, C. Troncoso, J.-P. Hubaux, and J.-Y. L. Boudec. "Protecting location privacy: optimal strategy against localization attacks". In: Proceedings of the 19th ACM Conference on Computer and Communications Security (CCS 2012). Ed. by T. Yu, G. Danezis, and V. D. Gligor. ACM, 2012, pp. 617–627. ISBN: 978-1-4503-1651-4 (cit. on p. 529).

[Smi09] G. Smith. "On the Foundations of Quantitative Information Flow". In: Proceedings of the 12th International Conference on Foundations of Software Science and Computation Structures (FOSSACS 2009). Ed. by L. de Alfaro. Vol. 5504. LNCS. York, UK: Springer, 2009, pp. 288–302 (cit. on pp. 501, 502, 504, 506, 513).

[Ste02] I. Steinwart. "Support vector machines are universally consistent". In: Journal of Complexity 18.3 (2002), pp. 768–791 (cit. on p. 521).

[Sto77] C. J. Stone. "Consistent nonparametric regression". In: The annals of statistics (1977), pp. 595–620 (cit. on p. 520).

[SV06] N. Santhi and A. Vardy. On an Improvement over Rényi's Equivocation Bound. Presented at the 44-th Annual Allerton Conference on Communication, Control, and Computing, September 2006. Available at http://arxiv.org/abs/cs/0608087. 2006 (cit. on p. 504).

[Vap13] V. Vapnik. The nature of statistical learning theory. Springer science & business media, 2013 (cit. on p. 507).

[Wol96] D. H. Wolpert. "The lack of a priori distinctions between learning algorithms". In: Neural computation 8.7 (1996), pp. 1341–1390 (cit. on p. 532).

Part V

Policy and Social Values

DOI: 10.1561/9781638284772.ch16

Chapter 16

Differential Privacy, Public Policy, and the Law

By Jeremy Seeman

Differential privacy research has coalesced around a relatively narrow conceptualization of data privacy, motivated by provable guarantees and impossibility theorems discussed earlier in this book. Outside of this literature, though, privacy law scholars have long studied the impacts of large-scale data processing systems on privacy in a broader set of social and political contexts. This research area encompasses numerous disciplines, including not only law but also political science, social sciences, economics, philosophy, and public policy. In this chapter, we discuss the intersection of DP and privacy law scholarship, namely how these different perspectives on privacy influence each other.

16.1 Introduction

Information privacy scholars seem to be everywhere, with established literatures in law [SS03], political and social sciences [Wes68], economics [Pos81], philosophy [Rac75], and public policy [Tho75]. However, the preceding chapters of this book focus exclusively on differential privacy (DP) and similar privacy-enhancing technologies (PETs) as understood for scientists and engineers, by scientists and engineers. Disciplinary perspectives approach the broad problems of data privacy using different epistemic viewpoints, conceptual frameworks, political values, and research tools. We may hope that there is cross-pollination between quantitative and qualitative privacy scholars; however, such cross-disciplinary engagement does not happen as frequently or substantially as we might like. Disciplinary-specific language barriers make communication difficult, and privacy scholars tend to center their work around a wide variety of conflicting political values and incentives. In this chapter, we'll discuss how these perspectives inform DP not only as a mathematical framework, but as a sociotechnical system which configures specific relationships between data curators, users, and subjects.

By "sociotechnical system," a term of art in science and technology studies (STS) [WSSJ08], we mean a system with different interacting social and technical dimensions that mutually influence each other. We've already seen throughout this book how DP introduces systems-level engineering considerations that change how data analysts interact with their query results, especially in Part III (Application Areas) and Chapter 14 (Challenges and Solutions to Deploying Differential Privacy). Similarly, our understanding of social values through law and policy will inform how we implement these technologies. Understanding the bilateral nature of this relationship is essential to viewing social and technical problems with privacy engineering as inextricably linked. When working in the realm of theoretical computer science, it's always tempting to abstract away messy social context when designing privacy-aware systems. Still, when the rubber meets the road and DP systems get deployed in the wild, we can no longer rely on these abstractions to solve the challenging normative aspects of privacy for us. Technologies contribute to our understanding of these normative aspects by configuring the terms of how we use them, sometimes known as "scripts of action" [Akr92]. Similarly, the way we choose to define a particular problem implies a particular set of solutions [Sel+19]. DP relies on a strict definition of privacy harms through the quantification of privacy loss, which represents only one of many possible harms under the umbrella of privacy. By looking more broadly and holistically at privacy as a social and political phenomenon, we can gain a more precise understanding of how to deploy DP in ways that best reflect privacy as a values-laden process.

Such a perspective reflects similar intertwining of information technologies and privacy regulation. When states enforce privacy regulations, there are multitudes of actors who participate in the process, ranging from lawmakers and regulatory agencies to advocacy groups and privacy engineers themselves. These actors reflect different regulatory forces on lived privacy experiences, not only including PETs but laws, social norms, and markets [Les+99]. In these spaces where contestation naturally occurs, the kinds of evidence privacy engineers value operate differently than in the realm of computer science. Technical scholars can determine whether a data processing system satisfies a particular definition of DP by theoretical analysis alone; this is the celebrated "provability" of DP that formalizes data protections as inherent to the system. Alternatively, in privacy law, whether a particular regulation is satisfied cannot always be directly inferred from theoretical analysis. Legal decisions of this form are contextually specific, subjective, and evolve over time concurrently with new laws and technologies. DP's formal guarantees in this new setting are now only *evidence* of whether a particular regulatory standard is met. Moreover, the resulting decisions are politically contested by different parties with competing incentives to strengthen or weaken the regulatory implications of the law. This shouldn't come as a surprise to anyone; after all, data privacy technologies allocate rights and responsibilities to different parties, making them essentially political [Rog15].

Despite the messy politics of qualitative privacy work, those working on PETs ought to embrace this complexity, as technologists and policymakers have much to learn from each other. DP technologists can show how a technical understanding of DP's privacy quantification can reveal alignments or misalignments between privacy law and privacy technology. Similarly, policy analyses can reveal the kinds of social values and political dimensions beyond the consideration by DP alone. It's incredibly important that technical scholars acknowledge this relationship, because it is quite tempting to view DP's neat formalism as a "solution" to the messy and ambiguous problems of privacy law. This approach echoes the common refrain that the law is perennially "outdated," and new technologies ought to help resolve these ambiguities. Instead, technology and the law co-evolve and mutually shape one another because technologists have always played a key role in producing privacy law [Coh19]. Just as we should be weary of "solving" issues of fairness and bias in machine learning [Pow18] using mathematical tools alone, we should remind ourselves that any PET can be used or misused, independent of whether it confers formal guarantees. DP is but one tool in a long lineage of statistical disclosure limitation methods [Hun+12]; while DP offers a multitude of quantitative improvements over these previous techniques, the underlying policy problems for using PETs have not fundamentally changed with the introduction of DP. Therefore, the sharing of knowledge across these disciplines will help us resist naive solutionism of all forms, be it technical, legal, or otherwise.

Due to the complex and multifaceted nature of these problems, we can barely begin to scratch the surface on the topics raised by this chapter. Entire literatures have been devoted to points which take up only a few sentences in the following chapter. Moreover, the intersection of DP and other qualitative theories of information privacy is a rapidly expanding but still nascent research area. The goal of this chapter is to provide a lightweight introduction to other privacy approaches and their intersection with DP. This will largely be a descriptive exercise of notable legal and social theories of privacy with an analysis of the role DP plays in said theories.

Above all else, this chapter ought to serve as an entry-point for technical scholars to substantively engage with privacy scholars at large. To achieve these goals, we will significantly and intentionally narrow the scope to focus on three aspects of DP and the law:

1. For this chapter, "DP" will refer *only* to definitions which share the same properties as the original formulation in [DMNS06]: namely, robustness to post-processing, semantic interpretations, and composition. There are hundreds of different formal privacy definitions that claim some relationship to DP [DP19], and we do not have the space to compare the social and political nuances of each definition.
2. When we say "privacy law," we refer to existing laws and guidelines shared among a wide variety of data processing laws frequently cited in data processing regulations throughout the US and EU. Our goal is to avoid pinning our discussions to any one law, as we do not attempt to do the work lawyers do; instead, we attempt to capture some core elements of legal reasoning reflected in data processing regulations, knowing such an approach lacks the nuance and specificity that detailed case studies can provide.
3. When we say "public policy," we refer to broad-scope scholarship that attempts to influence or reform the elements of legal scholarship as applied in the US and EU. We acknowledge that this Western-centric viewpoint omits comparative histories, cultures, and other systemic approaches to data privacy outside these geographic and cultural spheres of influence.

Organization of the Chapter

The rest of the chapter is organized as follows.

- Section 16.2 discusses the many kinds of privacy harms that concern qualitative scholars. We then discuss how the technical interventions posed by DP systems regulate these harms, noting that DP configures relationships between data subjects and data collectors in ways that home in on a narrow subset of these potential privacy harms. Even of that subset, DP addresses these harms in a particular way that strengthens or weakens the scope and magnitude of their protections.
- Section 16.3 discusses the guiding principles on which most current privacy legislation operates. By analyzing DP's relationship to the guidelines which undergird privacy laws, we can understand DP's relationship to legal design without relying on the minutiae of specific regulations. Like the previous section, we will see how DP systems interact with social conceptions of these guidelines, again focusing on compliance with some principles at the expense of others.

- Section 16.4 discusses recent developments in omnibus data protection policies, which centralize regulatory authority and directly regulate the threats of pseudonymization and reconstruction attacks which motivated DP. This feature has attracted the attention of quantitative scholars, as there are immediate connections between differential privacy as a formal guarantee and ambiguities in the broader definitions of "personal information" from these omnibus regulations.
- Section 16.5 discusses broader policy problems in existing data legislation, focusing on social and political values not currently reflected in privacy law and the way it is enforced. In this section, we discuss the role that DP plays in modulating these values.

16.2 Identifying Privacy Harms

16.2.1 Taxonomy of Privacy Harms

Early conceptions of privacy date back to the common law recognition of privacy harms, i.e., privacy violations as a tort. However, privacy's multifaceted nature makes it hard for us to understand what is meant when we refer to "privacy harms." PETs like DP were not intended to mitigate all possible privacy harms, so for this chapter, we need a common language to narrow the scope of our discussion. To make our harms of interest more concrete, we will rely on Solove's "Taxonomy of Privacy," which outlines four broad categories of privacy harms [Sol05]. Much as true with any taxonomy of social phenomena, the categories outlined are not neatly defined, nor exhaustive, and some legal theorists have been critical of this approach ([Bar06], among others). Still, the taxonomy serves as a helpful tool for focusing on what we mean by privacy harms in the context of DP. Moreover, it helps us concretize the kinds of harms that DP targets and those that DP omits from its consideration:

1. *Information collection:* practices that "create disruption[s] based on the process of data gathering, even if no information is revealed publicly."
    - *Surveillance:* "watching, listening to, or recording of an individual's activities."
    - *Interrogation:* "various forms of questioning or probing for information."
2. *Information processing:* "the use, storage, and manipulation of data that has been collected."
    - *Aggregation:* "The combination of various pieces of data about a person."

- *Identification:* The process of "linking information to particular individuals."
- *Insecurity:* "Carelessness in protecting stored information from leaks and improper access.
- *Secondary use:* "The use of information collected for one purpose for a different purpose without the data subject's consent."
- *Exclusion:* "The failure to allow the data subject to know about the data that others have about her and participate in its handling and use."

3. *Information dissemination:* practices involving the public dissemination of information.
    - *Breach of confidentiality:* "Breaking a promise to keep a person's information confidential."
    - *Disclosure:* "the revelation of truthful information about a person that impacts the way others judge her character."
    - *Exposure:* protections against information that "creates injury because we have developed social practices to conceal aspects of life that we find animal-like or disgusting."
    - *Increased accessibility:* the process of "amplifying the accessibility of information."
    - *Blackmail:* "[The] threat to disclose personal information."
    - *Appropriation:* "The use of the data subject's identity to serve the aims and interests of another."
    - *Distortion:* "The dissemination of false or misleading information about individuals."
4. *Invasion:* practice which invade people's private affairs which "need not involve personal information."
    - *Intrusion:* "Invasive acts that disturb one's tranquility or solitude."
    - *Decisional interference:* "The government's incursion into the data subject's decisions regarding her private affairs."

Conceptually, DP describes privacy as a technical property of the way data is *processed*, not of the way it is collected or disseminated. Moreover, because it is primarily concerned with personal information, DP deliberately brackets privacy harms like invasions, which do not strictly involve personal information. This is important for narrowing the scope of relevant privacy law; for example, many constitutional law scholars studying the Fourth Amendment focus primarily on decisional interference through the lens of state power (see [Stu98; Tok16] for examples). Such concerns, while certainly valid, are not immediately relevant for analyzing DP.

16.2.2 Situating DP in the Taxonomy

DP's technical properties aim to protect against many of the potential harms listed above, but in a very particular way. When viewed as a response to privacy threats from database reconstruction, DP provides defenses against harmful information dissemination, particularly disclosure. However, DP does not directly limit all possible disclosure risks because it quantifies privacy loss through relative risk measures, not absolute risk measures. In this way, DP is a harm-reduction project: since any useful statistic discloses some information about the data subjects whose information was used to produce it, DP can only limit additional information leaked through data processing [DN03]. Such a perspective also focuses specifically on disclosures attributable to how the data is processed, as opposed to how other sources of information could be combined with results published under DP; this feature has made it quite attractive to data curators hoping to demonstrate a lack of liability for disclosure harms emanating from data processing. On the contrary, if the potential for harmful disclosure was already quite high before the DP system was implemented, then DP alone cannot remedy that effect nor mitigate a preexisting potential for harms. This is especially important when assessing holistically whether a data curator's actions lead to such harms, as DP only quantifies information leakage directly attributable to the privacy mechanism.

Similarly, DP places restrictions on which kinds of information processing tasks fall within its framework, naturally restricting the space of processing tasks and therefore limiting some forms of identification and aggregation. Here, though, we ought to be more careful with our terminology when referring to "identification." DP was motivated by algorithmic attacks which attempt to reconstruct information about individuals, potentially in the absence of unique identifiers (see [DSSU17] for an overview of such attacks). Whether or not reconstructed records constitute re-identification in the legal sense tends to be contextually specific, as it depends on the mechanism through which descriptions of reconstructed records can be linked back to re-identified individuals. Sometimes, this mapping can be quite easy; for example, when the U.S. Census Bureau performed their reconstruction attack, they focused primarily on reconstructed records which isolated unique Census responses, allowing for easy matching to alternative data sources using naive deterministic record linkage tools [GAM19]. In other cases, the mapping can be quite hard; for example, descriptive statistics about large populations can technically fail to satisfy DP, but the amount of background information needed to demonstrate tangible re-identification harm can be infeasibly large. To demonstrate, suppose a hypothetical "oracle" data curator published the exact number of people in the United States who were vaccinated against COVID-19 at a specific point in time. While publishing this statistic technically violates DP, it would be hard to argue in court that this statistic could practically lead to a meaningful re-identification of one individual's COVID-19 vaccination status, even though the database reconstruction theorem proves it is technically plausible. Therefore, we must analyze DP based on evidence for or against satisfying individual privacy regulations, as the answer cannot stem inherently from the formal guarantees of the system.

While some privacy harms are directly or indirectly addressed by technical design, others are intentionally placed outside of DP's purview. By focusing on harms emanating from data processing outputs, DP does not consider harms in the information collection stage, nor harms from insecure computation. This caveat is especially important: DP cannot remedy a potentially harmful data collection process a posteriori because it intervenes at the information processing stage, not the information collection stage. Note that even in the more stringent local trust model, which sanitizes individual records before they are centrally aggregated, the act of surveillance alone can cause substantive privacy harms independent of whether the data is processed with local DP protections. For example, suppose users of a cell phone application accept a terms of service agreement which, unbeknownst to the users, collects data that users would not want collected under any circumstances. Local DP protections could not be used to ex post facto justify the surveillance, raising important questions about the relationship between DP and consent (which we will discuss later). In this way, DP intentionally abstracts away privacy harms emanating from how data is used after information dissemination.

The fact that DP does not address harms from surveillance at scale is particularly important, because DP relies on a quantification of disclosure risk that is, to some degree, independent of scale. On purely technical terms, this makes complete sense: the kinds of formal guarantees quantified by DP are agnostic to the size of the underlying database. Indeed, for many aggregate statistics, if a data collector wants comparable data utility when using a DP result, data utility can be improved simply by increasing the sample size while maintaining the same privacy guarantee. At the same time, there's something unusual happening when we say "to improve data utility while weakening disclosure risks, surveil more data subjects." In this way, DP pits two different privacy harms against one another, deferring one to the point in time immediately before DP intervenes in the system. Techniques to mitigate surveillance, often known under the umbrella term of "data minimization" [PH10], have proven to be a lightning rod for political discourse. Many technology and industry advocates argue that data minimization itself stifles innovation enabled by "big data" [TP11], directly conflicts with software business needs [SA18], and ought to be recast through the lens of secure and transparent data processing [Sch+18]. On the contrary, social theorists argue that normalized surveillance negatively influences our relationships to being known by the state [Har15] and performing for the state [Han20]; moreover, centering discussions around security and transparency help create these negative conditions instead of deterring them [Bir16]. Cohen notably writes that "commercial culture that sees privacy as threatening its own valued practices of knowledge production will register privacy regulation as a threat" [Coh12]. While we cannot resolve such debates here, we must acknowledge that DP enables a particular relationship to surveillance based on how it does (and does not) intervene in data processing systems.

Given the kinds of privacy harms DP centers and those DP brackets, assessing DP systems requires first asking whether DP targets the harms in question. For those harms DP targets, we must then consider whether the degree of protection proves sufficient for the laws, policies, or other regulations in place. This helps to align what DP is intended to do with how it could be used (or potentially misused) as a regulatory mechanism. Importantly, whether DP satisfies a particular law alone can sometimes fail to capture whether a particular harm is mitigated. We ought to remember that, especially in the U.S., many harmful technologies are entirely legal, and satisfying privacy laws need not imply no harm can be caused. Organizations may be incentivized to prevent harms holistically, or they may be incentivized to do the bare minimum to eschew liability. Regardless, it's essential that we identify harms as they map onto a data curator's goals, while recognizing DP can only address a subset of potential privacy harms.

16.3 Privacy as Individual Rights, Access, and Control

16.3.1 Guiding Principles for Privacy Law

Next, we'll briefly discuss how information technologies motivated existing laws and policies that aim to prevent privacy harms. Even since the late 1800s, developments in privacy law in the U.S. were often reactive to new threats enabled by new information technologies. Warren and Brandeis's seminal article "The Right to Privacy" served as a response to photography's threats from Yellow Journalism [WB90]. The expansion of the Fourth Amendment in Katz v. United States grew from demonstrated threats to the privacy of telephone conversations [Cou67]. The development of Fair Information Practice Principles, or FIPPs, originated from the growing use of automated data processing systems throughout the federal government and in private organizations [War73]. So, for over a century, technology has been the impetus for developments in U.S. privacy law.

Legal scholarship has responded to these developments by study privacy through the lens of how individuals manage information about themselves. The formalization of privacy as inseparable from individual autonomy can be traced to the seminal work of Alan Westin, who framed the right to privacy as an act of self-determination [Wes68]. The relationship between individuals and society-at-large was up to the individual, who would manage what they disclose about themselves and how based on their personal preferences for privacy versus disclosure. The process of equating the right to privacy with individual autonomy places privacy rights firmly within neoliberal political traditions, in that the information individuals choose to disclose about themselves has economic interpretations as individual property with its own particular set of market dynamics [Lit99; Sch03]. By centering privacy around individual rights and autonomy versus control, a new social theory of privacy was born which embedded itself squarely within projects of political freedom.

Today, when we think of data privacy law, we may mentally jump to specific regulations that focus on ways individuals can intervene in the data collection process. This includes U.S. examples such as the Fair Credit Reporting Act, the Right to Financial Privacy Act, and the Family Educational Rights and Privacy Act (FERPA). Yet aside from protections attributable to classes of sensitive data, privacy regulation was (and in many ways still is) guideline-based, notably with the introduction of Fair Information Practice Principles (FIPPs) which informed similar developments in the E.U. and further abroad. These principles originated within the Federal Trade Commission and their influence is so widespread that some scholars consider the FTC's regulatory power as a form of common law [SH14; Hoo16]. As privacy concerns grow to be more complex and multifaceted, FIPPs have been viewed simultaneously as outdated and indispensable, representing a "ground floor" for privacy regulation [Har16]. To concretize our discussion, we'll focus on FIPPs in this section to avoid tailoring this chapter too specifically to any one law. We recall the FIPPs here:

1. *The Collection Limitation Principle.* "There should be limits to the collection of personal data and any such data should be obtained by lawful and fair means and, where appropriate, with the knowledge or consent of the data subject."
2. *The Data Quality Principle.* "Personal data should be relevant to the purposes for which they are to be used and, to the extent necessary for those purposes, should be accurate, complete and kept up-to-date."
3. *The Purpose Specification Principle.* "The purposes for which personal data are collected should be specified not later than at the time of data collection and the subsequent use limited to the fulfillment of those purposes or such others as are not incompatible with those purposes and as are specified on each occasion of change of purpose."

4. *The Use Limitation Principle.* "Personal data should not be disclosed, made available or otherwise used for purposes other than those specified, except a) with the consent of the data subject, or b) by the authority of law."
5. *The Security Safeguards Principle.* "Personal data should be protected by reasonable security safeguards against such risks as loss or unauthorized access, destruction, use, modification or disclosure of data."
6. *The Openness Principle.* "There should be a general policy of openness about developments, practices and policies with respect to personal data. Means should be readily available of establishing the existence and nature of personal data and the main purposes of their use, as well as the identity and usual residence of the data controller."
7. *The Individual Participation Principle.* "An individual should have the right: a) to obtain from a data controller, or otherwise, confirmation of whether or not the data controller has data relating to him; b) to have data relating to him communicated to him, within a reasonable time, at a charge, if any, that is not excessive; in a reasonable manner, and in a form that is readily intelligible to him; c) to be given reasons if a request made under subparagraphs (a) and (b) is denied and to be able to challenge such denial; and d) to challenge data relating to him and, if the challenge is successful, to have the data erased, rectified, completed or amended;"
8. *The Accountability Principle.* "A data controller should be accountable for complying with measures which give effect to the principles stated above."

16.3.2 DP's Relationship to Fair Information Practice Principles

Like the relationship between DP and the taxonomy of privacy harms, DP situates itself as aligned with some of these principles listed above while directly or indirectly ignoring or negating other aspects of them. We focus first on use limitation, which aligns both implicitly and explicitly with DP's technical properties. In an idealized DP setting, each specified purpose for data processing has an associated set of output statistics, each processed with its own privacy loss budget. Optimal mechanisms, therefore, ensure the most information can be gained for a particular specified use while limiting other uses which leak identifying information. In this way, DP as a query system is designed to ensure use limitation from publicly disseminated statistics, assuming the data processor satisfies a reasonable standard for purpose specification.

The condition that data processors provide reasonable purpose specification to data subjects, however, can be more complicated for DP systems. Theoretically, DP encourages openness in how data processing operations through methodological transparency. One could argue the main benefit of provable privacy guarantees is in precisely the ability to disclose how data are processed without providing additional privacy risks. While certainly a virtue, there are other barriers to limiting the effectiveness of this transparency in practice, which largely depend on how much data processors are willing to embrace this transparency. To illustrate this, consider a scenario where a data curator specifies the DP data processing purpose as "personalization" with no additional information provided to data subjects. This is a common technique used in advertising technologies, and the relationship between personalization and privacy depends almost entirely on contexts where it either directly benefits and/or harms the subject [SRN19]. In this setting, the data curator's choice to disclose the use of DP statistics serves as attempt to reconcile the competing interests of personalized data processing with privacy protection, a fundamental issue at the heart of personalized technology. In this way, the transparency of using DP is something that data curators use to justify privacy as a social value in the act of data processing, granting the data curator what are known as "transparency affordances" [Cla21]. Organizations that appear transparent are viewed as more credible and more trustworthy, regardless of whether the information that's "transparently" disclosed has substantive meaning to data subjects. Naturally, data curators whose data processing techniques are proprietary would be reluctant to disclose that information; the concept of "trade secrets" has been weaponized by industry for ages [Men17]. So, while DP could hypothetically make organizations more substantively transparent, it could also entrench performative transparency and justify limited approaches to purpose specification.

Of the different principles presented throughout FIPPs, one could argue none attracts more confusion or controversy than the accountability principle. While most agree that the principles outlined by FIPPs are reasonable, the elephant in the room has always been how such principles are enforced to regulate data collectors. While we might think to turn to top-down approaches based on a hierarchy of federal, state, and local laws, a multitude of actors ranging from state regulators to privacy engineers and other privacy professionals make up the ground-legislating work of privacy law. These people are largely at liberty to determine what constitutes regulatory compliance (more on this later). For DP, privacy technologists and DP advocates often take a dominant role in this conversation by design, not necessarily intention. DP's technical conception of privacy risk and data processing requires a specialized set of skills beyond what most data processors have or can feasibly operationalize. As a result, using DP for the expressed purpose of regulation gives privacy engineers additional leeway in dictating these terms. This is neither strictly good nor strictly bad. On the one hand, DP's conception of privacy risk helps quantify harms directly attributable to data processing tasks; this ensures that should privacy harms emanate from the results, we have a formal understanding of how the data processor contributed to the harms [DN10]. On the other hand, data curators may be incentivized to dictate the limits of reasonable regulation, as ethical contestations tend be resolved in particular ways that do not challenge institutional power in data collection processes [MM+19]. At a high level, these issues are not unique to DP, but reflect deeper philosophical problems in using technical tools in self-regulation [Bla01].

16.4 Omnibus Privacy Law: Reforming the Legal Landscape

16.4.1 Relocating the "Personal" in Personal Data

In response to the patchwork of privacy regulations in the US and EU, recent developments in privacy law have centered around omnibus legislation that attempts to repair these holes within the patchwork. The most well-known of these regulations is the European Union's General Data Protection Regulation (GDPR), whose creation has heavily influenced similar legislation elsewhere, such as with California Consumer Privacy Act (CCPR). As the most-well studied and most influential of general data protections, GDPR fundamentally changes many aspects of privacy regulation beyond the principles enshrined in FIPPs-style regulations. Omnibus regulations like GDPR have massive implications for DP and other privacy-enhancing technologies because they are the first to legally enshrine strict, wide-spreading requirements on how data are processed. This has made such laws incredibly consequential for data subjects, collectors, and processors alike. Taken as a whole, these omnibus regulations are extremely dense, wide sweeping, and raise countless open questions about what constitutes their compliance.

We could easily dedicate an entire chapter to every intricacy and nuance of the leviathan that is GDPR. Instead, we will focus on how the quantitative thinking used by DP scholars helps to clarify the scope of where GDPR ought to apply. When it does, GDPR aims to guarantee very specific data subject rights when their personal information gets processed. The following are among the most consequential data subject rights:

- Article 7 (granting and revoking consent): users should be free to easily grant and revoke consent for data processing, and the terms for using a service should only depend on necessary data processing. Specifically, "when assessing whether consent is freely given, utmost account shall be taken of whether, inter alia, the performance of a contract, including the provision of a service, is conditional on consent to the processing of personal data that is not necessary for the performance of that contract."

- Article 12 (transparent notice): when personal data processing is authorized by subject consent, the user agreement must inform the data subject "in a concise, transparent, intelligible and easily accessible form, using clear and plain language, in particular for any information addressed specifically to a child."
- Article 15 (right of access): data subjects can request access to their personal information, including but not limited to "the purposes of the processing" and "where the personal data are not collected from the data subject, any available information as to their source."
- Article 17 (right to erasure): data subjects can request the erasure of their personal data in certain circumstances, including but not limited to when consent is revoked or when "the personal data are no longer necessary in relation to the purposes for which they were collected or otherwise processed."
- Articles 21 and 22 (rights to object): in certain circumstances, data subjects can object to data processing when "subject to a decision based solely on automated processing, including profiling, which produces legal effects concerning him or her or similarly significantly affects him or her." Notably, this does not apply when "the processing is necessary for the performance of a task carried out for reasons of public interest," specifically "scientific or historical research purposes."

All the data subject rights described above hinge on the precise definition of "personal information." Because data that falls outside this definition is no longer subject to the strict rules surrounding GDPR, clarifying the bounds of "personal" information has been a central source of tension for how to implement GDPR [FP20]. Let's look at how GDPR defines personal information (Article 4):

> "[Personal information is] any information relating to an identified or identifiable natural person ('data subject'); an identifiable natural person is one who can be identified, directly or indirectly, in particular by reference to an identifier such as a name, an identification number, location data, an online identifier or to one or more factors specific to the physical, physiological, genetic, mental, economic, cultural or social identity of that natural person."

In most other privacy regulations before GDPR, personal information was defined through the lens of what individuals specifically contributed to databases about their person. GDPR significantly expands this definition by including *identifiable* information, i.e., information which could hypothetically enable leakage of personal data. Interpreting this language correctly would be consequential for data processors, as Recital 26 uses it explicitly to determine the scope of GDPR's influence:

> "Personal data which have undergone pseudonymization, which could be attributed to a natural person by the use of additional information should be considered to be information on an identifiable natural person. To determine whether a natural person is identifiable, account should be taken of all the means reasonably likely to be used, such as singling out, either by the controller or by another person to identify the natural person directly or indirectly. To ascertain whether means are reasonably likely to be used to identify the natural person, account should be taken of all objective factors, such as the costs of and the amount of time required for identification, taking into consideration the available technology at the time of the processing and technological developments."

This language created space for confusion about what it means to properly pseudonymize data, requiring careful differentiation between two sources of information attributable to individuals: that which is directly attributable to how the data was processed, and that which could have been plausibly done with public information independent of future data processing [SK16]. Naturally, PETs like DP explicitly codify this difference in how privacy loss gets defined and quantified, eliciting a surprisingly organic connection between DP and the law, which we'll explore next.

16.4.2 Connecting Mathematical and Legal Formalisms in Personal Information

Between Article 4 and Recital 26, we see a major shift in the recognition of reconstruction harms that was only ever implicit in previous legislation. Article 26 goes much further, recognizing that pseudonymization can pose the same privacy threats as direct access to personal data *and* providing threshold tests for whether a data processing procedure "singles out" individuals. Because this language is so suggestive of differential privacy's worldview, numerous computer science scholars have formalized these concepts in a direct analysis of the law, adding mathematically formal structure to the concept of "singling out" [CD18; CN20; ACNW21] and connecting privacy attacks at large (e.g., [DSSU17]) to DP's ability to formally restrict statistical outputs. The language of Recital 26 bears immediate connection to the theoretical properties of DP: by quantifying relative disclosure risks attributable to the act of data processing, DP's particular risk quantification is immune to arbitrarily broad adversarial assumptions, taking a position that captures stronger notions than "the costs of and the amount of time required for identification" and "the available technology." Such work spotlights the important framing considerations that make DP a beneficial tool for interpreting GDPR. Taken to its conclusion, these scholars argue the beneficial properties of DP ought to be codified as principles which determine when processing is sufficiently pseudonymized [Alt+22].

In the last paragraph, we showed how the kinds of quantitative reasoning used to motivate DP align well with helping legal scholars codify inferences attributable to data processing operations. At the same time, we need to remember that DP governance requires addressing whether or not DP systems are implemented in ways that protect "all the means reasonably likely to be used." Much like the Katz test about "reasonable expectations of privacy," determining whether reconstruction vulnerabilities are "reasonable" remains the existential question of using DP to comply with GDPR and other omnibus legislation. Because DP focuses on relative harms, not absolute harms, a privacy loss budget alone lacks the context necessary to determine whether singling out has become substantially more feasible using the DP result. The database reconstruction theorem which motivates the relative conception of privacy harms does not "solve" the thresholding problem, but instead recasts it in terms of relative guarantees. Now, the question involves determining reasonable thresholds on prior information and affiliated privacy loss budgets. This brings us to modern problems about what broader purposes data privacy regulations are trying to serve, which we address next.

16.5 Modern Policy Perspectives: Towards Collective Rights

In this last section, we transition to policy work, focusing on what privacy law could be and not its current state. Many criticisms of existing privacy laws are not directed at the principles or laws themselves, but instead critiques of governance and organizational structures which attempt (and often fail) to properly implement or enforce them. At other times, public policy and privacy law research takes issue with the underlying philosophies dominant to privacy law in a few ways relevant to DP. This chapter investigates these modern developments and their connections to DP.

16.5.1 Consent and Data Subject Burden

Data privacy law is largely built around individual consent. Nearly every data protection in the FIPPs and associated laws has exemptions for cases when data subjects consent to their collection. This results in ballooned terms of service agreements and lengthy privacy policies that most end users ignore, often by design [OO20]. Because the burden of privacy self-management is often too onerous for data subjects, their privacy rights become a Kafkaesque paradox where data subjects are largely deprived of essential information needed for them to negotiate on whether to contribute their data [Sol12]. As a result of these policies, consent-based mechanisms for data collection exist less to empower users to make educated decisions, but instead largely to coerce consent and absolve data curators from liability for potential harms [Coh12]. Even on their own terms, terms of notice-and-consent often lack sufficient notice itself, creating conditions where data subjects fail to understand how their data is used in the first place [Sus19]. Despite these problems, it's exceptionally hard to imagine privacy law perspectives without notice and consent, as it's intended to directly help individuals manage their privacy.

DP is intimately related to consent, in ways that both empower data subjects and potentially extend the burdens of self-management. On a purely technical level, the privacy semantics associated with DP can be best understood through the lens of consent as a causal intervention [TSD17]. In colloquial interpretations of DP's guarantees, DP bounds whether one contributes to the database aligns with this causal interpretation, in that DP protects against learning about your individual data through consenting to data collection. Moreover, DP's methodological transparency hypothetically allows data curators to disclose how personal data more specifically is used. On the flip side, however, non-technical audiences may struggle with how to best interpret their personal privacy risks associated with using the technology through the lens of DP. Something that seems easy to a technical audience, like interpreting a privacy loss budget, requires expressing a complicated sociological trade-off that could only exacerbate problems with privacy self-management. So, although DP has strong connections to consent as the expressive regulatory mechanism, consent, there are underlying problems with the efficacy of the mechanism itself.

16.5.2 Contextual Integrity

Throughout this chapter, we've discussed privacy harms in relatively neutral, sterile language, which can fail to reflect the emotional context present when discussing lived privacy experiences [Sta16]. When subjects share information, the experience can be privacy-fulfilling or privacy-harming information sharing depends on numerous contextual factors. Data subjects share personal data for numerous reasons, but depending on the circumstances, the data curator, data subject, and data users may not be aligned on their motivations. Moreover, the kind of information collected and how it is collected play equally important roles in assessing social attitudes towards data processing. These dimensions of privacy as a contextually situated flow of information are outlined in Nissenbaum's framework of Contextual Integrity (CI) [Nis09]. Within a particular social context, CI defines information flows with five key elements: data subjects, sender of the data, recipient of the data, information type, and transmission principle. As a common example, when patients (data subjects and senders) share information about their medical history (information type) with their doctor (data recipient), there is an expectation of confidentiality unless explicitly consented otherwise (transmission principle). CI interrogates information flows as privacy harms depending on whether the contextual norms surrounding the information flow are respected. This highly influential theory has spawned a broad range of analyses, including those attempting to integrate DP and other algorithmic practices with CI [Nis16; BGN+17].

On purely qualitative grounds, it makes perfect sense to use CI to determine how best to implement any PET, including DP. Viewing privacy regulation through the lens of CI offers more nuance and complexity than consent-based or control-based perspectives, as it contextually specifies the normative expectations of information flows that these more traditional perspectives lack. At the same time, DP concerns itself with whether personal data is used in a personal matter, i.e., with the expressed intent of constructing information about an individual. Therefore, DP's agnosticism to downstream uses flattens one important contextual dimension of the data processing task. Similarly, contexts are socially co-constructed and understood among their participants through communication [Spo04]. Yet the contexts introduced by new technologies like DP are not necessarily grounded in lived privacy experiences because of their probabilistic nature. In general, typical data subjects consider personal thresholds for disclosure far differently than the way DP suggests, as demonstrated empirically through user research [CKR21]. Without a mutually shared understanding of the transmission principle, contextual integrity may not necessarily capture privacy expectations. To a degree, this is an existential problem with CI, not DP: as we discussed earlier, contextual norms are intertwined with and mediated by sources of power. So how to best integrate DP and CI remains an open question, but one worth pursuing to capture these connections.

16.5.3 Power and Accountability

As with all privacy-enhancing technologies, implementing DP systems requires significant effort and human organization among data curators, subjects, users, and regulators. Yet throughout this chapter, we haven't discussed much at all about how data privacy laws are enforced in the wild. It's often presumed that when a data processing system isn't "private" enough, some regulator would ideally intervene. However, a common misconception about privacy law (especially in the U.S.) is that it stems from traditional sites of top-down legal power, i.e., national, state, and local laws, authorities granted to regulatory agencies, and consequential court cases. When we trace the paper trails to see who's ultimately making the consequential decisions, the story becomes significantly more complicated.

In Ari Ezra Waldman's seminal article "Privacy Law's False Promise," he precisely documents these enforcement patterns by drawing on interviews with the groundworkers of privacy regulation [Wal19]. Past work had located sites of regulatory power in state attorneys general [Cit16] and corporate leadership roles [BM15], but Waldman demonstrates how this patchwork of external regulation and self-regulation has encouraged the "managerialization" of privacy law through symbolic corporate compliance and performative box-ticking. It turns out that data processors themselves play an outsized role in determining whether a particular system complies with privacy law, where the main decisions of consequences are performative: proper trainings, auditable (but not audited) records of past privacy decisions, etc. So long as someone within a data processing organization performs their duties within the formal confines of the bureaucracy, the decisions made do little to with their substance. This phenomenon, known as "legal endogeneity," represents a deep problem in how complex and politically contested regulations are enforced; privacy law is only one of many areas where the law suffers from this endogeneity [Ede16]. In some ways, this is to be expected based on the influence of data processors in creating the law. Regulatory agencies are often composed of former industry representatives, so the revolving doors of policymakers and data processing stakeholders can help precisely encourage these circumstances [Eng13].

This predicament poses an existential question for DP advocates: what role could DP play in the legal endogeneity of privacy law? As we've seen throughout this chapter, DP represents a particular framing of privacy harms which encourages generally stronger privacy protections than previous PETs. One could argue that if we temporarily ignore the thresholding problem of setting appropriate upper bounds on privacy loss budgets, systems which use DP as their "check-box" are still generally improved. On the contrary, because data processors have substantial leeway in determining what constitutes a reasonable threshold for "using DP," self-regulation may instead further encourage the legal endogeneity of privacy law. Furthermore, because DP requires a baseline understanding of its technical properties that most regulators do not have, this prerequisite knowledge alone could shift power to more technical stakeholders, giving them more leeway to self-determine if systems are implemented reasonably. Such a shift also makes auditing substantially more difficult: executing reconstruction attacks, let alone identifying possible reconstruction harms, can be burdensome for anyone involved. Formal privacy methods like DP largely aim to prevent such attacks from being necessary; at the same time, privacy loss budgets suffer from a lack of contextual specificity to realized harms. Like many of the social dimensions of privacy we've discussed before, the interventions posed by DP may or may not improve how power is allocated in these systems. Such a problem reflects deeper issues with the role of technical expertise in pivotal decision-making processes [Eya19].

16.5.4 Relational Data and Separability from Data Usage

DP focuses on an individualistic notion of data privacy through individual disclosure risks, a concept quite literally baked into the technical definition of privacy loss. As discussed earlier, this strengthens the connections between DP and political theories centered around neoliberalism, where privacy is defined through the lens of individual autonomy. Such a perspective ignores the numerous ways our privacy relations and decisions are not uniquely determined by individuals; [Coh12] writes that "the liberal self who is the subject of privacy theory and privacy policymaking does not exist...the self who is the real subject of privacy law and policy is socially constructed, emerging gradually from a preexisting cultural and relational substrate." By this, Cohen refers to social, cultural, and political forces which modulate our subjective and time-evolving experiences with boundary management in the broader sense. When we choose to "consent" to participate in a data processing task, we are not making individualized decisions in a social vacuum, but instead acting within a particular context in conjunction with broader forces playing a role in how we participate.

Such a perspective becomes important when we consider the kinds of privacy harms DP does not directly address, namely when we share information about others or used to determine our relationship to others. In Viljoen's "A Relational Theory of Data Governance," this idea is made explicit, writing that individualized notions of data privacy "miss the point of data production in a digital economy: to put people into population-based relations with one another" [Vil20]. Viljoen analyzes "horizontal relations" not between data subjects and data collectors, but among data subjects that mediate how their information is rendered at the population level. Because DP both homes in on individual disclosure risks and abstracts away potential harms from population-based relations by design (for example, see [Jon21]), these relations could be seen as falling outside DP's purview.

Such work invites questions about whether, and if so, how, we should consider the relationship between data collection and use. Like many aspects of data privacy, this too has proved to be a lightning rod of contestation. Some claim that issues of privacy should concern individual information leakage independent of use, whereas the concerns arising from "horizontal relations" more likely stem from issues of fairness and justice in how data are used [DM13]. Alternatively, others argue that we need to consider these data relations as privacy problems, where the relations in question are specifically enabled due to contextual information flows that fail to align with existing norms [BN14]. DP alone cannot resolve these issues, but it's important to acknowledge the kinds of data relations not strictly captured by individual privacy losses.

16.6 Concluding Remarks

Throughout this chapter, the following central themes have emerged in our discussions:

1. DP systems invoke interventions at the data processing stage in a particular way to target certain privacy harms while bracketing others. The way DP targets these technical risks DP does not delegitimize the real harms outside its scope.
2. DP, like any PET, requires contextual evaluation to determine when its use passes a threshold for satisfying a particular law. Who gets to determine this threshold remains one of the central challenges in enacting privacy regulations.
3. The formal properties of DP can help legal scholars concretize certain ambiguous aspects of privacy law, but this formalization alone does not provide a substitute for the contextual evaluation of DP systems.
4. DP's framing of disclosure risk is inherently tied to particular aspects and interpretations of data privacy regulations, and such ties may or may be not be representative of the legal mechanisms that best enshrine privacy as a social value.

Understanding the nuances and complexities of privacy law scholarship remains an important research goal and an exciting opportunity for new work at the intersection of quantitative and qualitative methods. We acknowledge that technologists who are excited by the promise of DP may be discouraged by the complexity of these problems or disheartened to hear so many legal scholars are skeptical or critical of these technological advances. Our goal with this chapter is not to sow disillusionment, but to describe how technologists are just as much involved in the production of privacy-mediated power relations as the multitude of actors we've discussed in this chapter. If anything, this chapter ought to encourage and excite technologists who wish to substantively engage with qualitative privacy literature in ways that can advance our social understanding of all privacy-preserving technologies, not just DP.[i]

i. This chapter was written and first submitted in early 2023. Since its submission, legal, ethical, and social studies of PETs like DP has emerged as a burgeoning research field. We hope that this book chapter continues to serves as an entry point into this exciting and rapidly expanding new literature.

References

[ACNW21] M. Altman, A. Cohen, K. Nissim, and A. Wood. "What a hybrid legal-technical analysis teaches us about privacy regulation: The case of singling out". In: BUJ Sci. & Tech. L. 27 (2021). Publisher: HeinOnline, p. 1 (cit. on p. 559).

[Akr92] M. Akrich. The de-scription of technical objects. 1992 (cit. on p. 546).

[Alt+22] M. Altman, A. Cohen, E. A. Markatou, F. Falzon, K. Nissim, M. J. Reymond, S. Saraogi, and A. Wood. "A principled approach to defining anonymization as applied to EU data protection law". In: SSRN (2022) (cit. on p. 559).

[Bar06] A. Bartow. "A feeling of unease about privacy law". In: U. Pa. L. Rev. PENNumbra 155 (2006). Publisher: HeinOnline, p. 52 (cit. on p. 549).

[BGN+17] S. Benthall, S. Gürses, H. Nissenbaum, et al. Contextual integrity through the lens of computer science. Now Publishers, 2017 (cit. on p. 562).

[Bir16] C. Birchall. "Shareveillance: Subjectivity between open and closed data". In: Big Data & Society 3.2 (2016). Publisher: Sage Publications Sage UK: London, England, p. 2053951716663965 (cit. on p. 553).

[Bla01] J. Black. "Decentring regulation: Understanding the role of regulation and self-regulation in a "post-regulatory" world". In: Current legal problems 54.1 (2001). Publisher: Oxford University Press Oxford, pp. 103–146 (cit. on p. 557).

[BM15] K. A. Bamberger and D. K. Mulligan. Privacy on the ground: driving corporate behavior in the United States and Europe. MIT Press, 2015 (cit. on p. 563).

[BN14] S. Barocas and H. Nissenbaum. "Big data's end run around anonymity and consent". In: Privacy, big data, and the public good: Frameworks for engagement 1 (2014). Publisher: Cambridge University Press, NY, pp. 44–75 (cit. on p. 564).

[CD18] R. Cummings and D. Desai. "The role of differential privacy in gdpr compliance". In: FAT'18: Proceedings of the Conference on Fairness, Accountability, and Transparency. 2018 (cit. on p. 559).

[Cit16] D. K. Citron. "The privacy policymaking of state attorneys general". In: Notre Dame L. Rev. 92 (2016). Publisher: HeinOnline, p. 747 (cit. on p. 563).

[CKR21] R. Cummings, G. Kaptchuk, and E. M. Redmiles. ""I need a better description": An Investigation Into User Expectations For Differential Privacy". In: Proceedings of the 2021 ACM SIGSAC Conference on Computer and Communications Security. 2021, pp. 3037–3052 (cit. on p. 562).

[Cla21] Clare Birchall. Radical Secrecy: The Ends of Transparency in Datafied America. University of Minnesota Press, 2021 (cit. on p. 556).

[CN20] A. Cohen and K. Nissim. "Towards formalizing the GDPR's notion of singling out". In: Proceedings of the National Academy of Sciences 117.15 (2020). Publisher: National Acad Sciences, pp. 8344–8352 (cit. on p. 559).

[Coh12] J. E. Cohen. "What privacy is for". In: Harv. L. Rev. 126 (2012). Publisher: HeinOnline, p. 1904 (cit. on pp. 553, 561, 564).

[Coh19] J. E. Cohen. Between truth and power. Oxford University Press, 2019 (cit. on p. 547).

[Cou67] U. S. Court. Katz vs. United States. Issue: No. 35. 1967 (cit. on p. 553).

[DM13] C. Dwork and D. K. Mulligan. "It's not privacy, and it's not fair". In: Stan. L. Rev. Online 66 (2013). Publisher: HeinOnline, p. 35 (cit. on p. 564).

[DMNS06] C. Dwork, F. McSherry, K. Nissim, and A. Smith. "Calibrating noise to sensitivity in private data analysis". In: Theory of cryptography conference. Springer, 2006, pp. 265–284 (cit. on p. 548).

[DN03] I. Dinur and K. Nissim. "Revealing information while preserving privacy". In: Proceedings of the twenty-second ACM SIGMOD-SIGACT-SIGART symposium on Principles of database systems. 2003, pp. 202–210 (cit. on p. 551).

[DN10] C. Dwork and M. Naor. "On the Difficulties of Disclosure Prevention in Statistical Databases or The Case for Differential Privacy". In: Journal of Privacy and Confidentiality 2.1 (2010), pp. 93–107 (cit. on p. 557).

[DP19] D. Desfontaines and B. Pejó. "Sok: differential privacies". In: arXiv preprint arXiv:1906.01337 (2019) (cit. on p. 548).

[DSSU17] C. Dwork, A. Smith, T. Steinke, and J. Ullman. "Exposed! a survey of attacks on private data". In: Annual Review of Statistics and Its Application 4 (2017). Publisher: Annual Reviews, pp. 61–84 (cit. on pp. 551, 559).

[Ede16] L. B. Edelman. "Working Law". In: Working Law. University of Chicago Press, 2016 (cit. on p. 563).

[Eng13] D. F. Engstrom. "Agencies as litigation gatekeepers". In: Yale lJ 123 (2013). Publisher: HeinOnline, p. 616 (cit. on p. 563).

[Eya19] G. Eyal. The crisis of expertise. John Wiley & Sons, 2019 (cit. on p. 563).

[FP20] M. Finck and F. Pallas. "They who must not be identified—distinguishing personal from non-personal data under the GDPR". In: International Data Privacy Law (2020) (cit. on p. 558).

[GAM19] S. Garfinkel, J. M. Abowd, and C. Martindale. "Understanding database reconstruction attacks on public data". In: Communications of the ACM 62.3 (2019). Publisher: ACM New York, NY, USA, pp. 46–53 (cit. on p. 551).

[Han20] B.-C. Han. The transparency society. Stanford University Press, 2020 (cit. on p. 553).

[Har15] B. E. Harcourt. Exposed: Desire and disobedience in the digital age. Harvard University Press, 2015 (cit. on p. 553).

[Har16] W. Hartzog. "The Inadequate, Invaluable Fair Information Practices". In: Md. L. Rev. 76 (2016). Publisher: HeinOnline, p. 952 (cit. on p. 554).

[Hoo16] C. J. Hoofnagle. Federal Trade Commission privacy law and policy. Cambridge University Press, 2016 (cit. on p. 554).

[Hun+12] A. Hundepool, J. Domingo-Ferrer, L. Franconi, S. Giessing, E. S. Nordholt, K. Spicer, and P.-P. De Wolf. Statistical disclosure control. Vol. 2. Wiley New York, 2012 (cit. on p. 547).

[Jon21] Jonathan Ullman. Statistical Inference is Not a Privacy Violation. 2021. URL: https://differentialprivacy.org/inference-is-not-a-privacy-violation/ (cit. on p. 564).

[Les+99] L. Lessig, L. Lessig, L. Edwards, Y. Akdeniz, C. Walker, and D. Wall. "Code and Other Laws of Cyberspace". In: (1999). Publisher: Vintage Books (cit. on p. 546).

[Lit99] J. Litman. "Information privacy/information property". In: Stan. L. Rev. 52 (1999). Publisher: HeinOnline, p. 1283 (cit. on p. 554).

[Men17] P. S. Menell. "Tailoring a Public Policy Exception to Trade Secret Protection". In: Calif. L. Rev. 105 (2017). Publisher: HeinOnline, p. 1 (cit. on p. 556).

[MM+19] J. Metcalf, E. Moss, et al. "Owning ethics: Corporate logics, silicon valley, and the institutionalization of ethics". In: Social Research: An International Quarterly 86.2 (2019). Publisher: Johns Hopkins University Press, pp. 449–476 (cit. on p. 557).

[Nis09] H. Nissenbaum. Privacy in context. Stanford University Press, 2009 (cit. on p. 561).

[Nis16] H. Nissenbaum. "Differential Privacy in Context: Conceptual and Ethical Considerations". In: Four Facets of Differential Privacy Symposium, Princeton, NJ, USA. 2016 (cit. on p. 562).

[OO20] J. A. Obar and A. Oeldorf-Hirsch. "The biggest lie on the internet: Ignoring the privacy policies and terms of service policies of social networking services". In: Information, Communication & Society 23.1 (2020). Publisher: Taylor & Francis, pp. 128–147 (cit. on p. 560).

[PH10] A. Pfitzmann and M. Hansen. A terminology for talking about privacy by data minimization: Anonymity, unlinkability, undetectability, unobservability, pseudonymity, and identity management. 2010 (cit. on p. 552).

[Pos81] R. A. Posner. "The economics of privacy". In: The American economic review 71.2 (1981). Publisher: JSTOR, pp. 405–409 (cit. on p. 545).

[Pow18] J. Powles. "The seductive diversion of "solving" bias in artificial intelligence". In: (2018) (cit. on p. 547).

[Rac75] J. Rachels. "Why privacy is important". In: Philosophy & Public Affairs (1975). Publisher: JSTOR, pp. 323–333 (cit. on p. 545).

[Rog15] P. Rogaway. The Moral Character of Cryptographic Work. 2015 (cit. on p. 547).

[SA18] A. Senarath and N. A. G. Arachchilage. "Understanding software developers approach towards implementing data minimization". In: arXiv preprint arXiv:1808.01479 (2018) (cit. on p. 552).

[Sch+18] S. Schiffner, B. Berendt, T. Siil, M. Degeling, R. Riemann, F. Schaub, K. Wuyts, M. Attoresi, S. Gürses, A. Klabunde, et al. "Towards a roadmap for privacy technologies and the general data protection regulation: a transatlantic initiative". In: Annual Privacy Forum. Springer, 2018, pp. 24–42 (cit. on p. 552).

[Sch03] P. M. Schwartz. "Property, privacy, and personal data". In: Harv. L. Rev. 117 (2003). Publisher: HeinOnline, p. 2056 (cit. on p. 554).

[Sel+19] A. D. Selbst, D. Boyd, S. A. Friedler, S. Venkatasubramanian, and J. Vertesi. "Fairness and abstraction in sociotechnical systems". In: Proceedings of the conference on fairness, accountability, and transparency. 2019, pp. 59–68 (cit. on p. 546).

[SH14] D. J. Solove and W. Hartzog. "The FTC and the new common law of privacy". In: Colum. L. Rev. 114 (2014). Publisher: HeinOnline, p. 583 (cit. on p. 554).

[SK16] S. Stalla-Bourdillon and A. Knight. "Anonymous data v. personal data-false debate: an EU perspective on anonymization, pseudonymization and personal data". In: Wis. Int'l LJ 34 (2016). Publisher: HeinOnline, p. 284 (cit. on p. 559).

[Sol05] D. J. Solove. "A taxonomy of privacy". In: U. Pa. l. Rev. 154 (2005). Publisher: HeinOnline, p. 477 (cit. on p. 549).

[Sol12] D. J. Solove. "Introduction: Privacy self-management and the consent dilemma". In: Harv. L. Rev. 126 (2012). Publisher: HeinOnline, p. 1880 (cit. on p. 560).

[Spo04] B. Spolsky. Language policy. Cambridge university press, 2004 (cit. on p. 562).

[SRN19] D. Susser, B. Roessler, and H. Nissenbaum. "Online manipulation: Hidden influences in a digital world". In: Geo. L. Tech. Rev. 4 (2019). Publisher: HeinOnline, p. 1 (cit. on p. 556).

[SS03] D. J. Solove and P. M. Schwartz. Information privacy law. Vol. 2. Aspen Publishers New York, 2003 (cit. on p. 545).

[Sta16] L. Stark. "The emotional context of information privacy". In: The Information Society 32.1 (2016). Publisher: Taylor & Francis, pp. 14–27 (cit. on p. 561).

[Stu98] W. J. Stuntz. "Distribution of Fourth Amendment Privacy". In: Geo. Wash. L. Rev. 67 (1998). Publisher: HeinOnline, p. 1265 (cit. on p. 550).

[Sus19] D. Susser. "Notice After Notice-and-Consent: Why Privacy Disclosures Are Valuable Even If Consent Frameworks Aren't". In: Journal of Information Policy 9.1 (2019). Publisher: Pennsylvania State University Press, pp. 148–173 (cit. on p. 561).

[Tho75] J. J. Thomson. "The right to privacy". In: Philosophy & Public Affairs (1975). Publisher: JSTOR, pp. 295–314 (cit. on p. 545).

[Tok16] M. Tokson. "Knowledge and Fourth Amendment Privacy". In: Nw. UL Rev. 111 (2016). Publisher: HeinOnline, p. 139 (cit. on p. 550).

[TP11] O. Tene and J. Polonetsky. "Privacy in the age of big data: a time for big decisions". In: Stan. L. Rev. Online 64 (2011). Publisher: HeinOnline, p. 63 (cit. on p. 552).

[TSD17] M. C. Tschantz, S. Sen, and A. Datta. "Differential privacy as a causal property". In: arXiv preprint arXiv:1710.05899 (2017) (cit. on p. 561).

[Vil20] S. Viljoen. "Democratic data: A relational theory for data governance". In: Available at SSRN 3727562 (2020) (cit. on p. 564).

[Wal19] A. E. Waldman. "Privacy Law's False Promise". In: Wash. UL Rev. 97 (2019). Publisher: HeinOnline, p. 773 (cit. on p. 563).

[War73] W. H. Ware. Records, computers and the rights of citizens. Tech. rep. RAND CORP SANTA MONICA CALIF, 1973 (cit. on p. 553).

[WB90] S. D. Warren and L. D. Brandeis. "The Right to Privacy". In: Harvard Law Review (1890). Publisher: JSTOR, pp. 193–220 (cit. on p. 553).

[Wes68] A. F. Westin. "Privacy and freedom". In: Washington and Lee Law Review 25.1 (1968), p. 166 (cit. on pp. 545, 554).

[WSSJ08] G. H. Walker, N. A. Stanton, P. M. Salmon, and D. P. Jenkins. "A review of sociotechnical systems theory: a classic concept for new command and control paradigms". In: Theoretical issues in ergonomics science 9.6 (2008). Publisher: Taylor & Francis, pp. 479–499 (cit. on p. 546).

DOI: 10.1561/9781638284772.ch17

Chapter 17

Relationships between Differential Privacy and Algorithmic Fairness

By Rachel Cummings

17.1 Introduction

Recent years have found growing interest in the overlap between the fields of differential privacy and algorithmic fairness. This includes both the question of when privacy and fairness can be achieved together in a learning system, and questions about the underlying technical relationship between privacy and fairness. While these questions are natural and simple to pose, they are substantially less straightforward to answer.

One major challenge is that there does not exist a universal definition of algorithmic fairness. This is in contrast to differential privacy, which is a single mathematical formalization of privacy[i]. At a high level, all fairness definitions take the form: "give similar treatment to people who deserve to be treated similarly," although there are many alternative formalizations of "similar treatment" and "people who deserve to be treated similarly." For example, should decision-making rules only consider an individual's observable, non-sensitive attributes (e.g., school admission based only on standardized test scores), or should it also consider protected

i. Although importantly, DP is not the only privacy definition one may ever wish to consider

attributes for the sake of de-biasing other measurements or as recompense for historical inequities (e.g., affirmative action)? To further complicate matters, analysts often must choose the set of attributes that deserve protection in their dataset, either because this set is not defined exogenously in the law, or because there are *proxies* that correlate with the sensitive attribute and can therefore be disclosive (e.g., shampoo choice correlates with race and gender). Additionally, the guarantee of "similar treatment" can be formalized with respect to many different performance metrics, such as precision or recall of a binary classifier, probability of a correct classification, closeness in distribution of outcomes, and more.

The fairness literature for the most part can be divided into three different classes of definitions:

1. **individual fairness** requires that "similar individuals are treated similarly,"
2. **group fairness** requires "fairness with respect to protected group membership," and
3. **multi-group fairness** requires "fairness with respect to membership in many, potentially overlapping groups".

These three classes are respectively explored in Sections 17.2, 17.3, and 17.4; each section presents formal fairness definitions, algorithms that achieve the desired fairness notions, and the relationship between the fairness notion and differential privacy.

In this chapter, we primarily consider the task of *binary classification*, where each individual i has some observable attributes X_i and a binary label $Y_i \in \{0, 1\}$; where appropriate, they will also have a protected attribute A_i. For individual fairness in Section 17.2, the fair algorithm only observes X_is, and must assign an outcome $\hat{Y}_i$ to each individual; for group and multi-group fairness in Sections 17.3 and 17.4, the algorithm takes in a training set of n observations containing (X_i, Y_i) pairs (and A_i in Section 17.3), and must produce a binary classifier for use on future observations that maps X_i to a predicted outcome $\hat{Y}_i$. In all settings, the mapping from X_i to $\hat{Y}_i$ must respect the fairness constraint.

As running examples of fair learning tasks throughout this chapter, we will use (1) school admissions and (2) evaluating loan applications. In each these tasks, binary decisions are made about individuals (i.e., acceptance/rejection at a school; approval/denial of a loan) based on that individual's submitted features X. In both of these settings, there are certain social, moral, and legal fairness obligations that should be respected in the decision-making processes. While we use these two examples for concreteness, we also emphasize that these are far from the only application domains where fairness requirements are relevant.

When combining differential privacy and algorithmic fairness in a machine learning system, a key observation is that these two constraints apply to different components of the learning pipeline. The classifier must be learned *privately* with respect to the training data, in order to not leak sensitive information about the training data when the classifier is applied in the future. The resulting classifier must also be *fair* when applied to new (test) data. That is, privacy is required in training, and fairness is required when testing. Of course, these requirements must both be considered together during training, to ensure that the privately learned classifier will be fair. Section 17.5 explores problems that may arise when fairness is *not* explicitly considered during training.

Before delving into the material, it is important to clarify that this chapter is *not* intended to be a comprehensive survey of the fairness literature, which is itself well-developed and rapidly evolving. Instead this chapter focuses only the parts of the fairness literature that are most relevant for differential privacy. The interested reader is referred elsewhere for a more comprehensive overview of the fairness field.

17.2 Individual Fairness

Individual fairness, first introduced in Dwork et al. [Dwo+12], is arguably the most natural of all the fairness notions considered in this chapter. At a high level, it requires that *similar individuals should be treated similarly*. In the language of our canonical running examples, this requires that students with similar academic aptitudes should be admitted to similar schools, and that loan applicants with similar likelihood of repaying their loans should receive loans with similar conditions. This adheres nicely to the primary high-level principle of differential privacy, that *similar datasets should be treated similarly* under differentially private algorithms. As we will see, this enables the tools of differential privacy to be brought to bear in a very organic fashion to achieve individual fairness—essentially by treating individuals with their many attributes as databases with their many entries.

The algorithmic approach of Dwork et al. [Dwo+12] described in Section 17.2.1 considers a classification setting, and relies on the existence of metrics over both individuals and outcomes to measure similarity for each. The individually fair classifiers they construct are mappings from individuals to outcomes that approximately preserve distances with respect to these metrics. They show that the use of differentially private algorithms is one such method for achieving this fairness goal, which is presented concretely here in Section 17.2.2.

As we will also see, this idealized fairness notion is unfortunately difficult to achieve in practice, as it requires a perfect metric of "distance over individuals" to measure similarity. For most—if not all—practical applications where fairness is desired, no such metric exists, and no such measurement of individuals can be made. What is a perfect measure of student aptitude or of willingness to repay a loan? We can use SAT scores and credit scores, respectively, but these are known to be imperfect measures that can be undesirably correlated with protected attributes such as race, gender, and family background, and using such imperfect measures risks further embedding existing societal biases. Recent work of Ilvento [Ilv20], Rothblum and Yona [RY18], and Jung et al. [Jun+20] have all explored more practical and query-efficient ways of learning a metric that can be used in the algorithmic individual fairness framework of Dwork et al. [Dwo+12]; these are discussed in Section 17.2.4.

17.2.1 Setting and Results

Consider a classification task over individuals (e.g., a bank must approve or deny loans based on applications). Let $\mathcal{X}$ be the set of individuals, and let $\mathcal{Y}$ be the set of outcomes (e.g., $\mathcal{Y} = \{0, 1\}$ for binary classification, as in our examples). The classification task is to predict an individual's $\hat{Y} \in \mathcal{Y}$ given their observed attributes $X \in \mathcal{X}$. Assume there exists a metric on individuals $d : \mathcal{X} \times \mathcal{X} \to \mathbb{R}$, which takes as input two individuals and outputs a "similarity score". That is, $d(X_1, X_2)$ quantifies the similarity of individuals $X_1, X_2 \in \mathcal{X}$.

We consider random classifiers $M : \mathcal{X} \to \Delta(\mathcal{Y})$, which map individuals to distributions over outcomes. That is, given an individual $X \in \mathcal{X}$, the classification mechanism will choose an outcome according to the distribution $M(X)$. Our fairness goal is for this mechanism to map similar individuals to similar distributions, so we also require a distance measure D on distributions to quantify similarity, for example D_∞ or D_{TV}, defined below.

Definition 17.1 (Total variation distance, D_{TV}). *Let P, Q be two probability measures over a finite domain A. The statistical distance or total variation distance between P and Q is:*

$$D_{TV}(P, Q) = \frac{1}{2} \sum_{Y \in \mathcal{Y}} |P(Y) - Q(Y)|.$$

Note that $D_{TV}(P, Q) \in [0, 1]$ for all distributions P, Q. If P and Q are similar, then $D_{TV}(P, Q)$ will be close to 0, and if P and Q are very different, then $D_{TV}(P, Q)$ will be close to 1.

Definition 17.2 (D_∞ distance). *Let P, Q be two probability measures over a finite domain A. The D_∞ distance between P and Q is:*

$$D_\infty(P, Q) = \sup_{Y \in \mathcal{Y}} \log \left(\max \left\{ \frac{P(Y)}{Q(Y)}, \frac{Q(Y)}{P(Y)} \right\} \right).$$

Note that $D_\infty(P, Q) \in [0, \infty)$ for all distributions P, Q. If P and Q are similar, then $D_\infty(P, Q) \ll 1$. If P and Q are very different, then $D_\infty(P, Q) \gg 1$.

We formalize the individual fairness constraint by requiring M to be a Lipschitz mapping with respect to the metrics D and d.

Definition 17.3 (Lipschitz mapping). *A mapping $M : \mathcal{X} \to \Delta(\mathcal{Y})$ is (D, d)-Lipschitz if for all $X_1, X_2 \in \mathcal{X}$,*

$$D(M(X_1), M(X_2)) \leq d(X_1, X_2).$$

Definition 17.4 (Individually fair classifier [Dwo+12]). *A classifier $M : \mathcal{X} \to \Delta(\mathcal{Y})$ is* individually fair *with respect to metrics $d : \mathcal{X} \times \mathcal{X} \to \mathbb{R}$ and $D : \Delta(\mathcal{Y}) \times \Delta(\mathcal{Y}) \to \mathbb{R}$ if it is (D, d)-Lipschitz.*

Note that, e.g., constant classifiers are trivially fair. Thus we want an individually fair classifier that also satisfies a notion of utility. Let $L : \mathcal{X} \times \mathcal{Y} \to \mathbb{R}$ be a loss function that measures the utility of assigning a specific outcome to a specific individual. In the example of loan applications, L may capture the expected probability that an applicant will default on their loan, or the (negative) expected revenue from awarding a loan to this applicant.

The goal of individual fairness is described in the following optimization problem:

Find a mapping M that minimizes expected loss subject to the Lipschitz condition.

This optimization problem can be stated mathematically as follows:

$$\begin{aligned} &\min_M \mathop{\mathbb{E}}_{X \sim \mathcal{X}} \mathop{\mathbb{E}}_{\hat{Y} \sim M(X)} L(X, \hat{Y}) \qquad (17.1) \\ &\text{s.t. } D(M(X_1), M(X_2)) \leq d(X_1, X_2), \quad \forall X_1, X_2 \in \mathcal{X} \\ &\quad M(X) \in \Delta(\mathcal{Y}), \quad \forall X \in \mathcal{X}. \end{aligned}$$

Assuming oracle access to $d(X_1, X_2)$ and $L(X, \hat{Y})$, and when D is D_∞ or D_{TV}, this problem can be written as a linear program and solved efficiently.

Theorem 17.5 ([Dwo+12]). *When D is either D_{TV} or D_∞, the optimization problem described in* (17.1) *can be solved with an LP of size poly*$(|\mathcal{X}|, |\mathcal{Y}|)$.

To see this, we can write the classifier M as a collection of distributions $\mu_X = M(X) \in \Delta(\mathcal{Y})$, which can each in turn be described by a collection of decision variables $\mu_X(\hat{Y}) = \mathbf{Pr}[M(X) = \hat{Y}]$, for all $X \in \mathcal{X}$ and $\hat{Y} \in \mathcal{Y}$. Then it is easy to see that the objective of (17.1) is linear in the $|\mathcal{X}||\mathcal{Y}|$ decision variables, and that the second constraint can be written as a collection of $|\mathcal{X}|$ linear constraints.

When $D = D_{TV}$, the first constraint of (17.1) can be re-written as $\frac{1}{2}\sum_{\hat{Y}\in\mathcal{Y}}(\mu_{X_1}(\hat{Y}) - \mu_{X_2}(\hat{Y})) \leq d(X_1, X_2)$ and $\frac{1}{2}\sum_{\hat{Y}\in\mathcal{Y}}(\mu_{X_2}(\hat{Y}) - \mu_{X_1}(\hat{Y})) \leq d(X_1, X_2)$, which requires $2|\mathcal{X}|^2$ linear constraints, given explicit access to the metric d.

When $D = D_\infty$, we can re-write the first constraint as:

$$\log \frac{\mu_{X_1}(\hat{Y})}{\mu_{X_2}(\hat{Y})} \leq d(X_1, X_2) \iff \mu_{X_1}(\hat{Y}) \leq e^{d(X_1,X_2)}\mu_{X_2}(\hat{Y}),$$

$$\forall X_1, X_2 \in \mathcal{X}, \ \forall \hat{Y} \in \mathcal{Y}.$$

Given explicit access to the metric d, this requires only $|\mathcal{X}|^2|\mathcal{Y}|$ linear constraints.

Other choices of metric D can also be plugged into this framework, and the same optimization problem of (17.1) still applies. The computational efficiency of solving this optimization problem will depend on on properties of the chosen metric, and how well the resulting instantiation of (17.1) can be solved using commercial solvers.

17.2.2 Relationship to Differential Privacy

The connection between individual fairness and differential privacy is immediate from the problem description. Individual fairness considers a mechanism that takes in an *individual* and outputs an outcome sampled from a distribution. Individual fairness requires that the distribution over outputs is similar when the the mechanism is run on *similar individuals*. Differential privacy considers a mechanism which takes in a *database* and outputs an outcome sampled from a distribution. Differential privacy requires that the distribution over outputs is similar when the mechanism is run on *similar databases*.

Using the language of differential privacy with the notation of individual fairness, consider a database $X \in \mathcal{X}$ and an analyst who wishes to privately answer a query $f : \mathcal{X} \to \mathcal{Y}$. The analyst will respond using a randomized mechanism $M : \mathcal{X} \to \Delta(\mathcal{Y})$. This mechanism will be ε-differentially private if and only if M is (D_∞, d)-Lipschitz for distance metric $d(X_1, X_2) = \varepsilon\|X_1 - X_2\|_1$. The utility loss function for producing answer $\hat{Y} \in \mathcal{Y}$ on database X is $L(X, \hat{Y}) = d_f(f(X), \hat{Y})$, which should capture the domain-specific accuracy notion. A common loss function for real-valued queries would be additive error: $d_f(f(X), \hat{Y}) = |f(X) - \hat{Y}|$.

In short, differential privacy can be seen as an instantiation of individual fairness, where databases are the individuals, and the neighboring relationship defines similarity. Hence many of the algorithmic tools developed for differential privacy can also be immediately applied to achieve individual fairness with the D_∞ metric over outcome distributions.

17.2.3 Pros and Cons of Individual Fairness

Pros

The biggest strength of individual fairness is that it is a very natural and strong fairness notion, which formalizes exactly what we would like our fairness notions to capture: people should be considered as individuals and receive treated in the way that they deserve, based on problem-specific merit-measures rather than irrelevant attributes; e.g., admit students to schools based on aptitude, not based on parents' income. The fairness constraint holds *for all* individuals, not just for some.

The natural connection to differential privacy allows existing DP tools to be used as individually fair mechanisms. Additionally, the general LP framework of (17.1) allows individually fair classifiers to efficiently computable if $|\mathcal{X}|$ is reasonably sized.

Finally, since fairness is considered at the individual level, algorithm designers do not need to pre-specify a class of protected groups as is required for group fairness (Section 17.3). This avoids problems of proxy variables which are correlated with the protected attribute (e.g., hair length as a proxy for gender). It also ensures fairness within groups, since "better" individuals receive "better" outcomes, independent of group membership. As we will see in Section 17.3, these are major challenges when applying group fairness.

Cons

The biggest weakness of individual fairness is that it requires complete knowledge of a perfect distance metric d over individuals. This is nearly impossible to achieve in practice, where the existing individual-level metrics are known to be imperfect and embed existing biases (e.g., standardized test scores and credit scores). Recent developments to address this challenge are discussed in Section 17.2.4.

Computationally, the population size $|\mathcal{X}|$ is not reasonably sized in many practical applications, and even $poly(|\mathcal{X}|)$ may be infeasible. Additionally, there are finite sample problems when learning M based on this approach: if an individually fair M is learned from a finite sample of a larger population, M is not guaranteed to remain fair when extended to entire population. These are due in part to the (desirable) strong fairness notion that requires fairness over all individuals. This also motivates the notion of group fairness presented in Section 17.3, which coarsely approximates individual fairness via group membership to achieve better computational efficiency and population-level generalization, at the cost of a less-perfect fairness notion.

The objective $\min \mathbb{E}_{X\sim\mathcal{X}} L(X,\cdot)$ minimizes average loss over the population, but does not optimize for individual loss. The objective could certainly be modified to consider minimax loss over individuals, $\min \max_X L(X,\cdot)$, but this would change the optimization problem and may harm some of the desirable algorithmic properties described above.

Upshot of Individual Fairness

Perfect in theory; extremely difficult to make practical.

17.2.4 Learning the Metric over Individuals

One of the main barriers to the practical deployment of individual fairness is the requirement of a perfect task-specific metric d over individuals, which is needed to apply the results of Dwork et al. [Dwo+12]. Naturally, access to such a metric is rare to impossible in practice. Instead, Ilvento [Ilv20] proposes approximating a metric for individual fairness using only a small number of queries to a human fairness arbiter, who is "free of explicit biases and possesses sufficient domain knowledge to evaluate similarity," such as a financial regulator or a college admissions officer. This approach builds upon tools from *metric learning*, which aims to automatically construct task-specific distance metrics from weakly supervised data, and also focuses on learning distance metrics from human feedback.

Ilvento [Ilv20] considers two types of queries that can be asked of the human fairness arbiter to learn the distance metric. *Triplet queries* ask whether point x is closer to point y or point z, and *real-valued distance queries* ask for the distance between two points x and y.[ii] It is assumed that comparative evaluations are easier for humans than absolute evaluations, and thus distance queries are considered more expensive to ask the arbiter than triplet queries.

A key observation is that individual fairness does not require distances between individuals to be maintained exactly by the Lipschitz mapping, only that the distances are not exceeded—note that the first constraint of (17.1) only requires a one-sided bound that $D(M(x), M(y)) \leq d(x, y)$. This motivates the notion of a *submetric* (Definition 17.6) which is a contraction of the original metric that does not overestimate any distance beyond a small additive error term. Substituting a submetric for the original metric d in [Dwo+12] will still maintain individual fairness and will prove easier to learn.

Definition 17.6 (α-submetric). *Given a metric d, we say that $d' : V \times V \to [0, 1]$ is an α-submetric of d if for all $u, v \in V$, $d'(u, v) \leq d(u, v) + \alpha$.*

---

ii. Relaxations of this framework are also considered, including settings where the arbiter is allowed to respond to triplet queries with "too close to call" if $d(x, y)$ and $d(x, z)$ are very close, and allowing noisy responses to real-valued queries. Similar relaxations were used in Jung et al. [Jun+20], which also considered how to incorporate human expertise into fairness evaluation.

The query-efficient submetric learning algorithm of Ilvento [Ilv20] first randomly selects a small set of representatives from V, then approximately learns the distances between each representative and all other points, and finally combines these to produce a single submetric hypothesis. To learn approximate distances to a single representative, first, points can be sorted in order of increasing distance from the representative using $O(|V| \log |V|)$ inexpensive triplet queries to sort the elements (i.e., "is x or y closer to representative r?"). Given this ordering, $O(\max\{1/\alpha, \ \log |V|\})$ expensive real-valued distance queries can be used to label the ordering with α-approximate (underestimated) distances.

These approximate distances alone are not sufficient to describe the underlying metric; for example, knowing only that x and y are equidistant from r, it is impossible to distinguish whether $d(x, y)$ is zero or twice their distance from r. Submetrics constructed based on different representatives preserve different information about the underlying metric, so information from all representatives are then aggregated to form a more expressive submetric. Ilvento [Ilv20] provides a method for combining the distances d_r from each representative, and shows that under certain technical assumptions, i.e., how tightly packed individuals are, this approach will result in a submetric with good distance preservation properties.

The approach of Jung et al. [Jun+20], which also focuses on engaging humans in the decision-making process via pairwise comparisons, sidesteps the issue of learning the metric over individuals by not even assuming that such a metric exists. Instead of trying to learn the true underlying metric, they seek to learn a classifier that is consistent with the pairwise fairness constraints elicited from the human arbiter.

Practical applications of these promising theoretical results are still far from immediate. Even though Ilvento [Ilv20] and Jung et al. [Jun+20] show that only a small number of queries are required of the arbiter, any practical system would first have to identify such an unbiased and qualified individual (or collection of individuals) to serve as the human fairness arbiter.

To address the challenge of extending the learned metric to a larger population, Rothblum and Yona [RY18] consider the problem of learning a predictor from a sample of labeled points $(\mathcal{X}, \mathcal{Y})$ that will generalize well to the underlying distribution, rather than learning a classifier for the input set of points. They show that applying the individual fairness definition of Dwork et al. [Dwo+12] as-is for this new goal makes even simple learning tasks infeasible. They instead develop a relaxed approximate metric-fairness notion—formalized as *Probably Approximately Correct and Fair* (PACF), which parallels the definition of PAC learning—that allows for both a small additive slack in the similarity measure of outcomes and a small probability of failure of the fairness guarantee. This allows them to show that (under certain technical conditions) learning an approximately metric-fair predictor on a sample generalizes to approximate metric-fairness over the underlying distribution.

17.3 Group Fairness

Group fairness focuses on *ensuring fair outcomes with respect to pre-determined protected groups* (e.g., race or gender). Specifically, it assumes that protected groups have been exogenously determined, and divides the attributes of each individual into those which are *protected* (e.g., race, gender) and those which are *unprotected* (e.g., zip code, SAT score). Group fair algorithms are free to use unprotected attributes arbitrarily, but must satisfy (approximately) equal treatment across groups, conditioned on any realization of the protected attribute.

Unlike differential privacy, there is no single unified definition of group fairness; the problem of defining group fairness is itself an active research area, with many natural definitions put forth, corresponding to different mathematical formalizations of "equal treatment across groups" [Nar18; Mit+21]. Unfortunately, several of the most popular definitions have been shown to be incompatible with each other, and it is impossible for any group fairness definition to achieve a short list of natural desiderata [KMR17]. As such, the appropriate formal definition of group fairness should depend on the use case and the analysis task.

The approach of focusing on fairness with respect to protected group membership is in part a response to the practical challenges of individual fairness: although it may be impractical to guarantee fairness across *all* individuals, we will see that standard machine learning tools are well-equipped to construct classifiers that guarantee similar outcomes across a small number of well-defined groups. The focus on group membership is also born out of the reality that in many practical contexts, fair treatment is legally or ethically mandated based on certain protected attributes, such as race, gender, sexual orientation, or disability status.

However, this approach also introduces new practical challenges when protected groups are not automatically defined, since fair treatment is *only* guaranteed with respect to the specified groups. Which groups deserve protection? How should correlations between protected and unprotected attributes be handled? The mathematical formalization of group fairness sidesteps this issue by assuming an exhaustive, pre-defined list of protected groups, which is input to the algorithm. This may be appropriate for applications such as housing or employment, where the set of protected attributes are legally defined, but poses a meaningful barrier for other critical applications, such as loan approval or recidivism prediction, where the division between protected and unprotected attributes is less straightforward.

Relationship to Differential Privacy

Unlike individual fairness, group fairness does not have an inherent technical connection to differential privacy. However, analysts who are concerned with the societal implications of their machine learning pipeline may want to simultaneously achieve privacy and fairness. In this framework, the analyst would require differential privacy for the training dataset that is used to learn the classifier, and fairness for the future test set (possibly the rest of the population) to which the classifier will be applied.

We emphasize that group fairness and differential privacy are orthogonal goals to be satisfied on separate portions of the dataset. The question becomes the compatibility of these two objectives, and whether they can be simultaneously achieved. While the design of algorithms for learning group-fair classifiers has been studied extensively in the fairness literature, we will focus here on the results of two papers [CGKM19; Jag+19] that provide a positive answer to this question by designing *differentially private* algorithms for learning group-fair classifiers. These two papers take a similar algorithmic approach (presented in Section 17.3.2) to achieve privacy for the training set and fairness for the test set.

17.3.1 Setting

Consider the problem of binary classification in a semi-supervised setting. Each individual's data forms a triple (X, A, Y), where X is an unprotected attribute, A is a protected attribute, and Y is a binary label (e.g., will repay a loan or not).[iii] These triples are drawn from an unknown joint distribution P, corresponding the underlying population. Given n i.i.d. samples from P, an analyst's goal is to learn a classifier $\hat{Y}$ that maps observable attributes (X, A) to predicted labels[iv] $\hat{Y}$ in a way that:

- is *differentially private* with respect to the database of n sampled training points,
- yields a $\hat{Y}$ that is *fair* with respect to the protected attribute A, and
- $\hat{Y}$ is an *accurate* prediction of Y given (X, A).

We emphasize that in contrast to the individual fairness setting, which sought predictions only for the given set of individuals, we move here to a more classical machine learning setting, where we have access to a finite sample from a larger

iii. On a (labeled) training dataset, the analyst will be able to observe all (X, A, Y) of an individual, but on the test set, the analyst will only be able to observe (X, A) and must predict $\hat{Y}$.

iv. To simplify presentation, we will abuse notation to let $\hat{Y}$ denote both the mapping and the outcome of that mapping on an implied (X, A).

underlying population, and we seek to learn a classifier that can be applied to the entire population.

As discussed above, there are many possible definitions of group fairness. In the setting of binary classification that we consider here, the most commonly used fairness notions are Equalized Odds (Definition 17.8) and Equal Opportunity (Remark 17.9), which require similar false positive and true positive rates across groups [HPS16]. We define these first.

Definition 17.7 (False Positive Rate, True Positive Rate). *Let $FP_a(\hat{Y})$ and $TP_a(\hat{Y})$ respectively denote the false positive rate and true positive rate of classifier $\hat{Y}$ on the group $\{A = a\}$:*

$$FP_a(\hat{Y}) = \mathbf{Pr}[\hat{Y} = 1 | A = a, Y = 0]$$
$$TP_a(\hat{Y}) = \mathbf{Pr}[\hat{Y} = 1 | A = a, Y = 1],$$

where the probabilities are taken over the distribution P and the randomness of the classifier.

We also define empirical false positive rate and true positive rate, $\widehat{\mathrm{FP}}_a(\hat{Y})$ and $\widehat{\mathrm{FP}}_a(\hat{Y})$ as the average rates evaluated on the labeled sample.

We use *Equalized Odds* as our fairness notion, which requires all subgroups $a \in A$ to have similar true and false positive rates. Similar *true* (resp., *false*) positive rates implies that conditioned on being a qualified candidate with $Y = 1$ (resp., unqualified candidate with $Y = 0$), the chance of getting the good outcome $\hat{Y} = 1$ is approximately equalized across groups.

Definition 17.8 (γ-Equalized Odds fairness). *A classifier $\hat{Y}$ satisfies γ-equalized odds fairness with respect to protected attribute A if $\forall a, a' \in A$, both the following conditions hold:*

$$|FP_a(\hat{Y}) - FP_{a'}(\hat{Y})| \leq \gamma \quad \text{and} \quad |TP_a(\hat{Y}) - TP_{a'}(\hat{Y})| \leq \gamma .$$

Remark 17.9. *A slightly relaxed fairness notion is that of* Equal Opportunity, *which only requires similar true positive rates across groups. This relaxation only requires that qualified candidates ($Y = 1$) receive fair treatment, and makes no fairness requirement for the unqualified candidates ($Y = 0$).*

To measure accuracy, define the *error* of a classifier $\hat{Y}$ to be its misclassification error on the population:

$$\mathrm{err}(\hat{Y}) = \mathop{\mathbf{Pr}}_{P,\hat{Y}}[\hat{Y} \neq Y].$$

We also define empirical error $\widehat{\text{err}}(\hat{Y})$ as the average misclassification error on the training set. Given a hypothesis class $\mathcal{H}$ (e.g., the set of all binary classifiers), we will consider randomized classifiers $\hat{Y}$ in $\Delta(\mathcal{H})$.

The analyst's formal goal is to find a classifier $\hat{Y}$ that minimizes empirical error subject to the equalized odds fairness constraint, which can be formalized as the following optimization problem:

$$
\begin{aligned}
&\min_{\hat{Y}\in\Delta(\mathcal{H})} \ \widehat{\text{err}}(\hat{Y}) \qquad\qquad (17.2)\\
&\text{s.t. } |\widehat{\text{FP}}_a(\hat{Y}) - \widehat{\text{FP}}_{a'}(\hat{Y})| \le \gamma \quad \forall a, a' \in A\\
&\quad\ \ |\widehat{\text{TP}}_a(\hat{Y}) - \widehat{\text{TP}}_{a'}(\hat{Y})| \le \gamma \quad \forall a, a' \in A.
\end{aligned}
$$

Solving the optimization problem of (17.2) will ensure a classifier that is accurate and satisfies γ-Equalized Odds group fairness. Of course, the analyst would prefer to minimize distributional error subject to distributional true and false positive rates, but they must instead settle for the empirical proxies evaluated on their finite sample. This gap will be accounted for in the final approximation bound given in Section 17.3.2.

If we additionally use a differentially private method for solving the optimization problem, then we will satisfy the desiderata of privacy and fairness. Fortunately, the requisite private machine learning and optimization tools exist, which we will see next.

17.3.2 Algorithmic Approach and Results

Since the optimization problem of (17.2) encodes the goal of maximizing accuracy subject to a group fairness constraint, the remaining task is only to solve (17.2) in a differentially private and computationally efficient way. Both Cummings et al. [CGKM19] and Jagielski et al. [Jag+19] take the same high-level approach to this task, with the following three steps: (1) re-write (17.2) as a linear program of finite size; (2) formulate the LP as a two-player zero-sum game; and (3) solve the game with differentially private no-regret learning dynamics.

This approach relies on a foundational result of Freund and Schapire [FS96], which states that in two-player zero-sum games, if one player plays according to a no-regret learning algorithm and the other player best-responds, then average play of both players will converge to a Nash equilibrium of the game. By strong duality, this equilibrium corresponds to an optimal solution of the LP, which must be a fair and accurate classifier. Since the learning algorithm is differentially private, this also satisfies the privacy requirement.

Below we present an informal statement of this main result, and then proceed with details of the algorithmic construction.

Theorem 17.10 (Cummings et al. [CGKM19] and Jagielski et al. [Jag+19]). *There exists an (ε, δ)-differentially private algorithm that runs in polynomial time (given access to an oracle), and with probability at least $1 - \beta$ outputs a random classifier $\hat{Y}$ that satisfies $err(\hat{Y}) \leq OPT + \alpha$ and $(\gamma + \alpha)$-Equalized Odds, for $\alpha = O(\sqrt{\frac{\log(1/\beta)}{n\varepsilon}})$.*

Step 1: Re-writing the Problem

First we observe that the optimization problem in (17.2) is a linear program with polynomially many constraints. Specifically, note that when a classifier $\hat{Y}$ is described explicitly by the probability of producing $\hat{Y} = 1$ given observable attributes $(X = x, A = a)$, then $\widehat{err}(\hat{Y})$, $\widehat{\mathrm{FP}}_a(\hat{Y})$, and $\widehat{\mathrm{TP}}_a(\hat{Y})$ can all be expressed as a linear function of the classifier.

For a given $\hat{Y}$, we can write the fairness constraints in matrix form, as $\vec{r}(\hat{Y}) \leq \vec{0}$, where,[v]

$$\vec{r}(\hat{Y}) = \begin{bmatrix} \widehat{\mathrm{FP}}_a(\hat{Y}) - \widehat{\mathrm{FP}}_{a'}(\hat{Y}) - \gamma \\ \widehat{\mathrm{TP}}_a(\hat{Y}) - \widehat{\mathrm{TP}}_{a'}(\hat{Y}) - \gamma \end{bmatrix}_{a,a' \in A} \in \mathbb{R}^{2|A|^2}.$$

Next we can Lagrangify these constraints by introducing a Lagrangian variable for each constraint:

$$\vec{\lambda} = \begin{bmatrix} \lambda_{(FP,a,a')} \\ \lambda_{(TP,a,a')} \end{bmatrix}_{a,a' \in A} \in \mathbb{R}^{2|A|^2}.$$

We assume $\|\vec{\lambda}\|_1 \leq B$ for a given B to ensure convergence of the no-regret dynamics.

Finally, our fair learning LP can equivalently be written as the following Lagrangian minimax problem:

$$\min_{\hat{Y} \in \Delta\mathcal{H}} \max_{\|\vec{\lambda}\|_1 \leq B} \widehat{\mathrm{err}}(\hat{Y}) + \vec{\lambda}^\top \vec{r}(\hat{Y}). \tag{17.3}$$

Step 2: Formulating as a Game

Kearns et al. [KNRW18] was the first to give a reduction from the problem of learning a fair classifier as formalized in (17.3) to the problem of computing an

v. $|A|$ is commonly assumed to be a small constant corresponding to the number of demographic groups in a population. However, if $|A|$ is infinite or otherwise too large for $2|A|^2$ constraints to be feasible, an alternative formulation relying on Sauer's Lemma requires only $O(n^{VC-DIM(A)})$ constraints.

approximate equilibrium of a two-player zero-sum game. This approach uses Sion's Minimax Theorem to write (17.3) as:

$$\min_{\hat{Y}\in\Delta\mathcal{H}} \max_{\|\vec{\lambda}\|_1\leq B} \widehat{\text{err}}(\hat{Y}) + \vec{\lambda}^\top \vec{r}(\hat{Y}) = \max_{\|\vec{\lambda}\|_1\leq B} \min_{\hat{Y}\in\Delta\mathcal{H}} \widehat{\text{err}}(\hat{Y}) + \vec{\lambda}^\top \vec{r}(\hat{Y}) = OPT, \tag{17.4}$$

where OPT is the optimal objective value to the fair learning problem.

This provides the payoff matrix for a two-player zero-sum game. The primal (minimization) player is a Learner who chooses a classifier $\hat{Y} \in \mathcal{H}$ to minimize empirical error (plus a fairness penalty term given by the Lagrangian). The dual (maximization) player is an Auditor who chooses a fairness constraint that is maximally violated. Intuitively, the Auditor is trying to identify a group $a \in A$ that experiences the largest fairness violation under the Learner's $\hat{Y}$, and puts all the weight on the dual variable corresponding to that constraint. Allowing both players randomized strategies in this game yields the full decision space for the optimization problem.

When these two players iteratively and repeatedly play this zero-sum game, and one plays according to a no-regret learning algorithm while the other plays a best-response, then the foundational result of Freund and Schapire [FS96] guarantees that average game play will converge to an approximate equilibrium. By (17.4), an equilibrium of this game corresponds to an optimal solution of the LP—i.e., a fair and accurate classifier.

Step 3: Private No-regret Dynamics

While the roles of "no-regret algorithm" and "best-responder" are interchangeable between players,[vi] both players must compute their action differentially privately. The Learner relies on the training data to evaluate classifier accuracy, and the Auditor relies on the training data to find a fairness constraint that is violated.

The player using the no-regret algorithm can use any of the numerous differentially private no-regret learning algorithms—such as Private Follow the Perturbed Leader or Private Multiplicative Weights—to compute their action. For the other player, Kearns et al. [KNRW18] show in the non-private setting that the best-response of both players can be reduced to cost-sensitive classification (CSC), where the cost of predicting a label depends on the label value. Thus the algorithmic results rely on the existence of a differentially private CSC oracle—such as the Exponential Mechanism or another private heuristic—to allow the best-response player to efficiently and privately compute their action.

vi. Cummings et al. [CGKM19] has the Learner play a no-regret algorithm and the Auditor best-responds, while Jagielski et al. [Jag+19] uses the reverse roles.

Thus we have privately learned a fair and accurate classifier, as desired. The additional approximation terms in the accuracy and fairness guarantees in Theorem 17.10 come from inherent noise in the private no-regret learner and the private CSC oracle. Additionally, Freund and Schapire [FS96] only guarantee an *approximate*-equilibrium, which corresponds to an approximate solution to (17.2). Finally, since (17.2) necessarily evaluates accuracy and fairness empirically based on the training data, there will be some loss that depends on the sample size when generalizing back to the original (infinite) population.

Remark 17.11. *Alabi [Ala19] provides improved sample complexity bounds for the problem of private and group fair learning, under the assumption of a slightly different oracle. Those bounds apply to Equalized Odds fairness, as well as other group fairness notions that can be expressed as a convex loss function.*

17.3.3 Pros and Cons of Group Fairness

Pros

The most obvious advantage of focusing on group fairness is that it integrates will with existing machine learning frameworks, and can be achieved in a computationally efficient way using existing algorithmic tools. This lowers the barriers for use, and makes it easier for theorists to design group fair algorithms, and for practitioners to implement them.

While this chapter focused primarily on Equalized Odds as a notion of group fairness, it is far from the only definition; dozens have been proposed, discussed, and used in the literature (see, e.g., Narayanan [Nar18] and Mitchell et al. [Mit+21] for surveys). Group fairness encompasses a family of fairness definitions, all sharing the same general flavor: "the treatment of individuals should independent of their protected attributes." This family ranges from attribute-blind policies (e.g., college admission based only on SAT scores), to attribute-aware policies such as affirmative action to make up for historical inequities, to dynamic policies that account for the many decisions made about an individual over the course of her life. The specific definition of group fairness used in any particular application can be tailored to suit practical needs, based on domain-specific fairness concerns and modeling choices.

Cons

The myriad of definitions is also a weakness of group fairness. There is no one single correct definition of group fairness that theorists or practitioners can use off-the-shelf across all application domains. Instead, they must understand the contextual and sociological requirements that give rise to fairness concerns in their specific application domain, and choose the appropriate mathematical fairness definition. This challenge is exacerbated by the fact that many common group fairness notions are incompatible, and provably cannot be achieved simultaneously [KMR17]. Thus while the field has readily available group-fair algorithms, the deployment of these tools does not scale easily to new use cases.

Relatedly, group fairness requires the analyst to pre-specify all groups requiring fair treatment as an input to the algorithm, and it does not provide any fairness guarantees with respect to other groups. In the absence of laws that explicitly enumerate legally protected attributes, determining the appropriate collection of protected groups is far from straightforward. This challenge is exacerbated when seemingly unimportant attributes may serve as a proxy for the protected attribute (e.g., shampoo choice may be highly correlated with race and gender). With high-dimensional training datasets and complex machine learning algorithms, it is easy to inadvertently encode bias through proxies. The selection of protected groups—like the choice of fairness definition—requires significant sociological research and domain expertise, which again slows the deployment of group-fair algorithms.

Finally, group fairness ensures fairness *on average* for a group, but does not provide guarantees across individuals within a group. Within a fixed group (corresponding to some $a \in A$), more qualified individuals may receive worse outcomes than less qualified individuals, even under a group-fair classifier. Within-group unfairness enables other types of unfair treatment such as reverse tokenism, where the least qualified members of a group are selected as positive examples (i.e., $\hat{Y} = 1$) to spuriously demonstrate lack of merit for the entire group, and it ignores intersectionality, where individuals may belong to multiple overlapping groups (e.g., based on race, gender, and disability status). Satisfying group fairness with respect to each group independently is not sufficient to guarantee fairness across the intersection of these groups, as we demonstrate next in Section 17.4.

Upshot of Group Fairness

Easy to achieve algorithmically; doesn't capture all fairness concerns.

17.4 Multi-group Fairness

Two of the shortcomings of group fairness as studied in Section 17.3 are that it requires all protected groups to be specified in advance, and that it does not capture notions of *intersectionality*, where individuals may belong to multiple overlapping groups—for example, a group corresponding to their race and a group corresponding to their gender. In the computer science literature, the latter concern is referred to as *multi-group fairness*.

As an illustration of the need for multi-group fairness, consider the following example. Imagine all people have two protected attributes: shape—round or square—and color— blue or green.[vii] Imagine that these attributes are uniformly distributed in the population and independent of an individual's ability or intent to repay a loan. Consider the classifier that awards loans to everyone who is round-blue and square-green, and denies all others. This classifier would satisfy perfect Equalized Odds fairness (Definition 17.8) with respect to shape and color separately, but not when the two features are considered together. In particular, this would be unfair to round-green and square-blue people under any reasonable definition of fairness, since they have no hope of a positive outcome, regardless of their merit. Similar examples were given in [DI19], which showed that group-fair classifiers do not *compose* in the way that differential privacy does. For example, making fair hiring decisions with respect to race and gender independently does not automatically ensure that combinations thereof will be treated fairly.

One solution for this simple example is to redefine protected attributes to include these intersections, and require group fairness across all four newly-defined groups. However, the computational complexity of this approach scales exponentially with the number of protected attributes, which may not be feasible in many practical applications, particularly when protected attributes take on non-binary (e.g., income) or continuous values (e.g., probability of developing a disease). Additionally, this would maintain the weakness of group fairness that one must pre-specify all possible groups that require fair treatment; in practice, the full set of protected attributes may not be known in advance, particularly due to correlations across attributes. E.g., hair color is not a legally protected attribute, but it can be a proxy for race due to correlations between race and hair color.

In this section, we will see approaches for multi-group fairness that do not require the set of protected groups to be known in advance, and are computationally efficient, even for an arbitrarily large number of protected groups.

17.4.1 Setting

In the multi-group fairness setting, each individual's data consists of a pair (X, Y) drawn from an unknown distribution P, where X includes all attributes, and Y is a binary label. Note that we no longer specify protected attributes A, but instead introduce an arbitrary attribute domain $\mathcal{X}$ that allows for high-dimensional attribute vector X. It will be the implicit task of the learning algorithm to determine which combinations of attributes require protection.

Our learning goal is a continuous *prediction task*—a relaxation of the binary classification task considered in Section 17.3. Given n i.i.d. samples from P, the

vii. For a more provocative example, consider these attributes to be race and gender. To avoid addressing complex social issues which are beyond the scope of this book, we use made-up attributes instead.

analyst would like to learn a predictor $p : \mathcal{X} \to [0, 1]$, where the prediction $p(X) \in [0, 1]$ can be interpreted as the predicted probability of the event that $Y = 1$ for an individual with attributes X.

Note that the Bayes optimal predictor $p^*(X) = \mathbf{Pr}[Y = 1|X]$ both maximizes predictive accuracy, and is perfectly fair to all individuals. That is, it is individually fair with respect to the metric over individuals $d(X_i, X_j) = |\mathbf{Pr}[Y = 1|X_i] - \mathbf{Pr}[Y = 1|X_j]|$. However, learning this optimal predictor is information theoretically impossible from a finite sample. Instead, we will seek to learn a predictor that seeks to maximize both predictive accuracy and the number of groups that receive fairness protections, given information-theoretic and computational constraints.

As we will see, the method for non-privately learning a multi-group fair predictor has natural algorithmic parallels to learning a group-fair classifier in Section 17.3, while known private methods for this problem take a substantially different algorithmic form. As a result, we will primarily focus here on algorithms for learning a multi-group fair predictor without a privacy constraint in order to better highlight this connection, with a discussion of differentially private techniques for learning a multi-group fair predictor deferred to Section 17.4.4.

17.4.2 Multi-calibration

A common fairness solution for predictors is *calibration*, which attempts to ensure that groups of individuals with similar risk, $\mathbf{Pr}[Y = 1|X]$, receive similar predictions, $p(X)$. Calibration is also commonly used (outside of fairness) as an accuracy notion in the statistics and forecasting literature (e.g., [SSV03]) to ensure that the probabilistic prediction of an event occurring is close to the true probability.

Definition 17.12 (α-calibration). *A predictor* $p : \mathcal{X} \to [0, 1]$ *is* α-calibrated *if for all* $v \in supp(p)$,

$$|\mathbf{Pr}[Y = 1|p(X) = v] - v| \leq \alpha,$$

or equivalently, in terms of the Bayes optimal predictor $p^*(X)$,

$$|\mathbb{E}[p^*(X)|p(X) = v] - v| \leq \alpha.$$

In words, calibration requires that of all the individuals who receive prediction v, their average positive outcome probability is close to v—e.g., among the people who receive a prediction of 70% chance of having $Y = 1$, 70% of them should truly have $Y = 1$. Note that for Boolean predictors, exact calibration ($\alpha = 0$) requires perfect accuracy.

However, while calibration is a desirable property, it is a relatively weak condition, and it alone is not sufficient to ensure fairness. Concretely, the *mean-predictor* $p_\mu(X) = \mu := \mathbb{E}_P[Y]$ is perfectly calibrated but uninformative: $\mathbf{Pr}[Y = 1|p_\mu = \mu] = \mathbf{Pr}[Y = 1] = \mu$. To relate this to fairness, consider two groups S and T with identical distributions of Y. Imagine that the predictor used for group S is calibrated and informative, where some individuals receive predictions above the mean, and that group T simply receives the (perfectly calibrated) mean predictor. Any reasonable decision-making procedure based on these predictions, will provide different outcomes to individuals with the same risk across different groups, due to their differently ranked predictions. This problem will be particularly exacerbated for minority groups who are underrepresented in training data, for whom an informative predictor will be more difficult to learn.

As with the binary classification setting studied in Sections 17.2 and 17.3, we observe that calibration as a fairness notion has a gap in treatment between individual and group fairness. Calibration across a small number of pre-defined groups is easily achievable, but does not provide sufficient fairness, as too many diverse individuals may be grouped together under one single prediction value. At the other extreme, individual calibration provides the guarantee that the prediction made for each individual is her true probability of receiving a 1-label: $\mathbf{Pr}[Y = 1|p(X) = v \wedge X] = p^*(X)$. However, this requires learning the Bayes optimal predictor, which is unattainable from a finite sample.

This motivates the definition of *multi-calibration*, which bridges between these two notions to provide multi-group fairness. Multi-calibration will guarantee calibration across a set of computationally identifiable groups, where the notion of *identifiability* will depend on a parameterized computational bound. This provides a computationally efficient relaxation of individual fairness, and it also strengthens the notion of group fairness by going beyond a small number of pre-defined protected groups.

Definition 17.13 (Multi-calibration [HKRR18]). *Let* $\mathcal{C} \subseteq \{c : \mathcal{X} \to \{0,1\}\}$. *A predictor* p *is* $(\mathcal{C}, \alpha)$-multi-calibrated *if* $\forall c \in \mathcal{C}$ *and* $\forall v \in supp(p)$,

$$|\mathbb{E}[Y|p(X) = v \wedge c(X) = 1] - v| \leq \alpha.$$

The class $\mathcal{C}$ describes the collection of subpopulations that require privacy protections, where for each subpopulation $\mathcal{S} \subseteq \mathcal{X}$, there should exist a function $c_\mathcal{S}$ such that $c_\mathcal{S}(X) = 1$ if and only if $X \in \mathcal{S}$. The class $\mathcal{C}$ should be chosen to be as expressive as the analyst can afford computationally—e.g., the class of functions that are implementable by depth-d decision trees. This gives the analyst explicit control over the balance between group and individual fairness—a larger and richer

$\mathcal{C}$ will result in fairness across more protected groups, but will be more computationally expensive.

An alternative interpretation of the role of $\mathcal{C}$ is that in order to claim that a predictor is unfair, multi-calibration requires a "witness" of a group that is treated unfairly. If $\mathcal{C}$ is large, this grants more computational power to find such a witness, which also requires fairness across more groups.

One benefit of multi-calibration is that it ensures that no qualified subpopulations in $\mathcal{C}$ are overlooked. For example, suppose there exists $c \in \mathcal{C}$ such that $\mathbb{E}[Y|c(X) = 1] > 1 - \alpha$. Then any $(\mathcal{C}, \alpha)$-multi-calibrated predictor should give high predictions on the group described by c. Thus $\mathcal{C}$ identifies the prediction-relevant structure in $Y|X$. This also ensures that multi-calibration is robust to under-representation, as predictions must be calibrated even if a group is small. Additionally, it requires learning *within* protected groups to identify qualified individuals a priori, thus avoiding the pitfalls illustrated in the example above with groups S and T.

17.4.3 Learning Multi-calibrated Predictors

The algorithmic process for learning a multi-calibrated predictor involves a similar primal-dual framework as the algorithm in Section 17.3.2 for learning a group-fair classifier, with some key technical differences. The high-level process is still: (1) write the problem formally as a constrained optimization problem; (2) formulate the optimization problem as a two-player zero-sum game; and (3) solve the game using no-regret learning dynamics.

As in Section 17.3.2, this approach will rely on the result of Freund and Schapire [FS96], that average no-regret play of a two-player zero-sum game converges to an approximate Nash equilibrium. With the appropriate game formulation in Step 2, an equilibrium strategy of the Learner (primal player) will correspond to a multi-calibrated predictor.

The main difference from Section 17.3.2 is that the underlying optimization cannot be written as an LP, but instead will be a non-linear feasibility problem. This new optimization problem leads to a modified no-regret learning set-up, and in particular, requires a reduction to weak agnostic learning for the Auditor to compute a best-response.

Nevertheless, the following theorem says that a multi-calibrated predictor can be efficiently learned using this procedure. The second part of the result tells us that the learned predictor can be described with a circuit of size not much larger than the complexity of representing the functions in $\mathcal{C}$.

Theorem 17.14 ([HKRR18]). *There exists an efficient algorithm that, if given access to a Weak Agnostic Learner, learns a $(\mathcal{C}, \alpha)$-multi-calibrated predictor p using*

$O(\log|\mathcal{C}|\text{poly}(1/\alpha))$ labeled samples in $O(|\mathcal{C}|\text{poly}(1/\alpha))$ time. Further, if membership in each set $c \in \mathcal{C}$ can be evaluated by a circuit of size s, then p can be implemented by a circuit of size $O(s \cdot \text{poly}(1/\alpha))$.

This result also says that learning a multi-calibrated predictor can be interpreted as a boosting algorithm, as weak agnostic learners can be boosted to strong agnostic learners after polynomially many iterations. The Auditor is a weak learner that identifies sources of unfairness in the Learner's current predictor. If the Auditor identifies a group that is treated unfairly, then this is used as an update that makes significant process towards multi-calibration. If the Auditor fails to identify such a group, then the current predictor must be multi-calibrated.

Now we proceed with details of the algorithmic construction.

Step 1: Framing the Optimization Problem

The major difference from Section 17.3.2 is that there is no explicit error objective in the optimization problem to be solved.[viii] Under group fairness, the goal was to maximize accuracy (that is, minimize error) subject to a fairness constraint. Here, multi-calibration is an accuracy notion—ensuring that average predictions on subgroups are correct—so we do not need to separately track accuracy and fairness. This leaves us with the following feasibility problem, where we need only to find a predictor that satisfies the multi-calibration constraint:

$$\begin{aligned} &\min_{p:\mathcal{X}\to[0,1]} \quad 0 \\ &\text{s.t. } |\mathbb{E}[Y|p(X)=v \wedge c(X)=1] - v| \leq \alpha \quad \forall c \in \mathcal{C} \text{ and } \forall v \in \mathit{supp}(p). \end{aligned} \tag{17.5}$$

Step 2: Formulation as a Game

While we can no longer explicitly Lagrangify the constraint in this formulation due to the the requirement that the prediction error must be below α for all $v \in \mathit{supp}(p)$, we can still view this as a two-player zero-sum game between a Learner and an Auditor.

The primal player is a Learner who chooses a predictor p, and the dual player is an Auditor who attempts to find a sub-population identified by $c \in \mathcal{C}$ that is treated unfairly under p. The payoff to the Auditor is the calibration error α on the sub-population c under the predictor p; the Learner's payoff is $-\alpha$.

Step 3: No-regret Dynamics

The Learner is facing a traditional online learning set-up when this game is played repeatedly: they can use any no-regret learning algorithm, iteratively update the

viii. This objective is not needed because the goals of multi-calibration are already aligned with regression accuracy, and imply standard loss minimization [Gop+22].

chosen predictor based on the bandit feedback from the Auditor, and (under the assumption of accurate feedback from the Auditor) this approach will converge to a solution where the Auditor cannot identify any (computationally-efficiently identifiable) violated sub-populations, which implies a multi-calibrated predictor. All that remains to be shown is that such an algorithm exists for the auditor.

Formally, the Auditor faces the following problem: Given $p : \mathcal{X} \to [0, 1]$, find a $c \in \mathcal{C}$ such that $|\mathbb{E}[Y|p(X) = v \wedge c(X) = 1] - v|$ is large, or equivalently, such that $|\mathbb{E}[c(X)(Y - v)]|$ is large. Note that this is exactly the problem of Weak Agnostic Learning for correlation detection, where a learner wants to identify correlations greater than α between X and $Y - p(X)$. This can be formalized through the following equivalence of auditing a multi-calibrated learner and Weak Agnostic Learning.

Theorem 17.15 ([HKRR18]). *If $\mathcal{C}$ is α-weakly agnostically learnable, then there exists a $(\mathcal{C}, \alpha)$-multi-calibrated learner. Similarly, if there exists a $(\mathcal{C}, \alpha)$-multi-calibrated learner, then $\mathcal{C}$ is α-agnostically learnable.*

Thus auditing multi-calibrated predictors is identical to weak agnostic learning (i.e., correlation detection), and by a reduction, we can go from auditing (or weak agnostic learning) to learning a multi-calibrated predictor. This gives us an algorithm to satisfy the learning goal of (computationally efficiently) identifying any function that satisfies fairness in the form of calibration for the sub-populations of interest, as specified by the class $\mathcal{C}$.

More concretely, in the repeated game, the Learner (primal player) can use any no-regret learning algorithm to learn a multi-calibrated predictor, and the Auditor (dual player) uses a Weak Agnostic Learning oracle to identify a sub-population in each round. No-regret dynamics and the result of Freund and Schapire [FS96] ensure that average play converges to an approximate-Nash equilibrium. The average predictor (i.e., averaged over all rounds of play) of the Learner corresponds to an approximately optimal solution to the original optimization problem (17.5), which will also be a multi-calibrated predictor.

Remark 17.16. *From a practical perspective, we note that while agnostic learning is computationally hard (i.e., it is equivalent to boosting), it can be efficient in some cases. For example, when predictions are in $[0, 1]$ rather than Boolean, this is a regression problem, which can be solved efficiently. More broadly, nearly all of machine learning is based on agnostic learning, so relying on a weak agnostic learner should work well in practice, despite theoretical hardness.*

Remark 17.17 (Individual calibration). *The framework in this section considers settings where each individual participates in this experience only once (e.g., applying for a* *mortgage), and experiences a single (high-stakes) binary outcome. Kearns et al. [KRS19] consider a variant setting where each individual instead participates in many low-stakes labelings (e.g., impressions of targeted ads). In this case, considering individual fairness in expectation may be justified since the individual can realize the outcomes of many personalized decisions.*

This set-up can be viewed equivalently as an average-case version of individual fairness as formalized in Section 17.2, or as an individual version of calibration as formalized here, where each individual's distribution of outcomes should be calibrated with respect to their personal ground truth.

17.4.4 Relationship to Differential Privacy

The algorithmic approach presented in Section 17.4.3 for learning multi-calibrated predictors is not differentially private as stated, although there are many indications that it likely could be made differentially private, to enable privately-trained multi-group fair predictors. Firstly, the original algorithmic construction for learning a multi-calibrated predictor "borrows ideas from the literature on differentially private query release and optimization" [HKRR18]. This suggests an underlying relationship between multi-calibration and differential privacy, even though the algorithm itself is not fully differentially private due to the use of other non-private subroutines. Secondly, the overall framework for learning a multi-calibrated predictor in Section 17.4.3 closely parallels the framework for learning a group-fair classifier in Section 17.3.2. Both involve first framing the fairness-constrained learning problem as a minimax optimization problem, then formulating the optimization problem as a two-player zero-sum game that can be solved by a no-regret learner, and finally showing that an equilibrium of the game corresponds to a solution to the original learning problem. In Section 17.3.2, this process is made private through the use of a private no-regret learner, which suggests that a private no-regret learner could similarly be used to privately learn a multi-calibrated predictor.

This open problem was answered in the affirmative by Kim [Kim20], which showed that multi-calibrated predictors can be learned in a differentially private way. Rather than adding differential privacy using the method above, Kim [Kim20] took an alternative approach that results in improved sample complexity of learning in some parameter regimes. This approach relies on statistical query (SQ) learning, and in particular, differentially private SQ oracles and differentially private density estimation oracles. The algorithm iteratively cycles through all classes in $\mathcal{C}$ and all possible outputs v, and (privately) checks whether the density at v is sufficiently high to be worth investigating the predictor's correctness at v. If yes, it calls a (private) SQ oracle to check whether the oracle gives an answer that is sufficiently far from the current prediction. If so, then this (private) SQ oracle is used to update the predictor; if not, then the algorithm continues checking classes and outputs.

This algorithmic approach is similar in structure to Private Multiplicative Weights (PMW) (see Section 4.6.1 of Chapter 4 for details), and its privacy analysis also follows a similar structure: it is shown that not too many update steps are required for convergence to a good predictor, and that each update step is differentially private; thus the the overall privacy guarantee follows from composition. Because the algorithmic approach is sufficiently different to other approaches presented in this chapter, and the analysis is quite subtle, it is not presented here; the interested reader is instead referred to [Kim20].

17.5 Impact of Privacy on Fair Outcomes

In an ideal world, privacy and fairness desiderata would be jointly considered to create algorithms that are private and fair by design. This is what we have seen in the previous sections, which focused on privately learning fair classifiers and predictors by considering these two objectives together. However, when privacy and fairness are considered separately—or, more generally, when they are considered independently of the complex system where they are used—the desired outcome may not be achieved. In this section, we will see several stylized examples of real-world applications where this occurs, as well as insights as to the causes and potential methods for remediation. While this is an active field of research that is rapidly evolving, we will survey what is currently known at time of writing as well as open research directions in the field.

Section 17.5.1 considers the impact of privacy noise on fairness of accuracy across groups, and shows that smaller groups tend to receive lower accuracy under a classifier learned via DP-SGD. This unfairness is due in part to fundamental limits of differential privacy which, by definition, limits the impact of small groups on learning, as well as due to specific details of the DP-SGD algorithm. Section 17.5.2 shows that adding differential privacy may cause unfairness in downstream decision-making tasks such as resource allocation, threshold comparison, and regression, all inspired by the U.S. Census Bureau's use of differential privacy. For each decision-making task, we see the cause of unfairness in terms of the privacy noise, and discuss potential solutions to address these disparities. Finally, Section 17.5.3 focuses on *fairness composition* as an analogy to privacy composition, and shows that unlike privacy, fairness does not compose. Several real-world examples are presented where fair classifiers do not compose into fair systems.

17.5.1 Differential Privacy's Impact on Model Accuracy Across Groups

When private learning tools are applied in practice without explicit fairness corrections, it is possible that differential privacy may have a disparate impact across subpopulations, with lower accuracy on smaller groups. [BPS19] demonstrated this effect empirically for deep learning models trained via a differentially private version of stochastic gradient descent (DP-SGD), where privacy of the gradient update step is achieved by first *clipping* the gradient to have a bounded norm, and then adding Gaussian noise that scales with $1/\varepsilon$ and the clipping parameter. See Section 6.3.1 for more details of the algorithm and its privacy guarantees.

[BPS19] found that accuracy of DP-SGD-trained models was not equal across all groups, but rather underrepresented classes in the training data received lower classification accuracy from the resulting model. They also found that while these accuracy disparities exist for non-private models, the extent of the disparity was worse under a privately trained classifier relative to a non-privately trained one. For example, an age and gender classification model trained using DP-SGD ($\varepsilon = 5.69$) had much lower accuracy for faces with darker skin tones (~59%) than for lighter skin tones (~78%), whereas the comparable non-private model achieved ~90% accuracy on lighter skin tones vs. ~85% on darker skin tones. Similar disparities and differences between private and non-private models persisted across other datasets and other classification tasks, suggesting that adding DP exacerbates existing unfairness in machine learning pipelines.

From a philosophical privacy perspective, this finding should be unsurprising. The goal of differential privacy is to hide the effect of one sample point; for populations represented by fewer points in the training data, the effect of this population on the model is more likely to be obfuscated by the group privacy properties of differential privacy, and thus private models are less likely to capture relevant features for accurately classifying statistical-minority[ix] groups. Even without privacy, one would expect machine learning models to have poorer performance on subgroups that are not sufficiently represented in the training data, because including additional training points generally lead to better performance of the learned model. The interesting observation of [BPS19] is that the additional disparity from privacy appears to be substantially larger than the disparity from just differences in sample sizes alone.

---

ix. It is important to distinguish between *minority groups* in society, corresponding to historically marginalized groups or protected social groups, and *statistical minorities*, corresponding to groups that are underrepresented in the dataset, which does not have any normative or social overtones.

To better understand how widely these phenomena will occur in general learning settings, future work is needed to disentangle how much of the observed effect is due to the algorithmic specifics of DP-SGD, versus fundamental limitations of the differential privacy constraint for accurate learning on minority groups. [BPS19] show that certain details the DP-SGD algorithm are one root cause of this disproportionate impact on model accuracy for underrepresented classes. First, points from underrepresented classes are simply less likely to be sampled in the gradient update step under uniform sampling. Even when they are sampled, these are precisely the points that will have a large gradient update and will be clipped, thus removing relevant update information. Without noise, these gradient updates would eventually converge to an accurate model, although perhaps at a slower rate. However, with both clipping and noise addition, the clipped gradients from the underrepresented class are not large enough to compensate for the noise and to allow the model to meaningfully update on this under-represented population. The highlighted text should be replaced with: [TDF21] also show that in DP-SGD, clipping and noise addition affect the gradient norms of different groups differently, which causes unfairness. It remains an open question to what extent the disparate performance across groups— beyond that which exists with non-private learning—is present and unavoidable under other private learning algorithms as well.

17.5.2 Differential Privacy's Impact on Downstream Fair Decision-making

The performance of a differentially private algorithm is traditionally measured in terms of additive accuracy between its output, such as distributional parameters estimated on the training dataset, and some ground truth, such as the empirical parameter value on the training data or the true value on the underlying distribution. However, the output of DP algorithms may be used for downstream decision tasks, where the domain-appropriate fairness notion may have a non-linear relationship with additive accuracy.

One notable and relevant use-case is the 2020 Decennial Census, where differentially private analyses of the collected data are used to allocate a fixed pool of federal resources. The noise added to preserve privacy inherently introduces small inaccuracies in the results; the related fairness question is whether some groups disproportionately bear the cost of these inaccuracies. [Puj+20] and [CDMS21] studied the downstream effects of the inaccuracies introduced by privacy noise in the Census use-case, with a particular emphasis on fairness in outcomes of decision-making problems.

[Puj+20] focused on three real-world *assignment problems* based on Census data products: (1) allocating funds to school districts, (2) voting rights benefits (i.e., translations of voting materials for minority language groups), and (3) apportionment of Congressional seats. The authors used public-use Census data as the ground truth;[x] they solved each assignment problem both using the non-private data and using differently private statistics computed on the dataset, and compared the outcomes using problem-specific fairness notions. They found that privacy noise can have a large impact, particularly when there is a misalignment of the upstream accuracy guarantees of the DP algorithms with the downstream fairness metric.

For educational funding, fairness was measured as a correct fractional allocation of funds relative to the ground truth. With privacy, smaller districts tend to get an inflated allocation of funds, at the expense of larger districts losing a small portion of their deserved funds. The effects were particularly noticeable for the smaller school districts, which may be due in part to the mismatch between the additive accuracy guarantees of most DP algorithms with the multiplicative fairness metric, which will cause seemly larger effects in smaller populations. Voting rights benefits is the problem of classifying minority language group populations as above or below the size threshold the receive benefits. Districts with minority language populations close to the threshold were the most affected by differential privacy, with some classified correctly less than half of the time. This is because changing only a few individuals' data would change the ground truth of the threshold comparison, which is precisely what differential privacy aims to protect. With legislative apportionment, fairness requires apportioning Congressional seats proportionally to each district's population. This cannot be achieved exactly, even without noise, because the number of representatives in a district must be integral. Adding small amounts of noise for privacy actually improves fairness in expectation, because randomization can reduce (on average) the deviation from the quota caused by the integrality constraint. However, ex-post, any realized outcome cannot achieve the expected (fractional) allocation, so this may be an unsatisfying guarantee in practice.

[CDMS21] empirically measured the accuracy impact of differential privacy in Census data for the task of *redistricting*, or redrawing the boundaries of voting districts based on population counts. They focused on the actual differentially private algorithm used by the U.S. Census Bureau, named TopDown, as well as a simplified and easier-to-analyze variant named ToyDown, which both involve geographical hierarchical constraints relating population counts of larger regions (e.g., states) to the smaller subdivisions contained therein (e.g., county, track, block).

x. Importantly, the Census Public Use Microdata is *not* the ground truth of the American population distribution, as these data already include disclosure avoidance measures, including (prior to 2020) *swapping*, where certain database entries have been swapped. Swapping has been shown to provide insufficient privacy protections, as substantial fractions of the true database can be reconstructed exactly, even after swapping has been applied [Abo21]. However, for the sake of analysis, the authors required a dataset that could be treated as ground truth, against which to measure the performance of differentially private algorithms.

These algorithms are first used to privatize the population counts in every relevant geographical region of the country, and then these private population counts are used to construct new voting districts which have approximately equal populations.

Among other results on TopDown and ToyDown—including the impact of privacy budget allocation across geographical hierarchy and the impact of the requiring geometric structure when constructing voting districts—the authors consider the robustness of linear regression to predict voting outcomes of each precinct based on demographics. This regression approach is commonly used to asses racial polarization of precincts for legal enforcement of the Voting Rights Act. The authors showed that standard linear regression based on privatized data introduces significant bias in the estimation parameters. However, simple post-processing of the private data, such as removing extremely small precincts or weighting precincts by population removes virtually all of this error.

Overall these results suggest that while differential privacy has been successful in providing accuracy *in aggregate*—e.g., additive accuracy between the ground truth value of a population statistic and the result of a DP algorithm to estimate that statistic—there has been less attention to accuracy in terms of disparity. This work highlights that more attention is needed to accuracy *as a fairness measure* of private algorithms—e.g., accurate allocation of funding or accurate classification of the existence of a minority population. A natural approach is the joint design of differentially private algorithms and decision-making processes to explicitly accommodate the noise from DP algorithms. For example, shifting down the threshold used in the comparison test for voting rights benefits would ensure that populations close to the true threshold are still likely to receive the benefits they deserve. While this might slightly increase costs of printing voting materials (i.e., increase false positive rate), it would substantially reduce disenfranchisement of minority voters (i.e., decrease false negative rate). More research is needed to develop richer tools for the growing number of practical use-cases where downstream decisions are made based on the results of differentially private data analyses.

17.5.3 Fairness Composition in Complex Systems

Differential privacy is known to enjoy *composition*, meaning that when multiple private analyses are performed, the privacy of the system is guaranteed by the privacy of its components. Unfortunately, [DI19] showed that fairness does not share this same property, and classifiers which are fair in isolation are not guaranteed to compose into fair systems. Additionally, unfair components can be used to build a system that is fair overall.

[DI19] give several practical examples of where fairness composition may fail:

- Settings where multiple tasks compete for individuals, e.g., online advertising for employment where bids must be individually fair with respect to job qualification. Due to competition with other advertisers, the cost to display the same ad may be different for similarly qualified individuals, so any fixed bid for a given qualification level will yield different outcomes between individuals who should receive similar treatment.
- Composing fair systems with other systems that legitimately differentiate based on the protected attribute, e.g., a diaper advertiser bids higher on women who are mothers, and an employment advertiser bids fairly across genders. In equilibrium, women who are mothers will see the diaper ad, while women without children will see the employment ad. This is distinct from the previous example because the (non-protected) diaper ad advertiser is free to bid "unfairly" with respect to parental status.
- Classifiers built as functions of fairly obtained values, e.g., getting into College A *OR* College B *AND* receiving financial aid, when each admissions decision is fair. In general, functional compositions of fair components are not guaranteed to be fair, although in certain cases, composition using only *OR*s can be fair.
- Approximate fairness with feedback loops, e.g., admission into a good high school will improve the chance of college admission, when each admissions decision is approximately fair. Slight unfairness early in the process may compound to have a large effect on fairness of final outcomes.
- Settings where each individual's classification is dependent on the classifications of others, e.g., sequentially interviewing candidates. Selecting an earlier candidate precludes later candidates from even being considered, even if each candidate is fairly evaluated.

While [DI19] give algorithmic solutions for achieving fairness in each example above, these results highlight that fairness of a system cannot be guaranteed simply by making fair decisions independently at each step of the process. Practitioners wishing to design fair complex systems must analyze and account for interactions between system components to ensure fair outcomes overall.

17.6 Concluding Remarks

This chapter has summarized the relationships between differential privacy and three different notions of algorithmic fairness: individual fairness, group fairness, and multi-group fairness. Each of these relationships takes on a very different flavor. The core definition of individual fairness is inspired by differential privacy, and techniques for achieving individual fairness include differentially private algorithms. Group fairness and multi-group fairness, on the other hand, are not inherently linked to the definition of differential privacy, but one can naturally ask whether these objectives can be achieved simultaneously with differential privacy. For both group and multi-group fairness, we see that this is possible. We also observed in Section 17.5 the potential negative impacts of differential privacy on fair outcomes if no explicit fairness interventions are taken. This suggests there is value to be gained from jointly considering privacy and fairness in learning systems.

Before these tools can be brought to bear to achieve privacy and fairness in machine learning systems in practice, there are a number of surrounding questions that must be addressed first. The most obvious is developing an understanding of when each fairness definition is appropriate for use. Naturally, it will depend on the application domain and the real-world fairness considerations that are being modeled in the algorithmic problem. As with any application of differential privacy, there is also the question of an appropriate choice of ε. The results surveyed in this chapter characterize the trade-off between privacy and fairness—as well as other desiderata such as accuracy or computational efficiency—as a function of ε, the sample size n, and other relevant problem-specific parameters. These insights should prove valuable to practitioners who wish to build and use systems that satisfy these desiderata, as well as to policymakers and regulators when developing new legislation to govern the use of AI systems.

Acknowledgements

The author would like to thank Michael Kim for extensive conversations and references on multi-group fairness, as well as comments on an earlier draft. Much of Section 4 and its framing is due to those conversations. The author would also like to thank Juba Ziani and Moon Duchin for conversations and references that were helpful in preparing this chapter.

References

[Abo21] J. Abowd. Third Declaration of John M. Abowd, Appendix B, Case 1:21-cv-01361-ABJ. https://www2.census.gov/about/policies/foia/records/disclosure-avoidance/17-1-abowd-decl-3.pdf [Last accessed 07/26/22]. Nov. 2021 (cit. on p. 600).

[Ala19] D. Alabi. "The Cost of a Reductions Approach to Private Fair Optimization". arXiv pre-print 1906.613. 2019 (cit. on p. 588).

[BPS19] E. Bagdasaryan, O. Poursaeed, and V. Shmatikov. "Differential Privacy Has Disparate Impact on Model Accuracy". In: Proceedings of the 33rd Conference on Neural Information Processing Systems. NeurIPS '19. 2019 (cit. on pp. 598, 599).

[CDMS21] A. Cohen, M. Duchin, J. Matthews, and B. Suwal. "Census Top-Down: The Impacts of Differential Privacy on Redistricting". In: Proceedings of the 2nd Symposium on Foundations of Responsible Computing. Ed. by K. Ligett and S. Gupta. FORC '21. 2021, 5:1–22 (cit. on pp. 599, 600).

[CGKM19] R. Cummings, V. Gupta, D. Kimpara, and J. Morgenstern. "On the compatibility of privacy and fairness". In: Adjunct Publication of the 27th Conference on User Modeling, Adaptation and Personalization. FairUMAP '19. 2019, pp. 309–315 (cit. on pp. 583, 585–587).

[DI19] C. Dwork and C. Ilvento. "Fairness Under Composition". In: Proceedings of the 10th Innovations in Theoretical Computer Science. ITCS '19. 2019, 33:1–20 (cit. on pp. 590, 601, 602).

[Dwo+12] C. Dwork, M. Hardt, T. Pitassi, O. Reingold, and R. Zemel. "Fairness through awareness". In: Proceedings of the 3rd Innovations in Theoretical Computer Science Conference. ITCS '12. 2012, pp. 214–226 (cit. on pp. 575–577, 580, 581).

[FS96] Y. Freund and R. E. Schapire. "Game theory, on-line prediction and boosting". In: Proceedings of the Ninth Annual Conference on Computational Learning Theory. COLT '96. 1996, pp. 325–332 (cit. on pp. 585, 587, 588, 593, 595).

[Gop+22] P. Gopalan, A. T. Kalai, O. Reingold, V. Sharan, and U. Wieder. "Omnipredictors". In: Proceedings of the 13th Innovations in Theoretical Computer Science Conference. ITCS '22. 2022 (cit. on p. 594).

[HKRR18] U. Hebert-Johnson, M. P. Kim, O. Reingold, and G. N. Rothblum. "Calibration for the (Computationally-Identifiable) Masses". In: Proceedings of the 35th International Conference on Machine Learning. ICML '18. 2018, pp. 1939–1948 (cit. on pp. 592, 593, 595, 596).

[HPS16] M. Hardt, E. Price, and N. Srebro. "Equality of Opportunity in Supervised Learning". In: Advances in Neural Information Processing Systems. Ed. by D. Lee, M. Sugiyama, U. Luxburg, I. Guyon, and R. Garnett. Vol. 29. Curran Associates, Inc., 2016. URL: https://proceedings.neurips.cc/paper/2016/file/9d2682367c3935defcb1f9e247a97c0d-Paper.pdf (cit. on p. 584).

[Ilv20] C. Ilvento. "Metric learning for individual fairness". In: Proceedings of the Symposium on Foundations of Responsible Computing. FORC '20. 2020 (cit. on pp. 576, 580, 581).

[Jag+19] M. Jagielski, M. Kearns, J. Mao, A. Oprea, A. Roth, S. Sharifi-Malvajerdi, and J. Ullman. "Differentially private fair learning". In: Proceedings of the International Conference on Machine Learning. ICML '19. PMLR. 2019, pp. 3000–3008 (cit. on pp. 583, 585–587).

[Jun+20] C. Jung, M. Kearns, S. Neel, A. Roth, L. Stapleton, and Z. S. Wu. "An Algorithmic Framework for Fairness Elicitation". In: 2nd Symposium on Foundations of Responsible Computing. FORC '20 2. Leibniz International Proceedings in Informatics, 2020, pp. 1–19 (cit. on pp. 576, 580, 581).

[Kim20] M. P. Kim. "A Complexity-Theoretic Perspective on Fairness". PhD thesis. Stanford University, 2020 (cit. on pp. 596, 597).

[KMR17] J. Kleinberg, S. Mullainathan, and M. Raghavan. "Inherent Trade-Offs in the Fair Determination of Risk Scores". In: 8th Innovations in Theoretical Computer Science Conference. ITCS '17. 2017, 43:1–43:23 (cit. on pp. 582, 589).

[KNRW18] M. Kearns, S. Neel, A. Roth, and Z. S. Wu. "Preventing Fairness Gerrymandering: Auditing and Learning for Subgroup Fairness". In: Proceedings of the 35th International Conference on Machine Learning. Vol. 80. Proceedings of Machine Learning Research. PMLR, 2018, pp. 2564–2572 (cit. on pp. 586, 587).

[KRS19] M. Kearns, A. Roth, and S. Sharifi-Malvajerdi. "Average Individual Fairness: Algorithms, Generalization and Experiments". In: Proceedings of the 33rd International Conference on Neural Information Processing Systems. 2019 (cit. on p. 596).

[Mit+21] S. Mitchell, E. Potash, S. Barocas, A. D'Amour, and K. Lum. "Algorithmic Fairness: Choices, Assumptions, and Definitions". In: Annual Review of Statistics and Its Application 8.1 (2021), pp. 141–163 (cit. on pp. 582, 588).

[Nar18] A. Narayanan. 21 fairness definitions and their politics. Tutorial at Conference on Fairness, Accountability, and Transparency. 2018. URL: https://www.youtube.com/watch?v=jIXIuYdnyyk (cit. on pp. 582, 588).

[Puj+20] D. Pujol, R. McKenna, S. Kuppam, M. Hay, A. Machanavajjhala, and G. Miklau. "Fair Decision Making Using Privacy-Protected Data". In: Proceedings of the 2020 Conference on Fairness, Accountability, and Transparency. FAT* '20. 2020, pp. 189–199 (cit. on p. 599).

[RY18] G. N. Rothblum and G. Yona. "Probably Approximately Metric-Fair Learning". In: Proceedings of the International Conference on Machine Learning. ICML '18. 2018 (cit. on pp. 576, 581).

[SSV03] A. Sandroni, R. Smorodinsky, and R. V. Vohra. "Calibration with many checking rules". In: Mathematics of Operations Research 28.1 (2003), pp. 141–153 (cit. on p. 591).

[TDF21] C. Tran, M. Dinh, and F. Fioretto. "Differentially Private Empirical Risk Minimization under the Fairness Lens". In: Advances in Neural Information Processing Systems. Ed. by M. Ranzato, A. Beygelzimer, Y. Dauphin, P. Liang, and J. W. Vaughan. Vol. 34. Curran Associates, Inc., 2021, pp. 27555–27565 (cit. on p. 599).

Index

About the Editors

Ferdinando Fioretto
University of Virginia

Ferdinando Fioretto is an assistant professor of Computer Science at the University of Virginia. His research focuses on addressing foundational challenges to advance artificial intelligence, privacy, fairness, and the intersection between machine learning and optimization. His work has been recognized with the 2022 Caspar Bowden PET award, the IJCAI-22 Early Career spotlight, the 2017 AI*AI Best AI dissertation award, and several best paper awards. Fioretto is a recipient of the NSF CAREER award, the Google Research Scholar Award, the Amazon Research Award, the ISSNAF Mario Gerla Young Investigator Award, and the ACP Early Career Researcher Award in Constraint Programming. He has been a member of the organizing committee of several workshops and events with focus on privacy, fairness, and optimization at premier AI and ML venues, including the AAAI workshop of Privacy Privacy Artificial Intelligence which inspired the development of this book.

Pascal Van Hentenryck
Georgia Institute of Technology

Pascal Van Hentenryck is an A. Russell Chandler III Chair and Professor in the H. Milton Stewart School of Industrial and Systems Engineering at Georgia Tech, the director of the NSF AI Institute in Advances in Optimization (AI4OPT), and the director of Tech AI, the AI hub at Georgia Tech. He is a Fellow of AAAI (the Association for the Advancement of Artificial Intelligence) and INFORMS (the Institute for Operations Research and Management Science). His research focuses on the fusion of Artificial Intelligence and Operations Research and, in particular, AI for Engineering. Van Hentenryck designed and implemented several innovative optimization systems, including the CHIP programming system (a Cosytec product), the foundation of all modern constraint programming systems and the optimization programming language OPL (now an IBM Product). Van Hentenryck runs the Seth Bonder summer Camps in Computational and Data Science for middle- and high-school students every summer.

Contributing Authors

James Anderson
Columbia University

Kallista Bonawitz
Google Research

Konstantinos Chatzikokolakis
University of Athens

Giovanni Cherubin
Microsoft Research

Graham Cormode
University of Warwick

Rachel Cummings
Columbia University

Damien Desfontaines
Tumult Labs

Liyue Fan
University of North Carolina at Charlotte

Ferdinando Fioretto
University of Virginia

Marco Gaboardi
Boston University

Marzyeh Ghassemi
Massachusetts Institute of Technology

Bryant Gipson
Google

Anna Goldenberg
University of Toronto

Michael Hay
Tumult Labs and Colgate University

Peter Kairouz
Google Research

Steven H. Low
California Institute of Technology

Ashwin Machanavajjhala
Tumult Labs

Brendan McMahan
Google Research

Catuscia Palamidessi
Inria and École Polytechnique

Nicolas Papernot
University of Toronto and Vector Institute

David Pujol
Tumult Labs

Reza Shokri
National University of Singapore

Jeremy Seeman
Urban Institute

Thomas Steinke
Google DeepMind

Vinith M. Suriyakumar
Massachusetts Institute of Technology

Yurii Sushko
Goolge

Yuchao Tao
Snap Inc

Christine Task
Knexus Research

Andreas Terzis
Google

Abhradeep Thakurta
Google Deepmind

Salil Vadhan
Harvard University

Pascal Van Hentenryck
Georgia Institute of Technology

Jiayuan Ye
National University of Singapore

Fengyu Zhou
California Institute of Technology

Juba Ziani
Georgia Institute of Technology

Printed and bound by CPI Group (UK) Ltd, Croydon, CR0 4YY

15/09/2026

14962366-0001